# BAPTISTS ON THE AMERICAN FRONTIER

# BAPTISTS ON THE AMERICAN FRONTIER

A History of Ten Baptist Churches
of Which the Author Has Been Alternately a Member

by
John Taylor

Annotated Third Edition

Edited and Introduced by
Chester Raymond Young

MERCER UNIVERSITY PRESS
Macon, Georgia

ISBN 0-86554-479-4


*Baptists on the American Frontier: A History of Ten Baptist Churches*
*of Which the Author Has Been Alternately a Member*
by John Taylor

Annotated Third Edition
Edited and Introduced
by Chester Raymond Young

Copyright © 1995
Mercer University Press
6316 Peake Road
Macon, Georgia 31210-3960

*Library of Congress Cataloging-in-Publication Data*

Taylor, John, 1752–1835.
    [History of ten Baptist churches]
    Baptists on the American frontier : a history of ten Baptist churches of
which the author has been alternately a member / by John Taylor.
—Annotated 3rd ed. / edited and introduced by Chester Raymond Young.
    xiv + 418 pp.                                   6 x 9" (15 x 23cm.)
    Includes bibliographical references.
    ISBN 0-86554-479-4 (alk. paper)
    1. Baptists—Virginia—History.  2. Baptists—Kentucky—History.
3. Virginia—Church history.  4. Kentucky—Church history.
5. Taylor, John, 1752–1835.  6. Baptists—Clergy—Biography.
7. Clergy—Virginia—Biography.  8. Clergy—Kentucky—Biography.
I. Young, Chester Raymond, 1920–   . II. Title.
BX6248.V8T33   1995
286'.1769—dc20                                          95-34931
                                                              CIP

# Contents

# Acknowledgments

The following publishing houses have graciously consented to permit the copying of brief excerpts from material for which they hold the copyright: The American Baptist Historical Society; the American Council of Learned Societies; the Franklin Trask Library, Andover Newton Theological School; Broadman Press; Glenmary Research Center; Heritage Papers; Judson Press; the Kentucky Baptist Convention; The Sunday School Board of the Southern Baptist Convention; The University Press of Kentucky; and the Virginia Baptist Historical Society.

As requested, specific acknowledgment is given for the following:

William L. Lumpkin, *Baptist Confessions of Faith.* © 1959, Judson Press. Reprinted with permission of the author., Judson Press, 1-800-458-3766.

*Encyclopedia of Southern Baptists*, Vol. 2. © 1958. Renewal 1986 Broadman Press. All rights reserved. Used by permission.

Larry Douglas Smith, "John Taylor and Missions: A New Interpretation," *Quarterly Review* (April-June, 1982). © 1982 The Sunday School Board of the Southern Baptist Convention. All rights reserved. Used by permission.

Reprinted from Otis Rice, *The Allegheny Frontier.* © 1970 by the University Press of Kentucky, by permission of the publishers.

The library of the Kentucky Historical Society has allowed the copying of a picture that first appeared in the 1948 issue of the organization's *Register*. The photograph shows the home that John Taylor gave to his youngest daughter. Also the library of Transylvania University has permitted the copying of a picture that shows Big Spring Baptist Church in Woodford County, Kentucky. This photograph is a part of the Photographic Collection of the late J. Winston Coleman, Jr.

I am grateful for each permission to use both words and images.

# Author's Preface to the First Edition

[iii]A romantic tale—if told with design to make you stare, weep, or laugh—is like bubbles from troubled water that soon die away. Or a tale told in truth that neither affects the understanding or conscience is no better as to us. And they are much worse when put on paper, and especially when men pay their money for them. Sacred history (the Bible) is best of all; because, most true. Without flattery, in awful majesty, it deals with men's minds and consciences and is worthy of its author—God. The brightest ornament of all history is the truth of its narration.

The facts stated in the following essay—some of them—are of more than fifty years' standing, and [there are] no written vouchers to guide. Many of the transactions have taken place in Kentucky and in the presence of thousands. The author is under no dismay in point of contradiction; his main object is, if possible, to benefit the young, rising generation. The old and wise may take part with them if they can.

The whole responsibility of default[1] in the book is with the author, for neither old or young has invited its publication—except papermakers, printers, and bookbinders. All this may be accounted for.

Part of the work will be in the style of history. The object in this is to encourage the Baptists, who are a numerous people in Kentucky, to publish their own history, which hitherto has been much neglected.

Would it not be the better plan for each association at their next annual meeting to appoint a committee of two or more to make out a history of their own [iv]association, returnable in one year—and by putting them al[l] together, [to] make a history of the Baptists more correct than has been [done] in any country?

As to the part consisting of expositions of Scripture,[2] though the author thinks highly of the opinions of other men, yet [he] takes the liberty, as Christ's free man, to differ from all when justice and truth demands it.

JOHN TAYLOR

---

[1]Here the noun *default* is an obsoletism meaning *fault*.

[2]Taylor includes four biblical expositions in the Appendix of the first edition. Covering pages 191-286, they deal with the following subjects: the Final Judgment (Matthew 25:1-46), anger without sin (Ephesians 4:26-27), David's fall and recovery (Psalm 51:17), and Job's captivity and enlargement (Job 42:10). These pieces are omitted from this present edition, because they do not concern Taylor's ten churches.

# Author's Preface to the Second Edition

[v]Indulgent reader (I thus accost you because it is probable I shall need your indulgence before you get through), I neither wish to make you merry nor mad, and yet perhaps both those passions of anger and mirth may be brought into action. Your patience also may be brought to the test. Indeed it may be [that] you already begin to laugh or frown when I tell you [that] I am about to publish a second edition of my *History of Ten Churches*. Should you ask, "What is that for?"; the answer would be, "The first is gone, and the people ask for more books."

The author is considered both by others and [by] himself but a very common man and not very proud nor modest and very poorly calculated to make books. And though [he is] now in his seventy-fifth year, and [though] from his boyhood [he] has endeavored to serve his generation in the gospel of his Saviour,[1] [he] is yet more than willing to serve on in any thing his conscience does not forbid, should it be even in bookmaking—a work so very much above his capacity.

It was an accidental thing that I ever made a book of any kind. First, beginning to write a little on some subjects for my own amusement without any design to go further, [and] after looking over the sheet and thinking [that] it might be of use somewhere, without invitation or leave from anybody [I] saw proper to send it abroad in print. All this, to be sure, seemed venturesome for a man of my description.

My editors, in the present edition, encourage me to go on; but this, no doubt, is more from a hope of remuneration for their labour[2] than [from] admiration of the work.

Some things in the first copy have been offensive to some of my friends and [to] myself to[o]. Some corrections will be made, but after all it will be, like the author, imperfect still.

Some things in the first copy [were] sneered at as romantic and [as] bearing the appearance of bravado—[such] as the killing [vi]of a great buck when I first settled at Clear Creek, the uncommon day's work about the same time in putting up new fence, [and] the mighty work done at Mount Byrd in so short a time.

"Strike it all out," says some of my friends.

But says myself, "They shall all stand and for the following reasons: the buck, with all his horns, shall stay where he is to show to my offspring the poverty of their father when he first came to Kentucky. The fence shall stand

---

[1]For the word *Savior* the author consistently uses the British spelling *Saviour*.
[2]For all forms of the word *labor* Taylor uses the British spelling *labour*.

where it is, with all the brush in which it was put up, as a reproach on all lazy men; and none will call the truth of this in question but some poor, idleing [*sic*] fellow that never did a good day's work in his life at that kind of business. And as to the mighty work at Mount Byrd, that shall stand as a lasting reproach on myself, not as a man of the world (for in that case it would be laudable) but as a gospel minister of the Lord and Saviour. And I refer the reader to the keen stings of soul I felt about the time and after I left Mount Byrd."

In this publication I have given my conscientious views of the gospel address and to whom the invitations of it are to be given by the ministers thereof, under the head of "The Gospel Supper."[3] Other ideas [that] I have given on some other subjects[4] perhaps will differ from [those of] all men. This I take the liberty to do as Christ's free man when I think justice calls for it.

But perhaps the greatest offence[5] I may have given in this whole work is in the additions of history I have made on some churches whose history I have been writing. The first is Hillsboro, as a daughter of old Clear Creek, when I take some notice of a new association lately sprung up under the appellation of Glens Creek.[6] The next item is the church at Frankfort, which has been progressing as a church in a checkered way about twelve years and seems on the brink of ruin by a violent discord between two of their leading members.

I would not wil[l]fully or wantingly [wantonly] hurt the feelings of or [un]justly offend any man or set of men, either friends or enemies; for when men are made mad there is no hope of their conversion from the error of their way. But my own thoughts are that historians should narrate faithfully, or how shall vice be made ashamed and virtue hold [vii]up its lovely head? This is one main

---

[3]This essay, based on Matthew 22:1-10 and Luke 14:16-24, deals with the unrestricted invitation of sinners to accept the gospel. It covers pages 233-48 of the second edition.

[4]Seven other theological pieces are found on pages 225-33, 249-77, and 283-300 in the second edition and make up the greater part of an addendum that comes next after the coverage of the ten churches. They concern the following subjects: baptism (Acts 22:16), anger without sin (Ephesians 4:26-27), blasphemy against Christ (1 John 5:16), vanity (Romans 8:20), bridled speech (James 1:26), the mammon of unrighteousness (Luke 16:9), and Peter's fall (Luke 22:31-32). The piece regarding speech takes the form of a circular letter written by Taylor at the request of the Franklin Association and is addressed to the North Bend Association.

The only exposition in the second edition that is carried over from the first is the one that has to do with anger.

All the theological essays of the second edition have been excluded from this present one, because they do not deal with Taylor's ten churches.

[5]Taylor consistently uses the British spelling *offence* for the noun *offense.*

[6]This union, known as the "Baptist Association," is discussed below in the text and also in its annotation.

object in all history: that men may be taught thereby to shun the evil and choose the good. Sacred history abounds in this. How many lives of both good and bad men are recorded at length [in the Bible] and even the sins of good men as a warning to those who shall come after!

Except in typographical blunders the whole default in this work is with the author, who so far as he knows has taken no method to conceal his own improprieties but rather has enjoyed pleasure in the confession of his own sins, for which he feels humiliation before the Lord; for I do not know (as to the workings of the secret corruption in my own nature) that there is any other man on the earth as bad as myself. But all this does not sink me into such deep despondency but that I very willingly make a comparison of actions with other men, and even prefer my own course.

I consider my greatest improprieties have been in the active pursuits of this world. But in one sense this is erring on the right side, for thereby I have supported my large family without spunging[7] on the people. And, if I mistake not, Paul at times preferred tentmaking to that of being a mean beggar among the people.[8] So that bad as my own course has been, I would prefer it to the course of some preaching men. To see a preacher, like a buzzard, sailing in the air from one country to another and from city to city to hunt for churches already built and, when he smells the carcass, [to] pitch down and fall to devouring—I say, when this seems to be the object of two evils I will choose that which seems to me the least.

I have been in the ministry just about fifty-four years, and of the many thousands of meetings I have appointed I do not recollect that worldly business ever stopped me from one of them. And I have been a man of such general[ly] uninterrupted health that I do not think I have disappointed half as many meetings in my life as I have been preaching years. Should this be called boasting, as Paul said in a similar case, "Bear with me in my folly."[9]

JOHN TAYLOR

---

[7]The gerund *spunging* is a misspelling of *sponging*, which is a colloquialism meaning "getting without cost."
[8]Acts 18:3; 2 Thessalonians 3:8.
[9]2 Corinthians 11:1.

# Editor's Preface to the Annotated Third Edition

It was in 1969 that first I began to teach collegiate students about the history of the westward movement in the United States. In the bibliography of that field I soon discovered John Taylor's *History of Ten Baptist Churches* and purchased a copy of it. The form that I acquired was an uncopyrighted, facsimile reproduction of the initial edition (1823). This copy had been issued in 1968–1972 by Art Guild Reprints, of Cincinnati. Later I obtained a copy of Taylor's second edition (1827). This one was a reprint published in 1980 by Arno Press, of New York City, as a part of its forty-volume collection titled *The Baptist Tradition*.

Upon its publication in Kentucky in the 1820s, Taylor's work had passed into the public domain, because the author had not copyrighted his two editions. He could have done so, however, at the federal district court located in Frankfort.

Some years after securing my reprints, Anne G. Campbell graciously supplied me with photocopies of the two editions of *Ten Churches* that are held in the Margaret I. King Library, at the University of Kentucky. The copy of the first edition that she gave me came directly from the 1823 imprint that is owned by the university; the copy of the second edition seems to have been made from a microfilm provided by some other institution. I am indeed grateful to Ms. Campbell for her kindness.

John Taylor, a preacher and a farmer, was also a frontiersman. He was especially fond of putting down his roots on the frontier, in "new countries" or "new settlements," by which terms he identified the places where initial occupants began housekeeping and farming. Years later Frederick Jackson Turner would define the frontier as the "hither edge" of land unencumbered by settlers and as the "outer edge" of westward expansion where "savagery and civilization" met. Taylor called such regions "back parts," "backwoods," or "wilderness." He was born on the frontier of the Virginia Piedmont, grew to maturity on the frontier of the Great Valley of Virginia, performed his first itinerancy as a missionary on the Allegheny frontier, and lived out his calling as a man of the cloth and as a tiller of the soil in numerous "settlements" on the Kentucky frontier.

Of a truth Taylor's writing lays out the metes and bounds of the religious landscape that he traversed throughout all his days. Because of the unparalleled content and quality of his narrational descriptions of Baptist activities on the frontier, I deem it appropriate to label this third edition of *Ten Churches* with the title *Baptists on the American Frontier* and to relegate Taylor's own title to the status of a subtitle for the purpose of identifying this book: *A History of Ten Baptist Churches of Which the Author Has Been Alternately a Member.*

Timothy Paul Hart, Larry Douglas Smith, and Norman Warnell, who have particular interests in John Taylor, provided me with photocopies of certain hard-to-find published works of the preacher that I otherwise might not have uncovered. I am especially grateful for the help they gave me.

Uniform assistance was afforded me by the staffs of the county clerks' offices of Fauquier, Frederick, Northumberland, and Shenandoah counties in Virginia and of Boone, Campbell, Fayette, Franklin, Gallatin, and Woodford counties in Kentucky.

Professors Charles Mayer Dupier, Jr., Robert Leland Palmer, and George Grover Ramey, colleagues of mine at Cumberland College, afforded help in numerous ways. Interlibrary loans of books and periodical materials were graciously provided for my use by Ronald L. Bunger, of the college library.

I have been encouraged in this work by two descendants of John Taylor: Dorothy Brown Thompson, a great-great-great granddaughter, and Sarah French Moore Clough, a great-great-great-great granddaughter. Mrs. Thompson merits praise for her remarkable series of Taylor articles that appeared in the two principal historical journals in Kentucky.

Carolyn H. Jett, a professional genealogist, is due special thanks for her help in untangling the lines of descent of early Taylors in Virginia. (She is in no way responsible for any error that I may have made in delineating the preacher's ancestry.) These persons also assisted in solving genealogical problems: Albert G. Craig, Lucy B. Geoghegan, Crockett A. Harrison, Margaret L. Hill, George L. Johnson, and Edward Russo.

The help of these individuals in answering general queries is gratefully acknowledged: Paul M. Debusman, Ronald F. Deering, Douglas W. Heare, Loyal Jones, Roscoe Keeney, Jr., Mark A. Keith, Harold G. Polk, Otis K. Rice, Bill Strickler, and Doris Yeiser.

I am thankful to Kandie Adkinson, Frederick J. Anderson, John R. Barden, Anita Chinn, Nelson L. Dawson, and Darlene F. Slater for their searching for certain manuscripts. Anne L. Rodick performed remarkable research in determining the landed activities of Taylor, who speculated in Indiana public lands. I appreciate her precise work.

Norma D. Hennigen deserves a word of appreciation for her gift of a photocopy of the manuscript minutes of the Bullittsburg Church for its first two decades.

The following persons gave me congregational histories or other published works pertaining to Taylor: Florence Puryear Campbell, Scott Cox, Lucy C. Kephart, Charles Tarrants, and Carol D. Palmgreen.

Gregory Scot Rose accompanied me on a trek into northern Kentucky, where we located the house that Taylor erected in 1803–1804 near Milton, in present-day Trimble County. Howard Long and Elaine, his wife, who own and occupy this national treasure, indeed made us welcome.

The following members of the staff of the Kentucky Historical Society rendered urbane help in providing books and information: Linda Anderson, Ron D. Bryant, James C. Klotter, and Diane Shelton.

To our son-in-law, David Kent Humphreys, I express sincere gratitude for the pieces of artwork that are used throughout the book.

Dr. David Turner Farrar, technology coordinator for the Williamsburg, Kentucky, City Schools, rendered invaluable service in transforming the manuscript from typed pages to a computer disk.

Thanks are extended to Professor Scott Nash, managing editor of Mercer University Press, and to the members of his staff for the profound interest they have expressed in the publication of the Taylor manuscript.

Without the help and encouragement of Florence Alice Baird Young, my wife, this project would never have seen the light of day. I am particularly thankful for her steadfast labor in typing the manuscript and in creating the computer disk.

Professors John David Broome and Rayford Watts have worked diligently as proofreaders. They gave personally of their own time. Their helpfulness in this regard is greatly appreciated. Dr. Broome also allowed me the use of a paper that he wrote during graduate school.

CHESTER RAYMOND YOUNG

To Our Children

Charlotte, Ray,
and Virginia

# Introduction

On a summer's day in 1835 four appointees of the Franklin County Court assembled in the home of the late John Taylor at the Forks of Elkhorn in order to evaluate his slaves and other personalty. When they sorted through the meager library of this Baptist minister, they found three copies of his *History of Ten Baptist Churches*.

While residing in Franklin County, Kentucky, in the heart of the Bluegrass, Taylor had produced two editions of this three-hundred-page book.

These appraisers—Bernard Dougherty, Isaac Wilson, Edward Herndon, and Alexander W. Macklin—had been neighbors of Taylor. They knew about this important publication and listed its title in their inventory. But, as circumstance would have it, they failed to set down its estimated value.

The selling price of the first edition of *Ten Churches*, which came from the press of Jacob Harrod Holeman at nearby Frankfort in 1823, is unknown. The second edition, which was printed by William H. Holmes four years later in Bloomfield, Kentucky, was advertised to subscribers at 87½¢ and to nonsubscribers at $1. It is not known to which edition the three remaining copies of Taylor's book belonged, but the evaluators of his estate may have determined their worth in 1835 as less than $1 apiece.

The value of this published work rose steadily. It was put at $15 to $20 as early as 1898. In the 1940s one dealer offered the volume for $40. In 1988 a West Virginia seller of rare books listed a copy of the first edition at $275.

Who was John Taylor, and what is there about this book that still demands attention? He was born and reared on the pre-Revolutionary frontier of Virginia. Converted to evangelical religion during the Great Awakening under the urgent preaching of dissenting Separate Baptists, he embarked forthwith upon the work of an itinerant missionary. Over the years he held membership in ten Baptist churches—two in Virginia and eight in Kentucky—and served as the stated preacher of seven of them. In addition to *A History of Ten Baptist Churches* he wrote two books that treat of religious controversy.

As for this Baptist preacher's significance, William Warren Sweet, the "Father of American Church History," characterized John Taylor as the one who "probably" exerted "a larger influence among Baptists in Kentucky during his generation than any other single individual."[1] William Vaughan (1785–1877), a younger colleague of Taylor, asserted, "Everything John Taylor ever wrote is

---

[1] "Taylor, John," *Dictionary of American Biography*, 18:331.

worth reading."[2] William Cathcart, a Baptist encyclopedist, held that Taylor "probably performed more labor, and was more successful, than any other pioneer preacher in Kentucky."[3]

Taylor's *History of Ten Baptist Churches* is important because it relates how the work of frontier congregations was conducted. In particular it is significant for its gripping account of a teenage boy's religious conversion, together with the portrayal of the terrors that attended his conviction of sin; its moving story of a slave woman's relation of her religious experience; its graphic description of baptismal scenes, one of which included the rite of the laying on of hands; its picture of church polity as seen in organizing a congregation, in calling and installing a pastor, in admitting and expelling members, and in maintaining discipline within the membership; its catalog of arduous tasks of clearing, fencing, and planting land covered by virgin forests; its depiction of difficulties and dangers encountered on preaching tours in the wintry Appalachians; its detailing of a neighborhood, house-to-house visitation by three teams of church officials; its chronicle of a Tidewater planter's embracing of heartfelt religion; and its record of the folk belief in dreams as portents.

In this new edition of *Ten Churches* careful attention has been paid in the annotation to uncovering and correcting Taylor's errors regarding events. The preacher was seventy years old when he penned the first edition. Given his age, he can be allowed a few mistakes. Even so, the presence of an error here and there does not mean that the whole narrative is flawed. Caution, however, is recommended in the use of his work and, for that matter, in the use of all reminiscences.

This third edition represents a consolidation of Taylor's two editions. When differences have been found in the 1823 and 1827 editions, the wording that seems more appropriate on the basis of context has been used here. In every important case, however, the reader is informed of the source of the accepted text.

This edition includes only the biographical and historical materials of the previous editions that pertain to Taylor or to the churches to which he belonged. Accordingly, thirteen sermonic and theological pieces and a sketch on Isaac Hodgen, which appear in one or the other or in both of the earlier editions, have been eliminated from the present one. On the other hand, the essay titled "The Author's Conversion and Call to the Ministry," a sketch on Lewis Craig, the "Appendix to the History of Clear Creek Church," and obituaries of Catherine

---

[2]John Henderson Spencer, *A History of Kentucky Baptists from 1769 to 1885*, 2 vols. (Cincinnati OH, 1885) 1:574.

[3]*The Baptist Encyclopedia* (Philadelphia, 1881) 1136.

Graves and Joseph Wilson, all have been interwoven with the text of Taylor's *Ten Churches*.

The pages of the previous editions from which the new text has come are indicated by bracketed and superscripted numerals inserted at proper places throughout the present text. Materials from the first edition are identified by a page number standing alone in superscripted brackets—for example, [62]. The second edition as the source is shown by a cardinal number for the page plus the ordinal abbreviation for the edition—for example, [142,2d]. In this regard, the pagination from the first edition constitutes the framework for the contents of this edition. References to the second edition are made here only when its materials are absent from the first edition or appear different in it.

Taylor structured his book to include one chapter for each church of which he had been a member. His ten chapters are retained as the basis of this edition also. Many of Taylor's lengthy paragraphs have been divided into shorter ones. Numbers of them exceed one page, some continue for four or five pages, and one goes for thirteen. Also many long sentences have been broken up into briefer ones.

To some sentences I have added words that complete the evident meaning or render the reading smoother. The additions made include nominative and relative pronouns, the conjunction *that*, and auxiliary verbs. In every such case, however, the added word or words are enclosed in brackets in order to indicate that they are not found in Taylor's text.

Modern capitalization of words and punctuation of sentences have been uniformly used.

The spelling of proper nouns has been made to agree with the orthography found in recent atlases or in denominational histories. Consistency in spelling verbs and common nouns has been harder to achieve. For such words a general rule was adopted: If Taylor spells a given word uniformly, his spelling has been left unchanged; if he uses multiple spellings for a particular word, its modern spelling is used throughout my text except in four cases: (1) the poetic spelling appears—for example, *stopt* (stopped); (2) one of the spellings reflects an early pronunciation—for example, *roppers* (wrappers); (3) his alternate spellings of the past tense or the past participle of a particular verb are given in an unabridged dictionary—for example, *past* (passed); and (4) a word appears as both a common noun and a proper noun—for example, *Beech Creek Church* and *beach* (beech). The double spellings are retained for words covered by these four categories.

It is impossible to determine whether an unusual spelling in the previous editions results from the work of Taylor, the printers, a typesetter, or a proofreader.

The author strikes the chords of memory and brings to life conversations in which he engaged, narrations of converts' religious experiences, and portions of prayers, sermons, and announcements. When this type of material appears in the direct words of the speaker, it has been set off by quotation marks. Also the alternating parts of conversations have been paragraphed.

Taylor's writing is plain and forthright. Nonetheless he uses many words that are now archaic, obsolete, dialectal, or colloquial. Occasionally his words are phonetic, sometimes poetic.

At times humor characterizes Taylor's work. In writing of Christians who had separated from one congregation and formed a new one, the author states, "Pure as they were, they soon fell out among themselves." A poor horse that had to cross and recross the frigid waters of a creek "could say nothing on that head." One minister who did well in the pulpit "would be better if he would leave off when he was done." A man who did not want to appear eager to attend preaching and who had been present at a day meeting said that he came to one after dark in order "to see what a night meeting was."

Sarcasm now and then crops out in the writing of Taylor. The leaders of Transylvania University are designated "the high powers at Lexington authorized to make doctors of divinity." The author writes, "For I allow Yankees to think faster and with more art than other men." When Taylor is accused of trespass, he scoffs, "The magnitude of the crime was hardly known, but it would come forward next term in all its glowing colours." The preacher's composition is skillful. His language is idiomatic. It is full of figures of speech—at least 138 metaphors, 86 similes, 28 uses of personification, and 9 instances of hyperbole.

Sometimes the author falls a victim to tautology, a common fault of writers and speakers. Once he finds "ocular witnesses before my eyes." Taylor ponders the question whether the elect can "finally be lost at last." He recounts his conversion for the benefit "of my posterity that shall come after me."

An extensive system of annotation has been devised in order to make Taylor's work more meaningful. The notes thus created fulfill several functions: to describe usage of words that is presently outmoded; to sketch biographies of persons mentioned in the text; to locate geographical sites, including counties, towns, glades, mountains, and streams; to define religious terms and theological systems; to provide biblical references; to demarcate regions of settlement and routes of travel; to identify congregations and associations; to distinguish between the texts of the first two editions; to correct errors; to solve problems of chronology; to make analogies; to document the sources of data, including quotations; and to cite additional bibliography.

## Ancestry

A descendent of Scottish and French immigrants, John Taylor was born on 27 October 1752 in the Virginia Piedmont in the part of Prince William County that later became Fauquier County. His father, Lazarus Taylor (born 1718), had moved there from Northumberland County, where an ancestor owned land as early as 1659. Lazarus' westward movement symbolizes the interest in the frontier that marked many members of this family.

The landowner of 1659 was John Taylor of Wicomico (1627–1702), who was a great-great-grandfather of John Taylor the author. While living earlier in Northampton County, John Taylor of Wicomico and one James Jones bought jointly a thousand-acre tract. It lay between the Wicomico and the Corotoman rivers in the lower end of Northumberland County in Wicomico Parish, which sat astride the border separating Northumberland and Lancaster counties. The immediate previous owner of this acreage had been Thomas Gaskins, who was perhaps the father-in-law of both Taylor and Jones and who had also lived in Northampton before settling in Northumberland. In 1688 Taylor became the sole proprietor. This land, located between the present-day villages of Browns Store and Wicomico Church, descended among the progeny of Lazarus Taylor (1668–1726/7)[4], a son of John Taylor of Wicomico and a great-grandfather of John Taylor the author. The plantation named Litchfield, a part of this larger estate, remained in the family until 1839.

Both John Taylor of Wicomico and his wife, Alice, died in 1702. His father may have been the John Taylor who migrated from Scotland to Virginia as early as 1638 and whom the widow Sarah Cloyden in Isle of Wight County claimed as a headright that year. She also listed Giles Taylor and Tobias Horton in her claims. In 1652 John and Tobias acquired adjoining tracts of land on Fleets Bay in Lancaster County. John died that year, and his widow married Tobias Horton.

Fleets Bay, an inlet of the Chesapeake Bay, is located just north of the mouth of the Rappahannock. It is the locale of a tradition that had come down to the family of John Taylor the author. This familial legend was recorded in the Bibles of two persons connected to this family. Both accounts agree that one John Taylor with his brothers Argyle and William disembarked from the *Amsterdam* at the head of Fleets Bay in 1650. These stories may have remained

---

[4]Throughout this work, the use of two consecutive years separated by a virgule indicates that the date fell within the period 1 January through 24 March, the closing portion of a Julian year, because the Julian New Year's Day was 25 March. In this "double dating" the first year is a Julian year; the second, a Gregorian year. For dates later than 31 December 1751 this system does not obtain, because British use of the Gregorian calendar legally began on the following day, which was called 1 January 1752.

unwritten for some 175 years. Even though this oral tradition is imprecise, it gives a measure of credibility to the conjecture that John Taylor of Fleets Bay may have been the father of John Taylor of Wicomico and the immigrant of the Taylor family from which John the author descended.[5]

Lazarus Taylor (1668–1726/7) and his brother John married daughters of George Vesey, Mary and Ann, respectively. Aaron, one of the six children of Lazarus and Mary, was a grandfather of John Taylor the author. Aaron died in Wicomico Parish in 1746, having willed his real estate to his son William. He gave his remaining slave, James, to Joseph, his son who would in time befriend John Taylor the author. Between his daughter Elizabeth and his son Lazarus (the father of John the author), Aaron's moveable property was to be equally divided.[6]

Aaron's brother Argyle executed this estate. Its debts totaled £82.7.5 in coin and tobacco. These expenses included shoemaking, rum for the funeral, the burial, clothing for the slave, cider, brandy, the stripping of tobacco, its drayage to a warehouse, and the purchase of four crops of the weed. The assets came to £82.4.8 and included sums owed by four debtors, income from a vendue, and the hire of the slave for one year. These assets, reported to the Northumberland County Court on 9 March 1752, amounted to a few coins less than the enumerated debts. Unless some hidden property figured in the settlement of their father's estate, Lazarus and Elizabeth received little or no patrimony.[7]

Aaron Taylor had perhaps distributed the bulk of his personalty among his children following the death of his wife, Betty Wilde. The inventory of his estate includes no furniture except three "old" beds. There are many small items, such as glass bottles, candlesticks, and pieces of earthenware and ironware. Equipment for a militiaman—three guns, a case of pistols, a sword, and fourteen pounds of shot—is listed. A supply of new feathers, cotton, and wool was found by appraisers.[8] Little wonder that Aaron directed that no appraisal be made. There was not much to record.

[5]Letters, Carolyn H. Jett, Heathsville VA, 19 Oct 1990, 21 Jan 1991, to Chester R. Young, Williamsburg KY; Dorothy Brown Thompson, "Ancestors and Descendants of the Rev. John Taylor (1752–1835)," *Register of the Kentucky Historical Society* 47 (Jan 1949): 22-23, 24-25; and Mrs. L. C. Anderson, "The Taylor Family of Northumberland and Lancaster Counties, Virginia," *Virginia Magazine of History and Biography* 35 (Apr 1927): 212, 213.

[6]Northumberland County (VA) Record Book, 1743–1749 (Office of the County Clerk, Heathsville) 167-A; and Anderson, "Taylor Family," 214.

[7]Northumberland County (VA) Record Book, 1747–1749 (Office of the County Clerk, Heathsville) 16, 96-98.

[8]Ibid., 16.

Lazarus Taylor (born 1718) had left Northumberland County for the frontier before 1746, the year his father died. He was residing in Prince William County as early as January 1744/5. In February two years later he purchased 149 acres on the waters of Marrs Run, a tributary of the Rappahannock River. In another two years Lazarus married Hannah Bradford, a daughter of John Bradford and Mary Marr Kingcart, a widow, both of Prince William County. In time Lazarus' brother William would marry a second daughter of this family, Sarah Bradford.[9]

John Bradford, a grandfather of John Taylor the author, had married the widow Kingcart about 1717. In March 1722/3 they were living in King George County on a fifteen-acre farm on the southeastern side of Marrs Run. Bradford's wife was a daughter of John Marr and the widow Elizabeth Fishback Rector. Marr, a French immigrant, had settled in Lancaster County by 1695. Five years later he was residing in the part of Stafford County that eventually became Prince William County.[10]

Several members of the Bradford family left the East and settled in Kentucky. Prominent among them was John Bradford (1747–1830), who cast his lot in Lexington, where on 11 August 1787 he established the *Kentucky Gazette*, the first newspaper in the Bluegrass. This printer was a grandson of John Bradford of King George County and a first cousin of John Taylor the author.[11]

## Childhood

In 1750 Lazarus and Hannah Taylor began their family, which in time would include six boys and three girls. At least three—maybe six—of these children were born in Prince William County. When John was born in 1752, a brother and a sister had already taken their places in the household.[12]

Lazarus and Hannah were convinced of the orthodoxy of Anglicanism, the state religion in colonial Virginia. Their home in Prince William County was perhaps located in Hamilton Parish. While a young child, John was christened

---

[9][Martha W.] Hiden, "The Bradford Family of Fauquier County, Virginia," *Tyler's Quarterly Historical and Genealogical Magazine* 27 (Oct. 1945): 136; and Northern Neck Proprietary (VA) Land Grant Book F (Virginia State Library and Archives, Richmond) 264; Dorothy Thompson, "Ancestors and Descendants," 28.

[10]Hiden, "Bradford Family," 115; M[artha] W. Hiden, "John Marr of Stafford Co[unty], Virginia]," *Tyler's Quarterly Historical and Genealogical Magazine* 26 (Apr 1945): 286-87.

[11]Hiden, "Bradford Family," 117, 118, 122, 123, 130, 132, 136, 137; Herndon J. Evans, *The Newspaper Press in Kentucky* (Lexington KY, 1976) 2.

[12]Hiden, "Bradford Family," 136; Dorothy Thompson, "Ancestors and Descendants," 29-30.

in the Church of England, so his parents would tell him later. As a boy, he was taught the "rules" found in the Book of Common Prayer, and thus he developed his "partialities" in "that way." Even so, there may have been no Anglican church or chapel on Marrs Run, "in the backwoods of Virginia where Indians often killed people not far from where I was." [13]

John's schooling, which was meager at best, was received during childhood. Later he would recall the time when he had been "a school boy" and had engaged in his share of "foolish fights" among his peers.[14] One of his coadjutors in Kentucky would record that Taylor's "early education" had been "much neglected." [15]

The region where the Taylors lived fell into Fauquier County, when in the spring of 1759 it was formed out of the upper part of Prince William County.[16] Five years later Lazarus and his growing family moved to the western side of the Blue Ridge Mountains, which separate the Piedmont from the Great Valley of Virginia.[17] He had chosen a site on a branch of Happy Creek, a tributary of the Shenandoah River, in the southeastern part of Frederick County. Safety in the Great Valley had been enhanced by the ending of the French and Indian War, in 1763.

Imagine the wonder that must have flooded the mind of John Taylor, now twelve years old but short in stature for his age, as he accompanied his parents, his older brother, Argyle, and his sister, Leanna,[18] on their trek out of Fauquier County and into the Shenandoah Valley, maybe going over Manassas Gap. Riding through that gap in 1764 was not as awesome as would be a trip by way of Cumberland Gap into Kentucky that John would make in the next decade. Even so, it was the lad's earliest venture into the alluring Appalachian Mountains, beyond which he was destined to act out the scenes of his manhood.

Not many miles from where the Taylors settled on the western slope of the Blue Ridge, there was a small village called "Helltown."[19] It was situated on the

[13]John Taylor, *History of Clear Creek Church; and Campbellism Exposed* (Frankfort KY, 1830) 44.

[14]J[ohn] Taylor, "Try the Spirits," *Baptist Chronicle and Literary Register* 1 (July 1830): 101.

[15]James E[ly] Welch, "John Taylor, 1772–1833 [*sic*]," *Annals of the American Pulpit*, ed. William B. Sprague, 9 vols. (New York, 1858-69; reprint ed., New York, 1969) 6:152.

[16]William Waller Hening, ed., *The Statutes at Large; Being a Collection of All the Laws of Virginia*, 13 vols. (Richmond VA, 1809-23; reprint ed., Charlottesville VA, 1969) 7:311.

[17]Letter, John Taylor to [Starke Dupuy], "The Rev. John Taylor's [Religious] Experience," *Kentucky Missionary and Theological Magazine* 1 (May 1812): 33.

[18]The birth dates of the other six children in the family have not come down to us.

[19]"John Taylor's [Religious] Experience," 33.

South Fork of the Shenandoah immediately above its juncture with the North Fork. The growth of this roistering community had come in part from locating a ferry over the river in 1738 at a site between its forks and the mouth of Happy Creek.[20] Helltown had developed into an important port for commerce by land and by water. Here produce from the field and furs from the forest were brought by pack train and by wagon to be loaded onto river craft for the voyage downstream to Harpers Ferry or elsewhere on the Potomac. Along the opposite route, manufactured goods were carried to Helltown for distribution within the Great Valley. The converging of boisterous river men and pack-train drivers at this place of transfer resulted in prosperity for the tippling houses and the brothels that sprang up on the waterfront. Heavy drinking, fighting, and other rowdy conduct were the activities of men who tarried in Helltown.[21] Here was the place in the backwoods near where John Taylor grew to adulthood and "where the settlers were chiefly like savages."[22]

Evidently when the Taylors arrived on Happy Creek, the community at the Forks of the Shenandoah bore two names. It was also called Lehewtown in honor of Peter Lehew, who ten years earlier had acquired two hundred acres that included the village. This Peter may not have been the same Peter Lehew who married Leanna, the eldest sister of John Taylor. When the town was incorporated in 1788 it was renamed Front Royal.[23] Today it retains this name and serves as the seat of Warren County.

When John was growing up on Happy Creek, his father required the household on Sundays to recite "a little church service" taken from the Book of Common Prayer. The rest of the day was generally given over to sports and gambling. "Other times were spent in what I call blackguard frolics," John would later record. On the creek, education and public worship were almost entire strangers.[24]

Even though the first grants of land in the Great Valley of Virginia (made in 1728) were located on Happy Creek,[25] the development of that community seems to have come on leaden feet. It may have taken Lazarus Taylor some years to accumulate the funds for the purchase of the Happy Creek land on which the family had settled in 1764. However that may be, he finally received from the

---

[20]Hening, *Statutes*, 4:531.
[21]Alvin R. L. Dohme, *Shenandoah: The Valley Story* (Washington, D.C., 1972) 25-26, 62; and Raus McDill Hanson, *Virginia Place Names* (Verona VA, 1969) 206.
[22]"John Taylor's [Religious] Experience," 33.
[23]Dorothy Thompson, "Ancestors and Descendants," 30; and Hening, *Statutes*, 12:672-73.
[24]"John Taylor's [Religious] Experience," 33.
[25]Richard L. Morton, *Colonial Virginia*, 2 vols. (Chapel Hill NC, 1960) 2:541.

Northern Neck Proprietary in 1770 title to 316 acres near the Blue Ridge.[26] This tract adjoined the Manor of Leeds, a vast estate of over 152,000 acres in Frederick, Fauquier, and Culpeper counties that Thomas Lord Fairfax had set aside as a feudal district.[27]

Nine years later Lazarus acquired another tract from the Northern Neck. This purchase consisted of 346 acres. The Manor of Leeds bordered this land also. Argyle Taylor, John's eldest brother, owned land on the southern edge of this acreage, which likewise was situated on Happy Creek.[28]

In most of Virginia, slavery generally went hand in hand with the ownership of land. John Taylor had become acquainted with black bondage at a young age. One of his early memories of slavery was the arrival at his father's house in Fauquier County in 1760 of the Negro woman Nan. She had been bequeathed to John's mother by her father, John Bradford, who had recently died.[29] John Taylor was then seven years old. He doubtless remembered other slaves willed by Grandfather Bradford, especially those left to his grandmother. (By the time of her death twenty-three years later, these slaves had increased to seven in number —the man Peter, the woman Lucy, and five children.)[30] Closer to home was John's acquaintance with two slaves owned by his father in 1767. They were named Moses, aged thirty-three years, and Judith, aged twenty-eight years. Lazarus mortgaged these two blacks that year as security for a debt of eight pounds sterling.[31] Here were a number of Africans who undoubtedly shaped this teenager's view of slavery—the basis of an economy that would provide John Taylor with untold financial benefits in years to come.

Although as a lad John had become familiar with the peculiar institution of slavery, introduction to an equally strange way of life awaited him. Evangelical Calvinism was making itself heard west of the Blue Ridge. The gospel of salvation was being sounded in the Great Valley by Separate Baptist preachers. And what unusual voices they were that trumpeted this good news. Most were

---

[26]Northern Neck Proprietary (VA) Land Grant Book O (Virginia State Library and Archives, Richmond) 321. Lazarus Taylor still owned a part of this land in 1805, when he sold twenty-six acres of it to a neighbor. Shenandoah County (VA) Deed Book O (Office of the County Clerk, Woodstock) 301-302.

[27]Gertrude E. Gray, comp., *Virginia Northern Neck Land Grants*, 2 vols. (Baltimore MD, 1988) 1:122; and Samuel Kercheval, *A History of the Valley of Virginia*, 4th ed. (Strasburg VA, 1925) 155n.

[28]Northern Neck Proprietary (VA) Land Grant Book R (Virginia State Library and Archives, Richmond) 297.

[29]Fauquier County (VA) Will Book 1 (Office of the County Clerk, Warrenton) 17.

[30]Fauquier County (VA) Will Book 2 (Office of the County Clerk, Warrenton) 1.

[31]Frederick County (VA) Deed Book 11 (Typescript, Office of the County Clerk, Winchester) 526-27.

melodic though sturdy, well-calculated to fetch tears from the eyes and to impress the heart. These voices could agitate the body and shake the nervous system.[32]

Virginia Separate Baptist preachers—New Lights they were called in derision —had been influenced by Shubal Stearns, of North Carolina. He had withdrawn from the fellowship of a Puritan church in Connecticut and had brought southward in his intellectual baggage elements of evangelicalism from the Great Awakening and Puritan aspects of polity and theology that would affect religion in the South for generations to come.

Fourteen years had passed since Stearns and his group pitched their tents on Sandy Creek on the North Carolina frontier. During that period newly converted Separate Baptists had advanced from Carolina into the Old Dominion, boldly proclaiming the gospel of grace to all who would listen. One convert among several hundred in Virginia was William Marshall of Fauquier County, who became a preacher in 1768. He itinerated into Frederick County, where he presented a striking appearance. He stood tall and well-favored. His movements were graceful and winsome; his eyes, dark and piercing.[33]

## Conversion

The time was perhaps the late fall of 1769 when John Taylor, having turned seventeen, first heard a sermon. Lazarus Taylor did not want his son to attend meetings at which New Lights preached, because he thought that they deceived the people. But boy that he was, John stole away to hear William Marshall. When he arrived at the site of the service the sermon was almost finished. John, however, reasoned that what little he had listened to was "the greatest bundle of foolishness I ever heard on any subject; and [I] intended never to hear any more of it."[34]

Such meetings continued throughout the rest of the autumn and into the winter. Reports circulated on Happy Creek that people were much exercised, that some fell down and shouted and cried. John was determined to go again for the sport of it. The preaching took place in the yard of an abandoned Anglican chapel about two miles southwest of Helltown. Winter had brought snow to the

---

[32]Morgan Edwards, *Materials towards a History of the Baptists*, 2 vols. (Danielsville GA, 1984) 2:93.

[33]W. M. Paxton, *The Marshall Family* (Cincinnati OH, 1885) 32.

[34]"John Taylor's [Religious] Experience," 33.

ground, and the people stood to hear William Marshall, who mounted an oak stump near a corner of the log meetinghouse.[35]

John attended the service that cold day and maybe had come with his friend Thomas Buck, who was four years his junior. John was disappointed because no one wept when Marshall began to preach. The first to respond was a Negro who cried out "in a doleful manner." John then wound his way through the crowd in order to watch and hear the black man. Others also reacted to the sermon. It was not until Thomas, who then stood at John's elbow, burst into tears and called for mercy that John began to listen to the preacher. The verses he quoted come from Revelation 6:16-17 and begin, "Oh rocks, fall on me." Like a dagger these words pierced the heart of John. He kept his feet and shed no tears, but he had been awakened.[36] Here was the beginning of some twenty-seven months during which he experienced a convincing travail that kept him keenly conscious of sin and guilt.

That day in the snow, maybe early in March 1770, John developed a strong attachment to Christian people. Even so, he continued to practice vice with his comrades for more than a year. He did so because he wanted to be accepted by them and he wanted to hide the anxiety of his soul. During the following spring or summer he attended the baptizing of the fifty-three converts who constituted the Lower South River Church. The number included his friend Thomas Buck.

Around May 1771 John began to forsake his companions in sin, to keep to himself, to read a good deal, and to pray at times. He thought that he would get to Heaven by doing good. He kept this course until about October, when Joseph Redding was converted and began to preach in the community. The Reddings were neighbors to the Taylors, and Joseph was only two years older than John. Redding's preaching showed John the difference between practical vices or sins of the flesh, on one hand, and sins of the spirit, on the other.[37]

For six months, beginning with November 1771, John's conviction of sin followed a higher level of intensity. The terrors of the law set in. John experienced exceeding anxiety, travail, and horror. His food was not tasty; he did not have a night of quiet sleep. For half of this period he labored under the mis-

---

[35]Ibid. The fact that a Baptist church was not constituted at this place until the following spring or summer lends credibility to the conclusion of J. L. Dickinson, of Front Royal, that the chapel had been erected by Anglicans. John Oliver, Jr., *The Treasure—The Earthen Vessels: A History of First Baptist Church, Front Royal, Virginia, 1839–1989* ([Front Royal VA], 1990) 18.

[36]"John Taylor's [Religious] Experience," 33.

[37]Ibid., 33-34.

guided impression that his day of grace had passed. He thought at times that he was worse than the Devil because of his unbelief.[38]

For John the terrors were horrific thoughts and agitations of the mind. God had always justly hated him, he maintained. It would be better for him to be in Hell now, because the longer he lived on earth the greater would be the store of wrath that God was accumulating against him. John later wrote that a "black destiny seemed to hover over my trembling soul." When he prayed, and he often did, he would not ask for mercy but would acknowledge that God's damnation of him was just. The thought struck him that God could not save him according to His justice and holiness and truth, and that no one ever realized this fact until just before he dropped into Hell. In that moment "a trembling desperation" laid hold of this nineteen-year-old boy, who thought that he would die immediately.[39] He had experienced total collapse.

For New Light preachers the length of the interval between the onset of conviction and the moment of conversion was of great significance. The intervening period of anxiety produced a breakdown and a valuable therapy that augured well for permanent transformation. Two months of travail, Separate Baptists calculated, produced the most favorable and lasting changes.[40] Over a century later William James, the pioneer psychologist of religion, would argue that "all the more striking instances of conversion . . . *have* been permanent."[41]

Relief and release for John Taylor came in the mountains. Near sunset on a spring day in 1772 he left his father's house for an uninhabited mountain two miles away. There he "intended to spend the little balance of my wretched life . . . expecting never to see the face of man again, nor the light of another day." But there he had what he called his "Hanging Rock experience." At a lofty formation he knelt to whisper the strange prayer that God's throne would become holy when he (John) was damned. At that point he suddenly acknowledged, "There is a Lord Jesus Christ able to save." It was then that the first ray of salvation beamed upon his benighted soul. It appeared to John that, through Christ, God had become reconciled to him.[42]

Within days John Taylor obtained a hope of his salvation. After the encounter at the Hanging Rock, he went to church on Saturday 2 May. It was his first time to attend a church service held in a Baptist meetinghouse. He also

---

[38]Ibid., 34.

[39]Ibid.

[40]Cedric B. Cowing, *The Great Awakening and the American Revolution: Colonial Thought in the Eighteenth Century* (Chicago IL, 1971) 71.

[41]*The Varieties of Religious Experience: A Study in Human Nature*, Modern Library ed. (New York NY, n.d.) 252.

[42]"John Taylor's [Religious] Experience," 34.

witnessed the baptism of eight converts the next day. On Monday morning he
went home and there experienced for the first time the sweet bliss of forgiveness
and grace. He was baptized thirteen days later by James Ireland, and he became
a member of the Lower South River Church—the first of the ten Baptist
congregations to which he belonged.

What teenage vices had weighed so oppressively on the youthful heart of
John Taylor? He mentions only two sins of the flesh in his writings—fighting
and gambling.[43] There were other such sins occasioned by the violence of the
frontier, by the immorality of the village nearest his home, and by the example
his father set. Then there were sins of the spirit, the most grievous of which was
unbelief. To be sure, the young man could enumerate both types of sins—vexing
his soul and mind and erecting a barrier between God and him.

In their preaching, Separate Baptist ministers in Virginia set forth a code of
conduct that disapproved of fisticuffing, card playing, horse racing, cockfighting,
gambling, drunkenness, slandering, quarreling, and dancing. Their designation of
such practices as sins produced in their listeners a sense of remorse. It has been
argued that the rules of behavior set by evangelicalism in pre-Revolutionary
Virginia were the common people's response to growing public disorder.[44] Be
that as it may, both religious and social factors impinged on the minds of the
unconverted, shaped their views of public and private morality, and moved them
toward conversion.

## Itinerancy on the Frontier

Only five months intervened between the conversion of John and the
beginning of his preaching in the homes of his neighbors. During the winter of
1772–1773 he visited Joseph Redding in South Carolina, whither the latter and
his family had gone in the hope of settling there. Disappointment prevailed, and
all of them returned to Virginia when winter passed.

That spring the Lower South River Church licensed John Taylor to preach
the gospel. He spent most of the next ten years laboring as an evangelist in the
backwoods of the Old Dominion. His tours took him onto the tributaries of the
Potomac and the Ohio rivers. Most of his trips were carried out on horseback but
a number were done on foot. Sometimes a fellow preacher—for example, Joseph
Redding—accompanied him, sometimes he traveled alone. As it turned out,
Taylor's going beyond the Great Valley put him out of harm's way from the

---

[43]Ibid., 33; J[ohn]Taylor, "Try the Spirits," 101.

[44]Rhys Issac, *The Transformation of Virginia, 1740–1790* (Williamsburg VA, 1982)
168-69.

religious persecution that was waged so vigorously against the Separates in the Piedmont and the Tidewater. Even though he was never imprisoned, at times in the mountains he was beaten and driven from his meeting place "by wicked mobs."[45]

Thus Taylor escaped the strictness of the civil law that was meted out to numbers of Separate Baptist preachers, only to run headlong into other dangers —problems related to mountain travel over unmarked paths and through sparsely populated regions; risks created by the Revolutionary War, including the likelihood of being scalped by Indians; and natural perils like floods, snow, and freezing weather.[46] His missionary travel and travail are suggested in a contemporary song:

> In these mountains let me labor.
> In these forests let me tell
> How He died, the blessed Saviour,
> To redeem a world from Hell.[47]

In the midst of such work the Lunies Creek Church sanctioned the ordination of Taylor to the ministry of an itinerant. He had moved his membership to this new congregation in Hampshire County shortly before. According to the Separate pattern, the ordaining ceremony was conducted by a council of ministers. They assembled at the Lower South River Church in 1776, possibly in October.

Baptists of Taylor's day were divided over what constituted a divine call to preach. Some looked for extraordinary visions or listened for miraculous voices.[48] Some, including Taylor, needed only the consent of a local congregation. He reasoned that when converted "every man receives a spirit of preaching, and if he has a talent thereto (which is only known by the voice of the good people), he need not doubt his call to the ministry." [49]

The payment of a preacher for his work was another question debated by eighteenth-century Baptists. In spite of their poverty the Appalachian people occasionally made Taylor "some little presents of the best they had, that I thought in my conscience was more than my poor preaching deserved, which perhaps never amounted to fifty dollars per year, exclusive of the food myself and

[45]John Taylor, *Thoughts on Missions*, 72-page ed. ([Frankfort KY], 1820) 27.
[46]Ibid., 27, 28.
[47]James Barrett Taylor, *Lives of Virginia Baptist Ministers*, 1st ed. (Richmond VA, 1837) 196.
[48]John Augustus Williams, *Life of Elder John Smith with Some Account of the Rise and Progress of the Current Reformation* (Cincinnati OH, 1870) 82.
[49]John Taylor, *Thoughts on Missions*, 44.

horse lived on."[50] Taylor generally opposed being paid for his preaching. In his early years, however, his own penury obligated him to accept the people's beneficence.

## Relationship to Father Substitutes

John's success in the mountains and his desire to visit a bachelor uncle, Joseph Taylor, impelled him to go over the Blue Ridge and into the Lower Northern Neck. In Northumberland County he met Uncle Joseph, whom he had not seen since his childhood. These two kinsmen soon became fast friends because they spoke the same language of religion. This visit by John to the county of his ancestors may have occurred in the summer of 1777. At any rate, 1779 found him in that region, and on 28 July he preached at the home of a Mrs. Lyne in Westmoreland County. His sermon dealt with the kingdom of God; Matthew 3:33 was the text. Richard Dozier, who heard him preach and who was the overseer on a nearby plantation, recorded that "the young man spake very well."[51]

During the following winter, which was known in North America as the "Hard Winter" of 1779–1780, John was introduced to the fertile lands of the Bluegrass under the most adverse conditions of weather. He and his preaching colleague Joseph Redding planned to settle in the West. Taylor traveled to Kentucky by way of Cumberland Gap. Redding, his family, and several members of the Lunies Creek Church went via the Ohio River.[52] For the most part John and Joseph intended to explore rather than to preach. The few Baptists whom they met lived under very disagreeable circumstances and faced hazards on every hand.[53] The freezing weather and the distress of the settlers in Kentucky resulted in "no opening for preaching."[54] Thus disappointed, the two preachers returned to their homes in the Great Valley.

Taylor was soon in the saddle again, and by May 1780 he was visiting in Westmoreland County once more. He went to see Robert Carter III, the most prosperous planter in the region. John preached on the twentieth to about three hundred people at Aries, one of Carter's plantations. The text of the address

---

[50]Ibid., 28.

[51]Richard Dozier, "Historical Notes Concerning the Planting of Baptist Principles in the Northern Neck of Virginia: Text Book from 1771," *Virginia Baptist* Register 28 (1989): 1397. See also Robert Carter III, Day Book 13 (Duke University Library, Durham NC) 197.

[52]John Taylor, *Thoughts on Missions*, 51-52.

[53]David Benedict, *A General History of the Baptist Denomination in America and Other Parts of the World*, 2 vols. (Boston, 1813; reprint ed., Gallatin TN, 1985) 2:228.

[54]John Taylor, *Thoughts on Missions*, 52.

came from Revelation 14:4. One listener wrote that he wanted never to forget that sermon. Eight days later Taylor, who was still in the neighborhood, preached to about five hundred at Nomony Hall. Maybe they congregated in the yard of this stately manor house of Carter. The sermon, which was derived from Jeremiah 15:19, caused the audience to be exercised, and many people cried out.[55] Taylor's reputation as a preacher who had ventured as far west as Kentucky helped to account for the presence of these large audiences in May.

On the eighteenth of the following November, John again preached at Nomony Hall, this time in its ballroom. His sermon was based on Malachi 4:2. One of Carter's overseers exuded gratitude: "O that I may ever remember that sweet sermon." That night at Aries, John preached about the kingdom of Heaven.[56] His next recorded sermon in the Northern Neck, which came from Hebrews 12:1, was delivered at Aries fourteen months later.[57]

## Marriage

In September 1782 John Taylor was married in Orange County. His bride was destined to follow him through many removals on the Kentucky frontier, to bear his children, and to serve as a dutiful minister's wife. Her name was Elizabeth Kavanaugh, commonly called "Betsy." She was born on 18 June 1761. Being twenty-one years old, she wrote her own consent when application was made for a marriage license. Her father, Philemon Kavanaugh, had died when Betsy was three years of age. Her mother, Nancy Cave Kavanaugh, as a widow of three years, took part in the organization of the Upper Spotsylvania Church, which was headed by Lewis Craig. In 1775 Nancy became the second wife of William Strother of Orange County. Thus, as a fourteen-year-old, Betsy had acquired a step-father.[58]

The first wife of William Strother had also been a widow. She was Sarah Bayly Pannill. By her marriage to Strother she mothered three children, the youngest of whom was named Sarah. In time both Sarah Strother and Elizabeth Kavanaugh—step-sisters—married Taylors who, however, bore no blood

---

[55]Dozier, "Text Book," 1399.

[56]Ibid., 1400.

[57]Ibid., 1402.

[58]Catherine L. Knorr, *Marriages of Orange County, Virginia, 1747–1810* (Pine Bluff AR) 87; W. W. Scott, "A List of Marriages Recorded in the Back Part of Deed Book No. 17, Orange County," *Virginia Magazine of History and Biography* 26 (Apr 1918): 196; Edwards, *Materials*, 2:57; and Dorothy Thompson, "Ancestors and Descendants," 31–32.

relationship. Sarah married Richard Taylor, and they became the parents of Zachary Taylor, the future president.[59]

Elizabeth Kavanaugh "fell in love with the blessed Jesus, and was baptized" by John Leland during the "Hard Winter" of 1779–1780.[60] Leland became her pastor in the Black Walnut Church in Orange County. He was noted for composing hymns. While a sermon was in progress one wintry day in Louisa County, Leland wrote a song about baptism, the second stanza of which follows:

> Jesus drank the gall for you,
> Bore the Cross for sinners due;
> Children, prove your love to Him,
> Never fear the frozen stream.[61]

A native of Massachusetts, Leland labored in Virginia during most of the Revolution and rendered yeoman service to the cause of religious liberty. Years later, while living in New England, he would recall his baptism of Betsy during the "coldest winter that America has ever known."[62]

A post-wedding tour of preaching carried John Taylor into the lower end of the Northern Neck. There he met with word that Uncle Joseph had recently died at Nomony Hall, where for several years he had been tutoring the children of Robert Carter III. John attended a worship service at the home of Robert Lyne of Richmond County on 11 October. Taylor's bereavement may account for the fact that he only prayed and spoke a few words on that occasion.[63] Three days later Taylor appeared before the Northumberland County Court and presented his uncle's will for probation. John Taylor, Lewis Lunsford, and Alexander Hunton were appointed the executors of the estate.[64]

By his will the bachelor Joseph Taylor made four token bequests, but the lion's share of his estate went to John Taylor.[65] Why was the uncle so munificent toward his preaching nephew? Perhaps other members of the family had resisted

---

[59]William Edward Railey, *History of Woodford County* (Frankfort KY, 1938; reprint ed., Versailles KY, 1968) 144-46; and Dorothy Thompson, "Ancestors and Descendants," 31-32.

[60]Letter, Leland, Cheshire MA, 10 Dec 1830, to John Taylor, *Baptist Chronicle and Literary Register* 2 (Jan 1831): 3.

[61]L. F. Greene, ed., *The Writings of the Late Elder John Leland* (New York NY, 1845; reprint ed., Gallatin TN, 1986) 28.

[62]*Baptist Chronicle and Literary Register* 2 (Jan 1831): 3.

[63]Dozier, "Text Book," 1403.

[64]Will, Joseph Taylor, 27 May 1778, in Northumberland County (VA) Record Book 11 (Office of the County Clerk, Heathsville) 273-74.

[65]Ibid.

Joseph's conversion from Anglicanism to evangelicalism. The adherence of the uncle to the Baptist position had produced a natural liking for his bold and vigorous younger "cousin" that manifested itself in an array of gifts.

John received the 260-acre plantation in Wicomico Parish on which Joseph had maintained his residence. This farm produced corn, cotton, and tobacco; cattle, sheep, and hogs. The eight slaves on the place, the livestock, the crops, and the household furnishings, all became the property of John Taylor.[66]

On 19 October, John was present at a meeting held at the Aries plantation, in Westmoreland County, at which he "spake a word of exhortation."[67]

Perhaps business concerning his newly acquired wealth brought John back into Northumberland County two months later. Nonetheless, on 20 December he attended another meeting at Aries. Being called on to preach, he allegorized his text, Revelation 22:2. The "tree of life" became Christ, and the "leaves of the tree" were the promises of God.[68] To uncover hidden textual meanings was a common way to sermonize in Taylor's day.

John Taylor decided, maybe during this Christmas season, to sell the Northumberland plantation that he had inherited. Lewis Lunsford, a Baptist pastor in that county, was to become the new owner. The price they agreed on was £320. This sum changed hands, and the title was conveyed on 15 July 1783. John's wife was not present in Northumberland to sign the deed. Undergoing the early distresses of her first pregnancy, she chose not to travel to the Lower Northern Neck in order to put her name to this indenture. At her home on Happy Creek in the Fork District of Shenandoah County on 6 August she consented to the transaction.[69]

## Settlement in Kentucky

The compelling reason for the sale of the Joseph Taylor farm was John's decision to move to Kentucky. He planned to depart late in September 1783. What motives impelled a Baptist preacher to leave a wide circle of friendship stretching from the Chesapeake Bay to the Monongahela River and to settle upon the sparsely populated, though fruitful, lands on "the western waters"?[70]

---

[66]Ibid.; Appraisal of Joseph Taylor's Estate, 10 Mar 1783, Northumberland County (VA) Record Book 12 (Office of the County Clerk, Heathsville) 14.

[67]Dozier, "Text Book," 1403.

[68]Ibid., 1404.

[69]Deed, Taylor to Lunsford, 15 July 1783, Northumberland County (VA) Record Book 12, 126-28.

[70]This was a common term for Trans-Appalachia in the eighteenth century.

The need for greater family income headed the list of factors for Taylor's westward propulsion. Here was a motive that drove numbers of Baptist preachers to move from eastern Virginia to the wilds of Kentucky. John considered it his duty "to seek a support in the fertile fields of the West, as, notwithstanding his toils in V[irgini]a, the churches contributed but little to provide for his necessities."[71]

The productive Bluegrass soil enticed many a migrant. Others left the Old Dominion because its agriculture tended to erode the ground. A drought in 1781 had caused many Baptists to seek economic improvement beyond the mountains. The departure late that year of Elder Lewis Craig and his Traveling Church, from Spotsylvania County, constituted the largest organized exodus of Baptists from Virginia to the Bluegrass.[72] On that occasion Elder John Waller composed an eight-stanza, celebratory song. The first two stanzas relate to the drought and the resultant migration:

> Let me sing of my best beloved,
> Whose vineyard a great while most fruitful prov'd
> But lately got blasted and now is earthbound.
> Lord Jesus, do plead for Thy poor cumber'd ground.
>
> Great sorrows of late have fill'd my poor heart,
> To think the dearest of friends soon must part.
> A few left behind, while many will go
> To settle the desert down the Ohio.[73]

For John Taylor the summer of 1783 was a busy season. Against his coming removal he resigned the care of the Lower South River Church, to which he had returned his membership a few years earlier. In August he made his first formal connection with the Regular Baptists by attending the annual meeting of the Ketocton Association, located in northwestern Virginia.

Taylor, together with Lewis Lunsford, John Sutton, and Henry Hagan (all Baptist ministers), appeared at Lunsford's Meetinghouse, in Lancaster County, on Sunday 21 September. About eight hundred people were present. Taylor did

---

[71] James B. Taylor, *Virginia Baptist Ministers*, 1st ed., 196.

[72] George Washington Ranck, *"The Travelling Church": An Account of the Baptist Exodus from Virginia to Kentucky in 1781* . . . (Louisville KY, 1891).

[73] *Desert* here means "an uninhabited, uncultivated land." The hymn is found in *A Sketch of a Journal of the Rev. Joseph Craig in Which Is Contained His Experience, a Sketch of the Gospel Labors* . . . (Lexington KY, 1813) chap. xi.

not preach, but he exhorted this vast audience. The service afforded him an opportunity to bid farewell to his friends of that region.[74]

Taylor and his small family left the Great Valley toward the close of September, going down the Ohio River to the mouth of Beargrass Creek near the Falls. A quick, overland trip brought them to Gilberts Creek and to Lewis Craig's Station, about nine miles from Logan's Fort. Christmas was almost upon them. Three months had passed since they left their Shenandoah home.

The birthing cry of Betsy Taylor's first child announced the arrival of Benjamin on 22 February 1784. It was not many weeks before John Taylor entrusted his wife and infant to two of her uncles and headed eastward to settle certain affairs.

Toward the end of April, Taylor had reached the Lower Northern Neck, and at Nomony Hall on the twenty-second he received from Robert Carter III a sight draft. It directed his agent Lewis Lunsford to pay John £51.4.9¼, the amount due the estate of Joseph Taylor. This payment represented the wages owed the deceased tutor and possibly covered his last school year in the Carter household. For some reason this sight order was not honored by Lunsford, because on 22 May, Carter himself paid Taylor the sum due.[75]

On Sunday 2 May before some six hundred worshipers at Lunsford's Meetinghouse, Taylor preached on the character of those who have partaken of the first resurrection, using Revelation 20:6 as the text. He equated "the conversion of the soul" to the first resurrection. Converts have a part in Christ and are holy and perfect in Him, even though they are sinful in themselves. Those in Christ who murmur show the "deadness, coldness, [and] hardness" of their hearts, but at the same time they give "evidence of their having grace." Taylor quoted David and Peter to show that, when such complaining appears, Christians might "be brought to [commit] sin." Such a circumstance, however, "would cause them to live more careful . . . [for] God would have them to be a holy people and [would] save them though they might doubt it and be afraid of death."

In the audience sat Richard Dozier, that untiring recorder of sermon texts. He saw the presence of Taylor that day as evidence of the goodness of God, who had caused him "to come from Kaintuck here as a messenger to me." Dozier extolled the preaching: "I think I never heard more feelingly my state and condition marked out in all my life, declaring such to be the Christian who had

---

[74]Dozier, "Text Book," 1405.

[75]Sight Draft, Carter, 22 April 1784, and Receipt, Taylor, 22 May 1784, in Dorothy Thompson, "Ancestors and Descendants," 2d unnumbered following 20. These manuscripts are a part of the Robert Carter III Papers, Virginia Baptist Historical Society, Richmond.

such exercise of mind. I thought I could join Simeon of old in saying, 'Now, Lord, lettest Thou Thy servant depart in peace.' "[76]

By the time John Taylor was ready to return to Kentucky, he had collected a party of six to accompany him—his sister Jane, his brother Joseph, John Hand, George McDonald, Abraham Dale, and a Negro woman who may have been his servant Mary (called "Moll"). At Pittsburgh the horses they rode, and perhaps some pack horses as well, were bartered for ironware to be delivered at the Falls of the Ohio. Also at the Forks they secured a pirogue for passage down the river. After fourteen days they arrived at Limestone. Within forty minutes after landing, John Taylor sold the canoe for eight dollars to William Wright, a surveyor who promptly directed his some twelve markers and chain carriers up the Ohio for Pittsburgh.

It appears that the preacher had planned to store in the fort at the mouth of Limestone Creek the eighteen hundred dollars worth of goods that he brought down the river, but Indians had burnt the fortified building and had driven away its occupants. As a result, John hid his property in the woods and with certain members of his party took off for Gilberts Creek in order to fetch his pack horses. They passed David Tanner's Station at the Lower Blue Licks. David was a brother of Elder John Tanner, a friend of John Taylor. David's strongly picketed house enclosed a hilltop of about three-fourths of an acre and guarded his four-kettle salt works, located where the path from Limestone to Lexington crossed the Licking River. His station was within a stone's throw of the salt works.

The Taylor party, on its way to Gilberts Creek, arrived in Lexington on 17 June 1784. Returning to the Ohio, they brought with them four or five pack horses on which to transport John's property that had been cached in the forest near Limestone. They recovered it and loaded the packsaddles of the animals. They headed down the trail toward Lexington. Upon reaching Tanner's Station, they learned that a party of about seven people from Fauquier County had arrived and, being infected with small pox, had not been afforded the safety of the fort. While this Fauquier group camped near the station, Indians attacked them at night and killed all but two. Even these survivors—a brother and a sister—had been tomahawked and scalped. The next morning Tanner allowed them to occupy a corner of his fort.

At David Tanner's Station the Taylor group also met Simon Kenton with a surveying party of thirteen. The two parties felt mutually protected and camped

---

[76]Dozier, "Text Book," 1406–1407. Dozier continued to record sermons in the Northern Neck until his death in 1818, but John Taylor appears no more in his Text Book.

together that night outside the fort. The next day John Taylor carried his goods to Benjamin Craig's Station, located about four miles from Lexington.[77]

Having transported to Kentucky his movable estate, Taylor now returned to Lewis Craig's Station in order to look after his family. It may have been his plan not to remain below the Kentucky River for any length of time, because the lands to the north beckoned him as they had done hundreds of other settlers.

John and Betsy transferred their membership from Virginia to the Gilberts Creek Church, the Traveling Church from Spotsylvania. But already Pastor Lewis Craig and the greater part of the members had removed north of the Kentucky in search of greener pastures. So it was that in July 1784 Taylor followed suit, crossing the river into Fayette County and settling on Clear Creek in an area that in time would become part of Woodford County. His farm was located two miles from John Craig's Station.

Taylor had hardly gotten located in his new surroundings that month, before he and his wife became charter members of the first Baptist church established north of the Kentucky River. It was called the South Elkhorn Church. A meeting was held by appointment on Saturday the last day of July at the home of Lewis Craig, situated where the path between Lexington and Harrodsburg crossed South Elkhorn Creek. The fourteen founding members, counting the Taylors, accepted the Philadelphia Confession of Faith as their doctrinal base.[78]

In the community where John Taylor lived, a revival during the winter of 1784–1785 resulted in the organization of the Clear Creek Church on the eighteenth of the following June. About thirty people became its constituent members, including Taylor and three other ministers.[79]

In an effort to exercise pastoral care for Baptists who lived north of the Kentucky River, a boundary was fixed between the South Elkhorn Church and the new congregation of Clear Creek, creating two "parishes" out of that vast region. Here was a remnant from the days of the Establishment, when every Virginian belonged to a parish and every church extended watchcare over the people within its vicinage. There may have been a number of reasons why such a parish-boundary plan, which was set up by Lewis Craig, William Hickman, George Stovall Smith, William Cave, and others, did not work. But one factor

---

[77]Joseph F. Taylor, Interview by [John D. Shane], Jessamine Co. KY, Draper MSS., 11CC228-29.

[78]S. H. Ford, "Kentucky Baptists," *Christian Repository* 5 (May 1856): 263; Phyllis Sharp Mattingly, *A Brief History of the South Elkhorn Baptist Church Lexington, Kentucky, 1783–1983* (Lexington KY) 54.

[79]Ford, "Kentucky Baptists," *Christian Repository* 5:267; Spencer, *Kentucky Baptists,* 1:59.

alone washed it away—within five years some fourteen Baptist congregations occupied the region north of the Kentucky.[80]

During those five years John Taylor participated with other ministers in the organization of four churches—Great Crossing, Boones Creek, Town Fork, and Forks of Elkhorn—and possibly of others.[81]

The first three churches established above the Kentucky River and two located below it set about to provide the means for corresponding and fellowshiping among themselves. They turned to what they had known in Virginia—the association, through which Baptist congregations cooperated. A convention assembled on 25 June 1785 at the home of Lewis Craig, in order to consider the wisdom of organizing an association. At least twelve preachers, including John Taylor, were present that day. The Philadelphia Confession was adopted as "the rule of our communion." For the time being, this action prevented the participation of Separate Baptists, who were generally opposed to confessions of faith.

Three months later on 30 September and 1 October this union was formally constituted as a Regular Baptist association at John Craig's Station, on Clear Creek. It was named Elkhorn after the stream on which it first met. Taylor again attended and with three fellow ministers represented the Clear Creek Church.[82]

The future prominence of John Taylor in the affairs of the Elkhorn Association was signaled by his election as its moderator in 1786.[83] His deep interest in its activities continued throughout his life and especially during its early years through 1801, the year before which his church affiliation took him into the Salem Association. This union had been founded only a few weeks after the beginning of Elkhorn. During the period 1785–1794 Taylor attended every annual meeting of Elkhorn except the autumn session of 1793. (In 1788, 1789, 1791, and 1793 the Elkhorn Association convened twice a year.)[84]

John Taylor took an active part in the work of the annual meetings of Elkhorn. He preached the introductory sermon in 1790, served on a committee charged to revise a proposed wedding ceremony, and collaborated in writing the

---

[80]Ford, "Kentucky Baptists," *Christian Repository* 5:264, 267; Spencer, *Kentucky Baptists*, 1:211.

[81]Ford, "Kentucky Baptists," *Christian Repository* 5:269; Spencer, *Kentucky Baptists*, 1:85, 115, 127; Ermina Jett Darnell, *Forks of Elkhorn Church* (Louisville KY, 1946; reprint ed., Baltimore, 1980) 19.

[82]Elkhorn Association, "Minutes," in William Warren Sweet, *Religion on the American Frontier*, 4 vols. (Chicago IL, 1931; reprint ed., New York NY, 1964) 1:417-19. Also see Ford, "Kentucky Baptists," *Christian Repository* 5:270-72; Spencer, *Kentucky Baptists*, 2:7-10; Ira [V.] Birdwhistell, *The Baptists of the Bluegrass: A History of the Elkhorn Baptist Association, 1785–1985* ([Lexington KY, 1985]) 20-22.

[83]Elkhorn Association, "Minutes," in Sweet, *American Frontier*, 1:420.

[84]Ibid., 417-66 *passim*.

circular letters in 1788 and 1789 and in arranging the order of business in 1794.[85]

Taylor also accepted the association's assignments that helped to occupy his time between its sessions—to preach at quarterly meetings; to attend "a yearly meeting for preaching and communion" in 1790; to serve on committees that inquired into the distress of the South Elkhorn Church, that helped two factions in the Great Crossing Church to reunite, and that conferred with brethren from the South Kentucky Separate Association regarding the affiliation of the two groups; and to represent Elkhorn at four annual meetings of the Salem Association.[86]

Whether by associational appointment or by local invitation, the tasks he performed took him far afield at times, as when he and Ambrose Dudley rode nearly two hundred miles and on 25 July 1791 constituted a church on the Red River at the mouth of Sulphur Fork. This congregation was located in the Cumberland settlement of Tennessee.[87] Then, there was the time in 1792 when Elkhorn appointed John Taylor and John Gano to visit the Columbia Church, the first congregation planted in Ohio. They did so and ordained a minister there.[88]

More often than not, Taylor's preaching in Baptist homes and churches throughout Kentucky was perhaps done of his own accord. For example, sometime after William Hickman arrived on Gilberts Creek in November 1784, Taylor went down from Clear Creek to visit in that neighborhood. While there Taylor preached in the cabin of one Robertson and used the text "Christ is all, and in all," from Colossians 3:11. Hickman, who was present, wrote: "I fed on the food; it was like the good old Virginia doctrine."[89]

To the slaves, the horses, and the household goods that Taylor brought into Kentucky, he soon added sizable holdings of realty. From the time he moved onto Clear Creek, in 1784, until he left for Campbell County, in April 1795, he bought some 3,300 acres located on Clear, Gum, and North Elkhorn creeks, and at the Forks of Elkhorn. About 1,550 of these acres were situated on Clear Creek.[90]

---

[85]Ibid., 420-65 *passim.*

[86]Ibid., 419-66 *passim.*

[87]Ibid., 442; Red River Church, Adams, Tenn., Minute Book, 1791–1826 (MF., Southern Baptist Historical Society, Nashville TN) 1; Benedict, *Baptist Denomination,* 2:220.

[88]Elkhorn Association, "Minutes," in Sweet, *American Frontier,* 1:451; Spencer, *Kentucky Baptists,* 1:570.

[89]William Hickman, *A Short Account of My Life and Travels* (n.p., 1828) 22. This page number is from the pagination of a typed copy of this work in the Kentucky Historical Society Library, Frankfort.

[90]Fayette County (KY) Burnt Record Book 5 (Office of the County Clerk, Lexington) 281-82; Fayette (KY) Circuit Court Deed Book B, 297-98; Woodford County (KY) Deed

A community soon developed at the place on Clear Creek where John Taylor settled. Among neighbors whose lands adjoined his were John Craig, John Arnold, Abraham Dale, Samuel Dedman, and William Powell. In September 1788 Taylor, these close residents, and other citizens petitioned the Virginia legislature to divide Fayette County and to form a new county that would include the area where they lived. They wanted this new jurisdiction in order to lower the costs of litigation, to speed the process of justice, and to enable the militia to pursue marauding Indians with greater vigor.[91] That fall the General Assembly responded by authorizing the creation of Woodford County out of western Fayette during the following May.[92] The church at Clear Creek became a vital part of the neighborhood that grew up on both sides of the stream. John Taylor was elected by the congregation in March 1786 as its "particular" pastor, and a log meetinghouse was constructed that year. When Taylor relinquished the pastorate three years later this four-year-old church numbered 294 members.[93]

By the fall of 1788 Taylor had erected on his Clear Creek farm a two-story log house with several rooms on the first floor. His family was growing, even though his sister Jane, having married Jechonias Singleton, had moved to her own home. Joseph, the Taylors' second son, was born on 17 August 1786. Betsy birthed her first daughter, Nancy, on 14 December 1788. One other child, Polly, would be born in Woodford County, on 17 June 1792.[94]

Discontented with the land he owned in Woodford and plagued with a landed dispute at the Clear Creek Church, John Taylor set his heart on a choice piece of realty on the Ohio River in what was then Campbell (soon to be Boone) County. John's brother Joseph had heard about this land from David Jones, a Baptist chaplain in the standing army. John David Woolper was granted this tract

Book A, 43-45; Deed Book B, 122-23, 400-402; Deed Book C-1, 21-22, 232-34; Deed Book E, 86-87, 342-44; Deed Book H, 487-88; Deed Book M, 371. (These Woodford County records are located in the Office of the County Clerk, in Versailles.) On the night of 31 January 1803 the courthouse of Fayette County was destroyed by fire. The records that were saved were copied into a number of volumes. Lewis Collins, *History of Kentucky*, 2 vols., rev. ed. (Covington KY, 1874; reprint ed., Berea KY, 1976) 2:173. Among these "burnt" documents only one deed to John Taylor survived. He may have purchased other lands, the deeds for which were destroyed.

[91]James Rood Robertson, *Petitions of the Early Inhabitants of Kentucky to the General Assembly of Virginia, 1769–1792*. (Louisville KY, 1914; reprint ed., New York NY, 1971) 114-16.

[92]Hening, *Statutes*, 12:663-64.

[93]Elkhorn Association, "Minutes," in Sweet, *American Frontier*, 1:431.

[94]Dorothy Brown Thompson, "John Taylor and the Day of Controversy," *Register of the Kentucky Historical Society* 53 (July 1955): 231, and "Ancestors and Descendants," 36, 37.

of two thousand acres in October 1788. He had been a sergeant in George Washington's First Virginia Regiment during the French and Indian War and later had become a lieutenant. Off and on Woolper had traveled on the frontier in search of ideal land. His tract on the Ohio had been surveyed in June 1775 by James Douglas, a deputy surveyor of Fincastle County. It began at the mouth of Woolper Creek and extended up the Ohio 4 1/8 miles to the mouth of Schranch (now Taylor) Creek, following an almost perfect ninety-degree bend in the river.[95]

## Life on the Ohio

For the purpose of buying Woolper's land, John Taylor formed an equal partnership with Elder John Tanner, who then lived at Boonesborough. It was a long, dangerous journey by horseback from the Bluegrass to Philadelphia, where Woolper lived; even so, Taylor took with him in old saddlebags £750 in gold and silver coins—the price agreed on for the acreage—and made the trip with safety. He left home around the middle of March 1791, reaching the City of Brotherly Love just as Woolper himself was preparing to leave town. On 12 April, Taylor and Woolper met at the city hall, where this landed transaction was closed, presided over by Mayor John Barclay, acting as a notary. The coins and the deed were exchanged, and now Taylor had at his disposal a large tract of frontier, riverfront land.[96]

During the years when John Taylor lived on Clear Creek, he disposed of his realty in that neighborhood piece by piece until only four hundred acres remained by the time he removed to the Ohio River. Some of this land had risen considerably in value. For example, he sold a tract for forty pounds per hundred acres for which he had paid only ten pounds per hundred.[97] The income acquired from the sale of his Clear Creek lands may have been invested in the Ohio acreage as well as in additional livestock. During 1787–1794 his herd of cattle

[95]Douglas Southall Freeman, *George Washington: A Biography*, 5 vols. (New York NY, 1948–1952) 3:408; Joseph F. Taylor, Interview by [Shane], Draper MSS., 11CC230; Military Warrant, Dunmore to Woolper, 4 Mar. 1774; Survey 6300, James Douglas, June 1775; Virginia Land Grant Book 15, 128. (These last three documents are housed in the Office of the Secretary of State, Frankfort, Kentucky.)

[96]Joseph F. Taylor, Interview by [Shane], Draper MSS., 11CC230; Woodford County (KY) Deed Book A, 259-62.

[97]Woodford County (KY) Deed Book B, 400-402; Deed Book M, 371; Woodford County (KY) Tax Lists, 1792 (MF., Kentucky Historical Society, Frankfort).

increased from nineteen to fifty, his herd of horses from six to ten. The slaves he owned grew in number from four to five during that period.[98]

In addition to the Woolper land, Taylor and Tanner around 1790 had bought from James Garrard part of a thousand acres adjacent to the Woolper grant. Known as the preemption of William Holliday, this land had been surveyed for him in 1785. Eight years earlier he had made some minor improvements on it. In 1785 Holliday assigned part of his interest in this acreage to Garrard; later the balance went to Philemon Thomas.[99] Tanner and Taylor knew that the Holliday land was overlapped by the prior claim of John David Woolper; even so, they had bought Garrard's equity in the preemption in order to eliminate the likelihood of lawsuits.[100]

In view of the fact that Woolper deeded his Kentucky land to Taylor alone, all the transactions of John Tanner regarding it went through Taylor's hands. Tanner's half of the Woolper tract was located in the upper portion of the acreage, while Taylor's lay down the river, both fronting on the stream. Tanner settled on the Ohio some five years before Taylor did. There Tanner established a station that bore his name and that was situated on the site of present-day Petersburg, in Boone County.[101]

When Taylor settled in northern Kentucky, he first lived on the bank of the Ohio about a mile below the mouth of the Great Miami River as this debouchment was then situated. He built his house on a mound that may have been located at the outlet of Schranch Creek and on the lower side of that stream. Today at that site is to be found an elevated tract some 130 feet above the river. It is about 1,000 feet long and averages about 200 feet wide. The site of his home was located across the river from present-day Lawrenceburg, Indiana.[102] Later the preacher settled in the upper end of Woolper Bottom.

By 1794 Tanner had sold 800 acres of his equity in the Woolper land. In 1798 Taylor, as the agent for the partnership, transferred the tax obligations on 1,955 acres of the Woolper and Holliday grants to six persons; these areas ranged

---

[98]Fayette County (VA) Tax Lists, 1787 (MF., Kentucky Historical Society, Frankfort); Woodford County (KY) Tax Lists, 1794 (MF., Kentucky Historical Society, Frankfort).

[99]"Certificate Book of the Virginia Land Commission, 1779-80," *Register of the Kentucky Historical Society* 21 (Sept 1923): 225; Joan E. Brookes-Smith, comp., *Master Index: Virginia Surveys and Grants, 1774-1791* (Frankfort KY, 1976) 95; Boone County (KY) Deed Book B (Office of the County Clerk, Burlington) 285-87; Joseph F. Taylor, Interview by [Shane], Draper MSS., llCC230.

[100]Boone County (KY) Deed Book B, 285-87, 464.

[101]Collins, *Kentucky*, rev. ed., 2:54.

[102]Joseph F. Taylor, Interview by [Shane], Draper MSS., llCC230.

from 100 to 850 acres.[103] By the following year Taylor's real estate in Boone County measured only 400 acres. The remaining portions of the Woolper and Holliday lands were held by fifteen or more assignees to whom Taylor would give deeds over the next two decades.[104] For each transaction the owner gave the purchaser a bill of sale or entered into a bond guaranteeing the delivery of a warranty deed. Payments made on the land were recorded privately, but the formal transfer of title by a deed awaited the buyer's full payment of the purchase price.

From all indications these two Baptist preachers carried on their landed partnership in an amicable way, from around 1790 until the death of Tanner, in 1812. Their compatibility was in stark contrast to the ways of many speculators in land whose complicated deals were spread across the dockets of the state's circuit courts for decades on end.

When the Taylor family moved in 1795 from Clear Creek to the North Bend area on the Ohio River, it numbered, besides John and Betsy, two sons and two daughters. During the seven years in Boone County, three children—Jane, John Wickliffe, and Cave—were born.[105] The number of slaves increased from five in 1794 to fifteen in 1801, the year before Taylor left Boone County.[106] Thus the larger Taylor "family" had grown considerably.

At least three of the eight slaves whom Taylor inherited from Uncle Joseph were transplanted from Virginia to the Bluegrass. They were Nanny, Asa, and Letty. Nanny had become a Baptist as early as the Woodford sojourn but had been excommunicated by the Clear Creek Church. In November 1800 she "made a satisfactory acknowledgment" to the Bullittsburg Church, the congregation in Boone County with which the Taylor family—both black and white—had aligned itself. Thus Nanny was restored to the fellowship of the church. Asa and Letty, who were brother and sister, were converted and baptized in August 1800.

---

[103]Boone County (KY) Deed Book B, 462-63; Campbell County (KY) Tax Lists, 1798 (MF., Kentucky Historical Society, Frankfort) 15; Campbell County (KY) Court Order Book A (Office of the County Clerk, Alexandria) 170-71.

[104]Boone County (KY) Tax Lists, 1799 (MF., Kentucky Historical Society, Frankfort); Boone Quarter Sessions Court (KY) Deed Book A, 45-46, 68-69, 115-16; Boone County (KY) Deed Book A, 97-99, 232-34, 268-70, 289-90, 311-14; Deed Book B, 403-409; Deed Book C-2, 389-90, 393-94; Deed Book D, 51-52, 224-25; Deed Book E, 172-73; Deed Book F, 28-29. (All of these deed books are located in the Office of the County Clerk, Burlington.)

[105]Dorothy Thompson, "Ancestors and Descendants," 40-42.

[106]Woodford County (KY) Tax Lists, 1794, 38; Boone County (KY) Tax Lists, 1801 (MF., Kentucky Historical Society, Frankfort).

During the next two months others of Taylor's slaves—Benjamin, Dublin, Jacob, and Judith—followed their example.[107]

The only black person belonging to John Taylor against whom a complaint was lodged in the Bullittsburg Church was Jacob. Eight months after his baptism he was accused of making "immodest attempts towards two black women, and other unseemly conduct, together with deviating from the truth when interrogated." The man failed to make an acceptable statement before the congregation and was suspended from membership; however, he was restored the following month.[108]

The religious atmosphere of the Taylor home had undoubtedly influenced these black people in numerous ways. In addition, their conversions took place in the milieu created by the Great Revival, which was sweeping across Kentucky at that time. During 1800 thirty-one blacks were accepted into the Bullittsburg fellowship.[109]

Sometimes Taylor acquired slaves by purchase, as was the case in 1801 with Curry and Sealy, who had belonged to Jeremiah Kirtley and John Graves, respectively.[110] Usually, however, it seems that the increase resulted from births within Taylor's black family.

On his farm in Woolper Bottom, with the use of slave labor Taylor produced—among other crops—corn, wheat, and apple trees.[111] James McIntosh, Jr., worked as the overseer on this farm as early as 1801; he may have occupied that post for the previous four years also. In any event, the employing of such a supervisor resulted from at least two factors—the increased number of slaves whom Taylor kept while living in Boone County, and the concomitant expansion of his agriculture.[112]

Sad to say, McIntosh and Taylor did not always see eye to eye regarding the operation of the latter's plantation. At one time Taylor would say that he held nothing against McIntosh. Later he would declare that the overseer had been "faulty in a number of instances." On another occasion the overseer was offended because the owner carried several hands from McIntosh's work gang down the river near the town of Milton to a tract of land called Mount Byrd. There in 1801 Taylor used these men to build log cabins in preparation for the removal of his

---

[107]Bullittsburg Church, Minute Book A (Office of the Church Historian, Burlington KY), 28, 30, 183.
    [108]Ibid., 38, 40.
    [109]Ibid., 183.
    [110]Ibid., 49, 67, 184.
    [111]Ibid., 68-69.
    [112]Ibid., 12, 13, 48.

family to that site the following spring. The overseer was displeased because Taylor had not consulted him about these workers' change of duty.[113]

Such an overbearing attitude on the part of McIntosh resulted in his discharge. John Conner took his place, perhaps early in 1802. That was the year when Taylor left Boone County for Gallatin County and for his land at Mount Byrd. It appears that for 1802 Taylor entrusted his farm in Woolper Bottom to the care of Conner and assigned two slaves—Benjamin and Sealy—and perhaps others to stay behind and work with the overseer. At any rate, the majority of Taylor's blacks went with their master to Mount Byrd. The year 1802 marked the last season that the preacher cultivated any of the Woolper lands.[114]

Taylor may have known this new overseer for some time, because he performed the wedding of John Conner and Mary Dicken in 1801.[115] The preacher had become in 1802 an absentee farmer, and during that year the overseer managed the Boone County farm in a heedless way. Taylor thought that Conner neglected his duties and caused the harvest that year to be diminished by 30 barrels of corn and 150 bushels of wheat. Also Conner's debts to his employer amounted to the value of 23 bushels of salt and 1 barrel of whiskey. In addition Taylor objected to Conner's method of selling apple trees to one Mills, including his use of falsehood about the seedlings. The preacher wanted to settle his complaints by arbitration, but the overseer was unwilling to do so.

When Taylor took these matters before the Bullittsburg Church in August 1803 even though he was no longer a member there, the congregation sided with Conner in each difficulty except the one related to the fruit trees. In that case the church suspended the overseer's membership. The handling of this particular accusation extended over the following five monthly sessions of the congregation. Finally Conner made an adequate acknowledgment of his fault, and the church acquitted him of the charge.[116] Nevertheless, having disposed of his last piece of Woolper land, Taylor terminated Conner's employment at the close of the harvest in 1802.

During the seven years that John Taylor maintained his membership in the Bullittsburg Church, he served several times annually as one of its moderators. Occasionally, as many as four moderators took their monthly turns.[117] These officials were ordained ministers. The usual pattern was that the moderator who

---

[113]Ibid., 48.

[114]Ibid., 67, 68-69; Gallatin County (KY) Tax Lists, 1803 (MF., Kentucky Historical Society, Frankfort).

[115]Boone County (KY) Marriage Book A (Photocopy, Office of the County Clerk, Burlington) 2.

[116]Bullittsburg Church, Minute Book A, 68-69, 70, 71, 72, 73, 74.

[117]Ibid., 2-53 *passim*.

served for a given month not only presided at the business session but also
preached or chose others to preach at the Saturday and Sunday meetings held
during a designated weekend.

In addition to preaching at worship services and moderating at business
meetings, other duties were assigned to Taylor by Bullittsburg from time to time.
Among such obligations were citing a member for absence from meetings,
inviting a Baptist who had recently arrived in the community to join the church,
"labouring" with a member accused of charging a second member an exorbitant
price for corn, helping to determine if organizing a congregation in a particular
neighborhood was expedient, and assisting in ordaining, at separate times, a
minister and a deacon.[118]

While Taylor lived in Boone County, his primary associational relationship
was to Elkhorn. As a messenger from the Bullittsburg Church he attended every
annual session from 1795 through 1801.[119] For three of those years he and
another minister wrote the Bullittsburg letter to the association.[120] While present
at yearly meetings of Elkhorn, John Taylor was given certain ministerial tasks
that bespoke his popularity, including preaching one of three Sunday sermons in
1799 and coauthoring letters to the Ketocton Association, in Virginia, and the
United Association, in Kentucky. On one occasion he was asked to attend a
quarterly meeting sponsored by Elkhorn during the period between annual
meetings. Elkhorn also sent him in 1797 and 1800 as a messenger to the Salem
Association.[121]

At the request of Elkhorn, Taylor helped to lay the ground work in 1797 for
forming an association of the congregations in Mason County. Two years later
these churches, located on the eastern side of the Licking River, organized the
Bracken Association. John Taylor and two other preachers were sent as Elkhorn's
representatives to the first annual meeting of Bracken.[122]

The peregrination and preaching of Taylor had made him a well-known
figure among Baptists of Kentucky. Because he could be counted on to invite all
sinners to receive the gospel, he was often asked to speak at one kind of event
or another. Such was the case early in the spring of 1800 when Benjamin Craig
requested Taylor to preach on a given night at his house in Port William, at the
mouth of the Kentucky River. That meeting turned out to be the beginning of the

---

[118]Ibid., 11, 13, 17, 18, 27, 41, 49, 53.

[119]Ibid., 2, 6, 10, 16, 20, 27, 42; Elkhorn Association, "Minutes," in Sweet, *American Frontier*, 1:468, 471, 475, 479, 482, 485, 488.

[120]Bullittsburg Church, Minute Book A, 2, 27, 42.

[121]Elkhorn Association, "Minutes," in Sweet, *American Frontier*, 1: 473, 477, 479, 783, 786.

[122]Ibid., 476-77, 483.

Kentucky Baptist phase of the Great Revival. Twice before—in the winters of 1784–1785 and 1788–1789—religious awakenings in the Bluegrass had occurred in connection with Taylor's evangelizing. The first revival promoted the organization of the Clear Creek Church and the Elkhorn Association; the second resulted in the baptizing of 146 converts at Clear Creek. The Great Revival produced even more profound effects—the baptism of 3,011 people by the churches of Elkhorn in 1801, and the healing of the only schism among Baptists in Kentucky.[123]

This division—between Regular Baptists and Separate Baptists—had originated in Virginia, whence most Kentucky Baptist preachers came. The genesis and development of these two groups were distinct. There were also differences in their doctrines. Regular Baptists, being predestinarians, did not address the gospel to all sinners, only to the elect. Separate Baptists called all men to repent. Regulars adhered to the Philadelphia Confession of Faith. In those days Separates did not subscribe to creeds or confessions.

John Taylor, having been converted among Separate Baptists, had adopted their evangelism and zeal from the beginning of his ministry. Years later, within a few weeks before his removal to Kentucky, the Lower South River Church, which he served as pastor, became affiliated with the Ketocton Regular Baptist Association, the oldest Baptist union in Virginia. In a strict sense, Taylor had become a Regular Baptist. If in fact he did not do so then, he became one when the Elkhorn Association in its incipiency adopted the Philadelphia statement. Thus Taylor drew from the deep wells of Separate ardor and of Regular order.

A number of factors prompted Regular Baptists in Kentucky repeatedly to attempt alliance with Separate Baptists—the desire for Christian unity, the need for denominational fellowship in a sparsely settled region, the merger of Regulars and Separates in Virginia in 1787, and the vigor derived from the Great Revival in 1800–1801.[124]

When union between Regular and Separate Baptists was achieved in Kentucky in 1801 and the name "United Baptists" was adopted, John Taylor was pleased with the outcome. He had taken part in the first and third of four Elkhorn efforts at consolidation. He approved the Terms of Union, which came from the fourth attempt. These terms set broad doctrinal boundaries that made possible the cooperation of immersionists who held to predestination and those who advocated free will. For the rest of his days, Taylor supported the General Union of Kentucky Baptists.

---

[123]Ibid., 431, 487-88; Spencer, *Kentucky Baptists*, 1:58, 425, 535-36, 538.
[124]Elkhorn Association, "Minutes," in Sweet, *American Frontier*, 1:432, 454, 488, 489.

Taylor became interested in the Corn Creek area almost two decades before he obtained title to the thousand-acre military survey known as Mount Byrd. Perhaps it was upon his return from Virginia in the summer of 1784 that he acquired the equity of Robert Johnson, a surveyor, in a twelve-hundred-acre tract lying on the eastern border of the Byrd land. The two grants were situated on the Ohio River in present Trimble County hard by the village of Milton. Johnson located and in 1786 laid out the twelve hundred acres for John Sutton, Sr., and for his services received half the land. It was this interest that Johnson had bargained away to Taylor. Sutton made an entry for this land, and in 1789 a patent for it was issued to him. Ten years later he deeded this property to his son John Sutton, Jr., and to John Taylor, each receiving equal parts. These two owners had already leased this realty to Richard Smith for thirty years beginning 1 January 1790.[125]

John Taylor purchased the Mount Byrd land also from Robert Johnson. The price was $2,300. The year was 1800. Even so, the seller did not give him a deed for the thousand acres until 13 August 1803, sixteen months after the Taylor family had taken up residence there. Johnson had bought this acreage from Patrick Henry, of Hanover County, Virginia. Richard Morris, of Louisa County, and John Carter Littlepage, of Hanover County, had been intermediate owners after the heirs of William Byrd III disposed of this military grant.[126]

Taylor's realty on the Ohio River now totaled sixteen hundred acres. But he was not to be left in its possession undisturbed, because three claimants stood ready to lay hold of parts of the Sutton grant. When Smith, the tenant of Taylor and the younger Sutton, complained in February 1806 to the Gallatin Circuit Court about the intrusion of one William Stiles, a suit in ejectment followed. It was titled *Taylor and Sutton v. Hogland*. The case dragged on until 21 July 1807, when a jury declared Moses T. Hoagland guilty of trespass and found for the plantiffs the land covered by the Sutton survey, one penny in damage, and their court costs.[127]

Having weathered this legal storm, the two owners proceeded posthaste to carry out an agreement that litigation had delayed. Fifteen days after the jury rendered its verdict the younger Sutton deeded his half of the land to John

---

[125]Joseph F. Taylor, Interview by [Shane], Draper MSS, 11CC228; Brookes-Smith, *Virginia Surveys*, 205; Gallatin Circuit Court (KY) Record of Proceedings, 1802–1810 (Kentucky State Archives, Frankfort) 131, 134, 136-38.

[126]Brookes-Smith, *Virginia Surveys*, 28; Gallatin County (KY) Deed Book A-l (Office of the County Clerk, Warsaw) 549; Kentucky Court of Appeals Deed Book H (Office of Secretary of State, Frankfort) 245-46.

[127]Gallatin Circuit Court (KY) Record of Proceedings, 1802–1810, 131-33, 134-35, 138-42; Order Book [1], 1807–1814 (Kentucky State Archives) 22, 25.

Taylor, who paid $280 for it.[128] Now the preacher owned twenty-two hundred acres on the Ohio River at Milton.

Here at Mount Byrd, Taylor had laid out his plantation with fields for corn, wheat, and flax and with an orchard and a pasture. In March 1802 the family had come down the river from Boone County and settled in the rough, log cabins that had been put up by his slaves. The land was then in Gallatin County.

In 1803–1804 a 1½-story house was constructed from bricks made on the site. This extant mansion, facing the south, fronted then on a steep road that came up from the river. It sits on a plateau that towers 400 feet above the bottom land. Such a handsome, wooded setting must have put Taylor in mind of the environs that enhanced Tidewater homes that he had seen on the Potomac and the Rappahannock rivers in the Old Dominion.

When Taylor moved from Boone to Gallatin County he owned fifteen slaves. That number increased to twenty by 1810. When he left for Franklin County five years later, his slaves numbered sixteen, six of whom were above sixteen years of age.[129] The contribution of these black people to the development of Taylor's Mount Byrd estate cannot be calculated, but it was indeed considerable. Nonetheless during the early years of his tenure at Mount Byrd, Taylor himself and his two elder sons labored side by side with the slaves in the forests and fields.

The Taylors had been given a letter of dismissal from the Bullittsburg Church on 6 March 1802. Beside the parents, the eldest son and five slaves were included. Fifteen months later the church granted a letter of transfer to two other slaves. These letters were lodged with the Corn Creek Church, near Milton. When this family left northern Kentucky in March 1815 only the parents and two black women were granted a letter of dismissal by Corn Creek.[130]

During the thirteen years that John Taylor belonged to the Corn Creek Church, he often preached at the monthly meetings and took his turn as the moderator at business sessions.[131] From time to time he paid his share of the apportionment for replenishing the treasurer's purse. The plan for the "fifth church fund," adopted in 1814, may have represented the usual quotas. Taylor's was seventy-five cents. Presley Gray, the father of Taylor's son-in-law John D.

---

[128]Gallatin County (KY) Deed Book B (Office of the County Clerk, Warsaw) 303; Kentucky Court of Appeals Deed Book L (Office of Secretary of State, Frankfort) 220-21.

[129]Gallatin County (KY) Tax Lists, 1803, 1816 (MF., Kentucky Historical Society, Frankfort); Census of 1810, Kentucky, Gallatin County, 194, records of the Bureau of the Census, Record Group 29, National Archives.

[130]Bullittsburg Church, Minute Book A, 49, 67, 182; Corn Creek Church, Minute Book B (The Southern Baptist Theological Seminary, Louisville KY) [81].

[131]Corn Creek Church, Minute Book B, [11, 12, 14, 15, 17].

Gray, was the only other man assigned this sum. Four persons were asked to donate fifty cents each; fourteen persons, twenty-five cents each.[132]

When John Taylor joined the Corn Creek Church in 1802, it was affiliated with the Salem Association. That fall he and two others went as messengers from Corn Creek to Salem. Taylor preached the introductory sermon, using 2 Corinthians 8:5 as the text. He was requested to attend a quarterly meeting at the Bear Grass Church in April 1803, to serve as one of Salem's messengers to the Elkhorn Association in August, and to be prepared to preach the introductory sermon at the organization of the Long Run Association in September in case the designated minister failed to attend.[133]

Because the Corn Creek Church was located north of Salt River, it joined in the effort to establish Long Run and in 1803 became one of the twenty-four affiliating congregations of the new union. At the constitution of Long Run on 16 September, John Taylor, as the alternate, preached the introductory sermon. The text was 1 Corinthians 15:58.[134]

As long as Taylor's membership remained at Corn Creek, he was usually sent as a messenger to the annual sessions of the Long Run Association.[135] The association used his talents in many ways. It honored him as the preacher of the introductory sermons in 1807 and 1813 also. He served once with a committee whose duty was to consider a charge of Arianism made against a church, he was chosen at least once to preach at a quarterly meeting between annual sessions, he represented Long Run during at least one annual meeting of Elkhorn, and in 1811 he was included in a group of ministers who agreed to make a circuit of certain Long Run churches and to preach to each of them once a year.[136]

Not only was John Taylor successful in the work of his divine calling, but also he accumulated a considerable estate through farming and through speculating in land. In Gallatin County he found himself near a convenient place at which to buy from the federal government public land located in the Jeffersonville Land District, of the Indiana Territory. The lands he purchased lay directly across the Ohio River from Mount Byrd.

---

[132]Ibid., [13-14].

[133]Salem Association, "Minutes," in Sweet, *American Frontier*, 1:617, 619, 621, 622.

[134]Spencer, *Kentucky Baptists*, 2:150.

[135]Ibid., 2:150, 156; Benedict, *Baptist Denomination*, 2:543; Corn Creek Church, Minute Book B, [10, 14].

[136]Ira V. Birdwhistell, *Gathered at the River: A Narrative History of Long Run Association* (Louisville KY, 1978) 21; Spencer, *Kentucky Baptists*, 2:151, 156; Elkhorn Association, "Minutes," in Sweet, *American Frontier*, 1:502.

The Jeffersonville Land Office opened its doors in Jeffersonville, Clark County, on 3 March 1807, and public sales began thirteen months later.[137] From Mount Byrd by a straight line down the river to Jeffersonville it is thirty-seven miles. During 1808–1812 Taylor or his agents made at least nineteen round-trips to the land office downstream in order to apply for lands or to pay installments on them.

During his sojourn in Gallatin County, Taylor was involved in the purchase of ten tracts of Indiana land, totaling 2,051.78 acres. Either he filed claims for the lands himself, or he was assigned the interests of other persons who had applied for them. In four cases he made the entries, paid the installments, and carried the process through to the receiving of land grants in his own name. In three other instances he made the payments on entries he had begun; later he signed over his certificates of payment to eventual recipients of the patents. Two additional purchases were represented by the entries of an individual and of a partnership and by the resulting patents secured by Taylor. A tenth tract was entered by his son Benjamin, and the patent was issued to a partnership, with John Taylor having been an intermediate owner. The lands Taylor bought were eight quarter sections of 160 acres each, plus five fractional sections of varying quantities, whose southern bounds were set by the meandering of the Ohio.[138]

Of these lands, 480 acres composed the northern half of Madison, the seat of Jefferson County, Indiana; 1,103.96 acres lay hard by to the west of the town; the balance of 467.82 acres was situated seven miles east of Madison and encompassed a zone from which the village of Brooksburg would be carved.[139]

These Indiana lands were priced by the national government at $2 per acre. The down payment on a quarter section, made at the time of applying for the land, was $80. A second like payment was due in two years. Payments three and four became due thereafter at intervals of one year. Discounts were given for early payments. Maximum discounts would lower the price per acre to $1.64. By the same token, delinquency in paying the installments resulted in penalties.

---

[137]William Forrest Shonkwiler, "The Land Office Business in Indiana" (M.A. thesis, Indiana University, Bloomington IN, 1950) 3, 21.

[138]Jeffersonville (IN) Land Office, Applications to Enter Land, 1810–1815; Register of Receipts, 1808–1813; Register of Certificates, 1808–1816, 2-7, 10-15, 30-31, 36-39, 52-53; Accompt of Public Lands Applied for by Individuals, sheets 2, 3, 31, 43. The above four manuscript volumes are located at the Indiana State Archives, Indianapolis. The following records at the U.S. Bureau of Land Management, Alexandria, Virginia, were also used: Card File of Final Certificates, nos. 41, 45, 62, 151, 244, 245, 249, 368; Register of Certificates, Jeffersonville (IN) Land Office, 3259, 3263.

[139]*Illustrated Historical Atlas of the State of Indiana* (Chicago IL, 1876; reprint ed. titled *Maps of Indiana Counties in 1876*, Indianapolis IN, 1968).

From all appearances Taylor's Indiana speculation was highly profitable. During 1812–1825 the preacher sold 1,051.78 of the total acres for $6,388. He had invested only $1,866 in this part of the acreage, his gross profit amounting to $4,522 (a gain on his investment of 242 percent). The patents for these lands had been issued to Taylor.

In addition he sold one quarter section for $1,068. This land had been acquired in 1810 by Taylor from an Ohio resident who at that time had paid only one of the four installments due the government. For this tract Taylor's gross profit may have been about $748.

Taylor disposed of four other quarter sections before their patents were issued. As a result, for this land, which is located in or near the county seat, Taylor's selling price is not recorded. If one assumes a profit of 242 percent (as above), the sale amounted to around $4,422, because the cost of the land to Taylor had been $1,293. For this reason, the gross profit may have been $3,129. Taylor gave the remaining 200 acres to his son John Wickliffe. This land had cost $349, but its worth was far greater.[140] Thus the venture of the preacher in something over two thousand acres of Indiana land rewarded him a gross profit of more than eight thousand dollars. His last five years at Mount Byrd were marked by the acquisition of this land; most of its disposition occurred in the early years following his return to the Inner Bluegrass.

The Ohio River, which rolled by the house of John Taylor at Mount Byrd, without doubt brought many unusual visitors to his front door, but maybe none was so interesting to the preacher as were John Freeman Schermerhorn and Samuel John Mills. They appeared at Taylor's home around the end of November 1812. Representing missionary societies in Connecticut and Massachusetts, these young ministers of the Dutch Reformed and Congregational churches, respectively, were surveying religion in the Ohio and Mississippi valleys. While they were upstream in Cincinnati, an acquaintance of Taylor encouraged them to visit him in Gallatin County. Instead of going directly to Lexington, they changed their course and went sixty miles out of their way in order to see Taylor.[141]

Taylor described these two youthful preachers, who spent at least one day and night at his house, as "respectable looking young men, well informed, and

---

[140]Jefferson County (IN) Corrected Deed Book A, 3, 9, 11, 71-72, 175-78, 395-97; Corrected Deed Book B, 5, 65-66, 101-102; Corrected Deed Book C, 160-61; Corrected Deed Book D, 120-22, 208-209; Original Deed Book E, 88-89; Original Deed Book G, 230-32. (These deed books are on microfilm at the Indiana State Archives.)

[141]Schermerhorn and Mills, *A Correct View of That Part of the United States Which Lies West of the Allegany [sic] Mountains with Regard to Religion and Morals* (Hartford CT, 1814) 18-20, 48; Clifton E. Olmstead, *History of Religion in the United States* (Englewood Cliffs NJ, 1960) 267; John Taylor, *Thoughts on Missions*, 5.

zealous in the cause in which they were engaged." They informed the Kentuckian about the Baptist ordination of Adoniram Judson and Luther Rice, whose work had had a "mighty effect" on the people of New England by arousing them to donate money for missions. Such contributions had spurred church members in the Northeast to give to all religious causes, so that even ministers who stayed at home were paid larger stipends for their preaching.[142]

The visitors were frank in asking personal questions. Especially did they want to know how Taylor "had got through the world, as they saw [him] then well settled and now old." They inquired about the "amount of supplies [that he] had generally received from the people for preaching." In their friendly way they blamed Taylor's "puny supply" on his bad policy.[143]

When these New Englanders learned that Kentucky Baptists were "a great people" spread out in fifteen associations, they became "quite impatient" with the "indolence" of Taylor and assured him that, if he would "only stir up the people to missions and Bible society matters," "a great change in money affairs in favor of preachers" would result. They asked, "Do you not know [that] when the springs[144] are once opened they will always run?" "Only," said they, "get the people in the habit of giving their money for any religious use, and they will continue to appropriate for all sacred purposes."

Taylor thought that his Cincinnati friend had given Schermerhorn and Mills the idea that his influence among the Baptists of Kentucky was greater than it "really was." He was confident that the visitors meant "friendship" to him and to preachers in general. Because these strangers were not Baptists and were guests in his home, "common modesty" kept the host from being as outspoken with them as he might have been at some other time and place. Later Taylor would record, "But surely it will not be thought uncharitable to say that I did begin strongly to smell the *New England Rat*."[145]

The big house at Mount Byrd and the surrounding acreage proved to be a haven for John and Elizabeth and their sons and daughters and slaves. The youngest two of the nine children who graced this family were born there. They were girls—Eliza, born 11 June 1803, and Sarah, born 22 November 1807. Also two of the children died there. One of these was Eliza, whose death came only fifty-eight days after her birth. The other was Cave, who bordered on ten years of age when he was drowned on 11 August 1810.[146]

---

[142]John Taylor, Thoughts on Missions, 5.

[143]Ibid., 5-6.

[144]Ibid., 6. The word *springs* comes from the 36-page edition. It is incorrectly printed *sponges* in the 72-page edition. See Page 6 in each printing.

[145]Ibid.

[146]Dorothy Thompson, "Ancestors and Descendants," 42, 43.

Benjamin and Joseph, the two eldest boys in the family, were packed off to Transylvania University for all or part of the 1807–1808 school year.[147] Joseph, at the age of twenty, had already been admitted to the bar of the Gallatin Circuit Court in July 1807.[148]

During Taylor's residency at Mount Byrd his three oldest daughters became brides. Nancy, the firstborn of these three, became the wife of John D. Gray, son of Presley Gray. In 1808 Mary (called "Polly") married William French, son of James French II. Jane (called "Jenny") was united in wedlock with William Plummer II, son of William Plummer. Joseph, the second son, was joined in matrimony to Elizabeth Van Pelt on 11 June 1812 in Gallatin County.[149]

A number of factors produced in Taylor's mind a growing dissatisfaction with his continuation at Mount Byrd—the departure of Elder Philemon Vawter from the Corn Creek community, the destruction by fire of Taylor's barn and the valuable grain stored in it, the death of his two small children at Mount Byrd, his slaves' selling goods stolen from his premises to people who lived across the Ohio in Indiana, the damage to his ministerial reputation amongst the people on Corn Creek, his being charged with trespass in the circuit court, the locking of the door of the schoolhouse that prevented Taylor's preaching in it during the wintertime, and the controversy in the Corn Creek Church regarding the Masonic order. Here were causes abundant, and in March 1815 they turned out to be enough to send Taylor, his wife, and part of his family down into the Inner Blue-grass. There in Franklin County at the Forks of Elkhorn the aging minister put down his roots for the last time.

Soon before Taylor departed from Mount Byrd and during the following decade a varied community arose on and near the lands that he had occupied. A steam mill and a liquor distillery were erected on a 501-acre tract given to Joseph Taylor by his father. Part of this land was sold to Israel T. Canby. In time this portion passed into the hands of the Bank of the United States and then to James McConathy & Company.[150]

[147]William Leavy, "Memoir of Lexington and Its Vicinity, with Some Notice of Many Prominent Citizens and Its Institutions of Education and Religion," *Register of the Kentucky Historical Society* 41 (Jan 1943): 55.

[148]Gallatin Circuit Court (KY) Order Book [1], 1807–1814, 18.

[149]Dorothy Brown Thompson, "John Taylor of the Ten Churches," *Register of the Kentucky Historical Society* 46 (July 1948): 570, and "Ancestors and Decendants," 36, 37, 40; Gertrude Earl Hewson, comp., "Marriages, Bonds, Consents [of] Gallatin County, Kentucky, 1799–1835," *Kentucky Ancestors* 14 (July 1978): 11, and 15 (Oct 1979): 79.

[150]Kentucky Court of Appeals Deed Book R (Office of Secretary of State, Frankfort) 343-44; Gallatin County (KY) Deed Book E, 453-57; Deed Book F, 345; Deed Book G, 52-54; Deed Book J, 392-93. These four manuscript county deed books are located in the Office of the County Clerk, Warsaw.

By 1817 Abraham King was occupying a 200-acre Mount Byrd tract fronting the river for 297 poles in the lower end of the military grant. Here he operated King's Ferry, crossing the Ohio to the town of Madison, Indiana.[151]

James McConathy & Company and King's Ferry may have grown out of the Gallatin Ohio Steam Boat Company, chartered by the legislature of Kentucky in 1815 and scheduled to be organized in March the following year.[152]

By 1823 a brick schoolhouse had been erected on a three-acre tract that was donated for that purpose by Joseph Taylor and that came out of the land given him by his father. It was first called Springfield Academy. When it was incorporated by the legislature in 1825 it was named Spring Creek Seminary, because it was located near the head of Main Spring Creek. The trustees appointed by the General Assembly received a deed for the school yard in February 1828. Joseph Taylor, the grantor, was also one of the seven trustees.[153]

On land west of Mount Byrd but not contiguous to it Michael Giltner established a tan yard as early as 1822.[154] A road running through the military grant to the Corn Creek Meetinghouse connected Taylor's farm and the growing community around it with the southern part of Gallatin County.[155]

Some years before the departure of John Taylor from the Ohio River he did for his sons and daughters what his father had been unable to do for him and his brothers and sisters. The preacher gave them pieces of land on which to locate their homes.

To Nancy Taylor and her husband, John D. Gray, went the uppermost corner of Mount Byrd, consisting of 500 acres and running for 175 poles along the shore of the river. After Gray died there on 1 October 1822 the Kentucky General Assembly provided for the sale of his land and for the use of the proceeds to buy a home for the widow and her six children and to pay the balance due on public land located in Indiana and Missouri, the purchase of which Gray had begun. This land in the public domain represented an investment for the rearing and educating of Gray's children.[156]

---

[151]Gallatin County (KY) Deed Book C (Office of the County Clerk, Warsaw) 439-40; Deed Book E, 343.

[152]General Assembly (KY) *Acts of 1815* (Frankfort KY, 1816) 538-41.

[153]General Assembly (KY) *Acts of 1825* (Frankfort KY, 1826) 100-101; Gallatin County (KY) Deed Book E, 453-55; Deed Book F, 384.

[154]Gallatin County (KY) Deed Book E, 262.

[155]Kentucky Court of Appeals Deed Book W (Office of Secretary of State, Frankfort) 134.

[156]Gallatin County (KY) Deed Book C, 278-B, 279-A; General Assembly (KY), *Acts of 1822* (Frankfort KY, 1823) 200-202.

The next riverfront tract, as one descends the Ohio, was given to Joseph, the second son, as early as 1812. It consisted of 501 acres and bordered the stream for 260 poles. It was in the northwestern corner of this land that the steam mill and distillery had been constructed. Joseph lived on a tract south of these 501 acres in a stone house that he had built. He had purchased this second tract from his father as early as 1817.[157]

Also John Taylor gave land to Benjamin (100 acres); to Mary French, his second daughter; and to Jane Plummer, who became a widow shortly after her father's removal to the Forks of Elkhorn. These farms were situated in the southern sector of Mount Byrd and perhaps spilled over onto the lands of the Sutton grant.[158] The elder did not bestow Mount Byrd land upon his youngest surviving son, John Wickliffe Taylor, but did give him 248 acres not far beyond the western boundary of Mount Byrd and 200 acres in Indiana.[159] In June 1820 at the age of twenty-two John Wickliffe married Jemima Gray in Gallatin County.[160]

John Taylor sold parcels of Mount Byrd and Sutton lands to Abraham King, George Kendall, Jason Overton, and John Gossam. Final payments were not completed by the last two buyers until after Taylor's death.[161]

## Life in the Inner Bluegrass

Taylor's tenure at the Forks of Elkhorn, in Franklin County, turned out to be twenty years. During that time he bought 1,162 acres, all of which may have been contiguous. At an average price of some $15 per acre, these lands cost him around $17,430. Stretching along the Frankfort-Georgetown Pike, the total acres he held ranged from as many as 750 in 1819 to as few as 100 in 1830.[162]

---

[157]Kentucky Court of Appeals Deed Book R, 343-44; Gallatin County (KY) Deed Book C, 278-B, 279-A; Deed Book H (Office of the County Clerk, Warsaw) 239-40; Gallatin County (KY) Tax Lists, 1812 (MF., Kentucky Historical Society, Frankfort).

[158]Kentucky Court of Appeals Deed Book W, 134; Gallatin County (KY) Deed Book C, 439-40; Deed Book E, 453-55; Deed Book H, 311-12; Dorothy Thompson, "Ancestors and Descendants," 37, 40.

[159]Gallatin County (KY) Deed Book D (Office of the County Clerk, Warsaw) 469; Jefferson County (Ind.) Original Deed Book E, 88.

[160]Hewson, "Marriages [of] Gallatin County," 79.

[161]Gallatin County (KY) Deed Book C, 439-40; Deed Book J, 65-66, 390-92, 446-48.

[162]Franklin County (KY) Deed Book E-2, 96, 330-31; Deed Book G-2, 173-74, 545-47; Deed Book N, 145-46; Deed Book O, 102-103, 267-68; Deed Book P, 16-17, 319-20, 334-36, 404-405; Kentucky Court of Appeals Deed Book Q (Office of Secretary of State, Frankfort) 2; Franklin County (KY) Tax Lists, 1816–1835 (M F., Kentucky Historical Society, Frankfort). The five county deed books are located in the office of the

John Taylor bought the first part of this land in the Forks of Elkhorn from George Rapene "Millpond" Smith on the next to the last day of 1814. Consisting of two adjacent tracts and totaling 237 acres, this land was located on the east side of South Elkhorn Creek and in the last great bend of that stream before it joins North Elkhorn Creek at the Forks. Before Smith came to Kentucky in 1804 and settled on this land, he had served as the pastor of the Separate Baptist congregation that met in Dupuy's Meetinghouse in Powhatan County, Virginia. His views in favor of emancipation rendered him generally unpopular among Baptists in Kentucky.[163]

In time Taylor built a gray stone dwelling on the Smith place. It stood about one hundred yards from a cliff above South Elkhorn Creek and about a half mile from the Forks of Elkhorn. Material for the house no doubt came from the quarry on this land. Within twenty years this residence contained, among other furnishings, a four-poster bed, an old bedstead, two other beds, two end tables, a third table, thirty-seven chairs, three pairs of andirons, two chamber pots, a bureau, a desk, a book case with some two dozen books, an old carpet, a press, a common press, a sideboard, a sugar box, a stove and pipe, a candle stand, a clock on the mantel, and a looking glass. Undoubtedly his twelve table spoons, twelve tea spoons, and a silver soup spoon were prized possessions. In the kitchen were to be found a coffee mill, two flatirons, a pair of steelyards, a lot of earthenware, a tea tub and box, a blue metal kettle, three other kettles, a bottle case, and a number of cooking utensils.[164]

John Taylor created around him at the Forks of Elkhorn a veritable settlement of his children such as he had laid out on Mount Byrd. Four of his daughters eventually resided within a mile or so of his stone house on the Smith farm.

Taylor constructed a brick house for his second daughter, Mary, and her husband, William French. It was located on the south side of the Georgetown Pike, across the road from "Bellsgrove," the farm of Clement Bell.[165]

---

Franklin County Clerk, Frankfort.

[163]Kentucky Court of Appeals Deed Book Q, 2; Darnell, *Forks of Elkhorn Church*, 261-62; Robert Baylor Semple, *A History of the Rise and Progress of the Baptists in Virginia*, rev. ed. (Richmond VA, 1894; reprint ed., Cottonport LA, 1972) 264, 474.

[164]Franklin County (KY) Deed Book P, 345-46; Franklin County (KY) Inventory and Sales Book A (MS., Office of the County Clerk, Frankfort) 347; Dorothy Brown Thompson, "Additional Notes on the John Taylor Family," *Register of the Kentucky Historical Society* 53 (Oct. 1955): 348-49; Jennie C. Morton, "Chronicles of the Old Neighborhood," *Register of the Kentucky Historical Society* 6 (Sept 1908): 66.

[165]Dorothy Thompson, "Ancestors and Descendants," 37; Morton, "Chronicles of the Old Neighborhood," 68, 70.

Perhaps it was soon after the death of her husband, John D. Gray, that Nancy Taylor Gray moved from Mount Byrd to Franklin County onto a 64-acre tract given her by her father. It lay directly south of the French farm. The preacher paid $1,088 for this land on which he settled his daughter and her four girls and two boys. In addition Nancy and her brother Benjamin swapped pieces of land in September 1829. She received 100 acres adjoining the 64 described above. He took part of the tract at Mount Byrd that had been the gift of John Taylor to John D. Gray.[166] Three months before these transactions, the widow Gray had remarried. Her new husband was Thomas L. Tate, a veteran of the War of 1812.[167]

Taylor's youngest daughter, Sarah (called "Sally"), married Joseph Smith in 1822. She was 15 years old; he was 30. Her father gave Sally a 191-acre tract, on which he built a stone dwelling for her and her husband. This farm was located on the south side of the pike and on the west bank of Buck Run. It lay to the east of the French place.[168]

A second widowed daughter, Jane Plummer, was given by her father a 145-acre farm, perhaps shortly after she was married to James Elliott in 1827. This land lay north of the road to Georgetown and on the waters of Main Elkhorn Creek. Taylor died before he got around to conveying to Jane title to this gift.[169]

Benjamin, the eldest son, lived only briefly in the Forks of Elkhorn—in 1818, 1821, 1822. Around 1815 he married Theodosia Payne, who died eleven years later. In 1827 he married Elizabeth Cotton. During 1828–1837 he lived in Woodford and Fayette counties. By 1840 he was residing again in Woodford County, at an estate named "Sugar Grove," near Versailles.[170]

---

[166]General Assembly, *Acts of 1822*, 200-202; Morton, "Chronicles of the Old Neighborhood," 70; Franklin County (KY) Deed Book P, 287-89.

[167]Dorothy Thompson, "Ancestors and Descendants," 37.

[168]Franklin County (KY) Deed Book P, 113-16; Dorothy Thompson, "Ancestors and Descendants," 43; Morton, "Chronicles of the Old Neighborhood," 74-75.

[169]Franklin County (KY) Deed Book Q (Office of the County Clerk, Frankfort) 2-5, 133-34; Dorothy Thompson, "Ancestors and Descendants," 40.

[170]Darnell, *Forks of Elkhorn Church*, 277; Dorothy Thompson, "Ancestors and Descendants," 32-33; Franklin County (KY) Deed Book G-2, 173-74; Deed Book I (Office of the County Clerk, Frankfort) 489; Deed Book L (Office of the County Clerk, Frankfort) 68-69; Deed Book M (Office of the County Clerk, Frankfort) 463-64; Deed Book O, 102-103, 333-34; Deed Book P, 113-16, 288-91, 319-20; Deed Book Q, 15-16, 133-34. See also Woodford County (KY) Deed Book Q (Office of the County Clerk, Versailles) 120-22, 274-75; Campbell County (KY) Deed Book N (Office of the County Clerk, Alexandria) 243-45.

Joseph, the second son, may have remained at Mount Byrd, in Gallatin County, until 1828. Sometime during the next four years he moved to Franklin County with his wife, Mary Fogg.[171]

It seems that John Wickliffe Taylor and his wife, Jemima Gray, continued to live at Mount Byrd until around 1833. They may have resided in Franklin County for a brief time during 1824, but they returned to Gallatin County the following year.[172]

What manner of man was John Taylor, who was known as a preacher across central Kentucky and who gathered his children about him and years before his death divided among them the abundant wealth he had accumulated? Within his family during his late years he was affectionately called "Daddy Taylor."[173] Friends who were familiar with him gave him the name "Johnny Taylor."[174]

Taylor was a man of strong constitution. Although he was short in stature, his bodily strength made him as bold as a lion, and yet at times he could be as meek as a lamb.[175] The manual labor to which he was inured on the frontier had hardened his muscles and widened his shoulders. He was marked by a broad face and high cheek bones. Heavy eyebrows overhung small, expressive eyes. His clothing was plain. His conversation was reserved, nevertheless he occasionally enjoyed a dry joke on his brethren.[176] John Taylor was friendly. He never saw a stranger. He actively sought the acquaintance of men whom he did not know. When such a person came under his roof, Taylor no longer considered him a stranger.[177] In spite of the fact that he was warmhearted, he was somewhat brusque in his manners, as was generally the case with most Kentuckians in those days.[178] Certain frontier circumstances had helped to shape the eating habits of the preacher. Because salt was often lacking during his early years in the back country, he forwent its use and developed an aversion toward salted food. Also, he was not much given to coffee or tea.[179]

As was true of almost all early Kentucky Baptist ministers, Taylor did not pretend to be a scholar. Even so, he possessed common sense, genuine piety, and

---

[171]Gallatin County (KY) Deed Book H, 236-40; Deed Book J, 39-40.

[172]Gallatin County (KY) Deed Book E, 262, 497; Deed Book H, 236, 311, 580.

[173]Darnell, *Forks of Elkhorn Church*, 277.

[174]"S[amuel] H[oward] F[ord], "Pioneer Preachers: John Taylor," *Christian Repository and Family Visitant* 8 (June 1859): 407.

[175]James B. Taylor, *Virginia Baptist Ministers*, 1st ed., 196.

[176]Welch, "John Taylor," *Annals of the American Pulpit*, ed. Sprague, 6:159.

[177]J[ohn] Taylor, "Try the Spirits," *Baptist Chronicle and Literary Register* 1:101.

[178]Thomas M. Vaughan, *Memoirs of Rev. Wm. Vaughan, D.D.* (Louisville KY, 1878) 71.

[179]John Taylor, *Thoughts on Missions*, 21, 28.

the native ability to reason and understand. At his death he owned at least two dozen books that he probably had put to good use. Among these volumes were Buck's *Theological Dictionary*, David Benedict's *General History of the Baptist Denomination*, and a biblical concordance. When his interest in a subject was sufficiently aroused, he might borrow and read a work, as in the case of his use of the two-volume history of Jesuit missions in Paraguay.[180]

Well-known among Taylor's traits were his friendly disposition toward young preachers and his eager desire to instill confidence in them.[181] Sometimes this encouragement took the form of public prayer. Once at Nicholasville in 1816 John Taylor, who was then sixty-four years old, heard a sermon by John Smith, a Baptist who later became a follower of Alexander Campbell. Taylor closed the morning meeting with this prayer: "Lord, we thank Thee that while many of us are growing old, Thou hast raised up this young man from the hill country. He is now thirty-two years old. Lord, grant that he may live yet thirty-two years longer."[182]

In other cases Taylor offered his friendship to fellow ministers. Chief among such preachers was William "Billy" Keller, who was sixteen years his junior. Even though Kellar was born in Shenandoah County, Virginia, in which Taylor had been raised to young manhood, the two had never met until Kellar moved to Kentucky and settled on Harrods Creek. Despite the fact that Taylor lived in Boone County at a distance of a hundred miles, he often visited Harrods Creek. At the first sight of Billy Kellar, Taylor "felt a partiality for him, as a devotional-minded, promising young speaker. It soon appeared that the attachment was reciprocal."[183] A nephew of Kellar wrote of his uncle and Taylor that "perhaps Jonathan and David never loved each other more."[184] Another close friend was William Vaughan, who was thirty-three years younger than John Taylor. Their intimate acquaintance was begun when Taylor was nearly sixty years old. John Taylor "did all he could to encourage him and hold up his hands," wrote Vaughan's son long after the older minister's death.[185]

Sometimes Taylor's method by which he inspired young preachers included the right hand of fellowship and an embrace in the pulpit. When Walter Warder attended the Elkhorn Association as a young messenger from the Green River Asociation, he met John Taylor for the first time. Taylor, who was thirty-five

---

[180]Thomas Vaughan, *Wm. Vaughan*, 71; Franklin County (KY) Inventory and Sales Book A, 347; John Taylor, *Thoughts on Missions*, 4.

[181]F[ord], "John Taylor," *Christian Repository* 8:408.

[182]John Williams, *John Smith*, 122.

[183]John Taylor, "William Kellar," in John Taylor, *Thoughts on Missions*, 59.

[184]Abram Kellar, "Of William Kellar," ibid., 56.

[185]Thomas Vaughan, *Wm. Vaughan*, 71.

years older than Warder, arranged for the newcomer to preach at a night meeting. After Warder finished his discourse, Taylor stood up and remarked that when Paul came to Jerusalem, and Peter, James, and John saw the gift that was in him, they gave him the right hand of fellowship. He proposed that all the older preachers there who perceived "the gift that was in their young brother" extend such a hand to Warder as a preaching novice. Soon Taylor's "venerable arms" encircled the younger man, and others followed suit "in a very solemn manner."[186]

Another technique by which Taylor encouraged a wavering young preacher was to insist vigorously that he stand before the people and make an effort to proclaim the gospel. One such incident occurred in September 1810 in connection with the annual meeting of the North Bend Association. The preacher was Wilson Thompson, then twenty-two years of age. He went to the home of one Ashbrook, where John Taylor was scheduled to preach. By nightfall the house, the doorway, and the yard were filled with people. Wilson was sitting near the table for the preacher.

At the time for worship, John Taylor arose from his seat near the fireplace, surveyed the crowd momentarily, and inquired, "Is young Brother Thompson in the room?"

Wilson became nervous and bowed his head very low. Several voices responded, "He is here."

Taylor approached Wilson, laid his hand on his shoulder, and said, "Go and preach."

The young man replied, "I have no appointment here, and I cannot fill yours."

Taylor quoted the Bible, "Children, obey your parents in all things."

"I do not think that command applies to this case," Thompson replied.

Taylor, who was thirty-six years older than the young preacher, answered, "I am an old man, and you are a young one. I want a seat, and good manners alone would require you to give me yours." In order to give Taylor room Thompson tried to shift to one end of the bench on which he sat. "You cannot make room that way, and an old man must stand unless you will give him your seat," the elder said. Wilson got up. Taylor took the vacated place and again said, "Go and preach."

Thompson had intended to go out the door, but the throng of people so filled the doorway that he could not exit. As he stood at the preacher's table, the idea came to him to open the meeting with singing and prayer and then to give way

---

[186]Letter, Walter Warder, Mayslick, [Ky.], 5 Mar. 1836, to Edmund Waller, in *Christian Repository* 5 (Mar 1856): 177-78.

to some other speaker. He took hold of a candle with one hand and a John Rippon hymnal with the other and led the assemblage to sing a hymn by Philip Doddridge, of which the first stanza follows:

> Ye little flock whom Jesus feeds,
> Dismiss your anxious cares,
> Look to the Shepherd of your souls,
> And smile away your tears.

During the singing, the text Luke 12:32 came to mind—"Fear not, little flock, for it is your Father's good pleasure to give you the kingdom." While prayer was being offered, Thompson felt impressed to say something on this passage. The young preacher expounded thereon with such force that all the house seemed to be in tears. He was followed by two elderly ministers whose emotions caused them to stop preaching.

Then John Taylor took the text Psalm 71:18. He spoke about how God was gracious to His people all the days of their lives. The promises of God were "the never-failing warrants to their faith and hope, and enabled them, in faith and assurance, to come boldly to a throne of grace, even when loaded down with the burden and infirmities of old age, and [to] pray as David did: 'Lord, remember me now I am old and gray.' "

Wilson Thompson never forgot this event, because it helped him to rid himself of "preacher-fearing embarrassment" that had theretofore sorely afflicted him.[187]

Not only did Taylor encourage young preachers but often in an abrasive way he publicly corrected what he considered to be their faults. On a summer Sunday at the annual meeting of an association a young man was preaching at an outdoor stand from the text Ezekiel 47:3-5, which recounts the prophet's vision of water coming from the temple and becoming deeper until it was a river fit for swimming. The preacher proposed to divide his address into four parts according to the depth of the water: ankle-deep, knee-deep, loin-deep, and the depth for swimming. He spent an hour on the first two points, spiritualizing their meaning. To him ankle-deep water represented repentance of sin; knee-deep water, assurance of salvation.

John Taylor, with his head bowed and resting on his hand, sat behind the young preacher. Taylor's dislike for such conjectural preaching was well known. His very posture revealed his disapproval of the sermon then underway.

---

[187]Wilson Thompson, *The Autobiography of Elder Wilson Thompson: Embracing a Sketch of His Life, Travels, and Ministerial Labors in Which Is Included a Concise History of the Old Order of Regular Baptist Churches* (Cincinnati, 1873) 108-13.

The young man, winding up his second point, said, "Thirdly, we go a little deeper where the water reaches the loins."

Taylor straightened his body and pointed his finger and sounded forth, "Young man, come ashore. You are deep enough, deep enough."

The other preachers on the stand bowed their heads in order to hide irrepressible smiles. The young man turned around and met the calm look of Taylor, solemn as the grave. Sitting down in confusion, he mumbled, "May the Lord bless truth and pardon error."

Even though the old man had been severe and abrupt, the long-winded young man had been taught a needful lesson.[188]

On another occasion, when the Elkhorn Association was in session at the Stamping Ground Church, a young preacher was among those filling the stand on Sunday. His text was "What is Man?" He announced three divisions for his sermon. It took him an exceedingly long time to cover his first part, regarding man as a physical being. It was plain to see that John Taylor, who was seated on the stand, was disgusted with the wordy performance of the young orator. Many were watching Taylor to see what action he would take.

The preacher finished his first part and introduced the second, which would deal with man as a moral being. At this juncture Taylor arose and slowly took out his pocket watch, maybe the one his uncle had given him years ago in Virginia. He moved toward the front of the stage and called out loud enough to be heard by the vast audience, "One hour gone, and gone forever, and nothing said." There was a painful pause, then the old man unhurriedly took his seat.

The young minister apologized because he had spoken so long, and abruptly sat down. The next scheduled speaker continued the outdoor exercises.[189]

Not only did Taylor now and then call a halt to a young preacher who was taking too much time, but he also used prayer as an indirect way by which to correct a long-winded brother. On one occasion, following a wearisome discourse by Joseph Buchanan, Taylor performed this pointed prayer: "Oh, Lord, teach Brother Joe what to preach, and how to preach, and to quit when he is done. Amen."[190]

---

[188]F[ord], "John Taylor," *Christian Repository* 8: 407. Ford recorded the fact that Ryland Thompson Dillard, who told him the story, sat on the stand beside Taylor at the service. Ibid., 407n. Even so, the account regarding such an event tends to become apocryphal. In 1876, when William Vaughn was delivering an address in Harrodsburg at the centennial celebration of the first Baptist preaching in Kentucky, he recalled the event concerning Taylor and the youthful minister and had Ezekiel riding a horse, whereas none is mentioned in the scriptural text. Thomas Vaughan, *Wm. Vaughan*, 270.

[189]F[ord], "John Taylor," *Christian Repository* 8:407-408.

[190]Thomas Vaughan, Wm. Vaughan, 270.

Thus the aging minister tried both to inspirit and to discipline young preachers.

Following a residence of twenty years on the Ohio, John Taylor returned to the Inner Bluegrass in the spring of 1815 and settled at the Forks of Elkhorn in Franklin County. During the twenty years that remained to him, he held his church membership in three congregations in that region: Big Spring, Frankfort, and Buck Run.

After his relationship of less than a year with the Big Spring Church, Taylor became a constituent member of the Frankfort Church on 25 February 1816. At that organizational meeting the church unanimously requested him "to exercise his privileges as a gospel minister" within the congregation. Two months later he was invited to preach on a regular basis.[191]

His tenure at Frankfort was one month less than two years. On 31 January 1818 Taylor, his wife, and a number of their neighbors at the Forks of Elkhorn constituted a church called Buck Run. In time its meetinghouse would be located at Woodlake, on the road between Frankfort and Georgetown. Taylor was the principal preacher here as long as his health allowed.

## Missionary Movement

By the time Taylor had returned to the Inner Bluegrass he habitually attended the annual meetings of seven or so Baptist associations. During the associational season in 1819, however, he was present at only five such meetings because of illness.[192]

The associational obligations that he fulfilled in these later years frequently included the annual sermon on Saturday. He participated in the constitution of the Franklin Association on 16 September 1815 by preaching the sermon. His text was Psalm 133:1—"Behold, how good and how pleasant it is for brethren to dwell together in unity!" This verse was frequently used for such addresses. Again, in 1823, Taylor delivered the introductory sermon at the Franklin Association, using Acts 3:6 as the text.[193] In 1816, when the Elkhorn Association met at the Great Crossing Church, he preached the introductory sermon from Matthew 17:10.[194]

---

[191]Frank Mariro Masters, *A History of Baptists in Kentucky* (Louisville KY, 1953) 113-14.

[192]John Taylor, *Thoughts on Missions*, 3.

[193]U. V. Williams and F. W. Eberhart, *History of Franklin Baptist Association from 1815 to 1912* ([Frankfort KY, 1912]) opposite [4], and 5.

[194]Birdwhistell, *Elkhorn Association*, 137.

As a younger preacher John Taylor had experienced much pleasure in attending associational annual meetings, but he thought that a number of circumstances had cast an "awful shade" over these assemblies in the years immediately preceding 1820. First, many messengers of "common rank" showed less humility at these meetings than did those who were legislators and state officeholders, of whom there were quite a number. Second, these ordinary people worked hard and long in order "to carry some favorite point" at the annual sessions. With all the cunning of an attorney, they overwrote and overtalked their opponents. "They seem much to exult when the vote is carried on their side."[195]

To Taylor's mind, a third evil was far greater than were the other two. It was the overbearing influence upon the associations of what came to be called "benevolent societies." He particularly had in view two such agencies—mission organizations and theological schools.[196]

In 1792 some mission-minded folk in England had created the Baptist Missionary Society, a successful, extra-ecclesiastical organization. Its purpose was to spread the gospel in non-Christian lands. When in 1814 the "General Missionary Convention of the Baptist Denomination of the United States of America for Foreign Missions" was formed in Philadelphia, it too was placed beyond the control of the churches. It met every third year and came to be known as the "Triennial Convention."

Luther Rice, who was appointed as the agent of the new convention, was sent to Kentucky in 1815 and arrived in Lexington while the Elkhorn Association was in session at the Town Fork Church. He preached one of the three Sunday sermons at this gathering on 13 August. His text was Matthew 6:10.[197]

John Taylor was present at Elkhorn that year and heard Luther Rice speak on his initial visit to the Bluegrass. Several thousand made up an attentive audience near Lexington. A well-dressed young man, the visitor stood tall on the outdoor stage. His face was pale and solemn. The people were orderly; all eyes and ears were open. Taylor thought that Rice expounded some meaningful ideas about the coming of Christ's kingdom, but it seemed to him that the sermon was geared toward the reception of a mission offering that came at the end. With great feeling Rice raised his arms as if he were seeing a vision. The preacher announced that angels were hovering over the congregation, ready to depart to Heaven with good tidings. He called out, "Stop, angels, till you have witnessed

---

[195]John Taylor, *Thoughts on Missions*, 3-4.
[196]Ibid., 4.
[197]Birdwhistell, *Elkhorn Association*, 54.

the generosity of this assembly."[198] Then some twenty appointed men arose and, using their hats, collected $147.75 for the Triennial Convention.[199]

The year before Rice's first trip to Kentucky a missionary society had been organized near Lexington. By 1816 five other such groups were located across the state at Bardstown, Mount Gilead in Green County, Mount Sterling, Shelbyville, and Washington.[200] Their most important contribution may have been the creation of sentiment favoring organized mission activity. Nonetheless, there developed at the same time a reaction against the missionary enterprise and its structured groups.[201]

In August 1801 at the request of the South Elkhorn Church the Elkhorn Association had established a mission to the Indians of the Great Lakes. The association appointed a committee of five preachers to select the missionaries and to gather funds for this venture. The following month the committee ordained John Young, of Jessamine County, as a missionary and sent him out. The next year Elkhorn continued the authority of the panel, but here the mission disappeared from the associational record.[202] This project was "the first organized mission by Kentucky Baptists to the Indians."[203]

Note the difference between this associational Indian mission and the work later sponsored by the Board of Foreign Missions of the Triennial Convention. Aside from the size of the two operations, the earlier project was requested by a congregation, authorized by an association, and financed under a plan originating with this group. The work of the Triennial Convention, on the other hand, was promoted by a society that the churches and associations did not control.

In order to preach the gospel beyond the Mississippi and at the same time to investigate the state of mission work recently begun there by John Mason Peck and James Ely Welch (missionaries of the Triennial Convention who arrived in Saint Louis in the fall of 1817), John Taylor made two trips to Missouri—in the

---

[198]John Taylor, *Thoughts on Missions*, 9.

[199]Ibid.; Baptist Board of Foreign Missions for the United States, *Second Annual Report*, 94.

[200]Baptist Board of Foreign Missions for the United States, *Second Annual Report*, 94; Luther Rice, *Dispensations of Providence: The Journal and Selected Letters of Luther Rice*, ed. William H. Brackney (Rochester NY, 1984) 89; John Taylor, *Thoughts on Missions*, 18.

[201]For a discussion of these contravening positions, see Larry Douglas Smith, "The Rise of the Missionary Spirit among Kentucky Baptists," *Quarterly Review* 40 (April-June 1980): 74-79.

[202]Elkhorn Association, "Minutes," in Sweet, *American Frontier*, 1:489, 494; Spencer, *Kentucky Baptists*, 1:570, 2:548.

[203]Larry Douglas Smith, "The Mission Work of the Elkhorn Association, 1785–1815," *Kentucky Baptist Heritage* 12 (July 1985): 3.

fall of 1818 and in the following spring. He found three associations in place in Missouri and one in Illinois, three of which antedated the advent of the two missionaries. The youngest Missouri association had been formed in July after their arrival. Taylor objected to the missionaries' solicitation of funds from people in that territory, to their construction of an exceedingly large meeting-house in Saint Louis, and to their description of Missouri and Illinois, with thirty-two Baptist churches, as "an almost blank as to religion."[204]

Taylor's observing of Rice when he first preached at Elkhorn,[205] his personal inspection of the work by the Missouri mission,[206] his recollection of the brief visit of Mills and Schermerhorn at his home in Gallatin and of their conver-sations with him concerning the use of money by churches and other religious societies,[207] and his calling up in memory the toilsome years he had spent on the frontiers of Virginia and Kentucky as an untrammeled, unpaid evangel,[208] all fixed in his mind an aversion toward organized mission work and its inherent dangers.

On 27 October 1819, his sixty-seventh birthday, John Taylor turned to the self-assigned task of putting on paper his ideas regarding the validity of mission organizations and their activities. Given the state of his health, it was an arduous chore to perform. For some months he had been suffering from a sickness from which he expected never to recover. His ailment was edema, or dropsy as it was called then. It was a swelling caused by abnormal accumulation of bodily fluids. Taylor thought that this illness was "likely to grow into a speedy rage and [to] make quick work of mortality." He was neither bedfast nor confined to his home, although during the past summer he had reduced the travel he customarily did.[209]

Taylor spent the late fall of 1819 and the succeeding winter producing a caustic polemic against evangelistic work conducted through organized and financed methods. His paper puts forth four principal reasons why he refused to sanction the work of the Triennial Convention and its auxiliary societies.

His first objection was the undue emphasis that agents and missionaries of the convention put on gathering funds for carrying out its mission work. It seemed to Taylor that no amount of money would ever be large enough to answer their purposes.[210] "The very many modes and artful measures of those

---

[204]John Taylor, *Thoughts on Missions*, 14, 24-25.

[205]Ibid., 9.

[206]Ibid., 12-16.

[207]Ibid., 5-6, 55.

[208]Ibid., 26-29, 50.

[209]Ibid., 3; John Taylor, "Intelligence from Kentucky," (Philadelphia) *Reformer* 21 (1 Sept 1821): 195. The quotation comes from the second source listed here.

[210]John Taylor, *Thoughts on Missions*, 10.

great men to get money are disgustful to common modesty."[211] Taylor thought that Rice was a modern Tetzel, because he insisted on taking mission offerings at associational meetings and doing so on Sundays in the prime part of the day, even against the rules of Elkhorn in one case.[212]

Taylor stated his second complaint against organized missions this way: "I consider [that] these great men are verging close on an aristocracy, with an object to sap the foundation of Baptist republican government." The convention sought to bring as many of the Baptist associations in the United States as possible into correspondence with the Board of Foreign Missions. The power thus acquired, Taylor reasoned, would constitute "a fine nest egg of gold [with which] to answer their future ambition."[213]

The author did not approve of the type of ministerial training that William Staughton, of Philadelphia, was dispensing to young men at his residence. Preachers who were educated in such seminaries would have to be paid salaries by their churches. The preachers who were then serving the twenty thousand Baptists in Kentucky did not come from theological schools, Taylor asserted.[214]

In the fourth place Taylor was offended by the missionaries' "noise about their privations, when the world knows how ill-founded these complaints are."[215] His mind traveled back fifty years to Virginia, where he had seen Baptist men buffeted and imprisoned and "counted the offscouring of all things."[216]

Why did John Taylor publish *Thoughts on Missions*? Let me construct an apology for him.

First of all, this outspoken Baptist preacher was opposed to a paid ministry. During his Virginia years Taylor had accepted small gratuities, usually in kind, at a time when he was without estate or income. Later, as the "particular pastor" of the Clear Creek Church, in Kentucky, he was promised produce as compensation, but for a two-year period he was paid only 23 percent of the amount that had been set. From then on, he never agreed to be designated as the pastor of any congregation, and he was not paid for the preaching he did. For the most part, he spent a lifetime of unpaid ministry within the churches he served. And now, given his personal wealth acquired through farming and land speculation, he had no need for a preacher's salary. At the age of sixty-seven it was too late for him to cancel an attitude that had been deeply ingrained in his mind since young manhood.

---

[211]Ibid., 11.
[212]Ibid., 10.
[213]Ibid.
[214]Ibid., 23-24.
[215]Ibid., 28-29.
[216]Ibid., 26.

Secondly, Taylor feared that associations and organizations connected with them would assert power over the churches. Article 28 of the Philadelphia Confession, to which he had assented a number of times, stated that churches' messengers who commune together "are not entrusted with any church-power . . . or with any jurisdiction over the churches themselves . . . to impose their determination on the churches or officers."[217] Taylor imbibed a double dose of freedom that came from his early years in the back country of Virginia and later from the Revolutionary era, through which he passed as an advocate of liberty. He had known preaching colleagues who had been subjected to corporal punishment, arrest, imprisonment, prosecution, and other legal restraints by both civil and ecclesial officers of the Old Dominion. Now that this type of control had vanished in the fires of war, he did not want any measure of ecclesiastical authority to take its place.

Thirdly, it was God's providence to create preachers and the congregation's privilege to call them forward to stand before the people. Taylor's own training did not include the kind offered by theological schools. For such institutions to turn out preachers would call for the gathering of funds and would thus create an endless cycle. Finally, Taylor reasoned that in his own itineration he had experienced as much danger and deprivation as had missionaries in foreign lands. With it all, he had never made much ado about his hardships. It never occurred to him that he had suffered unbearably in preaching the gospel.

In my apology for Taylor's writing of *Thoughts on Missions*, I have used stories and comments taken here and there from his writings. Now look at how he defended his work in an orderly, four-fold statement written to a friend in Philadelphia. This apology was penned during the summer of 1821, a year following the publication of Taylor's work.

In the first place, Taylor believed that all that had been spoken and much that had been printed regarding recent activities of the Triennial Convention had presented only one side of the question. *Thoughts on Missions* was his attempt to show its mission operations in their proper colors. He was a watchman obligated to blow the trumpet when the sword came upon the land. He was conscientious in what he did, because he thought that his physical affliction in 1819 was a sickness unto death. Two years later he had completely regained his health.[218]

His second apology dealt with the origin of the Triennial Convention and the missionary societies that were auxiliary to it. They were self-created, or they

---

[217]Quoted in William L. Lumpkin, *Baptist Confessions of Faith* (Philadelphia, 1959) 289, 349.

[218]John Taylor, "Intelligence from Kentucky," *Reformer* 2:196-97.

were organized by Luther Rice. Because they were not authorized by a congregation or an association, they constituted "an outrage on Baptist principles of republican government."[219]

The third defense of Taylor had to do with the connection between the Franklin Association, to which he belonged, and the Board of Foreign Missions. Because the association had revoked its correspondence with the Philadelphia board, Taylor thought that he could no longer treat the people of that group as if they were in fellowship with those of his association. Hence, he reasoned that he was at liberty to make "free with individuals by name in my book."[220] His last apology is the most important. For Taylor to have renounced all missionary activity would have been tantamount to rejecting his own work for nearly fifty years, because much of his "poor little preaching has been [done] in destitute places." He was not opposed to all mission efforts: "Under proper arrangements and with well-chosen instruments, nothing can be more laudable than to endeavour to spread the gospel and [to] bring [people] to the knowledge of the truth," Taylor argued.[221]

*Thoughts on Missions* was published in two editions in 1820 in Franklin County, Kentucky. What was perhaps the first one consisted of thirty-six pages, including the titular and the prefatory pages. This edition covered only his objections to organized mission work.

The other edition contained seventy-two pages. These were the title page; the preface; thirty-two pages bearing the text of *Thoughts*; a thirty-page section titled "Biographies of Baptist Preachers" and carrying short sketches regarding William Marshall, George Eve, William Cave, Richard Cave, Jesse Vawter, Philemon Vawter, Joseph Redding, Isaac Redding, and William Kellar; and Taylor's eight-page relation of his religious conversion.

Taylor may have embellished his second edition of *Thoughts* with the ministerial biographies in order to illustrate the kind of evangelical work that Virginia Baptist preachers conducted in their homeland and later in Kentucky. He began writing these vignettes as early as February 1816. The biographer showed what Baptist preachers a generation earlier had done on their own, unmoved by money or organization.

The first edition required thirty-four pages for the text; the second, thirty-two. This variance in pagination indicates a separate setting of the type for each edition. The same conclusion is suggested by other differences: capitalization, length of the line of type, and number of lines per page. The printer or printers involved are not known.

---

[219]Ibid., 198
[220]Ibid., 199.
[221]Ibid.

Some 450 copies of the book were published. After the supply was depleted, the question of another printing arose. Taylor's Philadelphia acquaintance wanted to buy 100 copies. The author discussed with some of his Kentucky friends the reprinting of the work. They concluded, however, that it would be better not to issue another printing, because "a dreadful tempest is already blowing in Kentucky on account of my little homespun book," the author wrote.[222]

Taylor offered his book for sale at least at the eight associations he attended in 1820. Traveling by horseback from place to place, he presented a copy to each of these unions. Elkhorn, one of the eight, discussed the book but returned it to Taylor without making a recommendation to the churches. Salem voted in his absence to return the book to the author. The other six unions cordially received the book, some with thanks.[223] One of these six was Licking Association, which was known for its strong Calvinism. It recommended that the brethren peruse the publication.[224]

In Taylor's time almost every Kentucky association at its annual meeting chose the preachers of Sunday sermons by the use of secret ballots. At six of the eight associations he attended in 1820, Taylor was honored in this way. He assumed that these private votes represented some degree of approbation of his book by 75 percent of Kentucky Baptists.[225]

However accurate Taylor's estimate may be, much opposition to his work had arisen. Such loud clamor and great displeasure were expressed that the author feared that the objectors would be glad to see him commit an offense by which he could be imprisoned for life. Taylor wrote that whenever a missions advocate met him "one of the best relished luxuries that he can enjoy is to insult me." Some of his Kentucky friends said that he had ruined himself by publishing such "a bad book."[226]

The adverse reaction took many forms. Elder Jacob Creath, Sr., for example, refused publicly in the spring of 1821 to serve on an ordaining presbytery if Taylor continued to be one of its members. During the following summer Taylor, who was conducting a meeting by candlelight in a Scott County home, called on a fervent supporter of missions to close the service. Even though the two ministers who had already preached had not uttered a word about missionary activity, the final speaker "rose with great warmth and . . . raved against those who would not send the gospel to the heathen." That preacher had a limited knowledge about

---

[222]Ibid., 193, 195. The quotation comes from page 193.

[223]Ibid., 195, 198; Elkhorn Association, *Minutes*, 1820, 6, 7.

[224]Spencer, *Kentucky Baptists*, 1:606, 2:242.

[225]John Taylor, "Intelligence from Kentucky," *Reformer* 2 195.

[226]Ibid., 195-96. The quotation comes from page 196.

mission work, "yet he glories in uplifted, loud voice, with clenched fist; and, to use his own term, he means to 'fight' for the good cause of missions."[227]

At an associational meeting a year or so after the publication of *Thoughts*, Taylor justified his writing of the book by impugning the motives of certain appointees of the Triennial Convention. A fellow minister interrupted the author's address with an inquiry: "If, sir, it were in your power to take back the money that has been expended for the support of missions among the heathen, and undo all the good that has been effected by the labours of those missionaries, would you do so?"

Taylor hesitated to reply directly but in the end answered in the negative.

The questioner then responded, "Never let me hear another word from you against missions."[228]

In addition to the four-fold apology of Taylor regarding *Thoughts on Missions*, what evidence has surfaced to show that he ever assumed any obligation to employ "means for the conversion of the heathen," to use William Carey's expression? First, at the annual meeting of the North Bend Association on 24 September 1815, Taylor contributed $1.50 to the Triennial Convention.[229] Next, he attended the yearly sessions of the Baptist Mission Society of Kentucky in 1818 and in 1819 at the Big Spring Church in Woodford County and at the home of Elder Silas M. Noel in Frankfort, respectively. This organization was not a statewide group but was centered in the Inner Bluegrass.[230] In the third place, in 1823 Taylor characterized Absalom Graves, a minister who belonged to the Bullittsburg Church, as having received "a missionary spirit in its warmest glow from the time of his first acquaintance with Luther Rice" that helped his spiritual nature to grow in a way that otherwise would never have been possible.[231] Fourthly, at the Great Crossing Church on 7 December 1828, John Taylor and his son Joseph, who was now a minister, took part in the ordination of Sampson Birch to the ministry. Birch, an American Indian, was a student at the Choctaw Academy, which was located at Blue Spring in Scott County and was operated under the direction of the Triennial Convention. An ordaining presbytery was composed of seven Caucasian preachers. After one of them had delivered the ministerial charge to Birch, John Taylor made some general remarks, took part

---

[227]Ibid., 196.

[228]Anonymous letter, in *Baptist Monitor and Political Compiler*, Bloomfield KY, 3 June 1823, 4.

[229]Baptist Board of Foreign Missions for the United States, *Second Annual Report*, 95.

[230]Baptist Mission Society of Kentucky, *Proceedings*, 1818, 10-11; John Taylor, *Thoughts on Missions*, 20, 22; Spencer, *Kentucky Baptists*, 1:579.

[231]John Taylor, *A History of Ten Baptist Churches*, 1st ed. (Frankfort KY, 1823) 98.

in the imposition of hands on the red man, and pronounced one of two closing prayers.[232]

In the fifth place, two years later when James Ely Welch, of Missouri, was visiting in Kentucky, he ran into John Taylor during the annual meeting of the Long Run Association at the New Castle Church and attempted to open a conversation about *Thoughts on Missions.*

Taylor replied, "Oh, Brother James, I hope you do not doubt that I *believed* I was telling the truth when I wrote that thing."

Welch asked, "How could you?"

The author answered, "Oh, never mind; let it sleep in silence." Taylor's attitude on that day showed regret that he had written the book.[233] Two other events bear on this matter. On 24 April 1831 Taylor joined the Buck Run Temperance Society, a type of "benevolent" organization. It had been constituted the preceding month at the Buck Run Meetinghouse.[234] Exactly three months before his death, Taylor attended on 12 January 1835 the adjourned session in Frankfort of the recently formed Kentucky Baptist Convention.[235] (This meeting seems to have been the convention's last coming-together. Its successor, the General Association of Baptists in Kentucky, would be established two years later.)

Here are seven pieces of evidence that testify in varying degrees that John Taylor held the spirit of mission activity dear to his heart even though he could not readily embrace all its methods.

Among Taylor's contemporaries who expressed a measure of dissatisfaction with benevolent societies was John Leland, a preacher famous throughout America who then was residing in his native Massachusetts. He had lived in Virginia during most of the Revolutionary War. There he had staunchly advocated religious liberty. In writing to Taylor in 1830, he contrasted what he heard at church services when he first became a preacher, on one hand, and what he heard now, on the other. In Leland's early days a minister set forth "the ruin and recovery of man," but now at "meeting" Leland heard "high encomiums on Sunday schools, tract, and missionary societies, antimasonic societies, etc., with a strong

---

[232]J. N. Bradley and Ellis M. Ham, *History of the Great Crossing Church* (Georgetown KY, 1945) 24.

[233]Welch, "John Taylor," 158. See also James Barrett Taylor, *Lives of Virginia Baptist Ministers,* 2d ed. (Richmond VA, 1838) 221.

[234]Buck Run Temperance Society, Minute Book, 24 April 1831 (Kentucky Historical Society, Frankfort) 11. Also see Dorothy Brown Thompson, "'James M. Bradford, Secretary': Pages from an Old Franklin County Minute Book," *Register of the Kentucky Historical Society* 48 (Oct 1950): 301-308.

[235]Kentucky Baptist Convention, *Minutes,* 1834, 27; and 1835, 27.

appeal to the people to aid with their money these institutions, which are to produce the millennium."[236]

When Leland's letter was published by Uriel B. Chambers, of Georgetown, Kentucky, in his *Baptist Chronicle and Literary Register*, the editor justified its appearance by concluding that Leland did not have "a fixed opposition to these societies, [that] he only designs to discourage an idolitrous [*sic*] devotion to them to the neglect of preaching the gospel, the primary means appointed by Heaven for the extension of Christ's kingdom in the world."[237]

Edmund Waller (1775–1842) was another colleague of Taylor. Counted among the able ministers of his day, he probably had no superior as a Kentucky pastor. His labor in bringing sinners to Christ had been "extraordinary." All the same, he opposed the methods used by missionary societies when they first appeared. In his later years, nevertheless, Waller warmly approved missions as well as higher education for ministers.[238]

Kentucky opponents of the methods used by mission societies were few in number, according to a resident of Great Crossing who attended the Triennial Convention in 1823, in the nation's capital. They were "found in the bosom of the Baptist churches and considered worthy members," even though they obstructed the progress of missionary organizations. Another reason for the lack of mission activity in the state was "defective organization."[239]

Since 1837 John Taylor has been categorized by historians and Baptist pastors as an opponent of missions. This misconstruction first appeared in the writing of James Barrett Taylor, a biographer of Baptist preachers and an administrator of a Baptist foreign mission board who charged John Taylor's "opposition" to his "ignorance." This accuser did not know that John Taylor was a reader of *The Latter Day Luminary*, the journal of the Baptist Board of Foreign Missions for the United States, which was issued five times yearly, and that he had read rather widely regarding the goals and progress of the mission projects of various denominations.[240]

In 1885 John Henderson Spencer, the principal historian of Kentucky Baptists, described John Taylor as the author of the book that "probably did more to

---

[236]Letter, Leland, Cheshire MA, 10 Dec 1830, to John Taylor, *Baptist Chronicle and Literary Register* 2:4.

[237]Note by editor, Chambers, ibid., 4-5.

[238]Spencer, *Kentucky Baptists*, 1:375.

[239]Anonymous letter, Great Crossing KY, June 1823, to unknown resident, Washington, D.C., in *Columbian Star*, quoted in *Baptist Monitor and Political Compiler*, 12 Aug 1823, 4.

[240]James B. Taylor, *Virginia Baptist Ministers*, 1st ed., 197; John Taylor, *Thoughts on Missions*, 4-5, 6-8, 18, 29-30.

check the cause of missions in Kentucky than [did] any other publication of the period."[241]

Benajah Harvey Carroll, Jr., saw Taylor in 1902 as "the victim of the prejudices engendered by his lack of education and [by] his early environment. Yet all his good qualities but served to give respectability and force to his opposition to the mission cause."[242]

Even William Warren Sweet joined the chorus of denigration in 1930. He laid "a good share" of the responsibility for the rise of the movement against missions at the feet of three men—John Taylor, Daniel Parker, and Alexander Campbell.[243]

In 1953 Frank Mariro Masters described Taylor's arguments as producing "hurtful effects" against "the Lord's work."[244]

Leo Taylor Crismon went so far as to assert in 1958, "Much of Taylor's activity was directed against Luther Rice and the missionary interests."[245]

A balanced interpretation of John Taylor's opinions about missions and antimissions had to await the writing of Larry Douglas Smith, of the University of Louisville. This teacher posited in 1982 the view that even though Taylor attacked the motives and methods of missionaries, he still held that "preaching the gospel to the unsaved was necessary and useful." Because Taylor opposed the monetary motive of missionaries did not mean that he was "totally against missions."[246] Smith holds that the "common caricature" of Taylor as an anti-missionary Baptist "does not fit the picture of him portrayed in his . . . Ten Baptist Churches."[247] "John Taylor was not antimissionary; he was against the means by which the Baptist missionary movement chose to structure and organize itself."[248]

Thoughts on Missions was not the only book that John Taylor wrote. Three years later he produced the first edition of his memoirs, A History of Ten Baptist Churches, the third edition of which is offered to the public in this present work. It seems that the basic purposes of Ten Churches were to counteract the opposition that the missions volume had met with in certain quarters and to preserve

---

[241]Kentucky Baptists, 1:575.

[242]The Genesis of American Anti-Missionism (Louisville KY, 1902) 87.

[243]The Story of Religion in America, 3rd ed. (New York, 1950) 256. Also see S[weet], "Taylor, John," in Dictionary of American Biography, 18:331.

[244]A History of Baptists in Kentucky, 194.

[245]"Taylor, John," in Encyclopedia of Southern Baptist, 2:1347.

[246]"John Taylor and Missions: A New Interpretation," The Quarterly Review: A Survey of Southern Baptist Progress 42 (April-June 1982): 58.

[247]Ibid., 54.

[248]Ibid., 61.

for all time the record of his work as a preacher and "missionary" in relation to the ten churches of which Taylor had been a member. The author wanted to show the nature of itinerating evangelism and the way by which he had conducted it—generally prompted and promoted by individual effort.

The missionary controversy was not the first disagreement to arise on the Kentucky scene. At least six disputes—some heretical, some schismatical— had disturbed the Baptist Zion in the Bluegrass State before contention over missions erupted.

The first wrangle had to do with uniting Separate and Regular Baptists. The addressing of the gospel to all mankind and the use of creeds or confessions of faith were troubling issues. Union was achieved in 1801 and United Baptists came into existence in Kentucky. This union, however, became unglued to some extent, and once more Separate Baptists appeared in the state, in 1804.[249]

Unitarianism reared its head in 1803 within the Coopers Run Church, which the Elkhorn Association excluded from its fellowship that same year.[250]

The emancipation of slaves was advocated by a few ministers, some of whom were expelled by churches and associations as early as 1805.[251]

An argument over the swapping of two slaves resulted in a schism in the Elkhorn Association in 1810 and the forming of Licking Association, which within ten years adopted the name "Particular Baptist" and generally retained the theology of John Gill instead of receiving that of Andrew Fuller. By this time Licking had become a Calvinist body, especially in regard to the atonement of Christ.[252]

Disputes over Masonry (as early as 1812 in Gallatin County) and Arminianism (in 1816) created other disorders among Kentucky Baptists.

## Campbellism

These six quarrels and the missions controversy paved the way for the Campbellite clash, which began in 1823, the year of Alexander Campbell's first visit to Kentucky. Despite the fact that John Taylor disclaimed any taste or talent for controversy,[253] he had taken part in the seven disputes or had obtained first-hand information about them.

---

[249]South Kentucky Separate Baptist Association, Minute Book A (MF., Southern Baptist Theological Seminary, Louisville KY) 41.

[250]Elkhorn Association, "Minutes," in Sweet, *American Frontier*, 1:494, 495, 499.

[251]Carter Tarrant, *History of the Baptised Ministers and Churches in Kentucky, etc., Friends to Humanity* (Frankfort KY, 1808) 6, 14, 16-17.

[252]Spencer, *Kentucky Baptists*, 2:240-43.

[253]J[ohn] Taylor, "Try the Spirits," 101.

Even though the doctrinal positions of the reforming movement headed by Alexander Campbell and his father, Thomas, were enunciated over a lengthy period, several dividing dogmas appeared quite early during the controversy and became bones of contention between Baptist leaders and Campbellite reformers.

Alexander Campbell, a native of Ireland who resided in Bethany, Virginia (now West Virginia), first appeared in Kentucky as a debater on the subject of baptism. Near the village of Washington he debated William Latta McCalla, a Presbyterian minister. This encounter lasted for nine days in October 1823.

John Taylor's first knowledge about Campbell came from a book regarding a previous debate that Campbell had held in Ohio with a Presbyterian divine named John Walker. Upon looking over this volume, Taylor felt pride that the Baptists of the West had in their midst such a man as Campbell.

Shortly after the Campbell-McCalla debate, the appearance of the reformer in the pulpit of the Lexington Church was advertised for a given Sunday. Taylor passionately longed to hear this renowned debater and in order to do so rode twenty miles from where he had been holding a meeting. Silas Noel, who lived near Frankfort, likewise came down to Lexington to attend the preaching of the Virginian. James Fishback, the pastor of the Lexington Church, was ministering that weekend to the Mount Vernon Church, in Woodford County, and thus John Taylor presided at worship in Fishback's stead.

It was on that day that Taylor heard Campbell preach in the morning and in the evening—the only times he ever listened to sermons by the reforming preacher. Campbell held forth for about three hours in the forenoon, using the last chapter of Matthew as an extensive text. He commenced his discourse well, touching the conversion of sinners and causing tears to flood the face of Taylor. But when Campbell came to a fuller explanation of his religion, he dried up Taylor's eyes "as barren as the heath of the wilderness." Seven years later Taylor remembered the sermon well: Campbell started his discussion of "religion with matrimony, and the duty of parents to breed up their children as believers in Christ. What belonged to the vital part, or religion begun by the Lord Himself, by an immediate influence from above, he left out; but did not speak against it, as he has done since."[254] What Taylor referred to as having been omitted by Campbell dealt with the work of the Holy Spirit in convicting transgressors of sin and guilt. Taylor never could forget his own conversion and the part that conviction had played in it.

A day or so later at Silas Noel's home, Taylor again encountered Campbell. Thomas John Chilton, a Separate Baptist preacher, was also present and with

---

[254]John Taylor, *Clear Creek Church*, 45.

these words commended a revival he had seen in a congregation: "Sin was weeping and crying aloud for mercy."

Campbell responded by raising his hand and loudly snapping his fingers. Looking scornfully at Chilton, he said: "I would not give that for it. If a sinner weeps when I preach, I know I have some way deceived him. Every sinner that hears the gospel, his countenance should brighten up, and he leave the place with joy!"[255]

That afternoon Campbell, Taylor, and the Noel family left the house and headed toward Frankfort, where the reformer was slated to preach. Taylor had decided not to hear Campbell again. So, when the party came to a crossroad, Taylor took his route homeward. Shaking hands, Campbell and Taylor parted with a kind of prayer for each other. Campbell said, "May your last days be your best days." Taylor looked the Virginian in the eyes and answered, "May you preach, and sinners weep; and when you next preach, use this text, and do it justice—James 4:8-9: 'Cleanse your hands, ye sinners; and purify your hearts, ye double minded. Be afflicted, and mourn, and weep: Let your laughter be turned to mourning, and your joy to heaviness.' "

Campbell stared into Taylor's face and replied not a word.[256]

When John Taylor published the second edition of his *History of Ten Baptist Churches* in 1827, he included an exegesis titled "Paul's First Work." He had written this essay in 1822, when he was preaching regularly at the Clear Creek Church and was baptizing great numbers of converts.[257] The biblical text covered by this piece is Acts 22:16—"Arise, and be baptized, and wash away thy sins, calling on the name of the Lord." These are Ananias' instructions to Paul following his conversion near Damascus. In his article Taylor holds that the guilt of Paul's sins was not removed until he was baptized. From the time of Paul's encounter with Christ until his baptism three days later, the new convert had travailed under a sense of guilt.[258] John Taylor wrote, "Though we believe nothing can radically remove the guilt of a man's soul but the blood of Christ, . . . this blood may be applied by the instrumentality of baptism, . . . through which the comforts of the Holy Ghost may . . . flow."[259] He was "far from believing" that water is useful in washing away sins except under God's "peculiar" arrangement—for example, the case of Paul. Even in such instances

---

[255]Ibid., 46.

[256]Ibid., 47.

[257]Letter, John Taylor, Oct 1830, to Alexander Campbell, *Baptist Chronicle and Literary Register* 1 (Nov 1830): 165.

[258]John Taylor, "Paul's First Work," in *A History of Ten Baptist Churches*, 2d ed. (Bloomfield KY, 1827) 225, 226.

[259]Ibid., 226.

it never happened except with regard to the blood of Christ. Be that as it may, Taylor had known many examples of baptism that were "marvelously efficacious in the comfort of poor, limited believers in Christ."[260] Here is a glimpse of the pastoral nature of Taylor's ministry.

Late in the spring of 1830 Joseph G. Norwood and Jacob Creath, Jr., editors of the recently established *Christian Examiner*, pictured John Taylor as advocating for at least the past three years what Campbellism was being denounced for teaching—namely, "Believers should be immersed for the remission of their sins." This reforming periodical, published in Lexington, Kentucky, carried an excerpt from Taylor's *Ten Churches* that contained the gist of his exegesis of Acts 22:16. The two publicists announced that they had been "charged with bringing in *'new fangled systems'* and *'damnable heresy,'* and are branded by our religious calumniators with the names 'Munster Fanatics,' 'Campbellites,' etc. etc."[261]

Even though the two and one-half-page extract from *Ten Churches* was cited by the two editors in what was probably an unfriendly way, Taylor thought that they did him a favor because they picked up "the most faulty part of the book." Had they borne all such parts away, as buzzards do, they would have shown even greater kindness to him.[262]

In the June issue of the *Millenial Harbinger*,[263] Alexander Campbell likewise accused John Taylor of expressing in the *Ten Churches* his (Campbell's) views on baptism as if he had gotten them from the reformer.[264] By then the followers of Campbell were clamorously voicing their belief in "baptism for the remission of sins."[265]

Rebuking Campbell in a public letter, Taylor wrote that the reformer was "very grossly mistaken." Taylor's purpose in exegeting Acts 22:16 had been "to encourage some timid believers to come forward." The exegete asserted that he never had considered "baptism a regenerating ordinance." "Though there are some instances in which sins have been forgiven at the time of baptism, . . . the

---

[260]Ibid., 227.

[261]"On the Remission of Sins in Baptism," *Christian Examiner* 1 (June 1830): 174-75.

[262]Letter, John Taylor to [Uriel B. Chambers], *Baptist Chronicle and Literary Register* 1 (June 1830): 93.

[263]1 (June 1830): 268.

[264]Letter, John Taylor to Campbell, *Baptist Chronicle and Literary Register* 1:165.

[265]Richard M. Tristano, *The Origins of the Restoration Movement: An Intellectual History* (Atlanta GA, 1988) 104.

most general drift of the Scriptures on the forgiveness of sins is without regard to baptism," Taylor maintained.[266]

Here were two doctrinal divergences between Baptists and Campbellites —the role of the Holy Spirit in effecting conviction of sin; forgiveness and regeneration by means of baptism. But these two only begin the list of differences. Baptists held that the followers of Campbell erred by proclaiming, among others, the following tenets: The moral law of the Old Testament was set aside by the Christian dispensation; it is not fitting to pray for sinners; the Holy Spirit does not operate directly upon the mind of a person before baptism; faith is a historical belief of facts given in the Bible; a person who presents himself to be baptized and who says that Jesus Christ is the Son of God need not be examined on any other matter; obeying the command to be baptized makes it possible for God to elect a person to salvation; any baptized person has the right to administer the ordinance of baptism; and the only creed the church needs is the Scriptures as they stand.[267]

Not only were such dogmatic differences developing between Baptists and the emergent reformers, but also points of ecclesial order were being ignored by some congregations to most of whom John Taylor had preached from time to time. Here are examples of disorder that occurred in churches in the Elkhorn Association: Without securing the approval of the congregation a group of nonmembers pledged to finance a Campbellite's monthly preaching at the Clear Creek Church; this party later celebrated the Lord's Supper in a grove near the meetinghouse; the minority membership of a Baptist congregation was constituted into a reformed church that met under the same roof as did the majority; one church retained as members the preachers who had helped the minority of a second congregation to become an organized church; and one church received into its membership a reforming minister who had been accused of creating disorder in another congregation.[268]

Such differing thought and action on the part of factions among Kentucky Baptists resulted in the most grievous conflict ever to occur in the denomination. John Henderson Spencer, the foremost historian of Baptists in the Bluegrass State, characterizes it in this way: "Never was there a time when religious controversy caused greater or more unremitting excitement on this continent than was manifested in Kentucky during the years 1829 and 1830. The contest was

---

[266]Letter, John Taylor to Campbell, *Baptist Chronicle and Literary Register* 1:165.

[267]Thomas Vaughan, *Wm. Vaughan*, 154, 170-71; Spencer, *Kentucky Baptists*, 1:626; John Taylor, *Clear Creek Church*, 10, 18, 21, 24, 26-27, 30-34, 42, 47, 52, 56-59, and "Creeds," *Baptist Chronicle and Literary Register* 2 (Aug 1831): 118.

[268]John Taylor, *Clear Creek Church*, 13-14, 16-18, 25, 28, 34, 37, 51; Birdwhistell, *Elkhorn Association*, 70.

a civil war. The contending parties were all members of the same churches and associations. The strife pervaded every department of society. The mad spirit of the hour entered the council chamber, pervaded the worshiping assembly, and invaded the sacred precincts of the hearthstone and family altar. Every form of public worship became a subject of wrangling and debate. Songs of praise, prayers for divine mercy, the regenerating power of the Holy Ghost, preaching from Scripture texts, exhorting sinners to pray, and relating the dealings of God with the soul, [all] were made subjects of jeering, contempt, and derision."[269]

The Campbell leaders in the Elkhorn Association developed a plan for securing members and congregations to the new position. Emerging strife in a church would be fomented until a division occurred. They would side with the party that favored Campbellism the more. If that party were in the majority, they would lead the congregation to reject its adherence to the Philadelphia Confession of Faith. If the side the reformist leaders chose were in the minority, they would organize it as a congregation "on the Bible alone."[270]

Another aspect of the overall scheme of the Campbell leaders was to conduct what Edmund Waller called "war dances." One such event was held at the Clear Creek Meetinghouse beginning on Christmas Day in 1829. John Taylor, who attended this three-day meeting, described it as a "feast" to the "new whims" of the "Baptist Reformers," a term that the promoters used when they advertised the event in the *Kentucky Gazette* during December. This was the first time that Taylor had seen this identifying name applied to the Campbellite leaders. Only four such reforming preachers—Jacob Creath, Sr., Jacob Creath, Jr., John Smith, and Josephus Hewitt—attended. Many had been expected.[271] These agents of change saw their mission as an effort "to remove still further the prejudices of that community [Clear Creek] against the 'Ancient Gospel,' and to confirm those who, through much evil report, were struggling to be free from the bondage of human authority."[272]

A third means for promoting the Campbell movement was the issuing of religious periodicals. In July 1823 Alexander Campbell printed the first number of the *Christian Baptist* at his homestead in Bethany, Virginia. For seven years it served as a vigorous advocate of the "ancient sect 'called Christians first at Antioch.'"[273] Its goal was to expose three flaws, as seen by the reformer, in nineteenth-century sectarianism: creeds or confessions of faith used as a means

---

[269]Spencer, *Kentucky Baptists*, 1:617-18.

[270]Ibid., 1:621.

[271]John Taylor, *Clear Creek Church*, 6-7, 42.

[272]John Williams, *John Smith*, 325.

[273]Prospectus, quoted in Robert Richardson, *Memoirs of Alexander Campbell*, 2 vols., rev. ed. (Cincinnati OH, 1897) 2:50.

to determine orthodoxy; clerical power not authorized by Scripture; and churchly organizations not sanctioned by the New Testament.[274]

In the summer of 1829 the Beaver Association, of Ohio and Pennsylvania, excluded from correspondence the association to which Alexander Campbell's Virginia congregation belonged. Shortly thereafter the neighboring associations followed Beaver's example. And thus a general movement got under way by which most of the followers of Campbellism and their churches were expelled from Baptist society during the next two years.[275] As a result, in January 1830 Campbell launched at his Virginia farm a second monthly periodical, named the *Millennial Harbinger*, by which to promote "a truly reformed church."[276] Six months later he stopped publication of the *Christian Baptist* and abandoned the denominational name it embraced.[277]

Once the effort to exclude the followers of Campbell from Baptist churches reached Kentucky, a monthly journal was begun in Lexington in November 1829 by Joseph G. Norwood and Jacob Creath, Jr., advocates of ecclesial reform. Called the *Christian Examiner*, this publication served as a mouthpiece for Campbellism in the Bluegrass. As early as June 1830 parts of John Taylor's *History of Ten Baptist Churches* came under fire in the new periodical. In the issue for that month the editors leveled their guns against two essays in the second edition of Taylor's book.[278]

The publication in May 1830 at Frankfort of John Taylor's blistering polemic against the reformers, titled *History of Clear Creek Church; and Campbellism Exposed*, gave rise the following month to a second Campbellite paper in Lexington. The editor was Jacob Creath, Jr.; the name of this twenty-four-page quarterly was *Budget*. In its first number, Creath accused Taylor of dividing the Clear Creek Church by his recently published history. Editor Creath mailed a free copy of this issue of the *Budget* to Taylor in care of the post office at Frankfort. When Creath posted the paper in Lexington, he had made the postmaster there think that it was double in size, or so Taylor surmised. One of Taylor's sons picked up the paper at Frankfort and was required to pay double postage.

Upon opening the paper at home, the father discovered that Creath had used eight of the twenty-four pages to display a public letter from the reformer to Taylor. In addition, other pages carried several extracts of Taylor's writings. Taylor

[274]Tristano, *Restoration Movement*, 94.

[275]Spencer, *Kentucky Baptists*, 1:610.

[276]Tristano, *Restoration Movement*, 105.

[277]Winfred Ernest Garrison and Alfred Thomas DeGroot, *The Disciples of Christ: A History*, rev. ed. (Saint Louis MO, 1958) 254.

[278]"On the Remission of Sins in Baptism," *Christian Examiner* 1:174-76; "Elder Taylor's Apostasy," ibid., 188-89; Garrison and DeGroot, *Disciples of Christ*, 254.

examined parts of the *Budget* and then consigned it to the flames of his fireplace. He had three reasons for burning it: He wanted to forget the folly of Creath's letter; he did not care to begin a correspondence with the editor; and he was disturbed by having had to pay extra postage on the paper.[279]

Such hard-hitting, religious journalism dealing with so particular a subject on the part of Campbell and his men was bound to call forth the establishment by Kentucky Baptists of countervailing papers. And so a veritable war of words erupted. While the Campbell controversy was at its height, in 1829 and 1830, two Baptist papers were being produced in the state. *The Baptist Chronicle and Literary Register*, published in Georgetown, was the more important periodical in opposing Campbellism as a departure from Baptist faith and practice, even though the paper was published for only three years (1830–1832). In March 1830 the *Baptist Recorder* (begun in 1826 as the *Baptist Register*) was merged with the *Chronicle*.[280] It was the *Baptist Chronicle* that published at least two letters and three essays by John Taylor dealing with the conflict.[281]

Baptists knew that they must count on more than the printed page if they were to turn the tide against Campbellism in the Bluegrass. It seems that a few Baptist preachers determined that the time had come for taking direct action in order to remove the reformers from the Elkhorn churches.

Following the passage of the resolution by the Beaver Association, in August 1829, regarding Campbellism, the minutes of that session were widely circulated in Virginia and Kentucky. The next month the Frankfort Church, of which Silas Mercer Noel was the pastor, urged the Franklin Association to publicize and protest the errors of Campbell and the disruptive tactics of his followers, which were directed against churchly order, sound doctrine, and the constitutions of churches and associations. Franklin was not ready for such a decisive move; instead, it voted to discountenance only the "corruptions" of Campbellism, thus identifying no perpetrators.[282] Such was too mild a relief for the deplorable problem at hand.

To set the stage for more remedial measures, John Taylor took up his pen again and produced his last book. He called it the *History of Clear Creek Church; and Campbellism Exposed*. It is probable that he began work on this

---

[279]J[ohn] Taylor, "Try the Spirits," *Baptist Chronicle and Literary Register* 1:101-102; Letter, John Taylor to Campbell, ibid. 1:164-65.

[280]Spencer, *Kentucky Baptists*, 1:217-18, 597; C. R. Daley, "Baptist Papers in Kentucky," in Leo Taylor Chrismon, ed., *Baptists in Kentucky, 1776–1976; A Bicentennial Volume* (Middletown KY, 1975) 186-88.

[281]1 (June 1830): 92-93; 1 (July 1830) 100-102; 1 (Nov 1830): 164-66; 2 (June 1831): 81-83; 2 (Aug 1831): 118.

[282]Spencer, *Kentucky Baptists*, 1:611-14.

sixty-page volume early in January 1830. The book came from the press of
Albert Gallatin Hodges in Frankfort the following May. Offered for sale at 12½¢
per copy, it was first available at the office of the *Frankfort Commentator*, where
it had seen the light of day. The next month it could be purchased in Georgetown
at the *Baptist Chronicle and Literary Register*.[283]

The appearance of Taylor's little book added considerably to the furor
already in progress. The reforming leaders in general opposed it with strong
passion. When the schismatic wing of the North District Association met in July
1830 at the Spencers Creek Church, the author appeared as the vendor of his
book. Covered with the dust of a droughty summer and laden with his saddlebags
stuffed with copies of this new book, John Taylor approached his erstwhile
fellow preacher John Smith and requested him to announce from the stand that
the work could be bought on the grounds. Smith demurred, saying that it was
wrong for Taylor to circulate such a book and for Smith to advertise it. Indeed
the author had ridden into the lion's den itself, for there on the stage sat, among
others, the two Jacob Creaths and Thomas Campbell, father of Alexander.
Despite his scruples, Smith ascended the platform and publicized the sale of the
book. He said that if all its slanders and lies were cut out there would not remain
in any part of it enough to make a thumb-paper for a schoolboy.[284]

On the other hand, many of Taylor's cohorts were delighted with his writing.
Uriel B. Chambers, of Georgetown, editor of the *Chronicle*, wrote that the
"pamphlet" breathed a spirit of candor and faithfulness, though it was often "a
cutting spirit" toward those who had rent Baptist churches. Taylor boldly
identified the leaders of this "new system of reform." Nonetheless, the booklet
stood aloof from personal invective and even from censure except so far as it
flowed from deep concern for the disruption that the reformers had caused,
Chambers continued.[285]

In the *History of Clear Creek Church*, Taylor dealt with points of order that
churches had disregarded. "Flagrant outrage on good order" committed by Campbell's followers had moved him to take up his pen.[286] Much of the disorder that
concerned the author had taken place in the Clear Creek Church and had been
committed by the two Jacob Creaths and by William Morton and William Rice,
all of whom were preaching men. The breaches of order consisted of preaching
against the congregation's creedal foundation, of inordinately prolonging heresy
trials, of the younger Creath's accepting a call to preach in the meetinghouse that

---

[283]*Baptist Chronicle and Literary Register* 1 (May 1830): 80, and 1 (June 1830): 89.
[284]John Williams, *John Smith*, 352, 362-64; Doran, ed., *Memoirs of Jacob Creath, Jr.*
(Cincinnati OH, 1872) 208.
[285]*Baptist Chronicle and Literary Register* 1 (May 1830): 80.
[286]John Taylor, *Clear Creek Church*, [iii].

was extended by nonmembers who had not secured the approval of the congregation, of this Creath's celebrating the Lord's Supper at an outdoor oratory a few hundred yards from the church house, and of the two Creaths' forming in the fall of 1829 a "Campbell church" composed of about forty members from the Clear Creek Church.[287]

The author might have treated some of these irregularities as questions of trespass or of heresy, but in formulating the grand scheme for Campbellism's exclusion he chose to emphasize points of order. Disorder pervaded not only the internal fellowship of the Clear Creek Church but also its connection with the Elkhorn Association. The two Creaths were members of the Versailles Church, which was, like Clear Creek, an affiliant of Elkhorn. The writer's broad view encompassed the covenant among the churches that composed the Bluegrass union, as well as the practice of correspondence that joined one association with another.[288] Taylor held that in a disorderly manner the "Creath men" (meaning the two Jacobs and their allies) had "broken the covenant with churches in their own close communion."[289]

Taylor proposed a course of action for the Elkhorn Association to take at its 1830 session at the Silas Church: to refuse to seat these disturbers unless they repented and restored what they had taken away; to remove from associational affiliation the churches to which the reformers belonged unless these congregations used their discipline and expelled these schismatics; to reassert the principle, first stated by Elkhorn in 1786, that when a church refused to take the advice of the association, it would be denied a seat at its annual meetings; and to act promptly on requests regarding Campbellism that came to the association from its aggrieved congregations. Taylor announced that these "Creath men" could expect to face charges at the next session of Elkhorn.[290] Until these procedures had been set in place, the writer urged the use of "a kind of *stay waste.*" This was the expedient of denying the followers of Campbell a place in Baptist meetinghouses.[291] By these calculated courses of action Elkhorn would say to the Campbell and Creath followers, "You have committed sacrilege on one of Christ's dominions on earth connected with us," and no longer can you occupy a seat with us.[292]

---

[287]Ibid., 9-21; Letter, John Taylor to Campbell, *Baptist Chronicle and Literary Register* 1:166.

[288]John Taylor, *Clear Creek Church*, 14, 37, 55.

[289]Ibid., 37.

[290]Ibid., 37-39.

[291]Ibid., 53.

[292]Ibid., 54.

In the overall plan, not only did Elkhorn have a role to play but Franklin did also. "What will Franklin Association do at her next session?" asked Taylor.

He answered his own question: "Break off her correspondence with Elkhorn except she rid herself of such filthy lumber [disorderly Creath followers]."[293]

By means of Taylor's *History of Clear Creek Church; and Campbellism Exposed*, the Baptists of Elkhorn and Franklin were informed of the procedure and the rationale of the plan by which the removal of Campbellite ministers from the churches of these two associations would be attempted.

The highhandedness of the two Jacob Creaths in organizing a church out of a discontented minority of the South Benson Church in January 1830 aroused the other Franklin churches to a sense of danger that they had never before felt. Its leaders decided as early as May to call a special session of the association.[294]

This unusual convention of the Franklin Association met on 9-10 July 1830 at the Frankfort Church. The John Taylor family had a prominent place at this session, which Spencer characterized as "probably the most important [Baptist] association ever held in Kentucky."[295] Not only did the aging father attend but his sons Benjamin and Joseph were also present, all as messengers from the Buck Run Church. Benjamin was appointed to the committee to arrange the order of business for the session; Joseph, to the committee to write a corresponding letter to Elkhorn; and John, to the committee to compose the circular letter to the Franklin churches. The letter to Elkhorn dealt with the objections of the Clear Creek Church and of the Franklin Association against the followers of Campbell. John and Benjamin Taylor, along with five others, were selected to carry this letter to the annual meeting of Elkhorn in August.[296]

The circular letter to the churches had been put on paper by Silas Mercer Noel well before the assembling of the brethren in Frankfort. This missive, which was adopted by Franklin, called on the congregations to "divest yourselves of the last vestige of Campbellism."[297] It contained the famous "Thirty-nine Articles; or, a New Edition of Old Errors, Extracted from Alexander Campbell's *Christian Baptist* and *Millenial Harbinger*." This letter filled eleven pages of the published associational minutes. It announced to Baptist society that the Franklin Association would no longer correspond with any association or church that tolerated the heresy of Campbellism.[298]

---

[293]Ibid., 37.

[294]Spencer, *Kentucky Baptists*, 1:622-23; John Williams, *John Smith*, 345.

[295]Spencer, *Kentucky Baptists*, 1:624.

[296]Franklin Association, *Minutes*, Special Session, July 1830, 3, 4, 5.

[297]Ibid., 6.

[298]Ibid., 5-15.

As a part of the published minutes of the Franklin Association, this circular letter regarding Campbellism was distributed to churches in the Bluegrass and elsewhere. A part of the concerted plan against the reformers had been the scheduling of Franklin's special session well in advance of the regular meetings of other Kentucky associations. As important as the Frankfort session had been in arousing the Baptist giant to action, the "Great Battle," as the older Jacob Creath called it, was yet to come in Elkhorn.[299]

John Taylor and his eldest son, Benjamin, as corresponding messengers from Franklin, attended the Elkhorn Association in August 1830 at the Silas Church, in Bourbon County.[300] Perhaps many people recalled that Taylor had written that Campbell's followers could expect to face challenges at Silas.[301] Indeed it became a place of reckoning. First, the Clear Creek Church and the Franklin Association complained that the Versailles Church had retained in its membership preachers who had formed the minorities of churches into regular congregations, the members within these minorities having departed from the faith and practice of Elkhorn.[302]

Next, the Providence Church stood accused of violating three points of order: the attempt at the current session to seat ten messengers instead of three as allowed by a rule then only one year old; the reception of Jacob Creath, Jr., as a member, even though he had abandoned the doctrine and order of Elkhorn; and the allowing of the younger Creath to remain in its fellowship in spite of the fact that he had helped to constitute churches out of congregational minorities that had also forsaken Elkhorn's faith and practice.

After lengthy debate, the association resolved to drop these two churches from its correspondence. The vote was forty-two to fourteen. In view of the fact that six of the fourteen noes came from members of the two churches being disciplined, only eight messengers from churches that remained in the union favored retaining the two reformed congregations.[303]

The following year Elkhorn excluded from its fellowship the South Elkhorn Church, of which Taylor had once been a member. At that annual meeting, John Taylor and his son Benjamin also attended as corresponding messengers from Franklin.[304]

In September 1830 John Taylor and his two oldest sons again represented Buck Run Church at the regular annual meeting of the Franklin Association. (The

---

[299]Spencer, *Kentucky Baptists*, 1:636.
[300]Elkhorn Association, *Minutes*, 1830, 3.
[301]John Taylor, *Clear Creek Church*, 39.
[302]Elkhorn Association, *Minutes*, 1830, 3-4.
[303]Ibid., 4.
[304]Elkhorn Association, *Minutes*, 1831, 2; Spencer, *Kentucky Baptists*, 1:622.

father was elected to serve as a messenger to nine associations during the forth-coming 1831 season.)[305] Franklin's published minutes for September 1830 announced to Baptist society that the two Jacob Creaths had been excom-municated from the "General Union of Baptists" by the Elkhorn Association and that Josephus Hewett had been suspended for a year.[306]

During the 1830 season John Taylor attended the meetings of eleven associations, as follows: July, two; August, four; September, four; and October, one. His horseback travel covered about one thousand miles in riding to and from the sessions of these unions. On the last day of his homeward return in October he rode fifty-one miles. His associational travel in 1830 compared favorably with his yearly record of riding nearly one thousand miles for that purpose over the preceding twenty-five years.

Kentucky weather in 1830 was hotter and drier than Taylor had before experienced. He described it thus:

> But on we went, through burning heat,
> With panting breath and trickling sweat.
> We mov'd on with hunger and thirst,
> Through the long lanes and clouds of dust.

In spite of adversity, Taylor traveled an average of about forty miles per day that summer and early fall.[307]

John Taylor did his duty regarding Campbellism that sultry summer not-withstanding his advanced age of seventy-seven years. Because Silas Mercer Noel and other ministers were likewise faithful, all the associations in central and northern Kentucky decided against the reformers during 1830.[308]

The membership of Baptist churches in Kentucky in 1829 numbered 45,442. Three years later this figure had fallen to 35,862. Here was a loss of 9,580 communicants, due to the apostasy of baptized converts from the revival of 1827 and to the expulsion of Campbell followers that came in the wake of the "Great Battle" at Silas in 1830.[309] It is improbable that John Taylor or any other Baptist minister anticipated such a remarkable decline in the ranks of their churches. But one thing is certain: The Campbell schism affected the faith and practice of Kentucky Baptists from that day until this.

---

[305]Franklin Association, *Minutes*, September 1830, 1, 3.
[306]Ibid., 4
[307]Letter, John Taylor to Campbell, *Baptist Chronicle and Literary Register* 1:165.
[308]Spencer, *Kentucky Baptists*, 1:637-41.
[309]Ibid., 1:642.

## Death

John Taylor lived out his last twenty years near the Forks of Elkhorn, in Franklin County, Kentucky. During the previous twenty years, while he resided on the Ohio River, he had met with fortune, and his estate had increased accordingly. While in Franklin County the value of his taxable property ranged from $21,625 in 1819 to $2,800 in 1830. This property included slaves, realty, cattle, horses, and carriages. The average annual evaluation was $9,871; the median, $10,000.[310]

It seems that a good deal of Taylor's possessions consisted of slaves. From 1787 until the year after his death, when his affairs were being settled, Taylor's estate had held a total of thirty-two blacks.[311] Their names and birth dates were recorded in his family Bible.[312]

During Taylor's Inner Bluegrass years the number of his slaves ranged from nineteen to three. The majority of these people were below seventeen years old.[313] During his last three years Taylor rented out one or two slaves.[314] Such was a common practice for the production of income.

When Taylor died he possessed eight slaves. Included were Philis and her children, William, Ann, and Gabriel, all of whom he bequeathed to his second wife. Taylor's other slaves were Essex (the only male adult he owned), Samuel, Hariott, and Nancy. These four, who were valued at $1,725, he required to be sold at his death.[315] Essex is remembered for joining the Buck Run Temperance Society, in 1832.[316]

The years 1832 and 1833 bore particular sorrow for the elderly minister, whose age had now reached fourscore. First, came the death on 19 July 1832 of his grandson John P. Taylor, the eleven-year-old boy of John Wickliffe Taylor.

---

[310]Franklin County (KY) Tax Lists, 1816–1835. These calculations are based on the lists for seventeen years. Some form of incompleteness has caused those for 1829, 1831, and 1832 to be set aside.

[311]Dorothy Thompson, "John Taylor of the Ten Churches," 571. Because Taylor acquired his first eight slaves in 1782, this total number of blacks is probably too small.

[312]The second owner of this Bible was the preacher's daughter Sally Smith (b. 1807). Her youngest son, DeWitt Wickliffe Smith (b. 1844) had possession of it in 1906. He passed the book on to his daughter Mary Temple Smith, wife of Dr. Stuart Broadwell. In time it was given to their adopted daughter, Mary Broadwell. Its subsequent owners are unknown.

[313]Franklin County (KY) Tax Lists, 1816–1835.

[314]Ibid., 1833–1835.

[315]Ibid., 1835; Franklin County (KY) Will Book 2 (Office of the County Clerk, Frankfort) 68; Franklin County (KY) Inventory and Sales Book A, 348.

[316]Buck Run Temperance Society, Minute Book, 20.

Then on Christmas Eve that year, Betsy, his beloved wife of fifty years, joined the choir invisible. The grave of Elizabeth Taylor became the first in a newly created cemetery about one hundred yards beyond the gray stone house where dwelt the dwindling John Taylor family. The burial site was located ten paces from the edge of the bluff overlooking South Elkhorn Creek. Nine days after the death of his wife, John Taylor lost a grandson, Temple Smith, a nine-year-old lad. This eldest child of Sally Smith was drowned at Churchs Ford in Main Elkhorn Creek. The accident occurred when his horse fell while crossing the stream. On 6 August 1833, death claimed another grandchild of the preacher. She was Elizabeth T. Gray Forsee, the second child of Nancy Taylor and John D. Gray. (Her husband was Peter Forsee, who married Elizabeth's sister Sally Ann Gray two years later.)[317]

Loneliness may have prompted the eighty-year-old John Taylor to take to himself a wife again. Whatever the motive, the widower was joined in wedlock on 16 August 1833 to Mary Nash, of Woodford County, an unmarried woman of half his age. The officiant was George Blackburn, a fellow minister of Taylor's and a staunch advocate for the short-lived Kentucky Baptist Convention.[318]

The second marriage of John Taylor was destined to be a short one. On 23 January 1835 he signed his will in the presence of his neighbors Isaac and Polly Wilson. He directed his executors to return to Mary, his wife of seventeen months, all the money and every other type of property she owned at the time of their marriage. In addition John bequeathed to her his Negro woman Philis and her three children, the sum of one thousand dollars, and her choice of any "riding horse or mare" on the premises. The remainder of Taylor's estate was to be auctioned off by the executors; the proceeds of the vendue were to be divided equally among his seven surviving children.[319]

John Taylor, hoary with age, laid down his burdens on the twelfth of the following April. When dying on that Sunday evening, he was "in quite a joyful state of mind. It was his desire to depart and be with Christ."[320] A colleague who was younger than Taylor wrote that "his death was peaceful and tranquil."[321] His

[317]Dorothy Thompson, "Ancestors and Descendants," 37, 42, 43, 44, 49, and "John Taylor of the Ten Churches," 570, and "Additional Notes on the John Taylor Family," 348, 349.
[318]*Commonwealth*, Frankfort KY, 20 Aug 1833; *Lexington Observer and Reporter*, 29 Aug 1833; Spencer, *Kentucky Baptists*, 2:31.
[319]Franklin County (KY) Will Book 2, 68.
[320]James B. Taylor, *Virginia Baptist Ministers*, 2d ed., 221. Also see *Commonwealth*, 18 Apr 1835.
[321]Welch, "John Taylor," 6:159.

weary frame was laid to rest in the family cemetery on his farm. The grave had been dug to the right of his dear Elizabeth and faced the rising sun. There he awaited the resurrection morn.[322]

A local newspaper eulogized John Taylor as "an old and faithful minister of the gospel."[323]

Eight days after Taylor's death, Benjamin, his eldest son, and William French, a son-in-law, appeared before the Franklin County Court, bearing the minister's last will and testament. The tribunal gave the execution of the will to the two presenters.[324]

When court-appointed appraisers of the estate filed their inventory with the justices on the following 17 August, it was disclosed that the deceased preacher had lent money to ten individuals and one business concern, totaling $3,185. These loans were secured by cash notes. Three sons-in-law had borrowed $355. Four land buyers owed $1,305. Uriel B. Chambers, the editor of the recently established *Cross and Baptist Banner*, had been lent $500, which perhaps went to finance this new denominational paper at Frankfort. The sum of $1,000 had shored up the business ventures of James McConathy, of Milton, Kentucky, who received both a private loan and a commercial loan. A loan of $25 went to an unidentified project. Besides these notes, $129.75 in cash was also found in his strong box. These liquid assets amounted to $3,314.75.[325] Taylor played the part of a money broker clear to the end of his career.

On his farm at the Forks of Elkhorn, the preacher had produced tobacco, wheat, corn, potatoes, hemp, honey, hay, cattle, sheep, and hogs. The total value of his personalty, excluding the four slaves given to his wife, Mary, was set at $6,188.80.[326]

---

[322]Dorothy Thompson, "Additional Notes on the John Taylor Family," 348. Within a quarter century Taylor's grave was called "neglected." Ford, "John Taylor," 400. In August 1950, Sarah French Moore Clough, who lived in Paris, Kentucky, rediscovered the unfenced Taylor cemetery with the graves of six persons connected with the family. Dorothy Thompson, "Additional Notes on the John Taylor Family," 348. In 1985, when the Elkhorn Association celebrated its bicentennial, Pastor Harold G. Polk, its director of missions, promoted a project by which these six graves were moved from Franklin County to the yard of the Clear Creek Church, in Woodford County. At a cost of ten thousand dollars, this undertaking was financed by the association. Polk, "John Taylor Gravesite," *Kentucky Baptist Heritage* 12 (July 1985): 14.

[323]*Commonwealth*, 18 Apr 1835.

[324]Franklin County (KY) Court Order Book K (Office of the County Clerk, Frankfort) 33.

[325]Franklin County (KY) Inventory and Sales Book A, 346-47.

[326]Ibid., 347-48.

When John Taylor died, four of his seven surviving sons and daughters still lived in Kentucky. The other three had moved to Illinois a year or two preceding his demise—Joseph, to Clinton County; John Wickliffe and Sarah, to Sangamon County.[327]

Benjamin, the eldest of John and Elizabeth Taylor's nine offspring, sat on the first board of trustees for Georgetown College, in Kentucky, and served as the principal executor of his father's will. Ben's own estate in the Bluegrass went into bankruptcy, and by 1841 he had settled on the Mississippi River about seventy miles from Vicksburg.[328]

Joseph Taylor, who became an attorney in 1807 and a Baptist minister in 1829, had moved to Illinois in 1834 and by the next year was seated on Shoal Creek in Clinton County. While visiting in Lexington in 1845 he succumbed to typhoid fever and was buried in the family cemetery on South Elkhorn.[329]

The eldest daughter, Nancy, was twice married. In 1823 she became a member of the Buck Run Church. She died of a protracted illness in 1847. Her obituary ran: "She bore her afflictions which were at times very severe with a great degree of Christian fortitude."[330] Her second husband, Thomas L. Tate, followed her in death five years later; both were buried in the Taylor Cemetery on South Elkhorn. Nancy bore six children by her first marriage; one, by her second. Her last child was James William Tate, who served as the state treasurer for twenty-one years beginning in 1867. He absconded with $350,000 of public funds and was never heard from again.[331]

Polly Taylor and her husband, William French, continued to live on the Georgetown Road in Franklin County. He died in 1863; she died sixteen years later.[332]

[327]Dorothy Thompson, "Ancestors and Descendants," 36, 43; John Carroll Powers, *History of the Early Settlers [of] Sangamon County, Illinois* (Chicago IL, 1881; reprint ed., Springfield IL, 1970) 668, 709.

[328]Spencer, *Kentucky Baptists*, 1:599; Woodford County (KY) Deed Book R (Office of County Clerk, Versailles) 89-90; *Baptist Banner and Western Pioneer*, 7 Apr 1842.

[329]*Baptist Banner and Western Pioneer*, 7 Apr 1842; Spencer, *Kentucky Baptists*, 2:298; Franklin County (KY) Deed Book Q, 2-5, 15-16, 133-34.

[330]*Baptist Banner and Western Pioneer*, 21 Oct 1847.

[331]Ibid.; Thomas D. Clark, Kentucky: *Kentucky: Land of Contrast*, Regions of America ser. (New York NY, 1968) 160-61; "Treasurers of the State of Kentucky," *Register of Kentucky Historical Society* 1 (May 1903): 46; Dorothy Thompson, "Additional Notes on the John Taylor Family," 349-50, and "Ancestors and Descendants," 37; Franklin County (KY) Deed Book P, 287-88.

[332]Dorothy Thompson, "Ancestors and Descendants," 39, 40. I was privileged to become acquainted with Sarah French Moore Clough, a descendant of this family who lived in Paris, Kentucky. She was a great-great-great-granddaughter of John Taylor. Sarah

Jane Taylor Plummer and her second husband, James Elliott, left Franklin County for Illinois the year following her father's death and settled in Sangamon County.[333]

John Wickliffe and his family had moved from Gallatin County to Sangamon County early in 1833.[334]

In 1834 Sarah Taylor and her husband, Joseph Smith, sold their stone dwelling and its 191-acre farm on the Georgetown Road to John Lewis, a teacher and poet, and the same year migrated to Sangamon County. Lewis conducted a school in the building and named the place "Llangollen" after his home in Virginia.[335]

Seven of the nine sons and daughters of John and Elizabeth Taylor achieved adulthood and begot forty-six children.[336] Only two of their grown children lived out their days in Kentucky. The other five migrated westward—one to Mississippi, four to Illinois. As did their parents and forebears they indeed loved a "new country."

## Dimensions of Taylor's Career

A final look at John Taylor outlines the scope of his career. It was multifaceted to be sure, but its chief aspect was his vocation as a preacher. Even though in some parts of this writing he has been designated as "John Taylor the author," his labor as a minister of the gospel of Jesus Christ towers above all else. It was to this calling that he gave himself with abandon in season and out of season. In the era in which Taylor's life fell and on the frontier where he lived, the most important dimension of a religious career was preaching.

What was the nature of his preaching? What were its essential elements? The theme of his sermons was the crucified Christ, presented as the only Saviour of

---

Clough, Interview by Chester R. Young, 25 Dec 1990, Paris KY.

[333]Dorothy Thompson, "Ancestors and Descendants," 41; Powers, *Sangamon County, Illinois*, 284; Franklin County (KY) Deed Book Q, 2-5, 133-34.

[334]Gallatin County (KY) Deed Book H, 580; Powers, *Sangamon County, Illinois*, 709.

[335]Franklin County (KY) Deed Book P, 113-16; Deed Book Q, 133-34. This house stood until early in the twentieth century when it was torn down. Dorothy Thompson, "Ancestors and Descendants," 43. It has been my pleasure to have corresponded with Mrs. Dorothy Allen Brown Thompson (b. 1896), who is a descendant of Sarah Taylor Smith. Mrs. Thompson is a great-great-granddaughter of John Taylor the author. Dorothy Brown Thompson, Kansas City MO, 18 Jan, [20] Feb 1990, to Chester R. Young, Williamsburg KY; Dorothy Thompson, "Ancestors and Descendants," 44-46.

[336]Dorothy Thompson, "Ancestors and Descendants," 33-47.

lost humanity.[337] He declared God's "whole counsel," including the doctrine of sovereign grace, which was generally conceived at that time to be a Calvinistic theme. But he did not believe that the likelihood of winning souls to Jesus would be reduced because grace was preached.[338]

Regarding the substance of his preaching, Taylor confessed in 1827 that during two-thirds of his career he had been "destitute of that tenderness of spirit that becomes the gospel ministry." He admitted that he had been busy at preaching all those years but that he had been concerned about "trifles": Was Adam a natural or spiritual man when he was created? Did Adam die a moral death when first he sinned? Can God's election be added to or taken from? Are regeneration and the new birth the same experience? Were the elect chosen before or after Adam's sin? Did Christ die for all mankind or for only a part of it? Were the elect sheep or goats before their conversion?[339]

Taylor's confession concerning the lack of compassion for sinners in certain periods of his ministry was seized upon by some Campbell followers as a sign of Taylor's apostasy. Taylor intended his statement to be a personal lament before God about the intermittent "coldness of his affections."[340] Taylor was saying that when his preaching was at its best he invited every sinner "to come to Christ whatever his guilt might be." From his own experience he knew what "o'clock it is with my soul" when he did not issue the call to heed the voice of Christ. The main object of the gospel was to secure "the repentance of sinners and the forgiv[e]ness of their sins," he insisted.[341]

How did Taylor regard the procedural elements of a sermon? It never went beyond three-quarters of an hour in length.[342] It was based on the Bible. Men like Taylor quoted the New Testament as if they knew all of it from memory. They often wept while they preached, and they did not hesitate to use language designed to arouse the emotions. In preaching "they usually threw the reins upon the neck of feeling and let her run full speed."[343] One of Taylor's coadjutors characterized his speaking: "He attempted nothing but scriptural plainness. The weapons of his warfare were wielded with much power. No man knew better

---

[337]James E[ly] Welch, "Early Preachers of Kentucky," *Christian Repository* 5 (May 1856): 291.

[338]Ibid., 290.

[339]John Taylor, "The Gospel Supper," *A History of Ten Baptist Churches*, 2d ed. (Bloomfield KY, 1827) 245.

[340]John Taylor, Franklin County KY, Oct 1830, Letter to Alexander Campbell, *Baptist Chronicle* 1:165.

[341]John Taylor, "The Gospel Supper," 236, 245.

[342]Ford, "John Taylor," 4.

[343]Welch, "Early Preachers of Kentucky," 292.

than he how to reprove, rebuke, and exhort with all long-suffering and doctrine. When he used the rod of correction, all were made to tremble. The Lord wrought glorious things by him."[344] Taylor was a very sensible and pointed man in his remarks and had very little patience with loose, disjointed discourses."[345]

Taylor's preaching was unusually successful. Ministers of his day subscribed to the idea that whoever caught the most fish was the best fisherman. One reason for their success in the pulpit was because they sought "to win souls to Christ." They were great preachers because they were great fishermen.[346] The preaching of men like Taylor usually turned out as they hoped because they "did not set themselves above their brethren as a sacerdotal class, deserving special attention and sumptuous accommodations." They identified themselves with the people. They took part in their labor and their privations.[347] Taylor entered into his pulpital duties with zest. A younger minister who worked with him but yet disagreed with his position on organized missions described his demeanor: He was an exceedingly "efficient preacher; his judicious zeal, strong faith, and remarkable industry qualified him to be useful to many souls. He was always cheerful, yet solemn, and willing to preach when requested."[348]

A missionary of the Triennial Convention who served in Missouri for a term classed John Taylor, William Hickman, Ambrose Dudley, and David Barrow as pioneer Kentucky preachers who faithfully proclaimed the gospel under adverse circumstances. They demonstrated "untiring industry and self-consecration."[349]

Judgments on the preaching of John Taylor began with his own in 1818 when he portrayed himself as "a worn-out, old, unprofitable servant." His friend William Kellar had died the year before, and Taylor was contrasting himself with Kellar, who had been "so profitable in the church."[350] Robert Baylor Semple, a contemporary Virginia preacher and historian, saw Taylor as "a preacher of weight, wisdom, and usefulness" in Kentucky even as he had been in Virginia.[351]

In 1888 John Henderson Spencer, a historian of Kentucky Baptists, grouped Taylor with Lewis Craig and William Hickman and described them thus: "Than these, a nobler trio of gospel ministers has seldom blessed any one community

---

[344]James B. Taylor, *Virginia Baptist Ministers*, 1st ed., 196.

[345]Thomas Vaughan, *Wm. Vaughan*, 71.

[346]Welch, "Early Preachers of Kentucky," 293.

[347]Ibid., 291.

[348]James B. Taylor, *Virginia Baptist Ministers*, 1st ed., 197.

[349]Welch, "Early Preachers of Kentucky," 290.

[350]John Taylor, *Thoughts on Missions*, 62.

[351]*Baptists in Virginia*, rev. ed., 415.

on our planet." Their names were familiar to Baptists over North America and in Europe.[352]

Professor Otis Kermit Rice called the influence of Taylor in western Virginia as "perhaps greater than that of any other Baptist preacher of his time."[353] A like judgment is extended to his work in Kentucky by Professor Larry Douglas Smith.[354]

Among the Baptists of Kentucky, John Taylor's renown as a pioneer Baptist preacher is well entrenched.

Not only was Taylor a famed proclaimer of the gospel, but he was also a volunteer missionary—an unpaid, unappointed evangel who went throughout the countryside leaving appointments regarding religious services that he proposed to conduct, who took the gospel to people who seldom heard it, and who kept his eyes peeled for ideal sites for the beginning of new congregations. He was "famous for planning new churches," wrote William Hickman.[355] Such voluntary work took him initially into the mountains of northwestern Virginia, where he and Joseph Redding were seen as the "daring spirits of that age."[356] One critic of Taylor's opposition to organized missions considered his later service as a missionary in Kentucky to have been "almost apostolic."[357]

Taylor's itinerancy carried him across northern Virginia from the Lower Northern Neck into the Upper Ohio River Valley. Later his parish encompassed central Kentucky and parts of Tennessee, Ohio, Indiana, and Missouri. At heart he was a true missioner.

As a denominationalist, Taylor sank his roots deeply into the Separate Baptist soil of Virginia. Shortly before he removed to Kentucky, the Lower South River Church joined a Regular Baptist association. In the Bluegrass he rejoiced in the merger of Separates and Regulars in 1801 and gave allegiance to the resultant General Union, which eventually spread throughout Kentucky.

A builder of Baptist society and a promoter of the work of its associations in Kentucky, Taylor was "famed for his success in reconciling contending parties and usually so directed his efforts as to be regarded the friend of both." On one occasion at the Elkhorn Association in 1805 a certain controversy caused much disagreement among the preachers. The determining vote pitted a minority of elder brethren against a majority of young ministers. At the Sunday preaching

[352]*Kentucky Baptists*, 1:160.

[353]*The Allegheny Frontier: West Virginia Beginnings, 1730-1830* (Lexington KY, 1940) 285.

[354]"John Taylor," 54.

[355]*Life and Travels*, 35.

[356]James B. Taylor, *Virginia Baptist Ministers*, 1st ed., 195.

[357]Carroll, *The Genesis of American Anti-Missions*, 104.

service Taylor, having been elected a speaker, took for his text "Let Reuben live and not die," from Deuteronomy 33:6. Considering that Reuben was the oldest son of Jacob, Taylor pleaded with the young preachers not to rejoice over their elders who were on the losing side. Such conciliation poured oil on troubled water.[358]

Taylor exerted a wholesome influence on the affairs of the Elkhorn, the Long Run, and the Franklin associations. Generally he attended the meetings of six to eight such groups each year.[359] James Ely Welch, who sometimes accompanied Taylor in the later years of the elder preacher's life, wrote that such travel required "persevering industry."[360]

Farming was the primary livelihood of John Taylor. During his early years in Kentucky he and his sons worked in the fields with his slaves. In his latter decades he seems to have hired overseers for his work force. Professor William Warren Sweet classes Taylor as an excellent example of "the farmer-preachers who were so largely responsible for the founding of Baptist churches in western Virginia, North Carolina, Kentucky, and Tennessee."[361] Taylor is credited with having been closely connected with the development of Franklin County, Kentucky, in which he died.[362]

Landed speculation was the second means by which the preacher made a living. He bought at least 14,944 acres in Kentucky, plus 2,051.78 acres of the public domain in Indiana. Almost all of these lands were sold for a profit. Tracts of generous size were given to his sons and daughters. The profits from farming and speculating made Taylor a wealthy man.

The role of a polemicist was another side of his multifarious career. The controversies he engaged in have been spelled out above. It was the strong will of Taylor that so often evoked trouble for him. He could not easily turn "from what he considered the path of duty. When once his mind was fully made up, he carried out his convictions with such unyielding tenacity as to render himself liable . . . to the charge of obstinacy."[363] On one occasion while composing a satirical piece, he confessed that he was expressing his views "with all the plainness that I think one friend should speak to another." Even so, he

[358]Welch, "John Taylor," 158.
[359]Birdwhistell, *Long Run Association*, 21; Sweet, "Taylor, John," *Dictionary of American Biography*, 18:331.
[360]"John Taylor," 158.
[361]"Taylor, John," *Dictionary of American Biography*, 18:331.
[362]L. F. Johnson, *The History of Franklin County, Ky.* (Frankfort KY, 1912) 243.
[363]Welch, "John Taylor," 158.

acknowledged his "sympathizing friendship" for all the men whose actions he was parading before the public view.[364]

Of the three books that John Taylor wrote, *A History of Ten Baptist Churches* (a duodecimo volume in two editions) has been the one that continues to fascinate students of religion. Unable to tolerate idleness,[365] Taylor wrote this history in order to fill the unoccupied hours at home and to record at the same time his connection with frontier churches. And this account of the origin and development of the Baptist denomination in the back country turned out to be very popular in the Bluegrass State.[366] John Henderson Spencer called the *Ten Churches* "the most valuable contribution that has yet been made to the history of the early Baptists in Kentucky."[367] A near half century later, according to William Warren Sweet, it remained "in many respects" "the best picture of pioneer Baptists."[368] Professor Ira V. Birdwhistell distinguishes the book because of its "marvelous first-hand descriptions of Baptist life on the Kentucky frontier."[369]

The career of John Taylor was disparate indeed. A venerable preacher of unusual ability and a faithful missionary of unflagging activity, he left behind a string of churches that he had nourished and in some cases had planted. He had tilled large tracts of land and by his speculation had opened up others for development. He had raised his voice when independence and orthodoxy were threatened by innovation and controversy. As an author, he penned valuable and irreplaceable reminiscences about ten Baptist congregations in Virginia and Kentucky to which in succession he had been so lovingly joined all the years of his adult life.

[364]John Taylor, *Thoughts on Missions*, 26.
[365]Welch, "John Taylor," 158.
[366]Railey, *Woodford County*, 242.
[367]*Kentucky Baptists*, 1:63.
[368]*American Frontier*, 1:106n.
[369]*Elkhorn Association*, 15.

# I
# [Lower] South River Church

[5]Being in the seventieth year of my age and according to David's standard of threescore years and ten[1] as the number of our days on earth, it is probable [that] this will be the last year of my pilgrimage here below; though [I am] in as much health now as I ever was in my life (age excepted), and though I yet travel a great deal, as well as attend to my own business at home. Having a few leisure hours while there which I mean to appropriate to a historical statement of [the] ten Baptist churches of which I have been in succession a legal member.

[287]I know of no trait in the human character more desirable than gratitude; therefore, no favor received from God or man should be forgotten. A favor received by one man from another (however inimical he may become afterwards) should have credit so far as the favor goes. True gratitude will rarely think that its debts are all paid even to men. And surely to God, from Whom we receive so many daily, unmerited blessings, how can our gratitude lay [lie] dormant?[2]

One of the greatest blessings we receive from the Lord is the pardon of our sins. Hence says David (Psalm 32d 1st and 2d verses), "Blessed is he whose iniquities are forgiven, and whose sins are covered"—so covered by the righteousness of another that sin is no longer imputed. Paul, in citing the same Scripture (Rom[ans] 4th chap[ter 6th verse]), says, "Blessed is the man to whom the Lord imputeth righteousness without works." Therefore, those mercies are unmerited. He who has received such favor, in his gratitude, should break silence with David in 66th Psalm [16th verse]: "Come, all ye that fear God, and I will tell you what He hath done for my soul," as also speak of the glory of His kingdom and talk of His power.

Paul's conversion was related three times—first by the historian (9th chapter of Acts), and then by himself when Lucius, the chief captain, bound him with

---

[1]Psalm 90:10.

[2]This paragraph and the four that follow are taken from the composition in the *Ten Churches* titled "The Author's Conversion and Call to the Ministry." Found on pages 287-300 of the first edition and on pages 212-24 of the second edition, this piece first appeared in print on pages 64-72 in the "Biographies of Baptist Preachers," which Taylor appended to his *Thoughts on Missions* (Frankfort KY, 1820). This essay has been divided into parts that are inserted at appropriate places in the accounts of the two Virginia churches to which the author belonged. The text of "Conversion and Call" used in this edition of *Ten Churches* is the one that appears in the first edition of Taylor's famous work.

two chains (Acts 21st chapter). He also relates his conversion before King Agrippa and Festus, the Roman governor (Acts 26th chapter).

Moses tells the Hebrews [288]to remember their coming out of Egypt and all the way the Lord had led them.[3] And as with the heart men believe to righteousness, so with the tongue confession is made unto salvation.[4]

And as I am now well stricken in years, and have professed hope in Christ,[5] and [have] been endeavoring to follow Him for near half a century, I think it not amiss to relate some of my trials through this long travel[6] [of my conversion and my call to the ministry], if it is only for the benefit of my posterity that shall come after me. As also perhaps some poor lamb of Christ may be encouraged thereby.

The place of my nativity was Fauquier County,[7] Virginia, and in the year of our Lord 1752 I was born.[8] Through the intemperate use of spirits and what is generally connected with that kind of vice, my poor father[9] had so far consumed his living that hard labour was my inevitable lot in my raising. My father had moved to Frederick County,[10] back of the Blue Ridge[11] on the Shenandoah

---

[3]E.g., Exodus 13:3; Deuteronomy 5:15.

[4]Romans 10:10.

[5]When eighteenth-century Baptists used such expressions as "obtain hope of conversion," "obtain hope in the Lord," or "profess hope in Christ," they were referring to a personal experience of regeneration and conversion. They used the word *hope* to mean "a trustful expectation of eternal salvation." During the past two hundred years the noun *hope* has lost a good deal of its emphasis on certitude and has come to mean *want* or *desire*. But for early Baptists "to obtain hope" meant "to lay hold on salvation with assurance and certainty."

[6]Except in Scotland, the word *travel* is the obsolete term for *travail*, which means (as Taylor used it) "agony of the spirit," "great emotional suffering," or "severe mental or physical pain." Such feelings the author experienced during his conviction of sins.

[7]Fauquier County, which was not established until 1759 and which encompassed the western part of Prince William County, lies east of the Blue Ridge. Hening, *Statutes*, 7:311.

[8]John Taylor was born on 27 October 1752. John Taylor, *Thoughts on Missions*, 3.

[9]Lazarus Taylor (b. 1718), the father of the author, was a son of Aaron Taylor and Betty Wilde and a native of Northumberland County, Virginia. Dorothy Thompson, "Ancestors and Descendants," 29.

[10]Frederick County was created by a law of 1738 and included the part of Orange County that was situated west of the Blue Ridge. County government was not erected there until 1743, because the area had been only sparsely settled. Hening, *Statutes*, 5:78-79; and Kercheval, *Valley of Virginia*, 171-72.

[11]The Blue Ridge traverses the Old Dominion in a northeast-southwest direction and marks the eastern boundary of the Great Valley of Virginia.

River,[12] where Mr. William Marshall came preaching the gospel of the king
dom.[13] At one of his meetings I became alarmed (as noted in his biography).[14]

[5] The first church of which I was a member, and where I was baptized, was
called South River Church,[15] being [located on] the southern branch of Shenandoah,[16] and near the Forks of said river, famous for the fertility of its soil, and
discharging itself into the Potomac River at Harpers Ferry, on the north border
of Virginia.[17] Said river spreads through and makes a part of the great rich valley
between the South Mountain (or Blue Ridge) and North Mountain. Said valley
is about twenty miles broad and several hundred miles long.[18]

[12]The Shenandoah River, a tributary of the Potomac, flows through the northern end
of the Great Valley of Virginia. For a history of this stream, see Julia Davis, *The
Shenandoah*, Rivers of America ser. (New York, 1945).

[13]William Marshall (1735–1809), who was an uncle of Chief Justice John Marshall,
was converted in Fauquier County, Virginia, in 1768 under the ministry of Separate
Baptists. When he began to evangelize, his preaching was like a "thunder-gust."
Assemblies numbering "one or more thousands" often heard him in the Great Valley of
Virginia. In those early, itinerant years he invited all sinners to embrace Christ and to
seek salvation. After he removed to Kentucky in 1780 and settled in Lincoln County, he
changed his belief, having "found eternal justification couched in the doctrine of
election." Later while serving the Fox Run Church (now called the Eminence Church),
in Shelby (now Henry) County, he refused to preach the gospel to sinners. The
congregation rejected his newly acquired dogma and eventually expelled him. He
remained outside the church for the rest of his days. John Taylor, *Thoughts on Missions*,
35-36.
    Biographies of him are found also in James B. Taylor, *Virginia Baptist Ministers*,
2d ed., 103-105; Spencer, *Kentucky Baptists*, 1:14-16, 285; and Semple, *Baptists in
Virginia*, rev. ed., 415n.

[14]The biography referred to is found in John Taylor, *Thoughts on Missions*, 35-37.

[15]This congregation of Separate Baptists, whose meetinghouse was located in
Frederick (now Warren) County, Virginia, in the vicinity of Front Royal, was more
properly known as the Lower South River Church but was sometimes designated as the
Shenandoah Church or the Lower Shenandoah Church. It is to be distinguished from the
Upper South River Church, situated farther up the South Fork of the Shenandoah in the
neighborhood of Luray. Semple, *Baptists in Virginia*, rev. ed., 412, 412n., 414, 414n.;
Asplund, *Annual Register, 1790*, 27, and *Universal Register, 1790–1794*, 26, 30; and
Garnett Ryland, *The Baptists of Virginia, 1699–1926* (Richmond VA, 1955), 50, 52.

[16]"South River" was a localism for "South Fork of the Shenandoah River."

[17]The Potomac River forms a state boundary for Virginia and West Virginia on its
south and for Maryland on its north. After running for 285 miles, it empties into the
Chesapeake Bay. As early as 1747 a ferry was maintained by Robert Harper on the
Potomac at the mouth of the Shenandoah, in Virginia.

[18]Taylor exaggerates the length of the Shenandoah Valley. It is about 160 miles long
and 25 miles wide.

The materials or converts of which this South River Church was first composed was [gathered] chiefly under the ministry of William Marshall, whose short biography I have given elsewhere.[19] Others also laboured in said bounds, as John Pickett,[20] whose sister[21] Marshall had married; Reuben Pickett,[22] brother of John; and the famous James Ireland,[23] [who], after being released from Cul-

---

[19]The biography referred to is found in John Taylor, *Thoughts on Missions*, 35-37.

[20]John Pickett (1744–1803), who was born in King George County, Virginia, was in early manhood a dancing master and a gaming enthusiast. He was converted in North Carolina under the preaching of a Separate Baptist in 1765. Back in his native colony, he helped to organize in 1769 in Fauquier County the Carters Run Church, the first congregation of the Separates in northern Virginia. Soon thereafter he became its pastor and continued in that post until his death. In 1771 he was kept in the Fauquier Jail for three months "for preaching contrary to act of Parliament," as the court order put it. Semple, *Baptists in Virginia*, rev. ed., 471-72; James B. Taylor, *Virginia Baptist Ministers*, 2d ed., 64-66; Ryland, Baptists of Virginia, 48, 49, 66; and Lewis Peyton Little, *Imprisoned Preachers and Religious Liberty in Virginia* (Lynchburg VA, 1938), 192-96.

[21]About 1766 in Virginia, William Marshall married Mary Ann Pickett, a daughter of William Pickett. W. M. Paxton, *The Marshall Family* (Cincinnati OH, 1885), 32.

[22]Reuben Pickett (1752–1823), a native of Prince William (now Fauquier) County, Virginia, was converted at the age of seventeen. Two years later he attended the General Association of the Separate Baptists in Virginia as a delegate from the Lower South River Church and at the age of twenty was ordained as a preacher. Most of his adult life was spent as the pastor of the Mayo Church, in Halifax County. Its building was called Pickett's Meetinghouse. Semple, *Baptists in Virginia*, rev. ed., 322-24, 322n.; James B. Taylor, *Virginia Baptist Ministers*, 2d ed., 171-74; and Ryland, *Baptists of Virginia*, 52.

[23]James Ireland (1745–1806), who was born in Edinburgh, Scotland, immigrated to northern Virginia, where he became a schoolmaster. By reason of his youthful vice, he entered a prolonged state of concern about his salvation but eventually obtained a hope for his soul. Almost at once he began to preach. In Pittsylvania County he was baptized by Samuel Harris and was ordained as an itinerant by eleven Separate Baptist preachers. His five-month imprisonment in Culpeper County, during the winter and spring of 1769–1770, stands out amidst the persecutions that Virginia county officials meted out to Separate Baptists from 1768 to 1778. While Jemmy Ireland was in jail, gunpowder was exploded under the floor, sulfur and hot pepper were burned beneath the door, and a scheme to poison him was plotted. When he preached through a small grating (maybe one foot square), some Negroes who listened were stripped and beaten, other persons were trodden under horses' hoofs, and miscreants urinated in his face. After Lord Botetourt, governor of the colony, gave Ireland leave to build a meetinghouse in Culpeper County, the magistrates could no longer hold him. James B. Taylor, *Virginia Baptist Ministers*, 2d ed., 114-25; Little, *Imprisoned Preachers*, 150-91; and Ryland, *Baptists of Virginia*, 63-66.

Of the forty-five Baptists who were jailed in colonial Virginia, Ireland is one of only two who left an autobiography—*The Life of the Rev. James Ireland* (Winchester VA,

peper Prison,for preaching,[24] laboured much and with great success on the waters of Shenandoah River. None of those ministers were ordained for [6]several years, so that [for] the first baptizing[25] in South River the noted Samuel Harris[26] traveled two hundred miles to administer this solemn ordinance. And an awfully[27] solemn thing it was indeed to thousands who had never witnessed such a scene before. I think fifty-three were baptized on that day. Several young ministers came with Harris, as Elijah Craig,[28] John Waller,[29] with a number of others.

---

1819). The other such prisoner was Joseph Craig.

[24]The words "for preaching" come from the second edition.

[25]Baptism was the immersion of a new convert in running water as a symbol of Jesus' death, burial, and resurrection and of the believer's dying to sin and rising to walk in a new life. Being converted and obtaining a hope in Christ preceded the ordinance of baptism. Adult baptism was the most outstanding of the nine rites of the Separate Baptists and admitted the convert into their closely knitted fellowship.

[26]Samuel Harris (1723/4–1799) was born in Hanover County, Virginia, but settled early in life in the part of Lunenburg County that in time became Halifax County and later Pittsylvania County. There he served as church warden, magistrate, sheriff, commissary, and militia colonel. He was also a member of the House of Burgesses. Converted in 1758, he was baptized soon thereafter by Daniel Marshall. Almost at once he began to preach but was not ordained as a minister until 1769. By then Colonel Harris, as he was commonly called, had relinquished his political and military posts. Later his itinerancy carried him throughout Virginia, and he became well-known as a preacher and as an organizer of churches. He played a part in forming at least twenty-six congregations. No other man during his lifetime accomplished among Virginia Separate Baptists as much as did Harris, whom a contemporary described as "like another Paul among the churches." Semple, *Baptists in Virginia*, rev. ed., 17-21; Little, *Imprisoned Preachers*, 44-50, 157; and Benedict, *Baptist Denomination*, 2:330-39. The quotation is from James B. Taylor, *Virginia Baptist Ministers*, 2d ed., 30.

[27]The adverb *awfully* is a colloquialism meaning extremely.

[28]Elijah Craig (1745–1808), a native of Spotsylvania County, Virginia, was converted in 1764, and he joined the Separate Baptists two years later. Ordained in 1771, he began to serve the Rapidan and the Blue Run churches. He played a vital role in communicating the views of Virginia Baptists to the new state government during the Revolutionary War. In Kentucky he was the pastor of the Great Crossing Church. He authored two pieces, which were published in Lexington, Kentucky. The first, *A Few Remarks on the Errors That Are Maintained in the Christian Churches of the Present Day* (1801), argued that a pastor was not entitled to compensation for his services. The other, *A Portrait of John Creath* (1807), was a tirade that took the part of a Lexington layman in his dispute with the pastor of the Town Fork Church over their exchanging of slave girls. Edwards, *Materials*, 2:59-60; Semple, *Baptists in Virginia*, rev. ed., 24, 90, 238, 240-41, 241n.; and Spencer, *Kentucky Baptists*, 1:87-89. Also see James B. Taylor, *Virginia Baptist Ministers*, 2d ed., 62-64.

[29]John Waller (1741–1802) was born in Spotsylvania County, Virginia. Noted as a profligate youth, he was called "Swearing Jack" and the "Devil's Adjutant." When he

[280,2d]Elijah was considered the greatest preacher of the three [preaching Craig brothers]; and in a very large association in Virginia, Elijah Craig was among the most popular for a number of years. His preaching was of the most solemn style. His appearance [was] as a man who had just come from the dead, of a delicate habit, a thin visage, large eyes and mouth, of great readiness of speech. The sweet melody of his voice, both to preach and [to] sing, bore all down before it. And when his voice was extended, it was like the loud sound of a sweet trumpet. The great favor of his preaching commonly brought many tears from the hearers, and many no doubt [were] turned to the Lord by his preaching. He was several times a prisoner of the Lord for preaching.[30] He moved to Kentucky at a later date than his other brothers. His turn to speculation did him harm every way.[31] He was not as great a peacemaker in the church as [was] his brother Lewis, and that brought trouble on him. But from all his troubles he was relieved by death, when perhaps he did not much exceed sixty years of age, after serving in the ministry, say, forty years.[32]

[6]The rite of [the] laying on of hands on the newly baptized[33] was practised[34]

---

became convicted of his sins, his anxiety lasted seven months. He was baptized in 1767 and was ordained three years later as the pastor of the Lower Spotsylvania Church. During his ministry in the Old Dominion he helped to plant eighteen churches and baptized more than two thousand persons. The authorities of Spotsylvania, Caroline, Essex, and Middlesex counties kept him in their prisons for 113 days for preaching the gospel contrary to the law. He spent the last nine years of his life in South Carolina. Edwards, *Materials*, 2:54-57; Semple, *Baptists in Virginia*, rev. ed., 24n.; James B. Taylor, *Virginia Baptist Ministers*, 2d ed., 77-84; Little, *Imprisoned Preachers*, 93-127, 404-17, 520; and Sprague, *American Pulpit*, 7:113-17.

[30]Two imprisonments of Elijah Craig can be identified. One took place in Orange County for seventeen days in July and August 1768; the other, in Culpeper County for one month at an unknown date. Edwards, *Materials*, 2:60; and Little, *Imprisoned Preachers*, 132-36.

[31]Elijah Craig moved to Kentucky in 1786 and settled in Fayette (now Scott) County. There he bought a thousand acres of land, laid off Georgetown on part of it, and built Kentucky's first saw and grist mill. He pioneered in the West in making paper and rope, in fulling cloth, and in distilling bourbon whiskey. Semple, *Virginia Baptists*, 241, 241n.; and Clark, *Kentucky: Land of Contrast*, 50.

[32]This paragraph comes from a piece in the addendum of the second edition titled "Biography of Mr. Lewis Craig."

[33]Imposition of hands at baptism was one of nine rites practiced by Separate Baptists in North Carolina and Virginia during their early decades. Even though a majority of these customs fell into disuse in time, the laying on of hands was continued by some churches until at least the second decade of the nineteenth century. Practiced as the final act of admitting newly baptized candidates into church membership, this rite had an ancient beginning among Baptists in various parts of Europe. As early as about 1670

by the Baptists in those days [in pre-Revolutionary Virginia]. This practice was performed as follows: Those upwards of fifty stood up in one solemn line[35] on the bank of the river, taking up about as many yards as there were individuals—the males first in the line. About four ministers went together. Each one laid his right hand on the head of the dedicated person, and one prayed for him, and after praying for three or four of them another proceeded [to pray] till they went through [the line]. It would appear as if that solemn dedication might be some barrier to future apostacy [sic], for the prayers were [uttered] with great solemnity and fervour[36] and [were designed] for that particular person according to their age and circumstances.[37]

On the same day, the church at South River was constituted under the style of a Separate Baptist church.[38] This was in 1770. It may be remembered that the

---

argument over its continuance arose in England. David Benedict, *Baptist Denomination*, 1:218, 2:107-108, and *Fifty Years among the Baptists* (New York, 1860; reprint ed., Little Rock AR, 1977), 160-62; and Spencer, *Kentucky Baptists*, 1:486, and 2:9, 12.

[34]In place of the verb *practice* Taylor consistently uses *practise*, the chiefly British spelling.

[35]The use on this occasion in 1770 of a fifty-yard line along the river bank instead of a circle as reported by Daniel Fristoe for a baptism in 1771 negates the significance that Professor Rhys Isaac draws from the latter configuration. He sees the Baptists' closed circle for laying on hands as their rejection of the Anglican concept of an all-inclusive parish that envelopes the entire population within its bounds. *The Transformation of Virginia, 1740–1790* (Chapel Hill NC, 1983), 166-67.

[36]Here the noun *fervor* is used with the British spelling *fervour*.

[37]Another Virginia account of the rite of laying on hands at baptism has survived. It was recorded by Elder Daniel Fristoe and dated 16 June 1771. In Fauquier County twenty-nine persons were immersed in a stream before a congregation numbering about two thousand. The newly baptized formed a circle in the middle of a nearby field; the preacher imposed his hands upon the head of each new member in a solemn, moving ceremony. The throng of people stood round about weeping with deep emotion, and when the popular hymn of Isaac Watts titled "Come, We That Love the Lord" was sung they lifted their hands and faces heavenward. Fristoe wrote that they "discovered such chearful [sic] countenances in the midst of flowing tears as I had never seen before." Fristoe, Journal, in Morgan Edwards, "Notebook," *Virginia Baptist* Register 18 (1979): 864. A second version of this diary entry is found in Benedict, *Baptist Denomination*, 2:305-306.

[38]Numbers of unregenerate members of Congregational churches in New England who were convicted of their sinfulness and who experienced God's sovereign grace left those churches during the Great Awakening and formed Separate churches. Many of these Separates were converted to Baptist beliefs, beginning about 1749. Their subsequent practice of believers' baptism followed closely on the heels of their embracing the principle that only regenerated persons should belong to their churches. Thus, some Separate churches became Separate Baptlst churches, and some Separates joined existing Baptist churches. C. C. Goen, *Revivalism and Separatism in New England, 1740–1800:*

word *Separate* here did not design a separation from what was called the "Regular Baptists,"[39] for it may be [that] they were not called Regulars till afterwards. The word *Separate* came from New England. The Presbyterians[40] there is called the "Standing Order."[41] All who desent [dissent] from them of whatever denomination are called and call themselves *Separates*, because they do not adhere to the Standing Order. Hence Shubal Stearns[42] and Daniel Marshall,[43] who

---

*Strict Congregationalists and Separate Baptists in the Great Awakening* (New Haven CT, 1962; reprint ed., Hamden CT, 1969), 36-44, 208-43, 258-67. For the story of the spread of Separate Baptists in the South, see William L. Lumpkin, *Baptist Foundations in the South: Tracing through the Separates the Influence of the Great Awakening, 1754-1787* (Nashville TN, 1961).

[39] After the rise of Separate Baptists in North Carolina and Virginia, the term "Regular Baptists" was applied to the members of churches in those two colonies that were related to the Philadelphia Association.

[40] Taylor should have used the word *Congregationalists*. It was easy to make this mistake because Congregationalists and Presbyterians were both Calvinistic in doctrine. The former were English Calvinists; the latter, Scottish Calvinists. For a discussion of their differing polities, see Benedict, *Baptist Denomination*, 2:495-96n.

[41] In all New England except Rhode Island, Congregationalism constituted the Established Church during the colonial era. In fact, in Massachusetts the Establishment continued until 1833.

[42] Shubal Stearns (1705/6-1771), a native of Boston who possessed singular zeal and ability, was converted in Connecticut in 1745 during the Great Awakening. Six years later he embraced Separate Baptist principles and was baptized and ordained on the same day. In 1754 he left New England and journeyed to Opequon Creek in Frederick County, Virginia (now Berkeley County, West Virginia). After a few months he moved westward to Cacapon River in Hampshire County (now West Virginia). There he was exposed to the ravages of the French and Indian War, then erupting on the frontier. Lack of response by Virginians to his preaching sent him in 1755 into North Carolina, where he settled on Sandy Creek in present-day Randolph County. There he formed the first church and the first association of Separate Baptists in the South. The itinerancy of him and his cohorts during seventeen years resulted in the conversion of hundreds of people and the organization of forty-two congregations. Edwards, *Materials*, 2 91-94; Semple, *Baptists in Virginia*, rev. ed., 12-14; James B. Taylor, *Virginia Baptist Ministers*, 2d ed., 9-14; and Goen, *Revivalism and Separatism*, 296-97.

[43] Daniel Marshall (1706-1784), a native of Windsor, Connecticut, and for twenty years a Congregational deacon, was converted in 1745 under the preaching of George Whitefield. Thereupon he separated from the Established Church. He was married twice. His second marriage was to Martha, a sister of Shubal Stearns. After evangelizing among the Mohawks for a brief time, he moved to Frederick County, Virginia (now Berkeley County, West Virginia). There he was baptized into the Mill Creek Baptist Church, was met in 1754 by Stearns, and the following year was fined for missing a muster of the militia. He removed with his brother-in-law to Cacapon River in Hampshire County (now West Virginia) and then to Sandy Creek in present-day Randolph County, North Carolina.

went from New England to the South, when they began society[44] there, called themselves—as they had been called before—*Separates*. Thus originated Separate Baptists. What was called the Regular Baptists had adopted for their creed[45] what is now called the Philadelphia Confession of Faith, with the discipline [7]annexed thereto.[46] The Separates had no public confession of faith but were generally constituted on a church covenant,[47] which to the best of my recollection was truly

He ranged far and wide as a Separate Baptist preacher. In time he settled in Georgia and founded the first Baptist church in that colony. Frederick Co. VA, Court Martial Records, 2 Sept 1755 (Photostat, Virginia State Library and Archives, Richmond); Edwards, *Materials*, 2:112, 143-44, 165; Semple, *Baptists in Virginia*, rev. ed., 13-14, 16-17, James B. Taylor, *Virginia Baptist Ministers*, 2d ed., 14-21; Goen, *Revivalism and Separatism*, 143n., 296-97; and Sprague, *American Pulpit*, 7:59-61.

[44]The term *society* as used here is an obsolete word meaning *union* or *relationship*. In this case, it takes the visible form of an organized congregation of believers. In other places in his *Ten Churches*, Taylor uses the word to signify "a religious denomination." At the turn of the eighteenth century in Kentucky the term "members in society" meant "church members" only. In New England it was more inclusive. Benedict, *Baptist Denomination*, 2:465.

[45]Taylor uses interchangeably the terms creed and "confession of faith." Also such usage is noticeable in the writings produced in Kentucky during the controversy regarding Campbellism. Spencer, *Kentucky Baptists*, 1:610, 613, 615, 617, 621, 622, 638.

[46]Some years after its organization, which occurred in 1707, the Philadelphia Association (the first of its kind in America) embraced the Second London Confession of Faith (1689), a Calvinistic doctrinal statement. In North America this statement—somewhat modified—became widely known as the Philadelphia Confession of Faith and appeared in a new edition in 1743. Annexed to this confession was a treatise on church discipline written by Benjamin Griffith (1688-1768). William L. Lumpkin, *Baptist Confessions of Faith* (Philadelphia, 1959), 349, 351-52.

[47]In 1783 the General Association of Separate Baptists in Virginia did adopt the Philadelphia Confession of Faith but agreed that a person was not obligated to observe every part of it. Semple, *Baptists in Virginia*, rev. ed., 92-93.
    A confession of faith, which was a doctrinal statement, was used as a means by which to gain religious toleration and freedom, to unify the churches, to win converts, and to teach doctrine. A church covenant, on the other hand, was the agreement upon which a congregation formed itself into a church. The members pledged to exercise care for one another, to follow certain moral standards, and to defend their doctrine and polity. *Encyclopedia of Southern Baptists*, 1:283, 306. Transcripts of five eighteenth-century church covenants are found in William L. Lumpkin, "Early Virginia Baptist Church Covenants," *Virginia Baptist Register* 16 (1977): 774-79, 780-82.

Calvinistic.[48] Their order of discipline was sum[m]ed up in the eighteenth chapter of Matthew.

At the time of this first great baptizing at South River, I was there the last two days. (Perhaps the whole meeting was near a week.) [I was] an ill-grown boy about seventeen years old. And though I would not then have been a Baptist for all the world, I was a close and serious observer of all that past[49]—first to the baptizing, which continued perhaps an hour for they went some distance [from the bank] to a proper depth of water and took only one at a time. I think the prayers for the newly baptized continued one hour more. I happened to be near when their church covenant was read. I remember concluding [that] no man on earth could comply with it. This church progressed on with rapid growth for several years.

[When William Marshall came preaching the gospel] [288]I was then about seventeen years old and went to that meeting[50] with the same view that I would have gone to a frolic, for I had heard of the great effect that was [produced] among the people under preaching (for he [Marshall] was a son of thunder indeed). I went to the meeting with no more concern about my soul than [did] the horse I rode on.[51]

About midway of his preaching (for I had not noticed a word he said before), the Word pierced my soul as quick and with as much sensibility as an electric shock. In a moment my mind was opened to see and feel the truth of all he said. I felt as if [I was] then at the bar of God, and as if condemnation was pronounced against me.

It may look strange, but I instantly loved the very truth that condemned me and [the] instrument that brought it, Mr. Marshall. I had never felt such an attachment to any human being before, and the whole [was] of a quite new quality. What knowledge I had of sin for [289]a considerable time was only what

---

[48]John Calvin (1509-1564), a French Protestant reformer, predicated the theological system that took his name on the doctrine of God's sovereignty, out of which grow all other doctrines of his system, including predestination and election.

[49]Here *past* is the rare, phonetic spelling of *passed*, the past tense of the intransitive verb *pass*.

[50]From a letter that John Taylor wrote to Stark Dupuy around April 1812, it appears that the teenager had attended the preaching of William Marshall on a previous occasion. He had arrived during the process of the sermon and had heard but little of its substance. "John Taylor's [Religious] Experience," *Kentucky Missionary and Theological Magazine* 1:33.

[51]This paragraph and the seven following ones are taken from the piece in the *Ten Churches* titled "The Author's Conversion and Call to the Ministry."

belonged to its practical part.[52] From that time I felt a particularly tender affection for all [persons who], I could think, were religious, though it might be an old African Negro. And had the world been mine, I would have given all to have been like one of them, though with it [I would have been] a slave for my life. Some things spoken of by Paul are as incredible as this. He often calls God to witness the truth of them.[53]

There is another thing as to myself which is strange. With all this desire [toward religion], perhaps for twelve months I lived in all the practical vice and folly that I had ever followed before, but with far other feelings as to the guilt of my actions than formerly. There were several reasons for this train of vicious living: As first, the attaining of true religion seemed so perfectly out of my reach and so great a thing that it never could be mine; and,[second], this heavy doubt sunk me into dark despondency.

Perhaps I never attempted to put up a prayer to God of any kind for six months together; and, as I was to be lost at last, [I thought that] I had better try to enjoy myself or at least [to] please my companions the best way I could. And though perhaps I much pleased them, yet, God help me, sin was a bitter cup to me, though I practiced it for fear they would laugh at me for being sanctimonious. So I continued for many days.

I seldom heard preaching and as seldom was in company with religious people, for all the connections I had in the world held the New Lights[54] (as they were called) in the utmost contempt.[55] But this early conviction gradually took deeper root, and sin grew more hateful; so that often (when I would be practising it) my guilt would become so heavy on my soul [that] I would be ready to roar out aloud. And to prevent my comrades from seeing the effect that was upon me [I] would abruptly leave the company and get by myself to bemoan my miserable case.

By this kind of compulsion, I forsook my companions [and] betook myself much to reading the Scriptures. But when I would think of prayer to God, it

---

[52]By the "practical part" of sin Taylor means a sin or vice that produces a momentary, fleshly benefit. In the *Ten Churches* he condemns swearing, theater going, bowling, dancing, horse stealing, and drunkenness as practical sins. Practical sins he contrasts with sins of the spirit. See 2 Corinthians 7:1.

[53]E.g., Romans 1:9; 1 Thessalonians 2:5.

[54]The derisive term "New Lights" had originated in New England during the Great Awakening about two decades earlier. It designated the people who favored this revival movement and who contended that a conscious conversion marked the entrance of Christ into an individual's life. Goen, *Revivalism and Separatism*, 33-34.

[55]In the Shenandoah Valley the New Lights were called deceivers. John's father was unwilling for any one in his family to attend their preaching. "John Taylor's [Religious] Experience," 33.

looked to me both [290]awful and dangerous—awful for a sinner to approach an infinitely Holy God, and great danger of offending God—more than to omit the duty.

Thus I worried on, I think a whole summer season [1771]. I began to reflect that I had forsaken all my old comrades and with them all my external vices,[56] and [that I] read the Scriptures a great deal. I foolishly began to conclude that I was much better than I was before, and that I might now begin to pray, for I was now good enough for the Lord to be pleased with my good prayers.[57] And [I] became abundantly pleased that I should get to Heaven as well as the noisy Baptists, and [I would] make no fuss about it. I now seldom went to hear preaching even when I had an opportunity, for the truth was [that] I thought myself as good as any of them. So I had cured all my former sores and was safe without a Jesus Christ. I had been my own physician and was safe and sound. Thanks and gratitude to the good Lord [that] he did not suffer me to continue there.

[7]For my own part, though I was solemnly affected at the time of the baptizing [1770] spoken of above (for some of my companions were in the number), I had such fellowship for sin that I seldom went to the meetings for a year or two, till Joseph[58] and Isaac Redding[59] obtained hope of conversion, was

---

[56]Taylor uses the term "external vices" as a synonym for "practical sins." See page 289, first edition.

[57]Taylor wrote in 1812: "I followed that track for more than a year, till through the constraints of guilt I forsook my companions and in a manner turned Pharisee." "John Taylor's [Religious] Experience," 34.

[58]Joseph Redding (1750-1815) was born in Prince William (now Fauquier) County, Virginia. Converted under the ministry of a Separate Baptist preacher, he was baptized in 1771 and, as John Taylor puts it, "immediately lifted up his voice like a trumpet and sounded out Hell and damnation at a most fearful rate." His preaching also possessed "the sweet charms of invitation." He was ordained as an elder in 1773 and as a pastor four years later. He became an indefatigable traveler in the work of the gospel, often with his family. He made two round trips to South Carolina and one to Kentucky, in addition to extensive journeys onto the northern Virginia frontier, before settling in Kentucky in 1789. In present Scott County, Kentucky, he served as the pastor for seventeen years at the Great Crossing Church and for five at the Dry Run Church. John Taylor, *Thoughts on Missions*, 47-55. See also Spencer, *Kentucky Baptists*, 1:85-86, 89-95; and James B. Taylor, *Virginia Baptist Ministers*, 2d ed., 208-209.

[59]Isaac Redding (d. ca. 1801), an elder brother of Joseph Redding, was also a native of Virginia. Isaac was aroused under the preaching of a Separate Baptist minister, but a month of conviction elapsed before he found a hope in Christ. His zeal for the salvation of sinners was greater than his ability to communicate the gospel. He eventually settled in Kentucky, where he died in Woodford County as a member of the Clear Creek Church. John Taylor, *Thoughts on Missions*, 48-49; and Spencer, *Kentucky Baptists*, 1:91.

baptized, and began to preach close in the neighborhood of my father's. By which I became stirred up afresh and was baptized (about two years after I had seen the first baptizing and near the same spot) in the twentieth year of my age and by James Ireland, then pastor of the church.

[290]Joseph and Isaac Redding (as noted in their biography)[60] lived neighbors to my father. Immediately after their conversion, they began to preach[61] with great zeal through the neighborhood—the purport of which was [that] ye[62] must be born again,[63] or be damned or never enter into the kingdom of God.[64]

I have perhaps more than once said that under the preaching of the Reddings the poor rags of my own righteousness[65] took fire and soon burnt me to death. For till now in reading the law of Moses I only understood its external demands, but by the removal of the veil of my heart[66] I discovered the sin of my nature. And that law which required truth and holiness in the inward parts[67] condemned me for the sin of my heart. The light and goodness I had thought of before was blown out as with a puff, and I was left as a perfect blank of darkness, from which dreadful darkness all manner of evil was constantly flowing and with a torrent which it was impossible for me to stop.

Amendment was now out of the question, for every [291]thing I could do was like the filthy fountain from whence it came. Every spring of my soul was now an unclean thing, and my best efforts [were] as filthy rags, and my prayers on which I had much relied appeared abhorrent both to God and [to] myself.

My practical sins that had been numerous (and many of them of [such] a magnitude that to this day I can never forgive myself) were in a manner removed out of sight by the late arrival of this mighty host of Hell-bred corruptions that seemed to swarm through my whole soul. Should you ask, reader, what these corruptions lay in, I could only state their outlines[68] as spiritual ignorance,[69]

---

[60]This reference is to a sketch of their lives in John Taylor, *Thoughts on Missions*, 47-55.

[61]Taylor seldom went to meeting "until the beginning of [his] twentieth year"—October 1771. Isaac Redding was baptized the preceding month and soon thereafter began to preach the gospel. "John Taylor's [Religious] Experience," 34; and John Taylor, *Thoughts on Missions*, 49-50.

[62]Here the word *ye* is an archaic form of *you*.

[63]John 3:3.

[64]This paragraph and the following thirty-three paragraphs are taken from the piece in the *Ten Churches* titled "The Author's Conversion and Call to the Ministry."

[65]Isaiah 64:6.

[66]2 Corinthians 3:15.

[67]Psalm 51:6.

[68]This enumeration by Taylor of the "mighty host of Hell-bred corruptions" indicates that he identifies them with the sins of the spirit.

unlawful desires,[70] hardness of heart,[71] and, above all, unbelief.[72] And each of these [was] generating their thousands. And my inability [was] such that I could not master any one of those thousands. My first thoughts under this new discovery were that my day of grace was past[73] (for this doctrine was much talked of in those days);[74] that time had been that I might have been saved, but having past[75] my day of grace it was now too late; and that I was given up of God to a hard heart and reprobate mind,[76] all of which marks I evidently found in myself.

Under these embarrassments I laboured for many months. I ate no pleasant food nor enjoyed one night's rest.[77] My father's family took the alarm that I had gone beside myself. And to tell the truth, I was driven to my wits' end, believing that I was as sure to be lost as if I was then in Hell. I was often on my knees day and night crying for mercy, if it could possibly be obtained.

At length a new thought struck me that was more distressing than all before, which was that I never [had] had a day of grace; that, as [with] Esau,[78] God hated me before I was born. And though some [people] quarrel with God about election,[79] it had a very different effect on me. I shall never forget where I was when this thought struck me. I was chopping firewood in the lap of a tree, and a deep snow on the ground. [It was] more than fifty years ago.[80] Under this thought [292]I was stricken with a tremor something like [what] Belshazzar [experienced] when the handwriting was [seen] on the wall.[81] While the axe dropped from my hands, I fell on my knees with trembling awe not to ask for mercy but to acknowledge God's justice in my condemnation.[82]

---

[69]Romans 10:3.
[70]Psalm 10:3.
[71]Mark 16:14.
[72]Hebrews 3:19.
[73]Psalm 77:7-9.
[74]Matthew 25:11-12; Hebrews 12:17.
[75]The two uses of the verb *past* in this sentence are rare, phonetic spellings of *passed*, which is the past participle of *pass*. The first usage is intransitive; the second, transitive.
[76]Romans 1:28.
[77]For six months, beginning about 1 November 1771, Taylor endured these difficulties regarding food and sleep. During about half of that period he labored under the impression that his day of grace had passed. "John Taylor's [Religious] Experience," 34.
[78]Malachi 1:3.
[79]The doctrine of election holds that God predestined certain people to be saved.
[80]The time of this incident was February 1772. John Taylor, *Thoughts on Missions*, 68.
[81]Daniel 5:24-45.
[82]Taylor recognized the perfection of God by which He preserves His holiness, despite

For about one month after this, I cannot describe the great variety of agonizing and vexatious thoughts that attended me.[83] I do not recollect for that space of time that I wittingly asked once for mercy, though I was often on my knees both day and night. The purport of my addresses to God were an acknowledgement of the justness of my doom. "O," said I often to myself, "that I was ever born, or that I was not some other creature than a man!" I really felt as if I had no friend in Heaven or [on] earth. But as wretched Cain, driven from God's presence with a marked fixed on him,[84] so felt I. Often did I think [that] I had better be in Hell than alive here, for life was only prolonged to aggravate Hell to myself hereafter.

The Scriptures say that it is impossible for God to lie or change.[85] I, therefore, thought my salvation impossible, for that it would counteract God's arrangement concerning me was then my belief. No spasm could more affect the body than [did] these awful thoughts, [which] alternately affected my soul about this time. Till at length, my conclusion was brought up to a point that no man ever saw and felt what I did till just before God cut them off and sent them to Hell, and that destruction was at the very door,[86] and that I should die soon.

And my impressions were, "This night thy soul shall be required of thee."[87] It was then near sunset. A lonesome mountain where nobody lived was in full view of my father's, and about two miles distant. There I intended to roam the balance of my wretched life, expecting never again to see the face of man. In what mode vengeance was to overtake me, whether by the violence of my own hands or by other means, was best known to Him Who thus decreed. Such were my impressions—that perhaps no criminal ever [293]went to execution with more agony of mind than [I had when] I left my father's house to go to this fatal mountain.

Before I got to the place and as it began to grow dark, in passing under a high, overhanging rock it occurred to me to fall on my knees and acknowledge —what I had often done—the justice of God in this awful sentence. To my knees

---

man's attempts to profane it. Theologians call this moral quality the "justice of God." God deals justly with mankind. Every person receives what is due him. Man merits the punishment allotted to him. Divine justice is obligated to punish wrongdoing. When Taylor acknowledged God's punitive justice, he was confessing his own sinful nature and accepting the fact that punishing evil fosters justice and right. L. Berkhof, *Systematic Theology* (3d ed., Grand Rapids MI, 1946), 74-76. See Psalm 51:4b.

[83]The idea struck Taylor that, because he was so much like the Devil in nature and unbelief, God had always justly hated him. "John Taylor's [Religious] Experience," 34.

[84]Genesis 4:14-15.

[85]Hebrews 6:18.

[86]Mark 13:29.

[87]Luke 12:20.

I went under this high rock, and as I began to whisper something like this: "Thy throne, O Most High, shall remain unsullied and unimpeached, when Thy wrath is inflicted on me."[88]

While thus speaking, my thoughts took a new and pleasing turn on the subject of salvation, which was that the great grace of Jesus Christ had extended to cases [as] desperate as mine, [such] as [cases of] Christ-despisers and Christ-killers who had been saved by this glorious Saviour. The truth was [that] I saw the fulness of the grace of Christ[89] and in a way entirely new, but [I] could not call it mine.[90]

The effect of that view was a sweet calm and peace of mind, such as I had never felt before. The mere possibility of salvation was to me like life from the dead, for I had long thought (for reasons given above) that salvation for me was not possible.[91] What I met with at the Hanging Rock, small as it might appear, was so great to me that I changed my resolution as to dying in the mountain or continuing there all night. I returned home as a new man this far—the style of my prayer was changed. I now began to cry again for mercy, as [I now believed that] the great grace in Christ had brought possible salvation to such a wretched sinner as myself.[92] I believe I shall never forget the Hanging Rock while I live, nor even in Heaven.

Unbelief soon overtook me again. This unwelcome intruder would force itself on me wherever I went, tempting me to discredit all the realities of religion. I did not hesitate to esteem myself the greatest sinner of humankind, but in unbelief I thought myself far worse than the Devil, for James says, "The devils believe and tremble."[93] But neither [294]mercies nor judgments could move me. Yet I continued a beggar for mercy from the encouragement I had received.

The Scriptures I read night and day. And among other parts I opened on the 9th chap[ter] of John, where the account is given of the man that was born blind. There appeared such a similarity in this man's case and my own that I read it

---

[88]Another version of his prayer goes like this: "O Lord! Thou wilt be righteous and Thy throne shall be holy when I am damned." "John Taylor's [Religious] Experience," 34.

[89]John 1:16.

[90]While at the Hanging Rock, an "unusual" thought, Taylor wrote years later, came to mind: "There is a Lord Jesus Christ able to save." "John Taylor's [Religious] Experience," 34.

[91]What Taylor underwent at the Hanging Rock was "the dawn of salvation on [his] benighted soul." It looked to the young man that, through Christ, God was "near and reconciled." He wrote decades later: "But my case was so singular and desperate (that it was only possible for me), but that itself was like life from the dead." Ibid.

[92]Acts 15:11.

[93]James 2:19.

with great attention. He was born blind literally; I was born so, as to spiritual eyesight. He was literally a beggar; I desired to be so at God's door.[94] He was cast out of the synagogue; I was despised by all my friends on earth on account of religion. His parents, through fear or ill nature, would not stand by him in his extremity; my parents[95] showed a great deal of sorrow and ill will on account of my late, great delusion. As I read, my conclusion was [that] if that man were now on earth I could have a companion, whereas all the comrades I had on earth and myself[96] had separated, our practices not agreeing together. I also much doubted whether I had any friend in Heaven. This man's eyes had been opened by Jesus, and he knew very little more of Him; at the Hanging Rock I [had] had some glimpse of Jesus Christ but did not know that He was mine.

But the Lord found him again and asked him a new question: "Dost thou believe in the Son of God?"[97] While I read that question, I began to feel as if I was at the bar of God and as if Jesus was near and asked me the question. I paused and tried to believe, but my heart failed.

But the next verse expressed the language of my soul: "Who is He, Lord, that I might believe on Him?"

And when I read the answer: "It is He that talketh with thee,"[98] though I neither saw nor heard anything, I began to feel as if the Saviour was talking to me in company with the blind man.

And when he answered, "Lord, I believe," and he worshipped Him,[99] the very language of my soul was expressed.

And if I did not speak out, my heart repeated it over and over, "Lord, I believe; Lord, I believe."

It is added: "And he worshipped Him." [295]My soul so ran in the same way that I understood more of Jesus Christ in one moment than I had learned in all my life before. I considered Him as both Lord and Christ, that He was the proper object of worship, and that it was no robbery to think of Him as on an equality with the Father.[100] The heavenly peace and joy that I felt for a season exceeds my expression.

---

[94]Taylor omits this sentence from his second edition.

[95]Hannah Bradford and Lazarus Taylor were married 1748. She was a daughter of John Bradford and Mary Marr. Dorothy Thompson, "Ancestors and Descendants," 28.

[96]Here the pronoun *myself* has the old meaning of *I*.

[97]John 9:35.

[98]John 9:37.

[99]John 9:38.

[100]Philippians 2:6.

But Satan was not far off and desired to sift me.[101] For I do not know that I ever had a more pleasing and rational religious exercise in my life than at this time, and yet within ten minutes I began to call the reality of it in question; indeed [I] strove myself to cast it away. For I soon rose up, laid down the Book, and walked hastily away, concluding [that] if it was the Devil deceiving me (which I strongly suspected) I had better be somewhere else.

But wherever I went my heart would keep talking as it had before: "Lord, I believe," etc. My lips would say so too. So that with all my strivings by pressing my bosom with my hands, rolling on the ground, biting lips, pulling hair, frowning, or groaning (all of which perhaps were used alternately); yet the same language of my heart would be, "Lord, I believe." This continued perhaps an hour. Had any person been looking at me, by my actions they would have thought me in the utmost distress, whereas I had never enjoyed such a peace of soul before.

You will think, reader, that I am more capable than any other person to account for this paradoxical, religious phrenzy[102] that has been narrated. In the first place, I was dreadfully afraid of being cheated by an unsound conversion, also as a very poor judge about it. Yet I had the whole affair carved out before me. It lay in something like being caught up to the third heaven,[103] a joy immense so that a man must walk tiptoe that [had] had it. What I now felt was only peace and rest of mind. And though I learned more of Christ than I had done before, I was not enabled to call Him mine; therefore, it could not be conversion. [296]And to take rest or indulge peace anywhere short of the new birth was losing conversion and settling on the sand.[104] From all this lack of knowledge in spiritual religion, we are able to account for the extravagance as stated above.

The conflict between hope and despair soon began again, for what I had yet received was only encouragement to seek the Lord. Meeting with Isaac Redding about this time, he (by extorting some answers from me) pronounced me a child of grace, according to his own experience, which gave me a very poor opinion of his religion.

About the first of May 1772[105] I went to a Baptist church meeting for the first time in my life. James Ireland was the pastor of said church. The house[106]

---

[101]Luke 22:31.

[102]*Phrenzy* is a misspelling of *phrensy*, which is an earlier spelling of *frenzy*.

[103]2 Corinthians 12:2.

[104]Matthew 7:26.

[105]This date was Saturday 2 May 1772.

[106]This log structure stood on a bluff on the right bank of the South Fork of the Shenandoah and overlooked the stream. Its location and an adjacent cemetery were still

being crowded, I took my stand outside, though near where the preacher sat to
examine candidates for baptism. By the help of open logs I could hear distinctly
all that was related. Eight were received for baptism, and my belief was that only
one out of the eight was converted. The others only related what I had felt
myself. This grieved me much. I doubted even the preacher himself being a
Christian for encouraging them[107] poor, deluded souls to join the church who
were in no better state than myself.

And to augment my vexation, Isaac Redding, whispering through the logs,
invited me to come in and tell my experience. I very abruptly answered, "No."
My private thought was, "You are sending people enough to Hell already,"
meaning the seven they had received that, in my belief, were not born again. This
was a sore day and night to me, being much distressed for others as well as [for]
myself.

The next day [Sunday] was also a grievous day to me to see these deluded
seven go into the water and from thence, as I thought, seal their own damnation
at the Lord's table.[108] I left the meeting with awful horror of mind on my own
account and [on] that of others. I slept but little that night.

When I got to my father's, though a fair, sunshine morning [Monday],
everything looked horrible. [297]All nature seemed to mourn. The very sunshine
looked to me sorrowful. Every breath I drew articulated to this amount, "Woe is
me!" I could neither sit down nor stand still five minutes together. [I was] with
pure distress of mind on account of myself and the poor, deluded seven I had
seen baptized the day before. My belief now is that my reason was giving way
fast, for the earth appeared to be trembling under me, or as running round with
me, [or] as unwilling to bear such a ponderous load of filth as I was.

Prayer to God was my main alternative, for He alone could help me.
Designing to go to a certain place for that purpose and casting my eyes on a
hymn book, a verse of a hymn occurred to me as follows:

> Jesus, my God, I know His name.
> His name is all my trust.
> Nor will He put my soul to shame
> Or let my hope be lost.

---

identifiable as recent as a half century ago. One tradition holds that this church house had
been erected by the Baptists. Another says that it had been the South River Chapel of the
Anglican Church, and that it had been abandoned by the Establishment and taken over
by the Baptists as a place of assembly. John Oliver, Jr., *The Treasure—the Earthen
Vessels: A History of First Baptist Church, Front Royal, Virginia, 1839–1989* ([Front
Royal VA], 1990), 18.

[107]Here the adjective *them* is a dialecticism meaning *these* or *those*.

[108]1 Corinthians 11:29.

This verse kept repeating in my mind till I got out at the door, when it kindled into a heavenly flame. It seemed as if the name Jesus never sounded so sweet before. Its fulness seemed as if it would fill earth and Heaven. And when this was added to it, "My God," my hope began to revive while this Scripture[109] rose up in my mind: "Reach hither thy finger and behold My hands, and reach hither thy hand and thrust it into My side, and be not faithless but believing."[110] I saw no man nor heard any voice, but according to my sincere belief the Lord Jesus spake[111] the words, and to me, and [He] was very near.

A tide of heavenly joy flowed into my soul, and [it was] of the rapturous kind far exceeding anything I had ever felt before [and] with a claim to Him far surpassing any evidence I ever had before. Which constrained me to answer as Thomas did in John 20th chap[ter] 28th verse, "My Lord and my God." This answer was repeating through my mind with such heavenly rapture that I scarcely knew whether I was in the body or out of the body.[112] I now believed [that] I was born of God, that Christ was my Saviour, and that I should never sorrow, [298] sin, or doubt again. But in part of this I was mistaken.[113]

I now could retrace my exercise and see that what I had received at the Hanging Rock was of the same quality and as saving in its nature as what I now received. And [I] had full fellowship for my seven, deluded Christians that had been baptized the day before.

Two weeks after,[114] I was baptized by James Ireland in the same church [Lower South River] where the Reddings had their membership.

I was now in my twentieth year [1772]. I found the church no place of ease to me, for among other distresses that attended me a new one occurred. I soon began to feel great anxieties to communicate what I felt and knew of Christ to my fellowmen. This was to me a great source of perplexity on account of my unpreparedness for so great a work. And how awful[115] it would be to run without [God's] sending [me]. And though I endeavored to look to the Lord by prayer for direction on that head, I could never get a satisfactory answer.

---

[109]Here is a rare usage of the noun *Scripture* to mean "a verse or passage from the Bible."

[110]John 20:27.

[111]*Spake* is the archaic past of the verb *speak*.

[112]2 Corinthians 12:2.

[113]When Taylor became a minister, he probably repeated the account of his conversion many times in his sermons, for it was the custom of a preacher in his day to line out in detail his own religious experience, his spiritual conflicts, and the weeks or months of alternate hope and despair that he had undergone. Thomas M. Vaughan, *Memoirs of Rev. Wm. Vaughan* (Louisville KY, 1878), 285-86.

[114]This date was Sunday 17 May 1772.

[115]The adjective *awful* is here a colloquilism that means "very bad."

Joseph Redding soon moved to South Carolina. Isaac Redding keeping meetings in the neighborhood, it came on as a thing of course [for me] to give him some aid in his meetings, so that in a few months I became a public speaker in the neighborhood where I lived.[116] My conclusions were that I could live nowhere but where Joseph Redding lived. The next winter [1772–1773], I traveled to South Carolina, either to live there or [to] get him to return with me. We returned in the spring, and the [Lower South River] Church called me forward to preach,[117] at which I have continued for more than fifty years.

[222,2d]But why the church did this is yet a wonder to myself; for although I was twenty years old, I was only a fit associate for mill[boys] or schoolboys. My lack of information filled me with dismay. My boyhood was such, even in stature, that seemed to forbid my addressing grown people. In a strange place I was taken to be about sixteen years old. In one place, it was said, my head came but a little above the pulpit.[118]

Near two years after I had been preaching, I was sent a messenger to an association. To be rid of the care of a horse, I went about twenty-five miles afoot. In those days the people went a great distance, took provision in their wagons, and campt[119] on the ground. I suppose there would be a thousand people about the meetinghouse all night.

On adjourning the first day, a preacher gave notice that I would preach at candlelight in the meetinghouse. Being much crowded when I came down from the pulpit, a very excentrick[120] man—Joseph Craig—came rushing through the crowd to give me his hand, exclaiming aloud: "Here is the ass['s] colt on which my Master rode to Jerusalem."[121] Laying hold of me, [he] called aloud to the people to "come and see the colt"; while a number pushed up as to see some strange sight. And I do suppose truly that neither Craig nor any of them had ever seen so unlikely an appearance[122] for a preacher. After this, Craig would introduce me to strangers as "the ass['s] colt," without telling my name.

---

[116]Taylor began to preach about October 1772—that is, five months after his baptism. John Taylor, *Thoughts on Missions*, 27. His preaching in private homes did not require the sanction of the church.

[117]To be "called forward to preach" meant that the congregation licensed Taylor to preach wherever opportunity was afforded.

[118]This paragraph and the two that follow, taken from "Conversion and Call," do not appear in the first edition.

[119]The word *campt* is the phonetic spelling of *camped*.

[120]For the word *eccentric* Taylor uses here the phonetic spelling *excentrick*.

[121]Matthew 21:5.

[122]*Appearance* is an obsoletism meaning *probability*.

[280,2d]Joseph Craig [was] a very singular man. His great excentricity[123] [281, 2d]drew the attention of all who knew him. No man in the bounds of our acquaintance manifested more zeal in the cause of religion than [did] Joseph Craig. At times his zeal seemed intemperate, as if the man had not common sense. And yet there was something in him more original than was found in other men. I will name a few instances of his singularity.[124]

I do not recollect, though a zealous preacher, that his persecutors [in Virginia] ever got him into prison. He had a method to baffle them.[125]

He was once preaching at a place, and the officers came after him. Stepping out at a back door, he ran into a swamp, supposing he was safe. But they took his track with a gang of dogs. To evade the dogs he betook himself to a tree, from which his pursuers shook him down (as if he were a wild beast) and demanded his going with them to court. After reasoning with them a while, he refused to go, but they forced him on a horse and perhaps tied his hands. On the way he reasoned thus: "Good men ought not to go to prison, and if you will put so good a man as Jo Craig in prison, I will have no hand in it." And [he] threw himself off of the horse and would neither ride nor walk, behaving perhaps as David did before Achish, king of Gath (1 Sam[uel] 21[st] c[hapter] 10[th] v[erse]). They let him go.[126]

His odd course was expressed in calling me the ass['s] colt his Master rode to Jerusalem.

---

[123]Here the noun *excentricity* is the phonetic spelling of *eccentricity*.

[124]This paragraph and the eleven that follow are taken from a piece in the addendum of the second edition headed "Biography of Mr. Lewis Craig."

[125]In Caroline County, Joseph Craig was arrested four times for illegal preaching. On one occasion he was put in the criminal jail, where he sang hymns for about an hour. Then he was given the bounds of the prison by which he was partially restrained for three weeks. At the time of another arrest Craig, being released momentarily by the constable, fled into the woods and escaped. *Journal of Joseph Craig*, chap. iv.

[126]This event occurred in Essex County. During the singing of a hymn, following a sermon by Joseph Craig, a constable laid hold of the preacher and led him some three miles off. There his captors put him in an upper room for the night and took away his fourpenny knife. The next morning Craig escaped but was pursued by a posse of eight men (some on horseback) and by a gang of dogs. He was captured and seated on his horse, and the constable made ready to ride to the jail. But Craig jumped off his horse and announced that he would have "no hand in carrying Joseph Craig to prison." Then the constable sat the prisoner on the horse again and tied his feet together under the animal. The officer led Craig's horse nearly ten miles to the county jail. As they neared the building, the rope around his feet became untied, and Craig took this circumstance as a sign that he would be freed. The constable put him in the prison, but the door would not lock. That night Craig set off for freedom and home. Ibid.

Walking the streets of Lexington one day, some young merchants followed on to have a little sport with Mr. Craig. Perceiving their object, [he] gave but one answer to all their questions, which was "Get thee behind me, Satan!"[127] And all this (done as if Craig neither saw nor heard them) turned a great laugh in the street on those young gentlemen.

[282,2d]He [Joseph Craig] was no speculator but [was] very punctual in all his commerce with men and particularly in paying his just debts, though seldom indebted to anybody.

On a journey one day he crossed a ferry, presenting his pay. The ferryman replied, "Mr. Craig, I will not take your money. You may pray for me."

Mr. Craig soberly walked out of the boat and asked the ferryman to come ashore that he might pray for him.

The ferryman replied, "I did not mean now, Mr. Craig. I am in a hurry. Do it another time."

But Craig seriously answered, "I will not go away in your debt!"

Little as the ferryman loved this kind of prompt payment, by this kind of compulsion he submitted. And Mr. Craig prayed for the salvation of his soul.

By vigorous industry and care of his property, Mr. Craig made a good estate. He raised many children, sons and daughters,[128] and taught them all the laudable trade of industry. Find a child of his where you may; they are surrounded with affluence, and [they are] of respectable standing among men. Nearly all of them have also a place in the church of Christ.

Mr. [Joseph] Craig was small of stature, stoop-shoulders, of a hardy complexion, active in business. [He was] persevering as a traveling preacher or rather exhorter, for there lay his greatest gift. He died of a lingering, debilitating complaint, after labouring in the ministry, say, fifty-nine years. [He was] aged nearly eighty.

[7]The first serious distress that took place in South River Church, as I was told afterwards, arose about who should be the pastor of the church. [William] Marshall and [James] Ireland, it seems, were the men about which the contest arose. Each man's children in the gospel chose their own father as the pastor of the church. But whether from Ireland's uncommon preaching talents or [from] some other source I am not informed, but so it was he became the pastor of the church. Though these men were complaisant to [8]each other, it is to be doubted whether the same tender affection existed after this pastoral struggle as before.

---

[127]Matthew 16:23.

[128]Joseph Craig was the father of six sons and four daughters. *Encyclopedia of Southern Baptists*, 1:327.

I think [that] the church consisted of about two hundred members[129] when I became one among them. It seemed my lot was to come into the church near the close of the harvest; for though several young gifts[130] rose up, ingathering[131] declined. Many were expelled for loose conduct, for to that they had been very much habituated before their religious profession.

Mr. Ireland, perhaps through prudence, took leave of the church as their pastor and took the care of one or more [other] churches. Soon after, Mr. Marshall was ordained to the pastoral care of the church. Joseph Redding, who had been preaching near a twelvemonth,[132] in the year 1772 moved his little family to South Carolina. While there he became a little dipt into Arminianism.[133] (See his biography.)[134] He returned the next spring and soon became ordained an elder[135] of the church with others also, for in those days some were ordained elders who were not preachers.

---

[129]In 1772, the year Taylor joined the church, there were 218 members. Edwards, *Materials*, 2:43.

[130]The word *gifts* is here an old usage meaning "persons who possess the ability to preach or teach."

[131]The archaic noun *ingathering* means *harvest* or "bringing into the church."

[132]Joseph Redding had been preaching for only about nine months when he migrated to South Carolina, John Taylor writes in another place. *Thoughts on Missions*, 50.

[133]Based on the teachings of Jacobus Arminius (1559/60–1609), Arminianism is a theological system that emphasizes human free will as opposed to predestination, the position of John Calvin.

In South Carolina, Joseph Redding was strongly influenced by David Martin (b. 1737), a Dunker preacher who held to Arminianism. John Taylor, *Thoughts on Missions*, 50-51.

For an essay on Arminianism in the Old Dominion, see C. Dirck Keyser, "The Virginia Separate Baptists and Arminianism, 1760-1787," *Virginia Baptist Register* 23 (1984): 1110-38.

[134]The biography referred to is found in John Taylor, *Thoughts on Missions*, 47-55.

[135]During the time when John Taylor lived in Virginia the term "ruling elder" designated an ordained man who did not preach but who performed other useful service within a congregation.

Around the beginning of the nineteenth century, most Baptists in the United States still designated their minister by the word *elder*, which indicated a person advanced in years. David Benedict, a Baptist historian, considered this term appropriate because the New Testament often applies it to ministers of God and because they "do or ought to possess the wisdom and gravity of seniors." *Baptist Denomination*, 2:466. As the nineteenth century wore on, other terms such as *brother* and *pastor* began to supplant the title *elder* among most Baptists.

[William] Marshall had gotten as much above the common style in divine decrees[136] as [Joseph] Redding was below it, and a heavy dispute arose between them about doctrines. Their grievances at length got into the church and produced great excitement there. This contest terminated as in the case of Paul and Barnabas.[137] Redding took a letter of dismission[138] and moved to Hampshire County,[139] adjoining the Allegheny Mountains,[140] where he had a great opening for preaching. The struggle in the church did not subside with Redding's removal. The contest continued till some of the parties got excluded.

In a few years Mr. Marshall moved into Culpeper County[141] and, I think, from thence to Kentucky in 1779 or [17]80.[142]

To where Redding moved, there was so great an opening for preaching that my time was spent chiefly there. And when a young flourishing church was raised on Lunies Creek,[143] I gave my membership there for several years[144] and

---

[136]According to Reformed or Calvinistic theology, the divine decrees or more accurate the divine decree is the eternal purpose of God by which God foreordained everything that takes place. For a discussion of this concept see Berkhof, *Systematic Theology*, 3rd ed., 102-105. For the way William Marshall applied the divine decree in addressing the gospel to sinners, see John Taylor, *Thoughts on Missions*, 35-36. For the origin of Joseph Redding's emphasis on free will, see ibid., 50-51.

[137]Acts 15:39-40.

[138]A "letter of dismission" was the instrument by which a person's church membership was transferred from one congregation to another. The noun *dismission* is an archaism for *dismissal*.

[139]Hampshire County, whose organization was provided for by a Virginia law of 1753, encompassed all of Frederick County that lay west of the Warm Spring and North mountains, ranges of the Alleghenies. Its early development was greatly hindered by the ravages of the French and Indian War. Hening, *Statutes*, 6:376-77; and Chester Raymond Young, "The Effects of the French and Indian War on Civilian Life in the Frontier Counties of Virginia, 1754–1763" (Ph.D. dissertation, Vanderbilt University, 1969), 406-408.

[140]In Virginia and West Virginia the Allegheny Mountains make up the largest and westernmost part of what geographers call the Appalachian Mountain Province. The Alleghenies lie immediately westward of the Great Valley of Virginia. These hills, whose highest peaks exceed forty-eight hundred feet, form on their eastern edge a steep escarpment called the Allegheny Front. They slope away southwestwardly and westwardly toward the Mississippi Valley.

[141]Culpeper County, which lies east of the Blue Ridge, was created in 1749 by a division of Orange County. Morton, *Colonial Virginia*, 2:548.

[142]In another place John Taylor puts the year of removal as 1780. *Thoughts on Missions*, 35.

[143]The Lunies Creek Church was organized in 1777. Benedict, *Baptist Denomination*, 2:521.

then returned and took my membership in my old mother church till I moved to Kentucky. [9]After my return to South River Church, Mr. Marshall having moved away, there was no minister in the church but myself.

The Revolutionary War[145] having not yet closed, [and] a number of the English prisoners being stationed through our country, those who had trades were permitted to disperse in the settlements to work for themselves. Two of whom, apparently respectable men and of good understanding, Duncan McLean[146] and Garsham Robertson, applied to our church for admission, having been baptized at Albemarle Barracks, while there stationed.[147] They, having no letters of dismission, came into the church by experience. McLean, being of Scotch[148] or Irish extract or a mixture of both, with fine use of his tongue, was soon invited to preach, which he readily accepted. And soon [he] surprised the most who heard him, for he spoke with great warmth and a mighty flow of eloquence. Robertson was a man of very deep understanding and of much modesty and sobriety.

Among others whom I baptized was one Donald Holmes, a Scotchman,[149] who was also a British prisoner.[150] He was a most excellent schoolmaster, a fine

---

[144]The materials that compose the remainder of this chapter fit chronologically at the end of chapter 2, because Taylor belonged to the Lower South River Church during two periods separated by the time of his membership in the Lunies Creek Church.

[145]The American Revolutionary War broke out in 1775 and essentially ended with the Battle of Yorktown in 1781.

[146]While a member of the Lower South River Church, Duncan McLean (d. ca. 1820) began to preach the doctrine of universal restoration, as advocated by Elhanan Winchester, a Baptist pastor in South Carolina. He was excluded from the Lower South River Church and became known as a preacher of universalism. Spencer, *Kentucky Baptists*, 1:190.

[147]The British prisoners of war who were confined at Charlottesville, in Albemarle County, in 1779 and later at Winchester, Virginia, were a part of the army of General John Burgoyne, who was defeated at Saratoga, New York, in 1777 by General Horatio Gates. Mark Mayo Boatner III, *Encyclopedia of the American Revolution* (New York, 1966), 275-76.

[148]*Scotch* is the colloquial form of the adjective *Scottish*.

[149]In Scotland the noun *Scotchman* is considered pejorative; *Scot* or *Scotsman* is preferable.

[150]Donald Holmes (1755–ca. 1820), a native of Resollas Parish, Scotland, became a Presbyterian at age eighteen. After a stint of teaching on a small island for about two years, he joined the British Army and arrived in New York in the fall of 1778. He participated in the Battle of Yorktown, in which he was taken a prisoner. He was moved to Winchester, Virginia, and released in order to teach school under the sponsorship of Thomas Buck. John Taylor baptized Holmes in the Shenandoah River in June 1782. Tarrant, *Kentucky Friends to Humanity*, 8.

scribe, and much of an English schollar [*sic*]. Having been raised a strict Presbyterian, he seemed to have studied every subject of religion.

With this European acquisition, the church seemed much encouraged, for among these three fine brothers, one of them was a non[e]such of a young preacher.[151] For though there were some odd things in him from the beginning, it was construed from charity only to be a little outlandish or [to be] overheated zeal.

Things moved on pretty well till I moved to Kentucky in the fall [of] 1783. The church at this time, I think, was about one hundred in number.

In the fall [of] 1782 I married my present wife,[152] about ten years after I had been a preacher. I lived one year with my little family in South River Church, who took up the subject of supply for me. The proposition was introduced with reasoning that I had been preaching for them off and on for ten years, and as a church they had never [10]given me anything. The sum being proposed, they voted to give me a hundred dollars for my past services in such things as my family needed. This thing seemed to be done with such readiness and pleasure by the church. It was received with equal pleasure and gratitude.

During this last year's stay in Virginia, there were many propositions from my old friends and mother church not to leave them, that I was going to a country of strangers and [of] savage rage. In a word, the importunities were such that I was almost prevailed on to stay, for it was a gloomy thing at that time of day[153] to move to Kentucky. But I had seen the place,[154] and when I found a growing family[155] to provide for, this overweighed all. And without a single friend or acquaintance to accompany me with my young, helpless family [and] to feel all the horrors that then lay in the way to Kentucky, [156] we took water at Redstone.[157] And from want of a better opening, I paid for a passage in a lonely, ill-fixed boat of strangers. The river being low, this lonesome boat was about

---

[151]The author refers to Duncan McLean here.

[152]His wife was Elizabeth Kavanaugh (1761–1832), a daughter of Philemon Kavanaugh (1732–1764) and Ann Cave (b. 1734). Elizabeth was born on 18 June 1761. Dorothy Thompson, "Ancestors and Descendants," 31.

[153]Inadvertently Taylor uses the term "time of day" rather than "day and time."

[154]Taylor had spent the winter of 1779–1780 in Kentucky.

[155]Here Taylor refers to the pregnancy of his wife, who was carrying their first child, and to his recent inheritance of seven black slaves.

[156]In 1783 only two convenient routes existed by which Kentucky could be approached from Virginia. The water route by way of the Forks of the Ohio River led downstream to the Falls at Louisville. The other course began in southern Virginia and followed the Kentucky Road through Cumberland Gap.

[157]Redstone, located on the Monongahela River at the site of present-day Brownsville, Pennsylvania, was the port of embarkation from which to descend to the Ohio River.

seven weeks before she landed at Beargrass. Not a soul was then settled on the Ohio between Wheeling[158] and Louisville,[159] a space of five or six hundred miles, and not one hour—day or night—in safety.[160] Though it was now winter, not a soul in all [the] Beargrass settlement was in safety but by being in a fort.[161]

I then meditated traveling about eighty miles to [Lewis] Craig's Station,[162] on Gilberts Creek,[163] in Lincoln County.[164] We set out in a few days. Nearly all I owned was then at stake. I had three horses—two of them was packed, the other my wife rode with as much lumber[165] besides as the beast could bear. I had four black people—one man and three smaller ones.[166] The pack horses were

---

[158]A fort was first built at Wheeling, in present-day West Virginia, in 1774 by the Virginia government. It was located on the left bank of the Ohio River about a quarter mile above the mouth of Wheeling Creek. Alexander Scott Withers, *Chronicles of Border Warfare* (Clarksburg VA, 1831; new ed., Cincinnati, 1895; reprint ed., Parsons WV, 1961), 220n.

[159]As a base for Colonel George Rogers Clark's expedition against the British-held Illinois country, Louisville (opposite the Falls of the Ohio River) was settled by erecting a fort on Corn Island in 1778 and by building its replacement at the mouth of Beargrass Creek the next year. Joseph O. Van Hook, *The Kentucky Story* (Chattanooga TN, 1959), 77, 86.

[160]Settled the following year (1784), Limestone (present-day Maysville, seat of Mason County) was the first Kentucky port that settlers arrived at as they descended the Ohio River.

[161]When Taylor reached Louisville, there were at least six stations on the waters of Beargrass Creek, which empties into the river a short way above the Falls of the Ohio. Z. F. Smith, *The History of Kentucky* (Louisville KY, 1892), 158.

[162]This station was built by Lewis Craig in the winter of 1781–1782. Its site is 2½ miles southeast of present-day Lancaster, in Garrard County, Kentucky. Ranck, "Travelling Church," 259.

[163]Gilberts Creek begins in Garrard County east of Lancaster and runs some seven miles before flowing into Dix (first written Dicks) River in Lincoln County.

[164]In 1780 the Virginia General Assembly divided Kentucky County into three parts—Lincoln, Fayette, and Jefferson counties. Hening, *Statutes*, 10:315-17.

[165]Here the noun *lumber* is not the Americanism for "sawn timber" but is the early usage meaning "old household articles" or *furniture*.

[166]These four slaves were from the group bequeathed to John Taylor by his Uncle Joseph. The man was named John (called "Jack"). Two of the three children were Asa and Letty, brother and sister. The other child cannot be identified. Northumberland County (VA) Record Book 11, 273; Record Book 12, 14.

The term "black people" to designate Afro-Americans is not of twentieth-century origin. For an essay on slavery and its relation to the Baptists of the Old Dominion, see Robert G. Gardner, "Virginia Baptists and Slavery, 1759–1790," *Virginia Baptist Register* 24 (1985): 1212-20, and 25 (1986): 1225-39.

led—one by myself, the other by my man. The trace,[167] what there was, being so narrow and bad, we had no chance but to wade through all the mud, rivers, and creeks we came to. Salt River[168] with a number of its large branches we had to deal with often. Those waters being flush, we often must wade to our middle. And though the [111]weather was very cold, the ice was not very troublesome. Those struggles often made us forget the danger we were in from Indians. We only encamped in the woods one night, where we could only look for protection from the Lord. One Indian might have defeated us, for though I had a rifle, I had very little skill to use it. After six days' painful travel of this kind, we arrived at Craig's Station a little before Christmas and about three months after our start from Virginia. Through all this rugged travel my wife was in a very helpless state, for about one month after our arrival my son Ben was born.[169]

We will return to South River Church. When I left them the only preacher they had was Duncan McLean. He soon became disgusted with the church, for, after applying to them to ordain him and they refusing to comply with his request, he went about his business and preached but little for them. But he pretty soon embraced the [doctrine of] restoration from Hell[170] [and] publicly preached it. Holmes followed his example.[171] Robertson went a little farther than either of them, for he openly professed deism[172] and disclaimed all revealed religion. Failing to be reclaimed by the church, she lost her three famous European brethren at one slam,[173] by expulsion.

Holmes, however, in process of time returned to the church, was restored, moved to Kentucky, joined the church at Clear Creek in Woodford County, by

---

[167]The word *trace* was an eighteenth-century Americanism for "a path beaten out by the traffic that went over it."

[168]The Salt River rises in Boyle County and runs northward and westward on its way to join the Ohio River at the town of West Point.

[169]Benjamin Taylor was born on 22 February 1784, in Lincoln County, Virginia (now Garrard County KY). Dorothy Thompson, "John Taylor of the Ten Churches," 570.

[170]The doctrine of restoration from Hell, known also as restorationism or universalism, holds that man will suffer remedially after death for his sins but will eventually be cleansed and delivered from them. For a discussion of this doctrine, see Edgar Young Mullins, *The Christian Religion in Its Doctrinal Expression* (Nashville TN, 1917), 494-503.

[171]Holmes remained a Universalist for only eleven months. Tarrant, *Kentucky Friends to Humanity*, 9.

[172]Deism is the belief in a personal God who is creator and final judge of man but who does not intervene in human affairs. It emphasizes reason and natural religion but rejects revealed religion and thus prayer, miracles, the Bible, and the divinity of Jesus.

[173]*Slam* is a colloquialism meaning *stroke*, *swipe*, or *blow*.

them was invited [to preach], and came out pretty much of a preacher.[174] He united with the emancipators,[175] seemed zealous in that cause,[176] and is now no more. I hear that he died a few years past in the Ohio state.

McLean, regardless of church censure, went on with great zeal through a number of the states [and to] Philadelphia and other great cities, and was considered a great champion to vindicate his Hell redemption; but after a while he gave up that point and openly embraced deism if not atheism. I need say no more than that it was the same Duncan McLean that came to Kentucky, settled near Bardstown, in [112]Nelson County,[177] and, as I hear, died a few years ago.

I know not whether any of these men became immoral in their practice. They all seemed to have esteemed me as a particular friend when I met with them. [Garsham] Robertson appeared like a man that feared God and talked as if he was conscious in his belief.[178] The Bible, he said, was a mere history of the Jewish nation, and no more validity in it than the history of Greece or Rome. Many parts of the Bible, he would say, was unworthy to have a Holy God for its author, and that other mediums more fully illustrated the eternal power and [the] Godhead.

He happened at my house in Kentucky one day when I killed a beef. He replyed [sic] in a most serious way. "Your Bible," says he, "indulges you in this. But what justice can there be in one animal's shed[d]ing the blood and taking the life of another?" He seemed to be a man of great sympathy of feelings, and his conduct [was] perhaps as clear of reproach as when he was in a Baptist church. He considered prayer to God a duty. Hence one night when I was from home, he went to prayer in the family.[179]

---

[174]In Kentucky, Holmes joined the Clear Creek Church in 1789 and was ordained as a preacher at the Griers Creek Church five years later. He served as the pastor of the Mays Lick Church, in Mason County, in 1797–1801. Tarrant, *Kentucky Friends to Humanity*, 8-9; Asplund, *Universal Register, 1790–1794*, 34; abd Masters, *Baptists in Kentucky*, 77.

[175]The question of emancipating slaves was debated in the churches and associations in Kentucky from 1788 to 1820. Donald Holmes was influenced by John Sutton to advocate emancipation. Spencer, *Kentucky Baptists*, 1:190, 484.

[176]In 1808 Holmes was a member of the Licking Locust Church, an emancipationist congregation. Tarrant, *Kentucky Friends to Humanity*, 9.

[177]By a division of Jefferson County, Nelson County was created in January 1785 under a Virginia law passed during the previous fall. Bardstown was made the seat of the new county. Hening, *Statutes*, 11:469.

[178]Taylor inadvertently uses the word *conscious* instead of the word *conscientious*.

[179]This paragraph was deleted by Taylor when he prepared the second edition.

"Lord, what is poor man?"[180] I understand this poor fellow got killed in Harmar's defeat many years ago.[181]

The church at South River became very much weakened[182] by many of my Baptist friends' moving to Kentucky a few years after I did.[183] I think Brethren John Price[184] and Lewis Corban[185] attended them. After they came to Kentucky, their old [meeting]house needed repairing or a new one built. They sold their old house to some Presbyterians who repaired and worshiped in it till they wore off another set of shingles.[186] The Baptists built a new house (about two miles from the old one) at a crossroads on a water course called Happy Creek,[187] which changed the style of the church.[188] And it is since called Happy Creek Church, after which their first pastor resumed the care of the church. This renowned man of God, James Ireland, continued this charge till he died, which took place about fifteen years ago, after which a Brother Benjamin Dawson[189] has taken the [13]care of Happy Creek Church and perhaps continues it to this day [1823].

---

[180]Here *poor* is a colloquial adjective meaning *pitiful* or *reproachful*.

[181]General Josiah Harmar (1753–1813) was thoroughly worsted by the Indians in 1790 on the headwaters of the Maumee River, in present-day Ohio.

[182]By 1790 the members of the Lower South River Church had dropped to twenty-two. Asplund, *Universal Register*, 1790–1794, 26.

[183]The adverb *alternately* appears at the end of this sentence in the first edition but not in the second.

[184]John Price (d. ca. 1805) became a Separate Baptist preacher in Shenandoah (first called Dunmore) County, Virginia. When he migrated to Kentucky he aligned himself with Regular Baptists. He was the most active participant in the dispute that split the Elkhorn Association and resulted in the organization of the Licking Association, in 1809. He was described as "a man of unpleasant temper [and] of great asperity of manners" and as one given to a "party spirit." Benedict, *Baptist Denomination*, 2:234. See also Spencer, *Kentucky Baptists*, 1:138-39.

[185]Lewis Corban was a ministerial associate of John Price in Shenandoah County, Virginia. In Kentucky, Corban served as the pastor of the Stony Point Church, a small congregation that entered into the constitution of the Licking Association. Benedict, *Baptist Denomination*, 2:234, 540; Spencer, *Kentucky Baptists*, 1:138, 213.

[186]One tradition holds that Presbyterians had helped to build this log house and had met there for worship. Oliver, *First Church, Front Royal, Virginia*, 18.

[187]Happy Creek, a small, right-hand tributary of the Shenandoah in Warren County, borders Front Royal on its eastern side.

[188]The change of name from the Lower South River Church to the Happy Creek Church took place about 1793. John Oliver, Jr., "The Baptist Meetinghouse in Front Royal, Virginia, 1830-1868," *Virginia Baptist Register* 13 (1974): 607.

[189]Before assuming the pastorate of the Happy Creek Church, Benjamin Dawson had ministered in Fauquier County and in other parts of the Northern Neck. He was highly esteemed by his brethren in the Ketocton Association. Semple, *Baptists in Virginia*, rev. ed., 415, 415n.

Thomas Buck[190] is one of the members of Happy Creek Church. He was one of the fifty-three that was first baptized in South River. Perhaps not one of the others are now alive, for it is more than fifty years ago. He was then a lad about fourteen years old. I believe he has never been a member of any other church.[191] He is wealthy as to this world and very liberal in the support of religion. His circumstance was such that when thirty pounds was made up by the church for my support before I came to Kentucky (by apportionment among themselves), ten pounds was levied on him, which he paid with the greatest cheerfulness.[192]

I was at his house eight or nine years ago. And riding in sight of the old meetinghouse (now all enclosed),[193] I proposed to ride in and take a look at the old skeleton, which he agreed to. One object with me was to see whether the great white oak stump, three or four feet over, and its mighty trunk that had always laid there when I resorted to the meetinghouse.[194] What made this great stump so sacred to me was [that] the preacher (Mr. [William] Marshall) stood on it when, I hope, spiritual life was preached into my soul, though it seemed like a blow of death to me.

The case was this: Report said that at these New Light meetings the people hallowed, cried out, trembled, fell down, and went into strange exercises. My object was to see and amuse myself at all this, as I would at other sport. The people were so numerous that the preacher went to this stump, about six feet from the end of the meetinghouse, that all might hear. The vast concourse of people took their stand in the snow, there being no seats to sit on.

---

[190]Thomas Buck, Sr. (1756–1842), a layman, was the clerk of the Ketocton Association for many years. He served as a trustee when the town of Front Royal was laid out in 1788, as a militia captain, and as the sheriff of Frederick County for three terms. In 1838 he and his second wife, Ruhamah, were excluded from the Happy Creek Church for disorders in their home. Oliver, "The Baptist Meetinghouse in Front Royal, Virginia," 608, 611; and Semple, *Baptists in Virginia*, rev. ed., 393.

[191]In 1810 Thomas Buck was a member of the Waterlick Church, located in the northwest corner of present Warren County. Semple, *Baptists in Virginia*, rev. ed., 413.

[192]For an account of Thomas Buck's relation to Baptists in the nineteenth century, see Oliver, *First Church, Front Royal, Virginia*, 19-24.

[193]Its logs had been weatherboarded.

[194]A *meetinghouse* was the building in which a church assembled for worship and business. By the use of this term, Baptists avoided the word *church* when designating the house where a congregation met. The expression *meetinghouse* was perhaps brought into the South by Separate Baptists, from New England, where it indicated a building of dual purpose in which a Puritan congregation worshiped and in which the residents of a town conducted their public affairs.

The intransitive verb *resort*, meaning *frequent*, is here an obsolete usage.

And while I was amusing and diverting myself, ranging through the company to see the exercise of the people, I had got in near the stump, when this Thomas Buck broke out into a flood of tears and a loud cry for mercy. He being my old[195] playmate, I stared at him for a while with awful[196] [14]wonder, and just at that time my eye and ear were caught by the preaching.

The minister was treating on the awful scene of Judgment, and while he dropt these words: "Oh rocks, fall on me; oh mountains, cover me from the face of Him that sitteth on the throne, and from the wrath of the Lamb; for the great day of His wrath is come, and who shall be able to stand?"[197] I felt the whole sentence dart through my whole soul with as much sensibility as an electric shock could be felt.[198] With my mind instantly opened to understand and love all that the preacher said afterwards and though every word condemned me, I loved the messenger that brought the awful tidings. I felt as if [I were] at the bar of God, and [as if there were] no mercy for me. How willingly would I have cried for mercy, if I could have hoped for any. From that moment every thing belonging to religion bore an entire[199] new aspect to me.

When we got to the old house, it was an entire, old waste. The trunk of the oak was quite gone; and the old stump on which the man had preached more than forty years before, but little of it was there. We stood there some time. I placed him[200] where I thought he stood when he with tears cried for mercy, [and] myself at his elbow where I received the Heaven-born stroke I have been speaking of. With grateful hearts we thanked the Lord that we [had] stood there more than forty years ago. Superstition would have said, "Take some of this old stump home with you to look at till you die."

The same kind of motive led me soon after to pay a visit to a lonesome, hanging rock in a rugged mountain. Not being able to get to it with convenience on horseback, I took it afoot. This rock was the place where I first received relief from my guilt forty years before. With grateful remembrance of the Lord's past kindness to me at that spot, I bowed my knees with thanksgiving to my God for past favors and [with] prayer to Him for preservation for days to come, and took final leave of that beloved, though homely, spot of nature.

---

[195]The adjective *old* is a colloquial term of affection.

[196]The adjective *awful* is here a colloquialism meaning *great*.

[197]Revelation 6:16-17.

[198]Years later John Taylor wrote of this moment: "My heart was touched as with a dagger! I felt as if God was near, and Judgment at hand, and I unprepared." "John Taylor's [Religious] Experience," 33.

[199]Here the obsolete adverb *entire* means *entirely*.

[200]I.e., Thomas Buck.

All this may look like a piece of superstitious rant, but perhaps [15]those contemplations are worthy of Heaven itself. For if Abraham would say to the rich man in Hell, "Remember, son, in thy lifetime,"[201] there will surely be a calling up into recollection, both in Heaven and in Hell, what transpired in life. While the poor, damned man, with horrid recollection, will remember every five-alley,[202] every ballroom, every gay festive season, with all the excuses [that] he plead[203] when called on to repent of his sins, with his uniform neglect of the great salvation of God promulgated in the gospel with all its precious invitations to him. While the Queen of the South and the men of Nineveh rise up in judgment against him,[204] while the torments of the cursed cities of Sodom and Gomorrah, [it] will be more tolerable in Hellfire [for them] than [for] gospel-despisers or gospel-neglectors.[205] All these will be sad reflections in the world to come, while it will be eternally vibrating through the soul, "Remember in thy lifetime thou hadst thy good things"; while the righteous will recollect their evil things with an everlasting reward of grace.[206] "Even so do, righteous Lord."

I have said that the church at South River[207] was first nominated a Separate Baptist church, but in August 1783 this with a church higher up Shanandoah River[208] joined the Ketocton Association, that was called Regular Baptists.[209] From the church above, James Ireland and others were messengers. From South River, myself and others were messengers to go into this union. Both churches

---

[201]Luke 16:25.
[202]A *five-alley* is a place, usually enclosed, for playing a bowling game in which five wooden pins are spotted.
[203]Here the word *plead* is the colloquial or dialectal past tense of the verb *plead*.
[204]Luke 11:31, 32.
[205]Matthew 10:15.
[206]Luke 16:25.
[207]In 1784 the Lower South River Church had seventy-five members. Robert G. Gardner, "The Ketocton and Philadelphia Associations in the 18th Century," *Virginia Baptist Register* 29 (1990):1486.
[208]Constituted in 1782 and located in the vicinity of Luray, in present Page County, this congregation carried a succession of names—Shenandoah, South Fork of Shenandoah River, South River, and Upper South River. Ibid.; William Fristoe, *A Concise History of the Ketocton Baptist Association* (Staunton VA, 1808; reprint ed., Stephen City VA, 1978), 5; Asplund, *Universal Register, 1790–1794*, 30; Semple, *Baptists in Virginia*, rev. ed., 387, 412, 412n.; and Robert G. Gardner, *Baptists of Early America: A Statistical History, 1639–1790* (Atlanta GA, 1983), 279.
[209]This association was formed in 1766 at the Ketocton Meetinghouse, in Loudoun County. It was the first Baptist association organized in Virginia. For the story of this union, see Fristoe, *Ketocton Association*.

were accordingly received and took seats in the association. This was done for convenience and not from contrast of doctrine.[210]

Thus I have surveyed a church of more than fifty years' standing. And though not blest with many remarkable revivals, [it] yet lives as a church of Christ.[211] Here I had my first standing as to church privileges.

---

[210]In his remarkable work titled *Baptists of Early America: A Statistical History, 1639–1790*, Professor Robert G. Gardner distributes the extant data concerning the two churches mentioned in this paragraph under three congregations instead of under two—Happy Creek (261), South River (276), and Upper South River (279). The two pieces of information that he associates with South River should be divided this way: the first to Upper South River, the other to Happy Creek.

The first datum relates to the contituting of a church and comes from the "Table of the Ketocton Association" in Semple's *Baptists in Virginia* (rev. ed., 387). In view of the fact that Semple uses 1783 as the year of constitution for both Happy Creek and South River, it is evident that he inadvertently enters in his table the year when these two churches joined the association but labels it the year of constitution. It was in 1770 and not in 1783 that Happy Creek was organized as the Lower South River Church. Thus, when Semple lists South River in this table, he means Upper South River because he also includes Happy Creek.

The second piece of information is the 1790 membership figure for a congregation found in Asplund's *Universal Register of the Baptist Denomination, 1790–1794* (26). In this instance Asplund names the church South River and means the Lower South River Church. At another place (30) he uses the name South Fork of Shenandoah River for a different congregation (Upper South River). Asplund lists Lewis Corban as the minister at South River. John Taylor recalls that after he and many of his friends left the Lower South River Church for Kentucky the minister who served the dwindling church was Lewis Corban. Thus, this second datum refers to the Lower South River (or Happy Creek) Church.

[211]The Happy Creek Church (formerly the Lower South River Church) continues today, being a Primitive Baptist congregation. Since 1881 its meetinghouse has stood at the corner of Stonewall Drive and Church Street in Front Royal, Virginia. *Advocate and Messenger* 129 (May 1990):back cover; and Semple, *Baptists in Virginia*, rev. ed., 414n.

In 1830 its meetinghouse, located on the verge of the town of Front Royal, burned to the ground. A brick structure was erected that year on what is now West Main Street. In 1833 the congregation joined the Primitive Baptist fellowship. Six years later a Missionary Baptist church was organized in the village, and both congregations used this meetinghouse until 1868 except during the period in which the Union Army occupied it as a hospital. The brick building was abandoned as structually unsound. The Happy Creek Church used the facilities of a Presbyterian church during 1868–1881. Oliver, "The Baptist Meetinghouse in Front Royal, Virginia," 607-609, 616, 618.

# 2
## Lunies Creek Church

[16]The second church of which I was a member was Lunies Creek, in Hampshire County, Virginia.[1] This Lunies[2] Creek is a branch of the main South Branch of Potomac River. The church was constituted near the river called the South Branch. On this river Lord Fairfax[3] in early times had laid off a large boundary of land called Fairfax's Manor.[4] This church was on or near this great manor, which nothing on our earth ever exceeded in point of soil. The bottoms were often a mile wide and continued so for many miles together. And the black soil [was] generally as deep as the banks of the river was high, but as yet they were barely free from Indian range.

Not long before the beginning of the Old Revolutionary War,[5] to this place [Joseph] Redding and myself paid a visit from eighty to an hundred miles from where we lived, soon after the contest between [William] Marshall and Redding. Through the country we found a few scattering Baptists, but in manners they differed but very little from other people. By encouragement Redding soon moved to the place. My great attachment to him led me to be much with him, for

---

[1]The Lunies Creek Church was located in the part of Hampshire that in time became Hardy County and later Grant County, West Virginia.

[2]The name that Taylor spells *Lunies* has appeared in print in several ways. Asplund puts it down in his two volumes as *Luneys* and then as *Lowneys*. The current map of West Virginia produced by the United States Geological Survey shows the stream as *Lunice*. Asplund, *Annual Register, 1790*, 27, and *Universal Register, 1790-1794*, 27. Because the author almost always uses *Lunies* to spell the name of the second church to which he belonged, and because the congregation has long been disbanded, the editor has not followed in this special case his rule to use modern spellings of geographical names in this edition. This stream is a small, left-hand tributary to the South Branch of the Potomac River in Grant County, West Virginia.

[3]Thomas Lord Fairfax (1693–1781), a resident of Frederick County, had owned the Northern Neck Proprietary for several decades when the Revolutionary War began. He was a grandson of Thomas Lord Culpeper, the first person to control the entire grant of land. Kenneth P. Bailey, *The Ohio Company of Virginia and the Westward Movement, 1748-1792* (Glendale CA, 1939) 45.

[4]Here Taylor refers to Fairfax's South Branch Manor, consisting of fifty-five thousand acres laid off in 1747 in Hampshire (then Frederick) County. That year the nobleman also developed in what is now Mineral County a tract of nine thousand acres called Patterson Creek Manor. Kercheval, *Valley of Virginia*, 50-51.

[5]Taylor thought of the recent War of 1812 as another "revolutionary war" against Britain. Thus he called the War for American Independence the "Old Revolutionary War."

he was my secondary father in the gospel so that Redding's company at that time was more to me than [that of] all other men in the world.[6] It was not long before the people became much affected. And [there were] some apparent conversions, but [there was] none to baptize them, for neither Redding or myself were ordained.

I prevailed on Mr. Marshall, the now ordained minister of South River, to take a travel[7] with me to see Redding and make some examination of the work we had been about. Him and Redding soon made up their difficulties. There were two men baptized. [One of them was] a David Badgley,[8] who some time after began to preach and is now, though old, a living preacher in Illinois near Saint Louis. The other man was Abram Clark, a warm Presbyterian who (when we first got acquainted with him) [17]became much affected and at times would say to us, "I love your preaching, but you shall never dip me." But when he obtained hope in Christ, he innocently broke that rash promise. Perhaps John Koontz,[9] a Dutchman,[10] attended there and baptized a number.

At Marshall's second visit a church was constituted, and Redding [was] ordained to the pastoral care of the church. I believe the church at Lunies Creek never amounted to quite a hundred members.

We ranged through almost every corner of the large county of Hampshire. On Patterson Creek,[11] a branch of the North Branch of Potomac River,[12] we

---

[6]The filial regard that John Taylor showed for Joseph Redding may have arisen because his father gave John but little support and encouragement.

[7]The noun *travel* is used here as a dialecticism meaning *trip*.

[8]David Badgley migrated from Virginia to Illinois as early as 1796. In 1818 he was living about fifteen miles east of Saint Louis near the Vincennes Road. By then he had been preaching for almost forty years. John Taylor, *Thoughts on Missions*, 13; and Sweet, *American Frontier*, 1:31.

[9]John Koontz (1739–1832) was converted and baptized in Frederick (now Warren) County, Virginia, in 1768. Soon thereafter he began to sound forth the gospel but was not ordained until around 1775. In the region that became Shenandoah County he was ill-treated by ruffians for a short season. For over half a century he ministered to churches in Culpeper, Fauquier, Frederick, Rockingham, and Shenandoah counties, Virginia, and in Hardy County, now West Virginia. Semple, *Baptists in Virginia*, rev. ed., 229-30, 242-47, 250-51; Little, *Imprisoned Preachers*, 224; Klaus G. Wust, *The Virginia Germans* (Charlottesville VA, 1969) 72-73; and James B. Taylor, *Virginia Baptist Ministers*, 2d ed., 96-101.

[10]The noun *Dutchman* was used colloquially in the eighteenth-century to indicate a "German-speaking man."

[11]Patterson Creek originates in Grant County, West Virginia, and flows northeast-wardly to join the North Branch of the Potomac River in the northern end of Mineral County.

found a few Baptists, where a church after a while was constituted.[13] Lewis Castleman,[14] now of Woodford County, and his wife [15] were baptized there.

At Lost River, the head branch of Cacapon River, where preaching had a great effect and a number were baptized, a church [has] since [been] erected that continues to this day.[16] There one Josiah Osborne[17] was baptized. And [he is] a respectable preacher now in Greenbrier [Association] who some years past published a large pamphlet on baptism (and much to the purpose) under the style of *The Giant of Gath and David*.[18]

In the North River and other parts of Cacapon River[19] a number were baptized, [including] one Levi Ashbrook,[20] a magistrate in the county, a man of great zeal in religion. And afterwards [he] became a respectable preacher but is

---

[12]The North and South branches of the Potomac River merge on the northern border of Hampshire County, West Virginia, to form the Potomac River, which flows southeastwardly into the Chesapeake Bay.

[13]The Patterson Creek Church was dismissed in 1775 by the Ketocton Association to enter into the organization of the Red Stone Association, which occurred the following year. Fristoe, *Ketocton Association*, 4; and Semple, *Baptists in Virginia*, rev. ed., 439.

[14]Because statehood came to the Bluegrass Region in 1792, Lewis Castleman lived in Fayette County, Virginia, in 1789 and in Woodford County, Kentucky, in 1800, but his place of residence had probably not changed. Charles Brunk Heinemann, comp., *"First Census" of Kentucky, 1790* (Baltimore MD, 1956) 19; and G. Glenn Clift, comp., *"Second Census" of Kentucky, 1800* (Frankfort KY, 1954) 50.

[15]The wife of Lewis Castleman was Jemina Pearsall. Darnell, *Forks of Elkhorn Church*, 99.

[16]The Lost River Church, organized in 1784, affiliated itself later with the Culpeper (now Shiloh) Association. Semple, *Baptists in Virginia*, rev. ed. 230, 250.

[17]Reared a Presbyterian, Josiah Osborne (b. 1750) was converted and became a Baptist at the age of twenty-eight. As a preacher he labored principally in Hardy and Greenbrier counties, now West Virginia. In 1807 he helped to organize the Greenbrier Association. Ibid. 421, 422-24, 430-31.

[18]Taylor mistakes in recalling this title. Osborne's work is named *David and Goliath: Or a Treatise on Water Baptism, Showing the Proper Subjects and the Mode of the Ordinance, with Observations on the Writings of Several Champions in That Cause* (Fincastle VA, 1807). It resulted from his debating publicly the subject of believers' baptism. Some of Osborne's contemporaries considered it "one of the best treatises on baptism that has ever been published." Semple, *Baptists in Virginia*, rev. ed., 431.

[19]The Lost and the North rivers head up in Hardy County, West Virginia, and merge to form the Cacapon, which empties into the Potomac in Moran County.

[20]Levi Ashbrook was a resident of Hampshire County, Virginia, in 1782. As a justice of the peace, he received the tax lists of the citizens of one precinct of the county that year. *Heads of Families, 1790: Virginia*, 25.

now gone to his long home.[21] A fine-looking, young man the name of Smith, of good family, was baptized by myself here. It was thought when baptized that he would soon make a preacher but, by getting into bad company and following on, was since hanged at Richmond,[22] in Virginia, for the sin of horse stealing, though [he] gave strong evidence (while in prison and at the place of execution) that he was a man of grace.[23] Poor man! What is he? [What is] even good Hezekiah when left to himself?[24]

A place called Georges Hills,[25] on the Maryland side—there we often went. Something uncommon generally attended the people here, which lay in profuse weeping—male and female. Their cries at [18]times would overwhelm our preaching, however loud. We did hope that a number of them found mercy of the Lord and followed Him in a watery grave. If I mistake not there is a church there to this day.[26]

After ranging through the large county of Hampshire a year or two, we contemplated passing the Allegheny Mountain[s] to the back settlements[27] on Monongahela River. The settlers there were much exposed to savage fury, for the English war had now gotten into full blast.

The first tour I went without Redding,[28] but a respectable brother the name of Whiteman,[29] who had acquaintance[30] over the mountain, went with me. The

---

[21]The idiom "go to one's long home" means "go to the place of the dead." Ecclesiastes 12:5.

[22]The capital of Virginia was moved from Williamsburg to Richmond in 1780.

[23]A "man of grace" is a person who, having recognized that he had no spiritual merit of his own, has depended on God's unmerited love and forgiveness and has received His gift of life through Jesus Christ. Before this event occurred, he had forfeited divine grace and had been under condemnation by reason of his sin.

[24]Isaiah 38: 1-18.

[25]The Georges Hills Church, an affiliate of the Red Stone Association, had a membership of twenty-nine in 1809. This church was located in Washington (present-day Allegany) County. Benedict, *Baptist Denomination*, 2:516.

[26]By 1816 the Georges Hills Church had become extinct. Gardner, *Baptists of Early America*, 246.

[27]The term "back settlements" indicates areas then on the frontier.

[28]When blind and aged and living in Nicholas County, Kentucky, David Crouch (b. 1767) recalled that at his father's house in Tygart Valley around 1775 he heard preaching for the first time. The "traveling" preacher was Joseph Redding. Crouch, then about eight years old, was impressed with the text of the sermon: "Behold the axe is laid at the root of the tree" (Matthew 3:10). He recollected that Redding "used to stop at my father's house and sometimes John Taylor [did]." Crouch, Interview by [John D. Shane, 1843], Draper MSS., 12CC225.

[29]Members of the Whiteman family were among the settlers of Tygart Valley in the years immediately preceding the Revolutionary War. Withers, *Border Warfare*, 126.

place of our destination was Tygart Valley, on the main branch of Monongahela and near its source.[31] This valley was estimated at fifty miles long and [was] newly settled by about one hundred families.[32] I found only one Baptist there and that one a woman, but I thought her a precious Christian. This tour was in the middle of winter,[33] and in the mountain[s] the snow about knee-deep. The distance from one settlement to the other was estimated at near fifty miles. The trace was so bad (perhaps a carriage has never past[34] there yet)[35] that we were two days getting there. Of course we camped out one night in the deep snow. When we got to this valley I became much discouraged. For the first time I now saw people living in a fort.[36] I had but very few meetings in the place, and those with a confused appearance.

We set out for Greenbrier.[37] From the upper end of the [Tygart] Valley settlement to the nearest part of the Greenbrier settlement[38] we traveled in one

---

[30]Here is a former usage of the noun *acquaintance* as a collective plural. Now it is usually singular.

[31]The Tygart Valley River merges with the West Fork River to form the Monongahela, which is one of the two streams that comprise the Ohio. Tygart Valley is named for David Tygart, who settled with his family in 1753 in that valley, which lies immediately west of the Cheat Mountain. The Tygart Valley River heads up in Randolph County, West Virginia, and flows northward. For a history of the Monongahela, see Richard Pike Bissell, *The Monongahela*, Rivers of America ser. (New York NY, 1949).

[32]The level part of Tygart Valley measures about thirty miles in length with widths varying from three-fourths mile to two miles. Its fertile soil and grassy range attracted the pioneers. After the quick exodus of the Tygart family following the massacre of the Robert Foyles family in December 1753, the valley remained unsettled until around 1770. The Westfall, Cassidy, and Crouch families were among the first settlers to put down their roots there. David Crouch, Interview by [John D. Shane, 1843], Nicholas Co. KY, Draper MSS., 12CC225; and Withers, *Border Warfare*, 125-26.

[33]This probably was the winter of 1774–1775. The Revolutionary War did not begin until April 1775, but Dunmore's War had occurred on the Virginia frontier during the fall of the preceding year.

[34]Here *past* is the rare, phonetic spelling of *passed*, the past participle of the transitive verb *pass*.

[35]During the Revolutionary War and at least up to the year 1787 there was no wagon road connecting Tygart Valley with the South Branch. David Crouch, Interview by [John D. Shane, 1843], Nicholas Co. KY, Draper MSS., 12CC225.

[36]Up and down Tygart Valley the settlers built in 1770–1787 a chain of ten or twelve forts that stretched some thirty miles. "All the forts were stockaded, with bast ends [bastions], for sentry to stand in of nights," one man remembered. Ibid., 12CC225-26.

[37]The Greenbrier River originates in northern Pocahontas County, West Virginia, and runs southward to empty into the New River in Summers County.

[38]The French and Indian War had destroyed early settlements on the Greenbrier River, but in 1769 John Stuart and several other young men had settled in the valley. They were

day. Every thing looked equally gloomy there. A few meetings pacified me there, and we returned back on a different rout[e]. The whole of this tour, disagreeable as it was, I considered an entire water haul.[39] All that I could say was that I had seen Tygart Valley and had seen Greenbrier, with but little desire ever to see them again. But it was not long before I felt deeply concerned about those poor, destitute people.

The next June [1775], I concluded to take a more extensive tour and [19] lower down than before. Monongahela River has five large branches—the first is Youghiogheny (commonly called Yoh), the second is Cheat River, the third and main one is the Valley Fork, the fourth is a river called Buckhannon, the fifth is the West Fork.[40] These were all peopled.

I set out with a young brother (who had been lately baptized) by the name of Wood. Our first settlement was Cheat River, where a little settlement of Baptists who had moved from Shenandoah were now living on a large bottom on the river called Dunkard Bottom.[41] All the settlement in the Great Glades[42] on

---

able to hold on to their improvements in spite of Indian incursions. Withers, *Border Warfare*, 58-59.

[39]"Water haul" is a colloquialism meaning an attempt that produces no results and derives from the hauling in of a net when no fish are taken.

[40]The Youghiogheny and the Cheat rivers empty into the Monongahela in Pennsylvania at points eighty-three miles apart, the way the crow flies. The Youghiogheny rises in Preston County, West Virginia; the Cheat is formed by the merger of Shavers and Black River forks at Parsons in Tucker County. The Valley (or the East) Fork River is now called the Tygart Valley River. Buckhannon River, which heads up in Randolph County, is a tributary of the Tygart Valley River. The West Fork River, rising in Upshur County, and the Tygart Valley River merge to form the Monongahela about one mile south of Fairmont, West Virginia.

[41]Dunkard Bottom was named for the Eckerlin brothers, Sabbatarian Dunkers from the cloister at Ephrata, Pennsylvania, who settled temporarily in this bottom around 1752. No one had tried to settle there again until 1772. The largest level area in present-day Preston County, West Virginia, this bottom is located on the right bank of the Cheat River about two miles southeast of present Kingwood. Thomas Condit Miller and Hu Maxwell, *West Virginia and Its People*, 3 vols. (New York NY, 1913) 1:50; Wust, *Virginia Frontier*, 30, 31; and Withers, *Border Warfare*, 126. To spell *Dunkard*, Taylor uses both *Tunkard* and *Tunchard*, transliterations of the German *tunker* (meaning "one who dips or baptizes").

[42]The Great Glades are situated in the western tip of Maryland south of the Big Sandy Creek Glades and in the area between the West Virginia-Maryland border on the west and the Youghiogheny River on the east.

Some glades were open, grassy spaces in the forest; others were brushy areas difficult to pass through. Regardless of their cover, all were probably flat and low and partly marshy. Hamil Thomas Kenny, *West Virginia Place Names* (Piedmont WV, 1945)

Youghiogheny River, between the South Branch and Cheat River, a space of sixty miles, had been broken up by the Indians.[43] At Cheat River we stopt[44] and worshiped awhile.

Our next stop was about thirty miles bearing down towards Redstone to the Forks of Cheat and Monongahela rivers,[45] where was a considerable settlement of people and a small Baptist church,[46] which had been constituted by Mr. John Corbley.[47] Here the people seemed to be in safety from the Indians; though after this, Mr. Corbley's family was killed by the Indians not far from this place.[48] We got to a Baptist house on Saturday evening, and on the next day his house was filled with people to hear preaching.

While the people were gathering, I found they generally took Brother Wood, that was with me, to be the preacher. He was well-dressed, had been lately baptized, and looked very serious. At length a respectable-looking man came to me [and], casting a respectful eye towards Wood, asked me where the preacher lived, what was his name, and the like. I replied his name was Taylor, where he lived, etc. Though I found he was deceived, I suffered the innocent deception to go on. He asked me to walk with him to the spring, where farther enquiries[49] were made about the preacher. I found he was no Baptist but showed respect for me, because I was traveling with a respectable-looking "preacher." This was not all the times [20]by many in which the people were deceived where I was a stranger.

---

270.

[43]Early settlers on the upper Youghiogheny River were hunters from the South Branch of the Potomac attracted there by the abundance of game in the glades. Withers, *Border Warfare*, 118.

[44]*Stopt* is the poetic form of *stopped*, the past tense of the verb *stop*.

[45]The term "Forks of Cheat and Monongahela rivers" is a misnomer, because the Forks of the Monongahela merge in Marion County, West Virginia. The term "Forks of Cheat," however, was used in the late eighteenth century to indicate the place where the Cheat River spills into the Monongahela. This site is located in present-day Fayette County, Pennsylvania.

[46]The Forks of Cheat Church was located in the vicinity of Uniontown, Pennsylvania, and near the mouth of the Cheat River. Simple, *Baptists in Virginia*, rev. ed., 440n.

[47]John Corbley (1732/3–1803), a native of Ireland, was baptized in northern Virginia by John Garrard. After he began to preach, he was imprisoned for a season in Culpeper County. He spent the last years of his life in the Redstone settlement in Pennsylvania. James B. Taylor, *Virginia Baptist Ministers*, 2d ed., 105-108; and Semple, *Baptists in Virginia*, rev. ed., 154n.

[48]For an account of this Indian attack in May 1782, see Withers, *Border Warfare*, 345-46.

[49]In the twelve instances of the verb and noun forms of the word *inquire* found in this book, the author uses the alternate spelling *enquire* or *enquiry*.

Traveling once in Virginia with my brother Joseph Taylor[50] and having a meeting appointed at Beeson Town,[51] near Redstone, a large assembly had gathered, and a man [was] preaching when we got there. When we got into the crowded house, a seat was soon made for his [Joseph's] reception. I worked off [52] to some back seat. By the wishful look of the people on him, with his fine black cloth[53] and clean neckband, he soon discovered their mistake. And though a wild rat[t]ling man, he perhaps put on more solemn looks than he would have done. And when the preacher was done, an opening was immediately made between him [Joseph] and the pulpit, which I had to scramble as I could—through and over the people—to get to the place.

However, with the man at the spring, he asked me if it was not time for the preacher to begin. We walked to the house, and I immediately went to the table and opened meeting. The people seemed to look on with wonder, and especially the inquisitive man. But they were all excusable, for, though I was now twenty-two or -three years old, I looked to be at least four years younger than I was. I was about twenty years old when I began to speak, but by those who did not know me I was taken to be sixteen. At twenty-five I was barely grown to my common stature.

When I opened meeting, I addressed the people as follows: "I am now nearly two hundred miles from home and an entire stranger to you all. It is probable you wish to know from whence I came and who and what I am." I then informed them where my home was when [I was] at it. I then told them my name, and as

---

[50]Joseph F. Taylor was one of the nine children of Lazarus Taylor and Hannah Bradford. He went to Kentucky with his brother John in the spring of 1784 and returned to Virginia in March of the following year. On the trip back home his company was attacked by Indians. Some years later at a dance in Versailles, Joseph scalped Bill Cornstalk, one of that marauding party, because the Indian was boasting how he had taken six scalps. Joseph settled in Clover Bottom, in Woodford County, and by 1799 had advanced to the rank of captain in the militia. Late in life "Old Joe" Taylor had the reputation of being an excessive drinker. Joseph F. Taylor, Interview by [John D. Shane], Draper MSS., llCC228, 232; A. Young, Interview by [Shane], ibid., llCC236; G. Glenn Clift, comp., The "Corn Stalk" Militia of Kentucky, 1792-1811 (Frankfort KY, 1957) 27, 154; Railey, Woodford County, 102; and Dorothy Thompson, "Ancestors and Descendants." 29, 31.

[51]Situated eleven miles from the village of Redstone, Beeson Town, on Redstone Creek, was settled about 1768 by Henry Beeson, a Quaker from Virginia. Its present name is Uniontown, the seat of Fayette County, Pennsylvania. A. Howry Espenshade, Pennsylvania Place Names (State College PA, 1925) 62; and William Darby and Theodore Dwight, Jr., A New Gazetteer of the United States of America, 2d ed. (New York NY, 1833) 535.

[52]The verb form "work off" is a slang expression meaning "put out of the way."

[53]The noun cloth is here an obsolete usage meaning apparel.

to profession I was a Baptist and of the Separate order. When I named Separate Baptists it produced some oblique looks, for the Baptists there were Regulars, and they considered the Separates a kind of heterodox people.

I took this for a text: "A man that hath friends must show himself friendly, and there is a friend that sticketh closer than a brother" (Pro[verbs] 18[th] chap[ter] 24th verse). [21]I ventured to transpose the words a little and read them, "A man that would have friends must show himself friendly." I then spoke of Jesus Christ, the eternal Son of God, Whose kind thoughts were turned to our race before the world began, as expressed in the eighth chapter of Proverbs.[54] And that our native enmity, which I dwelt on at large, did not prevent those early, kind designs from being put into practice by His kind visit to our world in His incarnation, [by] His active obedience to the law, [and by] His passive obedience in death. In which by help from Heaven, I was so expressive that there was a great gush of tears among the people. Then [I] added how the mighty enmity of our hearts were slain by a supernatural power from Heaven, with the cordial submission of the soul to Jesus Christ in friendship. The certainty of the salvation of that soul [was assured], because the friendship of the Saviour was more to be depended upon than any brother whatever, for that He was God and changed not.

My Regular [Baptist] brethren perhaps forgot that I was a Separate, for we parted that afternoon with tears of cordial friendship. And as an evidence on their side they made up among themselves and gave me three or four dollars which I received as a token of their friendship.

From thence we crossed over the main river [Monongahela] and ranged up its West Fork, where we had some happy meetings. Some of the people here were at home, others in forts.[55] I fell in at a meeting of Mr. [John] Corbley's, where we enjoyed a happy meeting together, it being the first time we ever saw each other.

From this settlement it was about one day's ride to Buckhannon River, where was about thirty families[56] [and] where (I think) preaching had never been [heard]. The people here were generally either forted[57] or a number of families

---

[54]Verses 22-31.

[55]This community on the West Fork River was located probably at the site of present-day Clarksburg, in Harrison County, West Virginia, having been planted shortly before the beginning of the Revolutionary War. *New Descriptive Atlas of West Virginia* (Clarksburg WV, 1933) 4.

[56]The settlement on the Buckhannon River had been planted in the spring of 1769 by Samuel Pringle and some thirteen other men from the South Branch of the Potomac. Ibid.

[57]It was not uncommon during the Revolutionary War for people on the Virginia frontier to be forted in for years on end. David Crouch of Nicholas County, Kentucky,

huddled together in kind of blockhouses[58] for their own safety. These poor things would risk all they had and their own lives to get together to hear preaching. To them it was a strong evidence of good will for a man to risk his [22]life to come and preach to them. There we had several meetings, and the people [were] much affected.

From Buckhannon, one day's ride more through a poor, gloomy forest brought us to Tygart Valley, which the winter before [had] looked so dreadfully gloomy to me. But dangerous as the times were, the summer season put a more pleasant aspect on the face of things.[59] I had several meetings there, beginning with Sunday in the thickest part of the valley settlement. The preaching was in the woods near the fort, where a great number of people gathered and [where they] seemed as perfectly composed as if they had no enemy in the world. For the first time, I preached twice in the day before the people broke.[60] The first text was: "The axe is laid at the root of the trees, and every tree that bringeth not good fruit is hewn down and cast into the fire."[61] The second text, I think, was this: "Come, for all things are now ready."[62] The people seemed to listen with interested attention, and some [were] much affected. There are some alive now in Kentucky who professes hope in Christ from that day's preaching.

On this visit I became acquainted in the valley with some warm-hearted Presbyterians who had embraced religion in the time of [George] Whitefield's[63] preaching [and] who seemed as kind to me as to a near relation. This with other things made an opening for another visit to Tygart Valley.

recalled that his family in Tygart Valley "were forted almost till I was a man grown." Crouch, Interview by [John D. Shane, 1843], Draper MSS., 12CC225.

[58]A blockhouse was a two-story log cabin in which the upper floor was cantilevered some eighteen inches beyond the walls of the first story. During an Indian attack persons in the second story could maintain surveillance through holes made near the outer edges of the floor. The blockhouses Taylor refers to were probably free-standing units. Such buildings, however, were often placed at two or more corners of a fort.

[59]When summer came the abundance of game and fruit changed the face of Tygart Valley. One settler recalled that it was the most bountiful region for wild fruit that he had ever seen. Plenty of serviceberries, huckleberries, and cranberries were found there during the Revolutionary War. David Crouch, Interview by [John D. Shane, 1843], Draper MSS., 12CC226.

[60]The verb *break* used here is an Americanism meaning "scatter in all directions."

[61]Matthew 3:10.

[62]Luke 14:17.

[63]George Whitefield (1714–1770) an Anglican priest from Gloucester, England, was "the greatest preacher" of the eighteenth century. He made several voyages to North America and significantly aided the Great Awakening in the British colonies there. Sweet, *Story of Religion in America*, 3rd ed., 131-33, 141-42, 169-71.

I returned to Lunies Creek, where [Joseph] Redding was now the pastor, and from thence to Shenandoah, where [William] Marshall was now the pastor. My designs were to spend the next winter in these back settlements, which I accordingly fulfilled.

This, I think, was in the winter of [17]75 and [17]76. The war was now increasing with mighty rapidity, and a number of regular troops were stationed in Tygart Valley to guard the frontiers. Some of the poor soldiers became much affected under preaching and were despised by their officers, declaring that my preaching disqualified them for fighting. Their fellow soldiers also derided their tears and sorrows. But I hope [that] the Lord blessed some of them. [23]The troops' being stationed at Tygart Valley made traveling less dangerous through that winter, and the people [lived] more at their homes. The great readiness in many of the people to hear the Word was an ample reward for all my troubles.

Through this dreary winter, I visited all the settlements where I had been before, but Tygart Valley was my temporary home. I here made up an acquaintance with a number of tender-hearted friends, some of whom were young converts. I took two tours from Tygart Valley to Greenbrier, one of which I will relate.

It was called thirty miles from the upper house in the valley to the first house in the Greenbrier settlement, and over a tremendous mountain that divided the Monongahela waters from Greenbrier River.[64] The trace was very dull, and [I was] a stranger to the way and without company. I was on a borrowed horse, and unshod; but the owner thought that would be no impediment, as a snow had lately fallen about ancle-deep [sic]. I went to the last house in the valley,[65] that by an early start I might prevent camping in the woods at night. The [Tygart Valley] River was from twenty to thirty yards wide when I sat out, to the source of which I had to travel before I took the mountain.

The freeze had been, and was then, so severe that [there was] scarce[66] a ripple of the river but was so blocked up with ice that it appeared impossible for my barefooted horse to cross it. I once thought of going back, but, after reflecting, the obstructions seemed too trivial to make a good excuse from. And,

---

[64]Taylor's route took him over the Tygart Valley River and Shavers Fork of the Cheat River, across Back Allegheny Mountain in present-day Pocahontas County, and onto the headwaters of the Greenbrier River.

[65]The house to which Taylor refers may have been John Warrick's Station, which was the most southern unit in the chain of forts and the one highest up on Tygart Valley River. Sometimes at that station as many as nine families were forted in. David Crouch, Interview by [John D. Shane, 1843], Nicholas Co. KY, Draper MSS., 12CC225, 228.

[66]The adverb *scarce* is the poetic form of *scarcely*.

not knowing what was ahead, I concluded to push on. I took my wrappers[67] from my legs and placed my horse's forefeet in the middle of the wrappers and then with my garters tied them round his legs, by which he might walk on the smooth ice. But after, I could not get him a step forward. My only remedy was to lead him onto some little steep bank on the river, two or three feet high, and by a sudden push, sprall [sprawl] him on the ice and then lead him on across the river. This was often repeated. And the cold [was] so sensible that I was [24]doubtful[68] my ears would freeze, and my hands [were] so numbed that I could scarcely tie my wrappers either on my horse's legs or my own. And so much time was spent in those several operations, though I had set out about sunrise I was pretty sure I should not arrive at any house that night. But my horse learned that it was better to take the ice at once after my wrappers were tied on his legs than to be dashed on it, for I suppose we crossed the river from ten to twenty times. The afterpart of the day became warmer, and I got to a house about sundown.

I had a number of meetings in what was called the Little Levels of Green-brier.[69] But [because of] the distracted state of the people by the war, or the barrenness of my preaching, or both, I became fully convinced that if the Lord ever intended to bless that people, the time was not come, or myself was not to be the instrument.

I returned to Tygart Valley and from thence paid another visit to the several different settlements, where was very hopeful appearances, and returned home in the spring [1776].

The hopeful prospects in the backwoods[70] induced me to take a letter of dismission from Shenandoah and join the church on Lunies Creek. After which [Joseph] Redding and myself took several tours. A part of one of them I think proper to state. Our first meeting was at Cheat River [in] Dunkard Bottom, sixty miles from Redding's, for this was the first settlement we came to. To this meeting there came a number [who had traveled] about fifteen miles from a place called Monogahela Glades,[71] where was a settlement of about twenty families.

---

[67]*Wrappers* is an old word for *leggings*. In two of his seven uses of this word Taylor writes it *roppers*, an indication of its common pronunciation.

[68]Here the word *doubtful* is an obsoletism meaning *fearful*.

[69]Set in a small valley that is hemmed in by high ranges, the Little Levels of Greenbrier are located near present-day Hillsboro in Pocahontas County, West Virginia. This name was given to the area by John McNeel, who settled near there about 1756. Kenny, *West Virginia Place Names*, 370.

[70]*Backwoods* is an Americanism for *frontier*.

[71]The Monongahela Glades are located in the western edge of present-day Preston County, West Virginia, near the village of Gladesville. Kenny, *West Virginia Place Names*, 270-71.

They importuned us to stop at their settlement and preach to them. Our other arrangements did not admit except[72] they could be together the next day about ten o'clock, on which we would spend about two hours with them. They set off on Sunday evening from meeting to give notice to their neighbors.

One James Brain, a Baptist, conducted us to the place next day.[73] We met about thirty or forty people and [25]began about the time designed. I went forward. There was nothing very visible while I was speaking. Redding dwelt on the awful subject of a Judgment to come. The first appearance was a young lady who began to weep[74] and tremble, sitting by her grandmother. The old lady for some time strove to stop her. At length she began to tremble herself, as if the Judge was at the door. From thence the effect spread through the whole house with solemn groans and lamentations; till at length a woman the name of Clark dropt on her knees in the middle of the house with the greatest appearance of agonizing guilt. And perhaps she did not leave that position for the space of three hours. When Redding stopt speaking, the only remedy I had to prevent [my] hallowing with all my might was to vent the tender feelings of my heart by exhortations[75] and feeling invitations to those apparently broken-hearted creatures. Whether Mrs. Clark had ever been concerned about her soul before, I disremember;[76] but she obtained deliverance from her guilt before she left her knees.

We had quite forgotten all the meetings that were ahead of us, and our worship continued perhaps six hours in prayers, praise, and exhortations among the people. I do not recollect that we took any sustenance before we left the place, for the family where the meeting was [conducted] seemed two [too] much affected to think of anything but the salvation of their souls. I solemnly surveyed

---

[72]The word *except* is an archaic conjunction meaning *unless*.

[73]This meeting was held at the home of William Powell. Page 30, first edition.

[74]In colonial Virginia it was said in derision that Baptists were always weeping and moaning. David Thomas responded, "It is true [that] lively Christians are apt to weep much, but that is often with joy instead of sorrow." *The Virginia Baptist* (Baltimore MD, 1774) 59.

[75]Exhortation is a type of preaching. Either it urges the unconverted to seek God, to flee from the wrath to come, and to turn from sin to the Saviour. Or it strongly advises the believer to walk in the path of the righteous and to perform the duty of the Christian. Preachers who carried Calvinism to an extreme could not find it in their hearts to exhort sinners, rather they believed that God would prod the lost person in His own time and by His own method. For fuller coverage, see Jerry L. Tarver, "Exhortation among Early Virginia Baptists," *Virginia Baptist Register* 5 (1966): 228-36.

[76]The verb *disremember* is a dialecticism meaning *forget*.

the house a little before we started, and it is a fact that the floor of it was as wet with the tears of the people as if water had been sprinkled all over it.[77]

Mr. Brain, our guide, the only Baptist that I know of at the place besides ourselves, went on to put us in the way,[78] while we made the lonesome forest ring with the praises of God, as if there was not an Indian in the world. Our guide parted with us late in the evening and not long after was killed by the Indians.[79]

This wonderful meeting at this little, glade settlement—the first that was ever [held] [26]there—if I judge from my own feelings and the effect afterwards, according to the number of people, exceeded any I was ever at in my life. I suppose one-third at least of the people present obtained hope in Christ afterwards and resorted to some churches thirty or forty miles off for baptism.

The husband of Mrs. Clark, at the time of her conversion at this meeting, was on a visit to the Jersies, where he had moved from. While there, as he told me afterwards, he had a dream of a meeting in his neighborhood, and about such an one as really was there. And at said meeting, he dreamed his wife was converted. He was struck with a sense of his own guilt from his dream. And when he found the reality of all his dream when he returned, [he] had no rest till he found it in the Saviour, and in a few months was baptized with his wife. At this place, I frequently called to worship with the people afterwards, and usually while there, [I] felt as, I think, Jacob did when at Bethel, where he had his dream of the ladder.[80]

[Joseph] Redding and myself went on our way (after leaving Mr. Brain) to visit chief [81] of the settlements where I had been before [and] where we found the people more affected than I had ever before seen them. And we soon became as much united to many of those poor, backwoods strangers as if they had been near relations. In those back settlements we constituted no church, for that to us appeared needless except there was some person stately to preach to them. Neither did we baptize any except where we found Baptists enough to make out at least a semblance of a church, for we had not yet grown up to apostolic style.[82]

---

[77]In the first edition, Taylor ends this sentence with the following words, which he omits from the second edition: "or with a shower of rain."

[78]The idiom "put us in the way" means "show us the road to take."

[79]James Brain lived on Snowy Creek in present-day Preston County, West Virginia. On 12 April 1779, as he proceeded to his day's work, he was shot, tomahawked, and scalped by Indians who had beseiged his house during the night. Withers, *Border Warfare*, 280-81.

[80]Genesis 28:12, 16-17.

[81]Here the noun *chief* has the archaic meaning of *most* or "the main part of anything."

[82]In his second edition Taylor omits the final clause of this sentence. He refers here

By this time Redding with the church at Lunies Creek counseled about my ordination, to which they agreed. And hearing of a council of ministers to meet at old Shenandoah Church[83] on some business, Redding took the certificate of Lunies Creek Church, and we attended this meeting of ministers at Shenandoah. This step to Redding appeared the more seasonable, because in this old [27]church, where both him[84] and myself had been baptized, my ordination could undergo another scrutiny. If I mistake not, the Baptists are much less careful now in ordaining ministers than they were in those past days. This was about four years after I had been a licensed preacher[85] and had traveled for that purpose about twice as many thousand miles as I had been preaching years, with tolerable approbation among the Baptists. The design of my ordination was in the itinerant way[86] and [also] to administer ordinances where the churches were destitute of a pastor and called for my service. The church at Shenandoah with the ministers present agreed to my ordination in this way, which was not uncommon for unmarried men in those days.

The presbytery who officiated in the ordination was Lewis Craig,[87] John

to the later practice of a Baptist minister's baptizing converts on his own authority rather than on the approval of the congregation of which they would become members.

Professor Otis K. Rice contrasts the permanency of Elder John Alderson's helping to found nine Baptist churches in the area from the Greenbrier River Valley to the Ohio River with Taylor's itinerancy in that region. *Allegheny Frontier*, 278-79. Alderson settled in the Greenbrier country in 1777, but Taylor worked as a traveling preacher.

[83]Here is another designation for the Lower South River Church or the Happy Creek Church.

[84]The pronoun *him* in the accusative case is here used ungrammatically in place of the nominative *he*.

[85]A licensed preacher is authorized by the congregation to which he belongs to exercise his gifts as a public speaker. He is said to be "liberated" to preach. But such a preacher does not administer the ordinances.

[86]As an itinerant, Taylor would do the work of a traveling evangelist.

[87]Lewis Craig (1737/8–1825) was born into a religious Anglican family of Spotsylvania County, Virginia. In time his parents, his six brothers, and his four sisters, all became Baptists. Lewis became a Separate Baptist in 1767. Two years later he was set apart as an elder. In 1770 he was ordained the pastor of the Upper Spotsylvania Church, which had 160 members. The first imprisonment of Baptist preachers in Virginia happened in Spotsylvania County in 1768 and involved Craig, who was held for four weeks. Also four other ministers were implicated. Three years later Craig was jailed in Caroline County for three months. He is renowned as the leader of a "traveling church" that migrated from Virginia to Kentucky in the closing months of 1781. Edwards, *Materials*, 2:54-55, 57-58; Semple, *Baptists in Virginia*, rev. ed., 472-73, 483; and Little, *Imprisoned Preachers*, 53. Lewis N. Thompson, *Lewis Craig, the Pioneer Baptist Preacher* (Louisville KY, 1910) is a eulogistic, poorly done biography of ninety pages.

Pickett, John Koontz, Joseph Redding, and Theodoric Noel,[88] then a young man. Being well acquainted with me made examination, in their esteem,[89] less needful. They proceeded in the common form, all of us kneeling down, with their right hand laid on my head.[90] Two or three of them prayed. Lewis Craig, I think, gave me a pertinent charge, while holding me by the right hand, with the right hand of fellowship from them and all the brethren that were present.[91] With me it was an awfully solemn time. I remember [that] young Mr. Noel, though an older man than myself, wrote the credentials they were pleased to give me.

[278,2d]The crowded pages of this little book leaves me but little room to furnish a biography of our lamented friend and brother Lewis Craig. We shall barely attempt a sketch of the most important events of his life.[92]

Mr. [Lewis] Craig became awakened, perhaps as early as 1765, by the preaching of Col[onel] Samuel Harris, who afterwards was ordained an apostle among the Separate Baptists.[93] Mr. Craig's great pressure of guilt induced him

---

See also James B. Taylor, *Virginia Baptist Ministers*, 2d ed., 84-88.

[88]Theodoric Noel (1750?–1813) began preaching soon after his baptism in 1773. His long suit was exhortation. He served several churches in Virginia, where few men excelled him in the ministry. Semple, *Baptists in Virginia*, rev. ed., 157, 160, 164, 165; and James B. Taylor, *Virginia Baptist Ministers*, 2d ed., 228-29.

[89]Here is used the archaic noun *esteem*, meaning *opinion*.

[90]In one Virginia association of Separate Baptists a dispute continued for a number of years, beginning in 1792, about the imposition of hands when a minister was ordained. Some preachers held that a presbytery or a "plurality of elders" ought to lay their hands upon the head of the candidate. Others contended that only a "solemn call" from the church was needful in order to effect ordination. Semple, *Baptists in Virginia*, rev. ed., 124-25.

[91]Giving the right hand of fellowship to the candidate for ordination confirms him in his new role. The right hand of fellowship, one of nine Christian rites used among early Separate Baptists, was also practiced at baptism and at the reception of members by other means. The other eight rites were baptism, the Lord's Supper, the love feast, laying on hands, anointing the sick, the kiss of charity, washing feet, and "devoting children." Edwards, *Materials*, 2:46; and Benedict, *Baptist Denomination*, 2:107. For an analysis of these rites, see B. C. Holtzclaw, "The Nine Christian Rites in the Early Baptist Churches of Virginia," *Virginia Baptist Register* 6 (1967): 243-60.

[92]This paragraph and the seven that follow come from a section in the addendum of the second edition titled "Biography of Mr. Lewis Craig."

[93]In 1774 the two Separate Baptist associations in Virginia set up the office of apostle, as listed in Ephesians 4:11. The southern group chose Samuel Harris for this post. On a day marked for fasting he was ordained an apostle, the hands of every ordained preacher present were laid on him, and the entire association gave him the right hand of fellowship. His duties were to visit the churches, to supervise ordination, to effect order where needed, and to report to the next association. In the northern group John Waller and Elijah Craig were elected as apostles. The plan failed after a few months because the

to follow the preachers from one meeting to another. And when preaching ended, he would rise up in tears and loudly proclaim that he was a justly condemned sinner. And with loud voice [he would] warn the people to fly from the wrath to come,[94] and [that] except they were born again,[95] with himself they should all go to Hell together. While under his exhortation, the people would weep and cry aloud for mercy.

In this manner, his ministry began before himself had hope of conversion. And after relief came to him, he went on preaching a considerable time before he was baptized (no administrator being near), many being converted under his labours.

When he was baptized, a church was constituted at once in Spotsylvania [County], Virginia, and Mr. [Lewis] Craig soon [was] ordained as their pastor.

His great zeal in preaching far and near soon drew the attention of magistrates, who were bound to keep good order. Mr. Craig was presented to the grand jury for keeping unlawful conventicles and [for] worshiping God contrary to the law of the land. A true bill was found against him but perhaps with the indulgence of another hearing.

The jury having withdrawn to a tavern for refreshment, Mr. [Lewis] Craig [also] attended. [He] called for a large bowl of rich toddy and politely invited them to partake of his treat, when a number of them pleasantly accepted (for Mr. Craig was truly a respectable men) [and] when he accosted them thus: "Gentlemen, I thank you for your attention to me. When I was about this courtyard in [279,2d]all kind of vanity, folly, and vice you took no notice of me. But when I have forsaken all those vices and warn men to forsake and repent of their sins you bring me to the bar as a transgressor. How is all this?"[96]

The great solemnity of this address filled the hearers with dismay. And Mr. John Waller, one of the jurors [and] a very wicked man, became so struck that he never got rest till he found it in the Lord. And [he] became one of the most

---

"spirit of free government ran too high" amongst the churches. It was agreed that this episcopal office "did not belong to ordinary times." Semple, *Baptists in Virginia*, rev. ed. 79-82. For more information, see John S. Moore, "Virginia's Three Baptist Apostles," *Virginia Baptist Register* 11 (1972): 498-502.

[94]Matthew 3:7.

[95]John 3:3.

[96]Treating the jury with toddy at the tavern may well have taken place, but it is not a part of the earliest account of this incident as found in Morgan Edwards, *Materials towards a History of the Baptists*, 2:54-55. According to Edwards, Lewis Craig said to the jurors as they left the courthouse, "I take joifully [*sic*] the despoiling of my goods for Christ's sake. I thank you, gentlemen, for the honor you did me. While I was wicked and injurious you took no notice of me; but now, having altered my course of life and endeavoring to reform my neighbors, you concern yourselves much about me."

successful preachers that was ever in Virginia and was oftentimes honored with
a prison for his preaching.

Whether Mr. [Lewis] Craig in these cases escaped a prison or not, he was
oftentimes with his son in the gospel John Waller imprisoned for preaching. Mr.
Craig was a great builder of churches in Virginia.

[So it was that], [298]about four years after I began to preach, I was ordained
as an itinerant preacher.[97] Theodoric Noel, the father of our Silas M. Noel,[98]
[was] a faithful servant of Jesus Christ who lived and died in Virginia. He began
to preach when young, continued in the ministry perhaps forty years, and was
one of the most successful preachers of his day. He [299]died a few years past.[99]

I was a traveling preacher about ten years (of which I have said something
elsewhere)[100] before I was married. Soon after, I moved to Kentucky in the fall
[of] 1783. There was no Baptist association[101] in this state when I moved to it,

---

[97]Based on the time Taylor first began to preach, his ordination took place in 1776,
perhaps in October. On page 27 of the first edition, however, he dates his ordination as
four years after his licensing, an event that followed his first preaching by six months.
There is no way by which to reconcile the difference.

[98]Silas Mercer Noel (1783–1839), a native of Henrico County, Virginia, migrated to
Kentucky, where he hung out his shingle as a lawyer. Soon after his conversion, he began
to preach and was ordained the pastor of the Big Spring Church. During 1813 he edited
the *Gospel Herald*, the second Baptist periodical to appear in Kentucky. An early
proponent of a statewide organization of Baptists, he served as the moderator of the
abortive Kentucky Baptist Convention during 1831–1835, the lifetime of this prototype
of the General Association of Kentucky Baptists. He was a circuit judge, a trustee of
Georgetown College, and the foremost advocate of the Baptist position during the
Campbellite struggle in Kentucky. Spencer, *Kentucky Baptists*, 1:316-18; and Sprague,
*American Pulpit*, 7:627-30.

[99]This paragraph and the following seven paragraphs are taken from the piece in the
*Ten Churches* headed "The Author's Conversion and Call to the Ministry."

[100]The reference here is to John Taylor, *Thoughts on Missions*, 27-29, 50.

[101]The Elkhorn Association, the first in Kentucky, was organized on 30 September and
1 October 1785, two years after Taylor's arrival in the West. Spencer, *Kentucky Baptists*,
1:109, 2:9-10.

For coverage of the origins of English and American Baptist associations, see Walter
B. Shurden, "The Baptist Association: A Historical Introduction," *Associational Bulletin*
(Atlanta GA) 17 (Nov–Dec 1983): 1-8.

and only five churches of that order.[102] I have gained an extensive acquaintance with the Kentucky Baptists, perhaps by being overly officious[103] among them.

I have said above I could get no satisfactory answer as to my call to the ministry. My present impressions are that the call lies in a good man's motives to the work and [in] the call of the church.[104] If a Christian has preaching talents and the church says "preach," he may go on safely. This is my call and for no other do I look at present, though in my youth I laboured long for evidences of my call, of which a visionary something would then have satisfied me.[105]

I have said [that] a good motive to the work and the call of the church is all-sufficient as to a man's authority to preach the gospel. By a good motive to the work, I understand, the man's own soul must be converted, for except he is born again[106] he cannot have a spiritually good motive. And [this] is what Paul designs by "the husbandman that laboureth must first be partaker of the fruit[s]."[107]

It is this [that] produces a desire in him after what Paul calls "a good work."[108] This is a feeling [of] sensibility in him that "one man's soul is worth more than all the world."[109] And while the love of Christ constrains him,[110] he will very gladly or readily spend and be spent for the salvation of his fellow men. All this I felt for many months to the amount of robbing me both of sleep and food, and adding to that the voice of the church. But all did not satisfy me,

---

[102]Here the memory of Taylor fails him. When he reached Kentucky shortly before Christmas in 1783, seven Baptist churches were conducting their organized "house-keeping." Their names and the dates of their constitutions follow: Severns Valley, June 1781; Cedar Creek, July 1781; the first Gilberts Creek, December 1781, gathered by Lewis Craig; Nolynn (now called South Fork) summer 1782; Forks of Dicks (now spelled Dix) River, 1782; the second Gilberts Creek, 1783, gathered by Joseph Bledsoe; and Providence, 1783. Spencer, *Kentucky Baptists*, 1:33, 34, 40, 41, 45; Masters, *Baptists in Kentucky* 24-33; and Ford, "Kentucky Baptists," *Christian Repository* 5:263.

[103]Taylor uses here the obsolete word *officious*, meaning *dutiful* or *formal*.

[104]George W. Truett's call to the ministry came through the Baptist church at Whitewright, Texas. Some aspects of that call comport with the ministerial call of John Taylor. Powhatan W. James, *George W. Truett*, rev. ed. (New York NY, 1945) 47-50.

[105]When Taylor published in his *Ten Churches* the story of his conversion and of his call to the ministry as it first had appeared in print in his *Thoughts on Missions*, he revised it at this point by dropping the final fifteen lines and by writing the conclusion that appears in the following five paragraphs. In this present edition I have omitted the original conclusion and have used his expanded one.

[106]John 3:3.

[107]2 Timothy 2:6.

[108]1 Timothy 3:1.

[109]Cf. Mark 8:36

[110]2 Corinthians 5:14.

for I was not called as the ancient prophets and apostles were. But to glorify God and [to] benefit men is the sole ground of the ministerial motive, and there is no self-serving in all this sacred business. In all this I have felt conscious for more than half a century.

[300]My own belief is that none properly understands the gospel or [the] voice of the Shepherd but His sheep or the true Christian. Therefore, the voice of the church is very essential in the call to the ministry. The Bridegroom is out of the way; what the bride does in His absence should be valid. The church ought to act under great responsibility, being accountable to the Chief Shepherd at His return. "So help us, Lord, that we may all have boldness in the Day of Judgment."[111] [As] the instruments of my encouragement in my early days, I had three gospel fathers, to wit: William Marshall, the instrument of my first awakening[112] and conversion; James Ireland, the man who baptized me and under whose pastoral care I lived for some time; and Joseph Redding, under whose care and with whom I traveled near ten years before I was a married man. All these men seemed tender towards me, as if I was their natural son.

But the greatest instrument of my encouragement after all was the Bible itself. There I saw the whole will of God at once. In point of both practice and opinion, what I saw in this Heaven-born Book I received as the voice of God to me, and [it] was the invaluable guide of my whole man both in motive and [in] actions. To this I appeal in all controversy, and by this I expect to be judged at the Last Day.

Of all the religious duties in which I have ever been employed, as to conscious satisfaction baptism takes the lead. And in that blessed work, three different days exceeds. The first was the evening after myself was baptized. The second was the same day fifty years after my own baptism [when] I baptized a number of people.[113] Lastly, on my birthday, when I was seventy years old, I baptized eighteen people. I suppose I have gone into the water hundreds of times[114] to baptize others, and in every case a sweet peace of conscience attended me.

[27][After my ordination Joseph] Redding and myself continued traveling in the back parts[115] and became acquainted with a number of ministers in the

---

[111]1 John 4:17.

[112]In the eighteenth century the word *awakening* from an individual standpoint indicated a period of travail and sorrow for one's sins that usually lasted for several weeks or, as in Taylor's case, for several months.

[113]See page 152, first edition.

[114]The term "hundreds of times" comes from the second edition and is a correction of the first-edition expression "more than a hundred times."

[115]I.e., on the frontier of Virginia and Pennsylvania.

Redstone country,[116] to wit: Isaac Sutton[117] and James, his brother.[118] At that time they had two more brothers that were preachers,[119] John[120] and David.[121] For family preaching they were pretty much like the Craigs in those days. We also became acquainted with John Corbley and William Wood,[122] very active servants of the Lord in building up churches in these backwoods, and from which Redstone Association [28]was created.[123] All these were Regular Baptists, but after becoming acquainted, though we were Separates, we found no difference as to doctrinal opinions.

[116]This term denotes the southwestern region of present-day Pennsylvania.

[117]Isaac Sutton became a charter member of the Morristown Church in his native colony of New Jersey in 1752. He helped to organize the Ketocton (1766) and the Redstone (1776) associations. His removals represent the westward movement in American history. From New Jersey he migrated to Frederick County, Virginia, and thence to the Redstone region in Pennsylvania. Edwards, *Materials*, 1:107, and 2:73; and Semple, *Baptists in Virginia*, rev. ed. 388, 439.

[118]James Sutton, a native of New Jersey, belonged first to the Scotch Plains Church, in Essex County. His westward pastoral trek took him from Somerset and Gloucester counties, New Jersey, to Kent County, Delaware, to the Redstone country of Pennsylvania, and to Kentucky. Edwards, *Materials*, 1:105, 124, 128, 129, and 2:14; Semple, *Baptists in Virginia*, rev. ed., 439; and Spencer, *Kentucky Baptists*, 1:189.

[119]The fact is that there were five of these brothers who were Regular Baptist preachers. Beside the four whom Taylor names, there was Abner Sutton (b. 1741) who was the pastor of the Mount Bethel Church, in Somerset County, New Jersey. Their father was William Sutton, of Middlesex County, New Jersey. Edwards, *Materials*, 1:124.

[120]John Sutton, Sr. (1732/3-ca. 1813), who was born in New Jersey, was educated in that colony at Eaton's Academy, in Hopewell. It was the first Baptist school in North America for the training of ministers. After a two-year pastorate in his native colony, he worked as a missionary in Nova Scotia during 1766–1769. Upon returning home, he began in 1770 a seven-year term at the Welsh Tract Church, in New Castle County, Delaware. For a few years he served churches in the Redstone area of Virginia and Pennsylvania. In 1788 he moved to the Bluegrass Region of Kentucky. There in 1806, as a means of promoting the emancipation of slaves, he organized in Woodford County the New Hope Church of the "Baptist Friends of Humanity." Edwards, *Materials*, 1:94 and 2:3, 10; Benedict, *Baptist Denomination*, 2:7, 449; Spencer, *Kentucky Baptists*, 1:188-89; and Tarrant, *Kentucky Friends to Humanity*, 7.

[121]David Sutton also was educated at Eaton's Academy. From 1764 to 1783 he served as the pastor of the Kingwood Church, of Hunterdon County, in his native New Jersey. Edwards, *Materials*, 1:97, 101-102.

[122]This William Wood may be the same person who later served the Limestone Church in Kentucky. See page 50, first edition.

[123]The Redstone Association was organized in October 1776 by representatives of Regular Baptist churches of Virginia and Pennsylvania. Semple, *Baptists in Virginia*, rev. ed., 439.

I remember we went to one new place called [Big] Sandy Creek Glades,[124] where we found some of these Regular Baptists. They looked a little shy at us, because of the name. For a new place there was a great gathering of people.

While I was speaking, I took notice of a small, pert-looking, old man who shed tears profusely while I was dwelling on the feelings of the heart under the influence of the grace of God. When preaching ended, he called me apart from the people to converse, his eyes being yet moist. I think he informed me [that] he had not heard preaching for several years. He had been baptized long ago by Benjamin Miller in the Jersies.[125] He thought proper to tell me his hope in Christ. He stated his long agony of guilt under which he laboured with the sensibility of his helpless case before he obtained relief. And while stating the glorious plan of salvation being opened to him by the Lord Jesus, he burst forth in a fresh flood of joyful tears, with perhaps smiting his hands together. In heavenly agitation [he] cried out, "O Brother Taylor, it was forty years ago, and it is now as plain to me as if it had taken place yesterday." My own sensibility could no longer be suppressed. While I partook of the same joyful torrent, [I] could not forbear reaching out the hand of Christian fellowship (which he was as ready to do) to a man I never saw before, and old enough to be my grandfather.

This man's name was Frasy.[126] He had a numerous offspring of children and grandchildren, and many of them living near him. I, one day after I became more acquainted with him, asked him how many children he had. He replied, "Nineteen." And after my remarking it was a goodly number, but he considered it only moderate, for that his father had raised twenty-nine children—nineteen by his first wife and ten by a second wife. But what gave him [29]most pleasure of all was the prospect of our preaching becoming useful among his children and neighbors, for some of them, I hope, found the Lord.

To this place I often went afterwards and was respected by the people as much as my character could possibly deserve. The place I have been just speaking of was called [Big] Sandy Creek Glades, where a considerable settlement was now living on the waters of Yoh River.

Higher up the same river was [a region] called the Great Glades, where for many miles together no timber grew. The whole extent of the Allegheny

[124]The Big Sandy Creek Glades are located near the northeastern corner of present-day Preston County, West Virginia. (This Big Sandy Creek should not be confused with the stream by the same name located in Roane and Kanawha counties, in the western end of the state.)

[125]For fifty-three years, Benjamin Miller (1716–1781) served the Scotch Plains Church, which was located in Essex County, New Jersey. Edwards, *Materials*, 1:104, 106.

[126]In 1782 one Samuel Fraze lived in Monongalia County, Virginia. He was a part of a family of seven. *Heads of Families, 1790: Virginia*, 35.

Mountains about this place was esteemed sixty miles across it. Those glades were a part of the distance and of course [were located] in the Allegheny Mountains. In the Great Glades there had been settlements but is now forsaken from Indian danger. Through these glades by different passways I had to go [in order] to pass from the eastern waters to [those of] the West. And the distance from one settlement to another [was so great] that a hard day's travel would not accomplish it, so that camping out often attended the traveler.

If these were inconveniences, I often met with them. I will name a few of them. Traveling once with a companion,[127] our lot was to take up quarters in a deserted cabin that had two apartments.[128] In one of them we put our horses for safekeeping; in the other we built a fire and slept. In the morning we found [that] our horses had broken out. And in the dry, glade grass it was impracticable to track them; however, we searched the chief of next day but found them not, in which time we ate up our provisions. It was about thirty miles to the first inhabitants ahead and nearly the same behind. We left our cabin in the evening to go on ahead with our saddles and all we had, on our backs. After a few miles dark compelled us to take up camp in the great, open glade. He having a gun, we obtained fire, but little or no fuel to supply it. But, though in the middle of winter, the weather was not very cold; so that we suffered as much from hunger as [we did from] cold, for we had [30]walked very hard to find our horses.

The next morning, without a mouthful to eat, we set out with all the cheerfulness we were master of to make this near thirty miles with all our luggage, before we got breakfast. The trace was very slashy[129] in these great, lonesome glades, besides [we had] Yoh River and many of its branches to wade through. After we left the glades the way was monstrous[130] mountainous. Before we got to Cheat River or Dunkard Bottom those mountains[131] appeared pretty hard on our hunger-bitten knees. We passed along by a hunters' cabin late in the day, but they were gone. We rumaged about after bones [that] they had cast away and [that had] perhaps been pillaged by their dogs, but [we] could not get one mouthful; however, [later] we got breakfast and supper together at night.

My partner who traveled with me in this little, rugged tour was a pleasant, little man the name of [William] Powell. It was at his house [that] our great meeting had been [held] (with but few people), where Clark's wife obtained

---

[127]His companion was William Powell. Page 30, first edition.

[128]Here the word *apartment* is an early usage meaning *room*.

[129]The adjective *slashy* is a dialecticism meaning *muddy* or *slushy*. B. W. Green, *Word-Book of Virginia Folk-Speech* (Richmond VA, 1899) 340.

[130] The adverb *monstrous* is here a dialecticism meaning *extremely*.

[131]The mountains that Taylor and his companion crossed westwardly are now called Briery Mountains, located in present-day Preston County, West Virginia.

conversion while on her knees. At the time of our travel Powell was a Baptist, and [he] now lives in Woodford County, Kentucky.[132] It is said [that] he now loves whiskey a little too much. Powell's horse went home. Mine I never got, which was a considerable loss to me.

Another similar tour I had about two winters after and partly on the same road. In the first instance I had no horse; in the last I had one too many, for I had one to lead. There had been snow on the ground, but a great rain had taken it chiefly off. I started from a place called the Crab Orchard, not far from Dunkard Bottom.[133] It was upwards of forty miles to the first house. I set out early to gain that object before night. I soon took a tremendous mountain called Laurel Hill, but in that place called Cheat Mountain.[134] My road was so small for eight miles that it could scarcely be followed by daylight.[135] When I came to the Great Glades, where the settlement had been, the road was plainer.

I soon after came to a creek[136] over which a bridge [131]had been made by the settlers. When [I got] there, I saw that the water was up to the planks of the bridge. I pushed on but soon found the planks were afloat. But hurrying forward, the le[a]d horse first fell through. And as the one I rode was going down, I sprang from him on the floating planks (with my saddlebags in my hand) and escaped clear to the opposite shore.[137] When I turned round, here were both my horses between the cills [sic] of the bridge and barracaded [sic] with floating planks on each side, and the water [was] about as deep as they were high.

The next thing was to counsel how to get them out, and none to counsel but myself; for the poor horses could say nothing on that head while they stood trembling in the cold water. Those glade creeks are generally deep, with steep banks lined with small willows on each margin and the water running very dead.

---

[132]Powell and Taylor later owned adjoining tracts of land in Fayette (now Woodford) County. At one time they had a dispute over a spring that watered both pieces of land. Dorothy Thompson, "Day of Controversy," 229.

[133]The community of Lenox in Preston County, West Virginia, is the present-day site of eighteenth-century Crab Orchard. It is located about nine miles northeast of Dunkard Bottom. Bill Strickler, Arthurdale WV, 9 Nov 1989, to Chester R. Young, Williamsburg KY.

[134]Here Taylor was crossing the Briery Mountains again. This time he went toward the east. The name "Laurel Hill" was applied more widely in the eighteenth century than it is today. In West Virginia the name used now is "Laurel Mountain," which forms the eastern border of Barbour County and then runs northward into Preston County. Cheat Mountain today is the range to the south of Laurel Mountain that extends along the western side of Shavers Fork in Randolph County.

[135]The phrase "by daylight" does not appear in the second edition.

[136]This stream is one of numerous tributaries of the Youghiogheny River.

[137]The noun *shore* is here a dialecticism for the word *bank*.

This stream was about eight steps across it, and timber laid on those planks and locked in the willows at each end had prevented their floating off. My plan was to stand on the cill [*sic*] of the bridge up to my knees in water, and [to] float the planks off till I got to my horses, and with mighty struggling with the poor animals [to] get them up the bank. My saddle was wet, the bridle caked with ice, and my hands so benumbed that I could not draw on my gloves. I suppose I lost a full hour of the day at this place.

With my feet [*sic*] wet to my knees [and] my bare hands to hold the frozen bridles (one to ride with, the other to lead), my saddlebags—being dry—kept me a little from the wet saddle. I hurried on lest Yoh River should rise beyond fording. I soon met with another creek which ran over my horses, where I got a fresh ducking. When I came to the [Youghiogheny] River, I found [that] it was impossible to cross it except by swimming, which I had often done in similar cases. I paused awhile. But when I found that I must go up the current to get to the opposite shore (and just below was an ivy[138] bluff for a long distance that was impassible [*sic*] but that I must inevitably be dashed [32]against it), viewing the muddy waves foaming over the great rocks which lay in the river and dashing against the icy rock on the other shore, I concluded that it was not proper to tempt the Lord my God[139] to work a miracle in my preservation.

What food I had for myself and horses we consumed, and about one o'clock [I] turned tail to get, if possible, to where I came from in the morning.[140] Riding on, I became so very cold in my wet, freezing clothes, I concluded a little walking would comfort me. It was usual to drive my horse before me in such cases, but the beast I led, being untutored that way, broke ground[141] to run back, and both [horses] together ran off in full speed. I ran with all my might to keep in sight of them in these great glades. I thus ran a mile or two in hopes the water ahead where they [had] had so hard a struggle would stop them, which it did. There I caught them.

I was now very wet with heat and sweat. "What shall I do?" was the next question. "Swim the creek immediately," which had risen higher, "or wait and cool first?" I had ten miles to go, the sun about two hours high, the road [would be] amazing[142] bad when I got to Cheat Mountain and so dim that I could scarce

---

[138]*Ivy* was the colloquial name applied by eighteenth-century settlers to "mountain laurel"—a flowering, evergreen shrub indigenous to eastern North America.

[139]Deuteronomy 6:16.

[140]When Taylor turned to retrace the day's journey, he had gone only about twelve miles, measuring by an east-west line between the Cheat and the Youghiogheny rivers.

[141]Taylor here uses the expression "break ground" figuratively to mean "take the first steps."

[142]Here the adverb *amazing* is a dialecticism that means *amazingly*.

follow it by daylight. The moon also [would be] dark. [I concluded] that there
was no alternative but to dash on or camp in the woods without fire. I mounted
my horse and swam the creek with all my sweat. The water ran up round my
middle, and soon after my clothes froze except what lay next to my skin.

About dark I got to where I [had] started from at morning light. Getting from
my horse, I could scarce keep my feet. I staggered on to the house and soon went
to bed. My hands were so swol[l]en with cold that I could scarce use them. After
some warm supper I slept sound. For several days I felt in a kind of listless
stuper [sic]. About one month after this I was stricken with a prodigious
surfeit[143]—a breaking out from head to foot in likeness of ringworm covered with
white scales, so that scarce a part under my clothes was free from it. And [it]
continues more or less to this [33]day, which has been a good deal upwards of
forty years.

I had many tours similar but none quite equal to the two last named in point
of difficulty.

It never sat well on my feelings to receive pay from the people for
preaching.[144] I, therefore, preferred my own exertions to supply my own wants.
My father[145] had given me a lot of broken land, on which I had cleared a field,
and [I] generally raised some corn[146] for my horse to eat when at home. With
other little mechanical arts, I nearly made a supply.

A few years after I had been called a preacher and while under great
misgiving of heart on that subject (fearing that I was running and the Lord had
not sent me), I had an uncommon dream, though I am not disposed to put
confidence in a mere vision of the night.[147] It was in the spring of the year and
when I was very busy in getting my little field in order to plant corn, my mind
being a little more on the the world than common.

---

[143]This surfeit was probably a form of urticaria, an inflammatory disease causing welts
to appear on the skin along with a redness. It is accompanied by a burning or itching
sensation.

[144]Taylor's views against his receiving payment for preaching coincided with those
of most Baptist preachers of his day in Virginia and Kentucky. Even so, the oldest
association of Kentucky held in 1787 that it was "the duty of churches to give their
ministers a reasonable support." Spencer, *Kentucky Baptists*, 1:492.

[145]Lazarus Taylor, the father of the author, still lived in Shenandoah (once Frederick)
County in 1805. Shenandoah County (VA) Deed Book O, 301.

[146]Rye, wheat, and Indian corn were the principal grain crops of the Great Valley of
Virginia during 1754–1763. Chester R. Young, "French and Indian War," 20.

[147]In the eighteenth century it was commonly held that dreams were vehicles for
revealing God's will. Reminiscences of preachers from various denominations contain
accounts that are much like that of Taylor's. Sweet, *American Frontier*, 1:144n.

I dreamed of being at a place of gathering of people where was a dead man. A blustering man present said [that] he could raise the dead man to life. A dispute arose between him and others who insisted [that] he could not do it. But at length the dead man did voluntarily rise up. When risen he looked very angry and turned his whole attention to me. With rage in his looks he informed me [that] he was sent from the dead to warn me never to preach any more. All this, though asleep, struck me with dreadful horror of mind. He further reminded me that I might treat his warning with neglect, "for," said he, "there are some who will not be persuaded though one rose from the dead."[148] All this I realized while asleep with dreadful anguish of mind. He further added, "I am not only sent from the dead to warn you never to preach any more, but [also to tell you that] when you die you will go to Hell. Damn you." By this time it seemed as if the pains of Hell had got hold on me while asleep. In this dumb agony I lay for some time not able to make any reply, nor dare I do it, for he [34]stood near me and looked as if he would tear me to pieces.

At length I began to reason while asleep. He told me [that] he was sent from the dead. "This," said I in my sleep, "does not assure me that he is a messenger of God." I further reasoned, "If he was a messenger of God, he would not be in such a rage of anger." I further thought, "If he came as His messenger, he would not use the language he did, either to curse or damn me." I then thought, "He looked more like a messenger from Hell than from Heaven, and of course nothing he has said is true." From which I came to the conclusion that Satan saw that my preaching would be against his interest among man and, therefore, strove to frighten me from it. And as to going to Hell when I died, this was all from the Father of Lies[149] too. And while my heart used an effort to go into a vow to God that I would preach more than I ever had done, the struggle waked me with uncommon agitation. [I was] reaching out my hand to lay hold of the man, for I yet conceited[150] [that] he stood by me to resist me, but [I] found it was a dream.

It is worth while to take notice how full the Scriptures are of dreams that are full of meaning. Witness Jacob's ladder.[151] Joseph had many dreams.[152] God often spoke to the ancient prophets by dreams.[153] The whole Old Testament is very full of the doctrine of visions from God this way. Job says [that] God speaks to men

---

[148]Luke 16:31.

[149]John 8:44.

[150]The verb *conceit* in this case is an obsoletism meaning *think*.

[151]Genesis 28:12-15.

[152]The Old Testament records only two dreams of Joseph. Genesis 37:7, 9. He sometimes interpreted others' dreams. Ibid., 40:12-13, 18-19, and 41:25-36.

[153]E.g., Daniel 7:1-14; Amos 7:1-9.

this way, by which he opens their ears and seals their instructions.[154] Pilate's wife had a striking dream. [155] Peter on the day of Pentecost cites up[156] Joel[157] on the subject of dreams, that their young men should see visions and their old men dream dreams.[158]

As I am now on [the subject of] dreams, I will relate one of a backwoods woman. Soon after my first visit to Lunies Creek, in Hampshire County, a respectable-looking man asked me to come to his house. [He said] that his wife had a particular desire to converse with me at a convenient time. I visited the family and tarried all night. Among other conversation, the poor, distressed woman related [35]to me a dream. A little before she first saw me, she dreamed that the awful Day of Judgment was come; that Jesus Christ, the great Judge, was present, preparing to decide the fate of the unnumbered world that was present. To each individual He gave a book to read. With the Judge were two men to direct the people how to use the books each person had.

When I rode up to the meeting where was a great assembly gathered, she knew at first sight that I was one of the men she had seen with the Saviour in her dream. After alighting from my horse, I had withdrawn a little to contemplate, which gave her the opportunity with deep concern to reflect on what she had just seen. There was all the features, complexion, age, and dress she had seen before in her dream. But one thing was lacking in the dress. The man she had seen in her dream had a pair of striped roppers[159] round his legs. This she had not noticed [on me]. When I returned from my contemplations, and she saw also the striped roppers round my legs, she said [that] she was stricken with such a trembling that she could scarce keep her feet. And when I rose up with the Bible in my hand to speak to the people and [to] direct them how to use the Book of God (and looking over the great and much-affected assembly that was present), it occurred to her that the great Day of God was at hand, and [that] she [was] unprepared. From this stroke this dear woman never recovered till she obtained peace through a Saviour.

To be sure, all this statement was as unaccountable to me as it was to this much-affected woman, and especially when I recollected that a few days before, I had called at a store and bought a pair of striped-ticking wrappers to tie round

[154]33:15-17.
[155]Matthew 27:19.
[156]The obsolete verb form "cite up" means *mention* or "call to mind."
[157]Acts 2:16-21; Joel 2:28-32.
[158]At this point in the first edition is found the following repetitious sentence that is omitted in the second edition: "While on dreaming, another occurs."
[159]Here the phonetic spelling *roppers* is used in place of the noun *wrappers*, which means *leggings*.

my legs. Solomon says [that] dreams comes through a multitude of business,[160] but some of them seem evidently to come from God.

There being no established priest in Hampshire County,[161] we met with no legal persecution while preaching there. But this did not prevent the rage of mobs, such as open contradiction while preaching, [36]for Satan is not fond of losing his prey.

We were only once driven from a place of preaching. Having a meeting appointed, perhaps on Christmas Day, in a rich and wealthy settlement, one of Satan's strongest holds in the county, the invitation for preaching was given by a man living in a large house and on his father-in-law's land. A large assembly met. But the old gentleman, the owner of the land, roused perhaps twenty rugged, young fellows—a number of whom came armed with instruments of death [in order] to drive all before them. A mighty uproar soon took place in the house, with some blows from the old man on his son-in-law. [Joseph] Redding and myself, standing by the side of the house [and] concluding to retire, for a deep snow had lately fallen [so] that we could not go into the woods. And but few of the people present was of a religious cast. After our departure they turned the meeting into a great Christmas frolic, so that Satan, the strong man, kept his palace and goods in peace[162] in this place as yet but became much frustrated afterwards.

After traveling three or four years in these back settlements (Mr. [William] Marshall having removed from Shenandoah River), by the importunity of my old brethren I took a letter from Lunies Creek Church[163] and again joined the old mother church, where I had been baptized and [had] had the pleasure of baptizing a number of people where myself had partaken of that blessed ordinance. I now became more acquainted with the man who had baptized me—James Ireland,

---

[160]Ecclesiastes 5:3.

[161]Since the creation of Hampshire Parish in 1761, the Establishment had maintained only a tenuous hold on the people of Hampshire County. In fact, dissenters occupied the whole of the Great Valley to such an extent that Anglican vestrymen in counties there served purposes more social and political than religious. Hening, *Statutes*, 7:430-31, 616-17.

[162]Luke 11:21.

[163]The Lunies Creek Church had a membership of 48 in 1790. In three years this number had dropped to 35. By 1810 only 11 people composed the congregation, which by then had no pastor. The church became extinct after 1836. Asplund, *Universal Register*, 1790–1794, 27; Semple, *Baptists in Virginia*, rev. ed., 230; and Gardner, *Baptists of Early America*, 284.

who now had the care of several neighboring churches.[164] He was not only a friendly companion but [also] an excellent guide to a young man.

After which I turned my attention to the lower parts of Virginia in the Northern Neck[165] thereof and near the Chesapeake Bay.[166] I had an uncle,[167] brother to my father who had been raised and now lived in those low lands. My object was to pay him a visit,[168] for I had not seen him from the days of my childhood.

Though kinsmen we met as strangers. Neither of us had ever heard [37]of a truly religious person among all our connections. And each of us had been held in contempt by them all, as men who had gone beside themselves. We each felt heavenly transports. After conversing together and finding that our language was the same (though esteemed that of madmen in that part of the world), had I been of the opinion of some I should soon have put my uncle in the water; for he was now waiting an opportunity, which soon after [was] offered by Lewis Lunsford[169] and other preachers, traveling and making a stand in that part of the world.

I stayed a week or two with my uncle and had several meetings in the place and made some acquaintance, for I found some who seemed desirous to seek the way to Heaven, as also a few Baptists who by traveling up the country had heard preaching and [who] after obtaining hope in the Lord had traveled far to receive baptism. I have seen people often who had traveled from one to two hundred miles to obtain baptism in those days, and they really seemed to enjoy more

---

[164]When Ireland died in 1806 he had the care of the Happy Creek, the Bucks Marsh, and the Water Lick churches in Frederick and Shenandoah counties. *Life of James Ireland*, 134-35.

[165]The term "Northern Neck" has two usages. A geographical use denotes the part of northern Virginia that lies between the Potomac and the Rappahannock rivers. Also the term designates politically the Northern Neck Proprietary, which comprised a vast, feudal domain covering the land (more than five million acres) situated between the said streams. It was owned successively by the Culpeper and Fairfax families. Bailey, *Ohio Company*, 45.

[166]The Chesapeake Bay is an inlet of the Atlantic Ocean that reaches northward into Virginia and Maryland for about two hundred miles.

[167]This unmarried uncle was Joseph Taylor (1722?-1782). Dorothy Thompson, "Ancestors and Descendants," 29.

[168]The time was perhaps the summer of 1777. It is likely that this initial visit occurred before Joseph Taylor drew up his will, on 27 May 1778, in view of the fact that he made John almost his sole heir. Northumberland County (VA) Record Book 11: 273-74.

[169]Lewis Lunsford (1755?-1793), a son of indigent parents of Stafford County, Virginia, was so eloquent that his teen-age preaching earned him the sobriquet "the Wonderful Boy." In time he became the founder of the Baptist denomination in the part of the Northern Neck that lies below Fredericksburg. Semple, *Baptists in Virginia*, rev. ed., 384, 473; and James B. Taylor, *Virginia Baptist Ministers*, 2d ed., 137-46.

satisfaction in baptism than others. It may be remembered [that] the Saviour traveled on foot from Galilee to Jordan to be baptized.[170] Some say it was two days' journey.

I could scarce get away from my uncle. He had a wish [that] I should make his house my home. He was never married but lived on his own farm with his black people. At parting, as a token of his good will he gave me his watch, which was the first I ever owned.

From this place to Fredericksburg[171] was called a hundred miles. I could now and then hear of some place in this long neck of land where [there] had been Baptist preaching. There I commonly called a halt [in order] to worship among the people and with surprising effect at times. I could give instances which I now think of with pleasure, but I forbear. The apparent call for constant traveling now bore with great weight on my mind [and] with great misgivings of heart, thinking[172] on my own inadequacy. I not only [38]kept up my range with [Joseph] Redding in the backwoods but [also] below the Blue Ridge on each side of the Rappahannock River,[173] where I became acquainted with a great number of the laborious servants of the Lord (chiefly all now gone home), as Theodoric Noel, Lewis Lunsford, Nathaniel Saunders,[174] all the Craigs,[175] Geo[rge] Eve,[176] Thomas

---

[170]Matthew 3:13.

[171]Fredericksburg, located on the right bank of the Rappahannock River, was the seat of Spotsylvania County until 1780. Hening, *Statutes*, 9:558; ibid., 10:228.

[172]The archaism "think on" means "give thought to" a matter.

[173]The Rappahannock River rises in the Blue Ridge along the border of Fauquier and Rappahannock counties and flows southeastly into the Chesapeake Bay, forming the southern boundary of the Northern Neck.

[174]Nathaniel Saunders (1735–1808) was an early Baptist convert in Orange County, Virginia. Ordained to the care of the Mountain Run Church in 1768, he suffered imprisonment in Culpeper County five years later for preaching the gospel. Semple, *Baptists in Virginia*, rev. ed., 234, 234n., 483-84; and Little, *Imprisoned Preachers*, 76, 368-73.

[175]In addition to Lewis and Elijah Craig, who have already been mentioned in the text, there was one other Baptist minister among the sons of Toliver Craig (d. 1796) and Mary Hawkins. This third preaching son was Joseph Craig (1741-1819), a native of Orange County, Virginia. Known for his eccentricities, he was more successful in the counting-house than he was in the meetinghouse, especially after he settled in Kentucky. Semple, *Baptists in Virginia*, rev. ed., 204n.; Spencer, *Kentucky Baptists*, 1:27-28, 81-84; and Draper MSS., 30CC49. Also see *Journal of Joseph Craig*.

[176]George Eve (b. 1748) was a native of Culpeper County, Virginia, and a charter member of the Rapidan Church, of which he was ordained the pastor in 1775. He settled in Kentucky in 1797. In his latter years he became addicted to strong drink and was twice dismissed from the North Fork Church, in Franklin County. Edwards, *Materials*, 2:60; Semple, *Baptists in Virginia*, rev. ed., 238; James B. Taylor, *Virginia Baptist Ministers*,

Ammon,[177] John Leland,[178] John Shackleford,[179] John Koontz, Anderson Moffett,[180] John Pickett, and many others—all of whom from my soul I preferred much higher than myself.[181]

It was more than a year[182] before I paid my uncle in the Northern Neck another visit, at which time I found a great revival of religion through the country where he lived. Himself[183] with many others had been baptized, and Lewis Lunsford [was] now living in that part of the world.[184]

In every direction there was now such a call for preaching day and night that it required the best of lungs in the preacher to bear the service. Though the nights were short, the houses would often not hold the people, when I have known the preacher stand in the yard by bright moonlight, and the sand on which he stood in a manner white as snow, and the light such without a candle that the preacher

---

2d ed., 223-25; Spencer, *Kentucky Baptists*, 1:294-95. See his biography in John Taylor, *Thoughts on Missions*, 37-39.

[177]Thomas Ammon (d. ca. 1820), a Separate Baptist preacher, was raised in the Crooked Run Church, of the Culpeper Association, in Virginia. He was imprisoned in Culpeper County for preaching the gospel. He migrated to Kentucky as early as 1790. Semple, *Baptists in Virginia*, rev. ed., 233; Spencer, *Kentucky Baptists*, 1:208.

[178]John Leland (1754–1841), a native of Massachusetts, was considered a very learned preacher. His remarkable career as an apostle of civil and religious liberty impinged upon Baptist life in Virginia during his stay in the new state, from 1776 to 1791, during which time he preached 3,009 sermons and baptized 700 people. He collected materials that were helpful to Robert Baylor Semple, who wrote *A History of the Rise and Progress of the Baptists in Virginia* (1810). Leland's most important publication concerning the Old Dominion is titled *The Virginia Chronicle* (1790). Greene, ed., *Writings of John Leland*, 19-30; *Encyclopedia of Southern Baptists*, 2:783; Sprague, *American Pulpit*, 7:174-86.

[179]John Shackleford (1750–1829) was a native of Caroline County, Virginia. Even before his ordination he was imprisoned briefly in Essex County. He removed to Kentucky, in 1792, so that he could support his family. In the West he served as the second pastor of South Elkhorn Church, for about thirty-seven years. Semple, *Baptists in Virginia*, rev. ed., 156n.; James B. Taylor, *Virginia Baptist Ministers*, 2d ed., 216-17.

[180]Anderson Moffett (1746–1835), a native of Fauquier (then Prince William) County, Virginia, served as the pastor of at least four Regular Baptist churches in the northern part of the Great Valley of Virginia. To one of them he ministered for over fifty years. For an unknown period he was held in the Culpeper jail for preaching the gospel. Semple, *Baptists in Virginia*, rev. ed. 246-47, 250, 250n., 252; Little, *Imprisoned Preachers*, 429, 433.

[181]Philippians 2:3.

[182]The time was perhaps in the fall of 1780.

[183]The pronoun *himself* occurs here, as well as in a number of other places in this work, as an Irish usage for the subject of the clause.

[184]In 1784 Lewis Lunsford resided in Northumberland County, in the Northern Neck. *Heads of Families, 1790: Virginia*, 74.

was capable to read. And hundreds, perhaps half a thousand, [were] attentive to the sweet voice of the gospel, while their sighs, groans, and cries for mercy would oblige every spectator to say that "God is here of a truth." I have known respectable, young ladies walk ten miles on those pleasant, sandy roads rather than miss being at one of those happy, night meetings. Perhaps our modern, young ladies who love carnal parties, novels, and theatres[185] more than they love the worship of God may blame them as imprudent, but God Himself has decided already in their favor and against those daughters of Diana and Venus.[186] This revival spread over a great part of the Northern Neck, and many hundreds were baptized.

The next visit[187] I paid to this part of the earth I found [Lewis] Lunsford a married man, to a relation of mine.[188] This circumstance [39]with others brought about a great intimacy between this useful servant of Christ and myself, which was interesting on my side at least.

Old Councellor [Councillor] [Robert] Carter[189] had now become a Baptist.[190] He, having a great family of children, had employed my uncle as a family

---

[185]In this work Taylor uses the noun *theater* twice, each time with the chiefly British spelling *theatre*.

[186]In Roman mythology Diana was the virgin goddess of the moon and of hunting; Venus, the goddess of love and of beauty.

[187]This visit may have occurred in the early summer of 1781. It is likely that by then John's Uncle Joseph had already been employed by Robert Carter III for a year or so. Dozier, "Historical Notes," 1400.

[188]In March 1787 Lewis Lunsford's second marriage occurred. He took for his wife Elizabeth Waddy Dameron, a third cousin of John Taylor on her father's side. Counting the lineage of Elizabeth on her mother's side, it is possible that she and John Taylor were also second cousins once removed. Letter, Carolyn H. Jett, Heathsville VA, 21 Jan 1991, to Chester R. Young, Williamsubrg KY. The visit that Taylor refers to may have been his trip from Kentucky to Philadelphia in 1791. Draper MSS., llCC230.

If Taylor, however, is dating this visit to the Northern Neck as coming on the heels of Lunsford's first marriage, the time was during an earlier, unknown year. Lunsford's first wife was Nancy Dameron, a first cousin (maybe a double first cousin) to his second wife. The paternal grandparents of these two wives were John Dameron and Elizabeth Taylor. Letter, Jett, 30 July 1991, to Young.

[189]Robert Carter III (1727/8–1804), master of Nomony Hall in Westmoreland County, owned at the age of twenty-one some seventy thousand acres of land and several hundred slaves. He was a member of the Executive Council of Virginia, a colonel in the militia, and a vestryman in Cople Parish in his home county. Lumpkin, " 'Col. Robert Carter, a Baptist,' " *Virginia Baptist Register* 8 (1969): 340-41.

[190]Carter experienced a mystical conversion in 1777. In September of the following year he was baptized by Lewis Lunsford and became a member of the Morattico Church. Ibid. 343-44, 348-49. For an evaluation of his tenure as a Baptist see ibid. 349-54.

teacher.[191] My uncle, being a very good English teacher, continued in Carter's family several years, and there he died.[192] My visits to see my uncle while at Carter's[193] brought about a great intimacy between the old councellor [councillor] and myself, for this great man's religion seemed to make him meek and lowly. Carter was fond of me because I could tell him a great deal about new countries and [about] the various effects I had seen among the people in the backwoods under preaching. And he was the more entertained after I had been to Kentucky.[194] He also being very zealous in religion, my preaching passed better with him than might be expected; for if nothing else attended it, there was plenty of noise.[195] Hence after preaching one night in his hall,[196] his old lady[197] remarked that before I came again she must remove her great, candle glass lest the sound should break it to shivers.

[Joseph] Redding started with his family to Kentucky by water in the fall of 1779 but did not arrive there till the next spring.[198] The same fall I went through

---

[191]Hunter Dickinson Farish, ed., *Journal and Letters of Philip Vickers Fithian, 1773-1774; A Plantation Tutor of the Old Dominion* (Williamsburg VA, 1957) gives an intimate account of a teacher who was employed at Carter's manor house a few years before John Taylor's uncle taught there.

[192]Robert Carter caused the body of his schoolmaster to be interred in the garden hard by Nomony Hall. Robert Carter III, Day Book, 1789-1790 (Robert Carter III Papers, Library of Congress) 8.

[193]Nomony Hall was a two-story rectangular mansion of stuccoed brick. At its corners at a distance of one hundred yards were located four dependent offices—schoolhouse, warehouse, washhouse, and stable. Twenty-eight other buildings completed a spectacular array. The five-room schoolhouse served also as the residence for the tutor and the boys of the family. Dorothy Thompson, "John Taylor of the Ten Churches," 551; and *Journal of Fithian* xxix, xxx.

[194]Here Taylor apparently refers to his first trip to Kentucky, during the winter of 1779-1780. His textual comment seems to imply that he had become acquainted with Carter before the journey to Kentucky took place.

[195]From 1779 through 1784 John Taylor preached in Westmoreland County at least eight times. Dozier, "Historical Notes," 1397, 1399, 1400, 1402, 1404, 1406-1407.

[196]Taylor preached at least twice at Nomony Hall—28 May and 18 November 1780. Ibid. 1399, 1400.

[197]Carter's wife was Frances Anne Tasker Carter (1735-1787), a native of Maryland. *Journal of Fithian* xxvii, 245.

[198]Joseph Redding's party included his burgeoning family and several members of the Lunies Creek Church, in New Hampshire County. Their route to Kentucky took them through northwestern Virginia to Redstone on the Monongahela, where they embarked on their trip down that stream and the Ohio. Somewhere in the Upper Ohio Valley their boat was wrecked. Such misfortune coupled with unsparing weather caused them to tarry for the winter. When spring arrived they continued their journey downstream, landing at Louisville in March or April 1780. One of the Redding children died soon thereafter. The

by land,[199] expecting to meet Redding in Kentucky and there to live if we were pleased. But all things bore such a gloomy appearance[200] as to preaching that we returned again to Virginia[201] and resumed our former travels for about two years.

Concluding that I should be more happy in this wilderness of sorrow by changing my station to a married life, I began the new business (to me) of wife-getting. I do not ascribe it to my own prudence that I became so well-suited in a bosom consort.[202] I am willing to say that Providence directed this thing. I married a girl[203] of good family[204] and a Baptist of Mr. John Leland's congre-

---

people at the Falls of the Ohio were "shut up in forts." John Taylor, *Thoughts on Missions*, 51-52.

[199]Taylor very likely traveled the Great Valley Road (often called the Philadelphia Wagon Road) that ran between the Blue Ridge and the Allegheny Mountains. This route crossed the New River at Ingles' Ferry and went by Fort Chiswell before arriving on the Holston River. On that stream was located the Block House, a tavern at which travelers waited for the gathering of a sizable group before plunging into the unsettled woods. Here was the beginning of the Kentucky Road (later known as the Wilderness Road) which led across steep mountains and through the Holston, Clinch, and Powell valleys before reaching famed Cumberland Gap. Through this saddle went the Warriors' Path, an ancient Indian trail connecting the southern Appalachians with the Ohio River. Taylor and his party would have used this path into Kentucky as far as Flat Lick (in present-day Knox County), located nine miles beyond Cumberland River Ford. At the lick he most likely turned to the northwest and followed Boone's Trace to the Kentucky River, or some distance beyond Flat Lick he cut off to the west at Hazel Patch onto Skaggs's Trace in order to go to Logan's Fort.

[200]In many respects the period covered by Redding and Taylor's travels in the West was unforgettable. That season, memorable for its length and severity, was fixed in the minds of the early pioneers as the "Hard Winter" of 1779–1780. The settlers had come to expect Kentucky winters to set in about Christmas and to continue for some six weeks. Around the first of December 1779, however, they were asserting that they had never experienced such severe weather at that time of the year. In Kentucky as well as in other parts of North America heavy snows and low temperatures brought extreme distress to human and beast over an extended time. Such dire weather partly caused the Kentucky venture of Redding and Taylor to turn out so exceedingly disagreeable.

[201]It appears that both preachers returned to Virginia in 1780 through Cumberland Gap but in separate parties. Redding did not reach his home in Hampshire County until June, whereas Taylor preached on 20 May at Aries, a plantation in Westmoreland County belonging to Robert Carter III. Dozier, "Historical Notes," 1399; and John Taylor, *Thoughts on Missions*, 52.

[202]Elizabeth Kavanaugh and John Taylor were married in Orange County in September 1782 shortly after the twenty-fifth, the day he posted a marriage bond. Knorr, *Marriages of Orange County, Virginia*, 87; and "Marriages, Orange County," 196.

[203]*Girl* is a colloquialism meaning "female of any age."

[204]The maternal grandfather of Elizabeth Kavanaugh Taylor was Benjamin Cave (b.

gation.[205] Before I married her, the acquaintance she had in Mr. Leland's family gave her full warning of the [40]difficulties of a traveling preacher's wife. For near forty years, patience and industry in her solitude has marked her way. In this conjugal contract I do not hesitate to think, as others will say, I had the best of the bargain. This took place about one month before I was thirty years old and about ten years after I had been a traveling preacher.

Having a little leisure after I was married and before I went to housekeeping, I took a tour[206] of preaching and to visit my uncle, then about sixty years old. When I got into the neighborhood I heard of his death. I also heard of a will he had left in the hands of an executor and that myself was another.[207] When the will was opened we found he had made me his heir. His estate was then worth about three thousand dollars, consisting of land, Negroes, stock of various kinds, household furniture, and several hundred dollars in money.[208] This was about ten times as much as I had ever owned before.

I reasoned with myself, "Why is this kind favor?" The secondary cause was my uncle's good will towards me, "but why [was the estate] not divided among

ca. 1688). His career included service as justice of the peace, sheriff, and vestryman in Orange County and as a member of the House of Burgesses. Benjamin's wife, Hannah, was a daughter of William Bledsoe, the first sheriff of Spotsylvania County. Dorothy Thompson, "Ancestors and Descendants," 31-32.

[205]The congregation to which Elizabeth Kavanaugh belonged was the Black Walnut Church, in the northeastern part of Orange County. Eight years later the church had a membership of three hundred. Asplund, *Annual Register, 1790*, 30; Greene, ed., *Writings of John Leland*, 29; and Semple, *Baptists in Virginia*, rev. ed., 206n.

[206]This tour was begun near the end of September 1782 or the beginning of the following month. Here Taylor covers the last of his four trips from the Great Valley into the lower part of the Northern Neck that he records through the time of his Uncle Joseph's demise. His listing, it should be said, does not coincide with Richard Dozier's recording of sermons preached by Taylor in the four easternmost counties of the Northern Neck.

[207]Alexander Hunton and Lewis Lunsford were also named as executors. Northumberland County (VA) Record Book 11, 273-74.

[208]Joseph Taylor, an uncle of the author, died in Westmoreland County, Virginia, but his estate was located in adjacent Northumberland County. His will had been written on 27 May 1778, and John Taylor presented it to the Northumberland County Court for record on 14 October 1782. The slaves of this estate totaled eight. One of them, Ephraim, was to be lent to the author's father, at whose death the slave was to become the property of John Taylor. The other seven blacks—Jack, Moll, Nann, Jemima, Letty, May, and Asa—were bequeathed directly to the preacher. The livestock included horses, cattle, hogs, and sheep. To each of two sisters and another nephew, Joseph gave one shilling; the nicety of the law was thus observed in order to nullify his favoritism toward John Taylor. Ibid.

his relations equally near to him?" My reply then was, "God would have it so, who has the hearts of all men in His own hands." When I came to examine,[209] I found [that] my uncle died about the time I was married. Perhaps there was not a day's difference. Here was more than compensation for my poor ten years' service, and at once repaid me by the Lord, and precisely at the time I needed it. I felt my heart bound with gratitude to the Lord with this kind of mental vow, "O Lord, I will be for Thee forever in whatever service Thou[210] mayst[211] demand."

For one year I continued at my usual travels with not quite as long tours as formerly. I have before stated [that] the kindness of my friends to me for the space of this year [confronted me] with the temptation [that] I had not[212] to move to Kentucky, at which place I found myself at the close of the year 1783.

[41,2d]The two churches of which I was a member in Virginia [42,2d]are so very distant from me, and of which I have heard so little for many years, I must pass them over with what has been said heretofore, tho'[213] from what I can learn they yet exist as a church.

---

[209]This intransitive usage of the verb *examine* is now obsolete.

[210]This sentence uses two forms of the personal pronoun *you*, second person, singular: *Thee*, the objective case; *Thou*, the nominative case. These forms refer to *God*.

[211]The verb *mayst* is the archaic present indicative of *may*, second person, singular.

[212]The expression "I had not" means "I ought not."

[213]*Tho'* is the clipped form of the conjunction *though*.

# 3
## Gilberts Creek Church

[41]The first winter in Kentucky [1783–1784], I took shelter in Lewis Craig's Station, on Gilberts Creek, south of Kentucky River, where my wife had some relations.[1] Soon after, my son Ben was born. Whether from the many frights my wife took on the journey or [from] some other cause is unknown; but when there was a call for a midwife, the alarm was such to her that she went perfectly out of her reason with violent, convulsive fits which continued about twenty-four hours, in which time she was delivered. But to this day [she] does not know that Ben is her son but from circumstances and information. This with other things much embittered Kentucky to me. Through this alarming crisis the life of my wife was so despaired of that all hope was gone, though I sent for a physician. Every thing appeared so hopeless that he soon left the place, despairing of any relief. But when all human aid failed, God Himself afforded help, and she was restored. And nothing of the kind has ever attended her since in similar cases.

The first opportunity I had I gave my membership to the church at Gilberts Creek. This had been one of the "traveling churches" from Virginia to Kentucky. Lewis Craig, with a great number of the members of his church in Spotsylvania [County],[2] had moved to Kentucky.[3] As I have been told, they were constituted when they started and was an organized church on the road. Wherever they stopped they were ahousekeeping[4] at once.[5]

---

[1]These relatives of Elizabeth Taylor were the families of Richard and William Cave, who were brothers of her mother, Nancy Cave Kavanaugh Strother (b. 1734). John Taylor, *Thoughts on Missions*, 40; and Dorothy Thompson, "Ancestors and Descendants," 31, 32.

[2]Spotsylvania County was organized in 1721 under a Virginia law enacted the preceding year. Hening, *Statutes*, 4:77.

[3]The Upper Spotsylvania Church, a Separate Baptist congregation, had been constituted in Spotsylvania County, Virginia, on 20 November 1767 with twenty-five members. When the majority of its members departed for Kentucky with Elder Lewis Craig in the fall of 1781, the remainder assumed the name Craig's Church (a designation that had already been in use as an alternate to the geographical name of the membership) and continued to do the work of a congregation. Edwards, *Materials*, 2:57; Semple, *Baptists in Virginia*, rev. ed., 186, 200, 200n.; and Ford, "Kentucky Baptists," *Christian Repository* 5:76.

[4]The verb *ahousekeeping* is a colloquialism meaning *housekeeping* or, in this case, "carrying out the internal functions of an organized congregation."

[5]Before this "Traveling Church" left Spotsylvania County it had constituted itself into a religious body. It brought along the pulpit Bible, the clerk's record book, and the Lord's

[279,2d]I think [that] he [Lewis Craig] moved to Kentucky in the fall of 1781. Here at that time, red men were waving the bloody hatchet against white men. Many thousands were killed after Mr. Craig came to the country. So many of his members came with him to Kentucky, bringing their clerk, church book, and all with them; they were a church as they came along. And where they settled down on Gilberts Creek in Lincoln County, they were an organized church at once, and perhaps the first establishment of the kind that was known in Kentucky.[6] At this place Mr. Craig continued about two years.[7]

[41]Just before I got to Kentucky, [Lewis] Craig, with a number of others, had left Gilberts Creek and moved to South Elkhorn [Creek][8] and set up a church there. The remnant left of Gilberts Creek [Church] kept up church order. It was this remnant [that] I united with. Among them was George [Stovall] Smith, commonly called "Stokes" Smith,[9] a valuable preacher; Richard Cave, then an

---

Supper service. In Kentucky it took the name of the stream on which it settled. Thus the Gilberts Creek Church—the first of two congregations to carry this title—dated from 9 December 1781, the Sunday when its members first met to worship on that water course. Ford, "Kentucky Baptists," *Christian Repository* 5:135, 137; and Ranck, *"Travelling Church,"* 30-31.

[6]In 1781 the Severns Valley and the Cedar Creek churches were organized during June and July, respectively. Thus these congregations had been in existence about a half-year before Craig arrived on Gilberts Creek. Spencer, *Kentucky Baptists*, 1:20.

[7]This paragraph comes from a piece in the addendum of the second edition titled "Biography of Mr. Lewis Craig."

[8]South Elkhorn Creek originates in Fayette County below Lexington; it flows northwesterly to join North Elkhorn Creek near the northeastern edge of Frankfort and to form Elkhorn Creek, a tributary of the Kentucky River.

[9]George Stovall "Stokes" Smith (1750-1810) was a son of Thomas Smith (1719-1786) and Martha Frances Stovall (1733?-1752). George S. Smith was among the seven Separate Baptist preachers raised up during the latter third of the eighteenth century at Dupuy's Meetinghouse, in Cumberland (later Powhatan) County, Virginia. In time he would migrate to Kentucky, participate in organizing the Elkhorn Asociation, advocate emancipation, and help to write Kentucky's first constitution. George Stovall Smith should not be confused with his elder half-brother George Rapene "Millpond" Smith (1746/7-1820), who did not settle in Kentucky until 1804. Semple, *Baptists in Virginia*, rev. ed., 264-65, 474; Spencer, *Kentucky Baptists*, 1:155, 191-92, 484, and 2:21-23; and Julie Trabue Yates and Charles C. Trabue IV, *The Trabue Family in America, 1700-1983*, (Baltimore, 1983) 95.

ordained minister; William Cave, who afterwards became a very good preacher;[10] and many other valuable members.[11]

I found with the [42]clerk of Gilberts Creek Church the old church book from Spotsylvania, that was of about twenty years' standing. It is probable [that] the clerk of that old church in Virginia had brought that book with him to Kentucky.[12] I was much amused at times in looking over the records of this old book [to see] the curiosity of their decisions.[13] A mere cap border or garments cut in any but a plain style was matter of complaint and expulsion.[14] One [complaint] I remember was entered by a preacher against Sister Such-a-One for delusion,[15] without any other explanation. This delusion, whatever it might be, cost this sister her membership.

All this [strictness] manifested the great zeal [that] the Baptists had in early times against the appearance of sin. It has also taught me ever since the great care [that] churches should take in their records that nothing foolish should be committed to record. Or at least, the whole [should be] made so explicit that afterages may understand it and not be compelled to use them as the books of curious arts by putting them into the fire.[16]

This George S. Smith was a man of great respectability as a man and [was] much of a doctrinal preacher. Simplicity and plainness attended his whole course.

---

[10]Richard "Dickey" (1750-1816) and William "Uncle Billy" (1738-1806) were sons of Benjamin Cave (d. 1762), of Orange County, Virginia. These brothers, together with their wives, came under the influence of the gospel when preached by David Thomas and Samuel Harris around 1766. They joined the Upper Spotsylvania Church. Both brothers moved to Kentucky, William accompanying Lewis Craig and his "Traveling Church" in 1781 and Richard following the next year. After a short while at Gilberts Creek they went their separate ways north of the Kentucky River, where they were prominent in the work of several churches. Edwards, *Materials*, 2:56-57; and Spencer, *Kentucky Baptists*, 1:293-94, and 2:23-24. For biographies of these two brothers, see John Taylor, *Thoughts on Missions*, 40-43.

[11]William Marshall, Joseph Craig, and Samuel Asher were also numbered among the members. Ford, "Kentucky Baptists," *Christian Repository* 5:141.

[12]As late as 1856 this record book of the Upper Spotsylvania Church was still being preserved by descendants of the clerk who had brought it to Kentucky. Ibid., *Christian Repository* 5:75, 135.

[13]Playing musical instruments (especially the fiddle) and attending parties or shows were not allowed. Ibid., *Christian Repository* 5:75.

[14]For other examples of objectionable dress, see [Woodford B. Hackley], "Baptist Dress in Olden Days," *Virginia Baptist Register* 9 (1970): 425-29.

[15]In this case, singing or whistling or repeating "fashionable or profane songs or ditties" was considered the sin of *delusion*. Ford, "Kentucky Baptists," *Christian Repository* 5:75.

[16]Acts 19:19.

His preaching operated but sparingly on the passions of his hearers, for though his voice was strong and sonorous (yet lacking that soft melody). As a Gibeonite in the house of God he was better calculated to hew wood than to draw water.[17] He continued preaching on with zeal and usefulness for about twenty years in Kentucky and died in the pastoral care of a large church in Jessamine County[18] called Mount Pleasant.[19]

[After] a temporary stay of about seven months at Gilberts Creek, I moved to the north side of the Kentucky River[20] about two miles from John Craig's Station,[21] on Clear Creek, now Woodford County. Soon after, George "Stokes" Smith and chief of the members at Gilberts Creek also moved to the north side of [the] Kentucky.[22] And a Separate Baptist church being set up at Gilberts Creek by Joseph Bledsoe,[23] the old [43]church became dissolved.[24] And the Separate Baptists chiefly took possession of the south side of the Kentucky River.

---

[17]Both a hewer of wood and a drawer of water are servants who do menial work. Thus the author has misused this metaphor here. Joshua 9:17-27.

[18]Jessamine County, established by law in 1798, lies in the heart of the Bluegrass.

[19]The Mount Pleasant Church, a present-day affiliant of the Elkhorn Association, was constituted in 1801. Kentucky Baptist Convention, *Annual, 1989*, 402.

[20]The Kentucky River became the line of separation among the three Virginia counties into which Kentucky County was divided in 1780. The area lying northeast of this stream was formed into Fayette County; the area lying southwest, into Jefferson and Lincoln counties. Hening, *Statutes*, 10:315.

[21]John Craig (1730-1815), who was the eldest son of Toliver Craig of Virginia, moved in 1783 from Bryan Station to Clear Creek, in Woodford (then Fayette) County. There John built a station at which the Elkhorn Association was organized two years later. This fortification was located on what later became the estate of Sowell Woolfolk near Elm Corner. Joseph F. Taylor, Interview by [John D. Shane], Jessamine Co. KY, Draper MSS., 11CC231; Spencer, *Kentucky Baptists*, 1:27, and 2:9-10; and Railey, *Woodford County*, 269, 396, 397.

[22]George Stovall Smith was still living on Gilberts Creek in the spring of 1785 when he was visited by Daniel Trabue, whose aunt was Smith's step-mother. By then Smith had made at least three trips into Kentucky. Chester R. Young, ed., *Westward into Kentucky: The Narrative of Daniel Trabue* (Lexington KY, 1981), 71, 73-74, 76-77, 81, 85, 89, 127.

[23]Before Joseph Bledsoe (b. 1738) moved to Kentucky and in 1783 organized the second Gilberts Creek Church, he was the pastor of the Wilderness Church, a Separate Baptist congregation in Spotsylvania County, Virginia. Semple, *Baptists in Virginia*, rev. ed., 202, 202n.

[24]When the Elkhorn Association was formed in 1785, a committee was appointed to inquire into the status of the first Gilberts Creek Church, the oldest congregation in the association. The following year the committee reported that the church had been disbanded. Spencer, *Kentucky Baptists*, 2:10.

I now moved to Woodford County[25] in the summer of 1784 and, rather than go into the fort, settled on my own land, with no family between me and the Indian towns and in the height of war. But we were not long in much danger, for the next winter the people settled out so that we soon began to hold night meetings at our little cabins in the woods. Our Sunday preaching was uniformly [conducted] at the station [of John Craig].

I now began to reflect seriously on my situation. For some time we [had] had to pack corn forty miles and then send a mile to grind at a hand mill[26] before we could get bread. As to meat, it must come from the woods, and myself no hunter. I would at times go out with hunters, and they, with the common generosity of hunters, would admit me to share in the profits so far as meat went.

Soon after I settled in my little cabin (sixteen feet square, with no floor but the natural earth, [and] without table, bedstead, or stool), I found that an old buck had his lodge a few hundred steps from my cabin among the nettles, high as a man's shoulders and interlocked with peavines. Those nettles the next winter we found very useful in getting[27] the lint, and with the help of buffaloe [*sic*] wool [we] made good clothing for our black people. However, I went many mornings to visit this old buck'[s] lodge, hoping to get a shot at him. I could some times see him but had not the skill to get hold of him. But I at length got a fire at him and accidentally shot him through the heart. This was a greater treat to my family than the largest bullock I have ever killed since, for he was large and very fat.

Embarrassed as my worldly circumstances were, the face of things as to religion gave me more pain of mind. There were a number of Baptists scattered about, but we all seemed cold as death. Everybody had so much to do that religion was scarcely talked of, even on Sundays. All our meetings seemed only the name of the thing with but little of [44]the spirit of devotion.

In short, we were such strangers to each other that confidence was lacking for want of more acquaintance. And our common calls were such that we had no time to become acquainted. Kentucky felt to me now as the quails did to the

---

[25]The area to which Taylor moved was then a part of Fayette County, Virginia. The formation of Woodford County in May 1789 was provided for by a legislative act passed the preceding November. Hening, *Statutes*, 12:663-64.

[26]Used for grinding cornmeal, the hand mill consisted of two round stones set one on top of the other—the bedstone and the runner—and kept in place by a hoop with a spout that discharged the meal. The mill was powered by hand by turning in a circular motion a staff of sturdy timber. The lower end of this staff was set in a hole in the upper surface of the runner, near its edge. The upper end of the staff was put through a hole in a board fastened to a ceiling joist. Grain was handfed into an opening in the center of the runner. Joseph Doddridge, *Notes on the Settlement and Indian Wars of the Western Parts of Virginia and Pennsylvania* (Wellsburgh VA, 1824) chap. xxv.

[27]Here Taylor uses the transitive verb *get* to mean *supply*.

Hebrews, who ate of them till they were loathsome and returned back through their noses.[28]

There was but one church now on the north side of [the] Kentucky [River], and this was South Elkhorn, where Lewis Craig had the pastoral care. Perhaps in the month of August 1784 I became a member of South Elkhorn Church,[29] where I was brought under the pastoral care of Lewis Craig, who was now in the prime of life as to the gospel ministry, of the age of between forty and fifty. Mr. Craig is yet living and about eighty-three years old. He is one of the old, gospel veterans in Virginia who often suffered imprisonment there for the crime of preaching repentance to sinners.

[186]The church I have been writing of at Gilberts Creek was swallowed up partly by Craig's members' moving away and partly by a Separate church settling there under the care of old Mr. Joseph Bledsoe. And though the old gentleman is dead; it seems, the church yet exists, and has succeeded for [187]near forty years, and has been alternately served by a number of different preachers.

[45,2d]Also the church on Gilberts Creek, south side of Kentucky River, having become extinct forty years ago, a Separate Baptist church (being organized at the same place that far back) yet continues in prosperity, so far as I know anything to the contrary.

---

[28]Numbers 11:13, 18-20.

[29]John Taylor and his wife became constituent members of the South Elkhorn Church on Saturday 31 July 1784, the day it was organized. The memory of Taylor slipped away from him in this case. In his serial history of Kentucky Baptists, Samuel Howard Ford quotes the minutes of the constituting session of South Elkhorn. He had obtained them "with considerable difficulty," he recorded. There were fourteen charter members, seven of whom bore the name Craig. When in her history of the South Elkhorn Church, Ms. Phyllis Sharp Mattingly follows Taylor's date of 1783 as the year the congregation was constituted, she ignores three pieces of evidence: (1) Ford's quoting the first church-record book as the source for Saturday 31 July 1784—the organizing day; (2) mentioning Saturday as the day of the week of 31 July 1784 by Richard Young, clerk of the constituting council (if the correct date had been 1783 the clerk would have written Thursday as the day of the week for 31 July that year); and (3) recording 31 July 1784—as the day of organization—in the historical portion of the church-record book begun in 1817. Ford, "Kentucky Baptists," *Christian Repository* 5:263, 263n.; and Mattingly, *South Elkhorn Baptist Church*, 50, 54-55.

# 4
## South Elkhorn Church

[44]South Elkhorn [Church][1] was eight miles from where I lived. I seldom went there but at monthly meetings.[2] I now became more acquainted with that old, successful man in the ministry Lewis Craig. This man's orthodoxy mainly lay in [his advocating] salvation through Christ by unmerited grace, with [his] urging repentance on all to whom he preached.[3] He had the most striking gift of exhortation that was perhaps ever in use in Kentucky. While [I was] with him in South Elkhorn, he treated me as a father would a son.

[279,2d][Lewis Craig] moved [from Lincoln County] to the north side of [the] Kentucky [River] and set up the first church there, on South Elkhorn [Creek]. By him as a leader, with others, all the churches on the north side were set up, till Elkhorn Association was created in 1785.[4]

From South Elkhorn, after eight or nine years Mr. Craig moved to Mason County,[5] near the Ohio River. There he set up a new church[6] [and] continued a

---

[1]The South Elkhorn Church was organized on 31 July 1784 and was located on South Elkhorn Creek in Fayette County. Lewis Craig was the magnet around whom the members of this congregation gathered, as it grew in size. Most of these Baptists had come with that elder from Virginia through the wilderness as the "Traveling Church" of 1781 and had formed the first Gilberts Creek Church. Ford, "Kentucky Baptists," *Christian Repository* 5:263, 263n.; and Spencer, *Kentucky Baptists*, 1:41-42.

[2]For Baptist churches of Taylor's day the monthly meeting consisted of a worship service and a business session on a stated Saturday of each month (for example, the third Saturday) and morning worship on the following day. This practice is retained today by all Old Regular Baptist churches and by some Primitive Baptist and United Baptist congregations.

[3]Lewis Craig's doctrinal creed (to use a term then in vogue) blended Calvinism and Arminianism. It is difficult to say with whom this harmony arose. John Leland expressed it in a pharmaceutical metaphor as compounding three grains of Calvinism with two of Arminianism. Andrew Fuller, of England, reconciled these two positions by coupling a special application of God's grace with a general atonement. By this reasoning, Fuller and many of his contemporaries, including Craig, justified their inviting all sinners to repent. Benedict, *Fifty Years*, 135-38, 141, 144.

[4]This paragraph and the eight that follow it come from a piece in the addendum of the second edition titled "Biography of Mr. Lewis Craig."

[5]Mason County was erected in May 1789 under a Virginia law of the previous year and by a division of Bourbon County. Around 1792 Lewis Craig moved to the part of Mason County that would become in four years a segment of present-day Bracken County. Hening, *Statutes*, 12:658; and Spencer, *Kentucky Baptists*, 1:31.

member of it many years till he died. He was a man of that influence that wherever he moved so many members followed him that they became a church at once.

Mr. Craig, though much persecuted in Virginia for preaching, through great industry had accumulated a good estate. And that in the end proved a snare to him. He reached out beyond what he could accomplish and thereby brought a shade over his ministry.[7] But with all his embarrassments, his zeal for religion and the interest of the church continued warm. If we ever saw a man that could serve both God and mammon,[8] it was Lewis Craig. The numerous anecdotes respecting this uncommon man would fill a [280,2d]volume.

He was in the gospel ministry near sixty years and was about eighty-seven when he gave up the ghost.[9]

As an expositor of the Scripture, he was not very skil[l]ful but dealt closely with the heart. He was better acquainted with men than with books. He never dwelt much on doctrine but most on experimental and practical godliness.

Though he was not called a great preacher, perhaps there was never found in Kentucky so great a gift of exhortation as in Lewis Craig. The sound of his voice would make men tremble and rejoice. The first time I heard him preach, I seemed to hear the sound of his voice for many months.[10]

He was of middle stature, rather stoop-shouldered. His hair [was] black, thick set, and somewhat curled. [He had] a pleasant countenance. [He was] free-spoken, and his company very interesting. [He was] a great peacemaker among contending parties.

He [Lewis Craig] died suddenly, of which he was forewarned, saying, "I am going to such a house to die." And with solemn joy [he] went on to the place and with little pain left the world.

Mr. Craig had two brothers that were preachers—Elijah and Joseph, both younger than himself.

---

[6]Within about a year of moving to northern Kentucky, Lewis Craig had gathered the Bracken Church, near the town of Minerva, in Bracken County. Lewis Thompson, *Lewis Craig*, 29.

[7]It was speculation in land that caused Lewis Craig to suffer mental anguish and financial loss. Spencer, *Kentucky Baptists*, 1:31.

[8]Matthew 6:24.

[9]The idiom "give up the ghost" means *die*. The word *ghost* in its original meaning of *soul* or *spirit* is now used only in the above idiom and in the term "Holy Ghost."

[10]Lewis Craig's voice was melodious and affecting. "Once heard it was seldom forgotten." Ford, "Kentucky Baptists," *Christian Repository*, 5:136.

[44]On my settlement at home I had nothing before me but hard labour, being entirely in the woods. I had [45]now been a housekeeper[11] about two years. And [with] but little done for family support, I felt great cheerfulness in laying away at work.[12] After getting another little cabin up and fixed for winter, our first work was to make fence rails and enclose all the land we intended to clear through the winter. I then had one Negro man and three black children. I employed a young man to work with us through the winter. The first fence that was put up on the place I did with my own hands.

I will state one of my day's work. I went out in a cold morning late in October or early in November [1784]. When I counted my ground work I found [that] fifty pannels [sic] were laid. "This," I thought to myself, "I must put up, and fifty more today." The rails [were] all lying where they were split at different distances. At it I went with nimble step. I only put up the fence six rails high, but this I found a full day's work. I concluded [that] I had often put my strength and activity to very bad purposes in my days of wickedness,[13] but that it was a very good work to get my fence up. About sunset I finished "my task," as I called it. In one day I had a hundred pannels [sic] of fence put up with my own hands, and the newly split logs [I had] moved from one to fifty steps through the brush and fallen timber (except the fifty pannels [sic] of ground work first laid). The rails were of a size for six of them to a pannel [sic] to make a safe fence. In this early day, their length was eleven feet.[14] I name this day's work that it may be accounted for how I have cleared near four hundred acres of land in the heavy forest of Kentucky, besides making other good improvements.

We had about twenty-two acres fenced in before Christmas, all of which we cleared and planted the next spring [1785]. By this time, in the neighborhood among my new acquaintances I had acquired the character of a very industrious man. But whether this adds to my credit as preacher is quite another question. But at this time, there were but very few people in Kentucky and but very little opening for preaching. Our crop of [46]every kind grew finely that year. And in the fall I had about 250 barrels of corn, the greater part of which I had to share to newcomers at a good price, for there was plenty of cane[15] and other good food

---

[11]Here the noun *housekeeper* is an archaism meaning *householder*.

[12]The idiom "lay away at work" means "labor with great zest and vigor."

[13]The phrase "in my days of wickedness" was omitted from the second edition.

[14]In the Great Valley of Virginia, where Taylor had grown up, rails were sometimes cut twelve feet in length and laid seven rails high. Such a worm fence was often supported at the corners (where the panels met) by long stakes driven into the ground. At times a chunk of wood the thickness of a rail was put under each fence corner in order to protect the bottom rail from rot. Chester R. Young, "French and Indian War," 21.

[15]Cane, a bamboolike grass, grew in many parts of eighteenth-century Kentucky.

in the woods for stock. When I first moved I had purchased two small sows with seven or eight pigs, from which the next year I killed about a thousandweight of pork. Salt was with us then about sixpence per pound.

Notwithstanding the exertions of the people in the woods to get something to sustain [themselves] on, there seemed to be some heart-melting move among the people. The first I recollect was at a night meeting at my little cabin. Though the night was wet and dark and scarcely a trace to get to my house, the little cabin was pretty well filled with people. And what was best of all, I have no doubt the Lord was there.

A Mrs. Cash,[16] the wife of Warren Cash,[17] was much affected and soon after was hopefully[18] converted. Others were also touched to the heart who afterwards obtained relief in the Lord. Warren Cash, though otherways[19] respectable, was a bold sinner, having spent several years in the Old Revolutionary War.[20] Seeing his wife much affected struck him with a great consciousness of his own guilt. They were both soon baptized. Perhaps Cash could not at this time read. I have heard [that] his wife learned[21] him to read. A few years after, he moved to a new settlement in Shelby County.[22] There he began to hold meetings, and Beech

(Even today it survives in a dwarfish condition along stream banks and in other places in the state.) The plant often grew as high as ten feet, occasionally measuring sixteen feet. Its stem sometimes reached a thickness of two inches. Livestock relished the leaves and shoots of this evergreen.

[16]Susannah Cash, a native of Goochland County, Virginia, was a daughter of Elder William Baskett and Mary Pace. In November 1783 she became the bride of Warren Cash. The young couple migrated to Kentucky in the fall of the next year. She may have been the first person converted to Christianity in the Kentucky Bluegrass. Spencer, *Kentucky Baptists*, 1:58-59, 329.

[17]Warren Cash (1760–1850) was born in Virginia, where he grew up as "a wild, reckless young man." Moving to Kentucky with his wife, he spent the winter of 1784–1785 at Grubbs's Station in present-day Madison County and settled in the spring in Woodford (then Fayette) County at the present site of Mortonsville. Ibid., 1:59, 329-30.

[18]Here is a correct use of the adverb hopefully, a word often misapplied today. Taylor means that when this woman was converted she was filled with hope in Christ. He does not mean that he hoped that she was converted.

[19]The word *otherways*, meaning *otherwise*, is now obsolete except in dialectal usage.

[20]A private in the Continental Army for four years, Cash began in 1831 to receive an annual pension of eighty dollars. Spencer, *Kentucky Baptists*, 1:58-59, 329; and *Kentucky Pension Roll of 1835*, 100.

[21]Here the verb *learn* is a dialecticism meaning *teach*.

[22]Shelby County was formed out of Jefferson County by an act of the Kentucky legislature passed in 1792.

Creek Church was soon raised.[23] He has moved several times and now lives in Hardin County.[24] For upwards of thirty years he has been a laborious, successful minister of the gospel. His tutoress and instrument of his conversion (his wife) is one of the most pious-minded and best-taught females in the religion of the heart I was ever acquainted with.

Soon after the awakening of Mrs. Cash, I had a meeting at Hillsboro[25] at John Whitaker's.[26] It being in the spring of the year [1786], I took a text from the Canticles about the winter [47]being past, and the flowers appearing, and the voice of the turtle[27] being heard in our land.[28] The people being affected, when I stopped speaking two men and their wives (as if they had previously consulted) rose up and with trembling came forward and asked me to pray for them, they being perfect strangers to me. And the thing [was] so new to the people that it spread a heavenly blaze through the assembly. They all [the two couples] soon after obtained hope in the Lord and was baptized.

But I am hurrying too fast to Clear Creek, for all those persons were baptized soon after Clear Creek became a church. I must return to old South Elkhorn. A revival soon took place there, and a number were baptized. Old Mr. [William] Hickman[29] in the spring of 1785 moved from the south side of [the]

---

[23]The Beech Creek Church, located in Shelby County, was gathered in 1796 with five charter members, two of whom were Cash and his wife. He was ordained to the ministry four years later and promptly became its second pastor. Spencer, *Kentucky Baptists*, 1:328-29.

[24]In 1802 Cash moved to Nelson County and four years later to Hardin County, which had been created by the division of Nelson County required by a 1792 legislative act.

[25]Hillsboro is located in the southwestern section of present-day Woodford County. It centers at the intersection of the Craig Creek Road and the McCowans Ferry Road.

[26]John Whitaker was the stepfather of Isaac Wilson, who in time became a charter member of the Buck Run Church of Franklin County. (He is not to be confused with the John Whitaker of Jefferson County who organized the Bear Grass Church in 1784.) Draper MSS., 16CC54-55; and Spencer, *Kentucky Baptists*, 1:52.

[27]*Turtle* is an archaism used in place of the noun *turtledove*.

[28]Song of Solomon 2:11-12.

[29]William Hickman, Sr. (1746/7–1834), who was born in King and Queen County, Virginia, first heard the gospel in 1770. He was baptized three years later. While exploring Kentucky in the spring of 1776 he preached his first sermon at Harrodstown (now called Harrodsburg). Returning home, he began to preach regularly and over the years served the Skinquarter Church, of Chesterfield County. He migrated in 1784 to Kentucky, where four years later he founded the Forks of Elkhorn Church. This congregation he served until his death except for a two-year expulsion, occasioned by his staunch advocacy of emancipation. See his autobiography titled *A Short Account of My Life and Travels: For More Than Fifty Years a Professed Servant of Jesus Christ* (1828). For a biography, see S. H. Ford, "William Hickman, Senior," *Christian Repository* 6 (Oct.

Kentucky [River] and lived in South Elkhorn neighborhood. A number of his children joined the church, one of whom was his son William (who is now the pastor of a respectable church on South Benson).[30] Under the labours of Lewis Craig, Sen[io]r Hickman, and other visitors, South Elkhorn soon grew up to a large and respectable church. They put up a framed meetinghouse not far from where the brick one now stands. And [it] was the first house of worship of any kind on the north side of [the] Kentucky [River]. Mr. [Adam] Rankin, a Presbyterian minister, soon after this settled in Lexington.[31] George "Stokes" Smith soon became a member at South Elkhorn. Of him I have said something before.[32]

Wm. Hickman, Sen[ior], though him[33] and myself were not members at the same time at South Elkhorn, we have both had our membership there and are now near neighbors. This man has had a great range in Kentucky, for here he has been a faithful labourer for near forty years. He is truly a '76 man, for in [17]76 he paid a visit to Kentucky, and here the same year he first began to preach. In early times and in the face of danger, he settled where he now [1823] lives.[34] For a number of years at the risk of his life from Indian fury, he preached to the people in Shelby County and [at] [48]other frontier settlements. So that he is one of the hardy, fearless sons of '76. For upwards of thirty years he has served the church at the Forks of Elkhorn,[35] in which congregation he has perhaps baptized first and last more than five hundred people. He has statedly served a number of

---

1857):600-612. Semple, *Baptists in Virginia*, rev. ed., 266, 267n.; and Spencer, *Kentucky Baptists*, 1:151, 152, 161. See also James B. Taylor, *Virginia Baptist Ministers*, 2d ed., 221-23.

[30]William Hickman, Jr. (1768–1845), a native of Virginia, moved to Kentucky with his parents in 1784. When about nineteen years of age he married Obedience Brown. In 1802 he was ordained as the pastor of the South Benson Church, to which he ministered for over forty years. This church was located south of the Kentucky River on South Benson Creek about five miles from Frankfort and was organized the year before Hickman's ordination. Spencer, Kentucky Baptists, 1:622, and 2:297.

[31]Adam Rankin moved in 1784 from Augusta County, Virginia, to Kentucky and shortly thereafter founded the Mount Zion Presbyterian Church in Lexington. Two years later he helped to organize the Transylvania Presbytery. Robert H. Bishop, *An Outline of the History of the Church in the State of Kentucky* ([Lexington, Ky., 1824]) 152; and Collins, *Kentucky*, 1:457, 461. This congregation functions today as the First Presbyterian Church of Lexington.

[32]See pages 41-42, first edition.

[33]The pronoun *him* in the accusative case is here used ungrammatically in place of the nominative *he*.

[34]William Hickman, Sr., lived then at the Forks of Elkhorn in Franklin County, Kentucky. Hickman, *Life and Travels*, 26.

[35]The Forks of Elkhorn Church was organized on 7 June 1788 in Fayette (now Franklin) County. Darnell, *Forks of Elkhorn Church*, 19.

other churches.[36] Perhaps no man in Kentucky has baptized so many people as this venerable '76 man. Though now about seventy-six years old, he walks and stands as erect as a palm tree. Being at least six feet high, rather of a lean texture, his whole deportment [is] solemn and grave. And [he is] like Caleb, the servant of the Lord of old, [who] at fourscore years old was as capable to go to war as when young.[37] This '76 veteran can yet perform a good part in the gospel vineyard, so that it is not strange that, like Abraham[38] of old, he should be now raising a young family by a second wife.[39]

His preaching is in a plain and solemn style, and the sound of it like that of thunder at a distance. But when in his best gears, his sound is like thunder at home and operates with prodigious force on the consciences of his hearers. His mode of speaking is so slow that the hearers at times get ahead of him in the subject before they get it from him. In this, his son Billy has not learned to preach from his father but speaks as much too fast as the old gentleman speaks too slow.

But to return to South Elkhorn, Lewis Craig continued their pastor for perhaps nine years and then moved to Bracken County, near the Ohio River. Having been well acquainted with John Shackleford in Virginia, who had lately moved to Kentucky, Craig advised the church at South Elkhorn to call him to take the watchcare of the church, which was done on Craig's moving away. I suppose Shackleford has been in the ministry at least fifty years and was one of the prisoners of the Lord in early times in Virginia.[40] He was a preacher of much respectability from his youth, and his labours commenced with great success before he came to Kentucky. He has been the [49]labourious pastor of South Elkhorn Church for more than thirty years. Under his ministrations there have been great additions to the church. Several great revivals have been there. About the beginning of the present century several hundreds were added in one year.

---

[36]At age eighty, Hickman was serving three other churches, completing a four-Sunday monthly cycle. Hickman, *Life and Travels*, 35, 36.

[37]Joshua 14:10-13.

[38]Genesis 21:5.

[39]John Taylor's note: "His wife has lately died and has left him in the care of four young sons." (Page 49, second edition.)

The first wife of Hickman was a daughter of John Shackleford, of King and Queen County, Virginia, to whom he was apprenticed for the learning of a trade. She died in Kentucky on 9 June 1813. Then on Christmas Day of the following year Hickman married the widow Elizabeth Abbett, of Scott County, a daughter of Benjamin Dicken. His second wife died on 25 September 1826. Hickman fathered eighteen children by these two marriages. Hickman, *Life and Travels*, 36.

[40]Shackleford was held in the prison at Tappahannock in Essex County during 13-21 March 1774. Little, *Imprisoned Preachers*, 399-400.

A few years past near two hundred were added in one winter, so that South Elkhorn has always been among the most numerous and respectable churches in Elkhorn Association.[41] Of late the church has suffered some devastation. A few years past, a numerous young church was constituted from them without the approbation of the old pastor.

The church at South Elkhorn has existed as such for near forty years. They have only had two pastors—[Lewis] Craig and [John] Shackleford. Both these men have often preached through iron grates in Virginia[42] and with great success in Kentucky. And now both [are] waiting to hear the applaudit[43] of "Well done, thou good and faithful servants."[44]

[185]Should we take notice of it [the use of the name Particular Baptist] at South Elkhorn, has it done good there? The first church on the north side of the Kentucky [River] and one of the [186]most prosperous in the state—what has rent it in twain?[45] [It is] not the General Union,[46] for that serves to unite in place of [to] pull asunder.

Compare the situation of that dear old prisoner of the Lord now to what it was when under the sunshine of the General Union. From what I can hear, how is he locked up as in the cage of death? [It is] far more distressing to himself than when preaching through iron grates in Virginia prisons and when at liberty

---

[41]In 1801 a total of 309 new Christians were baptized into the membership of the South Elkhorn Church. During the associational year 1816–1817 the number of people added to the congregation by various ways amounted to 180. Mattingly, *South Elkhorn Church*, 68.,89.

[42]When Lewis Craig and four fellow ministers were held in the Spotsylvania Jail at Fredericksburg in 1768, they preached through the grating over the prison window. Because their sermons had a telling effect upon many of the listeners, organized mobs did everything they could in order to keep the people from hearing. They sang obscene songs, started riots, beat drums, and threw objects at the preachers, but to no avail. While in the Essex Jail for eight days in 1774, John Shackleford and two compeers preached at least twice during the week. In their devotions, which were performed thrice a day, they were often joined by interested visitors. Edwards, *Materials*, 2:55; and Semple, *Baptists in Virginia*, rev. ed., 32, 40.

[43]The noun *applaudit* is an obsolete usage meaning *approval*.

[44]Matthew 25:21.

[45]*Twain* is an archaic variant of the word *two*.

[46]The cooperative fellowship between the Elkhorn and the South Kentucky associations, effected in 1801, is referred to in Kentucky Baptist history as the General Union. The setting up of this union is described elsewhere in the annotation.

baptizing his hundreds both there and in Kentucky.[47] "O my God, restore this man again to the children of his ministry, and let him die in peace."

Perhaps the Licking brethren can solve one doubt that rests on the minds of many. It is well known that one of the greatest barriers to a union with Elkhorn by the Licking people for many years was the recognizing of the minorities of the churches at Bryan [Station][48] and Dry Run[49] as the genuine churches of those places and admitting them as such to a seat in Elkhorn Association. The doubt is whether the disorder is not equally as great in [the case of] the Licking Association'[s] recognizing and admitting the churches at Friendship[50] and South Elkhorn to seats in Licking. Or does being a Particular Baptist sanctify every action that is done?

I had closed the history of South Elkhorn Church last year [1822], and some of the things named above having transpired since [then] I thought proper to add what is said above. There is no doubt [that] the once-flourishing church at South Elkhorn is divided—about fifty with the old pastor [John Shackleford] and more than three times that number on the other side (now served by Jacob Creath,

---

[47]The burdens of John Shackleford as pastor of the South Elkhorn Church were threefold. First, a financial dispute about two slave girls arose in the Town Fork Church, near Lexington, spilled over into the South Elkhorn Church, and divided the latter congregation. Shackleford sided against Jacob Creath, Sr., pastor of the Town Fork Church. Second, this conflict rent the Elkhorn Association and caused the forming of the Licking Association. A minority of the South Elkhorn Church under Shackleford joined the Licking group, while Creath headed the majority of the church, which remained with the Elkhorn Association. Both parties, however, continued to use the same meetinghouse. The third problem came in with the rising tide of Campbellism during the 1820s. Shackleford died in 1829. Two years later this doctrinal dispute led to the ouster of the South Elkhorn Church from the Elkhorn Association. Spencer, *Baptists in Kentucky*, 1:44, 116, 311-12.

[48]The Bryan Station Church, organized in 1786, was situated about five miles northeast of Lexington. Controversy within the Town Fork Church over two slave girls rent the Bryan Station Church into two congregations around 1810. For nearly a century these two groups occupied the same meetinghouse. Ibid., 1:112-13, and 2:240; Masters, *Baptists in Kentucky*, 74.

[49]The Dry Run Church, located in Woodford County, was organized in 1800. It was one of the organizing congregations of the Licking Association in 1810. By the next year the church had divided into two parts—one reported 105 members to the Elkhorn Association; the other, 116 members to the Licking Association. Spencer, *Kentucky Baptists*, 1:95, and 2:240; Benedict, *Baptist Denomination*, 2:539-40; and Kentucky Baptist Convention, *Annual, 1989*, 402.

[50]As an affiliant of the Licking Association, the Friendship Church had a membership of seventy-three in 1832. I. M. Allen, *The United States Baptist Annual Register for 1832* (Philadelphia, 1833) 181.

[Sr.]). [They are] perhaps to be each other's tormentors till some of their greatest warriors die. [50,2d]South Elkhorn, not far from Lexington, was the fourth church in which I had my membership. This was the first worshiping congregation of any kind organized on the north side of the Kentucky River, and early in the fall of 1783,[51] of course smartly[52] upwards of forty years ago. This, for near forty years, was among the most prosperous Baptist churches in Kentucky. As a church, they have had several great revivals.

But, alas, the sable wings of Sarron[53] has been hovering over them for many years. The division I spoke of before still continues, or so far as for two Baptist churches to be in one house. We will not doubt the truth of the Saviour, saying, "A house divided against itself must fall."[54] Paul also says, "If ye bite and devour one another, the natural consequence is to be consumed one of another."[55] The minority, so-called, at South Elkhorn calls themselves Particular Baptists.[56] And their old pastor [John Shackleford] is yet alive but very old, and a respectable young minister they have ordained in past days the name of Collins. So that the minor church as to the ministry is more comfortably fixed than the majority church. For though the two well-known Brother Creaths[57] have alternately served

---

[51]The South Elkhorn congregation was not constituted as a church until 31 July 1784. Ford, "Kentucky Baptists," *Christian Repository* 5:263, 263n.

[52]*Smartly* is a dialectal adverb meaning *considerably*.

[53]The word *Sarron* in the metaphor "sable wings of Sarron" is a Scotticism. Here Taylor misspells the word *sharry*, which means *dispute* and which contracts *Sharramoor* (or *Sherrymoor*). *Sherramoor* derives from the Perthshire place name *Sheriffmuir*, where the march of the Scottish Jacobites was halted during the rebellion of 1715. The word *Sherramoor*, a Scots word (and an English dialectal word), became in time a metonym for the rebellion itself, and a synonym for *turmoil* or *tumult*.

[54]Mark 3:25.

[55]Galatians 5:15.

[56]The term "Particular Baptists" distinguishes the second group of Baptists that arose in England early in the seventeenth century. The word *Particular* refers to a limited atonement and election—that is, the concept that Christ died for specific persons known as "the elect" rather than for all mankind.

[57]The Creaths were an uncle-nephew team who appeared separately on the Kentucky scene early in the nineteenth century. Jacob Creath, Sr. (1770?–1854), a native of Nova Scotia, grew up in Culpeper County, Virginia; served two churches in that state; and in 1803 migrated westward. In Kentucky he held short-term pastorates in at least seven churches. Some folks called him well-dressed; others, foppish. He was, however, a handsome, intelligent orator of remarkable power. When the Campbellite controversy broke into the open, in 1830, he put himself at the forefront of that movement and carried the Versailles Church and the majority of the South Elkhorn Church into the Reformed fold.

them, I know not whether they have any stated preaching at this time. But as no gifts can profit much but where charity abound, we must consider the South Elkhorn people uncomfortable, taking them in the aggregate.

What I said in print some years back [1823] about Particular Baptists gave them some offence.[58] And as I would not [un]justly offend any people or person, I have just now looked over what I then said! But after making all the allowance for self-partiality (more or less found in every man), I cannot see [51,2d] where anything was overwatched. If I called them Particular Baptists, was not that what they had called themselves? If I knew more than they did that this appellation gave their best friends disgust, ought I not (as one of their friends) have told them of it and in a way that they all might see it? The fact is [that] nothing should be ill taken that is not ill-designed. Being naturally a little venturesome and having made free with my friends some years past, I shall now go on a little further.

For [nearly] twenty years I was a sorrowful spectator of what was going on between Elkhorn [Association] and the Licking people.[59] I did not know a man among them that was an enemy to me, and I was intimate with all their leaders on both sides with a few exceptions. They were the companions of my youth. Living at that time a considerable distance from them all, only once a year did I witness what I esteemed a mighty forest of sin flowing from those I had esteemed the best of men. Many a night's rest have I lost after leaving them. At length, after pausing several years, I came to this result: Shall I lay[60] still, seeing my best friends so groosly [grossly] sin against God and fight themselves to

----

Jacob Creath, Jr. (1799–1886), a nephew of the elder, began to preach as a very young man. An early disciple of Alexander Campbell (1788–1866), he aided his uncle in the studied subversion of several churches in central Kentucky. After 1830 he followed his kinsman into the new denomination of Reformers. Semple, *Baptists in Virginia*, rev. ed., 172, 182, 183, 183n.; Spencer, *Kentucky Baptists*, 1:310, 312, 621-23, 636-37, and 2:32-34; and Masters, *Baptists in Kentucky*, 40, 114, 219. For a personal account of the nephew's work, see P. Donan, ed., *Memoir of Jacob Creath, Jr.*

[58]See under the Clear Creek Church for page 185 of the first edition of *Ten Churches* and under the South Elkhorn Church for pages 185-86.

[59]The Licking Association was organized in 1810 by representatives of eleven churches assembled at the Bryan Station Meetinghouse. It came into being as an offshoot of the Elkhorn Association but without its approval. Strange to say, this move resulted from a shabby dispute that erupted around 1804 in the Town Fork Church, near Lexington, over the exchange of two slave girls by two church members. Even so, for about a decade the Licking group corresponded regularly with its neighboring associations, including Elkhorn. For a history of this group, see Spencer, *Kentucky Baptists*, 1:310-12, and 2:239-50.

[60]Here is a dialectal usage of the intransitive verb *lay* meaning *lie*.

death? I wrote them a long letter, designed for the leaders on both sides. I should now be glad to see it, if it is not in the dust of ashes, for its manner and contents I have almost forgotten. But I suppose it was very incoherent, for hard as my heart naturally is I was often in tears while I was writing it. Was I to judge from its influence, provided they were perfect men, it must have been a very bad letter, for I offended both sides. And from warm friends they all became at least lukewarm friends. My whole object was lost, and they continued to fight on. The only thing I proved to them or others who knew of it was that I was no partisan in their war. I never saw a day in this long struggle but I would have gone almost any length (that my conscience would allow) to bring about a harmonious union between them. I shall now make as free as the best of friendship would dictate and inform my Licking brethren that the epithet "Particular Baptist" does not sit well with [52,2d]the brethren with whom they are in union.[61] Those who are less informed dislike it and say no more. Those who are more informed dislike it and are ready to give their reasons therefor.

As 1st. Why put on a badge of distinction from those with whom you are in union?

2dly. It is probable [that] the Licking Association acted premature[62] in adopting the appellation in the haste they did. For I think it did not exceed five minutes after Br[other Samuel] Trott[63] made the motion till it was adopted. Myself saw no evil in it; had I have been a member, perhaps I should have voted for it. Particular Baptist! Where do we find such a one this side of the Atlantic but in one part of Kentucky? Perhaps Br[other] Trott had his mind on the Baptists in England and particularly about the city of London. Perhaps he also thought as all the other Baptists in England were called General Baptists[64] and [sic] that they were all Arminians. And if he thought further should the Licking people call themselves Particulars that all the rest of the Kentucky Baptists would be Generals and of course Arminians. I say perhaps he thought all this before he

---

[61]In 1820 the Licking Association adopted the name "Particular Baptist" to indicate its holding to particular atonement and personal election. Two years later the group announced that it no longer considered itself an affiliant of the General Union of Kentucky Baptists. Spencer, *Kentucky Baptists*, 2:242.

[62]The adverb *premature* is a colloquialism meaning *prematurely*.

[63]Samuel Trott, a schoolteacher from New England, became the pastor of the Stamping Ground Church in 1817 and of the Dry Run Church two years later. He stayed only briefly in Kentucky before moving to Maryland. Spencer, *Kentucky Baptists*, 1:313-14.

[64]The term "General Baptists" designates the first of two groups of Baptists that developed out of Separatism in England early in the seventeenth century. The word *General* denotes that Christ's atonement for sins is available to all mankind.

made the motion. For I allow[65] the Yankees to think faster and with more art than other men. I presume [that] the Licking people did not think all this. And as an evidence [that] they did not think it, they desire to keep up the correspondence with the Baptists of the General Union [here in Kentucky].

Being an eye-and-ear witness of the haste in which this thing was acted on by the Licking people, I hope they will reconsider it, and especially when they consider that were they in England they would not correspond with the people [whom they] themselves are named after.[66] For if the majority [of a congregation in England] do not accord in it [the practice of Open Communion, for example], the minority ([which holds out] for Open Communion with Pedobapists)[67] is so strong that it is indulged in by their most leading preachers without complaint.[68] That we know of Mr. Ryland, of so high standing in London, [who] serves two congregations, worshiping at different times in the same house—one a Pedo[baptist], the other an Antipedobaptist[69] church. Though he does not baptize their children, yet [he] preaches for and administers the Supper to the Pedo[baptist] church, I think once [53,2d]a month.[70] My informant is a worthy

---

[65]The verb *allow* is a dialecticism meaning *think* or "express one's opinion."

[66]The Licking churches practiced Close Communion (the communing of only persons who have been immersed), but some Particular Baptists in England adhered to Open Communion (the communing of immersionists and Pedobaptists at the same table). Taylor implies that all Particular Baptists in England observed Open Communion. The truth is that English Calvinistic Baptists were divided on this matter. Close Communion had gained considerable ground during the eighteenth century, but by 1800 Open Communion was common among Particular Baptists of England but not among those of Scotland and Wales. A. H. Newman, *A History of the Baptist Churches in the United States*, rev. ed. (Philadelphia, 1898) 53-54.

[67]A Pedobaptist advocates infant baptism.

[68]On pages 52 and 53 of his second edition, Taylor mentions four pastors, all of whom deserve places in the pantheon of English Particular Baptists—Ryland, Hall, Booth, and Fuller. The denomination of which these preachers are representative originated the modern missionary movement, created a rich body of Christian literature, fought against antinomianism, and provided a ministerial corps characterized by considerable intellect and indefatigable pastoral work. John T. Christian, *A History of the Baptists together with Some Account of Their Principles and Practices* (Nashville TN, 1922) 336.

[69]An Antipedobaptist rejects the baptism of infants.

[70]Here in error Taylor probably refers to John Ryland (1753–1825), an English Baptist minister and a son of John Collett Ryland (1723–1792), who also was a Baptist divine. During the younger Ryland's forty-four years as a pastor, he ministered to only two churches—at Northampton and at Bristol.

There may have been more than one Particular Baptist preacher whose practices fit Taylor's story. One such person was Robert Hall, Jr. (1764–1831), the youngest of the fourteen children of Robert Hall (1728–1791), who also was a Baptist minister. From

Baptist minister living near the Great Miami [River], in Indiana, a few years from London and well acquainted with Mr. Ryland.

I have lately seen a pamphlet published by a minister of high standing among the Particular Baptists about London. I think his name is [Robert] Hall, [Jr.]. The whole dust of the work[71] is to prove the propriety of communing at the Lord's table with all Christians, whatever way they have been baptized or whether they have been baptized at all.[72] Part of his reasonings were the denial of John's[73] [baptism] as gospel baptism; the baptizing of Christ's disciples, when John was baptizing in Aenon,[74] of the same style; that the Supper of the Lord was instituted and administered before gospel baptism was; [and], of course, it was of no moment for any person to be baptized before coming to the Lord's table. He seems to despise [Abraham] Booth's[75] reasoning on that head. In his *Apology for the Baptists*[76] in not communing with the Pedoes,[77] he [Booth] owns [that] if Mr. [Andrew] Fuller[78] was living, he [Hall] should meet with opposition

---

1791 to 1831 the younger Hall served three churches, but none was located at London. At the second of these—the Harvey Lane Church at Leicester—there were two congregations under Hall's care. The congregation that met on Sunday mornings held to Open Communion. *Dictionary of National Biography*, 8:969-70, and 17:544-45.

[71]The idiom "the whole dust of the work" means "the commotion or confusion caused by the publication."

[72]Hall's work, titled *On Terms of Communion* (1815), is a defense of Open Communion.

[73]Luke 3:16.

[74]John 3:23.

[75]Abraham Booth (1734–1806) began his Christian life as a General Baptist but in 1760 was persuaded to accept the tenets of Particular Baptists. His piece opposing Open Communion was published in 1778. For thirty-five years he served as the pastor of the Little Prescott Street Church, a Particular Baptist congregation in London. *Dictionary of National Biography*, 2:835.

[76]The full title of Booth's work is *An Apology for the Baptists in Which They Are Vindicated from the Imputation of Laying an Unwarranted Stress on the Ordinance of Baptism, and against the Charge of Bigotry in Refusing Communion at the Lord's Table to Paedobaptists* (London, 1778).

[77]The noun *Pedoes* is a colloquialism for *Pedobaptists*.

[78]Andrew Fuller (1754–1815), Baptist theologian and advocate of missions, served as a pastor in England for forty years. In 1792 he helped to found the Baptist Missionary Society, the first such organization in modern times, and functioned as its initial secretary. His most important work was *The Gospel Worthy of All Acceptation, or the Obligations of Men Fully to Credit and Cordially to Approve Whatever God Makes Known* (1784). This piece maintains that the atonement of Christ was general in its nature but particular in its application. The "Fuller System," as this interpretation was called, justified a preacher's calling on all men to repent of their sins. *Dictionary of National Biography*, 2:835; and Benedict, *Fifty Years*, 135, 141.

from him [Fuller]. But Booth is dead; Fuller is dead; Hall as yet reigns champion among the Particulars, having written the last book in favour of Open Communion. Ink and paper is the best of evidence.

If Br[other] Trott knew all this, he imposed on the Licking people in his motion to call themselves Particulars, if his object was to imitate the English Particulars. But from charity, we believe he did not know it; therefore, excuse him.

But how far have I rambled from old mother South Elkhorn Church! For in a manner, she is the mother of all living on the north side of the Kentucky River; for directly or indirectly [the] chief of the Baptist churches in that district came from her. Let us yet hope that she will again look forth as the morning[79] and from the single circumstance of the happy end of contention between Elkhorn and Licking associations.

The consummation of this happy affair was somewhat aided by the mediation of Long Run[80] and Franklin[81] associations, whose committees met committees from Elkhorn and Licking at Town Fork,[82] near Lexington, last May [1826]. After two days' counsel, those parties who had been contending [54,2d]for twenty painful years met each other with the right hand of fellowship on the very spot of ground where the contention began. It seemed as much of Heaven as mortal man can bear on earth to behold the sight—the tears of joy and love and tenderness where some of those gray-headed committeemen met each other with their hands and arms and hearts. There was scarcely a dry eye in the congregation. I am almost unman[n]ed while I write, for myself was a spectator. What their committees had done in May,[83] their associations ratified the August and September following.

I will, therefore, hope for the best in case of old mother South Elkhorn. Though there are two churches there now, I hope the Lord will make them one

---

[79]Song of Solomon 6:10.

[80]The Long Run Association, organized in 1803, originally included the twenty-four churches of the Salem Association that were situated north of the Salt River. Spencer, *Kentucky Baptists*, 2:150. For a history of this union, see Birdwhistell, *Long Run Association*.

[81]The Franklin Association was constituted in 1815 by some six churches, most of which were located in Franklin County. Spencer, *Kentucky Baptists*, 2:290.

[82]The Town Fork Church was constituted in 1786 by John Taylor and others. Ibid., 1:115.

[83]The spring conference recommended that correspondence be resumed between the Elkhorn and the Licking associations. Ibid., 2:242.

in due time.[84] I care not which association they go to, so they can be one in the Lord. May we endeavour "to keep the unity of the spirit in the bond of peace."[85]

---

[84]It was not Particularism, however, that sundered the South Elkhorn Church from its moorage. Rather it was Campbellism that caused its expulsion from the Elkhorn Association in 1831. The church had been divided into two congregations for a number of years. The majority congregation, under the leadership of the two Creaths, lined up with the Reformers and inherited the property. After the death of Shackleford in 1829, the minority congregation of Particular Baptists erelong lost its strength and by 1861 became extinct. Claims have been advanced that a church organized in 1859 by William M. Pratt and John L. Smith at Slickaway (present-day Fort Springs) in Fayette County and called the South Elkhorn Baptist Church constitutes the historical continuum of Craig's old congregation. Ms. Phyllis Mattingly supports this position in her history of South Elkhorn. Larry Douglas Smith, of the University of Louisville, has demonstrated, however, that no connection exists between the Slickaway congregation and Craig's church. Mattingly, *South Elkhorn Church*, 108-112; Larry Douglas Smith, "How Old Is the South Elkhorn Baptist Church?" *Kentucky Baptist Heritage* 16 (Nov 1989):26-30; Spencer, *Kentucky Baptists*, 1:43, 44; Birdwhistell, *Elkhorn Association*, 70; Ford, "Kentucky Baptists," *Christian Repository* 5:265. Professor Ira V. Birdwhistell and Frank M. Masters argue that the Slickaway church in 1859 included a remnant from the Craig congregation. Masters, *Baptists in Kentucky*, 30; and Birdwhistell, *Elkhorn Association*, 81.

[85]Ephesians 4:3.

# 5
## Clear Creek Church

[49]From the heavenly buddings already named at Clear Creek, we began to think of having a church there. Through the winter and spring of 1785 several preachers had moved into the neighborhood, as John Dupuy,[1] James Rucker,[2] and Richard Cave. We held a council on the subject of a constitution, but we found a difficulty and in this way: A number of the members had been in the [Upper Spotsylvania] Church with Lewis Craig in Virginia, and in the "Traveling Church" through the wilderness [in 1781] and [during] its establishment in Kentucky. And, above all, if we had a new church, we might lose [50]Lewis Craig as our pastor.[3] And though we had four ordained preachers, all of us did not make one Lewis Craig.

But after several councils, we concluded [that] rather than not have a church convenient to us we would go into a constitution under the hope that Brother Craig would visit us and set us right when we got wrong. To this height of respectability was Lewis Craig in those days in Kentucky. We could only apply to South Elkhorn [Church] for assistance. And the helps[4] from that establishment agreed to acknowledge us a sister church. I think in April[5] 1785 about thirty members (to the best of my recollection) was in the new church under the style of Baptist Church of Christ at Clear Creek.[6]

---

[1]John Dupuy (1737/8–1831), a native of Virginia, was a son of John James Dupuy and Susanne Lavillain, both of French Protestant descent. He was the principal organizer of the Powhatan (first called Cumberland) Separate Baptist Church in 1771. Around 1774, Dupuy was ordained as the pastor of this congregation. He migrated to Kentucky in 1784 and settled in Fayette (now Woodford) County. Spencer, *Kentucky Baptists*, 1:166-69, 192; and Trabue, *Narrative*, 175-76, 189.

[2]James Rucker (d. ca. 1828), a native of Virginia, moved to Fayette (now Woodford) County around 1785. He spent the last quarter-century of his life in western Kentucky. Spencer, *Kentucky Baptists*, 1:425.

[3]These people, who lived on Clear Creek, were members of the South Elkhorn Church, whose pastor was Lewis Craig.

[4]*Helps* are men sent from sister churches to assist in ordaining or installing a pastor, in settling a dispute, or in organizing a new congregation.

[5]The South Elkhorn Church proposed on 23 April 1785 that a congregation be organized on Clear Creek and gave its final approval to the matter on 29 May. The new church was constituted on 18 June. Ford, "Kentucky Baptists," *Christian Repository* 5:266-67.

[6]For other accounts of the Clear Creek Church, see these histories: John Taylor, *History of Clear Creek Church; and Campbellism Exposed* (Frankfort KY, 1830); J. S.

We soon began to baptize our young converts, for some of them were waiting for an opportunity. We went on in great harmony through [the rest of] that year. We had four ordained preachers as named above. I think we baptized twenty[7] that year. Clear Creek was the second church on the north side of [the] Kentucky [River]. The same year others were constituted, as the Great Crossing,[8] Bryan [Station],[9] and a church near Limestone[10] under the care of W[illiam] Wood.[11]

We soon began to contemplate an association. For that purpose and partly to bring about a union with the South Kentucky [Separate] Baptists,[12] we held a conference at South Elkhorn [Church] in June 1785.[13] But failing in the union

---

Kirtley, "History of Clear Creek Church," Elkhorn Association, *Minutes*, 1887; "History of the Clear Creek Church," *Ashland Avenue Baptist* (Lexington KY), 19 Aug 1931; and Dennis E. Trimble, *Clear Creek Baptist Church: A Church History, 1785–1985* ([Versailles KY], 1985).

[7]In the first edition the expression "between thirteen and twenty" appears.

[8]The Great Crossing (first called the Big Crossing) Church, located in Fayette (now Scott) County, was constituted on 28 and 29 May 1785, according to a reconstructed church record made early in the nineteenth century. Bradley and Ham, *Great Crossing Church*, 8-9. Samuel Howard Ford, however, characterizes the May meeting as a time for the proposing to organize a church at the Great Crossing, which event occurred one month later. Ford, "Kentucky Baptists," *Repository* 5:269. Another factor that points to the founding of the Clear Creek Church before that of the Great Crossing Church is the division by the South Elkhorn Church on 29 May 1785 of the whole region north of the Kentucky River into two great "parishes"— South Elkhorn and Clear Creek—with no area being set aside for the Great Crossing Church. Ibid., 267.

[9]The Bryan Station Church was formed on Saturday 15 April 1786 and not during the preceding year. Spencer, *Kentucky Baptists*, 1:112.

[10]The Limestone Church, constituted in 1785, was located at the mouth of Limestone Creek, in Bourbon (now Mason) County. When its new meetinghouse of logs was built in Washington, the church was named after that town in 1792. Masters, *Baptists in Kentucky*, 36.

[11]William Wood, who served as the pastor of the Limestone Church from 1785 to 1798, founded the village of Washington, Kentucky. Around 1786 he visited John Gano, pastor of the First Church of New York City, and encouraged him in his moving to Kentucky. Spencer, *Kentucky Baptists*, 1:67-68, 125-26.

[12]The South Kentucky Association of Separate Baptists was organized on 5 October 1787 at the Tates Creek Meetinghouse in Madison County. In three years this union grew from eleven to nineteen churches. Ibid., 1:40, 147-48, and 2:80-82, 83; Asplund, *Baptist Denomination*, 1790, 32-34; and "Transcript of the Minutes of the South Kentucky Association of Baptists from 1787 to 1803," transcribed by George F. Doyle (Typescript, Margaret King Library, University of Kentucky, Lexington), 3.

[13]The conference was held on the twenty-fifth of the month, a Saturday. Spencer, *Kentucky Baptists*, 1:108.

with the South Kentucky Baptists,[14] we agreed to meet as an association at Clear Creek [on the] first of October 1785.[15] Six churches,[16] it seems, met. One of them was from Tates Creek,[17] south side of Kentucky. There and then Elkhorn Association was formed.[18]

We went on so prosperously at Clear Creek that everybody in a manner lost sight of Lewis Craig's particular watchcare over us. And sometime in the next winter the question began to be stirred among us about a pastor in the church from among our own preachers. When this talk came to my ears, it gave me alarm, thinking the peace of the church might be broken on this question [51]for I had seen much trouble at times in Virginia in choosing a pastor where there was a number of preachers. And my own opinion was that a church could do full as well without as with a particular pastor.[19]

Two of the preachers that were with us, [John] Dupuy and [James] Rucker, had been pastors in Virginia, and a number of their old flocks [were] then members of Clear Creek Church. My own fears were that between these men and their old friends[20] we should have a heavy church contest [over] which of them should be the pastor.

---

[14]Five Regular and five Separate Baptist churches were represented. When the conference voted to adhere strictly to the Philadelphia Confession of Faith, union was rejected by the Separates, whose congregations as a matter of polity had consistently refused to adopt a creed or confession. Ibid., 1:107-108, and 2:7, 8.

[15]The messengers of the churches met first on Friday 30 September 1785 and on the next day perfected the organization of Elkhorn Association. The sessions were held at John Craig's Station on Clear Creek in Fayette (now Woodford) County. Ibid., 2:8-10; and Hickman, *Life and Travels*, 23.

[16]These churches were represented in the constituting of this first Baptist association in Kentucky: the first Gilberts Creek, the first Tates Creek, South Elkhorn, Clear Creek, Great Crossing, and Limestone. Spencer, *Kentucky Baptists*, 2:9.

[17]The Tates Creek Church, organized in 1785, was situated in Lincoln (now Madison) County a few miles south of Boonesborough. It is not to be confused with the Separate Baptist congregation that was formed the next year in the same neighborhood and that carried the same name. Ibid., 1:96, 128.

[18]For a bicentennial history of this primal Kentucky association, see Birdwhistell, *Elkhorn Association*. An earlier, briefer account is Walter Mayberry Lee, *A History of the Elkhorn Baptist Association* (Leesburg KY, [1905]).

[19]Taylor uses the term "particular pastor" to indicate the man chosen from among the ordained preachers of a church and given the duties of preaching, of administering the ordinances, and of conducting the business of the congregation. He preferred that these responsibilities be distributed equally among all the ministers who held membership in a given church.

[20]The preceding prepositional phrase does not appear in the second edition.

But the question was brought into the church and the day fixed on to choose a pastor. Helps [were] sent for to [South] Elkhorn and the Great Crossing to install (as they called it) a pastor in the church. I think it was at our March monthly meeting [in 1786 that] the helps came, perhaps six or eight. Lewis Craig acted as the moderator.[21] His mode was to ask every member of the church, male or female, bond or free, "Who[22] do you choose for your pastor?"[23] I think the church was now about sixty in number. I must confess [that] it filled me with surprise when the first man that was asked answered that he chose me. And my astonishment continued to increase until the question went all-round. Only one man objected, but Lewis Craig soon worked him out of his objection, for it lay in thinking my coat was too fine. For my own part, I did think that no man in the church had the mind of Christ but this objector. Though the objection about my coat I considered trivial, yet to me [it] seemed as if the Lord directed it.

I could scarcely believe my own ears when I heard the two old pastors with the remnant of their former flocks give their voice that they chose me for their pastor. The objector soon acquiesced in the voice of the church. After which, I was called on to reply to the voice of the church I had just heard, to which I felt constrained to answer about as follows: That I had never thought myself adequate to the great responsibility of the pastor of a church, and especially in [52]the present case; that there were three ministering brethren in the church older than myself; that two of them had heretofore been pastors, and all of them [were] better calculated to fill that office than myself; and that it must have been the want of a better acquaintance with me which led the church to the present choice. And though I was ready by day or night to do anything in my power in a ministerial way for my brethren, yet I could not suffer my lips to consent in the present case to what my heart, conscience, and best, matured judgment contradicted. I, therefore, hoped that they would excuse me in the present negative. After some other, little business the church adjourned.

---

[21]In view of the fact that the Clear Creek Church had no "particular pastor" at this time, Lewis Craig's service as its moderator signified the respect accorded him as an elderly minister. In Old Regular Baptist churches in Appalachia today the term *moderator* indicates two functions filled by the same person: to serve as pastor, and to preside at church business meetings. Among Southern Baptists either the pastor or a specially elected layman bears the title *moderator* and conducts business sessions.

[22]The relative pronoun *who* is used in this question as a colloquialism instead of *whom*.

[23]This method of polling may have derived from the political elections of Virginia, in which the county sheriff called on each voter to express his choice audibly.

After meeting broke,[24] I took notice that a kind of silent, sorrowful gloom overspread the faces of the brethren in general, for they could scarce suppress tears when they spoke to each other and especially when they spoke to me. Though this operated somewhat on my feelings, my made-up resolution continued the same.

A number of the elder brethren went home with me that night. Their object was to labour further with me. Their mode of reasoning with me was that though Clear Creek was a young church it was made up mostly of old members who knew what they were about; that their judgments were not directed by blood connection or former local attachments; that I had baptized but few of the present church at Clear Creek; and [that], in a word, they had never seen a church so unanimous in the choice of a pastor at any place or time. At length one of them declared that he trembled for and at my obstinacy and that he looked for some heavy judgment from Heaven to overtake me. Those helps from a distance, thus reasoning with me, prevailed on me to agree that if the church was of the same opinion the next day I would submit.

A number of preachers from a distance, together with the design of the church's meeting, brought out [an] abundance of people, even from distant settlements. After preaching [53]had ended, the moderator, L[ewis] Craig, called the church together, informing them [that] if they were of the same mind they were the day before I had agreed to serve them. The voice of the church being unanimous, those helps proceeded to install me (as they called it) into the pastoral care of Clear Creek Church. Their mode was [for] three of them to kneel down with myself, while they all laid their right hand on my head. Two of them prayed, after which the moderator took my right hand into his and gave me the solemn charge to fulfill the duty of a pastor to the church. After which he called forward the church, each to give me the right hand of fellowship as their pastor.

This soon produced more heart-melting effect than we had ever before seen at Clear Creek. What wrought most on my feelings was [the fact that] almost every sinner in the crowded house pushed forward—either looking solemn as death or in a flood of tears—to give me their trembling hand.

From that day's meeting an instantaneous revival took place in the settlement of Clear Creek. That summer [of 1786] I baptized about sixty of my neighbors, and a number of them among the most respectable. I took notice that four experiences were received dating their first awakening from the day that I took the care of the church. We progressed on for [the rest of] that year with much peace and harmony.

---

[24]The intransitive verb *break* as used here is an Americanism meaning "cease for the time being."

This year Clear Creek Old Meetinghouse was built, a framed house forty feet by twenty. But we soon found [that] the house would not hold half the people that attended in good weather. I find the old house is yet standing. To me even at a distance the place looks rather sacred, because the Lord's presence has often been there. And there also I have alternately experienced great pleasure and pain. How checkered is human and especially the Christian life.

This year [1786] the church went into an agreement to make compensation to their pastor, as they now had one. Seventy dollars[25] was fixed on. Some said, "The pastor will be pacified with this small sum, as we [54]have our meetinghouse to build this year." The next year a $100 was voted for the pastor by the church, not knowing but [that] the first 70 had been all paid. The plan fallen on was to make out an apportionment on each member and [to] give the several sums drawn off into the hands of the pastor, and he [to] give the individual credit when the sum was paid. These several sums were in such produce as would answer for family use.[26] Out of this $170 I only received about 40. Those who did pay never knew but that all the rest paid also. The third year it was thought best to hire a man to attend to my business. This was done by commissioners appointed by the church who hired a man for a $100. The trustees took care to get their money from each individual. This produced a little flouncing. Thus ended my Peter's pence[27] at Clear Creek.

There were a number of conversions at Clear Creek soon after I became their pastor that was a little out of the common track. One was my own sister in the flesh[28] who has since married Mr. Jechonias Singleton,[29] in Woodford County, near Versailles.[30] I went to Virginia soon after I had moved to Kentucky.[31] My

---

[25]Until 1800 the maximum, annual salary for Methodist ministers in the United States was $64.00. Sweet, *American Frontier*, 1:155n.

[26]Members of another congregation in the Bluegrass pledged in 1798 to give their pastor the following items of produce as partial compensation for his services: corn, wheat, pork, beef, flour, salt, sugar, and whiskey. Kentucky Baptist Historical Society, *Publications*, No. 1 (Louisville KY, 1910) 27.

[27]Peter's pence was a tax that some English landowners paid annually to the papal see before the Reformation.

[28]Jane Taylor Singleton (1767?–1841), a native of Virginia, was one of nine children in the family of Lazarus and Hannah Taylor. Jane reached Kentucky in 1784. Dorothy Thompson, "Ancestors and Descendants," 30-31, and "John Taylor of the Ten Churches," 551n.

[29]Jechonias Singleton (1766–1836) was a son of Manoah Singleton and Sarah Craig, who was a sister of the preaching Craigs. Jechonias Singleton and Jane Taylor were married about 1786. Dorothy Thompson, "Day of Controversy," 230, 231.

[30]Shortly after the formation of Woodford County, Versailles became its seat of government.

sister, about sixteen or eighteen years old, applied to our parents to let her come with me to Kentucky.[32] I the more favored it, hoping that it was a religious object. But in Kentucky she soon formed an acquaintance with a number of gay, sportful young ladies. And in their alternate visits everything sacred was so far set aside that it was with difficulty that family worship could be kept up. I did now heartily wish her back with her parents.

A very devotional man the name of McDonald, and a stranger to my sister, had come to pay me a visit. He had great confidence in preachers, and when with them [he] would ask five times more questions than they were able to answer. And it would (in a manner) pain him to death if his questions was not answered. His object in those questions was to know to a certainty whether himself [55]was a Christian.

Sometime before we went to bed he asked me how I thought the foolish virgins felt.[33] Being obliged to give some answer, I entered on what I thought were the feelings of the foolish virgins. When I was done he broke out with doleful lamentations, and [said] that I had described his feelings so precisely that he was only a foolish virgin, and that the door of Heaven would be shut against him at last. Nothing that I could say afterwards would pacify him, for I had a very good opinion of his religion. My sister, who sat by and heard all that passed and [who was] ready to burst with laughter at (what she thought) this foolish man's talk, left the house to vent her levity to her satisfaction.

The next day we all started to meeting. My sister, riding on, took a look at this "foolish man," as her heart had called him the night before. It first occurred to her that he was the most holy-looking man she ever saw. The next thought was "This holy-looking man is afraid he will not be saved at last." The next thought was "If he is afraid, what will become of me?" With that thought this text occurred, "Woe is me, for I am undone, for I am a man of unclean lips."[34] The follies of her life so bore on her mind that her conclusion was that there was no mercy for her. Though there was a number in company, she left us all and fell

---

[31]The author visited the Tidewater during April and May 1784 and left Virginia for Kentucky shortly after 22 May. Dozier, "Historical Notes," 1406; Joseph F. Taylor, Interview by [John D. Shane], Draper MSS., 11CC228; and Dorothy Thompson, "Ancestors and Descendants," 2d after 20.

[32]Maybe with only a minimum of concern, Virginia mothers entrusted their daughters to Baptist ministers for the long trek westward into Kentucky. Keturah Moss, for example, was brought to the Bluegrass Country at the age of eleven by her uncle Augustine Eastin, a Separate Baptist preacher. *Biographical Encyclopaedia of Kentucky of the Dead and Living Men of the Nineteenth Century* (Cincinnati OH, 1878), 309.

[33]Matthew 25:1-13.

[34]Isaiah 6:5.

behind, weeping along alone. Others who overtook her she forbore to converse with, and they forbore to ask her what was the matter.

Lewis Craig that day paid us a visit. When he took his text it was the same that had occurred to her on the way, "Woe is me, for I am undone." Craig's sermon perfectly clinched the nail, for her conclusion was that God had sent Mr. Craig to show her that there was no mercy for her.

For about one month her agony and distress was such that at times it seemed as if she would go deranged. For that length of time she lived (in a manner) without food or sleep.

One day from the loom house she came rushing in with an apparent fright and a flood of tears. And not being [56]able to speak for a while, the first thing that occurred to me was Indians, for we were not then safe from Indians. But drop[p]ing on her knees, with heart-rending cries [she was] intreating[35] me to pray for her, for that God disdained her prayers, and she feared there was no mercy for her.

But the Lord soon gave her a happy deliverance, and with that [a] clearness that no doubt was left with any who heard the relation[36] of her hope in Christ. I do not recollect that a question was asked her by the church. She was among the first that was baptized in this happy revival. And [she] has given good evidence since, that the work is genuine and that she belongs to the Lord.

Another singularity in conversion about the same time was in George Dale. There being another man of the same name,[37] this [one] was called "Little" George Dale. I had been several years acquainted with Mr. Dale. In short, he had lived a good deal at my house.[38] My own opinion was that, as to morality, religion itself could make no amendment in him. And yet, [he was] destitute of spiritual religion. Many were obtaining hope in the Lord. At length a report came to me that "Little" George Dale was converted. I met with his brother Abraham[39] and asked him about the conversion of his brother George. He had heard nothing

---

[35]The spelling *intreating* is an archaic variant of *entreating*, the progressive form of the verb *entreat*.

[36]A convicted sinner who obtained hope in Christ was asked at a business session of the church to relate the experience by which he had arrived at his assurance of salvation. Such a public statement was called a *relation*. The word means either the content of the statement as in this case, or the act of making the statement.

[37]This man, known as "Long" George Dale, was a resident of Woodford County in 1810, had a family of eight, and owned two slaves. Riley, *Woodford County*, 11.

[38]"Little" George Dale may have been a hired hand.

[39]Abraham Dale accompanied John Taylor on his third trip into Kentucky in 1784. Joseph F. Taylor, Interview by [John D. Shane], Draper MSS., 11CC228.

of it, but he was sure [that] he was now in the state he was born [in], and he did
not presume he was born a Christian. But he had not seen him lately.

Soon after, George himself paid us a visit. Seeing my wife at the door, he
called to her, "How do you do, Sister Taylor? I am born again. I can now call
you-all[40] 'brothers and sisters.'"

Soon after, I came to the house and found George in the greatest rapture and
confidence in religion that I had ever seen any man [in]. As to anything he could
see to the contrary, he had at once arrived to a state of sinless perfection. Though
naturally a very silent man, he was now all-talk[41]—first, of his deliverance from
a great load of guilt; and [second], of the great grace in Christ Jesus, Who had
done all for him. I had often seen him at meetings [57]apparently as unmoved as
if he had no feelings, while others were weeping around him. In this, he soon
satisfied me that in all these cases he was inwardly mourning over his hardness
of heart; and that [he believed that] there was no mercy for him, and that God
in justice had passed him by and left him to perish in his sins.

The countenance of this man did not look as if he belonged to this world,
while he would exclaim, "O, the happiness that I shall enjoy both in this world
and [in] the world to come."

This man, about two weeks after, came forward with a solemn boldness to
join the church. Though he told a very good experience, many questions were
asked him on the subject of his great confidence. He was asked if he had felt no
trouble since his deliverance.

When he answered, "O, no, nor never shall! Why I am converted!"

He was further asked, "Have you had no temptations, evil thoughts, or
rambling of mind in the worship of God since that time?"

His answer was again in the negative, and rather expressing wonder at those
questions as he was born again.

There was some doubt expressed about receiving him as he was so much
better than other people, to which he replied with pleasant modesty [that] it made
no odds,[42] [for] God had received him; and [that] he should go to Heaven, for he
was born again. However, the church received him, and his course since has been
very even and orderly, though with not so much high sail[43] as at the beginning.

I have heard of but one complaint entered in the church against him, and that
was brought forward by himself. It seems [that] with some Baptist friends he
rode to Lexington. After which he came to the church and requested them to

---

[40]The pronoun *you-all* is an Americanism and a Southern colloquialism used instead
of *you*.

[41]*All-talk* is a colloquialism meaning *talkative*.

[42]This rare usage of the noun *odds* means *difference*.

[43]"High sail" is a colloquialism meaning *precipitancy*.

exclude him, for that he had gotten drunk when he went to Lexington. And though the company with him plead [*sic*] an excuse for him, and that they could barely discover intoxication in him, he insisted [that] there ought to be no plea for drunkenness. And for the honor of religion, [he] requested to be turned out of the church. But the church did not choose to grant his [58]request.[44] How very far from this is the hypocritical, sly Baptist who will cover his crime by falsehood till he dies a hidden drunkard!

There was a circumstance uncommon. I think it was on the day that George Dale joined the church. About twelve came forward to [join] the church with but one invitation. When the door was opened to receive members, there was no delay. For all of them, as one man, seemed eager to follow the Lord. Frequently two of them would step forward at once. To the best of my recollection there was neither female nor black person among them, but generally young men.

Among them, I think, was George Churchill,[45] an orphan lad who, in stating the consciousness of his lost and helpless condition, happened to say [that] he was willing to go to Hell. This expression was soon caught at by a number in the church as very improper. And [they] used endeavors by other questions to set the poor youth right, by reasoning that it was not possible for any person and especially a pious man (who knew what Hell was—a place of sin as well as sorrow) to be willing to go to Hell. Some perhaps insinuated [that] he need not speak any further, but [they] set him aside at once. The lad stood silent as if undismayed while these things were going on, but at length [he] replied that he saw at the time that it was just in God to send him to Hell and [that] he saw no way [by which] He could be just but in his destruction. He had no desire for God to change [in order] to do him any good. He saw no reason why He should be more partial to himself than to another person. He had no doubt that God would condemn the greater part of the world at last. And if he was willing for God to do right in that case, he saw no reason why he should be unwilling to be damned himself, and especially as he deserved it more than any other person. He had since seen that God could be just in saving a sinner through his Son, but without that consideration he was yet willing to be damned. The boldness in which this poor lad expressed his novel ideas [59]filled all who heard him with surprise and put to silence all who had objected against him. And of course he was received.

This was the same lad that, a month or two before, I saw standing at my style [*sic*] one morning as if afraid to approach the house. I walked out to him.

---

[44]Baptists of John Taylor's day counted as a sin the excessive drinking of alcoholic liquor but not the moderate imbibing of it.

[45]It may be that George Churchill was a son of Willoughby Churchill of Northumberland County, Virginia. Letter, Carolyn H. Jett, Heathsville VA, 19 Oct 1990, to Chester R. Young, Williamsburg KY.

He seemed about half-grown, poorly clad, an entire stranger to me. And his distress [was] such [that] he was scarcely able to speak. After [my] asking who he was and what he wanted, [he told me that] he had walked about three miles to request me to pray for him, for he felt himself a poor, lost sinner. We immediately withdrew into the woods and went to prayer.

I bore him much on my mind afterwards. After growing up he was very industrious. [He] married into a good family and is doing well in the world.[46] He has connected himself with the Emancipating Baptists in Kentucky and seems to walk uprightly.

There were several preachers [who] came out from this revival. I have already named Warren Cash. James Lee,[47] who was baptized about this time, became a good preacher afterwards. The rationality and sensibility of Brother Lee's experience, with his godly deportment and tenderness in the church, all foreboded future usefulness in the church some way. After a year or two he moved to Silver Creek, south of [the] Kentucky [River] about thirty miles from Clear Creek. There he began to hold prayer and exhorting meetings. This I had heard of for some time.

Having a night meeting with another preacher in my own neighborhood, soon after the other preacher began (the house being crowded) a brother informed me [that] Brother Lee was there. When the preacher ended, I called Brother Lee forward to close [the] meeting. He asked me for books. When I handed him my hymn book, he wanted a Bible too. Said I to myself, "Is he going to preach?" which I found a fact after he sung[48] a hymn. Said I further to myself, "If I think he can preach, he shall have my Bible." I do not remember the text he took. But I remember what I several times said to myself, "I am afraid [that] you will not get the [60]Bible," for he seemed embarrassed for a while. After which, he took the track so entertainingly that I with pleasure felt the Bible gone from me before he was half-done. He through mistake put the books in his pocket after he was done.

The next day he called to see me and [to] bring my books. The hymn book I received but informed him [that] the Bible was his and [that I] desired him to accept [it] and make use of it. But I did not inform him that he had won it last night, but afterwards he understood it. This was very acceptable to him, for in those early times it was not easy to get a pocket Bible in Kentucky.

---

[46]George Churchill married Sarah, a daughter of John Arnold and Elizabeth Hitt, and later moved to Illinois. Railey, *Woodford County*, 270.

[47]James Lee (d. ca. 1822) was baptized at the Clear Creek Church in the summer of 1786. In 1796 he moved to Campbell County, where he was ordained in September of that year by John Taylor and George Eve. Spencer, *Kentucky Baptists*, 1:295-96.

[48]*Sung* is a rare usage as the past tense of the transitive verb *sing*.

The Lord began to own this man's labours with his beginning to speak in public. A small church was soon raised where he lived.[49]

I was invited to baptize some people there. I think five were baptized at the time and among them an old man the name of Wilson, apparently far gone in a consumption. This became a great trial to my faith. I found [that] the old man could only speak a little above a whisper. And though he had been much of a singer and a prayerful man in his family, all had been laid aside perhaps for a twelvemonth for want of breath.

I had lately been reading Mr. [David] Rice's pamphlet on infant baptism,[50] where he had aver[r]ed that it was instant death to wet a man allover in the last stages of a consumption. If all this is true, thought I, which I did not know to the contrary, in this thing I had great perplexity.

This old man came foremost to the water. And I [was] almost ready to tremble with fear, but in we went. As quick as he recovered from the water, he raised his hands [and] with pretty strong voice cried, "Glory to God! Glory to God!"

The first thought I had was, "Old man, you are not yet killed."

A handsome, little revival of religion went on. This old gentleman's voice was so far restored that he resumed worship in his family and became a pleasant singer in public worship. And [he] lived after this for several years, so that wetting him allover did him no harm.

After my first year's pastorship at Clear [61]Creek, unhappiness began to make its appearance, and it lay very much in different views about discipline. We began with ruling elders according to the Virginia custom[51] and [Benjamin]

---

[49]The church that James Lee gathered was located on Silver Creek in Madison County. Spencer, *Kentucky Baptists*, 1:296.

[50]This tract by David Rice (1733–1816), a pioneer Presbyterian preacher in Kentucky, is titled *An Essay on Baptism*. Though written in Kentucky, it was published in Baltimore in 1789. Bishop, *The Church in Kentucky*, 113.

[51]The office of ruling elder was widely used among the early Regular and Separate Baptists of Virginia. When Morgan Edwards, a Philadelphia pastor, visited the Old Dominion in 1772 he discovered 34 Baptist churches there—13 Regular and 21 Separate. He recorded descriptive data for 8 of the Regular and for 15 of the Separate churches. All of the Regular churches and 73 percent of the Separate churches for which these data exist maintained the office of ruling elder. In 1806 one Kentucky church defined the duties of such an elder: to look after the "flock of God," to help members lead circumspect lives, to see that offenders are dealt with according to Christ's standard, and to promote unity and peace within the congregation. Edwards, *Materials*, 2:35-65; and Spencer, *Kentucky Baptists*, 1:485. (A distinction should be made between the terms elder and "ruling elder.")

Griffith's plan in the [Philadelphia] Confession of Faith.[52] Those men [ruling elders] were useful among us.[53] The emigrants from distant parts brought their former customs[54] with them, so that faction began in the church. We were now about a 150 in number, and the more the worse in case of confusion. We were often like the confused builders of Babel's Tower.[55]

James Dupuy[56] moved to Kentucky about this time. An old preacher, he became a member with us, so that we now had five ordained ministers in the church. Myself became very uneasy, for some, I found, considered the distinction of particular pastor a little more sacred than I had thought it to be. Each faction seemed displeased if I was not on their side of the question. Indeed some murmurs were heard that what partial influence I had in the church was not used to the best purposes. So that strong as the evidences were (in the beginning) of my pastorship['s] being of the Lord, I began strongly to doubt the propriety of its continuance.

About this time John and James Dupuy with a number of other brethren became a separate church, constituted on Buck Run, not distant from where now

---

[52]When the Philadelphia Asssociation adopted the Second London Confession, it requested two ministers to write an essay on discipline to be annexed to it. Benjamin Griffith, one of the two, responded with a treatise known as the "Discipline," his sources for which included the actions of the association regarding discipline, as well as the writings of four other Baptists. This "Discipline" spelled out how the doctrinal statement affected the relationship of the churches to the association. Lumpkin, *Confessions of Faith*, 349, 351-52; Robert G. Torbet *A History of the Baptists* (Philadelphia PA, 1950) 231-32.

[53]John Henderson Spencer, the principal Kentucky Baptist historian of the nineteenth century, differed with Taylor in this regard. Spencer saw the office of ruling elder as "wholly superfluous." *Kentucky Baptists*, 1:485-86.

[54]The nine Christian rites practiced by eighteenth-century Separate Baptists in Virginia have been listed above in the annotation. In 1772 Morgan Edwards recorded data concerning these rites for fifteen of the twenty-one Separate churches he found in that colony. The number of these ceremonies used per congregation averaged seven. *Materials*, 2:35-65.

[55]Genesis 11:1-9.

[56]James Dupuy (1744/5–1837) was an early member of the Cumberland (later the Powhatan) Church, which worshipped at the meetinghouse erected by his brother John. James and John were among an intimate group of seven converts who frequently met to encourage each other in their new faith. In time the seven became ministers. James followed his brother to Kentucky, going around 1788. He served as the first moderator of the Long Run Association. Spencer, *Kentucky Baptists*, 1:169-70.

Griers Creek Meetinghouse[57] stands. After a while faction tore out the bowels of this church, and it died a natural death.[58]

Factions did not yet die in Clear Creek, so that my former thoughts were brought to a point that yielding up my charge would be for the church's benefit, which I proposed to them at a suitable time. Though some of the church seemed alarmed and unwilling that I should do so, fearing that I would desert them. I assured them to the contrary that I hoped to render them the same service I had ever done, which so far pacified them that I gave up this sacred charge, after being under it about three years,[59] and [after I] had baptized among them about an hundred people. By this [62]act, my desires were by no means laxed[60] to serve the church to the best of my ability, but we were in a shocking pickle[61] as to coldness and barrenness. Faction and ill will had very much killed us, so that but few had been baptized for a long time.

But we were now calm and under a solemn pause. Two of our preachers were gone with the newly constituted church.[62] Only three now remained—James Rucker, Richard Cave, and myself. We had this to comfort us: We had now no heads and tails[63] among us—or in other words, we had no superiority and inferiority in the ministry. We were as equal match horses to lay our shoulders to the yoke at once. And I know not whether I was ever in better credit in the church than now. Those suspicions respecting my designs in the church became cured by this resignation act. We now met with the glow of affectionate brothers, longing to see another day of the Son of Man.[64] And blessed be God, we were not disappointed. There were some forebodings of the blessed work of the Lord [that] I am about to relate.

---

[57]In October 1802 the Griers Creek Church and thirty other congregations, all of which were located above the Kentucky River, formed the North District Association. The church on Griers Creek, in Woodford County, had been constituted during 1800–1802. Masters, *Kentucky Baptists*, 167.

[58]The first Buck Run Church was organized in October 1788 in Fayette (later Woodford) County but was dissolved within twelve years. Spencer, *Kentucky Baptists*, 1:166, 169, and 2:12, 15.

[59]Taylor's particular pastorship at Clear Creek began around March 1786 and ended around October 1788.

[60]The obsolete verb *lax* means *relax*.

[61]The word *pickle* is a colloquialism for *plight*.

[62]John and James Dupuy had entered into the original membership of the first Buck Run Church, of Woodford County.

[63]The idiom "heads or tails" here means "rank as to office" among the ministers.

[64]The term "Son of Man" seems to have been Jesus' favorite name by which he referred to himself. It derives from a prominent usage in the book of Ezekiel.

Soon after this resignation took place and we began to meet together in peace and love, our neighbors seemed to take [so much] pleasure in meeting with us that for several months our meetings were crowded by day or night. I found [that] this part of the Scripture bear[65] with great weight on my mind: "Lo these three years I come seeking fruit on this fig tree and find none."[66] Whatever the Saviour might have designed in this parable, I applied it to my neighbors, for it had been about three years from the close of our last revival.[67] As a dresser of the vineyard,[68] my soul often in tears cried, "Spare and save them, O Lord!"

Isaac Redding (brother of Joseph Redding, of whom I have said something elsewhere),[69] my near neighbor,[70] and a little before the work became obvious, came to and informed me with much assurance that God was about to revive His work among us. His confidence grew from a dream he [had] had and [from] its lasting effects upon his mind. Tears began to [63]flow while he narrated his dream.

He had lately dreamed that he was in Heaven. He supposed his vision continued several hours. He saw the Saviour in His glorified state. [He saw] the rewards of the just in that shining glory, which his eyes could barely behold. All his own language was with the most rapturous joy: "Wonderful! Wonderful!" Joel had said a great while ago that, as preludes to the greatest blessings on earth, "your young men should see visions, and your old men dream dreams."[71] However, in Redding's struggles to glorify God in Heaven, he waked himself [and] found he was lying on his back. And the profusion of tears which ran from his eyes and on each side of his face had so wet the pillow under his head as if [it had been] soaked in water.[72]

The first obvious effect that I now recollect was at my own house at a night meeting, perhaps in September [1788]. I remember [that] I had a hard job of

---

[65]The word *bear* is the phonetic spelling of the archaic past tense *bare* of the intransive verb *bear*.

[66]Luke 13:7.

[67]The first revival at Clear Creek had begun in March 1786 and lasted throughout most of the remainder of that year; therefore, from the close of that awakening until the outbreak of the next one in September 1788 only about two years had elapsed.

[68]Deuteronomy 28:39.

[69]A biography of Joseph Redding is found in John Taylor, *Thoughts on Missions*, 47-55.

[70]The area in Fayette County where Isaac Redding lived and paid taxes in 1789 became a part of Woodford County that year. Heineman, *"First Census" of Kentucky, 1790*, 79.

[71]Joel 2:28.

[72]The final clause of this sentence Taylor omits in his second edition.

work on hand in felling all the dead timber on a stubble field[73] and had employed a number of hands to assist me in that business. Among them was one Thomas Reese—esteemed the most hardened, bold sinner in the whole settlement. Towards the evening, it was my lot with Reese to be chopping down a very hard tree, one of us on each side. And sitting down a while to rest ourselves, I asked Reese what was to become of his soul hereafter. He was instantly struck with a serious look. He replied [that] he believed in a hereafter, and that he had a soul. And as to what would become of it, he had made a decision for several years past. That he was to be finally and forever lost. That in years past he had made some attempts to seek religion, but, finding it out of his reach, he had given it up forever. And his object long had been to take what pleasure he could while he was in this world, for that was all he should ever have. That he had no appetite to go to meetings. He, therefore, had declined that or prayer to God for many years. But in all this statement I found [that] he looked sorrowful, as if desperation was preying on his soul.

[64]I asked him to stay to meeting that night. And to oblige me—more than with appetite to do so—he consented. He expressed some gratitude for the freedom I had used with him, for his religious acquaintances had long given him up for the Devil.

That night the people came out to the amount of filling all the apartments of my little house. Whether from the absence of other preachers or what cause I misremember,[74] but it fell to my lot to speak to the people. The conversation with Reese led me to the text I took, which was "A certain creditor had two debtors. One owed five hundred pence and the other fifty. And when they had nothing to pay, he frankly forgave them both."[75]

By debts in this text I understood the sins of men, some of them of greater and some of less magnitude. That God, the Great Creditor, took notice of and remembered them all. That these debts could never be discharged by the poor, helpless debtor, however small the sum. That no man was able to discharge his account in God's book by his own services (seeing himself and all he could do belonging to God already), that [even] if he could do all that was commanded him in the Law. That God had taught him to say that he was an unprofitable servant. That no man knew or was sensible of this till God made him so. That in this case the poor, criminal debtor with agony of soul and contrition of heart

---

[73]On the frontier a common method of destroying the forest was to girdle the trees on a prospective planting area in order to prevent the growth of leaves. Girdling meant cutting away a strip of bark clean around the trunk of each tree. The resultant dead trees were removed after the first harvest of grain.

[74]The verb *misremember* is a dialecticism meaning *forget*.

[75]Luke 7:41-42.

acknowledged the truth of the case. That he had nothing to pay [with] and cried to God for mercy and forgiveness. And that the creditor God—in great grace, through the boundless merits of His Son, according to righteousness and truth—not only can but delights to abundantly pardon the greatest sinner of all Adam's race when they have nothing to pay [with]. So that none need to despair, however black or red as scarlet their crimes may be.

From the encouragement by the effect among the people I continued to speak much longer than was common, so that the candles all burnt out and no person moved to relight any. But the doors being all [65]open, through which and the windows, bright moonlight supplied the place of candles and seemed to heighten the solemnity of our devotion.

Reese had placed himself at some distance from where I stood. Or had he been near me, with the feelings of tenderness I then had for his salvation, I should have given him my hand with a cordial invitation to seek the Lord. I did call him by name—though I knew not where he sat—to come to the Lord with his mighty debt and receive forgiveness for all the sum.

Poor Reese became so far affected that he needed no more invitations to go to meetings but soon appeared to be a diligent seeker. About the middle of winter he obtained a hope and was baptized.

At our October [1788] meeting, I think, a few had obtained hope in the Lord and were baptized; at November meeting, a greater number. At our December meeting about ten were received on Saturday [the sixth].

That night—either through some indisposition of one of the children or some similar cause—I slept upstairs by myself. I awoke in the night with the most agonizing desire for the salvation of my neighbors that I perhaps ever felt in my life. I called up in my mind the situation of the people. It occurred to me—[that is], the diligence [that] we had been using in preaching for several months, day and night. I would try to pacify myself: "There is ten to be baptized tomorrow."

It would vibrate again through my soul, "But how many more are yet careless and yet in their sins!"

I would try to pacify myself with: "Oh Lord, what can I do for them?" My agony of mind became so increasing [that] I was constrained to leave my bed and walk the room. I would say to myself, "Oh Lord, I could die for them if that could do them any good."

I really was not able to account for this uncommon anguish of heart for the salvation of my neighbors. At length a Scripture occurred to me that I had never taken notice of before. It is in Acts 20[th] chap[ter] 20[th] verse, where Paul tells the elders at Ephesus, among other things, "I taught you publicly and [66]from house to house."[76] This fully accorded with the then feelings of my heart—to go from house to house, and [to] warn them to flee from the wrath to come,[77] and [to] pray the Lord to save their souls. Another thought sprang up in my mind: that when the Lord intended to bring the Hebrews from Egyptian bondage, he put it into the heart of Moses to visit his brethren as a prelude to their deliverance (Acts 7th chap[ter]).[78] This produced such confidence in my mind that the Lord would bless those visits to the people that I became bathed in joyful tears. And sleep departed from me the balance of the night.

A plan of those visits occurred to me in the following manner: There were three preachers in the church, as named before. There were also three ruling elders in the church, and each one so situated that he lived near to one of the preachers. Samuel Dedman,[79] one of the elders, lived central in the church and near to me. James Hiter[80] lived on one side and near to Richard Cave. John Whitaker lived on the other side and near to James Rucker. So that here were six men, making three couple[s]—a preacher and [an] elder—to go one after another to visit. Each couple [was] to go through the whole neighborhood.

But now arose with me one embarrassment: "Perhaps when I see my brethren, they will object to all my plans." If so, my reply was [to be], "I will go myself."

I set off early next day [Sunday the seventh] to meeting. I soon found that all the brethren in my arrangement were there. After calling them together and stating to them my own impressions of mind, I informed them of the plan I had in view [in order to see] if it met their approbation. Without a moment's hesitation they understood and accorded in it. And with joyful tears of brotherly love we were ready to embrace each other in our arms. I know not whether the disciples of the Day of Pentecost could have been more of one heart and one soul.[81] I proposed that with their approbation Brother Dedman and myself would take the first tour, which was cheerfully accorded [67]in.

This day we had a very crowded house for ten were to be baptized, and many of the people were much stirred up. When preaching ended I gave the following notice: "After a few minutes we will go to the water to baptize.

---

[76]Acts 20:20.

[77]Matthew 3:7.

[78]Verse 23.

[79]On 7 June 1788 Samuel Dedman and John Taylor represented the Clear Creek Church at the constituting of the Forks of Elkhorn Church. Darnell, *Forks of Elkhorn Church*, 19.

[80]James Hiter appears on the tax list of Fayette County dated May 1789. Heinemann, *"First Census" of Kentucky, 1790*, 46.

[81]Acts 2:46.

Meetings for the present week are to be at the following places." After which I informed the assembly that a number of us had agreed to visit every family in the neighborhood without regard to grade or quality. That the object of our visit was to pray and converse with each family and individual[82] on what belonged to the interest of their souls. That I desired a signal when we came to their houses. That where we were acceptable, they would lay aside their family business and prepare for the proposed worship. The other signal was to keep at their business when we came, and we would go about our own business, for that no family was to be interrupted but by their own choice. I remember [when] giving this last notice, the assembly seemed to be struck with a very solemn pause and [with] trembling[83] tears in a number.

Dedman and myself agreed to start on our tour next morning. A little after sunrise, a bitter[84] cold Monday morning [8 December 1788], Dedman was at my house to start on this holy campaign. Notwithstanding all my hopeful confidence before [and] my plans and propositions to my brethren (in which they had so cheerfully agreed), my mean, base heart began to hesitate, and [it] conferred with flesh and blood![85] My wife had been but a few days in childbed with my daughter Nancy[86] and was now poorly. My hogs were ready to kill and would admit of no delay. And above all, we should do more harm than good by offending the people we were about to force ourselves on. Unbelief has often been a masterpiece for me. I was ashamed to name any of those mental spasms to my partner, Brother Dedman.

After early breakfast we set out, but the Lord knows [that it was] with a heavy, fearful heart (as related to myself). But the ocular witnesses before my eyes soon removed [68]my gloom, for we seldom went to a house but we found the family in tears either of joy or grief. We had no exact, uniform mode when we came to a house. Sometimes one of us would strike some well-known song pertinent to the occasion, when the part of the family that could [do so] would join us, after which we would go into exhortation or examination.[87] At other times when we found chief of the young people in the family in tears when we came (which was often the case), we would take them by the hand and say, "Son (or daughter), why weepst thou?"[88] Which would lead on to the family

---

[82]Taylor deletes the remainder of this sentence in his second edition.

[83]This word is omitted in the second edition.

[84]The adverb *bitter* intensifies the adjective *cold*.

[85]Galatians 1:16.

[86]This first daughter of the John Taylors, Nancy, was born on Sunday 14 December 1788. Dorothy Thompson, "John Taylor of the Ten Churches," 570.

[87]The words "or examination" do not appear in the second edition.

[88]The question "Why weepest thou?" is an archaic expression that contains the present

examination. First [*sic*], our general custom was [for] both of us to pray just before we left the family.[89]

It would often be the case [that] when we left a family a number of them would go with us to the next house, and so on till at times we would have a kind of worshiping congregation as we moved along. But this would be mostly in the afterpart of the day.

We seldom used any food from morning till night. Neither the people or ourselves thought of that. We had a meat to eat such as the Saviour spoke of at the well when he pointed the disciples to the fields white already to harvest —when he saw the people from the city of Sychar flocking in great numbers to see and hear him preach.[90]

We went to but one or two places but the families received us cordially. But in those few instances we were not allowed to leave the place without reproach.

Among others, we visited the family of Tho[ma]s Reese, that I have spoken of before. I did not recollect of ever seeing Mrs. Reese before, but it seemed [that] the Lord had done His work with her before we got there. So far as a consciousness of guilt went, we found her overwhelmed in tears and sorrow. This we often found at other places. But Mrs. Reese was so suddenly driven to the borders of desperation that I feared from her talk [that] she might commit some personal violence on herself, which led me afterwards to frequently visit the family, for both she [69]and her husband seemed under deep anguish of soul.

In the course of these [home] visits we commonly held about two night meetings in the week, but no house in the settlement would hold the people. We had recourse in some instances to fires in the yards to keep the people from freezing. In getting to those meetings in time, in a few instances we passed by houses without calling. This led a number [of people] to conclude [that] there was no mercy for them, and that God had passed them by or the visitors would have called on them. Several experiences of this cast were told to the church.

Our tour of visiting continued about two weeks. I think [that] Richard Cave's was about the last house we went to. I remember his wife[91] asked me how the people seemed affected in our tour. My answer was [that] I thought [that] I had

---

tense, indicative mood, second person, singular of the intransitive verb *weep*, and the poetic form of the personal pronoun *you*, nominative, second person, singular.

[89]Taylor's idea of pastoral visitation agrees with that of Elder William Vaughan (1785–1876), who decades later visited in the homes of people in order to communicate the gospel to them and not to engage in idle gossip. Thomas M. Vaughan, *Wm. Vaughan*, 249-50.

[90]John 4:30, 34-35.

[91]Mrs. Richard Cave was the former Elizabeth Craig, a sister of Lewis Craig and his brothers. Spencer, *Kentucky Baptists*, 2:23.

seen five hundred people under conviction. I suppose we visited upwards of a hundred families.

Immediately after our tour was out, the other visitors proceeded with about the same length of time. About six weeks were spent in this profitable work. I call it profitable because about fifty experiences were told to the church from these visits. Indeed myself had become so foolish that I fancied [that] we had found out a plan that [by which] we could at least be lively in religion, when we pleased, by the visiting plan. But the trial of the same thing and in the same place a few years afterwards convinced me of my folly.

We found it needful to baptize twice in a month. There were several times we baptized near thirty at a time. Sometimes two of us went into the water at once to baptize. And to prevent confusion only one pronounced the ceremony[92] and that by the plural term. Standing near together and both [preachers] getting ready, one would pronounce, "We baptize you in the name of the Father," etc. I once baptized twenty-six myself on a cold, freezing day—the ice cut about six inches thick where the people stood close on the edge of the icy grave.[93] And though my clothes froze [*sic*] before I got on dry ones, I know [that] I speak safely [170]when I say [that] I suffered no inconvenience. And tho' this may be attributed to enthusiasm, I know not why enthusiasm may not be used in religion as [it is in] any other laudable work.

This revival continued seven or eight months and through a very severe winter [1788–1789]. About an 150 were added to Clear Creek Church,[94] which brought her number to upwards of 300. She was now the most numerous church in Elkhorn Association and continued so for many years.

We will notice a few particulars in this revival, [such] as the conversion of Reese and his wife. We left them in the time of our visits under great sensations of guilt. Mrs. Reese was first delivered and came to the church to relate her hope in Christ. I have often thought and sometimes said that if any experience I ever heard related exceeded all others it was Mrs. Reese's, if we take in the solemnity of her looks, the meekness of her spirit, her mighty temptations to infidelity and to discard the Scriptures, [and] the labour of her mind under those temptations (God's method of using the medium). She was tempted to disbelieve: first, as the instrument of her just condemnation; and secondly, in her relief by opening up

---

[92]Here the noun *ceremony* is a metonym meaning "the formula or the set form of words pronounced before the act of baptizing."

[93]John Leland, a minister who was a contemporary of John Taylor in Virginia, wrote about wintry baptizing: "I have seen ice cut more than a foot thick, and people baptized in the water, and yet I have never heard of any person taking cold, or any kind of sickness, in so doing." *The Virginia Chronicle* (Fredericksburg VA, 1790), 36.

[94]The converts of this revival numbered 164. Spencer, *Kentucky Baptists*, 2:61.

the plan of salvation through the Saviour [and by holding to] the pertinence of gospel promises to her particular case. The church had no need to ask her one question, except [about] her willingness now to be baptized. To which she meekly replied that her companion had been long under distress, she hoped for his relief, and therefore she was inclined to wait and be baptized with him.

But some zealot in the church answered, "Why tarryest thou?"[95] It may be of service to him." To which she yielded.

His consent being asked, the next day she was baptized. He, being present, was thrown into monstrous temptations. The roads were almost impassable at that time with mud. Reese and his wife had both rode[96] on one horse and had a child to carry. He being naturally a rugged man, he concluded [that] his wife [had] disregarded him and therefore had left [711]him and joined the Baptists, and they were all hypocrites together.

What added to his calamity [was that] he had a great bundle of wet clothes to carry home. This aggravated his rage. At length his wife having to get down to attend to the child, he broke out and declared [that], for the offence she had committed in leaving him, he would never live with her another day. [He] dashed down the bundle of clothes in the mud, and off he went as fast as his horse could go, leaving her the child to carry and the bundle of clothes to tug on as she could. From his own account, he rode on perhaps a half mile and stopped to reflect on what he had done. When he was so struck with a fresh sense of his guilt, [he concluded] that for him there could be no pardon. And being so far beside himself, he never thought of going back to relieve his wife. He took hold of the pummel [sic] of his saddle and began to roar out with all his might like a mad man till his wife came up. When he was ready to ask her a thousand pardons, [he] hoped she would forgive him. [He] left his horse, dropped on his knees in the mud, and entreated his wife to pray to the Lord for him.

Abundance of people, we hoped, had found the Lord, and many were yet under deep distress. At the water Isaac Redding came to me with smiling solemnity and said, "We shall hear of more conversions this week than we have yet known."

That day when meeting closed I made a curious appointment for a meeting about the middle of the week, for which I much reflected on myself afterwards. I named to the people [that] as there were many mourners[97] in the neighborhood and [as] we were directed to weep with them that weep,[98] I would appoint a day

[95]The expression "Why tarryest thou?" is an archaism that includes the present tense, indicative mood, second person, singular of the intransitive verb *tarry*.

[96]In this usage *rode* is the archaic past participle of the verb *ride.*

[97]Taylor means that there were many people distressed about their sins.

[98]Romans 12:15.

of mourning and fasting. And as "Long" George Dale and his wife[99] had been a considerable time labouring under great trouble, we would appoint his as the house of mourning. I also desired no person to come to the meeting but those who [had] abstained from food on that day.

I afterwards reflected how presuming I had been in such an appointment. I had not consulted [72]Mr. Dale about a meeting at his house nor counseled with any other person about such a meeting. So that for my own forwardness I began to mourn before this day of mourning came. I concluded that I deserved contempt and for no person to meet me when the day came.

When I got to the place I supposed [that] there were five hundred people, where I soon heard of about twelve persons obtaining hope in the Lord since last Sunday. And Thomas Reese was one of them, who was there himself. And [he] looked and conversed as the man did out of whom a legion of devils had been cast, when clothed and sitting at the Saviour's feet in his right mind.[100] Thus Isaac Redding's prophecy was fulfilled by such a number obtaining relief from the Lord within three or four days. And many more seemed [to be] not far from the kingdom of God.

Poor Dale and his wife were yet mourning. I took a text from the 51st Psalm: "Make me to hear joy and gladness, that the bones that Thou hast broken may rejoice."[101]

Another conversion a little singular in this revival was [that of] Charles Webb. This was an orphan lad, or the son of a widow who lived with his mother. This lad's conviction was long and pungent. His countenance bore the aspect of horror and desparation, and his conversation[102] was of the same cast. He had been so tempted with unbelief that it was long before he could be confident in his best evidences of eternal life. He had been made so sensible of his own helpless condition that he came out a strong predestinarian[103] at once, yet [he] doubted much whether such a wretch as himself could be a true believer. I remember when he related his experience to the church. He was asked whether he ever saw into the duty of baptism.

His reply was that he did not know that he ever had. He supposed he had not, but he had thought of it. He had thought that believers ought to be baptized

[99]Elizabeth Dale, the wife of George Dale, died in Woodford County on 31 May 1831. *Baptist Chronicle* 2 (June 1831): 96.

[100]Luke 8:30, 35.

[101]Verse 8.

[102]Here Taylor uses the archaic noun *conversation*, which means *behavior*.

[103]A predestinarian holds that God foreordained that certain souls would be saved and others would be lost; or that, on a wider scale, God determined beforehand everything that would happen.

because Jesus Christ was baptized in the River Jordan and had directed his disciples to follow Him. And he had further thought that it [73]was a wise thing in God in sending John the Baptist beforehand and [to] be here ready, by which Christ fulfilled that part of righteousness. But he could not say that he ever saw into it. And thus in all his religious exercises he would scruple their reality. But with all his doubts he was received by the church with great cheerfulness and fellowship.

I had once by the improper construction of a Scripture made this poor lad fast three days. At a night meeting I had taken a text in the chapter where Cornelius sent for Peter. And in that part "Four days ago I was fasting,"[104] I unwittingly construed into a four days' fast. I remarked that many of them seemed under great trouble and conviction, and then asked who of them like Cornelius had fasted four days. This lad had been long trying every method he could think of [in order] to obtain conversion, but all having failed. [He] became encouraged by this new project, hoping [that] at the end of four days' fast he should obtain the blessing of the Lord. And at it he went with great resolution. He continued three days without food and perhaps drink, following his daily labour. When his tender and religious mother became so alarmed for her son, [thinking] that he now intended to starve himself to death (for he had before been almost beside himself with soul distress), she put at[105] him with tears and importunities that for her sake and the Lord's sake to desist from his own destruction. Poor Charles was thus prevailed on to break his vow before the fourth day was out. This perhaps was the last gasp that legal hope drew in him.

The poor boy now became more distracted than ever. He had now lied to God. And what was that but the unpardonable sin?[106] This late act with the mighty swarm of corruption through his whole soul led him to think that he was fit for nothing but Hell, and [that] there was no mercy for him. But to him a better way was soon revealed: that it is not by keeping of vows that the inestimable blessing of the pardon of sin comes, but by the precious blood of the [74]Lamb of God is guilt removed.

Perhaps at the time of Charles Webb's baptism but few thought [that] he ever would become a preacher. And for several years he did not open his mouth in the Lord's name that way. But the religious world now says that the Lord has made Charles Webb a good gospel preacher and that he preaches by example as

---

[104]Acts 10:30.

[105]The provincial term "put at" means "chatter persistently."

[106]In the Reformed tradition, of which Baptists have partaken so freely, the unpardonable sin is seen as one's opposition to the Holy Spirit's revelation of God's glory and grace as shown in the life and death of Jesus Christ. Berkhof, *Systematic Theology*, 3rd ed., 253.

well as by precept. He now lives on his own land in Harrison County,[107] has become grey-headed in the service of his Divine Master, and for many years has served one or more churches in a pastoral capacity.

Martin Utterback[108] was baptized in this revival, and has come forward into the vineyard of the Lord, and labours with success in the ministry of the gospel. And though his style of preaching may not be so pleasing to the nice-tasted gentry of our base world, yet it is in that godly simplicity that [he] renders service to the generation in which he lives. He travels much with Warren Cash, preaching to their fellow men in the lower parts of the state of Kentucky.

I had once thought [that] if all the people on the earth could be Christians we should have a paradise here. But the circumstance of Clear Creek Church soon after this great revival is one item in the scale against this opinion, for the people were chiefly all religious now in the neighborhood. A circle from a center of three miles would now take in chiefly all the members of Clear Creek Church, which were upwards of three hundred in number.[109] The term of *brother* with everybody you met with became such a commonplace appellation that it in a manner lost its sacred quality. Human nature is of that base quality that it will not bear to huddle much of it together. We, therefore, soon found great difficulties in the church—by personal bickerings among the members, and for very trifling things quarrels were stirred up, and the sacred epithet[110] of *brother* [was] scandalized[111] while a man would use it when in bad temper. Two men can scarcely quarrel but others will take sides somewhere. [75]This produces faction and much destroys the peace of the church of Christ. These things not only made their appearance but sprang up in the church at Clear Creek. Accusations in the church became very common and [were made] for very trivial things.

Another thing which often awakened great excitement in Clear Creek Church was expelling their members by a majority of voices when a complaint was brought in, and especially when the case was somewhat doubtful. One side would

---

[107]The establishment of Harrison County was authorized by a 1793 Kentucky law.

[108]Born in Virginia about 1770, Martin Utterback was ordained as a minister around 1807 by the Bethel Church in Hardin County, Kentucky. Beginning in 1818, he served churches in Grayson County, Kentucky. He moved in 1835 to Richland County, Illinois, where he spent the remainder of his days. Spencer, *Kentucky Baptists*, 2:61; C. P. Cawthorn and Norman L. Warnell, *Pioneer Baptist Church Records of South-Central Kentucky and the Upper Cumberland of Tennessee, 1799–1899* ([Brownsville KY], 1985),359.

[109]In 1790 the membership at Clear Creek numbered 308. Asplund, *Universal Register*, 1790–1794, 34.

[110]Here *epithet* is an obsolete noun meaning *term* or *phrase*.

[111]The verb *scandalize* is here a rare usage meaning *defame*.

conclude, "If we do not exert ourselves a guilty man will be continued in the church."

The opposite side would think, "If we do not strive hard, an innocent man will be condemned."

So that we seldom had a trial of that kind but it was with great warmth of temper and, after all, but a cross-and-pile chance[112] as to the equity of the decision. Nothing is more rational than [the idea that] the way [by which] a man comes into the church [is the way by which] he should go out. Yet privileges may be curtailed by suspension through a majority of voices, while the member is yet retained under the admonition of the church (2d Thes[salonians] 3[d] chap[ter] 14[th] and 15[th] verses).

I know one of the most respectable members in Clear Creek Church [who was] improperly expelled by this majority plan. I suppose the free male members[113] at this time in the church was about 100. Perhaps 60 or 70 acted in this case. The case being a very doubtful subject, only 20 voted—10 on each side. One 10 voted for his guilt and expulsion; the other 10 voted him innocent. The moderator gave the casting vote against him, and the worthy deacon was thus slam[m]ed off[114] by this majority plan. The excluded man attended meetings as usual and with great calmness took his distance for a year or two, when the church reinvestigated the subject and unanimously voted the former decision wrong. And the deacon again took his seat by the invitation of the church without asking any questions.

Another instance of five or six complaints being brought into [76]the church [was] against one of the leading members about land claims. Only three members voted in this case—two against the member and one for him. One of the two rose up and insisted that, according to the rules of the church, he was expelled; and [he] demanded the record to be made. But the church would not admit this vote to stand and by a great majority in a second vote cleared the accused man.

This with several other similar cases convinced me of the majority plan of exclusion that it was improper, though myself had been a principal instrument to get it established in Clear Creek Church, then thinking that on any other plan we could never get clear of the bad people. But after [I altered] my conviction on that head, I could never get a change of the rule in the church, and perhaps Clear Creek uses this destructive rule to this day. Shall [the rights of] a religious man, whose privileges in a church are dearer to him than all other rights on earth, be

---

[112]."Cross and pile" is an archaism meaning "the obverse and reverse of a coin." Taylor's wording indicates "pure chance such as comes by the toss of a piece of money."

[113]In those days the governance of the congregation was exercised by the white, male members only.

[114]The term "slam off" is a colloquialism meaning "belittle severely."

all lost at once as by the toss of a penny? For twenty-seven years I have lived in the enjoyment of a more excellent way—that of final expulsion by a unanimity of voices, and by which we fairly get rid of all who ought to go out of the church. (See Buck Run rules of decorum.)[115]

A number of conspiring circumstances induced me now to think of moving from Clear Creek—as, first, the increase of my family. Though I had become possessed of about fifteen hundred acres of land in that neighborhood in early times, I had whittled it all off to one friend and another[116] to about four hundred —the farm on which I lived.[117] I now had four children and a prospect of more.[118] An opening offered on the Ohio River near the mouth of the Great Miami, now Boone County.[119] I purchased in different tracts near three thousand acres of land.[120] Here was aplenty[121] of soil for all the children I was like[122] to have. This was an almost entire unsettled country and much exposed to Indian danger.[123] This was of but small moment with me from the great propensity I had

[115]Pages 141-42, first edition.

[116]Purchasers of Taylor's land on Clear Creek included James Howard, John Arnold, Harris Hicks, John Rucker, William Christopher, Peter Bryant, Lewis Castleman, and Peyton Short. Woodford County (KY) Deed Book B, 211-15, 285; Deed Book C-1, 6-7, 232-34; Deed Book C-2 (Office of the County Clerk, Versailles), 419-21, 433-35; Deed Book E, 342-44; and Deed Book M, 371.

[117]On 4 December 1792 Taylor turned in his list of taxables, including four hundred acres of land. Woodford County (KY) Tax List, 1792, 15.

[118]The fifth child was born in Campbell (now Boone) County two months after the Taylors arrived there. Dorothy Thompson, "Ancestors and Descendants," 40.

[119]The region where Taylor purchased land on the Ohio River was then a part of Campbell County, Kentucky. Boone County was established with the opening of the county court on 17 June 1799. Boone County (KY) Court Order Book A (Office of the County Clerk, Burlington), 1. The Great Miami River empties into the Ohio in the present-day state by that name.

[120]Before the division of this land with John Tanner, it can be identified approximately as follows: 2,000 acres from John David Woolper; 620, Humphrey Marshall; and 300, James Garrard. Woodford County (KY) Deed Book A, 259-62; Campbell County (KY) Deed Book A (Office of the County Clerk, Alexandria), 117-51; and Joseph Taylor, Interview by [Shane], Draper MSS., 11CC230.

[121]The noun *aplenty* is a colloquialism (used chiefly in the United States) meaning "an abundance."

[122]Here the word *like* is a colloquial adverb meaning *likely*.

[123]The victory of General Anthony Wayne (1745-1796) over the Ohio Indians at the Battle of Fallen Timbers on the Maumee River in 1794 and his success in extracting the Treaty of Greenville from them the following year ended red incursions into Kentucky from the north.

to [77]live in a new country.[124] Where I lived in Woodford County was now thick settled, and but little cow range. A number of my religious neighbors were also desirous to move to the Ohio. All this well suited my then appetite, having this view that we could have a church there at once.

But another very prevailing reason with myself in leaving Clear Creek was [the fact that] a very respectable individual had withdrawn his membership from the church on my account. Delicacy itself will forbid going into a minute detail of all this business. I had brought money to purchase land for him in Kentucky. When he saw the land, he became displeased with the mode of the appropriation of his money. We left it to men as arbitrators. With their decision he was displeased. A very influential character[125] from another church prevailed on him to bring a complaint into Clear Creek, to which the church agreed by sending for helps from other churches.

The first decision of the church was unfavorable to the justness of my course with the offended man. On this result I stopped preaching a month or two. This gave great consternation to chief of the members of the church, [who were] not considering that their decision extended thus far. The fact was [that] they scarcely knew what they had decided on, for they were hurried into it by foreign[126] agents. I was ready to confess that in some things I had failed with the complaining man in point of generosity, but in point of justice I had never thought I had failed. The church, however, hasted[127] to the same churches for helps to reconsider what they had done.

The second decision of the church gave the offended man such dissatisfaction that he immediately withdrew from the church. All this was [taking place] while I had the pastoral care and of course [happened] before the last revival of religion I have been speaking of. And it may look strange that though several of his family were baptized in the time of the revival. His wife [was] a member. And I often had meetings at his house. He yet kept his distance from the church.

[78]All of which in process of time proved a painful spur to me to leave the place. I sold my land and made arrangements to move. Many of the brethren seemed much afflicted at my removal. But none of them all manifested such rational concern at my removal as [did] the man who was partly the instrument

---

[124]John Taylor was in every respect a frontiersman. "New country" is another of his terms for *frontier*

[125]The noun *character* is here a colloquial usage indicating an "odd or noteworthy person."

[126]Here the adjective *foreign* is an obsoletism meaning "not pertaining to one's congregation."

[127]*Hasted* is the past tense of the rare verb *haste*, which means *hasten*.

of my leaving Clear Creek. And though all this may look strange, it is the truth of the case.

Sometime before I moved he sent for me to come to his house, when he reasoned with me thus, "Many of your friends seem unwilling that you should move away, but as your land is sold they ought to remember that you cannot stay without a home." And then [he] proposed [to resell to me the] land that he had received from myself (which had risen in value at least double) on the same terms he had gotten it from me. And if it did not suit me to pay him the money (as I had laid out a good deal for land on the Ohio), he would take it [the land on the Ohio] on the [same] terms I had purchased [it] at, though the land lay about a hundred miles from him. This kindness I am bound to remember with gratitude till I die.

Things had been carried too far as to my removal to accept of his kind offer. And in the spring [of] 1795 I moved to the Ohio River, and near eleven years after I had settled on Clear Creek.

When I left the church they were well furnished with preachers, as James Rucker, Richard Cave, John Sutton, Donald Holmes, and a number of exhorters and prayerful men in public, so that it seemed I could be very well spared from that place.

John Tanner[128] had also lately moved into the neighborhood. [He was] much of a preacher but not a man of the most peaceable cast. Tanner had married [James] Rucker's daughter.[129] And [Tanner] soon stirred him [Rucker] up to think that the Baptists in Kentucky were too corrupt in doctrine and discipline [for them] to continue any longer in union with them. They, therefore, contemplated a new, pure, and separate church. John Penny, a respectable minister, had lately moved from Virginia and settled on Salt River south of [the] Kentucky [River].[130] These men prevailed on Penny to go into [79]this new church state with them.

---

[128]John Tanner (1732–1813), probably a native of North Carolina, served at least two churches in that colony. There he was shot through the thigh by an irate husband whose wife the preacher had baptized. For a short while in 1773 Tanner was imprisoned in Chesterfield County, Virginia, for preaching without a license. He moved to Kentucky around 1784 and settled in Woodford County near the Clear Creek Church about seven years later. Semple, *Baptists in Virginia*, rev. ed., 271n.; Spencer, *Kentucky Baptists*, 1:96-100; and Little, *Imprisoned Preachers*, 335-36.

[129]Sally Rucker and John Tanner were united in matrimony by John Taylor in July 1792. The groom was age 60; the bride, only 16. Railey, *Woodford County*, 327; and Joseph Taylor, Interview by [John D. Shane], Draper MSS., 11CC230.

[130]John Penny (1764?–1833) migrated from Virginia to Kentucky around 1790 and settled in the region that is now Anderson County. He served several congregations in the Bluegrass State, including the Salt River Church and the Salt River Reformed Baptist Church. Spencer, *Kentucky Baptists*, 1:370-73.

They constituted a church on Salt River under the appellation of "Baptist Reformed."[131] There were about ten members in this new church, and three of them ordained ministers. Their plan was to receive no member in this new, pure church but by experience and good character. A letter of dismission from any other church was with them only so much for nothing. But they had not progressed long before Penny began to think he had a hard bargain, though they had made him pastor of the new church. For pure as they were, they soon fell out among themselves. And this new fabric fell like Jonah's goard [sic].[132] Penny called for helps from neighboring churches and constituted what is now Salt River Church[133] and has continued a member thereof ever since. Tanner moved to Shelby County.

Rucker returned his membership to Clear Creek [Church]. But whether the confidence of his brethren became impaired or he lost confidence in himself after this Salt River enterprise, I cannot say, but his usefulness in Clear Creek was not so sensibly known afterwards. He moved to the lower end of this state and is yet living [as] a very old and respectable man.

John Sutton, who was now old, became what they called "a mighty scolder" in the church. Perhaps he was a Welchman, and high temper the more congenial to him thereby; but so it was, great as his preaching talents were. For in rich expositions from the Scriptures he had few equals, yet he scolded himself out of credit in the church. He was a principal leader in the emancipating question and became so turbulent that some of the members [were] treating with him in the church.[134]

Carter Tarrant,[135] who was of the same opinion with Sutton in emancipation,

---

[131]The Salt River Reformed Baptist Church, located in present-day Anderson County, existed for only two years after its founding around 1796. Ibid., 1:100-101, 425. The name "Reformed Baptist" as used here should be distinguished from the same name used two decades later by some congregations founded under the aegis of Alexander Campbell.

[132]Jonah 4:7.

[133]The Salt River Church was organized in 1798 as a Regular Baptist congregation. It was located on the north side of the stream for which it was named. In 1840 it affiliated itself with the Particular Baptists. Spencer, *Kentucky Baptists*, 1:368-70.

[134]By his vigorous opposition to slavery, John Sutton verbally abused some of the men of the Clear Creek Church. As a result, he was arraigned before the congregation. Ibid., 1:189.

[135]Carter Tarrant (1765–1816), a native of Virginia, was one of the organizers of the Green River Association, in 1800. Shortly thereafter he moved to Woodford County. After the War of 1812 ended, he served as an army chaplain in Louisiana during 1815–1816. Ibid.; Hugh P. Williamson, "A Chaplain [Carter Tarrant] in the War of 1812," *Daughters of the American Revolution Magazine* 91 (Sept 1957): 1038-40, 1114; and Charles Tarrants, "Carter Tarrant (1765–1816), Baptist and Emancipationist," *Register of the*

espoused his cause in the church, and by which a rent took place both in Clear Creek and Hillsboro[136] churches. A number of members uniting with Tarrant formed New Hope Church, where Sutton and Tarrant set up the first emancipating church in this part of the world.[137] Thus Clear Creek lost [80]John Sutton. He became blind but continued to travel and preach and died about eighty years of age.

Mr. Tarrant, [who] traveled and preached in Kentucky with great acceptance, had alternately served the churches at Clear Creek and Hillsboro. After his connection with the emancipators, he became reduced in his worldly circumstances, took a chapl[a]in's place in the army, went to New Orleans to fulfill his commission, and there he died.

[Donald] Holmes had also gone off with the emancipators, so that Richard Cave only was left at Clear Creek. But other visitors often attended.

In the Great Revival in Kentucky about the close of the last century,[138] Clear Creek greatly partook of this blessing, so that the church grew up to about five hundred members.[139] A principal instrument in this Great Revival was Richard Cave.[140]

For several years Clear Creek had kept up two places of worship at different meetinghouses.[141] They now contemplated a division. Hillsboro Church was constituted with perhaps a hundred and fifty members at the beginning.[142] Hillsboro

*Kentucky Historical Society* 88 (Spring 1990): 121-47.

[136]The Hillsboro Church, organized in 1802, was received into the Elkhorn Association that year. Elkhorn Association, "Minutes," 14 Aug 1802, in Sweet, *Baptists*, 1:492.

[137]Constituted in 1806, the New Hope Church soon built a two-story, brick meetinghouse measuring twenty-eight by thirty-six feet. Tarrant, *Kentucky Friends to Humanity*, 12, 12n.

[138]The Kentucky phase of the Great Revival took place during 1800–1803. *Encyclopedia of Southern Baptists*, 2:1162. For the story of this movement in six southern states, see John B. Boles, *The Great Revival, 1787–1805: The Origins of the Southern Evangelical Mind* (Lexington KY, 1972). For an early account of the Great Revival among the Baptists in Kentucky, see Spencer, *Kentucky Baptists*, 1:535-54.

[139]In 1799 the Clear Creek Church had 218 members; in two years the membership had grown to 558. Elkhorn Association, "Minutes," in Sweet, American *Frontier*, 1:481, 487.

[140]Since Taylor's departure from Clear Creek, Richard Cave had been the principal preacher for that church. Ibid., 1:466-90 passim.

[141]The second place of worship was situated at Hillsboro, also in Woodford County. In Kentucky today this second place would be called a mission; in Virginia in the 1770s it would have been known as a branch.

[142]When the Hillsboro Church first reported to the Elkhorn Association in 1802, it had a membership of 172. Elkhorn Association, "Minutes," in Sweet, *American Frontier*,

Church has been attended by different preachers, but by none of equal advantage as that laborious servant of the Lord [named] Edmund Waller.[143] Under his ministrations they have had several happy revivals, and [it] is now a growing, prosperous church.

But old Clear Creek has for many years seemed to be on the decline, though perhaps no place in Kentucky has been better supplied as to preaching talents. Mr. Jacob Creath, [Sr.], served them statedly for many years, in which time they were rich enough to build them[144] a large, brick meetinghouse. But they have found that the best of riches does not consist of a fine house. Mr. Henry Toler[145] for several years past has served them as a pastor, but things have not worked quite so well as was hoped for in the beginning. He has lately left them, and in a manner destitute. They have only one young preacher among them, and though he is a member there, he has not been ordained.

May this [81]old mother church pray the Lord of the harvest to send forth labourers.[146] They have yet a number of valuable members. And I was pleased not long since, among them to discover such a cry as this, "Lord, revive us!"

[147]The time when this cry was heard at Clear Creek was about Christmas 1821 and about four months after Mr. Toler had left them. Soon after this circumstance, a respectable brother informed me that the Clear Creek Church in her present destitute situation, he much feared, would lose her constitution or cease to continue as a church, for that he expected a number of the members would follow Mr. Toler. At this news I was much afflicted in mind. Perhaps I felt as

---

1:492.

[143]Edmund Waller (1775–1842), a native of Spotsylvania County, Virginia, was the son of William E. Waller, a pioneer Baptist preacher who moved in 1781 to Lincoln (later Garrard) County, Kentucky. Edmund was licensed to preach in 1802 and was ordained a few years later. With exceeding pastoral skill, he served several congregations in central Kentucky, including the Hillsboro Church, to which he was called in 1808. Spencer, *Kentucky Baptists*, 1:373-75.

[144]Here the pronoun *them* is the archaic, reflexive form for *themselves*.

[145]Henry Toler (d. 1824), a native of King and Queen County, Virginia, was educated for about three years at the academy of Samuel Jones, a Baptist minister in Lower Dublin, Pennsylvania, and was supported there mainly by Robert Carter III, of Westmoreland County, Virginia. Toler founded a church at Nomini in that county in 1786. During 1787–1795 its membership rose from 73 to 408. At the close of his some-twenty-year tenure with this congregation, the communicants numbered 875. Around 1816 he moved to Woodford County, Kentucky, where, strange to say, a lack of success attended the final years of his life. Semple, *Baptists in Virginia*, rev. ed., 175-76; Spencer, *Kentucky Baptists*, 2:26-28. See also James B. Taylor, *Virginia Baptist Ministers*, 2d ed., 264-69.

[146]Luke 10:2.

Nehemiah did in his first chapter[147] when the report came to him in Babylon of the distressed state of the Jews in Jerusalem. But the same barrier lay in my way that had done twenty-seven years back when I left Clear Creek, which had prevented my visiting that place for many years.

By apparent accident at Christmas on a visit with my wife to some friends in Woodford [County],[148] I had appointed a night meeting at Col[onel Jechonias] Singleton's, very near to Clear Creek Meetinghouse.[149] At the Christmas named above, Brother Edmund Waller, who had long served the church at Hillsboro and who had been much concerned for the state of Clear Creek Church, hearing of my [148]meeting, came to it.

Perhaps about thirty people attended, and chief of them [were] of the younger class. Our exhortations and prayers among them that night seemed to so arrest the attention of the youth that after meeting broke, Brother Waller so expressed the tenderness of his feelings: that he hoped the Lord would revive His work in that place. Brother L[ewis] Sullivan[150] tarried some time conversing on the longing desire of his heart for the Lord to revive His work among the rising generation, for that but few of them now professed religion in the whole settlement. His invitations were warm to repeat our visits.

A few nights after, I had a meeting at Brother J[ohn] Graves['s].[151] And though the weather was severely cold, the house was crowded with people, who gave great attention to the Word. When we set out for home next morning, Sister [Hannah] Graves[152] grasped my hand with great seriousness, intreating me to pray to the Lord for herself and children. This affected me much, with this resolve: That if the Lord would, I would soon visit the place again. The request of this

[147]Verse 3.

[148]At the time of this meeting Taylor had been living in adjacent Franklin County for six years.

[149]During the War of 1812, Singleton was promoted to the rank of colonel. He lived in 1821 about three miles from Versailles, his house being "across the pike" from the meetinghouse of the Clear Creek Church. Dorothy Thompson, "Day of Controversy," 230-31.

[150]Lewis Sullivan was serving as a trustee of the Clear Creek Church in 1815, when the church land was deeded to the congregation. Edna Wilson McAdams, comp., *Kentucky Pioneer and Court Records* (Lexington KY, 1929), 177.

[151]John Graves (1768–1824) grew up in a family of twelve children in Culpeper County, Virginia. His first marriage was to Hannah Cave. His second wife was Elizabeth Eve Graves, the widow of his brother Stephen. Darnell, *Forks of Elkhorn Church*, 155.

[152]Hannah Cave Graves (d. 1822) was one of five children who graced the home of Richard Cave and Elizabeth Craig. Benjamin Cave, her grandfather, was an emigrant from England who had settled in Orange County, Virginia. Ibid., 81.

sister followed me almost continually day and night with an uncommon awakening of prayer in my heart.

A few weeks after this, I had a peculiar dream. I had went[153] to a church meeting at the North Fork of Elkhorn [Church[154] on] the third Saturday of January[155] [1822]. [It was] very cold weather. I stayed all night at a Brother Sinclair's. [I] slept in a small, upper room when I dreamed I was fishing with another man in very clear water about middle-deep. We saw a number of large fish which we endeavored to take with a gig. Though they seemed gentle we caught none of them. A number of small fish began to skip out of the water and, using their fins as wings, came flying over our heads in abundance. When we became anxious to catch some of those very small fish, striking at them with my hat, I only caught one of them. The fins of this little captive looked the colour[156] of silver and, while fluttering, being entangled in the lining of my hat.

I awoke. [149]Being very drowsy, I turned over and soon dropt to sleep and as soon got to fishing again, and several others with me. Being very intent on success, we came to a water wherein was a vast number of very large fish, being very gentle. They were basking under a dark skum [sic] that was on the water. Only their tails could be seen waving near the surface of the very clear water. I grasped two of them near the tailfin in both my hands at once, and their weight was such that my whole strength could scarcely draw them out of the water. Laying them by, I prepared for another draft. Laying hold of only one, I now found it more difficult to draw it out of the water, owing to a number of smaller ones connected with it, all of which came out together. Though my comrades were engaged in other places, I said to one of them near me when I had made the last haul, "These small fish will make a fine fry." The idea was [that] the others were for future use.

I awoke from this second dream with feelings very different from the first. I sprang from the bed with an agonizing tremor through my whole soul and body. I could scarcely hold a joint still. The place seemed as dreadful as when Jacob saw the ladder.[157] A while I would walk the room, and a while [I would] be on my knees or sitting, weeping out my soul in prayers to God for a revival of religion among us.

---

[153]Here *went* is the past participle of the archaic, intransitive verb *wend*, meaning *go* or *journey*.

[154]In 1811 the North Fork of Elkhorn Church, an affiliant of Elkhorn Association, had a membership of 139. Benedict, *Baptist Denomination*, 2:539.

[155]The day of the month was the nineteenth.

[156]Here Taylor uses the British spelling of the noun *color*.

[157]Genesis 28:12, 17.

Habakkuk's prayer (3rd chapter)[158] seemed peculiarly adapted to the language of my heart. Sister Graves's last, tearful request revived afresh in my mind. And I know not whether I was ever more solicitous for my own salvation than [I was] to see a revival of religion at poor, old Clear Creek Church. All my prayers seemed to run particularly to that point. The pressing severity of the air in a room without fire compelled me to cover up in bed again. After about one hour, hoping for a revival of religion, and [praying] that the Lord would make use of me some way as an instrument in it (for I had not experienced such encouraging impressions as now for the space of twenty [150]years), the balance of the night was spent in awful anxiety and joyful hope. But this began to flag when daylight appeared.

I began to reflect on many things as to myself: first, my time of life, now in my seventieth year everything seemed out of repair; my lack of recollection through age; my fractured lungs, having been vigorously engaged for near fifty years in the ministry and now incapable to speak but little, for I found that a tour of preaching would soon break me down with hoars[e]ness; again, where my greatest desires ran (Clear Creek) embarrassments were in the way. So that I began to seriously believe that all my hopes respecting my own usefulness was built on vanity and presumption.

This sunk my spirits low and sealed my lips for a number of months, naming it to no flesh living—the encouragement I had received the night of which I have been speaking. This did not prevent my almost constant prayer to the Lord to revive His work by what instruments He pleased at Clear Creek, concluding that myself would visit there as a kind of auxiliary and preach at private homes.

About two weeks after those dreams spoken of, Brother William Rice,[159] a licensed preacher at Clear Creek, came to my house one evening about dark. Hearing him conversing with my wife in another room, I was struck with awful impressions that he had some serious message to me; and though I upbraided myself for the unlikely, foolish[160] thought, I yet felt an uncommon tremor of mind. Almost the first thing he said to me was that the church at Clear Creek with united voice requested me to preach among them;[161] that a letter had been written to that purport, but that he failed to get it when he left home. I agreed to attend their next monthly meeting, which was in February [1822].

---

[158]Verse 2.

[159]William Rice was a grandnephew of the preaching Brothers Craig.

[160]The adjective *foolish* does not appear in the second edition.

[161]On Saturday 19 January 1822 the Clear Creek Church had voted unanimously to call Taylor as its pastor.

And [I] prevailed on Brother James Suggett[162] to go with me, hoping that his attention would be turned to the destitute church at Clear Creek. After hearing [at that February meeting] the church record relative to myself, I [151]informed them that I had never attended statedly at any church but where I was a member; but as I saw their situation, I would be with them when I could make it convenient[163] till they could be otherways supplied. Of this loose agreement the church made a record.

In one respect, all the desire of my heart was accomplished. Now [there was] a free opening to express and communicate all the tender feelings of my soul for the salvation of the dear, young, rising race. I now began to contemplate the harmony of Providence in this apparently accidental thing. I was just writing the history of Clear Creek Church, with [an account of] the number of revivals that had been among them (and in which I had great interest) when the report reached me of their forloun [forlorn] situation. All this awakened my heart afresh.

The first night after the church's call for me to preach among them, I had the night visions I have been speaking of about fishing. A number of my beloved, preaching brethren, [who were] in the prime of life, with cheerfulness agreed to give agency to my Clear Creek enterprise. The barriers I dreaded at Clear Creek melted away like the mountains before Zerubbabel (Zech[ariah] 4th chap[ter] 7th verse).

In the three meetings [that] Brother Suggett and myself had, the effect became visible among the people. When we left the place, I appointed three other meetings. Brother [John] Edwards[164] cheerfully went with me. Brother [Edmund] Waller was with us at all those meetings. The effect was such among the people that no doubt was left with Waller and Edwards, for they thanked God in their prayers as seeing a revival. With myself there was more doubt, for I feared [that] the news was too good to be true.

---

[162]James Suggett (b. 1785), probably a native of Virginia, was brought to Kentucky the year of his birth. He married a daughter of Joseph Redding, who baptized him. Suggett was noted for his lighthearted conversation. Once John Taylor remarked: "When I see Suggett in the pulpit, I think he ought never to come out of it, and when I see him out of it, I think he ought never to go into it." He ministered to at least three churches in the Bluegrass country. During the War of 1812 he served in the military for a season. Spencer, Kentucky Baptists, 1:95, 312-13. (The quotation comes from Page 312.)

[163]Here convenient is the colloquial form of the adverb conveniently.

[164]John Edwards, a capable preacher, was probably a constituting member of the Six Mile Creek (now the Christiansburg) Church, organized in 1799 in Shelby County, Kentucky. Spencer, Kentucky Baptists, 1:430, 431.

Soon after this I had a number of meetings with Brother Waller in several of the churches he attended, as also about old Clear Creek, where we saw the effect greater among the people than we had seen before.

We had a meeting at an old, respectable widow's, Sister Arnold's,[165] where I have seen many happy meetings. This text was taken that night: "The effectual, [152]fervent prayer of a righteous man availeth much."[166] When preaching closed, a number of old professors rose up, male and female, and, in a flood of tears, desiring prayers to be put up to God for them and their children. This seemed to run through the people as an electric stroke. And while prayer was performed, the tears and groans of the people were not unlike the pangs of childbirth. "When Zion travaileth she bringeth forth."[167]

I now believed unhesitatingly that the Lord was at work among the people. At the April church meeting, none offered to the church, though I had heard that some had obtained hope in the Lord. At the May church meeting at Clear Creek was among the most pleasing days of my life, for while we were sitting hearing experiences, I recollected that just that day fifty years ago I had related my own experience and been received into the church.[168] This I named to the people with much satisfaction: that after trying the religion of the Saviour fifty years, it was now as precious to me as any day of my life. The same thing I named next day at the water: that just fifty years after myself was baptized, I [now] baptized five choice, young men and one young lady. Another thing was the more consoling —they had all lately obtained hope in the Lord Jesus.

Another very agreeable thing—Brother Abraham Cook,[169] from Shelby County, was with me at this time. We had a tour of preaching through Franklin,[170] Woodford, and Jessamine counties, but the most of our labours were about Clear Creek. This precious servant of the Lord preached with great effect among the people. Some souls will remember what he said in this [world] and [in] the world to come.

The people about this time turned out abundantly to meetings, and their looks on their way are as those [when] going to the funeral of a friend. Chief of the old Baptists about Clear Creek seemed now to be transformed by the

[165]This meeting was held at the home of Mrs. John Arnold.

[166]James 5:16.

[167]Isaiah 66:8.

[168]The third Saturday of May 1772 was the eighteenth day of the month; the third Saturday of May 1822, the sixteenth.

[169]Abraham Cook (1774–1854), a native of Virginia, was a charter member of the Six Mile Creek Church. He served as pastor of at least three churches in the Bluegrass before he moved to Missouri in 1851. Spencer, *Kentucky Baptists*, 1:432-35.

[170]Franklin County was created by a 1794 act of the Kentucky legislature.

renewing of their minds.[171] I pray that [153]they may continue in this harmony of soul till they die.

There were pleasing prospects at their June church meeting. Seven were received and baptized on the Lord's day. The most of these were females, only two males among them (one of whom was a black man).

Some of this old, forsaken church began to canvass the 54th chapter of Isaiah. And as that chapter begins with "Sing, O barren, thou that didst not bear," they are ready to go through the whole of it as a heavenly ditty or divine poem. While they lengthen their cords, may they strengthen their stakes[172] by good discipline.

It has been stated [that] at their first baptizing in May 1822 six were baptized; at their June meeting, seven. At their July meeting [there were] thirteen; at their August meeting, eleven; at their September meeting, fourteen; at their October meeting, eighteen. [There had been] seventy in all, taking in six baptizings. Of which about thirty were white males, all of them young men, though a number of them had families. About twenty-seven of them were white females, and thirteen [were] blacks, male and females. Mr. [George] Whitefield once said, "Whoever goes to heaven will see seven women for one man," but in this case the males are a little ahead.

At this last baptizing, prospects are obviously promising for a continuance of this blessed revival. Many of those young converts, both male and female, are delightful singers. The songs of Zion [that] they can now chant forth without a book seem in a manner endless.

The poor blacks, whose voices generally exceed [those of] the whites, have learned many of those precious songs. They are now abundantly stirred up to a devotional spirit. They flock together, and in the dead time of the night you may hear them at a distance praying to and praising God with charming sound. And as you travel the road in daytime, at their business you hear them singing with such heavenly melody that your heart melts into heavenly sweetness, while many in solemn pause [154]say:

> O happy days long looked for,
> The Comforter is come.[173]

---

[171]Romans 12:2.

[172]Isaiah 54:2.

[173]The verses that Taylor heard the slaves sing may have been the ones that are preserved in Edward W. Billups, *The Sweet Songster* (1854) as part of Hymn 180. There the song has ten stanzas, of four lines each. The first stanza runs like this:

> O happy time, long waited for,
> The comfort of my heart.

I have almost forsaken my home (at fifteen or twenty miles distance)[174] to be among them.

Another arrangement those young converts have gone into with each other is prayer meetings among themselves, meeting alternately at each other's houses. It is pleasant to be in some of those crowded meetings. Twice a week is now in practice. Their custom is to begin with singing and then prayer, and from three to five or six perform this service. And it is usual to sing about two songs between one prayer and another. The style of their prayers are that the Lord would keep and preserve them as young professors of His name, that His gospel and converting work may spread far and wide and by the means [that] Himself [175] may appoint, and that He would particularly bless the family where they are [meeting].

"Will not God hear his own elect who cry to him day and night?"

"Yea," says Christ, "He will answer them speedily."[176]

This happy work seemed rather to begin at Clear Creek. There, as yet, the most have been baptized. Neighboring churches are partaking of the same benefit. Edmund Waller has baptized upwards of forty at Hillsboro Church. Samuel Jesse has baptized a number at Griers Creek Church.[177] Some also have been baptized at Versailles Church.[178] It may be remembered that all these churches were included formerly in the bounds of old Clear Creek Church and may be esteemed her daughters.

[156]About this time the revival at Clear Creek began to spread more among the black people than it had done before, for at the church meeting in November [1822] twelve were received, and no white person among them.

---

Since I have met the saints once more,<br>O! may we never part.

[174]The distance between the site of Taylor's residence near the Forks of Elkhorn in Franklin County and the Clear Creek Meetinghouse in Woodford County is about thirteen miles the way the crow flies.

[175]The pronoun *Himself* (accusative case) is here an Irish usage as the subject of a relative clause and means He or *God*.

[176]Luke 18:7-8.

[177]Samuel Jesse was one of five trustees of the Republican Meetinghouse on Griers Creek. They received a deed to this property on 2 June 1817. This building was available for all denominations to use. Railey, *Woodford County*, 293.

[178]The Versailles Church, located in Woodford County, was established around 1816. Caught up in Campbellism, it was destined to be swept from Baptist ranks by that movement. The present Versailles Baptist Church was organized in 1842. Spencer, *Kentucky Baptists*, 1:635-37; and Kentucky Baptist Convention, *Annual, 1988*, 412.

A great many blacks attended the baptizing on Sunday. They, in a manner, took possession of the shore. And of the thirteen that were baptized only one was a white person who had been received a month before. The exulting joy among some of the blacks on that day went a little beyond moderation. For my own part, I do not recollect that I ever enjoyed such a heavenly feast among the black people before. For the sake of convenience I took two or three of them into the water at once. And when I would return them to the hundreds of their black friends on the shore, with tears of joy their friendly hands and arms would grasp them to their bosom. The air would ring with their thanksgiving and praises to God for His wonderful works of grace on the hearts of poor sinners.

When I brought out the last of them and got fairly on land among them, I partook with the utmost pleasure their manifestations of good will and Christian love, while I felt thankful that our God was no respecter of persons. I now remember a prophecy of David in [the] 68th Psalm 31st verse: "Ethiopia shall soon stretch out her hands unto God."

One of these poor, black men by the name of Essex, soon as his head was raised above water, began to praise God aloud and enquired for his dear master, who was then weeping on the shore. He wanted to give him his hand, which he soon did. Here master and servant[179] meets on perfect equality. James says, "Let the brother of low degree rejoice in that he is exalted, and the rich in that he is made low."[180] Jack and Harry or Essex has a master in the shop or on the farm but not so in the church of Christ. [157]There they all have a Master, and only one Master—Jesus Christ. And there they are all Christ's free men and [are] on perfect equality with each other. There as in the grave the servant is free from his master, and the oppressor's voice not to be heard. There [they] call no man master or father on earth.[181] There conscience is free.

This is 1 January 1823. At the last church meeting of Clear Creek seventeen had been received for baptism—six white persons and eleven blacks. Four of the white persons received (some from sickness and some from other causes) put off their baptism till another time. So that we now had, in a manner, another Negro baptizing. And though this was a day[182] of very cold rain and only two days from Christmas, the people in great abundance attended on the shore. Among the eleven blacks baptized on this day ten of them were males.

From some estimate now made at Clear Creek, within eight months and taking in eight baptizings, ninety-seven have partaken of that ordinance, and four

---

[179]In the time of Taylor the noun *servant* was a euphemism for *slave*.
[180]1:9-10.
[181]Matthew 23:9.
[182]Sunday 22 December 1822.

yet to be baptized. It seems about one-third of this number is blacks. Thus ends to Clear Creek Church the happy year of 1822.

This to me has been a year of great variety of sensation. If there is such a thing as sweethearted, painful anxiety, this has been my experience throughout the past year. For it will be remembered that the dream I had about fishing was early in January, and the very night after the church gave me the call to attend them, of which call I had no knowledge till afterwards. The prayerful anxiety of my soul when awaking from the latter part of this double dream has been expressed before. When nothing would pacify this expanded desire but an answer something like this: "You shall catch men."[183] This would often occur with sweet delight, not only at the time of the dream but through the year afterwards. Perhaps my feelings about this time were not unlike Ezekiel's [feelings about the] roll in Chapters 2d and 4th,[184] which he was to eat and [158]fill his bowels with and afterwards [to] speak to the people [about]. Or [I was] like John (Rev[elation] 10[th] chap[ter])[185] when he was directed to eat the little book that was sweet as honey in his mouth but bitter in his bowels, after which he was again to prophecy [sic] to the people. Those kind of feelings can only be understood by those who have felt the same.

Chief of the enjoyments of life, in a manner, lost their relish through the course of this year's anxiety. For weeks together I did not sleep perhaps more than four hours in twenty-four. And food itself seemed but a small object.

One painful thing to myself through the course of the year was [that] my preaching seemed more barren than common, though I practised as often as in any year of my life. It seemed to me like mere sounding brass.[186] So that I was both ashamed and sorrowful when I closed [a sermon]. And [I] could scarcely believe my own ears, when I heard anything about its utility.

From some hints I have heard at times, I find [that] some are much mistaken as to my instrumentality in the revival at Clear Creek. I am not considered either by myself or [by] perhaps any other person a man of much timidity or affectation; and [I] am, therefore, the better capable to judge in this affair. Other ministers have been instrumental (from what has been made manifest by the experiences that have been told to the church), as Jacob Creath, [Sr.], Edmund Waller, Abraham Cook, James Suggett, William Rice, and John Edwards. My being the only administrator of baptism at Clear Creek has probably produced the mistake as to my usefulness. But the truth is [that] God's set time to favor Zion

---

[183]Luke 5:10.
[184]Taylor's citation should be Ezekiel 2:8-10; 3:1-4.
[185]Verses 8-10.
[186]1 Corinthians 13:1.

was come,[187] and He seemed to use other means besides preaching to carry on His own work.

The several baptizings (and especially the first one) seemed to be the greatest medium of awakening sinners in this revival.[188] This is often seen in other places and is one evidence in favor of believer's baptism, by immersing the whole body under water. It is a usual thing for infant sprinklers to take up from three to [159]five hours in preaching on gospel baptism. But I do not recollect that I have spent ten minutes at any one time for seven years past on baptism. To a man with the New Testament in his hand, the best proof that can be given on gospel baptism is to see a man rise up and [to] hear him declare his faith in Christ, and [at] that moment for a proper administrator[189] to lead him into water of a proper depth, and [to] lean him back [in order] to figurate[190] a burial, and in the name of the triune God solemnly [to] immerse his whole body under water. This reduces the doctrine of baptism to practice before his eyes. In this the Baptists have the advantage of all the sectaries in the world in the article of gospel baptism. And to this is much owing their success in the world.

Another subject bore with much weight on my mind. This was the fifieth year of my ministry and [the] seventieth year of my age, and though I had no certain evidence that this was the last year of my life, the probability of it had its weight with me.[191] Before I was twenty years old, and [on] the day that my glimmering hope in Christ became confirmed I had a desire [for] and perhaps prayed the Lord to take me away at once that I might be with Christ. It occurred to me [then] with strong impression of thought that I was to continue on the earth fifty years longer. I now remember what trouble of mind it gave me and how often that day I looked at the slow motion of the sun, saying to myself, "How many days does it take to wear off fifty years?" And though that part of the exercise of that happy day had, in a manner, been long forgotten by myself. It now revived afresh, hoping (with awful weight upon my mind) that this was to be the last year of my life. But the year [1822] is gone, and I find myself here yet in good health writing what I now do. As to living longer or dying this

---

[187]Psalm 102:13.

[188]John Leland, a close Virginia friend and fellow minister of John Taylor, wrote of the effects of baptism on the unconverted, "At times appointed for baptism, the people generally go singing to the waterside, in grand procession: I have heard many souls declare they first were convicted, or first found pardon going to, at, or coming from the water." *The Virginia Chronicle*, 36.

[189]In order to carry out baptism acceptably, early Kentucky Baptists emphasized the need for a proper administrator—an ordained minister who himself had been immersed.

[190]The infinitive *figurate* is an obsolete verb meaning *portray*.

[191]Twelve years of Taylor's life still remained.

moment, I have but little choice. I have but one hope either in life or death, this being the Chief Cornerstone—Christ Jesus, the Lord. Paul says [that] for him [160]to live was Christ and to die was gain.[192] If I can but live to Christ and for Christ on earth, my days may speed their way to what length the Lord pleases.

I am just now pausing and reflecting with thanksgiving to the Lord for the happiness of the past year. This has been a year of great mortality. And while some preachers have died and a number more by disease has been brought to the gates of the grave,[193] I have mingled with diseases, traveled, and laboured much and through all kinds of weather without one hour's sickness. And though my fractured lungs (through fifty years' labour in the ministry) have this year been often reduced down to a mere whisper while speaking, I have recovered to as good plight[194] as I was at the beginning of the year.

In fifty years past I suppose I have traveled at least an hundred thousand miles and chiefly on the business of preaching. This would take me about four times round the globe on which we live. Had I have had no success in preaching before, what has taken place at Clear Creek and other places through the course of the past year more than compensates for the travels and all other distresses that I have met with through life (though my services, as stated before, at Clear Creek have been but partial).

If all this seems foolish to the reader, he is very welcome to his own thoughts. I expect very soon to see Jesus Christ. My preaching (as stated before) through the course of the past year seemed very far short of what I wished it be. To supply that lack I made it a point to visit the people at their own houses [and] to converse with them about the state of their souls. Those visits were so cordially received by the people, and so much confidence [was] manifested that they would generally converse with me freely. So that it was a rare thing for an experience to be related to the church but I had heard it before. Of course very few [people] that offered [their experiences] were rejected. In those domestic visits, I think, lay my best services.

[161]If an old brother or sister would give me their hand in tears (which was often the case), saying, "Pray for me and mine," it made an opening for a visit. If I saw a young person, male or female, weeping at meeting, my sympathy began to flow. And with heart yearnings [I would] desire to mingle my tears with theirs and would pay them a visit. If I heard of any that were offended or [were] speaking reproachfully of me, if I thought I could do it without giving greater offence, I would pay them a visit. Some one or more of the brethren would often go with me on those visits. And I think we shall never forget the happy, little,

---

[192]Philippians 1:21.
[193]The idiom "gates of the grave" means "verge of death."
[194]Here the noun *plight* is a rare usage meaning "state of health."

tearful, family meetings we had. When it was requested or appeared seasonable, we went to prayer; otherwise the time was spent on godly subjects or singing praises of the Lord.

Clear Creek Church has at present two teaching gifts—William Rice and Brother [David] Wafford. The latter has lately joined the church. Neither of them is yet ordained.

They have also three black teachers. Two of them is the property of old Brother [Lewis] Castleman. Their names are Marlock and James. They mostly teach among their own colour. In their meetings at times, I hear, there is much noise, but we have lately heard a number of good experiences from the blacks, as the fruit of their labours. Another black man [is] respectable both in looks and character. His age is perhaps fifty. He is styled both by black and white [as] Uncle Phil. He is tall, his countenance comely[195] and solemn as the grave. His preaching talents are such that for sometime back, by the help of the people, he has obtained his freedom. He travels considerably, and his preaching [is] acceptable wherever he goes.

Some circumstances a little uncommon in this last revival at Clear Creek will now be attended to. More than thirty-seven years past, I baptized a number of men and their wives at Clear Creek. Their children were then very young. In the course of last year I have baptized a number to the third generation.

[162]Old Mr. Joseph Collins[196] and wife were two [who were] baptized that long ago. They have kept their place in the church for this long time. He is now in his eightieth year. [He is] of a spare texture and can travel about, in a manner, like a boy. His old lady, something younger than himself [and] also of spare habit, can trip across the fields and along the roads afoot and seldom fails being at meeting. And her zeal in the cause of religion is such in her own circle [that] she preaches away in whatever company she is in. Their children were three daughters; they were all married. One is dead. The two surviving ones are the wives of those useful men in the church of Christ—Lewis[197] and James[198] Sullivan. One of those surviving daughters I have lately baptized and some of the grandchildren from all their daughters.

---

[195]The adjective *comely* is an archaism meaning *proper* or *decorous*.

[196]Joseph Collins was living in Woodford County as early as May 1790. Heinemann, *"First Census" of Kentucky, 1790*, 22.

[197]Lewis Sullivan was a son of Wyatt Sullivan and a first cousin of James Sullivan, Jr. Rainey, *Woodford County*, 88.

[198]James Sullivan, Jr., was a native of Virginia and a son of James Sullivan, Sr. Jane Collins was the wife of the younger Sullivan. Ibid., 85.

Also John Arnold[199] and his wife[200] were baptized about the same time of Collins and his wife. I have lately baptized some of their children[201] and grandchildren. Brother John Arnold, after keeping a respectable standing in the church of Christ, in the world, and in his own respectable family for more than thirty years, with great confidence of hope in Christ departed this life a few years past [1818].

This man, being a very near neighbor of mine[202] at the time of his conversion, laboured long under despairing conclusions that there was no mercy for him. Being raised under the light of the gospel, he concluded [that] he had some way committed the unpardonable sin and [that] that was the reason why his heart was so hard and wicked.

His deliverance took place when [he was] by himself and riding along the road, when he concluded [that] all the world round him was changed. While the comforts of love were vibrating in his soul as he rode along, he began to ask himself whether it was possible that John Arnold—Hell-deserving John Arnold—was converted.

While his conscience answered, "O yes, Hell-deserving John Arnold is born again and will nevermore see any trouble."

And looking at his hands, he really fancied they were not the hands [163]of the old John Arnold but of the new. After baptizing him, I lived long with him in Clear Creek Church, while he gave good evidence that this change was reality.

Old Sister Arnold is yet living. I remember she told a most interesting experience to the church and has long manifested a warm regard for the cause of Christ. And though she is now a widow and has lost one of the best of husbands, she is far from being sunk into the mopes. Her natural strength of judgment has great weight with her children as a counsellor. Her masculine fortitude bears her up under the most trying scenes. Her great aptitude to converse on things of religion, and seeing her zeal for the blessed cause, [and] being in her company, [all] would give you pleasure. You would perhaps say to

[199]John Arnold (1754–1818) was a son of Nicholas and Margaret Arnold, of Virginia. James and Lewis, brothers of John, were also pioneers in Kentucky. Ibid., 269.

[200]John Arnold's wife was Elizabeth Hitt (b. 1750/1), of Fauquier County, Virginia. She came to Kentucky as a member of the Traveling Church of Lewis Craig, in 1781. She and her husband lived briefly at Bryan Station. [Elizabeth] Arnold, Interview by [John D. Shane], Woodford Co. KY, Draper MSS., 11CC241-45; Draper MSS., 26CC42; and Railey, *Woodford County*, 269.

[201]John and Elizabeth Arnold were the parents of six sons and four daughters. Railey, *Woodford County*, 270.

[202]The land of John Arnold adjoined the farm of John Taylor, which was located on the waters of Clear Creek. Fayette County (KY) Court, Burnt Records Book No. 5, 281-82.

yourself, "Is not this Deborah, the prophetes[s],[203] risen from the dead?" She is truly a mother in Israel.[204]

At John Arnold's in old times we had many happy meetings. In my early visits last winter, one of the night meetings had been appointed at the widow Arnold's. When I got to the place I could not forbear fixing my eyes on the old house, where the Lord had done such wonders in former days. And naming that circumstance to the old sister, she replied with apparent strong emotion of mind, "Yes, Brother Taylor, God has converted many sinners in that old house." Expressing her prayerful desire that the Lord would again be merciful to poor sinners, the conversation ended.

That very night her prayer was answered, for a number of sinners, [who were] hopefully converted since, [now] profess their first awakening at that meeting. A niece of hers, Arrieny, daughter of James Arnold,[205] was among the number. James Arnold with his wife have long been Baptists. Though some of their children had been baptized before, the conversion of their daughter Arrieny proved a great blessing to the family. It is a pleasure to visit this now happy family. You will find three or four fine girls (among the best of singers), the old people with their son Garrard [164](a young man), all professing the Lord's name and joining in the heavenly melody. Before you were aware, you would think, "Surely I am in Paradise."

About three months after this night meeting at the widow Arnold's, her son Thomas[206]—a choice-looking young man—(unexpected[207] to his mother) stept[208] forward to relate to the church his hope in Christ, which he had obtained only the evening before, this being on Sunday forenoon. The house was much crowded. The relation was so much to the purpose and the young man so much affected while giving it that a general weeping took place through the great assembly.

And especially [was it so] when the old sister and her respectable-looking daughter Mrs. [Nancy] Rice[209] came pressing through the crowd (with joyful

[203]Judges 4:4, 6-7, 14.

[204]In 2 Samuel 20:19 the term "mother in Israel" refers to the town of Abel, located in the northern part of Israel and surrounded by dependent villages that were known as her daughters. Abel was regarded as a community of wisdom, conservatism, and sound judgment. Mrs. John Arnold's title "mother in Israel" denotes that she was a fountain of wise counsel.

[205]At least since June 1789 James Arnold, a brother of John Arnold, had lived in Woodford (then Fayette) County. Heinemann, *"First Census" of Kentucky, 1790*, 8.

[206]Thomas Arnold lived and died in Woodford County. Railey, *Woodford County*, 270.

[207]The adverb *unexpected* is a colloquialism meaning *unexpectedly*.

[208]The word *stept* is the poetic form of *stepped*, the past tense of the verb *step*.

[209]Nancy Arnold Rice was the wife of William Rice. Railey, Woodford County, 270.

tears) to give the hand of fellowship, while the one could only say, "O, my son! my son!" and the other, "O, my brother! my brother!" This gave fresh tide[210] to the feelings of sympathy among the people. And especially [was it so] when the old sister, turning from her son, reached out her hand to me, exclaiming loud enough to be heard all over the house, "O, Brother Taylor, God has answered our prayers." I confess my passions were wrought on above measure. This was the "beginning of days" with many. [See Hebrews 7:3.]

This being the first baptizing in this revival, thousands attended at the water. The persons baptized were William Singleton,[211] Thomas Arnold, James Jesse, Washington Jesse, Edmund Roper, and a respectable young lady Miss Hazard. All those young men were of respectable family. Singleton had been received into the church by experience at the March meeting, myself not present. At the April meeting others had obtained hope, but none came forward to join the church. When I asked Singleton if he would now be baptized, he was so confident that the Lord was working among the people, his reply was, "I will wait for company." At the May meeting he had the company I have just been speaking of, and himself took the lead and was first baptized.

[165]I have been talking of parents, children, and grandchildren. I have one more instance—the widow [Henrietta] Scearce. [97, 2d]She is now a widow of a great age. I baptized her and her husband [James Scearce],[212] in my early days of baptizing in Virginia, and nearly fifty years ago. [165]In this Clear Creek revival I have baptized some of her children[213] and grandchildren. A granddaughter of hers, Martha Scearce,[214] is the daughter of Mr. William Scearce.[215] Though he has many children, Patsy[216] is his only daughter and the youngest child.[217] Per-

[210]The idiom "gave fresh tide" means "cause a renewal of tears."

[211]This William Singleton may have been one of the six children of Jechonias and Jane (Taylor) Singleton. The author was an uncle of their four sons and two daughters. Jechonias' son William was born in 1798. Dorothy Thompson, "Ancestors and Descendants," 31, and "Day of Controversy," 231.

[212]James Scearce migrated from Virginia and settled near John Craig's Station in Woodford County. Railey, *Woodford County*, 423.

[213]Henrietta Scearce was the mother of four sons and two daughters. Ibid., 424.

[214]Martha Scearce married Caleb Baker. Later they settled in Missouri. Ibid.

[215]William Scearce (b. 1771) was a native of Virginia and a taxpayer in Woodford County as early as August 1800. Ibid., 422; Clift, *"Second Census" of Kentucky, 1800*, 260.

[216]*Patsy* is the diminutive form of the proper name *Martha*.

[217]William Scearce was the father of four sons and one daughter. Railey, *Woodford County*, 424.

haps parents cannot be more deservedly attached to a child than [is true] in the present case. I had baptized Patsy's mother[218] before she was married.

Mr. William Scearce lives in high style and looks as independent as any man in Kentucky. Though he is a friendly man, he seems to take but little pains to please anybody. It is probable [that] he is a religious man, but himself thinks [that] he does not always give the best evidence of it. Being well acquainted with him from a child, my visit seemed acceptable to the family. After some friendly conversation with Mr. Scearce, Miss Patsy and her mother walked into the room where we were to take share in the conversation. Though I had never known the young lady before, the solemnity of her countenance bespoke [that] the Lord is there. Her consent was soon gained to relate her hope in the Lord Jesus. After sitting down for that purpose, the tears for some time began to flow from her comely eyes. And though her father mildly chid her childish weakness when she began to talk, his strongest philosophy could not bear him up. Big as he was, he retired from the room (though not out of hearing) that he might give vent to the tender emotions of his own heart. This is perhaps one evidence that himself has felt religion.[219]

I remember the purport of her experience. [She was] at a meeting where Edmund Waller had preached [166]from this text, "Martha, Martha, thou art cumbered about many things, but one thing is needful."[220] Perhaps her own name being Martha made the text and preaching the more striking to her, reflecting [that] she had never done anything for the Lord in all her life. But to serve herself had been her whole object. She determined now to try to seek the Lord. Her first attempt was prayer to God. In the first effort this part of the Scripture occurred to her: "He will have mercy on whom He will have mercy, and whom He will He hardeneth."[221] This proved a killing word to her, for in all her cries for mercy that killing word "whom He will He hardeneth" would strike her dumb, for there was no mercy for her. When she read the Book of God, it all justly condemned her, for she was hardened and helpless. She had no rest day or night for about one week.

When walking abroad to meditate and condole[222] her lost state, these words applied to her mind with sweet relief: "Fear not, little flock; it is your Father's good pleasure to give you the kingdom." Returning to the house in peace, love,

---

[218]Anna Thompson was the wife of William Scearce. Her father was David Thompson, a Baptist minister of Louisa County, Virginia. Ibid.

[219]Taylor means a religion characterized by feeling. The word *felt* is used as an adjectival participle.

[220]Luke 10:41-42.

[221]Romans 9:18.

[222]The transitive verb *condole* is an archaic usage meaning "show grief for."

and joy and picking up the Book of God (not knowing that these blessed words were there), by apparent accident she soon opened to the very spot (Luke 12th chap[ter] 32d verse).

Finding these to be the words of Christ to his disciples, the whole plan of salvation opened up to her. From her own statement, in joyful tears she pressed the open Book (where this cordial[223] of her heart lay) to her palpitating bosom, saying in her soul, "This beloved Saviour is mine, and I am His forever."

Very shortly after this, she was baptized in the month of July with many others. The very clear deliverance[224] [of the account] of Patsy's conversion proved a discouragement to a number of other young converts whose evidences were not so clear.

John Adkins[225] and family—this subject I would touch with some delicacy. Mr. Adkins [was] a worthy man and a licensed preacher, being much attached to the late pastor at Clear Creek, [Henry Toler], who had left the [167]church there and joined the church at Griers Creek. Adkins had applied for a letter of dismission at Clear Creek to join where the old pastor had gone. This favor was denied at Clear Creek. The causes of this denial was [that], whether by the influence of the old pastor or some other cause, the church at Griers Creek had assumed a new style. [The members were] calling themselves Particular Baptists, by which, if not expressed, [it was] fully understood [as] a denial of the General Union of Baptists in Kentucky. The church at Clear Creek concluded [that] they could not legally dismiss their members to join a church by which they immediately went out of their own communion.

Adkins, considering himself a free man, joined this church at Griers Creek without this legal dismission. The church at Clear Creek, though much attached to Adkins, made record that this conduct of his did not correspond with good order.[226] This was virtually exclusion. Adkins' wife, being a member at Clear Creek, did not choose to go with her husband.

The Lord in great mercy broke in on Adkins' family and without doubt converted four of his children—their eldest daughter, married to a Richard Barnes; their son Jonathan, a young man; their daughter Polly, a fine-looking girl, free-spoken, and very ready-witted; and a pleasant, well-favored, younger daughter the name of Martha. Those children being very desirous to unite among

---

[223]The noun *cordial* is a rare usage meaning "stimulant of the heart."

[224]The noun *deliverance* is here an archaic usage meaning *delivery* or *utterance*.

[225]One John Adkins, a veteran of the Revolution, was living in Woodford County in 1810. Railey, *Woodford County*, 21.

[226]Kentucky Baptists of the early nineteenth century were much concerned with various aspects of "good order," including the proper transfer of church membership from one congregation to another.

the people of God, the question was: Where shall they join—the church where their father was a member; or at Clear Creek, where their mother's membership was? This produced a little halting, but in a family council among themselves, and leaving it to the children, they came on to Clear Creek, the parents and the three eldest children. There was no delay when the door was opened to hear experiences. The youngest of them,[227] Polly, came forward first. The solemnity of her looks, her readiness of expression, and the whole at times mingled with tenderness of tears (without doubt), putting all together, placed the relation [168][of her conversion] on an equality with any I ever heard related to a church. Perhaps the whole of the assembly, numerous as they were, heard this interesting statement distinctly, which their contenances and eyes manifested. In turn, the other two children immediately followed. And it is a rare thing for three such experiences to be told to a church together at any time. Martha was baptized sometime afterwards.

This was one of our happiest days at Clear Creek, both at the meetinghouse and at the water. O happy parents! My soul overflows with pleasure while writing.

I have said that one of those daughters was the wife of a Richard Barnes. As he is connected with the family of Adkins, I shall make some statement of him and his brother Washington Barnes.

The first time I ever saw Richard Barnes to know him was at his own house. His brother Washington then lay sick of a fever. In conversing with these two brothers, I believed [that] they were not far from the kingdom of God. At the time of the baptizing of Mrs. Barnes, I believed Richard to be a converted man. But finding his mind under great anxiety, I forbore to give him my opinion, thinking [that] the Lord had something more in store ready to be revealed to him in a short time, which came to pass. For when I saw him again, he informed me of a very clear deliverance he had received. But the poor man was now ruined, for he had lost it all again and found [that], with all the comfort he had felt, he was yet a sinner, which would not be the case if he was born again.

I now encouraged him to come forward to the church.

"This," he concluded, "would be presumption."

The church sat at a private house about one hour after this conversation. He sitting very near to me, I asked him by name to relate to the church what he had done to me about an hour before.

He replied, "O sir! I cannot do that here, for it would be offering myself to the church, and I am too great a sinner to be among the people of God." Thus saying, he burst out into a flood of tears.

---

[227]The author means the youngest of the three oldest children.

After [169]asking him a number of questions, the brethren left their seats to get round him to give their hand of fellowship with the greatest cordiality.

Washington Barnes had been sick with fevers. He would recover a little and relapse again. When I first saw him the fever of his mind under a sense of the guilt of his sin seemed the greatest distress he had. But relief came soon after his brother was received by the church. He attended the September church meeting. He looked, in a manner, pale as a corpse. After a number of others had related their hope in Christ, he rose up from a remote part of the meetinghouse. His deliberate, slow movement towards the table arrested the attention of the crowded assembly, while they with great intenseness looked on a young man more than six feet high, who barely looked like a living man [and] whose countenance seemed [as] solemn as if he had just risen from the dead.

Those who could [do so] strove to get nearer. But they need not have done that, for when he began he spoke loud enough to be heard all over the house. I do not recollect seeing an assembly more attentive to any address made to them than when this young man was telling his experience. No part needful seemed to be left untouched, so that there was no need for any church to ask one question. When he was received, some brother with great warmth began to sing:

> Come, we that love the Lord,[228]
> [And let our joys be known;
> Join in a song of sweet accord,
> And thus surround the throne.]

And indeed it was a time of love.

When the song ended, another young man came forward the name of Harrison, who had been under distress of soul about two months. And having conversed with him a few hours before (he then professing no hope), I [now] asked him when he had obtained his hope. He answered, "Just now, while they were singing." He was received and baptized the next day with many others.

This instance seemed a little more like the Day of Pentecost[229] than anything I had seen before—those two Barneses. My own belief is that Richard had as good an experience as Washington, but lack [170]of confidence in the evidence [that] God gave him threw Richard in the background. And [he] can only be received by extorted answers to questions, while Washington is received without one question. Both these brothers were baptized the same day, while Richard seems as much comforted as Washington.

---

[228]Here is the opening line of one of the stately hymns of Isaac Watts (1674–1748), called the "Father of English Hymnody." This song was written in 1707.

[229]Acts 2:1-4.

Washington's long and obstinate fevers would alternately change to the fever and ague. The day he was baptized he took a relapse, and his ague came on just before he went into the water. But his zeal to do his duty pushed him on. And while [he was] under a violent ague I put him under the water, leaving that entirely with his conscience and the God he served. I had once baptized others when myself had the fever and ague, but till now [I] had not baptized a man shaking with the ague. I was immediately called off on a long tour and did not hear from my shaking, young brother for several weeks, but I often thought of him with great solicitude. When I enquired after Washington by his brother, he replied [that] he believed I had cured him by baptizing him. But I think [that] he relapsed again several times, till Capt[ain] Frost, under Providence, was his doctor.

Two females deceased. Those departed friends were [Mary] "Polly" Rice and Hannah Graves. These, being sisters,[230] were the daughters of Mr. Richard Cave. He lived long in the gospel ministry. And his labours at times [were] very useful. Some years past he was taken away by death. I have said something elsewhere of his biography.[231]

Their mother, [Elizabeth Craig Cave], was a sister of the old, preaching Craigs. [She] has been a Baptist more than fifty years and now, as a mother in Israel, is a member at Clear Creek. Her daughter Polly, both small and handsome,[232] was married very young to Mr. Richard Rice.[233] Soon after becoming a mother, she became alarmed of her awful danger by sin.

This awakening was by the preaching of Thomas Ammon, always a mighty son of thunder. He had been a great, practical sinner. His conversion was as visible as his wickedness [171]had been. He began to preach in the time of hot persecution in Virginia [and] was honored, as many others were, with a place in Culpeper Prison for the testimony of his Divine Master. He died some years past in Kentucky.

Mrs. Rice was long under great anguish of soul about her lost and helpless state. All her prayers and tears left her justly condemned before a Just and Holy God. At length [she] concluded [that] there was no mercy for her, for the sinfulness of her own prayers condemned her.[234] At a night meeting at Dudley

---

[230]These two Cave sisters had three brothers—John, Richard, and Jeremiah. Darnell, *Forks of Elkhorn Church*, 81.

[231]A biography of Richard Cave is found in John Taylor, *Thoughts on Missions*, 42-43.

[232]The author omits from his second edition these descriptive words about Polly.

[233]Richard Rice handed in his list of property on 26 February 1790 to a magistrate of Fayette County. Heinemann, *"First Census" of Kentucky, 1790*, 80.

[234]Mrs. Rice meant that the sins for which she sought forgiveness were an affront to

Mitchum's,[235] this text pressed on her mind: "We know that God heareth not sinners," etc.[236] Lewis Craig being at the meeting, it occurred to her in the time of preaching that he and myself were worshipers of God and that He would hear our prayers for her. Therefore, with great appearance of contrition she requested our prayers. And while prayer was thus offering up to God, she obtained a happy deliverance, which she openly professed, and was soon afterwards baptized. She soon manifested her great zeal and sprightliness in the cause of religion.

It was not long till she [Mrs. Rice], requested her husband, who had been a Baptist before he married her, to worship God in his family. This being declined by her husband, she seriously proposed (with his consent) to do it herself. This was yielded to [by him] for awhile and perhaps would have been more sufferable if company did not come. Her mode was to read the Scriptures, sing, and pray with her husband, little children, and servants.

Whether from the reproaches of his own conscience or [from] some other causes, we cannot say, but it seems [that] he threw discouragements in her way. Yet nothing could prevent her earnest prayers to God for her little children. It is said [that] she would leave her bed and kneel down in the dead time of night by the beds of her sleeping children, in tearful prayers to God to save them. Her oldest son, William [Rice], now an ordained preacher at Clear Creek, says [that] when [he was] a small [172]boy his mother would lead him out to a secret place to pray for his salvation. There was no visible evidence that her prayers were answered before her death. At which time none of her children was grown, and herself [237] (though the mother of seven children)[238] bore the appearance of a girl not grown or that [of one who] had never been married. Her death was very unexpected and much lamented by her acquaintances.

To converse on religion seemed to be the theme of her soul, and with the utmost freedom [she] expressed her mind though it might differ from all that were around. In company nothing seemed to escape her piercing eye. And in any dereliction from correctness, either in action or opinion, you might expect to hear

---

the Holy God. This is a high view of God's eternal holiness but a low view of God's readiness to heed the prayer of a sinner.

[235]Dudley Mitchum (b. 1759) was a taxpayer in Woodford County as early as 1800. His daughter Martha (1797–1888) married Joseph Harris Woolfolk (1788–1860), a son of Sowell Woolfolk. Clift, *"Second Census" of Kentucky, 1800*, 205; and Darnell, *Forks of Elkhorn Church*, 148.

[236]John 9:31.

[237]The pronoun *herself* occurs here as an Irish usage for the subject of the clause.

[238]In the first edition Taylor puts the number of Mary Rice's children at eight and indicates that there were "an equal number of sons and daughters." In the second edition he sets the number at seven.

from her. And though in great pleasantness, her reproofs would reach the quick like a sharp needle.

Shortly before she [Polly Rice] breathed her last, a neighbor on a visit remarked to her friends that he thought it improper to flatter her about a recovery, that she had but little time to stay, and [that] he would be faithful to warn her to use that little time the best way she could to prepare for eternity.

She, overhearing what passed, calmly replied with a smile, calling him by name, "I am not afraid to die," and as to preparation for eternity it was not with her but in the Saviour, Whom she had trusted long ago; and that it was rather her choice to depart and be with Christ, which was far better.[239] No doubt she thus went to her beloved Lord and Saviour. She left seven children.[240] Her husband has since died and left those children without living parents. The most of the children are since married, and in good families. All her children are hopefully converted and [have] joined the Baptist church.[241] Her prayers are [still being] answered after her death.

Hannah Graves was baptized about the time her sister [Polly] Rice was, and [she was] then about fourteen years old. She had a very intimate companion about her own age. And both of them [were] under deep distress of soul at [173]the same time. This companion was Polly Woolfolk, the daughter of Col[onel] Sowell Woolfolk,[242] yet living.

The revival of religion was so universal at Clear Creek at this time that meetings were progressing day and night. These [two] poor, distressed girls were generally together. And when (after long sitting up at meetings) [they were] in bed together, they would weep and converse together chief of the night. And if one should drop to sleep, the other with bedewing tears, raising her warning voice, would say, "How can you sleep when every drawing breath may terminate in eternal destruction?" Those dear girls continued a considerable time in this distressed state.

Hannah [Graves] obtained deliverance first. [It happened] at a meeting where old Sister Arnold[243] now lives, in the same old house spoken of before where

---

[239]Philippians 1:23.

[240]Again in the first edition Taylor gives the number of Mrs. Rice's children as eight, a number that is changed to seven in the second edition.

[241]Here is the first of Taylor's three uses of the term "the Baptist church" to indicate "the Baptist society or denomination."

[242]Sowell Woolfolk (1744–1830), who migrated from Albemarle County, Virginia, was appointed in December 1792 as the major of the 11th Militia Regiment, located in Woodford County. Clift, *"Corn Stalk" Militia*, 12; and Darnell, *Forks of Elkhorn Church*, 148.

[243]She was the widow of John Arnold.

many sinners had been converted. These girls [were] sitting together. And Polly [Woolfolk], seeing something unusual in Hannah's countenance, exclaimed, "What ails you?" Receiving no answer, she then replied, "Hannah, you are converted! O Hannah, you are converted!"

Joyful Hannah, after a little, replied [that] something had taken place [that] she could not well account for. But [she] hoped it might be that great blessing.

This sunk poor Polly into deeper horror and despair than ever, concluding [that] the Lord had cast her off forever. This proved the killing blow to this dear girl. It seems [that] they did not meet again for several days. Soon after this, Polly received deliverance. And the tide of joy having not subsided, [she] could say, "Dear Hannah, I have found the Lord," at their next meeting.

To the best of my recollection, they were baptized on the same day. I remember [that] the church sat at my house when Polly told her experience. The relation of her hope in Christ was of the most striking kind. [It was striking] to see a comely virgin—about fourteen years old [and] from one of the most respectable families in the county—rise from her seat with all the apparent solemnities of Heaven; [to see her] set forth by the tender feelings of heart in the presence of a crowded, attentive assembly; [and] with all the [174]judgment of mature age [to hear her] relate her hope in the Lord Jesus, which she had obtained the day before. It is no wonder that the whole assembly was much affected. I remember [that] a respectable, old lady broke out aloud with tears and trembling, exclaiming, "The Lord is doing such wonders for children. What is to become of me? There is no mercy for me." Her sorrow seemed not to subside through the whole day's meeting.

Though this was in the dead of winter, about twenty-six were baptized the next day. Ice or snow in those days were no barriers to the young disciples. And though all this was betwixt[244] thirty and forty years past,[245] I yet retain it with sweet recollection.

A few years after this, both these girls were married. Polly Woolfolk was married to a respectable, young man Benjamin Garnett.[246] She has been the mother of many children and is yet living in Shelby County.

Hannah Cave married the well-known John Graves of Woodford County.[247] Hannah Graves, from the time of her conversion, always manifested a warm

---

[244]The preposition *betwixt* is an archaism meaning *between*.

[245]In the second edition Taylor sets this time as "near forty years past."

[246]In June 1789 John Taylor united Benjamin Garrett and Polly Woolfolk in marriage. Railey, *Woodford County*, 324.

[247]John Graves and Hannah Cave were married by John Taylor on 1 August 1790. Ibid., 325.

attachment to the cause of religion. She was the mother of six sons and two daughters.[248] She was a fine singer, and to praise the Lord was her daily delight.

What belonged to gay appearance she esteemed painted folly, but [she] was among the most provident wives. She possessed much shrewdness of mind and what may be called "plain sailing" in all her conversation. The Bible and hymn book she most resorted to for information. She had gained a considerable understanding in the Scriptures, so that she was a nice critic on preaching and a good judge of Christian experience. Flattery was no trait in her character. She never sought friendship at that expense, and yet [she] possessed a sympathizing, benevolent soul. To see religion revive and sinners come to Christ was the delight of her heart. If she had any favorite preachers, she esteemed those highest whom the Lord most used that way. This was a pretty good rule to go by.

A small appearance of a revival would [175]fill her with such prayerful anxiety that she almost foresaw what was coming to pass. This was exemplified some months before her death. The church of which she was a member had long been in rather a declining state, which some of her brethren naming to her expressed a fear that their church would come to nothing. She with great confidence affirmed to the contrary, and she hoped to soon see better days. She was among the very first who gave evidence of the forebodings of the late, happy revival at Clear Creek.

Her blount dealings with preachers at times seemed as if she ran some hazzard [sic] of violating a saying of God Himself, "Touch not mine annointed [sic], and do my prophets no harm."[249] One instance, among many others, was not long before her death. A minister who had served the church several years where she was a member had declined his service any longer. She asked him if he was going to prove that he was only a hireling, seeing he fled when the wolf came and seemed not to care for the sheep.[250] While at the same time she esteemed this man among the best of preachers.

As age advanced she [Hannah Graves] grew very infirm and was often struck with heavy sickness. That of which she died was a complication of disease. She was happy to see her predictions as to a revival come to pass. By day and night she would attend meeting and perhaps by that means exposed herself too much. She was not happy enough to attend any one of the baptizings. The first baptizing was in May, at which time she was confined in her bed, where she continued near three months before she breathed her last.

---

[248]Another source lists Hannah Graves's children as six sons and one daughter. Darnell, *Forks of Elkhorn Church*, 155.

[249]1 Chronicles 16:22.

[250]John 10:12-13.

[281, 2d]Hannah Graves, of whom I have said something before, seemed at the point of death by sickness. She being a sister's daughter of Mr. [Joseph] Craig, he paid her a visit. And after earnest prayer to God for her recovery, in taking leave, [he] gave her his hand with this charge: "Now, Cousin[251] Hannah, don't die. You have a good husband, many fine children, some of them yet to raise. It will be the meanest thing you ever did in your life if you die now. 'The Lord bless you.' Don't die."[252]

Poor Hannah could barely remember what her uncle said but at another time asked him, "Uncle, what did you mean by charging me not to die? [282, 2d]Did you think I could prevent it?"

His answer was, "I feared, cousin, you would get willing to die, and I knew if you did, the Lord would take you home at once."

[175]When she [Hannah Graves] was able to bear it, we often had meetings where she was. Notwithstanding her rack of misery, it was entertaining to be in her company. The solidity of her conversation on her then pains, [on] death itself as a useful medium to be better understood another day, [on] the grave as a house of rest much to be desired, [and on] the resurrection and [the] blessed immortality [176]beyond the grave (in which she had the strongest confidence), all of which she seemed as familiar with as with us who sat around her bed.

In some of her fainting, strangling spasms in which we would think she was gone, when recovering she would say, "I wonder I cannot die, as I desire it so much." Her whole trust seemed to be in the Lord Jesus in this trying hour, being reduced to a skeleton.

Her husband asked her if it would not be her choice to be restored to health again.

With all the apparent deliberation of a judge making up his decision, she replied [that] it was her choice to go now. And soon after, [she] did go. Thus died Hannah Graves.

Having gotten to 1823, at the January meeting at Clear Creek fifteen were received for baptism, and all them black people. Some having offered [themselves] on Sunday morning and not being prepared, only ten were baptized. This being a day of cold rain without intermission, our clothes and heads were much sprinkled before we went into the water.

We do not give in to that prodigious whim that sprinkling is gospel baptism, though the sprinkling came in a shower from heaven [and] though we had much

---

[251]Here the noun *cousin* is loosely used to indicate "any relative." Hannah Cave Graves was a niece of Elijah Craig, whose youngest sister—Elizabeth Craig Cave—was Hannah's mother.

[252]This paragraph and the two following ones come from a piece in the addendum of the second edition titled "Biography of Mr. Lewis Craig."

better evidence that we were sprinkled that day than the Hebrews had in the Red Sea. For as the water was congealed in the sea when they passed over (as expressed in Moses' song immediately after), there could come no sprinkling from congealed water. And as the cloud spoken of was always a pillar of fire at night; this being in the night, had there been any sprinkling it must have been fire and not water.[253] We are not left to such poor, dark makeshifts for gospel baptism. And it is, if possible, a greater incongruity to administer gospel baptism in any mode whatever to unconscious babes. Those who have any use for those scraps of popery[254] are very welcome to them, as we have no use for these childish playthings.

Among the fifteen named above [who were] received the last meeting, two were black children, the property of old [177]Brother [Lewis] Castleman. One of them was about ten years old, the other about eight. What they related to the church could not be objected to. Their mistress being a member of the church in whom great confidence was placed and being present, the children were received for baptism.

When the church convened next morning, some hesitation was expressed about the reception of those children the day before, fearing [that] they might some way have picked up what they stated to the church. Their baptism, by the unanimous voice of the church, was deferred till they could be reexamined. The mode fallen on for that purpose was [that] two ministers in whom the church confided (with as many other brethren as chose to attend) [were] on a day then named to meet with the family where the children lived. And altogether [they were] to make up a decision whether they should be admitted to baptism.

Thus far the church at Clear Creek is careful in the reception of their members. Jemima, sister of the above-named children, had been baptized one month before this time. She is about fourteen years old. By her good, old master and mistress she has been learned to read. This perhaps gave her some advantage in relating her experience. But it is very uncommon for any age—black or white—to give as interesting a statement of a hope in Christ as this poor, black girl did in her relation to the church.

O happy family! This old Brother Castleman and his companion have been together perhaps fifty years. Soon after they embraced religion, [they] were both baptized together. They have raised many children. A number of them are in the Baptist church, also their grandchildren in different parts of our common-

---

[253]1 Corinthians 10:1-2; Exodus 15:8.
[254]*Popery* is a hostile term referring to the dogma and practices of Roman Catholicism.

wealth.[255] The family at home is a pretty respectable church among themselves. They have many black people, [and] a number of them have been lately baptized. Two of their black men, Marlock and James, can not only read but have been preachers for a number of years. The old gentleman has long [178]kept a great tannery. His apprentices have been numerous. Many of them have become professors of religion, so that this family has been a great nursery to the Baptist church for near half a century. The old lady being truly a mother in Israel and a fine tutoress of children, we have the best hopes that these poor, black children spoken of above will be taught the way of the Lord.

But their baptism is put off till we see what another day may bring forth. At the February [1823] church meeting at Clear Creek a very deep snow had fallen, and such a mighty freeze ensued that baptizing could not be performed. And as only two were now received by experience, we fear the revival is declining at Clear Creek. But close at hand in the Versailles Church nine were ready for baptism, but the freeze prevented.

We are now come to the March meeting at Clear Creek. About two weeks past, I had a night meeting at Mr. Martin Nall's[256] about four miles from home. By a heavy fall of rain I got very wet going to the meeting. But few people attended, the night being dark. I set out for home before nine o'clock. After riding about three miles and on a hillside, my horse fell into a gully about two feet deep. His first fall was on one of my legs. In his struggling to rise and falling back, he dashed me into the bottom of the gully, and himself on me. Not being yet alarmed at my danger [and] having a small switch in my hand, to make him rise I gave him a few stripes.[257] But the situation of the ground prevented his rising. And with every effort he made, he fell back on me. And with his head it seemed as if he would knock out my brains, for both of our heads lay in the same direction, and down the hill.

By this time I was buried in mud and water as deep as his weight could sink me, so that my naked head (for I soon lost my hat) was buried in the soft mire till my ears and mouth were filled with mud. This old workhorse, about sixteen [179]hands[258] high and very heavy, was thus fixed on me in a gully about large enough to receive us both. I lay somewhat on my side, his breast and forelegs lay

---

[255]The noun *commonwealth* is an Americanism meaning *state*, referring here specifically to *Kentucky*.

[256]Martin Nall, Jr. (d. ca. 1806), who was a native of Culpeper County, Virginia, lived in Scott County, Kentucky, as early as 1800. He and his wife, Ann, were the parents of four sons and five daughters. Clift, *"Second Census" of Kentucky, 1800*, 214; and Darnell, *Forks of Elkhorn Church*, 213.

[257]The noun *stripe* is an archaism meaning "a stroke with a switch or whip."

[258]*Hand* is a four-inch unit used to measure the height of a horse.

across under my armpit, his greatest weight was on my hips, my legs lay under his hips and thighs.

My lungs were so depressed that I only could respire as with a dying breath. A house being a few hundred yards from where I lay, I now hallowed with what strength I had, but none answered or came to my relief. Perhaps what noise I made bore but little resemblance of a human voice, for I found that I could articulate nothing plain. Though a number of houses were in sight of where I lay, all was silent as the grave, only the blowing of the wind and [the] blackness of the clouds foreboding a storm at hand. I now silently composed my mind the best way I could and[259] think a while before I died.

I was as perfectly collected as to my thoughts as I now am. I thought of my time of life, now more than seventy years old: That it was now time to die; that I had no hope for eternity but what I had been preaching to men for more than fifty years; and that all those labours bore no part of the ground of my acceptance with God. The obedience unto death of the Saviour Christ Jesus, His glorious resurrection, and [His] intercession with the Father for me was the only ground of my hope for Heaven.

With these thoughts I could that moment breathe my last. But another thought occurred: "Tomorrow I am to set out on a ten days' tour of preaching about Versailles and Clear Creek." A number of people there had been received and not yet baptized. I had anticipated pleasure by an interview with my young brethren and old ones too, also [with] those who were enquiring the way to Zion. "But all this," said I to myself, "is over, for here I must die." Indeed my thoughts were, "This is my destiny. God has appointed it." But not knowing fully the will of God, I put up a very short, broken, and doubtful prayer to Him about to this amount: [180]"O Lord, I beseech Thee. Suffer me not to die in this gully."

About this time I felt strength [enough] to draw my feet from under the horse's hips. And by the help of my feet [I] worked my hips a little front under the heaviest weight of the horse. My thought then was [that] if he attempted to rise and [if he] fell only one foot lower down the hill (which was most likely), my breath would be stopped in a moment. Or with his knees or feet, if he could even get up, he would tread me to death; for through weakness and depression I could barely now breathe.

My right hand was the only limb through the course of this struggle that I had the use of, that being a little below the horse's shoulders as he lay on me. With my little whip I began to crack[260] the horse again. When he began to struggle, I thought, "Now death is coming." It was so dark I could not see the

<hr/>

[259]Here the word *and* seems to be a substitute for the expression "in order to."
[260]The transitive verb *crack* is here a colloquialism for "hit with a sharp blow."

horse. But reaching out my hand to feel, I found [that] he was gone. When I examined further, he was standing where my feet had lain.

Though I do not ascribe this to miracle, it was surely the most striking interposition of Providence in my favor of any other in my life. I lay there a while to rest and [to] thank God. And then with much struggle [I] got out of the mud. With the help of the fence I got on my horse, leaving my hat, saddle, one shoe, and a mitten in the mud. And [I] got to my son-in-law French's[261] [house] about eleven o'clock. From estimation I must have been one hour at least under the horse. A great part of the next day I kept my bed. The greatest injury I seemed to have received is in my hips, which will perhaps never be restored.

On Friday morning I set out on the tour of preaching and unexpectedly fell in with the beloved Brother Absalom Graves,[262] who attended with me on this late, happy tour. And though at the February meeting I [had] feared [that] the work was declining, seventeen were baptized last Sunday.

Though this blessed revival has been progressing more than twelve months at Clear Creek, and in which a hundred and between twenty and thirty have been baptized, we hope [that] the [181]Lord is yet converting sinners in this place. If there is joy in Heaven by angels and the inhabitants there,[263] with what pleasure must angels for a year past have been hovering over the southwest corner of Woodford County!

Only for something like this or [in order] to be some way useful in the church of Christ, do I desire to live longer on earth. It is possible [that] for something of this kind the Lord suffered me not to die in the gully spoken of above. I say possible, for I do declare that when I look at myself [and see] what a poor, worn-out, weak, and sinful old man I am, it does not appear probable that the Lord would use me as an instrument in His work. But His footsteps none can

---

[261]In 1805 William French (1785–1863) married Polly Taylor (1792–1879), the second daughter of the author. William was the eldest son of James and Keziah French. Keziah's father was Richard Calloway, of Boonesborough. William and Polly French lived in a brick house built by her father and located on the Georgetown Road. They were the parents of eleven children. Dorothy Thompson, "Ancestors and Descendants," 37-39.

[262]Absalom Graves (1768–1826) was born in present-day Madison County, Virginia. He moved to Kentucky in 1797 and settled in Boone County. In 1801 he was ordained a deacon in the Woolper Creek Church. Nine years later he was licensed to preach by the Bullittsburg Church, and in 1812 he was ordained to the ministry. Spencer, *Kentucky Baptists*, 1:297. For biographies of Graves, see J[ames] A. Kirtley, *History of Bullittsburg Church* (Covington KY, 1872), 41-46; and "Life and Death of Absalom Graves," in Absalom Graves, ed., *Hymns, Psalms, and Spiritual Songs* (Frankfort KY, 1825).

[263]Luke 15:10.

know. He often uses the most unlikely instruments to fulfill His great designs. Only[264] for this I should sink into hopeless despondency.

I have said that there are three neighboring churches to Clear Creek that may be called her daughters—Hillsboro, Griers Creek, and Versailles.

Hillsboro is about four miles from Clear Creek. She has existed as a church for more than twenty years. Except [for] some trouble in her beginning about emancipation, she has been a very properous church. A number of preachers have served this church in a temporary way, but her most permanent servant has been Edmund Waller. Under his administrations she has had several precious revivals. One of them has been in the course of the past year. In the course of ten months about eighty have been baptized. Her number now is between two and three hundred members.

Griers Creek Church, about five miles from Clear Creek, was originally called Buck Run. Buck Run, by contention, lost her existence. With the same old materials of Buck Run and some additions, Griers Creek was constituted by Joseph Craig, Robert Asher, and Isaac Crutcher.[265] The only platform of this constitution was the Scriptures of the [182]Old and New Testament[s].

In process of time Brother Samuel Jesse, a respectable minister, living convenient, took his membership in Griers Creek Church. At which time they made an addition to their constitution, or rather an explanation of certain doctrines of grace understood by themselves as plainly drawn from the Scriptures. Though no confession of faith is named in those articles, all who saw [them] or heard them read considered the divinity as sound as if coming from headquarters itself (Philadelphia).[266]

Brother Jesse, through infirmity, cannot preach much. Of course much of the supply that way comes to Griers Creek from abroad. When Brother [Henry] Toler left Clear Creek, he was invited to take his membership at Griers Creek, which, it seems, he agreed to do provided they would make some further addition to their constitution. All the items of the proposed amendment I do not recollect, but the main one was that for the future they would go under the appellation of "Particular Baptists." To get one of the most interesting[267] preachers in Kentucky

---

[264]*Only* is a colloquialism meaning *but* or *except*.

[265]Isaac Crutcher (1767–1837), a Separate Baptist preacher, was ordained around 1797. He entered into the General Union in Kentucky in 1801. In August 1800 he was enrolled as a taxpayer in Woodford County. Spencer, *Kentucky Baptists*, 1:304-305; and Clift, *"Second Census" of Kentucky, 1800*, 69.

[266]*Philadelphia*, as used here, is a metonym for the Philadelphia Association, which had adopted a written confession of faith about a century earlier.

[267]The adjective *interesting* is here used as an obsoletism meaning *important*.

as their pastor was such an object with the church that they carefully submitted to all of the proposed amendment. And Brother Toler becomes their pastor.[268]

This change gave such offence to some of the members that about five of them took letters and joined at another place. But to be under the care of this favorite pastor six or seven members left other churches and joined at Griers Creek, [even though] not being able to obtain letters for that purpose. How far the churches were wrong in not giving those letters and how far the church at Griers Creek was wrong in receiving members without letters, the reader will judge for himself. I'm only giving facts in the history of Clear Creek and her neighboring daughters.

It seems [that] it was expected that Griers Creek would leave Franklin Association and join Licking Association, who had before styled themselves "Particular Baptists." [183]But when it came to the trial, the church chose not to leave Franklin Association. And, moreover, they struck from their records that part of their amended constitution which distinguished them as Particular Baptists and chose to stand as they had done before [as] United Baptists.[269] Upon which the old pastor [Henry Toler] and chief of his brethren who had joined at Griers Creek on his account immediately took letters of dismission and set themselves afloat as to any church station.[270]

This left Griers Creek in a prodigious[271] crippled situation. Their whole number perhaps never exceeded thirty members. They had lost five for calling themselves "Particular Baptists." And now for saying [that] they would no longer be of that particular order, they have lost their pastor and chief of their male strength. Perhaps from four to six is all the free male strength they have. But if God be for us, who can be against us?[272] [No one], for one month after this

---

[268]Soon after Henry Toler assumed the pastorate of the Griers Creek Particular Baptist Church, he published a tract under the name *Union—No Union*, in which he defended this congregation against a charge of schism for its having left the Elkhorn Association. In 1822 James Fishback, pastor of the First Church of Lexington, rebutted Toler in a pamphlet of 185 pages titled *A Defence [sic] of the Elkhorn Association in Sixteen Letters Addressed to Elder Henry Toler . . .* (Lexington KY). Fishback, *Defence of Elkhorn Association*, copy in Franklin Trask Library, Andover Newton Theological School, Newton MA; and Spencer, *Kentucky Baptists*, 2:28.

[269]By mergers of Regular and Separate Baptists, United Baptists came into existence in Kentucky (1801), in Virginia (1787), and in North Carolina (1772). *Encyclopedia of Southern Baptists*, 2:1435.

[270]Henry Toler and a faction left the Griers Creek Church and in 1822 formed the Versailles Particular Baptist Church. He served that congregation until his death two years later. Spencer, *Kentucky Baptists*, 2:27.

[271]Here *prodigious* is a colloquialism used in place of the adverb *prodigiously*.

[272]Romans 8:31.

explosion seven were received by baptism. Perhaps more than that number have been baptized since, [and] others have joined by letter. Brother John Edwards preaches for them statedly.[273] Brother [Samuel] Jesse also is much more capable to perform ministerial service. They have an elegant, new, brick meetinghouse to worship in. That I suppose Griers Creek Church was never so prosperous as at the present time. "The Lord preserve his little vine."

Versailles—I consider this church the youngest daughter of Clear Creek. They have existed as a church six or seven years. The well-known Jacob Creath, [Sr.], was constituted with them, and his membership [is] still there. They have had no other pastor from the beginning. They were but few in number when constituted. They progressed but slowly for some time, worshipping God in the courthouse or [in] some other shelter as they could find. They now have a large, well-finished, brick meetinghouse, where the people attend in crowded assemblies to worship the Lord in solemn devotion. The truth is [that] God is converting sinners here. The gospel now sounds here [184]with sweet invitation to every sinner to seek the salvation of his soul. A considerable number have been baptized quite lately in this place. The greatest conflict this church has had has been about Particularism. More members went from this church to join the Particular Baptists than from any other neighboring church.

And since Mr. [Henry] Toler took his leave of Griers Creek, he has constituted a little church of Particular Baptists in the Baptist meetinghouse at Versailles. The reason, I understand, for [his] using this freedom is [that] some of the members with him have paid pretty liberally for building the meeting-house. Where this kind of thing will end, time will better explain. But the reader will judge for himself how two Baptist churches [can] set up in one house who will not commune together at the Lord's table and [who] in many instances [are] not so friendly together as wicked men generally are. And it is the more to be lamented that this is not the only case in Kentucky.[274] Of this I should incline to say nothing, but it is interwoven in the history of the churches I am writing.

Whatever other object Particularism may have in view, with some there is no doubt that the destruction of the General Union[275] of Baptists in Kentucky is its main object. If so, let it be remembered that in 1801 when the Baptists were in better order than they ever were before or since in Kentucky, Elkhorn

---

[273]John Edwards became the pastor of the Griers Creek Church around 1809. Spencer, *Kentucky Baptists*, 1:431.

[274]At least three other churches—Bryan Station, Dry Run, and South Elkhorn—had been divided over Particularism into two congregations each. Ibid., 1:95, 113, and 2:240; and Birdwhistell, *Elkhorn Association*, 53.

[275]The first nine of the twelve terms of this General Union are given by Taylor in the last chapter of his *Ten Churches*. See Page 140, first edition.

Association appointed a committee of five men to make the first advances for a union with the Separate Baptists.[276] The men were David Barrow,[277] Ambrose Dudley,[278] Joseph Redding, John Price, and William Payne.[279] Those men were well chosen. They made the advances [and] obtained the hand of the Separate brethren[280] on terms now extant.[281] In 1802 this committee made their report.[282]

---

[276]Taylor means that the Elkhorn Association initiated the fourth attempt by which the union of Regular and Separate Baptists in Kentucky was finally effected. The first essay took place in June 1785, when Taylor, among others, represented the Clear Creek Church at a specially called convention. This effort failed because the Regulars, who were in the majority, adhered to the Philadelphia Confession of Faith. Regulars and Separates united in Virginia in 1787; two years later Baptists in Kentucky made the second effort at union. Their trial came to naught because the Regulars had adopted the Philadelphia statement, and the Separates rejected "any creed but the Bible." The third attempt was made in 1793. Taylor was one of five Regular Baptists who arranged with the Separate Baptists for a convention to meet in July. At that assembly a majority of the messengers agreed on terms of union, but the opposition of some Separates defeated the plan. Spencer, *Kentucky Baptists*, 1:107-108, 175-76, 277.

[277]David Barrow (1753–1819), who was a native of Virginia and an unusually accomplished preacher, served in the Revolutionary War, brought order to the General Baptist churches in North Carolina along the Virginia border, took part in uniting Regular and Separate Baptists in North Carolina, and emancipated his slaves. In 1798 he settled in Kentucky and there served as the pastor of several churches. At Lexington he published *The Important Doctrine of the Trinity* (1803) and *Involuntary . . . Slavery* (1808). Spencer, *Kentucky Baptists*, 1:192-97; and McMurtie and Allen, *Kentucky Imprints, 1787–1810*, 95, 157. See also James B. Taylor, *Virginia Baptist Minutes*, 2d ed., 155-59.

[278]Ambrose Dudley (1750–1825), a native of Virginia, served as a captain in the Revolutionary War. While stationed at Williamsburg, he was converted. Shortly after his military discharge, he was ordained a minister. Arriving in Kentucky in 1786, he soon became the pastor of the Bryan Station Church, near Lexington. Some twenty years later the church divided over the question of predestination, and the majority took the name Particular Baptist. Dudley served that faction for the rest of his days. Spencer, *Kentucky Baptists*, 1:112-14; and Sprague, *American Pulpit*, 7:202-204. See also James B. Taylor, *Virginia Baptist Ministers*, 2d ed., 214-16.

[279]William Payne, a member of the Town Fork Church (near Lexington) as early as 1790, took part in the constitution of the Goshen Church, in Clark County, in 1797. He served that congregation as pastor and later the Washington Church, in Mason County. Even though he was appointed in 1801 by the Elkhorn Association as a member of the committee to treat with Separate Baptists regarding union, his name does not appear as a subscriber to the resultant "Terms of General Union." In 1810 he became a Particular Baptist. Spencer, *Kentucky Baptists*, 1:345, 545-46.

[280]On 21 August 1801 the South Kentucky Association appointed Robert Elkin, Daniel Ramey, Thomas J. Chilton, Samuel Johnson, and Moses Bledsoe as its representatives. Doyle, "South Kentucky Association," 19.

Elkhorn was now at its zenith [with] forty-six churches, including between five and six thousand members.[283] In this great body consummating this union there was only one dissenting church—Town Fork. Means were used to pacify this church without a murmur.[284]

[185]We had enjoyed this happy union for about twenty years, until personal jangling took place with a few preachers. This jangling came to public view in preaching introductory sermons. The first was at Hillsboro in the year 1817. The second was at the Big Spring[285] in the year 1819. The third was at the Great Crossing in 1820. And especially in the two last cases no men perhaps ever preached more personal without calling names. Shall the Baptists [in order] to gratify a few imprudent men tear themselves asunder?

The first we hear of Particular Baptists in Kentucky was by a respectable preacher from New England, a Brother [Samuel] Trott. His question in Licking Association was that [because] "we hold to particular redemption, particular election, and particular calling," he thought it proper to be known in future by the appellation of "Particular Baptists." It was soon agreed to by the association, but with this generous reserve that it should not affect the correspondence they had gone into with the brethren of the General Union. However innocent this thing appeared at the beginning, in its progress its features look more alarming.

---

[281]Building upon the foundation laid by the three earlier attempts at union, the two associations finally effected an agreement during 1801. The Elkhorn Association of Regular Baptists began this fourth attempt at its annual meeting in August 1801. Its committee met with a similar group appointed by the South Kentucky Association of Separate Baptists. While that association was in session the joint committee agreed on mutually acceptable terms of union. The South Kentucky Association unanimously approved these terms and joined with the Elkhorn Association in calling for a convention to gather at the Howards Creek Meetinghouse, in Madison County, on 10 October 1801. At that convention the General Union of Regular and Separate Baptists was consummated. Much of the impetus toward this union came from the Great Revival, then sweeping mightily across the state. Doyle, "South Kentucky Association," 19, 20, 26-27; and Spencer, *Kentucky Baptists*, 1:544-46.

[282]Here Taylor refers to the final report made by the Elkhorn committee of five when the association met in 1802.

[283]At the first annual meeting of Elkhorn following the consummation of the General Union, the clerk of the association listed forty-eight churches as affiliates, including twelve received at that session. These congregations carried on their rolls the names of 5,223 members. Elkhorn Association, "Minutes," in Sweet, *American Frontier*, 1:490-93.

[284]The Elkhorn Association appointed James Garrard, Ambrose Dudley, Robert Johnson, and David Barrow as the "helps" to give the Town Fork Church "all the friendly aid" they could. Ibid., 1:494.

[285]The Big Spring Church was an affiliate of the Elkhorn Association. Spencer, *Kentucky Baptists*, 2:31.

At a distance, when a corresponding Licking brother presents his letter to be read in the association under the new style of a "Particular Baptist," many are at a loss to know its meaning; while others who know more about it smile with contempt. Were they to call themselves "Regular Baptists," they would be better understood. And [even] then it would be wondered at, seeing all names of distinction are lost in the General Union. If we look at it nearer home, every spectator will judge for himself whether [the name] "Particular Baptist" recommends itself to any but its own votaries. Should we survey it in Woodford County, to what advantage does it appear there to saint or sinner, though its professors are equally respectable as men as [are] any in the county?

[187] I have this day returned from the April [1823] monthly meeting at Clear Creek. I had a tour of preaching about one week while there, and a painful time it was with me for I was stricken with a severe pain in my hip the night before I left home. [This pain resulted] from the effects of lying in a gully.[286] So that from first to last of my meetings I was not able to stand up to speak but did the best I could sitting down.

My greatest burden was on the Lord's day, having no ordained brother with me to assist at the Lord's table, including preaching. The whole service continued about three hours, at the close of which I felt very much broken down. I suppose more communicants surrounded the Lord's table this day than I had ever seen at one time. Perhaps there was more than three hundred, and by accounts from the deacons very few kept back from partaking. This was esteemed a precious season. To see that number of people, after solemnly sitting and communing with their dying Lord, and many from floods of tears, rise to their feet as one man with sonorous melody (and many of them with all the warmth of young converts) [and] sing the closing hymn was pleasant indeed.

A brother lately from Virginia said to his friend on that occasion, "I have not been at so happy a meeting for more than two years."

For more than twelve months no complaint had been brought into the church at Clear Creek, but in this meeting two complaints were brought against transgressors, and both of them men who had been baptized last year. When new armies are raised we are to look for some deserters as a thing of course. But three more came forward with new experiences. Their baptism was put off for want of time.

I have lately returned from the May [1823] meeting at Clear Creek. On the day of business there were some sorrowful things. While we were treating with these young deserters spoken of above, some were [188]restored; while two others are still suspended with design to labour further to reclaim [them] if possible.

---

[286]This sentence is not included in the first edition.

Several painful hours were spent on these subjects of discipline. The great harmony of the church somewhat sweetened this cup of sorrow. But the best of all came afterwards, for a number of late Heaven-born experiences were told in the church, while a tide of heavenly joy flowed from heart to heart. And many could say with David, "My cup of joy abundantly run[n]eth over."[287]

The next day eleven were baptized. This is just one year since we began to baptize in this revival.

The Ropewalk Gang.[288] About midway between Versailles and [the] Clear Creek Meetinghouse, Mr. John Mitchum[289] has a large ropewalk.[290] The people around this place, though respectable, had scarce a professor of religion among them. James McQuiddy and wife[291] were among the first converts in this place. Having heard of a lady of that name who had obtained hope in Christ, [and] James having several brothers, and from lack of acquaintance, I knew not one from the other. And being in company with James and a friend coming in, I asked which of the McQuiddys' wives had obtained this hope of conversion, who replied, "This is the man." Turning and conversing with him on that subject, though a bold man he seemed stricken with concern, for he had not heard of it before.

On his way home he began to reflect on what he had just heard and [to] call up into recollection the many instances of distress he lately had seen in his wife, and the means he had used in flouting her on that occasion, [and] his former life of sin with this late addition of unpardonable guilt. His heart being soon uncovered to him with the depth of its corruption, he began to think [that] there was not so bad a man as himself in the world, and that God had so justly set him apart for destruction that he ought (in righteousness) immediately to [189]go to Hell. That night he scarcely slept at all.

And for several days [he was] in a mighty whirlwind of distress. And his deliverance [was] equally uncommon. In less than one week from the beginning of this conviction, he was ranging among his neighbors and [was] warning them

---

[287]Psalm 23:5.

[288]In the second edition Taylor designates these people as the "Brethren at the Ropewalk." 117.

[289]John Mitchum (b. 1789) was numbered among "the most respectable members" of the Clear Creek Church. John Taylor, *Clear Creek Church*, 10.

[290]A *ropewalk* is a long, narrow building or a covered walkway where ropes are manufactured.

[291]On the day before Christmas in 1811, Edmund Waller united James McQuiddy and Jane Perry in wedlock. Railey, *Woodford County*, 332.

in tears to flee from the wrath to come.[292] The effect was such, I suppose that thirty of his near neighbors has since been baptized.

Those young converts soon began to meet together among themselves for the purpose of praise and prayer. Their older brethren at a distance (with great pleasantness) has given them the appellation of the "Ropewalk Gang." The zeal and good order in their meetings are such that the church last winter took up the subject and by way of encouragement nominated four of them to lead on in their meetings, of which a church record is made. I very lately attended one of their Sunday evening meetings. Perhaps two hundred people came out. Their mode is alternately to sing and pray. Should any of them have a word of exhortation to speak to the people, they rise up and say on. Great effect appears at times in their meetings.

Among the number last baptized at Clear Creek was a very small boy under twelve years old. His name is Benjamin Shouse. The great solemnity and intelligence with which this youth related his experience drew more tears from the assembly of both old and young than we have seen here for many days. This lad's sister, a little older than himself, was baptized the same day. Some time back their grandmother, the wife of Mr. Lewis Perry,[293] and two of her daughters were baptized. So here is three generations of the same family baptized near together. This looks a little like the old business of household baptism.[294]

At the June [1823] church meeting at Clear Creek four were baptized, and a few days after they had obtained hope in the Lord Jesus. This happy revival at Clear Creek began about eighteen months ago, and [190]in a little more than one year about a hundred and forty have been baptized. This is the thirty-ninth year since Clear Creek Church was constituted. "While she lengthens her cords, may she strengthen her stakes[295] by well-directed and wholesome discipline [so] that in generations to come God's name may be worshiped here is my prayer for Jesus' sake."

[118,2d]Clear Creek is a respectable church, the first daughter of South Elkhorn —a mother church whose standing [119, 2d]is near forty-two years.

In her last revival of 1822–[182]3 upwards of a hundred sixty were baptized. We suppose [that] since her beginning she has baptized not much under a thousand members. Perhaps half of them has been baptized by the writer hereof. We suppose [that] she has seen the time that her number contained five hundred

---

[292]Luke 3:7.

[293]Lewis Perry (b. ca. 1754), a native of Culpeper County, Virginia, migrated to Kentucky in 1784 and settled in Woodford County. Jane Bourne was his wife. Railey, *Woodford County*, 198.

[294]Acts 16:33.

[295]Isaiah 54:2.

members. At the close of her last revival she was about three hundred in number.

But there is one thing [that] afflicts Clear Creek and all other churches in the thick settlements of Kentucky. The opening to the west of new countries to fill up very much dreans[296] churches of their most efficient members—the young and active. In this way Clear Creek has been much weakened.

Many men have [become] good preachers who were baptized at Clear Creek, but it has mostly been after they moved away to other parts. For after the church had stood near ten years, it was found from her records [that] she had never ordained a minister. David Wafford was the first, who having preached in the church a year or two. Being about to move to Indiana, the church took up the subject of his ordination, and without a dissenting voice committed that sacred trust to him, and immediately dismissed him to a foreign land.

Soon after Wafford, William Rice was ordained. He had been baptized at Clear Creek and [had been] a public speaker about ten years when this trans-action took place. The church was not unanimous in this affair; though afterwards, the minority submitting, he was put into office. The church having not received the exercise of Mr. Rice's office among themselves with that cordiality that could be wished for, he leaves them in seeming disgust.

Thomas Minsic[297] was baptized in their last revival. By the church's invi-tation and afterwards[298] license he went forward a while to preach (and with entertainment to the people).[299] But his great backwardness to go forward (and when they most needed his services), this much afflicted his brethren. And from some strange turn of discontent, unexplained by himself, he and Rice the same day both requested letters of dismission, and neither of them going to move from where they lived. And since that, neither of them scarcely can be prevailed on to even pray in meetings. And though a number of months has past,[300] I know not of any other place where they have become members. These men are but little alike [120,2d]in their course except one thing. For whatever other defaults they may have, each of them seems to have a plentiful stock of self-will.

---

[296]*Drean* is the phonetic spelling of the transitive verb *drain*.

[297]Thomas Minsic, a kinsman of Taylor, later transferred his church membership from Clear Creek to Versailles. Because he had belonged to three congregations without having moved his place of residence, Taylor writes that "in religion he gads about a little too much." John Taylor, *Clear Creek Church*, 60.

[298]The adverb *afterwards* is used here colloquially as an adjective to mean *subsequent*.

[299]Here the expression "with entertainment to the people" is an obsoletism meaning "with a demand upon the attention of the people."

[300]Here *past* is the rare, phonetic spelling of *passed*, the past participle of the intransitive verb *pass*.

Mr. Minsic has a pretty good understanding in the Scriptures. [He is] moral in his deportment [and] mild in conversation on religious subjects, but his choice ones are those of a controverted nature.

Henry Hill,[301] a choice, young man, seemed to have promising gifts but suddenly moved off to Missouri. James McQuiddy [is] of a ready mind in the Scriptures [and is] communicative in his address. And though naturally a bold man, his timidity keeps him from doing his best when he speaks to the people.[302] Robert Scearce,[303] stud[d]y[304] as an ox [and] always ready to do his part in the worship of God, very seasonable addresses the people at times.

Old Uncle Phil, a brother of colour, is a good preacher. Marlock and James also [are] preachers but mostly among the black people. Poor, old mother Clear Creek now seeks her supply of preaching from abroad. After their last revival James Suggett served them one year. The well-known Theodoric Boulware[305] is now their preacher.

I have above called Clear Creek a mother church—a mother church because she has three neighboring daughters, to wit: Hillsboro, Griers Creek, and Versailles.

Hillsboro is a large and respectable church, now upwards of two hundred members.[306] She has long enjoyed almost uninterrupted prosperity under the labours of the well-known Edmund Waller. He yet continues his service there once a month statedly. She has had several happy revivals. Her last was about four years ago, in which about a hundred were baptized.

---

[301]Henry Hill, an ordained minister, was working in Missouri within the bounds of the Fishing Creek Association as early as 1833. "Sketches of Baptists in Missouri," *Christian Repository* 6 (July 1857): 417.

[302]Three years later, when the Campbellite controversy began to seethe within the Clear Creek Church, Taylor would wonder aloud why McQuiddy and others did not rise up and tell Jacob Creath, Jr., that he was walking in a disorderly way. John Taylor, *Clear Creek Church*, 16-17.

[303]Robert Scearce was commissioned a lieutenant in the 11th Militia Regiment of Woodford County in August 1797. Clift, *"Corn Stalk Militia,"* 54.

[304]*Studdy* is the phonetic spelling of the adjective *steady*. Green, *Virginia Folk-Speech*, 371.

[305]Theodoric Boulware (1780–1867), a native of Essex County, Virginia, was named after Theodoric Noel, under whose ministry Boulware's parents had become Baptists. The parents of Boulware brought him as a young child to Kentucky, where they settled at Lewis Craig's Station. Theodoric was firmly established in his faith during the Great Revival and was ordained a minister in 1812. He held a number of pastorates in the Bluegrass. Spencer, *Kentucky Baptists*, 1:314-15.

[306]The membership of the Hillsboro Church had totaled 161 in 1811. Benedict, *Baptist Denomination*, 2:539.

A course taken by this respectable church very lately makes her neighbors stare at her. The case was uniting with three other churches to set up a new association[307] contrary to common order and against the counsel and advice of their best friends. To be sure, four churches [as] respectable as the four who set up this new establishment might safely venture in a new country, and where the wrath of man was not at the bottom of it.

It seems [that] the grounds of offence which produces this new establishment was at the meeting of Elkhorn [Association] in 1825[308] and by and for the adoption of a circular letter.[309] The subject was on the nature and power of a Baptist association. There were a few hands up against the passage of the letter. [121, 2d]It is said that one of the men soon left the house with great resentment. And [he] openly declared [that] he would never come to Elkhorn again, for they saw his hand up against the letter and yet they would send it.

Not being present myself, I cannot vouch to the exact truth of all this. Though unanimity is best in all cases, yet this seems to be a case that might be put up with, as those letters are commonly sent by a majority of voices. The letter is now extant, and perhaps nine Baptists out of ten will say that it is the best they ever saw on that subject. I suppose [that] there was at least ten to one on that vote. And why not be submissive on a question of so little moment?

There are two things men ought to be guarded against: one is straining at gnats, the other is swallowing camels.[310] Let it always be remembered that "the wrath of man worketh not the righteousness of God."[311]

Should friendly advice have no weight? What was the advice of Franklin Association on this head? Three of our churches have asked a dismission to form a new association.[312] All this they have a right to as free and independent

---

[307]Messengers from the Hillsboro, the Salt River, the Glens Creek, and the Fox Creek churches established the "Baptist Association" in October 1826 in Woodford County. Spencer, *Kentucky Baptists*, 2:419.

[308]John L. Johnson, James Fishback, and Rhodes Smith were appointed by the Elkhorn Association on the first day of its session in 1825 to write the customary circular letter. This committee produced a letter that was adopted on the third day, a Monday. Ibid., 2:418.

[309]A circular letter is a printed communication from one association to the associations corresponding with it and to its affiliated churches. Appearing annually in the minutes of the association and approved by it, the letter may take the form of a didactic essay on a particular subject, such as prayer, baptism, or grace. Or it may be an admonition to exercise the Christian graces. In some cases the circular letter represents the association's stand on a given issue.

[310]Matthew 23:24.

[311]James 1:20.

[312]The three congregations from the Franklin Association that sought letters of

churches of Christ; therefore, their request is granted. But as we see no necessity for such an establishment at this time, we do in the most cordial friendship and brotherly love advise our brethren not to go into this arrangement. I suppose fifty men raised their hands to this friendly advice, with no opposing vote recollected.

A question to the same purport was brought into Elkhorn Association,[313] but the mover thereof, finding some excitement stirred up, withdrew his motion. It was obvious [that] the advice would have been the same [as that] of Franklin.

What can a few brethren expect in this heady, if not high-minded, course? I say few brethren, not setting at naught these respectable churches. Far from it. But in those cases ministerial aid is always contemplated. And in this case three at least was expected—[John] Penny, [John] Edwards, and [Samuel] Jesse. For some cause Jesse backs out. Edwards [is] to move away in one week.[314] Only one seventy-years-old [sic] man [is] left.

Would not common prudence have dictated, "Pause awhile"? I was informed that some individuals said [that] if they would make their constitution so that they who joined them afterwards could not alter it, the church at North Elkhorn, he thought, would join them. What sort of work would this be [with] churches crossing each other [and] going [122,2d]a greater distance, and all of the same order? Is this mere whim or something worse? I understand [that] this rigor of constitution gave Mr. Jesse the alarm, and no wonder. For whose conscience could bear any human instrument to be like the laws of the Medes and Persians —unalterable?[315]

But the constitution is gone into by whom? We "the authorized delegates" of the churches,[316] not messengers but delegates. This is the first leap they made in their constitution that was to be so unshaken that none who came after them should alter it. No wonder these men so much objected to the circular [letter] adopted by Elkhorn [in 1825], for that disclaims all such power belonging to an association as those men seem to claim in the beginning. Delegates are men

---

dismissal in 1826 were Salt River, Fox Creek, and Goshen. The latter church, however, did not take part in forming the new association. Spencer, *Kentucky Baptists*, 2:419.

[313]The Hillsboro, the Glens Creek, and the Clover Bottom churches obtained letters of dismissal from the Elkhorn Association, but the latter congregation did not follow through with its intention to enter into the new union. Ibid.

[314]John Edwards moved from Kentucky to Missouri in the fall of 1826. Ibid., 1:431.

[315]Daniel 6:8.

[316]The Baptist Association based its organization on the Philadelphia Confession of Faith, but the preamble of the consititution called the founders "the authorized delegates of the Baptist churches of Jesus Christ." The neighboring associations were pleased with their new sister's plan of union, but they were aroused by the four churches' claim to delegate their powers or a portion of them to the new union. Spencer, *Kentucky Baptists*, 2:419.

authorized to make laws for those who send them. No Baptist association ever went into existence on this ground, that I know of; for only advisory [*sic*] counsel did they ever claim. Therefore, their messengers are not delegates, for they are no lawmakers for the churches.

Nothing is more preposperous [preposterous] than to imagine that a Baptist association can make a constitution for the churches, for the churches have their own constitutions before they make an association, which is a mere creation of the churches. If a church can delegate her power into other hands, she can have no power with herself till it is restored back by those delegates. This may do for other societies, but as yet it will not do for the Baptists, for their belief is that associations can make any rules for their own government while together, and no more.

Perhaps it is very well that this little establishment has come into existence in the way it has, [so] that all associations may sink into disrepute and die a natural death at once, or crumble up four churches together and die by degrees. For I do declare, "If associations are to have more power than mere advisory [*sic*] counsel, I wish them all dead at once."

If I have said one word calculated to chafe feelings anywhere, I may be believed when I say, "It was not designed. It has been lack of skill in the choice of words. For as an individual in this whole affair, I have nothing to lose. Moreover, a number of the very best religious friends I have on this earth is involved in this little affair. I hope that the respectable church at Hillsboro will reconsider the course she has taken. Nothing is more [123,2d]common to mortal man when he thinks he is insulted than to retort again."[317]

The church at North Fork of Elkhorn had received one of the circulars from Glens Creek [Church] [318] on the subject of this new association. In their response it came out in print. I never read the letter either in manuscript or print. From what I have heard, it was pretty severe. [Silas M.] Noel, it seems, was thought to be the author; if he was, I suppose he would not deny it. Glens Creek [Church], it seems, considered herself insulted. Shall her resentment determine her to make an association? Should she get but four churches in place of five, according to her letter? Or could she have gotten two churches instead of four, would she have rushed on as two would have made an association? Perhaps Noel might have felt himself insulted as the moderator of Franklin Assocaition and, therefore, retort[ed] in his long letter in print.

---

[317]Today the Hillsboro Church is a prospering congregation within the fellowship of the Elkhorn Association. It has a resident membership of 340. Kentucky Baptist Convention, *Annual, 1989*, 402.

[318]The Glens Creek Church was constituted in 1801. Ten years later its members numbered thirty. Ibid.; Benedict, *Baptist Denomination*, 2:539.

For whoever till now knew two men to determine to have a new association without consulting others? First, lay the thing before their own church, and then send out their invitation to fourteen churches to meet them on a certain day to go into this new establishment.

Eight of those churches invited belonged to Franklin [Association], where Noel presided as moderator. The bounds laid out by these two surveyors went to the central church in Franklin, leaving the other twelve churches in such a zigzag form that they could not with convenience have met together. What encroachments were made on Elkhorn [Association] was quite another thing. Perhaps Noel considered all this insult, and that Glens Creek [Church] was the first ag[g]ressor, and that he must retort.

I say all this, if possible, to mol[l]ify and soften resentments that may be among brethren. I know not a better-tempered man in the world than Silas M. Noel. It is also well known what a shaver[319] he is with his pen when he turns his hand that way. Should this new establishment hold on their way, it is not expected that they will offer a correspondence to Elkhorn, against whom their resentment run[320] so high; nor to Franklin, whose friendly advice they have so much contemned.

I have dwelt much longer on this disagreeable subject than I intended [to do]. But I have therein had the opportunity of giving my views of a Baptist association, for which we have very little authority from the Scriptures. I also much [124,2d]doubt their utility in this day, for by the pride or wrath of man they are often like the synagogues of Satan.[321] Though I suppose no man on earth ever traveled so much to them as myself. On the frontiers they are much more comfortable than [they are] in the thicker settlements.

I fear [that] they will some day overturn the simple, easy government of the church of Christ among the Baptists, for there is now a number of the poor Baptists [who] incline to use them as a kind of appellate court. Their being brought into existence should be with the greatest care, the extent of their power [being] understood in the beginning. And so long as they are only advisary [sic], they can do no harm. Remove them from that [role], and they are destruction at once.

Perhaps the disorders and divisions among the Baptists in Kentucky has prevented the writing of their history, for (though they have been the most numerous society in the state) their divisions, factions, schisms, and herecies [sic] both in doctrine and practice has brought them very low. Faithfulness binds a

---

[319]*Shaver* is an archaism meaning "a person who drives a hard bargain."
[320]Here *run* is the dialectal past tense of the verb *run*.
[321]Revelation 2:9.

narrator to tell the truth, and it is a painful thing to tell a tale unfavorable, and especially of a friend. Therefore, the historian lies still about the poor Baptists in Kentucky.

The most frivolous thing will stir up faction among them, as exemplified in the new association of which we have been speaking.[322] I would ask my good friends of this connection to look at the word *faction* and then look at the word *schism*, against which Paul speaks so much[323] and [to] see how far those words are adapted to the course they have taken; and then [to] ask themselves how far they can calculate on permanent society. Provided their example is followed, some other factious individual may become dissatisfied with some trivial decision [*sic*] of theirs, and break off, and set up another establishment without their approbation. Where are such things to end but in a breach of confidence between man and man and [in] the violation of all good order among the Baptists?

Griers Creek is a second daughter of old Clear Creek. So little change has been in this church since I last wrote of her that I need say but little. [John] Edwards has moved away. He formerly preached for her statedly. [Samuel] Jesse, their preacher, who lives among them, is rather frail than otherwise. Some of their members have moved away [125, 2d] or joined other churches, so that we suppose she is rather declining than otherwise.

Versailles Church is the third daughter of Clear Creek, and their places of worship [are located] about three miles distant from each other.

This is one of the unhappy spots where there are two Baptist churches in one house. One [church] belonging to Elkhorn Association, their pastor is the well-known Jacob Creath, Sen[io]r. The others call themselves "Particular Baptists," and belong to Licking Association, and have Thomas [Parker] Dudley[324] for their pastor, a son of the well-known Ambrose Dudley, deceased. The division and painful struggles of these two churches of different names have been considerable, though all [are] Baptists. So much for the history part. Shall an old man venture to give advice to the Baptist church at Versailles? There is a happy

---

[322]The Baptist Association continued under its original name from 1826 to 1956, when it designated itself as the Anderson Association. Wendell Holmes Rone, Sr., comp., *Baptist Associations of Kentucky* (Louisville KY, 1967), 13.

[323]E.g., 1 Corinthians 12:25; Romans 16:17.

[324]Thomas Parker Dudley (b. 1792), a native of Fayette County, was one of fourteen children in the house of his father, Ambrose Dudley—a pioneer preacher in Kentucky. Thomas served as an army commissary during the War of 1812 and worked fifteen years as a banker. Ordained to the ministry at the age of thirty-one, he was the pastor of several congregations. As his father had ministered to the predestinarian wing of the Bryan Station Church, so did the son for more than fifty-five years. Thomas also filled the post of moderator of the Licking Association for a number of years. Spencer, *Kentucky Baptists*, 2:247-48.

opening before them, if they can have prudence to improve it. The happy accommodation of differences between the Elkhorn and Licking associations may be the beginning.[325]

My personal acquaintance with the most leading members of both churches gives me hope that they will soon be one church, and especially if the preachers will try to bring about this great object. Should they be backward in this good thing, I would advise the church to dismiss them from any further service among them. Say to them, "We will be one in the Lord. Consider the union in the adorable Godhead. The Father is one, the Son is one, and the Holy Ghost is one. And these three are one in essence, eternity, power, and glory. Fellowship with the Triune God will lead you to love one another. Remember the Saviour's prayer for his Disciples (John 17[th] c[hapter]) and not only for His then Disciples but for all who should afterwards believe through their word.[326] Not to be in love and union one with another is to frustrate this prayer of the Saviour."

Paul exhorts, endeavoring to keep the unity of the Spirit in the bond of peace (Eph[esians] 4[th] c[hapter] 3[d] v[erse]). To effect this, there must be much meekness [and] long-suffering (2[d] v[erse]). Much forgiv[e]ness is needful. And he that forgives most shall have the most forgiven from the Lord; "condemn not and ye shall not be condemned; forgive and you shall be forgiven" (Luke 6[th] c[hapter] 37[th] v[erse]). And this shall be to you good measure—shook[327] together, heaped up, running over.[328] Religion is like nothing else in the world, for the [126, 2d]more we lose the more we gain. And he who makes the first sacrifice will have the first remit[t]ance from Heaven.

About the beginning of this year [1827] a conversion took place in Woodford County and [in the] neighborhood of Clear Creek [Church] that was something out of the common course. The person I allude to is Captain Lewis Arnold.[329] Mr. Arnold was raised by religious parents[330] and under the ministry of the Word from his childhood. From his own account, from seven years old to nineteen he was much employed in prayer. He now turned his attention to the pleasures of the world, married when young, [and] in eager pursuit to make an estate turned his attention to many mechanical arts. In his last three years he was studying and working at the [theory of] perpetual motion. And after straining his reasoning and

---

[325]This reference is to the resumption of correspondence between these two associations in 1826. Ibid., 2:242.

[326]Verse 20.

[327]*Shook* is the dialectal past participle of the verb *shake*.

[328]Luke 6:38.

[329]Lewis Arnold (b. ca. 1777) was married three times. Railey, *Woodford County*, 270.

[330]His father was John Arnold.

thoughts to their utmost stretch, [he] concluded [that] none could teach him what he desired to know but the First Cause of all things.

Well, who and what is this First Cause? Vulgar opinion said [that] it was God. Having strove[331] for thirty years to rivet himself in infidelity, [he] had disdained to read the Bible or [to] yield to vulgar opinion. He now had a subject on his mind of much greater magnitude than the perpetual motion. To find out this unknown God, perhaps he sent to his mother's for a Bible, having none of his own. [He thought about] the awful greatness of this Holy One, with his beaming justice to crush him and all the sinful sons of Adam to utter destruction. But another thought occurred—the amazing goodness of this infinitely wise God in His preservation of him all his life, and he now about fifty years old and so Hell-deserving. Another thought sweetly surprised him—God's marvelous plan of salvation by His well-beloved Son, and all this contrived before the world began. He comes out a strong predestinarian at once.

After all these cogitations of thought, it occurred to him to pray to God. Being alone (perhaps upstairs), he threw himself on a bed, and covered himself up, and began the Lord's Prayer.[332] He told us [that] he had not put up a prayer to God for thirty years. This prayer—"Our Father, which art in Heaven"—suited him best of all. [He thought] that God in Heaven was his Father for Jesus' sake. He had lain on the bed but a short time till it occurred to him, "Arise, sluggard. What doest thou here? And what thou doest do quickly."[333]

When his mind asked, "What must I do?" the reply was, "Be baptized." [127,2d]He set out a bitter cold afternoon to ride near twenty miles to find the man in whom he had confidence, having sat under his ministry when in childhood. And should he think him worthy, [he wanted that man] to baptize him before he returned. Some friends in Versailles informed him [that] the way was hard to find; and [that] if he knew the way, it would be ten o'clock at night before he could get there; [that] likely the preacher was not at home; and [with] such a mighty freeze in the waters that hardly a place could be found to baptize him. Being dissuaded from going on, he applied to other friends for counsel.

The noted old Sister Arnold, his mother, of whom I have said something before, and most of his other relations' belonging to Clear Creek perhaps determined his choice to join there, though Hillsboro Church was rather more convenient. When he was received by experience, I think [that] there was more joyful tears shed over this poor, believing, eleventh-hour sinner than I had seen

---

[331]Here in a rare usage *strove* is the past participle of the verb *strive*.
[332]Matthew 6:9-13.
[333]John 13:27.

at the place for several years. He preferred not to put off his baptism till the next day and was baptized the same evening[334] in dead of winter.

---

[334]In this usage the noun *evening* is a colloquialism meaning *afternoon* (from noon to sunset).

# 6
## Bullittsburg Church

[81]I have already stated that one reason of my removal [to Bullittsburg] was [the fact that] a good man, as I esteemed him, had left the [Clear Creek] Church on my account. My desire was that he might enjoy what I esteemed the greatest of all privileges on earth—a place in the church of Christ. Some years after my removal he took his place in the Clear Creek Church and has continued a member there ever since.

The summer before I moved to the Ohio [River], I was present at the constitution of a small church there of eight members.[1] Most of them had moved from Clear Creek. This little church, though constituted on the margin of the Ohio River, was in the wilderness; and not one family [was] free from Indian danger. This little, new church in the wilderness was far from any establishment of the kind. Its appellation was the Baptist Church of Christ at Bullittsburg,[2] where I moved in April 1795 and [to which] we took our membership.[3] I think [that] the church was thirteen in number,[4] all of whom I was well acquainted with.

I was invited the day I joined the church to take the care of it as a pastor, which I declined, for my mind was now fully made up as to my pastorship anywhere. As there was a man in the church the name of [Lewis] Deweese[5]

---

[1]The church at Bullittsburg was formed in June 1794 by Elders Joseph Redding and John Taylor and was composed of seven charter members, not eight. It was then the custom among Baptists in Kentucky that only ordained ministers should preside over the constituting of a congregation. The church's minutes from June through the following January were soon misplaced. When the first record book was begun, with the minutes of 7 February 1795, a statement about the founding of the church was formulated, showing Joseph Redding and William Cave as its organizers. In so far as this record relates to Cave, it is in error, because he was not set apart as an ordained minister until November 1801, as the church record shows. Bullittsburg Church, Minute Book A, 1, 47; John Taylor, *Thoughts on Missions*, 41-42; and Spencer, *Kentucky Baptists*, 1:292.

[2]When this congregation was organized, it was called the Great Bend of Ohio Church. It was located in Campbell (now Boone) County. Sometime between August 1795 and August 1796 its name was changed to Bullittsburg. Elkhorn Association, "Minutes," in Sweet, *American Frontier*, 1:468, 471; and Spencer, *Kentucky Baptists*, 1:292.

[3]John and Elizabeth Taylor joined the church on 2 May 1795 by a letter of dismissal from the Clear Creek Church. Bullittsburg Church, Minute Book A, 1.

[4]John Taylor and his wife became members no. 15 and no. 16. Ibid., 168.

[5]Two years would elapse before the church agreed to ordain Lewis Deweese as a

(young in the ministry though a [82]man in years), I informed the church [that]
if they would examine into the character and talents of Brother Deweese and
thought proper to ordain him, I should be ready with him to render any
Gospel service [that] the church called for [and] that we were capable to do.
In this the church seemed quite satisfied.[6]

The first year I felt my state awfully wretched and more so when the
Lord's day came than at any other time. I had long been in the habit of
worshiping the Lord in various directions among thousands of His people.
But now [I was among only] from twenty to forty hearers[7] and nearly the
same people every time we met together. And all of us as to religion [were],
in a manner, [as] cold as Canada.

The space of country between us and the settlements on Elkhorn [Creek
was] seventy or eighty miles. And the country [was] so generally rough that,
in my estimation, it would never fill up or at least in my time. Some small
villages across the [Ohio] River had lately began, as North Bend and others
in Symmes['s] late purchase. Cincinnati had lately sprung up a new town.[8]
But all looked gloomy to me. Every thing seemed to bear the aspect of
sorrow. I could not, in good conscience, invite anybody in good circumstances to move to the country. And yet as to this world, my all was there.

I remember writing a letter to a friend in which I stated my case to be as
[that of] Cain when driven from the presence of the Lord and [while]
dwelling in the land of Nod.[9] And as to my own feelings [I] seemed to have
no more comfortable religion than Cain himself [had]. It is said by the Jews
that when God pronounced the sentence against Cain that [*sic*] he [Cain] was

---

minister. Ibid., 10, 11.

[6]The clerk recorded this arrangement tersely: "John Taylor [was] invited to officiate
as minister in this church, which he is willing to do." Ibid., 1.

[7]From a membership of seven at the time of its constitution the church at Bullittsburg
had grown to twenty-three members by August 1795. Elkhorn Association, "Minutes," in
Sweet, *American Frontier*, 1:468.

[8]John Cleves Symmes, a New Jersey resident, secured from Congress a large grant
of land between the Great Miami and the Little Miami rivers, on the right bank of the
Ohio. Late in the summer of 1788 he and some of his cohorts arrived in that region. In
November, Columbia was settled a short distance below the mouth of the Little Miami.
Losantisville was established opposite the mouth of the Licking River. In time this village
would become the city of Cincinnati. Early in 1789 Symmes himself planted a settlement
at North Bend, the northernmost thrust of the Ohio River between the territories of Ohio
and Kentucky. Ray Allen Billington, *Western Expansion*, 4th ed. (New York NY, 1974)
214; and Thomas D. Clark, *Frontier America* (New York NY, 1959) 153.

[9]Genesis 4:16.

struck with a trembling and a particular nodding with his head which always attended him till his death. And this was the mark[10] that God set on him, and that nobody should kill the man that was always nodding with his head. Therefore, the country to which he went was called the land of Nod.[11]

[83]But as poor, wretched Cain had plenty of work to do in his new country and went at it and built him a city,[12] so we had the same remedy at hand. It now [was] late in the spring [1795] and we [were] in a new,[13] heavy forest.[14] We went to work with all might and main and made a fine, little crop and considerable improvement[15] the first year.

Through the course of the next winter and spring [1795-1796], a large connection of respectable people moved from Virginia by the name of Graves and settled in our neighborhood, which was a great acquisition to our settlement.[16] As also the second year after my removal [1797], a number of respectable families [came] from Scott County [17] and other parts of Kentucky, and a number of them being Baptists of the first class as to religious character.[18] Our little Bullittsburg Church received such a reinforcement that

---

[10]Genesis 4:15.

[11]There may be some substance to this tradition, because the Hebrew noun for *flight* or *exile* is transliterated *nod* and derives from the verb that in its intensive, reflexive form means *wag* or *nod* (the head).

[12]Genesis 4:17.

[13]By the adjective *new* Taylor means that it was a *virgin* forest.

[14]This land in Woolper Bottom, of present-day Boone County, was part of a two-thousand-acre tract purchased by Taylor and John Tanner from John David Woolper, of Philadelphia. Bordering on the Ohio River, it was forested with an abundance of species, including the following: black ash (hoopwood), white ash, beech, buckeye, cottonwood, dogwood, box elder, American elm, slippery elm, hackberry, hickory, hornbeam, black locust, honey locust, maple, mulberry, red oak, Spanish (southern red) oak, white oak, poplar, sugar, and sycamore. Boone County (KY), Boone Quarter Sessions Court, Deed Book A, 115-16; Boone County (KY) Court, Deed Book A, 268-70, 289-90, and Deed Book B, 288-90, 403-407, 407-409.

[15]*Improvement* is here an Americanism meaning "cultivation or construction that renders realty more valuable."

[16]Three Baptists by the name of Graves were received into the church on 1 July 1797 by letters of dismissal. Bullittsburg Church, Minute Book A, 9, 10.

[17]The establishment of Scott County was provided for by an act of the Kentucky legislature in 1792.

[18]From 1795 to 1797 the number of tithable persons in Campbell County grew from 541 to 794. Probably nearly 50 percent of these tithers lived in the area that became Boone County in 1799. (During its first year the newly formed county had 311 tithables, and the parent county of Campbell had 375 remaining.) Campbell County (KY) Court, Order Book A, 28, 78, 124, 217; and Boone County (KY) Court, Order Book A, 8-9.

we became much more comfortable in a church way. The settlement soon filled up so thick about Bullittsburg that the church increased entirely[19] by newcomers to about sixty[20] members, and many of them good-old,[21] peaceable disciplinarians.

About this time the church took up the subject of Brother [Lewis] Deweese's ordination at my request. I think there was now about twenty free, male members in the church, and their seats [were] seldom vacated at church meetings.

In no similar case did I ever see members act with so much plainness, faithfulness, and friendship as in this [instance]. For each one was asked his or her mind on this ordination. To the best of my recollection, not one was willing to ordain him, and their reasons given. I remember [that] one of the objectors [spoke] as if in the presence of God and with the utmost friendship to the man in question. He had known and been intimate with him from the time he began to preach, which had been several years. He could not see that he had improved any from the beginning, that he [Deweese] was now getting old, and [that] he [the objector] did not look for improvement hereafter. Others had similar reasons, but all agreed that he preached sound doctrine. Last of all I was enquired of. I also [84]objected to his ordination[22] but not from the same source that others did. My objection lay in an overbackwardness when he was called on to preach. But the whole church encouraged him to continue preaching.[23] Himself, [while] under all the investigation, seemed meek as a lamb, believing, as the church did, that he ought not to be ordained.

But the voice of the church [for Deweese] to go on gave him fresh activity. I do not recollect that he ever said, "No," after this when I asked him to preach. A few months after this the church took up the same subject and without a dissenting voice ordained him.[24] And he soon became one of the

---

[19]Taylor omits the word *entirely* in his second edition.

[20]By the close of 1797, sixty-four whites and one black had joined the church. Bullittsburg Church, Minute Book A, 168-69, 181.

[21]Here Taylor uses the adjective *good-old* as a colloquialism of affection.

[22]In view of the fact that Taylor brought the subject of Deweese's ordination before the church, it is strange that the elder opposed it.

[23]On Saturday 12 November 1796 the church debated the ministerial ordination of Deweese with "much conversation." Even though it was postponed, he was encouraged "to go forward as a preaching man." Bullittsburg Church, Minute Book A, 6.

[24]The ordination of Deweese was unanimously approved by the church on 2 September 1797 and scheduled for 15 October at the meetinghouse. Ibid., 11.

most acceptable preachers in Boone County.[25] After this he moved over to White Water[26] and is now generally the moderator of White Water Association.[27]

About this time James Lee had moved into Campbell County[28] and came some distance to join Bullittsburg Church. This was the same Lee that I had baptized at Clear Creek [and] who afterwards won my Bible by preaching. His reason for going some distance to join at Bullittsburg was, from his own account, that the church from which he was licensed to preach was young and weak in judgment.[29] He, therefore, desired to be under the close inspection of Bullittsburg as related to his ministry.

This heavenly man was soon called forward to ordination.[30] I call him "a heavenly man" because in his deportment there was a greater image of the Saviour in him than was commonly seen. With his great power of self-government[31] he never seemed caught off of his guard. He was often in tears, and his very smiles seemed to have something of Heaven in them. After his ordination he removed to the state of Ohio,[32] where he preached many years with great success. [He] has lately gone the way of the earth[33] and not in a very advanced age.[34]

---

[25]On 15 July 1799 the Boone County Court authorized Lewis Deweese to solemnize marriage. Boone County (KY) Court, Order Book A, 3.

[26]The church gave Lewis Deweese a letter of dismissal of 6 October 1810. Bullittsburg Church, Minute Book A, 136, 172.

[27]The White Water Association was constituted in 1809 in the Indiana Territory. Benedict, *Baptist Denomination*, 2:547.

[28]Campbell County was established by an act of the legislature passed in 1794.

[29]James Lee and Mary, his wife, were admitted to membership at Bullittsburg on 9 July 1796 on the basis of their statement that the congregation to which they once belonged had dissolved its organization. Bullittsburg Church, Minute Book A, 5.

[30]When the church had met in November 1796, it postponed the ordination but encouraged Lee "as a preaching man to come and see us as often as he can for better acquaintance." Almost ten months later the congregation unanimously consented to his being set apart for the ministry and scheduled the ceremony for Sunday 17 September 1797. Ibid., 7, 11.

[31]Here the noun *self-government* is a rare usage meaning *self-control*.

[32]Ohio entered the Union on 19 February 1803 as the seventeenth state.

[33]Joshua 23:14.

[34]James Lee was dismissed by letter from membership in the church in November 1797. Bullittsburg Church, Minute Book A, 169.

Mr. George Eve moved from Virginia and took his membership at Bullittsburg.[35] After Mr. Eve's arrival we had great hopes of a revival of religion, [85]for he had a great talent in stirring up the people that way. By some of the members the question of [a] particular pastor was thought of. Perhaps those who brought the question forward had their mind on Mr. Eve. But the church was of [the] opinion that they were better off as they were,[36] for they now had three ordained ministers.[37] Though Mr. Eve continued with us perhaps two years,[38] we had no ingathering by baptism. God's time to favor Zion that way had not yet come.

But the church at Bullittsburg, through this apparent[39] wintry season, exceeded anything I had ever seen in peace and good will among her members. She exceeded also in strength of counsel and [in] well-tempered zeal in the cause of religion. The brethren were often together in different kinds of meetings and always seemed to part with reluctance. God's praises often rang among them with heavenly melody, for we had a number of good singers among us.

For five long years only one man was baptized; and he perhaps was not sound at core, for two months after his baptism he was excluded from the church.[40] Yet through all this season the church with steady zeal in the cause of religion and [with] love to each other went forward. Perhaps their number now was from sixty to eighty.[41]

---

[35]On 8 April 1797 George Eve joined the church by a letter of dismissal. During the following month his wife, Elizabeth, became a member. Ibid., 8, 9, 169.

[36]On 2 December 1797 the church took up the question of calling a pastor but decided that one was "not necessary at present." Ibid., 13.

[37]The three ministers were John Taylor, Lewis Deweese, and George Eve.

[38]George Eve and his wife left the church by a letter of dismissal granted on 1 February 1800. Through the moderator, John Taylor, the congregation at that meeting invited Eve to remain in the vicinage of Bullittsburg, but he chose to move to Franklin County. Bullittsburg Church, Minute Book A, 24, 169; and Spencer, *Kentucky Baptists*, 1:294.

[39]The adverb *apparent* is a colloquialism used in place of *apparently*.

[40]Taylor miswrites here because during his first five years at Bullittsburg three people were baptized—Isaac Carlton, Lettice Peck, and William Cloud, Jr. Cloud was the person who was excluded from the church. At a called meeting on Saturday 14 December 1799 he was excommunicated for the offense of using "harsh and unsavory speeches and railing." On that day, as at a meeting the previous month, Cloud refused to express regret and to seek the forgiveness of the church. He had been baptized only three months earlier. Bullittsburg Church, Minute Book A, 21, 22, 23, 168-69, 172.

[41]During the five-year period that began with May 1795, seventy-five whites and one black had joined the church. Twelve of that number had been excommunicated, had been

Very early in the spring of 1800 Mr. Eve left us. And though there was some weeping at his parting sermon (as I heard, for I was then on a tour from home), yet many feared they should never hear again the joyful tidings of the conversion of sinners or see any more people baptized. Indeed myself was very much overwhelmed with those kind of feelings, for the removal of Eve was, in a manner, like death to me. Yea,[42] death itself about that time would have seemed a relief to me and great gain.

A few days after Mr. Eve left us, I received a letter from Benjamin Craig,[43] at the mouth of [the] Kentucky [River],[44] that they had a great revival of religion there,[45] desiring me to pay them an immediate visit, and [informing me] what night there would be a meeting at his house. [86]Sometime before this, I had purchased a tract of land at the lower end of Gallatin County[46] and [had] fixed on a day to meet the man I had purchased of or his agent on the land [in order] to trace up the lines.[47] [Even] had not Craig sent his letter (which was near fifty miles), I had intended to have been at his house the very night that the meeting was to be there [in order] to meet my business below; so that I deserve no credit for being at the meeting at Craig's.

The house being much crowded with a number of preachers present, they requested me to preach. This I did with much reluctance. From the dull feelings of my heart I took a text which suited my own state: "Lord, help

---

dismissed by letter, or had died. The membership at the end of April 1800 amounted to sixty-four. Ibid., 168-69, 181.

[42]*Yea* is an archaic adverb meaning *moreover*.

[43]Benjamin Craig (b. 1751), who was not a preacher, was the ninth child of Toliver Craig and Polly Hawkins, of Orange County, Virginia. At the organization of the Elkhorn Association in 1785, he represented the South Elkhorn Church. Spencer, *Kentucky Baptists*, 1:27; and Masters, *Baptists in Kentucky*, 52.

[44]At this site was located the village of Port William, now called Carrollton, the seat of Carroll County.

[45]This meeting in the early spring of 1800 marked the beginning of the Baptist phase of the Great Revival in Kentucky. Spencer, *Kentucky Baptists*, 1:536, 538.

[46]Gallatin County was created under the terms of a 1798 act of the General Assembly.

[47]See page 88 of Taylor's text for his comments on this tract of one thousand acres. Adjoining this acreage on the east side was a tract that measured twelve hundred acres and in which Taylor owned a half undivided interest. On 5 August 1799 John Sutton, Jr., and John Taylor had received a deed from John Sutton, Sr., and his wife, Temperance, for this second piece of land. It had been first surveyed on 4 October 1786, and the elder Sutton had been granted this land three years later. Patent to John Sutton, 30 Oct 1789, in Gallatin (KY) Circuit Court, Record of Proceedings, 1802-1810, 136-37; and Deed to John Sutton, Jr., and John Taylor, 5 Aug 1799, ibid., 137-38.

me."[48] I continued but a short time, for I felt myself very worthless. After which they continued on in prayer, praise, and exhortation with much noise at times till late in the night. Some were rejoicing, having lately obtained deliverance; others groaning in tears under a pensive load of guilt; while myself silently musing on what I saw or heard.

My own heart [was] so barren and hard that I wished myself out of sight, or lying under the seats where the people sat, or trodden under their feet. And yet I was so base at times [as] to call in question the reality of the work that was before me. For there was a mixture of Methodists and Baptists together. Having now forgotten all their differences, [they] were now worshiping God together. This mixture disgusted my jealous heart a little, thinking that this union would not last long, which did come to pass soon after when they came to dividing the fish they had caught together. However, the result as to myself was that, be this work what it may, I was too unworthy to bear the name of Christian minister. My soul felt sad indeed.

Many of the people tarried all night. One object with them was to converse with me. I never heard the question "What shall we do to be saved?"[49] more prevalent at any time of my life than now. Or had I ever so many questions asked me for the same [87]length of time as through the balance of this night, while the text I had taken would reverberate through my whole soul—"Lord, help me"—for I felt unworthy to be in their company. A number of them neither lay down nor slept through the whole night and seemed disappointed when near the break of day I lay down to take about one hour of broken rest.

About sunrise next morning I took my leave of this blessed company of young disciples, which seemed a great grief to them. My excuse was that I must meet some men in the woods next day for the purpose of surveying and that it became my duty not to disappoint them. But with myself I had one more secret reason, which was to get by myself and mourn over my own barren soul.

I had no desire to use food that day. I rode on with pensive reflection, calling up in my mind past days when I had hoped [that] the candle of the Lord shone on me. But by the multiplicity of the business of this little world, my affections had been stolen off from the Lord. My eyes would not only swim, but overflow, with tears as I rode along by myself. That afternoon I came to a Captain Gray's [farm] on Corn Creek, now Col[onel] Presley

---

[48]Matthew 15:25.
[49]Acts 16:30.

Gray.[50] He treated me very respectfully; but, with the small acquaintance I had with him before, I considered him a great critic on the Baptists and rather deistical in his principles. As I expected to be several days in the woods surveying not very distant from Gray's, I concluded to appoint three night meetings one after the other at different places. Mr. Gray through complaisance agreed to circulate the notice.

I felt uncommon desire for the salvation of that family when I took leave of them that evening. My desire had so far enlarged on the same object that at my second night meeting, being near Mr. Gray's, I invited myself home with him and was made happy to find this freedom to be very pleasing both to him and Mrs. Gray.[51] It being near bedtime when we got home, though supper came on, an almost entire, solemn silence pervaded us all. I had but little [88]appetite for food through the anxiety of my soul. Yet [I] feared to ask them how the state of their souls were, lest they should take offence and my object be lost. But at length I broke[52] my mind with the feelings of my heart for their eternal interest. I found [that] they were equally willing with myself to converse on that subject, for their minds had been considerably touched that night at meeting.

At my last night's meeting they took some trouble to hunt me up in the dark to take leave of me, and perhaps both of them in tears. This gave me more pleasure than men feel when the oil and wine increases.[53] Several others became stirred up at those night meetings. This part of the world becoming my home after this, I will take some notice of this land I was now surveying. It was an old military tract of a thousand acres that had been surveyed about forty years before for a Col[onel William] Byrd [III].[54] And it, being one of

---

[50]Presley Gray (b. 1764) became a captain in the Franklin County Regiment in July 1800. The 51st Militia Regiment, planned for the new county of Gallatin, was not laid off until December of that year. Gray was commissioned a major during that month. Two years later he was given the command of the new regiment with the rank of colonel. Clift, *"Corn Stalk" Militia*, 88, 90.

[51]Mrs. Presley Gray was the mother of at least three sons—John D. (d. 1822), Benjamin, and William. Dorothy Thompson, "Additional Notes," 350.

[52]Here the transitive verb *break* is an old usage meaning *disclose* or *divulge*.

[53]2 Chronicles 32:28.

[54]William Byrd III (1728-1777) was generally known as Colonel Byrd of Westover, the name of the mansion built by his father on the James River. The younger Byrd, like his father, was a member of the Executive Council of Virginia. During the French and Indian War he commanded the 2d Virginia Regiment. He became a Tory when the Revolutionary War erupted; in time he squandered his estate and committed suicide. Richard L. Morton, *Colonial Virginia*, 2:713n., 715; and Louis Knott Koontz, *Robert*

the highest bluffs on the Ohio River, was called by the surveyor "Mount Byrd," by which name it has been called ever since.[55] Though nothing of the kind could be more pleasing to the eye than this situation— the levelness and fertility of the soil together with the plenty[56] and purity of the water (all calculated to invite)—my mind was but sparingly elated under its anxieties otherways, while we were doing this surveying.

Notwithstanding the little apparent success at Corn Creek, I left the place with an aching heart, thinking on my past delinquency and unprofitableness in the Gospel ministry. I went from thence to Clear Creek, the place of my former residence. The object was to be at their church meeting. This was among the calamitous times of Clear Creek Church. On Sunday, I took another text suited to myself: "I have put off my coat. How shall I put it on? I have washed my feet. How shall I defile them?"[57] This text perhaps suited others as well as myself, though I felt at present great, heart yearnings for my old neighbors.

I almost dreaded to go home, fearing I should be, as I had been, unprofitable among them. [89]Poor Bullittsburg now appeared like a forsaken cottage in the wilderness, for Mr. Eve was now gone. I had heard of his removal while on this tour.

When I got home, a new scene very much afflicted me. A Captain [Abraham] Depew,[58] who had married a relation[59] to my wife [and] being of a gay turn, had been for some time encouraging balls at his house, which had

*Dinwiddie: His Career in American Colonial Government and Westward Expansion* (Glendale CA, 1941), 183n.

[55]The one-thousand-acre tract called Mount Byrd was surveyed on 24 May 1774 by John Floyd (1750-1783), assistant surveyor of Fincastle County, Virginia. It is situated on the Ohio about eleven miles below the mouth of the Kentucky River. This parcel was assigned by the executors of William Byrd III to John Carter Littlepage, who received a grant for it in December 1780. In the previous month the area where this tract is located had been incorporated into the newly created Jefferson County. Society of Colonial Wars in the Commonwealth of Kentucky, *Year Book, 1917* ([Louisville KY, 1917]), 72; and Brookes-Smith, *Master Index: Virginia Surveys and Grants, 1774-1791*, 28.

[56]The term "the plenty" is an early use of the noun *plenty* with the article *the* to mean "sufficient supply."

[57]Song of Solomon 5:3.

[58]Abraham Depew was commissioned in 1799 a militia lieutenant in the 21st Regiment, of Campbell County; a year later, a captain; in 1803, the adjutant. In 1806 he became a major in the 67th Regiment, of Boone County; in 1811, its commanding lieutenant colonel. Clift, *"Corn Stalk" Militia*, 68, 169, 170.

[59]Abraham Depew married Elizabeth Mountague (d. 1808), daughter of William Mountague, Sr. Power of Attorney, 27 Jan 1800, Boone County (KY) Deed Book A, 28.

grown to such a height about this time that chief of the youth in the neighborhood had become distracted with the pleasure of Depew's dances. And what gave me most pain of all was [that] many of the good-old Baptists had not restrained their children from these frolics. Their plan was to advise their children and then [to] let them take their own course. In vain did I remonstrate from the example of old Eli and his sons.[60] Some of them were ready to laugh at my scrupulocity [*sic*]. This made me wish heartily that I had never seen Bullittsburg, notwithstanding all my earthly interest was there. But I had some glance of hope by a removal to Mount Byrd, about sixty miles down the river, for in that neighborhood I had lately seen some buddings of a revival of religion.

About this time [March 1800], a brother of Mrs. [Elizabeth] Depew's, William Mountague, [Jr.],[61] got married to a young lady[62] in the neighborhood. And this made a great opening for several days' dancing at the wedding and several infares.[63] From Thursday till perhaps Sunday morning they were in the sweet enjoyment of these pleasures of sin. Their last day of mirth was at Capt[ain] Depew's on Saturday. That night I had a meeting near the place, where but few attended, though I heard they had a crowded house at the infare [and] though two young ladies left the dance and came almost alone from thence to the meeting. This was some encouragement [to believe] that the Devil did not reign sole monarch of this lower world.

The next day was preaching at our meetinghouse. It was a usual thing, notwithstanding the vanity of the youth, for all to come to meeting and

[60]1 Samuel 2:22-25.

[61]William Mountague, Jr., who was converted during the Great Revival, joined the Bullittsburg Church. From his ordination in 1817 until his defection in 1830, he worked diligently within the bounds of the North Bend Association. In the latter year, however, the Campbellite tidal wave swept him from his Baptist anchorage. Spencer, *Kentucky Baptists*, 2:148.

[62]William Mountague, Jr., and Polly Robinson were married in Boone County in March 1800 by Lewis Deweese. Boone County (KY) Marriage Book A, 2. Even though the groom was a kinsman of Elizabeth Taylor, he did not choose John Taylor to officiate at his wedding. We do not know why he chose Deweese. It may have been that the marriage occurred while Taylor was gone on tour to Mount Byrd and Clear Creek. Or it may have been that the groom took umbrage at Taylor's opposition to his sister's promotion of dances in the Bullittsburg community.

[63]The dialectal word *infare* means "dinner served after a wedding." For an account of infares and the accompanying conviviality and dancing common to eighteenth-century frontier weddings, see Doddridge, *Western Virginia*, chap. xxii.

especially on Sundays. We had a crowded meeting; perhaps all the dancers were there.

[90]Mrs. Depew had endeavored to strengthen her female disciples before they went to meeting by saying to them, "Girls, we shall hear enough of our dancing today, but let us not mind that Mr. Taylor says. We are at liberty and will do as we please, let him say what he will."

I never had been so thoroughly cowed down by discouragement through the course of my ministry as now, though it had been in action for twenty-five years. And [I] really thought [that] I had better be dead than alive, for I felt as if Satan had gotten the mastery where I lived. So that I could say from my soul, "Woe is me that I sojourn in Mesech, and that I dwell in the tents of Kedar!"[64]

My eyes had for several years often glanced over a text of Scripture, and [I] often had a desire to preach from it. But [I] never had till this day, fearing that I had not the feeling [that] the author had when he wrote the text, which was Rom[ans] 10[th] chap[ter] and 1st v[erse]: "My heart's desire and prayer to God for Israel is that they might be saved."

Soon after I began, a set of feelings overtook me that exceeded anything I ever felt in public speaking. They consisted of a profuse weeping that I could not suppress, while I made a comparison of the then state of Israel with my poor neighbors [and] while the whole assembly seemed to reciprocate the same feelings. Perhaps there was not a dry eye in the house.

Mrs. Depew, who had braced herself and others before she came to meeting, exceeded in weeping, so that it was some time before she could get from the place after meeting broke. She went weeping all the way home. And nothing that her affectionate husband could say could pacify her, because nothing but the blood of Jesus can relieve a wounded conscience.

What the Lord did at this meeting entirely broke up all the dancing in the settlement. And about three months after this, Mrs. Depew was baptized and her husband soon after.[65]

---

[64]Psalm 120:5. Before the outbreak of the Great Revival, spiritual barrenness characterized nearly all the churches throughout Kentucky. Even so, William Vaughan described John Taylor as being among the few ministers "who still maintained their integrity to heaven" and who "moaned over the desolation of Zion." Thomas M. Vaughan, *Wm. Vaughan*, 120.

[65]On the basis of her experience of grace, the church received Elizabeth Mountague Depew as a candidate for baptism on 5 July 1800; her husband, on the seventeenth of the month following. Bullittsburg Church, Minute Book A, 27, 28, 170.

Immediately after this meeting, some business called me down to the mouth of the [91]Wabash River,[66] and [I] was absent three or four weeks. Arrangements [that had been made] before I started down the [Ohio] River hurried me home so speedily that though I came through Corn Creek settlement I did not stop to hold a meeting.

I hastily called at Captain [Presley] Gray's and took breakfast. And while at the table, Mrs. Gray informed me that some of her family, since I was there last, had expressed a great desire to see me again. But my heedless soul seemed to take no notice of what she said, though her husband was sitting at the table [and] looking very serious. But in my headlong way [I] hurried off, and saying but little about religion, except in common enquiries, while there. And [I] did not reflect on the purport of Mrs. Gray's statement till I had traveled ten miles, when I had a strong excitement to turn back as a chastisement for my neglect. But I afterwards concluded [that] I would soon come back to Corn Creek and spend a week worshiping among the people.

Arriving at home, I was happily informed that a number of the people were under very serious impressions. This was early in May [1800]. Our meetings became more crowded by day or night, till our monthly meeting in June, which was on the first Saturday and Sunday, at which time five respectable men (and they only) came forward and related their experiences and were baptized. They were men with families and [were] permanent settlers in the place. Their names were John Graves, [Sr.],[67] William Cave, [Jr.],[68] Jameson Hawkins,[69] James Cloud,[70] and Edward Webb.[71] Mr. Graves

---

[66]The Wabash River empties into the Ohio where the boundaries of the present-day states of Illinois, Indiana, and Kentucky converge. It heads up in western Ohio, flows clear across Indiana, and forms the lower half of the western border of the latter state.

[67]John Graves, Sr., was the father of Absolom Graves. Some of John's descendants even to the fifth generation were still members of the Bullittsburg Church in 1872. Kirtley, *Bullittsburg Church*, 8-9.

[68]William Cave, Jr. (1768?-1825),was a son of William Cave, Sr., the preacher, and Mary Mallory, the first of his three wives. Dorothy Thompson, "John Taylor as a Biographer of Pioneer Baptist Preachers," part II, Filson Club *History Quarterly* 63 (Oct 1963): 343, 348, 356.

[69]On 15 September 1800 Jameson Hawkins listed his property with a justice of the peace in Boone County. Clift, *"Second Census" of Kentucky, 1800*, 129.

[70]The name of James Cloud appears on the tax roll of Boone County for 1800. Ibid., 56.

[71]Edward Webb turned in his list of property to a magistrate of Boone County on 20 August 1800. Ibid., 312. Webb presented himself before the congregation on Saturday 7 June 1800; the other four, on the following day. Bullittsburg Church, Minute Book A, 26,

was between sixty and seventy years of age. [He] had obtained hope in Christ thirty or forty years before but could never have courage to join the church till now.

I have spoken of this as a happy day. I consider it so from the mighty effects of this day's baptizing [on 8 June]. Perhaps many present had never seen baptism before. And [for] others it had been so long since they had seen it, it seemed as if it had just come from Heaven. None seemed to leave the place but with great moisture of heart and eyes.

[92]On the road, I traveled [by] myself. About a half mile from the water I overtook the well-known George Gaines,[72] who was afoot. From his philosophical mind and firmness as a man, it would seem that nothing of a common nature could move him. [He] had been weeping all the way from the water. When I came near him, with all the apparent agony of soul as if the Day of Judgment had come, [he] forced out a dolerous [sic] cry with this enquiry: "Can you feel or find a heart to pray for me?" We clasped each other's hands, and for some time neither of us seemed able to speak.

I moved on about two miles and overtook another man who was also walking alone. He seemed to stagger as he moved on through [a] weighty burthen[73] of soul, for I saw and beheld him several hundred yards before I came up with him. This was Christopher Willson, the now well-known preacher.[74] This man, though the son of a preacher, had seemed as far from God as any man in the county. He had been long striving, through love of vice, to rivet himself in infidelity and [to] throw away the Scriptures as a book unworthy of his confidence.

At that time he was doing some cabinet work at my house. On Saturday morning I had asked him to go to church meeting. [I told him] that I expected some people would offer their experiences, and that perhaps the Lord would do something for his soul. And though I looked for nothing but some jeering answer, he seemed struck with a sober appearance and replied [that] if I

---

170.

[72]Around 1812 George Gaines donated the two-acre tract to the church on which its meetinghouse had been standing since 1797. This land the congregation has continued to occupy to this day. William Bruce Campbell, Sr., *Bullittsburg's Ministry of Faith: 175 Years* ([Burlington KY], 1969), 6.

[73]The archaic noun *burthen* means *burden*.

[74]In 1812 Christopher Willson was serving as the pastor of the recently constituted Forks of Gunpowder Church, affiliated with the North Bend Association. Benedict, *Baptist Denomination*, 2:540-41.

desired him to go he would. And immediately [he] laid down his tools and prepared for meeting.

However, when I overhauled him in the road [that Sunday], he seemed to be trembling in tears as if the joints of his loins were loosed.[75] We reached out hands to each other, not being able to speak, and parted in solemn silence, while I reciprocated all his then tender feelings.

About two months after this, Willson was baptized[76] and soon began to preach.[77] Mr. Gaines was also soon baptized.[78] From this happy [93]baptism, I took notice [that] about twenty experiences were received in the church.[79]

My secret vow to visit Corn Creek, at the lower end of Gallatin County about sixty miles from home, had been put off a week or two on account of this looked-for baptism. I had previously agreed with my very respected friend Mr. [William] Cave, though an old man [but] now a young preacher, to take this Corn Creek tour with me. On Monday morning [9 June 1800] we set out for Corn Creek with all the encouragement and heavenly warmth excited at this late baptizing. We passed by the mouth of [the] Kentucky, leaving appointments on our return.

On the second day we came to Captain [Presley] Gray's, he not being at home. My first work was to acknowledge the fault of my abrupt departure when I was there last. To atone for which (as one reason) I had rode sixty miles over a very rough road, as also to worship some days among the people and [to] warn that settlement of people to flee from the wrath to come.[80] On which Mrs. Gray burst forth into a torrent of tears, and at times exclaiming, "Mr. Taylor sees the ruin we are in and is come to warn us of it!" And [she] seemed to feel as if Sodom's fire[81] was hovering over the place. Perhaps this became a death blow to this dear woman, as Paul says, "Sin revived and I died."[82] But I have ever thought [that] she died to live again. After becoming

---

[75]Daniel 5:6.

[76]Christopher Willson was added to the church on 3 August 1800. The account of his experience was heard on the previous day. Bullittsburg Church, Minute Book A, 28, 170.

[77]On 1 August 1801 the church voted to encourage Willson in the use of his "public gifts" as a preacher. Ibid., 44.

[78]George Gaines was received by the church as a candidate for baptism on 22 June 1800. Ibid., 26, 170.

[79]From the time of the baptism of the five men on 8 June 1800 through the following August twenty-two whites and twelve blacks were baptized into the membership of the congregation. Ibid., 170, 181.

[80]Matthew 3:7.

[81]Genesis 19:24.

[82]Romans 7:9.

a little composed, she expressed her grief at the absence of her husband, who was then on a tour after runaway horses and not likely to return before we left the place. But she informed us that he had been under an increasing concern about his soul from the time of my surveying my land in the neighborhood, and [that she] was much more hopeful of her husband's salvation than her own.

We immediately made appointments in the settlement for several days. And not expecting to see Capt[ain] Gray, I wrote him a friendly letter. I meant to express all the friendship and tenderness that one man could to another; but, finding that I came very far short of the feelings of [94]my heart, I now recollect [that] I closed with a single verse following:

> Now to conclude, my dear friend Gray,
> It is but little I can say;
> But, 'tis a truth, I wish you well
> More than my pen or tongue can tell.

At our last evening meeting Mr. Gray came home and was present when it was agreed that we would take breakfast with him next morning, when none of us had much appetite for eating. He seemed solemn and pensive as if the sentence of death had lately been passed on him by an earthly judge. I was soon inquisitive about the state of his mind or [about] what view he had of himself as a sinner. He replied [that though] he had never committed a practical sin he was a sinner in heart, and that he was nothing but sin throughout, and that he could see but little difference between his best and worst things in the sight of a holy, heart-searching God, [and] that he was such a lump of moral corruption in the sight of God that he could not rise from his then seat and walk out at the door but [that] there would sin enough naturally flow from him to damn a world, if imputed to them. And all this [was] expressed in such a pensive strain that it was enough to awaken sympathy in the hardest heart.

This doctrine may look strange to a blinded heart, but I defy the man who has [made] such a discovery of himself ever to fall in with Ariainism[83] or

---

[83]Arianism is the teaching of Arius (d. 336), a Greek patriarch of Alexandria who held that Jesus Christ was not of the same substance as was God the Father but that he was a created being occupying a place above all other creatures. Arius thought that Jesus was neither fully God nor fully man. Williston Walker, *et al.*, *A History of the Christian Church*, 4th ed. (New York, 1985), 131-32, 133.

Socinianism[84] or any other ism of the kind, for only an Almighty Saviour will suit his case. But superficial conviction of sin may lead a deluded soul to make use of a superficial saviour of some sort, but Jesus Christ did not come to our world to save self-helpers but the lost and helpless.[85]

Sometime after this I baptized both [Presley] Gray and his wife but not at the same time. These were among the first fruits at Corn Creek. We took our leave of the family, attended our meetings at the mouth of Kentucky, and moved on our way to Bullittsburg.

The revival [95]from this [June] baptizing became very general through the settlement [of Bullittsburg]. I remember [that] when Elkhorn Association came on in August [1800] we had baptized twenty, and but few young people among them and only one man of colour.[86] [The latter was] a young fellow who I had raised myself by the name of Asa.[87] I had learned him to read very well. He afterwards became a preacher. Asa and Christopher Willson were both baptized the same day, and they only.[88] After they both became preachers, Mr. Willson took great pleasure in taking Asa with him when on a tour of preaching.

This revival differed a little from the common, for people of years and of the male kind took the lead, as I have stated in our first baptism of five men. This revival continued about one year (with pretty even pace), in which about a hundred and twelve were baptized.[89]

It will be remembered [that] the settlement in Boone County was but sparingly filled up as yet. Bullittsburg church had now grown up to about two hundred members,[90] and they were very compactly settled with their meeting-

---

[84]Socinianism is the doctrine of Faustus Socinus (1539-1604), an Italian reformer who denied the divinity of Christ and who rejected the total depravity of man, the authority of the church, and the satisfaction theory of the atonement. Socinus held that the Scriptures are the source of religious truth but that they must be rationalistically interpreted. Ibid., 536, 538.

[85]Cf. Matthew 18:11.

[86]Taylor means that up to the time the Elkhorn Association convened, only one black had been baptized during the three months under study. During the last ten days of August, however, eleven blacks were baptized. Bullittsburg Church, Minute Book A, 181.

[87]Asa was one of the eight slaves bequeathed to the author by his uncle Joseph Taylor in 1782.

[88]These baptisms occurred on Sunday 3 August 1800. Bullittsburg Church, Minute Book A, 28, 170, 183.

[89]The church roll shows that 111 persons (80 whites, 31 blacks) were baptized during the fourteen months beginning June 1800. Ibid., 170-71, 175, 181, 183.

[90]When the movement for forming a church on Woolper Creek began, the

house in a central place. Only some members about Middle Creek and
Woolper Bottom were a little scattered off. Those members began to contemplate a new constitution. And on a paper for this purpose about twenty names
were set down and petitioned Bullittsburg to constitute them.[91] Robert Garnett,[92] a young preacher, was among them.

Bullittsburg now had six or seven preachers, but only [Lewis] Deweese
and myself were ordained. I now lived at the upper end of Woolper Bottom
and about middle ground between the new [church] and [the] old church, who
immediately appointed helps to examine into and, if need be, [to] constitute
this new church. They appointed several others with all their preachers but
myself to constitute this new church.[93] After this arrangement I soon began
to feel as if I was in a sweat house, for I was not on their paper as a peti-
tioner for a new church.

"And why [was I] not named in their council," said my [96]proud heart, "to
constitute this new church?"

membership of Bullittsburg stood at 162 (130 whites, 32 blacks) on 8 March 1801. Ibid.,
168-71, 181.

[91]On 7 February 1801 some members who lived on the southern edge of the
Bullittsburg Church sought its approval to constitute a separate congregation in their
neighborhood. The church agreed to the request provided that the helps who would be
called in also thought that the proposition was necessary. Ibid., 32.

[92]The author may have mentioned Robert Garnett by name as a young preacher
because of the notoriety he later acquired as the accused in a case before the church.
Probably a native of Virginia, this migrant with his wife, Eleanor, had joined the
Bullittsburg Church on 22 June 1800. In May 1801 the man but not his wife united with
the newly constituted congregation on Woolper Creek. The following month when the two
churches merged under the old name, his membership returned to Bullittsburg. As a
speaker, Garnett had impressed his brethren, who in August encouraged him to exercise
his "public gifts" as a licentiate. But all did not go well, for in March 1803 he was
charged with making "immodest attempts towards a woman," and his membership was
suspended. A month later, still not giving the church satisfaction, he was
excommunicated. In August, however, Garnett atoned for his wrongdoing, and the church
forgave him and restored him to its fellowship. In March 1804 he and his wife were
furnished letters of dismissal, and they probably joined the Middle Creek Church, which
in time ordained Garnett to the ministry. Ibid., 26-176 passim; and Spencer, *Kentucky
Baptists*, 2:148.

[93]In March 1801 the church appointed Lewis Deweese, William Cave, John Hall, John
Conner, and Cave Johnson to help in the constitution of the proposed congregation.
Bullittsburg Church, Minute Book A, 33.

The answer in myself was, "The old church designs some way to hook you into the new church and thereby get clear of you. And the new church has no desire to have you, or they would have invited your hand to their paper." All this made my sweat house the more hot.

The time for the constitution[94] was on our monthly meeting day in a house at the lower end of Woolper Bottom. (The Sunday's preaching was to be at my house.) I went to the meeting. That business being taken up, all went on smoothly.[95] Myself was perfectly silent, for I was partly in the dumps. There was then an agreement that all who chose to be in the new church might say so the next day after preaching and save the trouble of after applications for letters of dismission.

"This," said I to myself, "is to be the mode of hooking." My sweat was about its highest pitch when I left the meeting, being at the utmost loss to know what to be at, for to me there was plenty of evidence that neither church wished me to be among them.

But after I got home and my sweat began to evaporate (being naturally fond of new establishments) [and] after consulting my family[96] (who then consisted of eleven members[97] of the church), we unitedly agreed to fall in with the new establishment, though it was only the skirts and mere little shanks of the old church both in members and local situation.

Accordingly, after preaching the next day I made known the choice of myself and family.[98] On which about forty of the members of the old church rose up and made the same declaration. And some of them [lived] beyond the meetinghouse and [were] among the most respectable members of the church. Perhaps the new church acquired fifty members on that day.[99]

---

[94]The date of the constitution was Saturday 14 March 1801. Ibid., 33, 37.

[95]The new congregation was named the "Baptist Church of Christ at Woolper Creek." Ibid., 37.

[96]Evidently the family council, composed of both whites and blacks, was held before Saturday the fourteenth of March 1801, because the record of the Woolper Creek Church shows that the constituting members presented themselves on Saturday and not on Sunday. Ibid., 37-38.

[97]Taylor, his wife, and his oldest child were part of this number. Seven slaves—Asa, Ben, Dublin, Lettice, Jacob, Judith, and Nanny—who belonged to the preacher were members at Bullittsburg. Ibid., 181, 182.

[98]The black woman Nanny did not move her membership to Woolper Creek; the other six of Taylor's slaves did. Taylor and his wife and their first-born son, Benjamin, then a lad of seventeen years, also transferred their membership. Ibid., 34, 181, 182.

[99]John and Elizabeth Taylor's names head the list of constituent members. Altogether forty-five whites and twelve blacks composed the new congregation. Ibid., 34.

And in a few meetings after, by dismissions the new church became about on an equality as to number[100] [with the old church] and perhaps equal in strength either in counsel or property. The new church had three or four licensed preachers and one ordained. The old church had one licensed preacher [97]and one ordained.[101] Absolom Graves was also in the new church —a man of fine counsel in a church. And afterwards [he] became a famous preacher.

The new church, after selecting their officers, proceeded in haste to build them[102] a meetinghouse. [It] raised about five hundred dollars and began to build a framed meetinghouse of size sufficient to hold all the worshipers in the settlement. And [it was located] about two miles below the old meetinghouse.[103] The old church intended building a new house higher up and [at] a greater distance from the new church.[104] But after a solemn pause [the old church] appointed a committee to wait on the new church and [to] propose reunion of the two churches, which was cheerfully agreed to by the new church.[105] And the materials prepared for their meetinghouse[106] [were]

---

[100]As to the number of white members at the time the two churches merged, the old one had seventy-three and the new one seventy-two. Ibid., 172-75.

[101]John Taylor was the ordained minister in the new church; Lewis Deweese, in the old. Ibid., 34, 168.

[102]The pronoun *them* is here an archaic, reflexive usage meaning *themselves*.

[103]On 14 March 1801 the Woolper Creek Church agreed to locate its meetinghouse at a spring near the Richard Tanner farm. It seems that the site was on Ashbys Fork of Woolper Creek at the crossing of the road leading from John Tanner's Station to Newport. A month later the congregation decided on a framed meetinghouse twenty-four by thirty-six feet. Its construction would be principally financed by the members' contributions of "certain species of property." Bullittsburg Church, Minute Book A, 36, 38, 39, 40.

[104]Since October 1800 the Bullittsburg Church had been toying with a proposal to construct a new meetinghouse. The members agreed a month later that a framed building twenty-four by forty feet with a thirteen-foot pitch to the roof would meet their needs. Money would be required for nails, hinges, locks, and window glass, but lumber could be obtained by bartering the members' gifts in kind. The following January the congregation chose the ford on Ashbys Fork as the site, provided someone donated a piece of land there. Ibid., 30-31, 32. After the Woolper Creek Church was formed, the mother church evidently changed the intended location to one higher up in Woolper Bottom.

[105]On 6 June 1801 Chichester Matthews suggested to the Bullittsburg Church that it be consolidated with the Woolper Creek Church and that the two congregations meet for that purpose on the twenty-seventh at the Crossing of Ashbys Fork. Bullittsburg agreed with this motion and designated Matthews and Lewis Deweese as its agents to carry this proposal to the next meeting of Woolper Creek. When the Woolper Creek Church

taken to the old cite [*sic*], which remains the place of worship for Bullittsburg to this day and [which] is often called Old Jerusalem.

I never did enquire very closely why myself was not named in the council to constitute this new church, for it must have been a concerted thing among the brethren, thinking perhaps that I should not approve of what they considered a good work.

[141,2d]A little before this circumstance a number of Baptists had moved from Virginia and settled [on Dry Run] about ten miles from Bullittsburg. They sent to us and other places to come and constitute them into a church.[107] A number of helps met from different quarters. I think there was seventeen members [who] thus applied for helps, and nearly half of them [were] respectable, free, male members.[108] And the distance [was] considerable from any other church. Perhaps there was no doubt with any of us of the utility of a church in that place.

While in that investigation, I asked the brethren a few questions, such as "Do you think if you are brought into a church state you can meet together and worship God independent[109] of any person coming from a distance to worship with you?" [I told them] that I considered every church of Christ as a candle of the Lord wherever it was set up[110] [and] as a city on a hill that

---

assembled on the twentieth, it consented to its dissolution and to the returning of its members to the Bullittsburg Church. One week later at the joint meeting of the two congregations, their unification was formally ratified. Ibid., 36-37, 41.

[106]The new church had collected materials at a building site at the Crossing of Ashbys Fork, but construction had not yet begun by the time the two congregations were unified. Before the merger occurred, the old church agreed to abide by the choice of the site already made by the new church. In July 1801 the unified church completed the formation of a building committee. The next month the church voted to raze the meetinghouse at Bullittsburg and to use the materials thus secured as a part of what was needed for the new construction. In September the united church abruptly changed the site of the new building from Ashbys Fork to Bullittsburg and provided for hauling to the old location "the timbers" already collected on Ashbys Fork. Seven months later the new meetinghouse was completed, and the building committee received it. The finished structure cost Ł157.5.0, of which sum Ł18.10.6 was still owed the "undertaker." Ibid., 41, 42, 43, 45, 52.

[107]This meeting was scheduled for 16 September 1797. Bullittsburg appointed John Taylor, George Eve, Lewis Deweese, William Cave, and John Hall to help with this proposed constitution. Ibid., 10-11.

[108]In 1800 seventeen Baptists living on Dry Creek in Boone County purposed to consitute a church. Spencer, *Kentucky Baptists*, 1:454.

[109]*Independent* is a colloquial adverb, which Taylor uses instead of *independently*.

[110]Revelation 1:20.

could not be hid.[111] I then added, "Who among you can go forward in worship when you come together?"

Several of them answered in the affirmative. And then [they] named who, while that one would name some other for [he said that] he could not.

Which led me to ask, "Which of you brethren now prays in your families, for it is vain to expect if you do not pray there that you will when you come to meeting?"

After a serious pause, one replied who had been in the habit of public speaking in Virginia while there. Said he, "I used to pray in my family, but in moving here we became so confused that I have never resumed it since." So said a number of them, by which we found [that] there was not a man among them that prayed [142,2d]to God in his family.

The helps soon withdrew to consult about constituting them, when I remarked to them thus: "Brethren, there is aplenty of you here to constitute this church without me. And notwithstanding the promising opening in this case, I cannot agree to set up a church of Christ anywhere except they can meet together and worship God independent of any person coming from a distance to join with them."

It was not long before all the helps fell in with my opinion. And, returning, we informed them that we could not constitute them in their present, debilitated condition. This very much afflicted them. And before they parted they agreed to meet the next Sunday to counsel further what they should do.

When they met, they had a very small, poor man among them. He was also decriped [decrepit], for he limped as he walked, who was rather a stranger among them. His name was Moses Vickers.[112] He was a good singer and a man of good religious fame. When they convened, Vickers began to sing and weep among them and proposed to go to prayer, after which he exhorted them in tears to trust in the Lord. Several of them, I think, went to prayer. They had such a tender, weeping meeting that they concluded to meet the next Sunday. And in fact a revival of religion soon took place among them. They became constituted.[113] Vickers [became] a respectable preacher

---

[111]Matthew 5:14.

[112]Moses Vickers (1764-1820), a native of Maryland, migrated to Kentucky in 1784 and settled in Boone County over a decade later. On 10 December 1796 he joined the Bullittsburg Church and in time served the Dry Creek Church as its first minister. Bullittsburg Church, Minute Book A, 7, 169; and Spencer, *Kentucky Baptists*, 1:454-55.

[113]Sometime after this attempt at constitution in 1797, the Baptists on Dry Creek built a meetinghouse where they convened from time to time. Their progress earned the

among them. They soon called him to ordination, and he baptized many that were the fruits of his own labours. He is now gone the way of all the earth. His son Samuel Vickers[114] seconds[115] his father in the ministry, so that lively devotion to God has been kept up at Dry Creek, Campbell County, about thirty years. The church is called Dry Creek.

My overnicety at Dry Creek perhaps was the reason why my brethren did not invite me to the constitution of the new church spoken of above.

[97]Bullittsburg has produced more preachers from first to last than any other church I ever knew. Sometime back one of their preachers being at my house, we counted up about fifteen or sixteen, chief of whom have been ordained. Four of them were invited forward at my request, about the time that Mr. Eve left Bullittsburg and Depew's dances were in their highest blast in the neighborhood, and just before this happy revival of religion began. The names of those men I have spoken of before,[116] which were [William] Cave, [Chichester] Matthews,[117] [Jeremiah] Kirtley,[118] and [Philemon] Vawter.[119]

---

approval of the Bullittsburg brethren. John Taylor was among the ministers whom Bullittsburg appointed on 5 July 1800 as helps for the constitution of Dry Creek. The others were William Cave, Jeremiah Kirtley, and John Conner. Two weeks later the Dry Creek Church was organized with twenty-two members, five of whom came from Bullittsburg. The same year the new congregation affiliated itself with the Elkhorn Association and three years later helped to form the North Bend Association. Bullittsburg Church, Minute Book A, 27, 28, 169; and Spencer, *Kentucky Baptists*, 1:453-54.

[114]Samuel Vickers was one of ten children in the household of Moses Vickers. Spencer, *Kentucky Baptists*, 1:455.

[115]The transitive verb *second* is an obsolete usage meaning "succeed to the place of."

[116]On page 42 of his *Thoughts on Missions*, Taylor lists these four would-be preachers.

[117]Chichester Matthews (1756-1828), a native of Fauquier County, Virginia, was a charter member of the Bullittsburg Church and its first deacon. He was ordained as a minister in 1812. Spencer, *Kentucky Baptists*, 1:296-97.

[118]Jeremiah Kirtley (1754-1806) was reared in Virginia as an Anglican. Under the preaching of George Eve he was converted in 1788. He migrated with his family to Kentucky in 1796. Soon after joining the Bullittsburg Church, he was ordained a ruling elder. In 1800 he was licensed to preach but never was ordained a preacher. Ibid., 1:299.

[119]Philemon Vawter (1765?-1815?), a native of Virginia, lived for awhile in the Holston Valley on his westward trek. In Kentucky, he belonged in succession to three of the churches in which John Taylor held his membership—Clear Creek, Bullittsburg, and Corn Creek. He was ordained a preacher by the latter congregation. Around 1810 he moved to Indiana, where he spent the remainder of his days. Ibid., 1:461-62; and John Taylor, *Thoughts on Missions*, 45-47.

Three of them are no more in this world. The surviving one[120] is now a good-old gospel minister.

Christopher Willson takes the next lead. He became a preacher both useful and popular.[121] [He] was much beloved by the people and well calculated to preach association Sunday sermons. But ah me! May he preach by example as well as [98]by precept, and [may he] remember afresh the day I first saw him staggering under a mighty sense of his guilt.

Asa, the black man who was baptized with him, may he be useful among his fellow blacks, as there is the greatest sphere of his action.

Absalom Graves [was] every way genteel and decent in his personal appearance, whose regular and pleasant deportment offers conviction[122] to all who are in his company. There is no thanks due this man for preaching. For though a man of good information, he (through native modesty and timidity of mind) kept him[123] back so long that it seemed as if agony of soul would kill him. And it was preach or die. Being thus forced out, the Lord has greatly blessed his labours in different places, but a little less timidity might be a benefit to him yet. But by receiving a missionary spirit in its warmest glow, from the time of his first acquaintance with Luther Rice,[124] has given

---

[120]Chichester Matthews outlived the others in this quartet of preachers.

[121]Christopher Willson was ordained to the ministry by the Bullittsburg Church on Saturday 2 May 1807. Bullittsburg Church, Minute Book A, 116.

[122]The obsolete noun *conviction* means *demonstration*.

[123]Here *him*, an obsolete (or rare), reflexive pronoun, is used redundantly with the intransitive verb *keep*.

[124]Luther Rice (1783-1836), a native of Massachusetts, has been called the "Father of American Baptist Foreign Missions." A Pedobaptist, he went to India as a missionary of the recently organized interdenominational American Board of Commissioners for Foreign Missions. Following the lead of Adoniram Judson (1788-1850), who had preceded him to the Orient, Rice adopted the Baptist view of baptism. He soon returned to America and promoted the support of Judson and his wife, who had by then moved to Burma. The resultant society, formed in 1814 and known as the "General Missionary Convention of the Baptist Denomination in the United States for Foreign Missions," became the first nationwide organization among American Baptists. In 1815 Rice visited most of the associations in Kentucky, which cordially welcomed him. The contributions for missions that he gathered in Kentucky or Tennessee were larger than those received in any other state. In the nation's capital Rice also called into being Columbian College, which in time became George Washington University. Spencer, *Kentucky Baptists*, 1:568-69, 571; *Encyclopedia of Southern Baptists*, 2:1164-65; and Sprague, *American Pulpit*, 7:602-607. See also James B. Taylor, *Virginia Baptist Ministers*, 2d ed., 431-41.

him a growth that he never would have had only for that circumstance.[125] He is now their first preacher at Bullittsburg.

Time would fail me to speak of all the preachers that has come out from this church. She has been not only the mother and nursery of many preachers but of many other churches. Her two nearest and most flourishing daughters are Middle Creek[126] and Sand Run,[127] as also Forks of Gunpowder. [128]

We will take some notice of several conversions that were out of the common course, beginning with Captain (or afterwards Col[onel]) Abraham Depew[129] and his wife. We have heard how Mrs. Depew went to meeting prepared to brook and forestall all the arrows of God[130] but found them to be weapons that would not be denied and [that] forced their way to her heart. Her loving husband did all he could to charm away her grief and [to] restore her spirits to what they were before, but all in vain. When God gives the wound, only Himself can heal it. After she had obtained relief from the [99]Lord, she consulted her husband's approbation to be baptized and join the church. His reply was about to this amount, "My dear, all this is a thing of late date with you that perhaps will not last long," and that she had better try[131] herself longer, lest she fell away as many others had done.

Her reply was [that] as to falling away she was very fraid[132] of that herself, but that [her] being under the care of the church would be at least some remedy against that evil. So that with his consent she desired to make the experiment.

---

[125]Absalom Graves became a pioneer in Kentucky in espousing the cause of foreign missions. "Life of Absalom Graves," 5, in Graves, ed., *Hymns, Psalms, and Spiritual Songs.*

[126]The Middle Creek Church, located in Boone County and constituted in 1803, consisted of seventy-two members in 1832; seventy-three, in 1835. I. M. Allen, *Annual Register, 1832,* 183, *The Triennial Register, 1836* (Philadelphia PA, 1836), 238.

[127]The Sand Run Church, which was constituted in 1819 and was affiliated with the North Bend Association, reported fifty-five members in 1832. Allen, *Annual Register, 1832,* 183; and Spencer, *Kentucky Baptists,* 2:149.

[128]The Forks of Gunpowder Church, organized in 1812, had a membership of seventy-seven in 1832, sixty in 1835. Allen, *Annual Register, 1832,* 183, and *Triennial Register, 1836,* 238.

[129]John Taylor's note: "This man was afterwards excluded."

[130]Job 6:4.

[131]Here the obsolete verb *try* means *prove.*

[132]The aphetic form of *afraid* is used here.

He not only gave his approbation but came with her on the suitable day.[133] The church was sitting when they came to the door and was just then inviting candidates to come forward. When she came in at the door, she made no stop to take a seat but came straight forward to the table (with her mind fully collected, and [with] a countenance apparently [as] calm as Heaven itself, [and] with a solemn boldness as if it was a pleasure to do her Lord's will), when without embarrassment she related an excellent work of grace lately wrought in her soul.

I reminded the church of her husband, who sat near the door, [and of] the utility of his approbation in her joining the church. He rose up before the question was asked him and gave his consent. But [he] soon shrunk back to his seat to vent the tender emotions of his heart.

At the baptizing[134] he stood near the water. Not taking notice of Mrs. Depew's hat on her head till I had gotten to a proper depth of water, I [then] gave it a cant to the shore, it falling at her husband's feet. He picked it up with an uncommon gush of[135] tears. Leaning his head against a tree, [he] was not able to leave the place till all the company was gone. Not long after this, himself was baptized.

Moses Scott:[136] This is a small man in stature, but before his conversion [he] was a very great captain for the Devil. And though somewhere in the East he was raised by a religious Presbyterian father, he came to Kentucky and threw off even the form of godliness. Among other things he was a great fiddler, and [100][he was] fond of all the amusements connected with that practice. It may generally be taken for granted that what is called "a good fiddler" is the Devil's righthand man. This Scott gloried in his native strength of intellect, [which was] connected with his wit [and which] capacitated[137] him to make wickedness acceptable to men (and that of higher ranks). An appointment of county surveyor[138] brought him to Boone [County]. I had a

---

[133]The date was Saturday 5 July 1800. Bullittsburg Church, Minute Book A, 27, 170.

[134]The baptizing was probably conducted after preaching on the day following her public confession of faith.

[135]The words "an uncommon gush of" are omitted from the second edition.

[136]Moses Scott listed his property on the tax roll of Boone County as early as 1800. Clift, "Second Census" of Kentucky, 1800, 261.

[137]The verb capacitate is here a rare usage meaning qualify.

[138]Having been commissioned by Governor James Garrard as the first county surveyor of Boone County, Moses Scott assumed the post on 17 June 1799. Boone County (KY) Court, Order Book A, 1.

very near neighbor both rich and wicked. On his land Scott settled for a while. He at once had a fine partner in vice.

He [Scott] very seldom came to meeting at all, but when he did he looked about as shy and wild as a buck in the woods. After the revival had progressed some time, [his] curiosity (like [that of] Zacchaeus)[139] led him to go to a church meeting to see and hear what was designed by "telling experiences." This obliged him to get nearer than he was accustomed to. With great attention he stood and heard an experience related, which was so much to the purpose that it brought forward a moving exhortation from some other person. From whatever it might be, the buck was shot, and tears began to trickle from Scott's eyes. But being willing to hide (as bucks generally do when they receive the deadly ball) by sitting down, he concealed himself. That or the next evening a meeting being appointed at Maj[or Robert] Kirtley's,[140] Mr. Scott came to it. The major expressing great satisfaction at seeing Scott there, he [Scott] strove to laugh it off by saying [that] he came to see what sort of a thing a night meeting was, as he had never yet seen one of them. With apparent seriousness, he attended meeting for a while with a seeming willlngness to converse about his soul.

A number of Cincinnati gentry (male and female), paying a visit to this near, rich neighbor of mine and desiring to have a dance, could not do it without Scott's agency with his fine fiddle. In this he accommodated them, and they had a long dance. And with this, away went all Scott's religion apparently.

He forsook meetings for several months till a monthly meeting being at my house in dead of [[101]]winter.[141] Mr. Scott, living almost in sight, came to the meeting. One of the finest young ladies that I knew in the county as to dress was also there. A companion of hers came forward and related her experience, which so much affected this fine girl, which [affection] she strove to suppress for some time. At length [she] broke forth in plaintive sorrow. By some call, I had stepped into another room of the house, when a heart-broken

---

[139]Luke 19:13.

[140]Robert Kirtley (1786–1872), a native of Madison (then Culpeper) County, Virginia, was a son of Jeremiah Kirtley and Mary Robinson (1753–1837). His parents brought him to Boone (then Campbell) County, Kentucky, at the age of ten. He was an officer in the War of 1812. He was converted in 1811, ordained a deacon in 1817, and licensed to preach two years later. In 1822 he was ordained a preacher. From 1826 until his death he served as the pastor of the Bullittsburg Church. He was the moderator of the North Bend Association for thirty-two years. Spencer, *Kentucky Baptists*, 1:299-302.

[141]This meeting probably occurred in January or February 1801.

sound called after me by name. When I came in, the young lady intreated me to pray for her as a poor, lost sinner, while she trembled from head to foot [and] while all her flouncery,[142] jewelry, curls, and feathers trembled as if an earthquake was under her feet. What was most affecting [was that], after I had closed my prayer, with tremorous voice before she left her knees [she] prayed herself at some length for the Lord to have mercy on her guilty soul. Perhaps no preaching could have affected the assembly more. This circumstance opened Mr. Scott's wound afresh. This young lady was baptized about a month afterwards. That bitter cold evening I baptized about ten persons among the fleeks [flecks] of ice.

Being very busy the next day killing my hogs [at a place] about half the distance from my house to Scott's and on the direction there, he came to where we were at work. He no more looked wild but meek as a lamb. After obtaining a little leisure I sat down to converse with him. With all his striving he could scarce keep his tears within his eyes. He soon spoke of the weeping, young lady at the meeting the day before, wishing he could be as she was.

To which I replied, "But, Mr. Scott, what will you do with your fiddle?"

His reply was [that] on that head his mind was made up: That he intended to make a present of it to me to do with it as I thought proper.

However, soon after, his house got burnt with chief of his effects—fiddle and all. He was a considerable time labouring under a consciousness of his helpless condition, which brought about the most intimate friendship between us.

[102]Our old, rich neighbor, of whom I have been speaking, strove hard to draw Mr. Scott off but at length became hopeless. Being now bereaved of his associates in sin through the whole settlement, [he] became disconsolate and said to me one day, seeming more serious than I ever saw him: "Mr. Taylor, I really am afraid that Scott will leave me too."

To which I replied, "O sir, you had better go with him." But perhaps he lived and died as he was born.

Mr. Scott was much afraid of a mistaken conversion, refusing to be comforted till the Lord spoke peace in his soul. After which he hesitated awhile on the validity of his former baptism, which led him to the close study of the Scripture on that point. But his way being cleared, he followed his Lord in baptism.[143] When I put him in the water, I hoped that I had gotten a

---

[142]The archaic noun *flouncery* means *flounce* or *ruffle*.
[143]Moses Scott was received for baptism by the church on Sunday 26 July 1801. Bullittsburg Church, Minute Book A, 43, 175.

preacher. And he certainly would have been numbered among the Bullittsburg preachers, but he is a little too proud. He has made some attempts [to preach] by the invitation of the church, which gave great satisfaction to others. Being a good judge of preaching himself and not being able to please his own taste that way, [he] lays it all aside. Let him remember the man that laid up his lord's money in the napkin.[144] Perhaps his popularity in the county hangs as a clog to his heels, for he has been elected several times to the state legislature.[145] But this will be a poor thing in the Day of Settlement with his Lord. Moses Scott is one of the men with whom I agonized in birth till Christ was formed within him.[146]

John Ryle[147] was one of the happy subjects of sovereign grace in this revival. He was a tall, rawboned, giant-looking man, and his countenance at times [was] like the blazing lightning. It would seem as if devils of different complexion attended this man. For at times he would be very merry with his shrewd kind of fun and [then would] quickly change into the appearance of a mad bull, scraping the earth as if he would tear up everything before him. Or with cursing [he would] make the air ring like the roaring of a lion.

[103]This tiger of a man betook himself to coming to meeting, while his countenance looked awfully sad as if he was much troubled with a hard heart. For some time I forbore conversation with him, believing from some previous evidence that he hated me more than [he did] any other man on earth. At length falling in and riding together, I enquired about the state of his soul. I found [that] he was far pushed on the verge of desperation. Though he seemed to tremble as we conversed, there was no tear of tenderness about him. When I asked him if he ever prayed to God, he answered in the negative: For that he was afraid to attempt prayer, [because] he was such a monstrous lump of sin before God; that should he attempt the sacred work of prayer it would offend God more than anything he had ever done. And for the presumption, the Lord would with some visible breach[148] of His displeasure cut [him] off and send him to Hell at once.

---

[144]Luke 19:20.

[145]During 1819 and 1820 Moses Scott served in the state House of Representatives as the member from Boone County. Collins, *Kentucky*, rev. ed., 2:771.

[146]Galatians 4:19.

[147]John Ryle became a taxpayer in Boone County as early as 1800. Clift, *"Second Census" of Kentucky, 1800*, 256.

[148]The archaic noun *breach* means *assault*.

All this awakened great sympathy in my heart, remembering the wormwood and gall[149] my soul had felt long before. I encouraged him [Ryle] all I could to call on the Lord [and to] believe and trust in the Saviour for his eternal salvation. This poor man through deep distress of soul did after this, like the publican in the temple, cry for mercy;[150] and the Lord sent him speedy relief. When he related his hope in Christ, though he hoped the Lord had forgiven him, he could not tell whether some in the church could forgive his former conduct towards them, seeing for the same conduct he could not forgive himself. Knowing whom he meant, I was ready to say, "That was done long ago."

When we went into the water, I said, taking him by the hand, "Come, Brother Saul."[151] And I know not whether I ever baptized a man with more pleasure in my life.[152] A number of his connections were baptized about the same time,[153] while another of the connections said [that] all the rest would hold out, but John Ryle would soon fall away. This he judged from his past wickedness, but he ought to have remembered that sin shall not have dominion [104]where grace reigns.[154] More than twenty years have elapsed, and he yet stands.

Edward Webb was one of the converts of this revival. As named before, he was one of our first day's baptizing.[155] He was perhaps about thirty years of age, and his character as a man [was] very different from the two last named. About the time Mr. [George] Eve left our country, I had a night meeting at old Mr. Webb's, where I stayed all night. His son Edward was there, and after meeting broke, he tarried till late bedtime. I apparently by accident asked him if he ever [had] prayed to God in his life. He answered [that] he never had made such an attempt except when joining others when they went to prayer. The thing passed off for perhaps an hour, and other conversation came in the way. When I asked him if I could get him to go to Cincinnati for me, he replied [that] he would if I needed his service that way.

---

[149]Jeremiah 9:15.

[150]Luke 18:13.

[151]Acts 9:17.

[152]John Ryle was received for baptism by the church on Sunday 31 August 1800. Bullittsburg Church, Minute Book A, 28, 170.

[153]During the last five months of 1800 three members of the Ryle family— Elizabeth, Sarah, and James—were baptized. Ibid., 170, 171.

[154]Romans 6:14.

[155]Edward Webb, received for baptism on Saturday 7 June 1800, was baptized, probably the next day. Bullittsburg Church, Minute Book A, 26, 170.

I then said, "I do not want you, Neddy, to go to Cincinnati for me, but there is a little piece of business I wish you to do for me that is much easier than going to Cincinnati. Will you in one week from this time go by yourself and kneel down and pray to God?"

He readily answered, "Yes," without any reserve, for he was a man of that cast that he could not readily say no when a favor was asked of him.

He soon reflected on what he had promised, concluding, "It must be done before the week is out." For I do suppose [that] he never had told a willful lie in his life. As days passed on, he more seriously thought on what he had promised. I had said [that] it was lighter than going to Cincinnati. But if that would relieve him from his promise, he had rather go there many times or [do] any other hard labour he ever did in his life.

He became so tormented after a few days [that he decided] that he would go and do it and be done with it. He would then say, "What am I going to do? To gratify a man like myself, I am hypocritically going to mock God Almighty, Who declares [that] He will not be mocked.[156] I am going to commit the greatest sin I ever committed in my life (or perhaps any [105]man ever committed, thus to trifle with his Maker)." He tried to examine what God required of those who drew near to Him, nothing of which was found in him. After all these painful reflections, he set off to some lonesome and selected spot in his own mind. As to practical sin, he could not so much impeach himself, but his heart was full of hypocricy [sic] and [was] a den of pollution. His knees [were] barely able to bear the weight of his body as he walked along, through apprehensions that a Just and Holy God would strike him dead at the place. The truth of the case [was that] he was a heavy-laden sinner, whom the Saviour invites to Himself [even] before he got to the place of prayer. Till this day he has been a man of prayer. Perhaps about a month after this, the Lord appeared to his relief.

William Ramey and [Elizabeth], his wife, obtained hope in the Lord in this heavenly revival. They lived in the new settlement over the Ohio River. For some time they had been coming across the river to meetings and appeared to be under much concern. I crossed the river in a vessel and walked a mile to converse with, encourage, and comfort these mourners. When I got to the place, Mr. Ramey was not at home. I found his wife in a very curious way, being in a kind of trouble which bordered on distraction. Her tears and lamentations excited my pity with a secret pleasure, as her mistake could easily be removed. She had been about two weeks that she had

[156]Galatians 6:7.

partaken of but little sustenance. She had laid aside all her family business, even to that of cooking for her husband and little children.

When the whole was explained (which she was very ready to do): About two weeks ago she had obtained a relief from the Lord, at which time her heart and tongue had made a vow to the Lord which she could not fulfill without committing one of the greatest sins. Her great strait lay in this: Being under a great weight of guilt at the time spoken of, some words had occurred to her mind that [106]had relieved her, and at which time she had great ecstacy [sic] of joy. The words were "Believe and be baptized and thou shalt be saved."[157] Her thoughts had been (at the time) that those words came from the Lord and that baptism was connected with believing and with salvation.

And that in her ecstacy [sic] she had answered, "O Lord, I will! I will! I will!"—that is, be baptized. But soon after, she had found that it was all a mistake and delusion, for she was not yet changed. And as evidence of it, her heart was yet [as] base and vile as it ever was, which would not be the case if she was born of God. And that if the church would receive her (which she knew they ought not), it would be a great sin against God to be baptized in her unrenewed state. And then [she] exclaimed with tears and trembling, "O Mr. Taylor, what shall I do? What shall I do?"

The religious reader will judge of my then feelings. My advice to her was that at the first opportunity she had, to comply with her vow to God—that is, get baptized. And then [I] informed her that a few days hence there would be a baptizing convenient to her, adding for her encouragement [for her] not to think it strange concerning the fiery trials she had met with,[158] for they were common to the people of God. I then added, "As I see your wheel is idle, do you go to spinning. And as your family has suffered some time through your neglect, clean your house and cook food for your husband and little children. Trust in the Lord and be at rest."

It is probable that Ramey had been in some fret about his wife's conduct and neglect in her family, for they were a very pushing and industrious people. A heavy shower of rain coming on, he came home in a rage, with heavy curses and imprecations against some of his hands for not taking in some hemp [that had been] set up in the yard [and] that should not have gotten wet. But after he came into the house, he seemed a little mortified at finding me there, and especially [107]when I asked him if I was mistaken or did I hear cursing in the yard.

---

[157]Mark 16:16.
[158]1 Peter 4:12.

With much modesty he confessed the impropriety of the practice. He afterwards said [that] the Devil had used him so ill[159] in that case that he would never curse for him again, which vow he has perhaps never broken to this day.

His wife, however, came to the meeting[160] in hopes [that] the church would not receive her. And that would free her from her vow, for she was yet overwhelmed with doubts about her own state. Making no delay (as the church was sitting when she came) [and] moving right forward, she began to tell the church what a dreadful[161] bad creature she was. And [she] would have kept back what she esteemed her best evidences for fear the church would receive her. But they were drawn from her by questions. When the moderator reached out the hand of fellowship to her, she put her hand behind her. And after reaching round and getting hold of her hand, [he] desired[162] her [to] take her seat. Which she only did a minute or two, when she rose up with this affecting remark, being much affected herself, "O my friends, you are mistaken. Do examine me further. O, do give me the opportunity to convince you how bad I am." The moderator kindly hushed her to silence, and perhaps the church never received any person with more fellowship.[163] A great tremor attended her till after she was baptized. In these cases much water does much good to tempted believers.

Sometimes the Devil entirely overleaps himself as he did in [the] case of Mr. Ramey's cursing. For this—with the baptizing [of] his wife—became as a dagger to his heart, from which he did not get delivered for several months. The same Devil that tempted him to curse men now tempted him to curse God, his Maker; and not only [to] call in question but [to] condemn all the religion that was brought to men in the Bible. This mighty torrent of temptation drove him into the extremes of despair for a long time. It was the joys of Heaven on earth to hear him tell how the [108]Lord Jesus took him

---

[159]Except in dialectal English the adverb *ill* is an obsolete usage. Here it means *grievously* or *painfully*.

[160]The date of this meeting was Sunday 27 July 1800; its location, John Tanner's Station. Bullittsburg Church, Minute Book A, 27, 170.

[161]The adverb *dreadful* is a dialecticism and a colloquialism used in place of *dreadfully*, which means *very*.

[162]The verb *desire* is here an obsolete word meaning *invite*.

[163]Elizabeth Ramey was received as a candidate for baptism at John Tanner's Station on 27 July 1800. Bullittsburg Church, Minute Book A, 27, 170.

from the deeps of sin and [the] gates of gaping Hell and fixed his standing on the Rock of Ages. He was baptized in dead of winter.[164]

Mrs. [Susanna] Allen, the wife of Thomas Allen,[165] was hopefully converted about this time. She had been a very constant attendant on preaching and at times seemed very much affected. On a return from a tour of several days, my wife informed me that Mrs. Allen was like[166] to die and had a great desire to see me. I quickly went. When I entered the door she was laying on the bed. Seeing me, she rose up with a great gush[167] of tears and loud weeping. I stepped forward and gave her my hand to enquire how she was. She laid hold of me as with a dying grasp, as if the agonies of death were on her. After she became a little composed, I asked her how she was and what the state of her mind [was].

As to her bodily complaint, she could not well describe [it], but she was certainly going to die and very soon. As to her [spiritual] state, [she said that] inevitable destruction was at hand and that Hell was to be her final doom forever. And as an evidence that she believed what she said, it seemed as if she would weep her life away.

I waited for her composure again and asked what was her request of me.

She replied, "Your prayers." In this she was particular: She had no desire that I should pray for her life if it was to continue as it had been. She feared that I should be deceived in thinking [that] this was a work of God on her, for she said, "It is only a Hell-fright[168] and not conviction of sin, for I have been so before and promised the Lord great things and was afterwards bad as ever. And it would be better to die and go to Hell at once than live longer in sin." From which I gathered what she wished [that] I should pray to the Lord for.

I often visited this poor, afflicted woman to pray with and for her, having a much better opinion of her state than she had herself, believing her a changed woman [and] that whether she lived or died she would never love

---

[164]William Ramey was received for baptism on Saturday 7 February 1801 and was immersed, probably the following day. Ibid., 32, 171.

[165]Thomas Allen was enrolled on the tax list in Boone County as early as 1800. Clift, *"Second Census" of Kentucky, 1800*, 4.

[166]The dialectal verb *like* is here the intransitive form and means "be about" or "be on the verge."

[167]The term "a great gush of" is omitted from the second edition.

[168]*Hell-fright* is an archaism meaning "fear of perdition."

sin again. Her husband also became deeply distressed about his soul and obtained a hopeful deliverance.[169]

[109]It was at length rumored about that Mrs. Allen had obtained hope in the Lord. This news was so good to myself that I soon paid her a visit. And informing her what I had heard, she positively denied the truth of the report and [said] that it could be no friend to her or religion that had started it. After hearing that her cousin Betsey Mosby[170] was the author, she burst into a flood of tears that her cousin should serve her so. And [she said] that she never told her that she had a hope but only that her trouble was gone which she had been greatly afraid of. [She had said] that her trouble would leave her where she was before [and] that her case was worse than it ever was, for her trouble was gone and left her a poor, unrenewed sinner still. With tears trinkling from her eyes she would exclaim, "Oh that I had my trouble again!"

For fifteen or twenty minutes I preached[171] to her the glorious plan of salvation by a Redeemer's atonement, and that it was not the quantum of our trouble that was a recommending qualification for which God saved a sinner.

To this she listened with great attention, looking straight at me and [with] the tears drop[p]ing from her chin. When I ended, she replied, "This is good news, but it is not for me for my trouble is gone."

The Lord after this gave her plainer testimony that Himself took away her trouble, and she gained confidence enough to be baptized.[172] After which she lived in the comfortable hope of eternal life for a number of years, till by death the Lord took her home to rest.

Letty,[173] a poor slave: Lest I should be considered partial to those of higher rank, we will state the conversion of this poor, black woman. I had owned Letty as my property from a child, and she was now the mother of children. She had ever manifested the greatest aversion to anything like religion, so that she could not be ruled (except by harsh means) to family worship, but otherways [she was] the most faithful servant I ever owned. Her masculine strength made her equal to any black man on the plantation. Her

---

[169]On Saturday 6 September 1800 Thomas Allen was received for baptism. Bullittsburg Church, Minute Book A, 29, 170.

[170]Elizabeth Mosby joined the church by means of a letter of dismissal on Saturday 14 May 1796. Ibid., 5, 169.

[171]Here the transitive verb *preach* is an obsoletism meaning *teach*.

[172]Susanna Allen was received for baptism on Sunday 20 December 1801. Bullittsburg Church, Minute Book A, 48, 175.

[173]Letty was among the eight slaves whom the writer acquired in Virginia upon the death of his uncle Joseph Taylor.

high [110]spirit and violent temper often brought her in contact with them [black men] in bloody blows. As her body was strong so was her mind. Nature had done more for her than common. She was an own sister[174] to Asa, that I have spoken of before [and] who after his baptism became a preacher.

Whether through the conversion of her brother (which was very striking) or some other means, she became alarmed of her lost state and laboured long under great consciousness of guilt before she obtained relief. The relation of her experience to the church one Sunday morning (with a number of other black people) was more striking to the assembly present than the loudest preaching. The solemnity of her looks with the style in which she spoke I can only give a faint description of. I would give her own phraseology, of which I only recollect a part.

The hour of sorrow being come with a woman in the neighborhood, which has killed many of our Mother Eve's poor daughters for her first sin,[175] my wife had sent Letty to give assistance in this distressing crisis. The husband of this afflicted woman was the name of Carrol, an Irishman and perhaps a Catholic as to religion. But be him what he would, otherways he was a monstrous wicked man as to swearing and drunkenness. And on this occasion [he was] perhaps in his highest gale,[176] though his wife [was] very like to die immediately.

And while Letty stated the case, she made this remark, "I looked at Mr. Carrol and thought he was the wickedest man I ever saw in my life and wondered [that] the Lord did not strike him dead at once. But after reflecting on myself a while, I really thought I was worse tham Mr. Carrol, for all he does is only outward sin, but I am a sinner through my whole soul.[177] And my heart is worse than Mr. Carrol's, and [I] had rather have been him with all his wickedness than myself. I then began to wonder that the earth did not open, or [that] some other vengeance [would] send us all to Hell together, which I looked to take place immediately." But she hasted away [ill] from Mr. Carrol's and found herself not yet in Hell.

She went to converse with her brother, Asa, to know what she should do in her present, lost, and helpless condition. After examining of her a while,

---

[174]The term "own sister" indicates a direct relationship as opposed to that of "half sister" or *sister-in-law*.

[175]Genesis 3:6, 16.

[176]The noun *gale* is an Americanism for "loud outburst."

[177]The final clause of this sentence is omitted from the second edition.

he pronounced all the work she talked of to be of the Devil, and that she was not under true conviction at all.

She went to the overseer,[178] a very good, religious, old man, who, as she thought, treated her with scorn and contempt.

She then thought of going to her master and mistress for advice. But thinking of the contempt she had treated them with heretofore as to religion, [she said], "They will think of me as my only brother and the good overseer do."

Then said she, "I thought I had no friend in the world. [I said], 'I will go to God and beg Him for mercy and to be my friend.' But when I tried to pray to Him, I saw that He was angry with me, for I had done nothing but sin all my life. And there was no mercy for me."

Then said she, "I thought of Jesus Christ, who had died for sinners. I prayed to Him to be my Saviour and friend. But I thought [that] Jesus Christ was angry with me, for I had despised Him all my life in despising His people. I then thought," said she, "that I had no friend in Heaven nor earth, and that no creature was ever in my case before."

Living on the [Ohio] River bank, she concluded to run down to the river, perhaps to drown herself. As she went down the steep bank, it occurred to her [that] she ought to fall on her face to the ground and confess the justice of God in her eternal damnation. She concluded [that] this ought to be done with her head down the steep bank, as she was immediately to go to Hell.

"When I fell down," said she, "with my face to the ground, some words came into my mind, which were: 'Come, ye blessed of my Father, inherit the kingdom prepared for you from the foundation of the world.'[179] When," said she, "I began to think, 'O blessed God, what do these words mean, and who speaks them?'" Then remembering [that] they were the words of Christ, and that they were spoken to her, for she felt their influence through her whole [112]soul, "I then saw," said she, "that the anger of God was turned away from me, and that Jesus Christ had made an angry God my friend. I said, as I rose up, 'Jesus Christ is my Saviour, and God is my friend.'" Thus she went on still repeating till she came to the top of the bank with that heavenly rapture, not knowing for some time but [that] she was going straight on to the heavenly kingdom, to which the Saviour had invited her.[180]

---

[178]The overseer in 1800 may have been James McIntosh, Jr., who was Taylor's employee the following year. Bullittsburg Church, Minute Book A, 48.

[179]Matthew 25:34.

[180]Letty—or Lettice, the way her name was entered on the church roll— was received

For more than twenty years this poor, black woman has given good evidence that the work I have been stating was a reality. It is probable [that] this riverbank will never by her be forgotten. We may see verified in this instance what the voice said to Peter that "God is no respecter of persons."[181] And it is probable [that] more slaves will go to Heaven than masters.

About the close of the revival spoken of above and at which time the church consisted of about two hundred members,[182] [because of] the great affliction of my family by summer and fall fevers which had continued for several years together, I thought it my duty to remove from where I was to Mount Byrd. The church at Bullittsburg being so well supplied with preachers, as I have named before,[183] there was not so much call for my service at this place as there appeared [to be] at Corn Creek, to which I moved in the spring of the year 1802, after living seven years in Bullittsburg Church.[184] This mother church has continued from the beginning about twenty-eight years.

Not long after my departure from them, the churches in that quarter thought proper to form themselves into an association, consisting of nine churches. Their appellation is North Bend Association.[185] In the beginning and for a number of years, Bullittsburg contained about as many members as all the rest of the churches in this new establishment.[186] About seven or eight years after my departure from this church, they had a second great revival,

---

for baptism by the church while it was assembled at John Tanner's Station on Sunday 24 August 1800. On the same occasion Benjamin and Dublin, also slaves of John Taylor, along with four other blacks, were likewise accepted for membership in the church. Bullittsburg Church, Minute Book A, 28, 183.

[181] Acts 10:34.

[182] By the end of June 1801—when the revival of 1800-1801 had come to a close and the Woolper Creek venture was over—the membership of the Bullittsburg Church stood at 177 (145 whites and 32 blacks). Bullittsburg Church, Minute Book A, 172-75, 182-83.

[183] Pages 96-97, first edition.

[184] On 6 March 1802 the Bullittsburg Church granted letters of dismissal to John Taylor, his wife, his eldest son, and five of his slaves. Bullittsburg Church, Minute Book A, 49.

[185] The North Bend Association was organized in July 1803 by nine churches at the Dry Creek Meetinghouse in Campbell (now Kenton) County. Spencer, *Kentucky Baptists*, 2:144.

[186] When the North Bend Association was formed, the membership at Bullittsburg stood at 167 (141 whites, 26 blacks), while the members of the new union's eight other churches totaled 262. Ibid.; and Bullittsburg Church, Minute Book A, 172-76, 182-83.

and in which they had about a 150 baptized in the course of one winter.[187] About [113]four years past they had a third, most heavenly season. This blessed work began to be very obvious at North Bend Association which was held at Bullittsburg. A number of the preachers present took the fire there and spread it abroad like Samson's foxes,[188] for the work spread to a great distance. Bullittsburg baptized more people than she had done in any other revival. And though several churches had been constituted from her, she now contained upwards of four hundred members, and [they] lived in very compact bounds.[189] But being so numerous, it was thought most suitable to divide and constitute a large, young church called Sand Run.

Since their division each church has built a spacious, brick meetinghouse (and about three or four miles apart) and now lives as a loving mother and daughter, while their own sons in the ministry serve them in rich supply. Each church having several, good preachers and no lordly king among them, for Bullittsburg has never had a particular, selected pastor among them from the beginning. And I have never seen so much harmony and good order in any other worshiping church of Christ as [there is at] Bullittsburg. An uniform rule in their discipline has been the eighteenth chapter of Matthew.[190] And for many years, in final expulsion they acted by unanimity, but I hear they now expel by majority of voices.[191] Whether this rule may not some day do them injury is yet to explain.[192] But where brotherly love continue, any

---

[187]During the winter beginning 21 December 1810 a total of 117 converts (96 whites, 21 blacks) were received for baptism. Bullittsburg Church, Minute Book A, 137-40.

[188]Judges 15:4-5.

[189]During the ten months beginning with August 1817, the church experienced a revival in which 165 persons were baptized. Its membership climbed to 365. Kirtley, *Bullittsburg Church*, 18.

[190]In 1797 the Bullittsburg Church first adopted the three-step, disciplinary procedure laid down by Jesus and found in Matthew 18:15-18. It was used by Bullittsburg for handling all "transgressions" except extraordinary, public ones, in which cases the congregation set a special plan to follow. Eight years later this earlier rule was amended by separating private and public offenses. The process of Matthew 18 would still be followed in cases of private trespass; in cases publicly known, a member who had counseled with the offender and notified him that he would be charged at the next church meeting was at liberty to hand in such an offense to the church. Bullittsburg Church, Minute Book A, 11, 90.

[191]In April 1797 a rule was adopted requiring unanimous consent for the excluding of a member. It was amended in September 1803, when expulsion by majority vote was allowed. Ibid., 8, 71.

[192]The verb *explain* is here an obsolescence meaning *unfold*.

church rule may be innocent; but where that is wanting, no rule can supply its place.

A very shrewd member of Bullittsburg some years past, being up on Elkhorn [Creek] and seeing the mighty devastation made in the churches by the preachers, remarked thus: "Where we live we are blessed with preachers of smaller growth, and each one esteems another greater and better than himself."[193] And then [he] expressed thankfulness that his lot was not cast among overgrown preachers. If this man was right, talents of any grade will not fill up the vacuum where brotherly [114]love is lost.

I never knew Bullittsburg Church stalled at any difficulty that came before them. Each one seemed to pull the right way to get the carriage out of the mud.[194] They seem to have learned how to behave themselves in the house of God[195] by treating each other with brotherly respect and receiving the reward as they go. They seem to love going to church meetings. Faction among them was perhaps never known. No man has his favorite [preacher] there that he must go with, contrary to the dictates of his own judgment. And as the prophet said formerly, "The name of that place is 'The Lord is there.'"[196] And all this is not a temporary thing when religion is in lively flow, but [they] seem more like their Saviour than many other churches, for He is "the same yesterday, today, and forever."[197] And the truth is: They never seem very cold and barren in their religious profession, if we are to judge from their actions in general. Considering their number, they lose but very few members by exclusion. As a people they are highly respectable in the eyes of all sorts of spectators. To some they are [as] terrible as an army with banners;[198] hence, there is scarcely such a thing as other religious sectaries through that whole region.

Whether human nature can bear all this long together or always, we will not say. As the Lord has thus kept them for many years, may Heaven prevent those high privileges from terminating into a Laodicean lukewarmness.[199]

---

[193]Philippians 2:4.

[194]The idiom "get the carriage out of the mud" means "solve a difficult problem."

[195]1 Timothy 3:15.

[196]The clause "The Lord is there" translates the Hebrew noun of which *Yahweh-shammah* is the transliteration. See Ezekiel 48:35. As the means by which to account for the harmony that prevailed in the Bullittsburg Church, Taylor uses what the prophet Ezekiel saw in the New Jerusalem.

[197]Hebrews 13:8.

[198]Song of Solomon 6:4.

[199]Revelation 3:16.

[161,2d]This church, above any I ever knew, has been prosperous. She has existed about thirty-two years [from] her beginning in the wilderness with only eight members.[200] Her additions have been great. I suppose not less than six hundred first and last have been added by baptism. More preachers have been raised there than [at] any other [church] that has ever come under my notice.

In this church's constitution, she had reference to the Philadelphia Confession of Faith. They have been uniform in doctrine, discipline, and practice. Their rule of discipline is the short lesson of the Saviour in the eighteenth chap[ter] of Matthew. Their doctrine is sovereign grace with a universal invitation to all mankind to seek the salvation of their souls.

I suppose to this prudent, godly course is much owing the numerous revivals they have had among them. They have had four extensive revivals among them.[201]

In Boone County there are many Baptist churches, and Bullittsburg [is] the mother of them all. This place is yet, by way of compliment, called Old Jerusalem. It has been a rare thing for [162,2d]religious strife to be known in that part of the world. Neither is there many of any other denomination but Baptists through several counties; and where there are others, there is but little falling out by the way. I lived many years among them in early times and now [1827] mingle more among them than [at] any other place the same distance from me.

North Bend Association is now respectable [with] upwards of twenty churches.[202] They have very seldom had an annual meeting (from their beginning) but I have been among them. Contention there is but little known. Though one contentious man may breed much disturbance, such an one there—by the moderation and good example of so many—would soon be frowned down to silence.

Though Bullittsburg Church has long been so happy a people, and a late instance of prosperity was about two years ago [when] they had a great revival in which upwards of a hundred was added by baptism. Their whole number at present we suppose to be upwards of three hundred,[203] but the great

---

[200]Page 8, first edition.

[201]In this paragraph the archaic, reflexive pronoun *them*, meaning *themselves*, is used twice.

[202]In 1827 the North Bend Association had seventeen churches within its fellowship. Spencer, *Kentucky Baptists*, 2:144, 145.

[203]During the nine months beginning with November 1833 the church was blessed by a revival in which 118 persons joined the congregation. Its membership rose to 359.

opening to the west[204] may have drained them off to a less number. [After] the great, late revival at Bullittsburg and after such very long prosperity as a church, a very disastrous calamity has overtaken them as a church in the past year of 1826. Within about two months three of their choice ministers died—to wit, Absalom Graves, James Dicken,[205] and Landon Robinson,[206] all close in the same neighborhood.

Graves, it seems, died with a liver complaint, of which he had been lingering about six months.[207] Dicken, it seems, died by a violent fever after an illness of a week or two. Robinson died by a lingering decline.

Graves was perhaps something under sixty years old when he breathed his last.[208] He had been baptized in his youth in Virginia. [He] moved to Kentucky with a young family, and as a private man in Kentucky he seemed to grow in favor both with God and man.[209] Being a man of prudence [and] good understanding, and also a good pensman [sic], he was appointed to the office of clerk to the [Boone] Circuit Court.[210]

In the church his usefulness was sensibly felt. As a private man he had so much the power of self-government that he seemed an example to all men. He was seldom unguarded even in the article of levity, and yet [he was] of the most pleasant manners. One prominent [163,2d]trait in his character was to do good for others. His native modesty and humility recommended him to all his acquaintances.

---

Kirtley, *Bullittsburg Church*, 22.

[204]Indiana, Illinois, and Missouri, to which Kentuckians migrated in great numbers, had become frontier areas.

[205]James Dicken (1785-1826), a native of Culpeper (now Madison) County, Virginia, migrated with his parents to Boone County, Kentucky, around 1800. He was ordained a minister by the Bullittsburg Church in 1820. Spencer, *Kentucky Baptists*, 1:298.

[206]Landon Robinson (d. 1826) was ordained as a preacher by the Sand Run Church in 1820. Ibid., 1:298-99.

[207]Graves's infection of the liver was first noticed in November 1825 and resulted in severe pain for nine months. "Life of Absalom Graves," 10, in Graves, ed., *Hymns, Psalms, and Spiritual Songs.*

[208]Graves died at the age of 57 years. Ibid., 11, 15.

[209]Luke 2:52.

[210]Absalom Graves was designated the temporary clerk of the Boone Quarter Sessions Court on 19 August 1799. Nine months later this appointment was regularized. When the Boone Circuit Court took the place of the earlier tribunal, Graves was named the clerk of the new court on 1 April 1805. Boone Quarter Sessions Court (KY) Minute Book (Kentucky State Archives), 1, 9; Boone Circuit Court (KY) Order Book A (Kentucky State Archives), 1, 2.

His readiness in the Scriptures and the devotion of his mind to the Saviour's cause induced his brethren and the church to invite him out as a preacher. Only the agony of his own mind on that subject impelled him to obey the church. His own timidity was a disadvantage to himself. It led him to speak too hesitatingly. And though he was a very good, edifying preacher, he for a long time fancied he was in the background of all that bore the name of preacher. Let it be remembered [that] this is much the safest side to err on. And in no case perhaps has it been more exemplified than in Absalom Graves, for in [sic] this kind of unaffected humility awakened sympathy in the hearer and recommended all the sacred truth he delivered.

Perhaps the gospel of the Saviour never came better recommended by human character of any mere man than [by] this humble servant of the Lord. His preaching talents did not exceed the middle grade. And his labours were abundantly blessed in various directions. He traveled a great deal. He attended several churches and at a great distance from home. The county in which he lived was so naturally rough that he could not go one mile in any direction but he had to deal with very bad roads. And through all kinds of weather and seasons of day and night [the bad roads] would not stop him from attending his appointments, and for no other reward than a peaceable mind. And serving (David-like) his generation according to the will of God; and after that David fell asleep,[211] so has Absalom Graves. His ministry thus continued upwards of twenty years, but he rests from his labours and his works do follow him.[212] And (Abel-like) he being dead yet speaketh.[213]

He [Graves] departed the evening before North Bend Association met at Bullittsburg, about three miles from his place of residence.[214] He was buried the evening of the first day's meeting. Perhaps five hundred people attended. And James Suggett addressed them on the solemn occasion, [speaking] from [the text] "Blessed are the dead that die in the Lord," etc.[215] Mr. Graves had commonly acted as the clerk or moderator of the association from its

---

[211]Acts 13:36.
[212]Revelation 14:13.
[213]Hebrews 11:4.
[214]Graves died on 17 August 1826.
[215]Revelation 14:13.

beginning.[216] All the members bore a solemn, sad aspect, for their beloved Graves was dead. They now felt their loss.

Mr. Graves has only [164,2d]had one wife, now a sorrowful widow but a serious, devotional mother in Israel.[217] Four living children are their offspring —three daughters[218] and a son. All of them, I think, [are] members of the same church of their parents. The children are or all have been married. The son, Willis Graves,[219] [is] an amiable young man of good information, who served in the clerk's office when his father declined it. May his soul be so impressed that he may serve in the gospel ministry, now [that] his father has gone the way of all the earth.

James Dicken was a choice young minister who had been baptized and ordained in the same church with Graves, his fellow worker, and to serve in the same church with Graves. Hence, I was once there in their last revival and twelve or fourteen people to be baptized. And both the men went into the water to baptize. This perhaps may need some explanation. The church at Bullittsburg, great and prosperous as she has been, has never had a particular pastor. I think she has raised and ordained about fifteen preachers and has never had any belled or horned ram among them. Should a man have qualifications for the ministry, the church ordains him according to common form among the Baptists, and he goes to work as a servant of the church and on full equality with his sinner brethren. The prosperity of this church is one item against this special pastoral work. A pastor that is only with the flock once a month is but a poor thing at best—only the name of the thing. And it is often seen that churches in this situation only have a name to live while they are dead.[220]

I call Dicken young comparitively [sic], for I suppose he was more than forty years old. I think Dicken and Graves were kinsmen, but there was some

---

[216]Graves was elected the clerk of the North Bend Association when it was constituted, in 1803, and filled that office until 1823, at which time he was chosen the moderator. He continued in that post until his death. "Life of Absalom Graves," 8, in Graves, ed., *Hymns, Psalms, and Spiritual Songs.*

[217]Mrs. Absalom Graves (d.1851) was the former Felicia White, of Virginia. Spencer, *Kentucky Baptists,* 1:297.

[218]One of the daughters of Elder Absalom Graves and Felicia White was Elizabeth, who married Absalom Graves, the eldest son of John Graves and Hannah Cave. Darnell, *Forks of Elkhorn Church,* 155.

[219]Willis Graves (d. 1834), the only son of Elder Absalom Graves, served as the clerk of the Bullittsburg Church and of the North Bend Association from 1826 till the time of his death. Kirtley, *Bullittsburg Church,* 24, 25. 220.

[220]Revelation 3:1

desparity [*sic*] in their looks. Mr. Graves seemed to be of a delicate habit and not able to bear hardship, but this he disregarded, rushing on, which perhaps brought on his end. Dicken bore the picture of health. [He was] of a ruddy complexion [and] personal[221] to look on. [He] bid fair for a long life, but the First-born of Death[222] [comes as] a violent fever [and] cuts him down as in a moment, leaving a number of rising children, a sorrowful widow, and an afflicted church to bewail their loss.

As to preaching talents these men were about on a par. Perhaps in voice [and] readiness of speech Dicken was ahead, [165,2d]but in solidity and godly simplicity but few were equal to Graves. Mr. Graves not long before his death published a selection of hymns, for which (I find) he obtained a copyright.[223] A thousand of them was more quickly circulated than anything of the kind I have known.[224]

Landon Robinson died about this time. Perhaps he and Dicken began to preach about the same time and had been thus employed about ten years. It appeared doubtful for some time whether Robinson's preaching gift would be profitable, but his purity of manners much recommended him. From delicacy of constitution he often taught a school for a livelihood. Though he was baptized at Bullittsburg, from which a young and prosperous church had been constituted called Sand Run, about four miles distant from the church. There Robinson had his membership. By the use of books and [by] traveling much (as he had no family) he had so far improved [that] the church saw proper to ordain him a few years before he died.

This well-disposed, inoffensive, young man had traveled and been so much with Graves that he seemed a second edition of the same man. Indeed there was a personal favor,[225] and the gestures and speech [were] so much the same that to be in his company you would fancy you was with Graves. Similar things are often seen in others without the least design of affectation

---

[221]Instead of the word *personal*, the author intended to use the adjective *personable*, which means *handsome* or *attractive*.

[222]The expression "First-born of Death" means some epidemic visitation as a henchman of death. Job 18:13.

[223]Absalom Graves edited a hymnal titled *Hymns, Psalms, and Spiritual Songs* (Frankfort KY, 1825).

[224]Other Baptist hymnals published in early nineteenth-century Kentucky include Starke Dupuy, *Hymns and Spiritual Songs* (Louisville KY, 1812); Silas Mercer Noel, *A Hymn Book* (Frankfort KY, 1814); and William Downs, *A New Kentucky Composition of Hymns and Spiritual Songs* (Frankfort KY, 1816).

[225]The noun *favor* is an archaism for *appearance* or *countenance*.

or the man himself knowing anything about it. And in fact, I have seen no example among men more safe to imitate than Absalom Graves.[226]

Thomas Whitaker,[227] an old and respectable member of this church, died about this time. Perhaps three months would have covered the death of these four men, close in the same neighborhood. I had baptized Whitaker and his wife in Woodford County before they were married about forty years ago.[228] And to me they always felt as children. Whitaker, being a very industrious man, was in good circumstances of life. He sometimes spoke in public, but this was in the more warm seasons of a revival. The most of his children have died, only three sons now living. They all profess religion. The oldest son, William,[229] has come forward in the ministry and lately been ordained in the church at Sand Run.

This [Sand Run] Church has two other preachers. Chichester Matthews [is] a good preacher both in precept and example, [but] now old and very infirm, and is [166,2d]thought to be one of the best men that ever walked this earth. His wife[230] also [is a saintly person]. A very pleasant, old sister, [she is] closely attentive to her infirm husband, [who is] yet trying to do what he can in a preaching way. They have had no children of their own but have raised many orphan children whom they treat as their own. And in that way [they] now have many grandchildren. William Mountague, [Jr.], has been the most active preacher in this church. He has moved some distance from them, married a second wife, but yet (I think) tends them stately. So we see Sand [Run] following the example of the old mother Bullittsburg in having no pastoral preeminence among them.

Bullittsburg Church is now in a lower condition as to the gospel ministry than at any other time for more than thirty years past. She has but one preacher in this very large church—Robert Kirtley, who was baptized among

---

[226]A sixteen-page eulogy, titled "A Short Account of the Life and Death of the Late Rev. Absalom Graves," appears in Graves's hymnal as the final section of the edition produced after his death.

[227]Thomas Whitaker (d. 1826) settled in Woodford (now Scott) County as early as 1791. By 1800 he had moved to Boone County. Railey, *Woodford County*, 326; and Clift, *"Second Census" of Kentucky, 1800*, 315.

[228]John Taylor had conducted the wedding of Thomas Whitaker and Elizabeth Conner on 6 May 1791. Railey, *Woodford County*, 326.

[229]William Whitaker (1793-1872), a native of Scott County, Kentucky, was ordained as a preacher in 1826. He served the Sand Run Church for forty years. Spencer, *Kentucky Baptists*, 2:148.

[230]Her maiden name was Agnes Walters. She and Matthews were married in Virginia in 1780. Ibid., 1:296. 231.

them. [He is] a respectable man and [has] respectable preaching talents. He is rich in this world. [He has] aplenty of servants, and aplenty of children, and a very great plenty of work to do both at home and abroad. It is very well, that from his looks he is able to bear it. [He is] now about forty years old [with] a robust, bold appearance. His trunk looks like a sturdy oak. [He has] plenty of lungroom (and the sound of his voice may be heard afar off) to preach and sing.

But poor fellow, I feel for him. I say I feel for him, for I have known him from a child. For what man or son of man can bear up under all the mighty responsibility that now rests on him? "Kind Saviour, help him, for Thou art able." I don't doubt but this dear man feels, in the death of Graves and Dicken (who were his near neighbors), that two-thirds of the world was swept from him at once. My dear Brother Robert, I commend you to God and the Word of His grace, which can not only build you up but bestow the everlasting inheritance in the end.[231] "May the Lord of the harvest send more labourers."[232] There are a number of members in this church [who are] capable to go forward and assist their desolated Brother Kirtley. "May the Lord stir them up."

I have dwelt longer on Bullittsburg than common. And the fact is [that] my thoughts and affections seem so strong to the people of this part of the earth than I am ready to indulge in this kind of innocent pleasure. But a few more remarks shall close.

[167,2d]At the funeral of Absalom Graves though there were many good preachers there, James Suggett and myself (living at a greater distance) were requested by the family to address the people. When Mr. Suggett was done,[233] I named a text of Scripture and gave some ideas that are precious to myself. And finding that some good people differ from my views, I will now state a few of them.

The text that I named was in Isaiah 57[th] c[hapter] 1[st]-2[d] v[erses]: "The righteous perisheth and no man layeth it to heart: and merciful men are taken away, none considereth that the righteous is taken away from the evil to come. He shall enter into peace: they shall rest in their beds, each one walking in his uprightness."

---

[231]Acts 20:32.

[232]Luke 10:2.

[233]The text for Suggett's sermon was Revelation 14:13. "Life of Absalom Graves," 16, in Graves, ed., *Hymns, Psalms, and Spiritual Songs*.

By "the righteous perishing" I understood their death, and as [in the case of] other men their bodies mouldered[234] to their mother dust. By "no man layeth it to heart" I understood that the value of the righteous on the earth was not appreciated as it ought to be, for they were the salt of the earth, the lights of the world.[235] And as salt and light were valuable articles among men, so were the righteous in this dark world. By "merciful men being taken from the earth" they were called off by death. And [I understood] that none was truly merciful among men but the righteous; that their tender feelings towards their poor fellow sinners much imitated their Divine Master, Who died for poor sinners; and [that] by that circumstance they were known to be righteous. They were "taken away from the evil to come": that this is a world of evils or troubles always here and always coming with sorrow upon sorrow, but from them all the good man was taken away forever.

They "shall enter into peace": [that] the day the soul leaves the body it enters into Heaven; that it does not die with the body, neither does it sleep. "They shall rest in their beds": [that] their graves [are] the peaceable resting place for the body, where the servant is free from his master and the oppressor's voice is no more heard [and] where kings and slaves are on a perfect equality, and though they rest in their beds each is "walking in his own uprightness." It is not in this world they now walk, but [it is] in the place Christ went to prepare for his disciples—sometimes called Paradise or, in other words, Heaven itself.

That departed spirits do converse we will not doubt, for the souls of them who were beheaded did enquire under the alter [sic], "How long?" and [168,2d]was kindly answered by the angels.[236] Moses and Elijah did converse with Christ on the mount concerning His sufferings, which He was to accomplish at Jerusalem.[237] Some think that the messenger conversing with John was the departed spirit of a saint, as he called himself John's fellow servant.[238] We know to a certainty that departed spirits do converse in Hell and cry for mercy.[239] A departed spirit can lose nothing of its rationality or sensibility in the world to come but much [sic] enlarge in both, "for then," says Paul, "we shall see face to face and know we are known."[240]

---

[234]The intransitive verb *moulder* is the British spelling of the word *molder*.
[235]Matthew 5:13, 14.
[236]Revelation 6:9-11.
[237]Luke 9:30-31.
[238]Revelation 19:10.
[239]Luke 16:23-24.
[240]1 Corinthians 13:12.

After remarking to this effect, I took up the four near neighbors that had so lately left this world [and who had] had so long and happy [an] acquaintance, having been members of the same church so very long together. I did not doubt at all but [that] they were that evening in Heaven together, that they knew each other full as well as they ever did when they met together to worship at Bullitsburg, and [that] at that moment [they were] recounting all the troubles through which they came.

Graves had only left his painful tenement[241] of clay about twenty-four hours [earlier], but, quick as thought, some kind, ministering spirit (as in case of Lazarus)[242] bear[243] him away [and] announce[d] his arrival at Heaven's gate, while the Saviour says, "Enter into rest, my laborious servant."

The Lord Jesus is as kind and sympathizing now as when He was on earth, as He is the same yesterday, today, and forever.[244] His Disciples once returned from a laborious tour of preaching, and the throng was so great [that] they had not [had] leisure to eat bread. He then directed them to withdraw into the desert and rest awhile.[245] So when their labour of love is done on earth, He calls them to Heaven to rest forever.

I closed my short subject by stating that I knew no rational ground on which punishments and rewards can be administered in the world to come but by knowing each other and [by] calling up into recollection what had transpired in life.

The Lord told Zechariah (ll[th] c[hapter] 8[th] v[erse]) that He had or would cut off three shepherds in one month. Three shepherds or preachers the Lord has cut off from Bullittsburg in a month or two. With those in Zech[ariah], God had a controversy and cut them off for their wickedness,[246] but I cannot think thus of the Bullittsburg shepherds.

That it is a scourge on the church I have no doubt, and God's rod cause-less does not come.[247] Let each one examine closely, [169,2d]"Why is it we are thus chastised?" Perhaps duty to the preachers some way was neglected,

---

[241]Here the noun *tentement* is used as a poetic word meaning "dwelling place."

[242]Luke 16:22.

[243]*Bear* is here the phonetic spelling of the archaic past tense *bare* of the transitive verb *bear*.

[244]Hebrews 13:8.

[245]Mark 6:7, 12, 30-31.

[246]Zecariah 11:15-16.

[247]Proverbs 26:2.

either in not reasonably communicating[248] to them or in failing to pray for their prosperity, or [in] neglecting their ministry in some way.

Should the Lord call away [Robert] Kirtley, what goes then with your public worship, speaking as men?[249] It might look strange to some that I should think his lot so very responsible. Men who can preach once a month to three or four churches may think strange of this. But Kirtley has not yet got into that vague method of serving churches. "May the Lord send forth more labourers."[250]

---

[248]Here the intransitive verb *communicate* is an archaism meaning "share in common" (one's material blessings).

[249]Taylor's fears in this regard were unfounded because Robert Kirtley continued to preach at Bullittsburg for forty-five years and was succeeded there by his son James A. Kirtley (1822-1904). Spencer, *Kentucky Baptists*, 1:302; and Masters, *Baptists in Kentucky*, 451.

[250]Matthew 9:38.

# 7

# Corn Creek Church

[115]I had gotten a flat-bottom[1] boat to move my household furniture and year's provision down the [Ohio] River sixty or seventy miles to Mount Byrd. This provision seemed needful as I was going into the woods. My boat sunk in the river with chief of my effects in it; and though the clear loss was only about a hundred dollars, yet many of my things were much injured by getting wet.

We had some rough cabins prepared to go into,[2] but [we were] surrounded by one of the heaviest forests I ever saw. It was now late in March [1802], and our bread to get the next year. Only about four acres [were] cleared and no fence around it. [That] was our beginning at Mount Byrd.

I had acquired some acquaintance with the people from my visits there, but my wife was a perfect stranger to all. A young church of perhaps twenty members had been constituted not long before I moved and was called Corn Creek Church.[3] The place of worship was about four miles from Mount Byrd. The opposite shore of the Ohio was Indian title,[4] and the Indians [were] hunting on their own land about a mile from my house, but they were at peace.

At the first monthly meeting of the little church (Corn Creek) after our arrival at Mount Byrd, myself and family gave our membership to the church. After I was received by the church, I informed them that I had joined them as a member and with no office authority among them;[5] that, though I had been long a preacher, it was not by their sanction as a church; that I was now at their disposal as one of their members; that, if they required any ministerial service

---

[1]The adjective *flat-bottom* is a dialectal usage meaning *flat-bottomed*.

[2]At least two cabins had been constructed on Mount Byrd as early as December 1801, using hands from the work crew of James McIntosh, Jr., Taylor's overseer. Bullittsburg Church, Minute Book A, 48.

[3]The Corn Creek Church, located in Gallatin (now Trimble) County, was organized by William Taylor and Joshua Morris on 14 October 1800. Eight charter members adopted the Philadelphia Confession of Faith with three reservations: God is not the author of sin, an oath before a civil magistrate is not an act of worship, and the use or nonuse by other churches of the laying on of hands at baptism does not constitute a bar to fellowship. Corn Creek affiliated itself with the Salem Association the next year and with the Long Run Association in 1803. Corn Creek Church, Minute Book B, 1-2; and Spencer, *Kentucky Baptists*, 1:461.

[4]Here the noun *title* is an archaism meaning the "land that a particular group claims to own."

[5]Taylor omits this clause from the second edition.

from me, I expected them to signify it, otherwise I should not make free[6] among them in that way.

Perhaps what myself said brought on the same day a request [for me] to take the pastoral care of the [116]church. Perhaps I had baptized more than half the members that were in the church (at the times of my visits there before I moved). The older brethren did not hesitate at that request, as they had no other preacher in the church but myself. I then opened up my own views of particular pastorship; That myself was never calculated for it [and] that I was ready to do any service I was capable [of], without that particular charge. With which the church was perfectly content and has had no particular pastor since.

As to our earthly concerns, we had never seen such heavy labour before us [by which] to obtain support as [we did] now. We had no time to pause and think but [had to] go right on to work. The timber [was] quite green and standing very thick, consisting of various sorts as poplar, beach [sic], [black] walnut, ash, and other kinds,[7] with the largest kind of buckeye, three or four feet through with their trunks an hundred feet long.[8] It was usual to get from three and four to seven and eight cuts of rails from a tree. Many of the poplars were six or seven feet through, and their length [was] an hundred feet without a limb.[9] The looks of the soil encouraged us to rush on in hopes of future reward.[10]

I had at that time three strong, black men and a boy and as many black women, who could help us burn brush and roll logs.[11] My two sons [were] one eighteen and the other sixteen years old,[12] and myself [was] now in a manner in

---

[6]The idiom "make free" means "take liberties."

[7]In addition to the five species of trees that Taylor mentions, the following were also found: hickory, linden, white oak, sugar, and white walnut. John Floyd, Surveyor's Certificate, 24 May 1774, in Gallatin Circuit Court (KY), Record of Proceedings, 1802-1810, 138-39.

[8]Today the largest kind of buckeye in Kentucky, which is called the yellow or sweet buckeye, grows up to ninety feet in height. Mary E. Wharton and Roger W. Barbour, *Trees and Shrubs of Kentucky* (Lexington KY, 1973) 300.

[9]Taylor omits the final clause of this sentence from his second edition.

[10]The species that Taylor called the poplar is commonly known as the yellow or tulip poplar. This hardwood tree has a straight trunk, often today reaching 200 feet in height. The distance from the lowest limb to the ground varies from 80 to 100 feet. Its diameter may be from 8 to 10 feet. When early settlers saw the poplar tree in the forest they thought that it meant fertile soil. Its lumber was used in houses and barns. Ibid., 522, 523.

[11]Taylor's tax list for 1803 includes seven blacks above the age of sixteen years, fifteen for the total number. Gallatin County (KY) Tax List, 1803 (Microfilm, Kentucky Historical Society).

[12]Benjamin Taylor was born in 1784; Joseph, in 1786. Dorothy Thompson, "Ancestors and Descendants," 32, 36, 42. The father overlooks his two young sons—John Wickliffe, born in 1798, and Cave, born in 1800—because he is thinking in terms of the laborers at

the prime of life, though upwards of fifty years old. The sound of our axes made entertaining music in this mighty forest.

My wife and daughters[13] with a black woman or two in the house made the wheels roar in our large cabins. With also the use of a loom there, [all] made it probable that we should get food and raiment. Another thing in our favor [was that], though for several years we had been afflicted with sickness, the sweet air and water of the lofty bluff of Mount Byrd restored us all to good health again. We first enclosed twenty-five acres of land in two apartments,[14] thirteen of which we planted in corn and two in flax and vegetables. [117]We had ten barrels of corn per acre that year [1802]. That with the help of a good beachmast [sic] made us bread enough and to spare. After laying by[15] our corn, we cleared our ten acres we had enclosed and put it in wheat. We then enclosed twenty-five acres with a design to clear it next winter, and twenty acres more we enclosed for the use of a pasture. After we had cleared our intended ground the next winter, we had taken down so much timber that we found the logrolling[16] prodigious heavy. I took notice that we spent thirty days in logrolling, and after which it was more trouble to burn up this green timber than to roll it.

However, after we had planted our corn [1803], we concluded to go to building. We did but little at brickmaking till after harvest, when we moved on with rapidity. We made about an hundred thousand bricks. [We] put up a house seventy feet by twenty-two [with] a stone cellar under the whole of it and forty feet of it two stories above the cellar. Before Christmas [we] had it all covered in, and [we] moved into one end of it in February [1804].

We then cleared the ground we had enclosed, and [we] enclosed twenty acres more for pasture. So that when we had been at Mount Byrd two years we had seventy acres of cleared land [and] twenty more enclosed. [We were] living in the house I have described and [had] a very great orchard of apple, peach, and other kinds of fruit. So that in Gallatin County, I was a little like Job when he lived in the East in the early days of his prosperity.[17]

It is probable [that] I was the richest man in the county where I lived, but wise Providence has found a way to put me in different circumstances since that

---

his disposal.

[13]There were three daughters in the family at this time—Nancy, born in 1788; Polly, 1792; and Jane, 1795. Ibid., 36, 37, 40.

[14]In this case the noun *apartment* is a Scotticism meaning "a distinct portion of land, such as a field."

[15]The verbal term "lay by" is a dialecticism meaning "cultivate for the last time."

[16]The noun *logrolling* is an Americanism signifying the frontier practice of rolling felled trees into one place in order to clear a field.

[17]Job 1:1-3.

time. I do not recollect paying one dollar for labour in making all this improvement except to mechanics.[18] If it be asked if our labour was not too severe, I should no doubt answer in the affirmative. But it was all done with great pleasantness, for I have found both by experience and [by] observation that when master goes all the rest goes cheerfully to business.[19]

[118]Through the course of this two years, I preached but little except on Saturdays and Sundays or of nights. I was commonly at church meetings on those days somewhere. And in the time of the year for associations, I commonly went to a number of them. The settlement in which I lived did not admit of much preaching. Fifty families perhaps were the amount of all the people, and they had much to do to get their living in this heavy-timbered country.

The settlement, however, increased, and the church at Corn Creek grew, though but slowly. There had been a revival in the place, as I have named, before I moved there. And perhaps in two or three years after I joined the church, at different times, I baptized about twenty people, the church being then about sixty in number. And I think she never grew higher than about eighty till I moved from the place.[20]

A year or two after I moved to Mount Byrd, Philemon Vawter moved from Bullittsburg and joined Corn Creek Chruch.[21] He was a respectable preacher and one of the best of men. His example preached loud to the world. Soon after his arrival at Corn Creek, the church thought proper to ordain him. This gave me great pleasure to have a fellow labourer in the Lord. And in the church he was of great usefulness till he moved to Indiana. (Something of his biography I have given elsewhere.)[22]

Corn Creek Church, though they treated with all their members according to the eighteenth [chapter] of Matthew so far as was practicable and though their final exclusions were by unanimity of voices, yet there was not that harmony of sentiment as might be wished for. They often differed as to the mode of doing church business; this at times brought about bickerings between the members in harsh speeches and sulky looks. And though it did not come to tumults, yet their

---

[18]Here the noun *mechanic* may mean "worker who uses tools," or it may be an archaism meaning "manual laborer."

[19]The author implies that on the plantation he and his two teenage sons worked side by side with his black slaves.

[20]In 1812 the Corn Creek Church had seventy-seven members. Benedict, *Baptist Denomination*, 2:543.

[21]On 4 February 1804 a letter of dismissal was granted by the Bullittsburg Church to Philemon Vawter and his wife, Anna. In July 1802 he had been licensed to preach by the congregation. Bullittsburg Church, Minute Book A, 55, 76, 173.

[22]For a biography of Philemon Vawter, see John Taylor, *Thoughts on Missions*, 45-47.

forerunners were sometimes seen, which Paul calls *swellings*—which is another word for *poutings* [and] which is a very unbecoming thing among [119]the followers of the meek and lowly Saviour.[23]

Methodist influence began in Corn Creek settlement soon after Baptist worship was set up there. This divided the people at large, and the contest between the parties was the warmer as the strength of members was about equal on each side.

With all my attachment to my fine Mount Byrd, some things began to turn up to embitter the place to me. In the first place, Vawter moved away, which was a great drawback on my peace and happiness.

I had built a great barn first of brick and added to it with timber,[24] so that it was very spacious. I had filled it with the greatest crop of small grain[25] I had ever raised. Soon after I had housed it, the same kind of fire that killed Job's sheep and servants[26] destroyed my barn. A flash of lightning as in a moment burnt it down. Perhaps a thousand bushels of grain were burnt with the barn, the whole loss at least a thousand dollars. This was done when I was on a tour of preaching from one association to another. This bespoke to me that the Author of this fire would have me leave the place. So that if I was a little like Job in one case, I was also a little like him in another. And though my children were not all dead, yet two of them had died at Mount Byrd.[27]

Another strong reason for leaving the place [was that] the town of Madison sprung up opposite to where I lived,[28] and its inhabitants [were] trafficking with the Negroes for all that they brought to market. And my absence from home (and always on Sundays) placed everything I had in jeopardy.

But the greatest reason of all was a partial loss of my repute among the people. This thing worked like the spreading of leaven. And a number of the people seemed to have the strongest malice against me. I was presented to the grand jury as having committed a trespass on the public good.

A schoolhouse had been built at the meetinghouse, for which I had paid my quota of money and where we often preached in the winter. The door was locked, and I had reasons to think it was to keep me from [120]preaching in it.

---

[23]2 Corinthians 12:20.

[24]The noun *timber* is a Briticism meaning *lumber*.

[25]The meaning here is such grain as rye, wheat, oats, or barley as opposed to corn.

[26]Job 1:16.

[27]Eliza Taylor died in 1803 at the age of eight weeks and one day. Cave Taylor was drowned in 1810. Dorothy Thompson, "Ancestors and Descendants," 42.

[28]Madison, a town on the Ohio River, is located in the southeastern corner of Indiana in Jefferson County.

I often thought of what the Lord said to Ezekiel (2d chap[ter] 6th verse) about dwelling among scorpions. Some of the church, I found, was prejudiced against me. It was some time before I could conjecture what root of bitterness all this had sprung from. But be it what it would, my mind was made up to leave the place, and that from the Saviour's direction: where [Jesus said], "If they persecute you in one city, flee to another."[29]

I knew that some of the best friends I had in the world were in Corn Creek Church, who, from the storm of vengeance they saw among some of the people, gave it as their opinion that it would be best for me to move away.

The origin of all this mighty spleen came from one single circumstance. A member of the church and a man of considerable influence had joined the Freemasons[30] about forty miles from home. And [he] was in that connection some time before the church had any knowledge of it. A complaint being brought into the church against him for that act,[31] the business for a decision was laid over till their next meeting. Knowing that I as one should have to give my voice in the church on this affair, I procured the constitution of the lodge at Shelbyville[32] and gave it a reading for my own information. A large gathering of people came to the next meeting to hear a trial in the church about Freemasonry.

I took the liberty to make a pretty long speech on the mysteries of that subject in the hearing of a member of the Masonic brethren, for they were increasing fast at this time in our settlement. I confessed, as they claimed, its great antiquity: That it probably existed before any of the Scriptures were written,

---

[29]Matthew 10:23.

[30]Freemasons are members of an international society that practices brotherliness, charity, and mutual aid. For a recent interpretation regarding the origin of Blue Lodge Masonry, see John J. Robinson, *Born in Blood: The Lost Secrets of Freemasonry* (New York NY, 1989).

[31]The Long Run Association, with which the Corn Creek Church was affiliated, had declared seven years earlier that "any member of our Baptist society is condemnable in joining a Freemason lodge." Birdwhistell, *Long Run Association*, 13.

Baptists were not alone in their aversion toward the Masonic order during the first third of the nineteenth century. Congregationalists in the Northeast, Presbyterians in the West, and Methodists throughout the nation also entertained strong feelings against Freemasonry, primarily because it was viewed as a secret society. This intense hostility against secrecy reached its height with the advent of the Anti-Masonic Party, which played a role in the presidential election of 1832 as the country's first "third political party." Sweet, *American Frontier*, 1:170n.

[32]The Masonic organization at Shelbyville, the seat of Shelby County, was named Solomon Lodge No. 5. When it was begun in 1800, the other lodges in Kentucky were located at Lexington, Paris, Georgetown, and Frankfort. George L. Willis, Sr., *History of Shelby County, Kentucky* (Louisville KY, 1929) 261.

that it was an excellent institution when first introduced among men [in order] to bring them from barbarism to some degree of civilization and [to] unite one man to another and [to] a number of men into a kind of civilized community, and [that] by their compact they were bound to do each other good and [to] moralize their own [121]behaviour.[33] All of which was very good and had been of great use to ancient beings of our race, but that it was of as little use now as the moon and stars are when the sun is shining. And [I suggested] that their modes of tuition,[34] even in their lodges, were so dark and figurative that weak minds could not easily get into it.

If the pupil looked at an operative Mason with his apron on, his hammer in his hand, his compass, his trowel, his square, or all this figure on paper for his contemplation, he studies the hammer by which the uneven parts of the stone is taken off and with the square shaped off at right angles to fit it for the building. So the schollar [sic] must moralize himself by smoothing in his conduct as the operative Mason did the rock.

Again, the square [was made] with exactly as many inches as hours in a whole day, and then going off with an exact square. So all his conduct must be regular to fit him for society.

When he [the pupil] studied the compass with its exact circles or the trowel in using the morter [sic] or cement to unite one rock to another, [it was] teaching the consolidating of affection and interest between man and man, and smoothed off as with the trowel in brotherly friendship.

[I stated that] as morality was the highest object of the whole establishment, the Author of our being has given us a more excellent way in the Bible and especially in the New Testament, in which the brightest morality and spirituality of heart is made known in the most explicit style. And moreover, Freemasons in general, with all their fine system of morality, were not the most moralized men as to their actions. I consider it a very weak thing for a Christian to give up his privileges in the church of Christ for the half-handed morality that was found in a Masonic lodge. Though I professed no knowledge of any of their byelaws [sic], yet the doctrine I had propagated was a natural deduction from their constitution. I know not whether I ever had a more attentive assembly of hearers in my life.

I then made a proposition [122]which was agreed to by a majority of the church: to give the man in question two months to give an answer whether he would finally leave the Masonic lodge or lose his place in the church. To this a number of the church objected, saying [that] he ought to repent for the sin he had

---

[33]*Behaviour* is the British spelling of the noun *behavior*.

[34]The noun *tuition* is now a rare word meaning *instruction* or *teaching*.

committed. (To this proposition at the given time he affected to comply but was not as good as his word afterwards.)

I knew of no Masonic man present that was offended at my remarks in the church, but their progress[35] was rather with friendly overtures. To these I made but little reply, till at length a judge of a court from the opposite side of the river waited on me with overtures so explicit that I was compelled to be plain. This friendly judge was very zealous in the cause and, no doubt, had friendship for me, such as it was. After illustrating the utility, advantages, and excellency of Masonry, [he] plainly importuned me to cast my lot among them.[36]

The only, short reply I made was about as follows: That "it would by no means suit me to be a Mason"; that "if it was a good thing, I would not keep the secret; and if it was a bad thing I would not keep the secret but would warn the people against it; and if there was neither good nor harm in it, of course it was not worth having."

Finding a number of the church [members] dissatisfied about the man who had joined the Masons; and he being a deacon of the church, they could not receive the ministration [of the Lord's Supper] from his hands. I made a proposition in the church: to dismiss him from his office under existing circumstances. This the church immediately accorded in.[37] This, I soon found, stung him to the quick. Esteeming me the instrument of his degradation in the church, [he] seemed determined to be revenged, if we judge from his actions afterwards. And the generality of his Masonic brethren cooperated with him, which brought forward the whole sweep of vengeance spoken of above. For though he had given his word to the church to [123]forsake the lodge, he did not do it. The influence of the man may be known by his being twice elected after this by the county to the

---

[35]By *progress* Taylor means "invitation to join the order."

[36]Masons consider it a breach of propriety for one of their own to invite a man to take membership in Freemasonry, which by custom must originate with the application of the novice.

[37]In that part of Kentucky where the Corn Creek Church is located, the prevailing Baptist view regarding Freemasonry would be greatly altered within thirty-four years. In 1846 the Sulphur Fork Association, with which Corn Creek had been affiliated since 1827, took a neutral position and advised its churches not to make one's approval or disapproval of the Masonic order a test of fellowship. Spencer, *Kentucky Baptists*, 2:404.

legislature of Kentucky.[38] Others who united with him for my destruction were men of much influence.

With deep concerted and secret counsel, the presentment was laid before the grand jury, while to my face they were fair and mild. I was at the court and in friendly conversation with the men the day that this transaction took place, but I had left the courthouse before the presentment was made.[39] I understood it was brought forward by a harmless, old Dutchman. These cunning men made him think, though they were on the grand jury themselves, that he would be forsworn if he did not bring on this kind of indictment.

The great crime committeed against the commonwealth: A man who lived with me, in taking in a bit of new ground, had run a corner of his fence over an old, forsaken road which they called a public one. I was, of course, legally called on to answer for the crime. It soon spread through my neighborhood and perhaps through the county. Some said [that] I was indicted; others, that I was presented.[40] The magnitude of the crime was hardly known, but it would come forward next term in all its glowing colours.

The attorney for the commonwealth and the judge himself, neither of whom had ever been at my house before, came about six miles out of their way on Saturday night[41] before the court assembled. Their object, I presume, was to see the spot themselves where the trespass was committed. They passed by the place in the morning, myself with them going to a meeting I had.

When the business came on, a respectable man of the bar of my acquaintance who knew the whole affair of this trespass volunteered his services to make a

---

[38]This Mason was David Owen, who served in the state House of Representatives as the member from Gallatin County during 1814 and 1815 and who was one of the eight charter members of the Corn Creek Church. Collins, *Kentucky*, rev. ed., 2:287, 775; Willis, *Shelby County*, 263. Owen remained a member of Corn Creek until February 1819, when he removed from the bounds of the church. On the sixth when his letter of dismissal was granted, the congregation voted to add the following statement to his letter: "There is a number of members in this church whoes [sic] fellowship is hurt with Brother Owen on account of his haveing [sic] joined the Freemason lodge long since he was a Baptist." Corn Creek Church, Minute Book B, [53].

[39]In the Gallatin Circuit Court a grand jury of twenty-two men appointed on 13 July 1812 made a presentment on the following day against John Taylor. He was charged with obstructing a public road. Gallatin Circuit Court (KY), Order Book [2], 1810–1814 (Kentucky State Archives) 309.

[40]An indictment by a grand jury comes after an investigation and recommendation by the prosecutor. On the other hand, a presentment is handed in by a grand jury on the basis of its own knowledge and observation regarding an alleged offense, but without a bill of indictment.

[41]The date was 10 October 1812.

short statement to the court, to which the commonwealth's attorney scarcely replied. And the charge [was] dismissed by the judge in perhaps ten minutes after it was taken up,[42] to the great mortification of those vengeful [124]men. This, as might be looked for, was very far from curing their malicious fever, which I might give in many more instances, but time would fail.

I have no doubt that thousands among the most honorable men in our nation are what is called Freemasons, but it did not happen to be of that kind into whose hands I fell. Neither have I ever known a Baptist who joined that order of people that was ever of much use in a church afterwards. The man spoken of is a striking instance.

In this mighty blast some [members] of the church became prejudiced against me, for those active men were very influential, and some of their kindred belonged to the church. One of the members said to another who was prejudiced that it was the same spirit that was working against me in the neighborhood that had put Jesus Christ to death long ago.

I had now been a preacher upwards of forty years and had never been in the same situation I now was: being in less credit[43] as a preacher at home than abroad. Being now in the habit of traveling the greater part of my time on long tours and by visiting many associations, [I had] acquired an extensive acquaintance with the Baptists.[177,2d]Had a stranger attended our meetings at Corn Creek, he would have thought that I was popular in the place, for even those who disliked me frequently came to meetings, though perhaps from no better motive than [did] the Pharisees [who] followed the Saviour.

[124]Not long before I left the place, at one of our Sunday meetings I took this text: "The harvest is great but the labourers are few: pray ye the Lord of the harvest," etc.[44] My own soul was enlarged with prayerful desire that the Lord would send preaching there that would be more useful to the people than mine had been. And [I] also urged the people to thus pray. It was soon reported that I got so mad with the people that I even wept when I was preaching.

The reader has seen already that the origin of all this storm seemed to be from Freemasonry. But it may be remembered that [125]only a few men of that order was at the bottom of the whole of it, for others of the same connection treated me with the affection of a brother, holding those others in contempt for their conduct. One instance was the gentleman of the bar already spoken of who

---

[42]This case, *Commonwealth v. John Taylor*, came before the Gallatin Circuit Court on 12 October 1812. Circuit Judge Henry Davidge, assisted by Judges Garland Bullock and Presley Gray, reached the "opinion that the defendent [should] be acquited." Gallatin Circuit Court (KY), Order Book [2], 1810–14, 333, 334.

[43]Here the noun *credit* in a rare usage means "the quality of being believable."

[44]Luke 10:2.

volunteered [to plead] my case in court and [who] would afterwards receive no compensation.

When I reflect soberly, my own opinion is that the root of all those difficulties was with God himself, as a just visitation for my sins. I esteem the deceitfulness of sin in its subter[r]aneous and serpentine windings an overmatch for any man on earth. Where the fear of God is but little removed from his heart, a jealous God will not admit a rival.

When we [had] moved from Bullittsburg to Mount Byrd, we soon emerged from great family affliction into a state of great health. And though we did a great deal of hard labour, yet prosperity attended our efforts for a number of years; till with my fine Mount Byrd and two thousand acres of valuable land on the river connected with it (besides other valuable lands at a distance),[45] I owned about twenty slaves clear of debt.[46] And [I] had a considerable amount of stock in different banks. My children [were] growing up, and [they] bid fair to recommend themselves to the world.

Putting all together no doubt became a thief on my heart, though unperceived by myself or others. For I do not know that any person considered me in any other light than a zealous man in religion, for I do not recollect that worldly business ever prevented my attending one of my thousands of meetings that I have appointed for near fifty years past.

But a Holy God does not see as man sees. Three times He was displeased with holy Moses: first, for not circumcising his son, and [he] sought to slay him at the inn;[47] secondly, for pleading an excuse, desiring Aaron to be sent to Pharaoh instead of himself, and for which it is probable [that] God deprived him of an eloquent tongue as long as he lived;[48] and thirdly, his intemperate spirit and unadvised [126]lips at the waters of Meribah,[49] for which he was forbid[50] going into the promised land. All of which might seem innocent in the eyes of men. With many other instances in the Scriptures confirming this saying: "I the Lord, your God, am a jealous God."[51]

---

[45]Beside 1,960 acres in Gallatin County, Taylor owned land in Boone, Hardin, and Henry counties that totaled 2,177 acres in September 1811. Gallatin County (KY), Tax List (Microfilm, Kentucky Historical Society), 1811.

[46]In 1811 Taylor owned twenty slaves, only seven of whom were above the age of sixteen years. A twelvemonth later his total number of blacks had decreased to fifteen with the number above sixteen years remaining the same. Ibid., 1811, 1812.

[47]Exodus 4:24-25.

[48]Exodus 4:10-16.

[49]Numbers 20:10-13.

[50]Here *forbid* is the archaic past participle of the verb *forbid*.

[51]Exodus 20:5; Deuteronomy 5:9.

For David's sin of pride (unperceived by himself) in numbering the people, which was a very common thing in Israel, seventy thousand men lost their lives.[52] And for another sin of his, the son of his own loins stole the hearts of the people, and God bid Shimei to curse him.[53]

For the idolatry of Solomon and the folly of his son Rehoboam, God raised up a Jeroboam, by whom ten tribes were rent from the house of David.[54] So true is that saying of Solomon that "When a man's ways please the Lord, He maketh his enemies to be at peace with him."[55] David (in the 17th Psalm 13th verse) speaks of the wicked as God's sword and hand or rod of correction.

And though I felt as if I dwelt among scorpions; and though, as to my course among men, I could with all my examination see nothing of which I could accuse myself. Yet from the apostacy [sic] of my affections from the Lord, I concluded that God's own way of chastising[56] was the best. And [I] was almost ready to excuse these men and [to] pray the Lord to pardon their folly and sin.

I left Corn Creek in March 1815 after living at Mount Byrd thirteen years.[57] The church at Corn Creek while I lived there had grown but slowly. I had baptized while there perhaps about thirty people. I think [that] they were about eighty in number when I left them, after which they invited supplies from abroad for a year or two.

A young speaker moving into the bounds of the church was licensed to preach among them. His name was [John] Wallace.[58] A George Kendall,[59] who was baptized at Corn Creek, began also to speak in public and was licensed by

---

[52]2 Samuel 24:1, 10, 15; 1 Chronicles 21:1-4, 14.

[53]2 Samuel 16:5-13.

[54]1 Kings 11:31, 33-35; 12:12-15, 20.

[55]Proverbs 16:7.

[56]Here Taylor uses the gerund *chastising*, which is a verbal noun whose present participial form derives from the archaic verb *chastise* meaning *chasten*.

[57]On Saturday 4 March 1815 the Corn Creek Church approved the application of Taylor for letters of dismissal for himself, his wife, and two of his slave women, Judith and Sealy. The transfers were to be ready for delivery to him on the following day. Corn Creek Church, Minute Book B, [18].

[58]On 5 August 1815 John Wallace (d. ca. 1828) and his wife, Ruth, joined the Corn Creek congregation by a letter of transfer from the New Providence Church, which had licensed him to preach. His new church unanimously continued this license. During 1816–1818 Corn Creek considered on at least eleven occasions the ordaining of Wallace as a minister but delayed the matter each time. Ibid., [23-50] passim; and Spencer, *Kentucky Baptists*, 2:181.

[59]George Kendall succeeded William Buckley as the preacher at the Corn Creek Church, in which the former had been raised up to the ministry. Spencer, *Kentucky Baptists*, 1:463.

the church. But, by what I could learn, the people at large, as also some of the church, paid but little attention to those young preachers for some time, till at length a William [127]Buckley[60] was invited to attend[61] them. And from appearances of success he moved and lived among them two or three years.

Under his labours and the zealous efforts of the younger preachers, a considerable revival took place, so that in one year Mr. Buckley baptized upwards of a hundred people.[62] Mr. Buckley attended several other churches about this time and was successful at them all. But at length [he] moved his family to the lower end of the state[63] and, like my poor self, left the church in less credit as a preacher than when he came to it.

The church was again left with their two young preachers, but they had grown, so that public worship was kept up with respectability. However, they soon contemplated a new church for the sake of convenience. They constituted a church called Hunters Bottom,[64] on the river. This new establishment included Mr. [John] Wallace, whom the new church has ordained since their constitution.[65]

Corn Creek has only George Kendall as a preacher among them. His correctness of opinion in gospel doctrines, his orderly deportment in general,[66] his zeal for the cause of gospel religion, and his aptitude to explain the Bible (which is almost the only book he reads), [all] has led the church to take up the subject of his ordination. But it was found that the church was much more willing to ordain

---

[60]William Buckley (b. 1772), a native of Frederick County, Virginia, was ordained as a preacher by the Glens Creek Church of Woodford County, Kentucky, around 1807. He became a member at Corn Creek about 1816. Ibid.

[61]In this case Taylor uses the rare verb *attend* to mean "look after" or "minister to."

[62]In 1818 during the first eight months Buckley baptized 108 people into the membership of the church. Corn Creek Church, Minute Book B, [35-50] passim.

[63]In later years Buckley labored in Livingston and Caldwell counties, where improvidence led to poverty, drunkenness to excommunication. Spencer, *Kentucky Baptists*, 1:463.

[64]The Hunters Bottom Church was organized in 1819 and was disbanded about 1830. Ibid., 2:160, 181, 336.

[65]After John Wallace left Corn Creek, it was as a preacher at the Hunters Bottom Church that he was finally ordained to the ministry. The Corn Creek Church sent four men in November 1820 to take part in his ordination. Corn Creek Church, Minute Book B, [69].

[66]The term "his orderly deportment in general" is omitted from the second edition.

than he was to receive it.[67] Corn Creek has existed as a church upwards of twenty years. Perhaps their number at present is an hundred and thirty or forty.

When I left Corn Creek the sensation with myself was entirely of a new stamp. When I [had] left any other place before, the solicitous voice of the people was for me to stay, and this gave me pain of mind. The thing was quite reversed [now], and this gave me greater pain, for I knew not whether I had a friend under existing circumstances that wished me to stay longer.

[154]On the evening of this last baptizing [in October 1822][68] at Clear Creek [Church], I set out on a tour of about seventy miles to Corn Creek Church, in Gallatin County, where I had formerly lived for many years. On Friday night I had meeting at an old Brother Jessee Connell's.[69] The text was "It is high time to wake out of sleep, for now is our salvation nearer than when we believed."[70]

A number of the people after preaching tarried, perhaps for the purpose of conversing on their religious impressions. [155]One woman in great seriousness related her hope in Christ. The next day being church meeting at Corn Creek, she was received for baptism.[71] The church sat again at night, when a crowded assembly came out, and three more [were] received for baptism.[72]

----

[67]When George Kendall's ordination to the ministry was taken up by the church on 1 September 1821, John Taylor, who was visiting Corn Creek that day, "offered his light respecting the matter." With nearly complete agreement the congregation approved his being ordained. Because Kendall had some objections, the question was laid over for a later time. Having considered this subject at one other meeting that year, the church on 2 November 1822 agreed to his ordination and scheduled it for the following May. Two months before the ceremony the congregation invited helps from at least four churches to attend. Kendall was finally set aside as a gospel minister on Saturday 3 May 1823. John Taylor and other helps came from five churches. "Entire harmony appeared in all parties, unanimity seemed to prevail through the day, and love seemed to flow from breast to breast. The ordination was gone through with great solemnity." Corn Creek Church, Minute Book B, [74, 75, 84, 88, 90]. The first quotation comes from page [74]; the second, from page [90].

[68]Here the author skips seven years in his narration.

[69]This Jessee Connell (b. 1748), a charter member of the Corn Creek Church, was not the same man as the person by that name who served as the foreman of the grand jury that charged John Taylor in 1812 with obstructing a public road. Gallatin Circuit Court (KY), Order Book [2], 1810–1814, 297. The date of this meeting was 1 November 1822.

[70]Romans 13:11. This paragraph and the following five paragraphs are taken from Taylor's "Appendix to the History of Clear Creek Church."

[71]This new convert was Polly Connell, who was received on Saturday 2 November 1822. Corn Creek Church, Minute Book B, [84].

[72]The clerk recorded only the names of Wyatt Coulman and Charlotte Nicholson as being received as candidates for baptism on Saturday evening 2 November 1822. The meeting was held at the home of William Wood. Ibid., [85].

Agreeing to sit again at 10 o'clock on Sunday morning, two more were received [then]. This morning the neighborhood flocked out early. In relating these experiences, the people seemed much affected, for the candidates[73] (though females) spoke so as to be heard all over the house. And [they] gave such evidence that God was in them of a truth that joyful tears flowed profusely from the old disciples of Christ, while those destitute of religion appeared solemn as death.

The church at Corn Creek has been without an ordained minister for several years, though the voice of the church has been united for the ordination of George Kendall. As yet he has declined being ordained, esteeming himself un-qualified for so great a trust.[74] For this cause baptism had not been performed here for a long time, except [for] one man [whom] myself had baptized last spring.[75]

Our old baptizing place at Corn Creek had become filled up with drift. And the whole assembly seemed anxious to see baptizing again; we all progressed on down the creek through the brush and fallen timber a long distance before we found suitable water. One of the women failed to come forward to baptism (who had been received), perhaps on account of her husband.

Here I baptized five of my old acquaintances,[76] whose salvation I had long prayed for, while my heart was filled with paradisiacal [sic] peace and joy. This afternoon bore the appearance of a revival of religion among the people. How it will terminate is only with the Lord to know. The respectable, old Brother Connell, now in his seventy-fifth year and [who] has been a Baptist about fifty years, remarked to me with great joy of heart as we were going to the water, "Now I see why it is I did not die sooner." For all the people now [being] received in the [156]church were his own connection and offspring—to wit, one son-in-law, one daughter-in-law, three daughters, and one granddaughter.

[180,2d]Corn Creek Church is pretty respectable as to members. I think they count [in 1827] smartly upwards of a hundred, and they have a number of respectable male members. But their official men who seem to take much con-cern for the church are very few. Hence, you may go to their monthly meeting on their days of business and not find ten people there.

---

[73]These candidates were Betsy Collier and Cynthia Coulman, accepted on Sunday 3 November 1822. Ibid.

[74]Taylor wrote this sentence before 3 May 1823 and failed to correct it after attending Kendall's ordination on that day. Ibid., [90].

[75]On Sunday 5 May 1822 Taylor baptized Farrow Bowman at Corn Creek. Ibid., [79].

[76]Following the Sunday morning preaching on 3 November 1822, "old Brother" Taylor baptized Polly Connell, Betsy Collier, Charlotte Nicholson, and Wyatt Coulman and wife, Cynthia. Ibid., [85].

But for all their neglects, they have what they call good excuses. A little bad weather will keep them off. Or if they entirely forget the day—this must be a very good excuse, for they could not come if they did not think of it. Or if they have some business on hand, that should it be neglected, they might lose twenty-five cents. And it will not do to come off loser. Or if they have been labouring very hard among the great poplars through the week, they cannot go Saturday nor Sunday, for they must have some time to rest. "The Lord help us." Corn Creek is not the only place where those frivolous excuses are made by Baptists. But with what awful surprise will those kind of virgins be struck when the midnight cry is made.[77]

Another troublesome thing at Corn Creek: Some of their members are self-wise and very contentious, and [they] stir up strife on very trivial occasions.[78] And this is perhaps one reason why many fail to fill their places. The two sons of Eli caused the offering of the Lord to be abhorred,[79] and a contentious man in a church never fails to do the same thing. Says Solomon, "One sinner destroys much good."[80] And just so it is with a contentious man. Those kind of men often glory in what they do, calling it faithfulness in the house of God. But through all these barriers, Corn Creek has [181,2d]kept up their discipline, but oft[t]imes[81] feebly executed.

A Baptist church has been at Corn Creek about twenty-seven or -eight years. Soon after they became a church, they had a handsome revival, and they pretty soon grew up to fifty or sixty members. About seven years ago they had a revival in which more than a hundred were added. A Brother George Kendall, who was baptized among them, is now their preacher. A few years ago he was ordained and now [1827] administers among them.

I was longer a member of Corn Creek Church than any other of the ten with which I have been connected.[82] And my mind is yet annoyed to think how useless my ministry was there. For though first and last, I suppose, I have baptized fifty or sixty people in that place. And the church grew, as I have said, before I left the place with sorrow of heart. For though I got rich at Mount Byrd, there also I sustained losses. There I lost my children and something more dear than

---

[77]Matthew 25:6.

[78]The obsolete noun *occasion* means "matter of discussion" or *subject*.

[79]1 Samuel 2:17.

[80]Ecclesiastes 9:18.

[81]*Oftimes* is the poetic form of the adverb *oftentimes*.

[82]John Taylor held membership in the Corn Creek Church for thirteen years. He could not know that he would serve for seventeen years as a member at the Buck Run Church, the last of his ten congregations.

children.[83] My prayer to the Lord is that Corn Creek may yet prosper as a church, that her wilderness may become an Eden and her waste places like the garden of the Lord.[84]

A small church was constituted from Corn Creek in a place on the river called Hunters Bottom. How they progress I am not fully apprised. They have some prime members and a worthy man among them ordained as their preacher the name of [John] Wallace.

With the most tender affection I would willingly encourage my more active, worthy brethren at Corn Creek not to be weary in well doing, for in due time they shall reap if they faint not.[85] Many will be their temptations to decline their activity, but, says Paul, "Be ye steadfast, unmoveable, always abounding in the work of the Lord, forasmuch as ye know that your labour is not in vain in the Lord" (1 Cor[inthians] 15[th] c[hapter] 58[th] v[erse]). Remember harvest day is coming, when the Lord will gather all things out of his kingdom that offend. The tares shall be bound in bundles and cast into the fire, but the wheat shall be gathered home to Heaven.[86]

Neither would I be willing to despise the absenters or the contentious, which is commonly the worst men in a church, for the Saviour directs not to despise one of these little ones.[87] For I esteem a contentious man in a church the least one there, though the [182,2d]greatest in his own conceit. For, said Christ, "He that would be greatest among you, let him be least in his own opinion and servant of all."[88]

It is worthwhile to remember what Paul says (1 Cor[inthians] ll[th] c[hapter] 16[th] v[erse]): "But if any man seem to be contentious, we have no such custom, neither the churches of God." Paul did not allow a man to seem to be contentious, that even small symptoms of it was wicked. And he allowed of no such custom in any church of God.

Ask such a man if he is the husband of a wife, whom he loves as his own life. And [ask] how it would set on him, in his absence, for a ruffian to come and breed disturbance in his family [and] use his children ill, to the great distress of his beloved wife. Just thus I look on a contentious man in a church. The Saviour

---

[83]By "something more dear than children," Taylor means his usefulness as a minister of the gospel.
    [84]Isaiah 51:3.
    [85]Galatians 6:9.
    [86]Matthew 13:30.
    [87]Matthew 18:10.
    [88]Matthew 20:27.

is absent. O consider the millstone about a man's neck for offending one of the little ones.[89]

---

[89]Matthew 18:6.

# 8
## Big Spring Church

[128]When I had gotten [in 1815] to the Forks of Elkhorn,[1] I was brought to a pause where I should put my membership, for churches were plenty[2] in various directions. The nearest church was where Mr. [William] Hickman had the pastoral care at the Forks of Elkhorn. But, considering this an old church and the pastor an older man than myself, having been always fond of new establishments, and finding that Brother Silas M. Noel (a young minister and a man in the prime of life) had the care of a young church called Big Spring[3] (in Woodford County and about five miles from where I lived), my wife and myself cast our lots at Big Spring under the pastoral care of Brother Noel.

Here we had but a slight acquaintance[4] with the members of the church, and though they were not numerous, after more acquaintance, I became warmly attached to the worthy brethren. Being well-advanced in years, my conclusion was: "Here I shall live and die." I felt happy with my pastor and brethren, though we were (in a manner) new to each other. Our acquaintance was increasing into brotherly love, so that I was as happy as the nature of my own condition would admit.

For some of the stings from Mount Byrd and Corn Creek would haunt me at times, as if all (some way) had not been right as to my proceedings there. For I began to take notice that, from the time of the burning my fine barn with fire from Heaven, my substance in life had been crumbling away. When in my travels, I would call at Mount Byrd. Though my affectionate children lived there, it would present itself to me as the theatre of my past folly.

Zophar's reproach on Job (chapter 20) seemed as if it applied to me more than to Job: "He hath swallowed down riches, and he shall vomit them up again."[5] But above [129]all, it was painful to me to believe what appeared most obvious that my usefulness in the gospel ministry was laid aside, [and] that

---

[1]At the Forks of Elkhorn, on the eastern edge of Frankfort, South Elkhorn and North Elkhorn creeks merge to form Elkhorn Creek.

[2]The colloquial adjective *plenty* means *plentiful*.

[3]The Big Spring Church was organized in October 1812 at present-day Spring Station in Woodford County. A large, stone building was constructed for its meetinghouse. Darnell, *Forks of Elkhorn Church*, 30.

[4]The term "a slight acquaintance," used in the second edition, replaces "spareing [*sic*] acquaintance" of the first edition.

[5]Verse 15.

in that sense I had become a castaway[6] and especially in that part of it always most dear to me—the conversion of my poor, fellow sinners. This has often made me feel that death would be a relief.

Judge [Henry] Davidge—a man of high standing, both as a judge of law[7] and [as an advocate of] moral deportment—had been baptized a few months before I joined the church at Big Spring. Being intimately acquainted with the judge and believing him to be a religious man, I had no scruple in becoming a member with him in the same church, though I knew him to be much tinctured with Arminianism. For the constitution of Big Spring Church was not of that cast. Not long after I became a member there, the judge published a pamphlet[8] in which the Arminian doctrine was strained to its utmost link. This filled me with surprise, for I had thought that the judge was on the change of sentiment, as he had voluntarily joined the Baptists. And I knew they had treated him very respectfully. But it is probably [that] the judge was not fully apprised of the order of the people with whom he had lately connected himself.

The judge's book soon spread far and wide and began much to arrest the attention of the Baptists. And the more so as he was a licensed preacher in the Big Spring Church.

Traveling about, I found many of the Baptists much disgusted with this new book. And [I found] that Big Spring Church was like to be brought under an odium, if she did not in some way act on that affair. This led me to converse with the pastor, [Silas Mercer Noel], on that subject. But whether from the judge's influence being greater with him than my own or from some other source, so it was [that] what I said was treated with neglect. Under this I could not in good conscience lie still, for I could not tell but that the judge and our pastor [130](both of them being great men) intended to try their

---

[6]1 Corinthians 9:27.

[7]As early as 1812 Henry Davidge had served as the circuit judge for the Fourth Judicial District, which included among other counties both Gallatin and Franklin. He was reappointed to this post from time to time—for example, in 1817 and 1820. Gallatin Circuit Court (KY), Order Book [2], 1810–1814, 297; and Office of the Governor of Kentucky, Executive Journal, 1816–1820 (Kentucky State Archives) 14, 33, 132, 219.

[8]In 1816 Henry Davidge published a tract titled *An Address to the Advocates of a Partial Gospel*, which was considered by many Baptists as a defense of Arminianism. Spencer, *Kentucky Baptists*, 2:19. The same year at Frankfort the judge also issued a 147-page book that is Part II of *Reflections, Moral and Theological*. (A copy is located in the library of Transylvania University, Lexington, Kentucky.) It may be that the first-mentioned work is Part I of *Reflections*.

strength in the society for a new organization of things both in doctrine and other ways. For indeed I found some of the Baptists who were pleased with the judge's book, though there were but few of that cast.

About this time a number of Baptists in and about Frankfort[9] were contemplating the setting up a new church in the town. Some individual overtures being made to me on that head, and on some accounts it being more convenient to me than the Big Spring. And especially as no society kept up stated worship in Frankfort at this time, I was prevailed on to unite in a new establishment of this kind in Frankfort.

I found the church at Big Spring somewhat divided as to the contents of the judge's book. And having a desire to know the doctrinal sentiments of my new brethren I had lately become connected with, I thought proper to introduce a question into the church of the follow purport: "Does this church approve or disapprove of the doctrine contained in the above-named pamphlet?" This was at a January [7, 1816], meeting held at a schoolhouse, and but few people there. Having the highest opinion of the judge every other way but in his doctrinal points, having lived a friendly neighbor to him several years before I moved.[10] His wife also I esteemed among the most amiable of her sex, and from charitable hope I also esteemed her a Christian. So that I could not have had ill design against the judge in this query. My design was that he should by the voice of the church receive a gentle admonition, so as not to indulge in the same kind of practice hereafter.

On the day of the introduction of this query into the church, before our business closed I applied for a letter of dismission, expecting to become a member of the new constitution at Frankfort before the next meeting. The pastor of the church at Big Spring did not arrive till just before the reading of the business [131]of the day. And on reading the item of the query (which had been laid over till next meeting), he seemed to manifest considerable displeasure, expressing to this amount: That queries in a church were generally mischievious things, and that the present one would never be answered in the church. In all of which I felt unmoved, believing that I had done my duty. For I felt entirely easy, making some allowance for my pastor's age.

---

[9]The establishment of the town of Frankfort was provided for by a 1786 Virginia law. It was located in the part of Fayette County that in time became Franklin County. Hening, *Statutes*, 12:390-92, 597.

[10]Henry Davidge was the judge who presided in 1812 at the Gallatin Circuit Court when John Taylor was acquited of the charge of obstructing a public road.

Various methods were used to prevent the answer of this query in the church. Other men of influence combined with the pastor to effect this mighty important work, which was done at length by a committee of picked men to the amount of from ten to fifteen sent for from other churches. Their decision was that the query was brought into the church contrary to good order [and] that if I had a complaint against my brother I should have used the eighteenth [chapter] of Matthew. These committeemen also advised that it was contrary to good order to answer the query at all. Thus the business seemed settled smooth and easy.[11]

As to myself, I was at none of those council-holding meetings. My presence was not very acceptable in those days. Their last council day I heard of by chance. Previous to [receiving] the information, I had about ten days' preaching appointed from home that I did not think proper to disappoint on account of this choice meeting.

The judge went home from this celebrated meeting in high spirits but, being a man of great generosity and sympathy, expressed much pity for the blunder I had made in this breach of good order.

But the Baptist society became so much concerned for his breach of good doctrine in his book that at the next session of Elkhorn Association, they took up this business very nearly in the same style that I had introduced it into Big Spring Church and with almost a unanimous vote condemned the doctrine in the book.[12]

William Kellar,[13] being at Elkhorn Association, [132]purchased one of the judge's books. He went home and first investigated it in the church where he lived, who sent a request to Long Run Association, where the book met with

---

[11]The adverb *easy* is here a colloquialism meaning *easily*.

[12]The Elkhorn Association adopted a resolution regarding Davidge's book. Presented by Silas Mercer Noel, it obliquely condemned John Taylor's method of trying to secure the censure of the publication by the Big Spring Church. Noel wrote that that congregation should "treat with the author in a gospel way" if it were grieved by the pamphlet. According to Matthew 18:15, this means that Taylor should have first talked privately with the judge about the matter. On the other hand, the resolution discountenanced "the doctrines and sentiments therein contained." Spencer, *Kentucky Baptists*, 2:19.

[13]William Kellar (1768–1817), a native of Shenandoah (then Frederick) County, Virginia, was first aroused under the preaching of James Ireland. Kellar migrated to Kentucky and settled on Harrods Creek, where he lived the rest of his life. Ordained as a preacher, he spent the greater part of his ministry serving four churches aligned with the Long Run Association. During the War of 1812 he commanded a unit of mounted riflemen. Ibid., 1:349-51; and John Taylor, *Thoughts on Missions*, 55-64.

a second association[al] condemnation with a united voice, except [for] one man who voted in favor of the book [and] who had been very strongly suspected as an Arian.

General [Joseph] Lewis,[14] of Bardstown, being at Long Run Association, had the same book investigated in Salem Association,[15] where it met with the same fate as at [the] other places.

So that we see [that] three of the most respectable associations at that time in the state decided against the judge's book. And all [these actions were] in consequence of the excessive friendship of his friends who thought at first they were doing a great favor for him. I much question whether one of them thought more highly of the judge than myself, and it is probable [that] had the plan I first had in view been followed, the judge would now have felt himself happy in the Baptist society. It seems [that] the judge by these several association decisions felt himself illy[16] treated, obtained a letter of dismission from Big Spring Church, and has never joined any religious society since. Neither does he now preach any more.

Mr. Noel, sometime after this, relinquished the pastoral charge at Big Spring, though he preached [for] some time for them after this. He at length took a letter of dismission and joined the church at Frankfort. After which being appointed a circuit judge for a season,[17] he desisted from preaching altogether and resumed the practice of the law, to which he had been raised. He forbore the sacred office of gospel minister about two years, being very unhappy in mind in this elapsed state. About one year past he came forward

---

[14]Joseph Lewis was commissioned the major general of the 4th Militia Division on 11 July 1805. A preacher who visited him at Bardstown in January 1810 described him as "a man of great simplicity and apparent sincerity." David Benedict, Journal (Franklin Trask Library, Andover Newton Theological School, Newton MA), 14 Jan 1810. See also Clift, "Corn Stalk" Militia, 156.

[15]On 29 October 1785 the Salem Association was organized by messengers from four churches who met on Coxs Creek in Nelson County. The second Baptist association in Kentucky, it was formed twenty-eight days after the Elkhorn Association had been brought into being. Spencer, Kentucky Baptists, 1:109-10, and 2:44-46.

[16]The adverb illy is a dialeticism meaning ill or badly.

[17]Silas Mercer Noel had become an assistant judge of the Franklin Circuit Court in July 1813. This appointment was renewed in December of the following year. In August 1818 Noel succeeded Henry Davidge as the circuit judge of the Fourth Judicial District, which included Franklin County. By January 1819 Noel had resigned from this post and was promptly replaced. Office of the Governor of Kentucky, Executive Journal, 1812–1816 (Kentucky State Archives), 82, 109 and Executive Journal, 1816–1820, 133, 150, 167.

again as a preacher with more zeal, consistency, and apparent stability than at any time of his life before. And [he] is now one of our first-rate Baptist preachers in Kentucky and has lately taken [133]the pastoral care of the Baptist church in Frankfort.

After Mr. Noel, Mr. [Jacob] Creath, [Sr.], served the church at Big Spring one year. For about two years past they have very acceptably been served by the well-known Mr. John Edwards. This church has only had a gradual growth from the beginning. They do not now perhaps exceed fifty in number, but they are a well-disposed, loving body of brethren.

[186,2d]Big Spring Church is in Woodford County and perhaps of fifteen years' standing. The first preacher I knew of in this church was Silas M. Noel. There, I think, he was ordained as their pastor when only a young preacher.[18] In that capacity he served the church for several years. He was in that station when my wife and [187,2d]self[19] became members there, in 1815. There we continued only about ten months and took leave to unite in a young church in Frankfort.

The church at Big Spring for several years past has been served by the respectable, well-known John Edwards. But very lately he took leave of several respectable churches that was under his care and moved to Missouri.[20] This church now [1827] have two young preachers, but men somewhat advanced in years. One is George Blackburn,[21] a pretty good preacher. His delivery is not quite so ready as some men, but his ideas are very good. The other is a Brother [Thomas] Suiter,[22] a man of great devotion of mind and [a man of] zeal in his Master's cause. [He is] a pretty good preacher, but some of his hearers say [that] he would be better if he would leave off when he was done. [They say] that after he has gone through his subject, [in order] that the people may not forget or [may] better understand it, he will go over it again. If this is an error in preaching, Suiter is not alone. But who knows that this is not the best way of preaching, for the prophet [Isaiah] said that

[18]Silas Mercer Noel was ordained as the pastor of the Big Spring Church in 1813. Sprague, *American Pulpit*, 5:628.

[19]Here the pronoun *self* is a colloquialism that means *myself*.

[20]In 1833 John Edwards was numbered among the ordained ministers in the Fishing River Association of Missouri. "Sketches of Baptists in Missouri," *Christian Repository* 6:417.

[21]George Blackburn (d.1837), a constituent member of the Big Spring Church, was ordained to the ministry in 1825. Spencer, *Kentucky Baptists*, 2:31-32.

[22]Thomas Suiter was ordained a minister about 1834. Ibid., 2:38.

line should be upon line and precept upon precept, here a little and there a little?[23]

The church at the Big Spring has not had a rapid growth, but they have progressed on with uncommon peace among themselves. Their number at present does not much exceed fifty. It is hoped that, though their shepherd is gone, they have a greater Shepherd that will not forsake them, and [that] according to His own heart [He will] raise up undershepherds that will feed them with knowledge and understanding. "O Saviour, take care of Thy own flock."[24]

Silas M. Noel, their first pastor, is now a great traveler and one of the most successful preachers the Baptists have in Kentucky. This man's sun went below the horizon for a season. For after he had been ordained several years, he laid aside his gospel ministry for a year or two for the honors of this world. And while in that interval he seemed as a kinsman of Demas.[25] His mind was so wracked by the chastening of the Lord [that] he sprang again above ground as [did] Jonah from the bowels of the whale.[26] And his sun rose again in brighter lustre[27] than ever it shone before. For about three years past, I suppose [that] he has baptized more people than any other man in Kentucky. His labours seem blest in whatever direction he [188,2d]takes.

The conversion of sinners to the Lord seems to be the greatest object of his address to men. Repentance and faith, or faith and repentance, connected with a godly life, is the main drift of his discourses—with profuse invitations to every one to come to the supper. Speculative trifles are barely found in his exhibitions. "God, bless the heavenly man. May he thus press on to the end."

Mr. Noel's literary accomplishments—together with his zeal in the gospel [and] with his great success therein—has procured him the high appellation of double [D] (D.D.). The high powers at Lexington [that are] authorized to make doctors of divinity a year or two back has saluted him with a flowing diploma.[28] But it is pleasant to see that these high-flying trifles does not

---

[23]Isaiah 28:10, 13.

[24]The Big Spring Church ceased to exist as a worshiping congregation in 1846. Seven years later it disposed of its property. As recently as 1946 the stone meetinghouse was being used as a farm building. Darnell, *Forks of Elkhorn Church*, 30-31.

[25]2 Timothy 4:10.

[26]Jonah 2:10.

[27]*Lustre* is the British spelling of the noun *luster*.

[28]In 1822 Transylvania University awarded Noel the honorary degree of Doctor of Divinity. Sprague, *American Pulpit*, 6:629. For a history of the institution, see John D. Wright, Jr., *Transylvania: Tutor to the West* (Lexington KY, 1975).

prevent his yet going into the thickets—or, according to his own term (while at his work), the highways and hedges—to invite the poor, the halt, the blind, and [the] lame, with every other soul to seek the salvation of God.[29]

Who is so far destitute of the wedding garment[30] and his poor, little soul so crampt[31] up by little creeds that he cannot reach out his hand of love and say, "Brother Noel, go on and prosper"? Mr. Noel has visited some towns with great effect. It is very lately reported that he is soon to move to Louisville to take care of the Baptist church in that town. "May the Lord prosper him through life."

---

[29]Luke 14:21, 23.
[30]Matthew 22:11-12.
[31]*Crampt* is the phonetic spelling for the word *cramped*.

# 9
## Frankfort Church

[133]The same month (7 January 1816) that I took a letter from Big Spring, after being a member there ten months, we met in Frankfort to go into a new church establishment.[1] Several ministering brethren were with us, and Silas M. Noel [was] the acting moderator. Perhaps the number who were constituted into a church were seventeen, male and female. And it is probable that no Baptist church ever came into existence exactly in the same style. We met in the Assembly Hall[2] and there became a church of the humble Lord Jesus with all the rich paintings around us. At that time the town of Frankfort as to stated public worship was an entire blank. This [circumstance] was some inducement with us to become a church there. A Presbyterian minister came into the hall while we were at the business of constituting. And though [he was] invited to take a seat with us, he declined using that privilege but sat and looked on.

Passing through Frankfort a very few days after this, I was informed that six or seven hundred dollars had been subscribed in these few days for a Mr. [Eli] Smith,[3] who had [134]some time before preached in Frankfort but was now at the distance of several hundred miles. It was said also that almost every man in Frankfort had been invited to put his hand to paper. It was thought by some that on account of our constitution the Presbyterians were thus led to bestir themselves. Be that as it may, so it was Mr. Smith did come and has set up a congregation in and about Frankfort, and where he continues to this day. Between these two congregations there has not always been that harmony that could have been wished for.

---

[1]To prepare for the founding of the Frankfort Church, two meetings were held during January 1816 at the home of Simon Beckham, in the state capital. The new congregation was organized on the twenty-fifth of the following month with thirteen constituent members. Masters, *Baptists in Kentucky*, 113-14.

[2]This hall was one of the two rooms in which the houses of the General Assembly convened. They were located on the first floor of the temporary state house that was constructed in 1814. Collins, *Kentucky*, rev. ed., 2:246.

[3]Eli Smith moved to the capital in 1816 and became the first pastor of the Frankfort Presbyterian Church, which had been constituted the previous year. Remaining in that office for about ten years, he promoted in 1823–1824 the construction of a brick meetinghouse on Wapping Street. Carl E. Kramer, *Capital on the Kentucky: A Two-Hundred-Year History of Frankfort and Franklin County* (Frankfort KY, 1986) 87, 108-109.

The Baptist church in Frankfort progressed but slowly. Indeed among some of her own members, there was not that harmony that makes religious society desirable. During my stay there in a church way, I had never been so poorly shipped[4] in my life. When I would set out from home (even at a monthly meeting), it was often unknown where it would be held till we got to Frankfort. Sometimes [we met] in the Assembly Hall, Senate Chamber, or courthouse. And sometimes neither of the places could be gotten. Then we had to seek a byecorner[5] somewhere else.

My preaching also seemed of but very little benefit among them. Then thought I, "Woe is me that I ever came to Frankfort."

The church at length invited Mr. [Henry] Toler to preach for them, which he did. And though [he did so] with much acceptance for one year, there was yet but little increase in the church. After Mr. Toler, Mr. [Jacob] Creath, [Sr.], served the church in Frankfort stately for two or three years. Under his ministrations the church began to move. And there were additions both by baptisms and [by] other ways, so that their number grew up to perhaps upwards of fifty. Since Mr. Creath has declined preaching there, the church has chosen as their pastor Mr. Silas M. Noel. They now bid fair to be more interestingly served for the future. There are also two other men of sprightly preaching talents who are members of the church at Frankfort: a Mr. Philip [Slater] Fall[6] and Mr. Porter Clay.[7]

[4]The verb *ship* is an old usage here and means *shift* or "move from one place to another."

[5]The noun *byecorner* is an obsoletism meaning "secondary place."

[6]Philip Slater Fall (1798–1890) served as the pastor of the First Church of Louisville during 1822–1825. When the Campbellite dispute reached its height, he aligned himself with the Reformers. Spencer, *Kentucky Baptists*, 2:182.

[7]Porter Clay (1779–1850), a native of Virginia, was a son of Elder John Clay (1742–1781) of Hanover County and a brother of the statesman Henry Clay. After migrating to Kentucky, Porter began to practice law at Versailles. About 1820 he was ordained a minister. He later served churches in Illinois and Arkansas. Ibid., 2:298-300; and Mary Rogers Clay, "The Genealogy of the Clays," in *The Clay Family* (Louisville KY, 1899) 90.

The Baptists [135]also have now in Frankfort (either by compromise or law) a partial use of a house[8] called "the church," which is alternately used by them and the Presbyterians. The Methodists have also gotten foothold in Frankfort.

When I united in the constitution at Frankfort, I did not conclude that my continuance there would be very long. One reasons was [that] I did not consider myself calculated[9] for a town preacher. My restlessness became so increasing as to my church state that I contemplated an escape when the church was well provided for under the ministrations of Mr. Toler.

A number of brethren—near neighbors of mine within the Forks of Elkhorn —had for several years contemplated a church there for their own convenience. After some individuals' naming this thing to me, it met with my full approbation. And after holding a council on that subject, we made arrangements to go into a constitution.

I, therefore, applied to the church at Frankfort for dismission. I became much afflicted when I discovered great backwardness in my brethren to give me up to leave them. This I had not looked for, thinking my service so very small among them, but I had gone into agreement with my brethren in the Forks. And, like Jephthah,[10] having opened my mouth, I could not go back. I then thought of visiting the brethren at Frankfort, more than I have had it in my power since. They not being able to deny what was my right, I took leave of the church in Frankfort, having been a member there two years.

I was never fond of an old, musty, worm-eaten letter of dismission. When such letters come to market[11] where I am, it is no great recommendation to the bearer of them. For whether through overcarefulness or carelessness, it is about the same with me. Some foolishly fancy [that] if they have a letter of dismission they are now free and belong to no church. This is overcarefulness of Number One—I mean, their poor, little selves. Some are so careful of their [136]letters that they will not take them to market for fear [that] they will not get into as good a church as they came from and [for fear] that they may be imposed on by a

---

[8]The "House of Public Worship" stood in Frankfort on the southwestern corner of the Old Capitol Square on Broadway. Its construction was completed in 1818 with funds from a lottery authorized by the legislature. Soon thereafter the Frankfort Baptist Church began to use this building on the fourth Saturday of each month. Until it burned on 12 December 1825, it had been occupied at various times by Presbyterians, Baptists, and Methodists. Masters, *Baptists in Kentucky*, 114; Darnell, *Forks of Elkhorn Church*, 31; and Collins, *Kentucky* rev. ed., 2:247.

[9]In this past participle of *calculate* the idea of *design* has disappeared and only the sense of *suit* remains.

[10]Judges 11:30-35.

[11]The idiom "come to market" here means "be presented to a congregation as a means to verify one's church status."

ministry a little inferior to the good-old, orthodox preacher they left behind. They must have a very nice[12] cooked dish, or they cannot eat at all. And they had rather the worms should eat their letter than to run these risks. Poor, nice, careful things! They ought to remember that jealousy, as other things, begets its own likeness and is the destruction of confidence between man and man. Besides, there is a little Pharisaism in this thing. Or why should a man think another not as good as himself?

A man is always interested in the friendship and confidence of the people among whom he lives. And if a man is so superior that others can do him no good, why should he be so churlish as not to be willing to do others good? And [he should] not wrap up his little, musty letter, as the man did his talent.[13] And [why should he] not put it to usury[14] in that heavenly commerce that the Lord has directed between one Christian and another? Besides, a man keeping up a letter of dismission, his name is known nowhere, for the church who dismisses him has taken his name from their book—except by accident he is brought back by complaint [for] having joined no other church. Such a man as this, as to society or church membership, is what Paul speaks of the man without charity. He is nothing.[15] He much resembles a mere cypher, a little o. Putting a hundred of them together would not make 1 [one] without another figure.

Among these overcareful ones who keep up letters, there are careless ones who have letters if they have not lost them [and] who are too much of libertines to use them, except something is to be made by them.[16] Sometimes a revival of religion will bring forth their letters. And, like the ancient cowards in Israel, [they will] fight hard when the enemy is running.[17] As my usual custom has always been (when I had a letter of dismission) to embrace the first opening, I took mine from Frankfort to Buck Run in one week after I had gotten it.

[191,2d]I have before stated the high style in which the church in Frankfort came into existence. And she has almost from her beginning been attended by the best preaching talents we have; yet she from the whole has progressed but slowly. Somehow it seems [that] the Lord does not take delight in high things. None shall be high but His Almighty Self, Who is the high and lofty One inhabiting [192,2d]eternity. Yet [He] much regards the lowly in mind; while on the

---

[12]Here the colloquial adverb *nice* means *well* or *excellently*.
[13]Luke 19:20.
[14]Luke 19:23.
[15]1 Corinthians 13:2.
[16]The final clause in this sentence does not appear in the second edition.
[17]1 Samuel 7:7, 10-11.

proud in spirit He justly frowns. Solomon says that pride goes before [destruction],[18] and a haughty spirit before a fall.[19]

A farce of the most outlandish kind that I ever knew played in a Baptist church was acted a few years ago in Frankfort.[20] The subject was the installing a pastor and the ordination of a young minister. To perform this great solemnity, ministers were sent for twenty or thirty miles distant and in various directions to the amount of five or six most ripe and orthodox men. I was not there myself for common men were not invited, but I had the honor afterwards to see at least part of their records.

From what I could learn, the examination was very close. All the questions and answers [were] recorded, but they were all on deep subjects in divinity. But few questions [were asked] on practical godliness, for this would come of course if men were right in doctrine.

I recollect only one of the solemn questions that was asked of the candidate for ordination, which was: "Do you recollect, brother, that you ever knew a sheep turned into a goat or a goat into a sheep?"

After a long and solemn pause, the candidate replied, "I do not recollect that I ever knew such a circumstance."

What could common spectators think of such dark, mysterial[21] questions and answers? But the design of this question was whether the elect before conversion were not the sheep of Christ, and whether these sheep of Christ by election ever could become goats and finally be lost at last.

After a very pompous perade [*sic*], they installed the pastor and ordained the minister. The pastor was Silas M. Noel; the minister ordained was Porter Clay—both of them now members at Frankfort. What church, as to the ministry, could expect more than [what] Frankfort now has in their possession? About one year after this, Noel gives up the pastoral care and goes to better business —preaching the gospel far and wide with marvelous effect, as stated above. Porter Clay, by the call of the church, takes on him[22] the solemn charge of pastor of the church at Frankfort, which has continued for several years and with good acceptance, so far as I know anything to the contrary, till about one year ago.

A heavy dispute arose between the pastor [Porter Clay] and one of the most leading members [193,2d]of the church [Jephtha Dudley]—both of them filling high offices in the state: one of them a senator, a lawmaker; the other [the] auditor of

---

[18]Here Taylor inadvertently uses the word *distinction*.

[19]Proverbs 16:18.

[20]This event took place in 1824. Masters, *Baptists in Kentucky*, 114.

[21]Here the rare adjective *mysterial* means *mystic* or *mysterious*.

[22]The obsolete (or rare), reflexive pronoun *him* is here the object of the preposition *on*.

all the revenue of the state.[23] The first rupture, it seems, between these men was about politics, that has run so very high in Kentucky. Other things soon sprang up which widened the breach between them. The pastor thinking it his duty to treat with his brother according to the law of Christ.[24] Either from lack of skill in the pastor or [from] the violence of his brother, in their interview together they nearly came to blows. Not all the labour of their friends could bring them together. Noel, with all his pacific measure, could not bring them together. Being a member at Frankfort, he [Noel] strove hard with all the help he could get, but all in vain.

At length their distresses must come into the church. It seems the plan fallen on was [for] each one to prepare his written charges against the other and [to] present them at the next meeting. The pastor had three or four against his brother; the other had thirty-one exceptions or charges against his pastor, who must have had his approbation in his first ordination and also his voice to put him in the pastoral office in the church. At this dreadful business, the poor, distressed church laboured for many days and nights, and twenty-three charges yet behind. They send abroad for helps; and so far as I yet know, things are no better.

I only witnessed about ten hours of this violent trial. It overgoes all the calculations I can make to reconcile it to the religion that comes from the Saviour. How a disciple of Christ can make a book of several sheets and deliberately for several weeks be setting down charges against a brother (his pastor), and the chief of them so frivolous that wicked ingenuity must be put to the wrack[25] to make them out [as] charges! And then with such angry violence, [how can he] contend for them for days together? I confess [that] if this is the religion of Christ, I know nothing about it. I wonder, while a man is making out so long a list of charges, that it does not occur to him what sort of a being the Devil is. [He is] an accuser of the brethren.[26]

After the thirty-one charges were gone through, an unwritten one seemed more destructive than all the rest (as to the pastor's interest in life), for it was a charge of insanity. The other charges were calculated to destroy his peace and comfort as a Christian and his usefulness as a preacher; [194,2d]but this last, to

---

[23]Jephtha Dudley, a state senator, objected to the selection of Porter Clay as the Kentucky auditor and attempted to have him removed from this post. When he could not unseat Clay, the dispute spilled over into the Frankfort Church. Spencer, *Kentucky Baptists*, 2:299.

[24]Matthew 18:15-17.

[25]Here the noun *wrack* is an archaism (or present-day Scotticism) meaning *ruin* or *calamity*.

[26]Revelation 12:10.

destroy his office[27] from which all the supplies of his family came. This last charge made many of the spectators impatient and sorrowful; but when they heard the replications of the pastor to all those charges, which put to the blush this last charge of insanity, their spirits seemed revived again. However justified the pastor might have been in clearing himself from the last charge as a man, he did himself no credit as a Christian in his tart replies. These men are now at the church's bar as strangers. For nine months they sinned against each other by wholesales [sic]; they now repent by halves. They sinned fast; they repent but slowly.

God's way is in the sea, His path in the great waters, and His footsteps are not known (Psalm 77, 19[th verse]). A few months past the church in Frankfort seemed on the brink of dissolution by contention between two of her leading members. The church had suspended them both from church privilege. One of them being the pastor, of course his preaching was stopped, and the church left destitute of preaching. Mr. S. M. Noel being a member among them, they invited him to preach for them statedly, which he has done with very good effect.

The man [Jephtha Dudley] who had thirty-one written charges against his pastor made some partial confessions and was restored to privilege in the church. And now [he] seems zealous in a happy revival of religion lately sprung in the church. A number of respectable people have very recently been baptized, and a prospect of many more; but this depends on the will of God alone.

The old pastor [Porter Clay] attends meetings closely and seems delighted at what he considers the work of God among the people. But [he] is so deeply stung with what he thinks were false charges against himself, he has not as yet taken his place in the church.[28]

---

[27]I.e., his office as state auditor.

[28]Porter Clay served as the auditor of Kentucky from 1820 to 1836. "List of Auditors of the State of Kentucky," *Register of the Kentucky Historical Society* 3 (Jan 1905): 37.

About the time the Saviour was put to death, it seemed as if His religion was extinguished in the world. It is probable that for about fifty days not a preacher He had made or called opened his mouth in that way. One of His leading disciples [Judas] had sold Him for thirty pieces of silver.[29] And another [Peter] denied that he knew Him.[30] And the balance of the flock was scattered when the Shepherd was smitten.[31] But O what marvelous works when He turned His hand again on the little ones at the day of Pentecost! [195,2d]So it somewhat seems at this time in Frankfort. "May the Lord turn our wilderness into Eden and make our waste places as the garden of the Lord."[32]

---

[29]Matthew 26:14-16.
[30]Matthew 26:70.
[31]Matthew 26:31.
[32]Isaiah 51:3. The Frankfort Church, known today as the First Baptist Church, is a prospering congregation in the capital of Kentucky.

# 10
## Buck Run Church

[137]The constitution of Buck Run Church. As there has been a good deal of likeness in the faith and practice of the ten churches of which I have alternately been a member for fifty years past, I think proper to give the constitution and rules of decorum of Buck Run Church at length.

Church covenant, unanimously agreed to by the church. As, we hope, a number of us have long since given ourselves to the Lord, we do this day in the Divine Presence give ourselves in a church compact to one another and do solemnly covenant and agree to fulfill the duty of brethren to each other [and] not to expose each other's faults but in the true letter and spirit of the gospel. That we will not forsake the assembling ourselves together[1] but fill our seats, both in meetings of business and public worship, except providentially hindered. That we will watch over each other in brotherly tenderness, each endeavoring to edify his brother [and] striving for the benefit of the weak of the flock; to raise up the hands that hang down and [to] strengthen the feeble knees, making strait[2] paths for our feet, least[3] that which is lame be turned out of the way.[4]

That we will bear each other's burdens, and so fulfill the law of Christ.[5] And as the Lord has prospered us,[6] [we will] bear a proportionable part of the expense to keep up the worship of God in decency.

And in token of our above agreement, [we] give each other our hands and hearts. And as it is needful to have some epithet to distinguish our church from another, our appellation and the future style of our records shall be "The Baptist Church of Christ on Buck Run." And our monthly meetings to be held the last Saturday [138]in each month, with the Lord's day following—31 January 1818.

Met at Brother [Isaac] Wilson's,[7] day and date above, according to

---

[1]Hebrews 10:25.

[2]The word *strait* means *narrow*. Taylor intends to use the adjective *straight*.

[3]Here the author means to use the word *lest*.

[4]Hebrews 12:12-13.

[5]Galatians 6:2.

[6]1 Corinthians 16:2.

[7]In 1800 John Taylor sold a tract of land to Isaac Wilson, Sr. (1775–1863). It was located in the Woodlake neighborhood of Franklin County near where the Buck Run meetinghouse would later be erected, on the Georgetown Pike. Darnell, *Forks of Elkhorn*

appointment, for the purpose of constituting a Baptist church. Elder William Hickman [was the] moderator; Elder Silas M. Noel, clerk. With the above ministers [and the following ones also]: James Suggett, John H. Ficklin,[8] Mordecai Boulware,[9] Theodoric Boulware. All those ministers agreed to give agency in the constituting of the above-named church.

Names of the members in the constitution: John Taylor, Elizabeth Taylor, Benjamin Taylor, Presley Neale,[10] Fanny Neale,[11] Julius Blackburn,[12] Elizabeth Blackburn,[13] Frances Castleman,[14] Isaac Wilson, Lucy Wilson,[15] Lucy Nall,[16] John Graves,[17] Catherine Graves,[18] Elizabeth Gatewood,[19] John Price,[20]

---

*Church,* 304.

[8] John Herndon Ficklin (1771–1826), a native of Spotsylvania County, Virginia, migrated to Kentucky and settled in Scott County. He was ordained a preacher by the North Fork Church in 1807. A mechanic by trade, Ficklin aligned himself with the emancipating movement but retained his membership in North Fork. Tarrant, *Kentucky Friends to Humanity*, 15; and Spencer, *Kentucky Baptists*, 2:28.

[9] Mordecai Boulware was then the pastor of the North Fork Church. Spencer, *Kentucky Baptists*, 2:30.

[10] Presley Neale was a son of Daniel Neale (1735–1804) and Jemima Kitchen, of Fairfax County, Virginia. Darnell, *Forks of Elkhorn Church*, 216.

[11] Frances Neale (d. 1826), the first wife of Presley Neale, was the mother of at least two children. Ibid.

[12] Julius Blackburn (d. 1821) was enrolled as a taxpayer in Scott County as early as 1800 and lived near the Woodford County line. Clift, *"Second Census" of Kentucky, 1800*, 24; and Darnell, *Forks of Elkhorn Church*, 74.

[13] Elizabeth Scruggs married Julius Blackburn and bore him at least seven children. Darnell, *Forks of Elkhorn Church*, 74.

[14] Frances Gatewood married John Castleman. She was a daughter of Augustine Gatewood (d. 1802), who lived in Jessamine County. Ibid., 32, 99, 100.

[15] Lucy Morton, a daughter of Jeremiah Morton, married Isaac Wilson, Sr., in Woodford County in 1801. Ibid., 304.

[16] Lucy Finnell married Martin Nall III and mothered ten children. Ibid., 213.

[17] John Graves (1776–1848), a native of Maryland, settled at Woodlake in Franklin County around 1805. He was married four times. Ibid., 154.

[18] Catherine Graves (d. 1826), a daughter of Richard Thomasson, was the second wife of John Graves, to whom she bore at least nine children. Ibid.

[19] This Elizabeth Gatewood may have been a daughter of Augustine Gatewood. Ibid., 100.

[20] John Price, Jr., was perhaps a son of Elder John Price. Ibid., 230.

Susannah Price,[21] Lewis Nall,[22] Jane Nall,[23] Love B. Fuller,[24] Sarah Head,[25] Nancy Triplett.[26] In all, twenty-one agreed to go into a constitution.

The following articles [of faith], after examination, were unanimously adopted:

1st. There is but one true and living God, the Maker and Preserver of all created things, visible and invisible; and that in this adorable Godhead there are three personal relations, as Father, Son, and Holy Ghost; and these three are one—equal in glory, dignity, eternity, and power. Though, as to the true humanity of Jesus Christ, He is often spoken of in the New Testament as inferior to the Father.

2d. That the Scriptures of the Old and New Testament[s] as stated in their canonical books, is the uniform doctrine of faith; and that this sacred volume is the only infallible rule of all our faith and practice.

3d. That by the disobedience of the first Adam, [139]all his posterity became guilty and sinful in every part and helpless as to any aid they can give in the great work of converting their own souls.

4th. That according to God's foreknowledge, previous to time He did predestinate His people to life, and being chosen in Christ before the world began; He [Christ] did, as our second Adam (the Lord from Heaven), assume human nature, yet without sin; and by His obedience in His incarnation, making an atoning sacrifice for sin, [He] brought in an everlasting righteousness for the rebellious; and when said blessed merit is imputed or applied to them through faith in His blood, they are thereby justified before God, and, being effectually called by His grace and Holy Spirit, [they] shall finally persevere therein to happiness and eternal glory.

5th. Since the day of the Apostles, there is no higher ecclesiastical authority on earth than the congregated, worshiping church of Christ, being

---

[21]Susannah Gano Price was a daughter of Elder John Gano and the second wife of John Price, Jr. Ibid., 230-31.

[22]Lewis Nall was a son of Martin Nall, Jr. Lewis was living in Scott County, Kentucky, as early as 1800. Ibid., 213; and Clift, *"Second Census" of Kentucky, 1800*, 214.

[23]Jane Nall and Lewis Nall, who were first cousins, were married in Woodford County on 22 December 1791. They became the parents of eight children. Darnell, *Forks of Elkhorn Church*, 213; and Railey, *Woodford County*, 325.

[24]Love B. Fuller was granted a letter of dismissal in 1818 by the Forks of Elkhorn Church in order to join Buck Run. Darnell, *Forks of Elkhorn Church*, 32, 139.

[25]In 1801 Sarah Head became a member of the Forks of Elkhorn Church. Ibid., 32, 167.

[26]Nancy Triplett (1764–1836) was dismissed in 1818 from the Forks of Elkhorn Church in order to become a charter member of the Buck Run Church. Ibid., 32.

God's heritage here below. Their right is to govern themselves by their own voices [and] select their own officers, as bishops and deacons—the only officers now known in the church of Christ. These are their servants for Christ's sake. So that no conclave of bishops or any council appointed by themselves or even their own officers have a right to lord it over the church.[27]

6th. As it is appointed for men once to die, there shall also be a resurrection both of the just and unjust; on which awful day Jesus Christ will judge all men in righteousness, when the wicked shall go into everlasting punishment and the righteous into life eternal.

7th. We consider baptism valid only by profession of faith and [by] immersing the whole body under water.

8th. We do most seriously consider the preaching of repentance and the invitations of the gospel to all characters of men to be one of the most interesting [140]subjects of the gospel ministry; and that they who persecute, neglect, or disobey the gospel more highly aggravate their own guilt.

To manifest our good will and charitableness towards our brethren who may somewhat differ from us in some of the above doctrines, we do most cheerfully accord in the terms of the General Union of Baptists in Kentucky, which are as follows:

1st. That the Scriptures of the Old and New Testament[s] are the infallible words[28] of God, and the only rule of faith and practlce.

2d. That there is but[29] one only true God, and in the Godhead or Divine Essence there are Father, Son, and Holy Ghost.

3d. That by nature we are depraved, fallen[30] creatures.

4th. That salvation, regeneration, sanctification, and justification are by the life, death, resurrection, and ascension of Jesus Christ.

5th. That the saints will finally persevere through grace to glory.

6th. That believer's baptism by immersion is necessary to receiving of the Lord's Supper.

7th. That the salvation of the righteous and[31] the punishment of the wicked will be eternal.

---

[27]1 Peter 5:3.

[28]This word was singular in the original agreement. North District Association, Minutes, 2 Oct 1802, in Doyle, "South Kentucky Association," 26.

[29]The word *but* does not appear at this place in the original agreement. Ibid.

[30]The words "depraved, fallen" appear in the original as "fallen and depraved." Ibid., 27.

[31]The word *the* does not appear at this place in the original agreement. Ibid.

8th. That it is our duty to be tender and affectionate to each other; and [to] study the happiness of the children of God in general; and to be engaged singly to promote the honor of God.

9th. And that [the][32] preaching "Christ tasted death for every man" shall be no bar to communion.[33]

Whereupon, Buck Run Church was pronounced constituted. Rules of decorum for said church:

1st. The business of the church [is] to be done the last Saturday of every month, beginning at twelve o'clock. Any free male member failing to attend shall be accountable to the church for such neglect.

[141]2d. A moderator [is] to be chosen by a majority of voices. And until another is chosen, he is to preside in the church while at business. He is to keep order but always under the control of a majority of the church. He is to withhold his own opinion until all other members who wish to speak have spoken, except by the request of the church. He shall take the voice of the church when called on for that purpose.

3d. When the church is met, after prayer, members of sister churches [are] to be invited to seats, who may give their light on any subject but not vote in the decision of the case. The moderator [is] to then enquire, "Are all in fellowship?" or "Has any a matter of complaint to bring forward that has been treated in gospel order?"

4th. The unfinished business of the church, if any, [is] to be now attended to, after which a door may be opened for the reception of members.

5th. Any brother having a motion or speech to make in the church shall rise from his seat and address the moderator with brotherly respect. A motion thus made [is] not to be attended to without a second.

6th. No brother [is] to be interrupted while speaking, except he depart from the subject, on which the moderator or any other brother may call to

---

[32]The word *the* appears at this point in the original agreement. Ibid.

[33]The Buck Run Church omitted the last three terms of the General Union, which are associational in nature and which appear below:

10th. And that each may keep up their association and church as to them may seem best.

11th. That a free correspondence and communion be kept up the churches thus united.

12th. And that a convention of the churches be called at Howards Creek Meetinghouse the second Saturday in October next [1801]. That the churches send two members to said convention to carry said Union fully into effect, August 22d 1801. Unanimously agreed to by the Joint Committee. Ibid.

order. Of which point of order the church may judge when applied to for that purpose.

7th. No brother shall speak more than twice on any subject without leave from the church.

8th. There shall be no laughing, talking, or whispering in the time of a public speech, nor shall there be any ungenerous reflections on a brother who has spoken before.

9th. Any business in which particular fellowship is not affected may be done by a majority of voices.

10th. Any member being accused and found guilty of a crime and unanimity cannot be had for exclusion, a majority may suspend [him] from privilege till satisfaction can be given.

[142]11th. In the great affair of receiving into membership or of final exclusion, unanimity is required.

12th. That brotherly love may continue, the direction given by the Saviour in the 18th [chapter] of Matthew's [Gospel] is to be attended to in all cases so far as practicable in treating with our brethren. And in all uncommon cases the church [is] to be the judge. And in all public transgressions, acknowledgments are to be made to the church.

13th. We consider it the duty of members in removing their residence to distant bounds to apply to the church for a letter of dismission and [to] join some other church with speed or as soon as duty and prudence may dictate.

Having given the constitution of Buck Run Church with its mode of government at length, by which the creed of my own heart on these subjects is very fully expressed. And these are not the mere ideas of a day but my unwavering opinion from my youth. That whoever may look on the items above may see the complexion of my whole soul in theology. I had thought of making some enlargement on those constitutional articles, but they stand explicit for themselves. By them I have lived long. By them I expect to die, which I hope is not far distant; but always with this reserve in that article: "The will of the Lord be done." As to the terms of the General Union of Baptists in Kentucky, as named in the constitution of Buck Run Church, I as fully accord in them as I did in the beginning. A few imprudent individuals shall not drive me from that salutary measure.

At the time of the constitution of Buck Run Church there was a small revival in the neighborhood, and spreading more largely through many parts of Scott County. At the Great Crossing [Church] they baptized many about this time. At the North Fork and the Forks of Elkhorn, two neighboring churches and [143]very near on each side of Buck Run, a number were baptized.

After we became a little composed as a church at Buck Run, I named to them what I have generally done when I became a member of a church: that I had united as a mere member in a church capacity with them and with no office hanging round me, as to them in their now church state; that though no other preacher belonged to them as a member but myself, I could not make free in any office work among them as a church except they some way signified it by their own voice.

I was a little amused when some of them proposed for me to walk out while they counseled on that subject.

To which I replied [that] if they could not look me in the face and speak what they thought on that occasion, they did not deserve a name in the house of God; and if I could not bear with patience whatever they might say, I did not deserve the name of gospel minister.

However, it was taken up in my presence and myself acting as their moderator, in which I was equally officious as if they were talking of another man, while they seemed to act and converse in that independent, godly simplicity which gave evidence that they neither designed to cringe or [to] flatter. But so it was [that] there was no dissenting voice at my serving them as a preacher. But they had forgotten to ask my consent, but it is probable [that] they concluded [that] I would not deny.[34]

When the business of the day was read at the close, the clerk had recorded that I was called to the pastoral care of the church. After hearing my explanation and my aversion to that kind of charge as to myself, the record was changed [to read] that I had agreed to preach for them once a month and [to] administer [the] ordinances till they could be otherways or better supplied. We have been on the same footing on that head for upwards of five years.

I have named a little revival when Buck Run became a church. We soon began to baptize some, but this has but sparingly continued. I suppose, [144]first and last, we have baptized between twenty and thirty since Buck Run became a church, and these were mostly soon after our constitution. We have grown up to the number of about sixty members. We have very few black members among us. And another thing in our favor: We have very few rich men among us. For very often by rich men and Negroes the cause of religion suf-

---

[34]The intransitive verb *deny* is an archaism meaning *refuse*.

fers much, for while one is above, the other is below its native, godlike simplicity.[35]

Buck Run has built a snug, little, brick meetinghouse, forty feet by thirty. It is comfortable to worship in.

From the local situation of Buck Run it is not likely to become a numerous church. It is adjoining and surrounded by a very thick Catholic settlement with their priest and great cathedral,[36] not far from Buck Run. Neighboring Baptist churches [are] also very near and in all directions. But taking this little church by and large, they are rather a happy people than otherwise. And though that warm glow of brotherly love is not often seen among them, they are peaceable among themselves. There has been but one legal complaint ever yet brought into the church, and that was against a poor Negro who was excluded.

When Buck Run had gotten their meetinghouse prepared to worship in, they concluded to have more preaching than once a month. Therefore, they invited the well-known Father [William] Hickman, [Sr.], who filled up another Sunday in a month. After which, they invited Theodoric Boulware to fill up another Sunday in the month. They were now pretty full of Sunday preaching.[37] Mr. Boulware soon after this gave himself a member of Buck Run, when Mr. Hickman concluded that his labours would be more useful in more destitute places and withdrew his services after preaching at Buck Run something more than one year. Mr. Boulware continues his preaching one Sunday in the month. He is much of a preacher and [is] considered very orthodox by all the high-toned[38] predestinarians.[39] His preaching bears the

---

[35]In the first edition the word *dignity* appears in place of *simplicity*.

[36]The building of the Saint Pius V (now the Saint Francis) Church still stands in White Sulphur in Scott County on Federal Highway 460, which connects Frankfort and Georgetown. This congregation, known as the mother church of the Catholic Diocese of Covington, was established in 1793 by Stephen Theodore Badin, the "Father of the Catholic Church in Kentucky." For a history of this congregation, see Ann Bolton Bevins and James R. O'Rourke, *"That Troublesome Parish": St. Francis-St. Pius Church of White Sulphur, Kentucky* (Georgetown KY, 1985).

[37]For the Buck Run Church to have had preaching three Sundays per month was unusual in the early 1820s, because as late as 1835 only a few Kentucky Baptist churches provided Sunday worship twice a month. Once each month was the prevailing rule. Spencer, *Kentucky Baptists*, 1:660.

[38]The adjective *high-toned* is a derisive colloquailism meaning *fashionable*.

[39]The predestinarian bent of Theodoric Boulware is seen in the principles of theology that he laid down early in his Christian walk: the eternal and immutable purposes of God, the ultimate and complete accomplishment of God's purposes, the measured and unhin-

[145]semblance of a man snuffing a candle,[40] as if he would take away from true religion all the superfluities that could possibly mingle themselves with it. Some are of opinion that at times he snuffs a little too deep. He has a greater aptitude to trim hypocrites than to invite poor sinners to come to Christ. In Mr. Boulware's own way, perhaps no man exceeds him. He has a fine voice both to speak and [to] sing. [He] speaks with uncommon elocution and is very popular with a certain cast of Christian men. Whether lambs fare as well under his ministrations as [do] older sheep is doubted by some.

[202,2d]Buck Run Church [is] now among the most happy little churches of my acquaintance. I call her little because comparitively [*sic*] speaking she is so as to numbers, and for reasons given before [she is] like to continue small; but she is in a growing state. To be growing is a pleasant thing, tho' the growth may be but slow. We have had smart[41] additions to Buck Run for a year or two past, both of white and black members.

We had but few black members until about three years past. A number joined us by letter, among whom was an old Brother Jack, of colour, a preacher, now a free[d]man. He is now called by white and black "our good-old Uncle Jack." He is deservedly very popular among the blacks; they sometimes debate among themselves which is the greatest preacher, Uncle Jack or [Jeremiah] Vardeman.[42] They mostly say that Uncle Jack is the greatest, but others agree that Vardeman is his equal. About two years ago under the labours of Uncle Jack, we baptized about twenty black people with perhaps no white person among them. They have fine singing voices, and it is a kind of heaven on earth to see and hear them on a baptizing shore.

Uncle Jack has a fine voice [both] to sing and [to] speak. His exhortations are very affecting. He is also a text taker. In my opinion, I never heard any man put up a better prayer to God. He is now perhaps fifty years old.

About one year [1826] ago, a move began among the white [203,2d]people. The first I knew of it was [in regard to] one Isaac Wingate, a magistrate in

---

dered pace of His program, and the sovereign agency of God in the salvation of the sinner. Spencer, *Kentucky Baptists*, 1:314-15.

[40]Here the idiom "snuff a candle" means purge or "make clearer or brighter."

[41]The adjective *smart* is a dialecticism meaning *numerous*.

[42]Jeremiah Vardeman (1775–1842) was celebrated in Kentucky, Tennessee, and Missouri as an accomplished Baptist preacher. For his biography, see Spencer, *Kentucky Baptists*, 1:232-40; J. M. Peck, "Rev. Jeremiah Vardeman," *Christian Repository* 6 (Jan 1857): 14-24, 104-l09; and "Jeremiah Vardeman," in Sprague, *American Pulpit*, 6:417-28.

the county.[43] He progressed on very secretly with great agony of mind till he obtained relief but yet kept very silent. The people flocked out to meeting more than usual through the winter of 1825–[182]6 and [were] very much affected at times. I heard of a few that had obtained a hope in the Lord, but they (like Wingate) kept very silent.

A zeal more than common was very discoverable among the preachers, and particularly in Theodoric Boulware. Some said he had changed his doctrinal opinions, but that was a mistake; for he had only got better to understand the harmony between the doctrine of election and the invitation of the gospel to all mankind. And from the tender feelings of his heart [he] went on accordingly. He was the principal instrument in the late revival at Buck Run.

A delicate young lady, daughter of Capt. [Isaac] Wilson, [Sr.][44] near the meetinghouse, had married a young man by the name of James [S.] Martin.[45] About middle of winter Mrs. Martin was delivered of a child; and, as many others of old Mother Eve's daughters,[46] one month after her delivery she died [1826]. The death of this respectable young lady had great effect in the neighborhood, for the smokeing [*sic*][47] flax that was among the people before, from this circumstance, broke out into a flame. And strong conviction among numbers became very obvious. Several experiences have been told to the church from the death of Mrs. Martin, and her husband was one of the number. The sovereign Lord, our God, works by means as He will in the conversion of sinners. That when He pleases, the death of one shall be the life of another. Mrs. Martin's religious mother also thought that her daughter Nancy Martin went to Heaven, though she did not profess religion before her death.

Going to our March monthly meeting, 1826, I passed by a Mr. [William] Hubble's, and hearing [that] his wife[48] had a hope in the Lord, I stopped

---

[43]Isaac Wingate (1791–1876) was a son of Smith Wingate, who with his brother Joseph migrated to Kentucky from Delaware. Darnell, *Forks of Elkhorn Church*, 284.

[44]Isaac Wilson, Sr., was commissioned a lieutenant in the militia of Franklin County in 1804. Later he was advanced to the rank of captain. Clift, *"Corn Stalk" Militia*, 90; and Draper MSS., 16CC54-55.

[45]Nancy Wilson was probably the youngest of the seven children of Isaac Wilson, Sr., and Lucy Morton. Nancy was the first wife of James S. Martin, a son of James H. Martin. Their wedding took place in 1825 in Franklin County. Darnell, *Forks of Elkhorn Church*, 204, 304.

[46]Genesis 3:16.

[47]Isaiah 42:3.

[48]William Hubbell married Elizabeth Price, a daughter of John Price, Jr., and Susannah Gano. Darnell, *Forks of Elkhorn Church*, 230.

awhile, not knowing that my company would be acceptable, and especially to Mr. Hubble (for I had somehow concluded that he was a pretty great lover of sin). But beginning to converse with him first, I soon concluded that I never met with a more penitent man in my life. He had lost several nights' sleep through distress of soul, and the day before [he] had received a relief [204,2d]that he knew not what to make of. And himself and wife had concluded to go to meeting that day and consult the church on what course they should take. They both came forward and was received by the church with great joy, and a pleasing effect on the assembly. Great solemnity attended the crowd next day at the baptizing.[49] As Mr. Hubble and wife took the lead in the late, happy revival at Buck Run, several other men and their wives were baptized afterwards—as [Isaac] Wingate and wife,[50] Price[51] and wife, [Thomas] Casey and wife.

I shall now take a little notice of several families belonging to Buck Run Church—as Price, Wilson, Wingate, and Casey.

Mrs. Hubble was a daughter of the noted, old Mr. John Price, [Jr.], who had married a daughter of the well-known, late Father [John] Gano[52] by whom he [Price] has a swarm of respectable children.[53] A number of them has been baptized in the last revival. "The Lord grant that the balance may follow." Mr. Price is a deacon of the church. Whether his wife should be numbered among the deaconess[es], we may examine a little. A deaconess was an early appointment in the church of a worthy female of age to officiate in sacred rites and thereby serve the church. All this was drawn from what Paul said of widows [in] 1 Tim[othy] 5[th] c[hapter].[54]

Mrs. [Susannah Gano] Price professed the Lord's name from her youth, [is] the mother of many children, [shows] uncommon ripeness of judgment in what belongs to good order, takes great interest in the church where she

---

[49]The date was Sunday 26 March 1826.

[50]Isaac Wingate married Jane N. Sneed in Shelby County in 1816. They lived at Woodlake, in Franklin County. Jane was one of the ten children of Patrick Sneed, a native of Virginia. Darnell, *Forks of Elkhorn Church*, 267, 284.

[51]This Price was perhaps one of the seven sons of John Price, Jr. Ibid., 230-31.

[52]John Gano (1727–1804), a native of New Jersey, served as a missionary in Virginia and North Carolina and as a chaplain during the Revolutionary War. Following pastorates in Pennsylvania and New York, he migrated in 1787 to Kentucky, where he wrote his *Biographical Memoirs* (Providence RI, 1806). *Encyclopedia of Southern Baptists*, 1:524-25; and Sprague, *American Pulpit*, 6:62-67.

[53]Susannah Gano Price was the mother of ten children. Darnell, *Forks of Elkhorn Church*, 230-31.

[54]Verses 9-10.

is a member, [and] has some gift in poetry, as some of the hymn books will show some of her poems in print. Her mind [is] more devotional to the Lord than common and particularly in those highest strains on earth—prayer and praise to God. She now rejoices in the Lord that He has answered her prayers in the conversion of her children and neighbors. She is, by way of compliment, among us at times called "the seed of Abraham," not merely being the daughter of old Father Gano but by faith the daughter of old Abraham, the patriarch.[55]

Query: Should not a woman of this cast be invited to prayer or prophecying[56] [sic] in the church? Answer: Nothing but the pride or folly of man would object to it. (See 1 Cor[inthians] ll[th] c[hapter]).[57] All that is demanded of Paul here is that a woman should have power on her head (10th v[erse]), which only designs a veil[58] or covering. A cap itself would do, showing [205,2d]that a woman praying or prophecying [sic] in the church manifested due respect to her husband, or that the government of the church mainly lay with the male members. Though in some churches the greatest strength of intellect and counsel is the females, prudence in those cases should direct. But it is a pity a church should lose any gift that is among them merely because it is found in a female.

Isaac Wilson is another deacon in the church. His and Price's family are connected by marriage.[59] In these two families the revival was first apparent. A number of the children from both were lately baptized. Mr. Wilson through prudence and industry has accumulated a good estate. His family [is] in high credit. It is probable [that] through affluence his mind was too much drawn off to the perishable things of this little world. The death of his daughter [Nancy] Martin deeply affected him. He betook himself more to prayer both in his family and closet and in prayer meetings. For nine months past he seems transformed by the renewing of his mind.[60] His wife, [Lucy], also [is] calmly resigning her best things, when the Lord calls them away and especially when finding [that] the death of one child is the life of many. Both of these families for months past have been happy indeed.

---

[55]Galatians 3:29.

[56]In an incorrect spelling, here is a rare usage of the gerund *prophesying*, which means "teaching matters of religion."

[57]Verses 5-13.

[58]*Vail*, the obsolete spelling of the noun *veil*, is used here by Taylor.

[59]In 1819 America Wilson, the eldest daughter of Isaac Wilson, married John G. Price, whose father was John Price, Jr. Darnell, *Forks of Elkhorn Church*, 230, 304.

[60]Romans 12:2.

Isaac Wingate and family: His children are young, but himself and wife, [Jane], and a servant woman is lately, hopefully converted to the Lord. This man in his natural cast is high-minded and resentful [and] rather distant in his manners than otherwise. His understanding is penetrating, and he is a nice observer of all the words and actions of men. If a preacher does not go pretty strait,[61] he will spy out his blunders. And in due time he [the preacher] will hear from him, though not in an ill-natured way. The worth of these kind of men are seldom appreciated as they should be, for by this means many gross mistakes are corrected. Mr. Wingate seems to be of the most affable, pleasant turn.

To show the stripe of Mr. Wingate and wife I will give one single item: He comeing [*sic*] home one evening, his wife informed him of a meeting close at hand that night and asked his company with her. After hearing who was to preach he refused, saying, "You know I have a bad opinion of that man. I consider him a hypocrite, and you must [206,2d]excuse me." But to accommodate his wife, he went [but] with the design to pay no attention, as he disliked the man. But that night the arrows of God reached his soul, [so] that he could not extract [them] till he found relief in the Lord. This hypocrite, in Wingate's esteem, was Theodoric Boulware—now his dear brother in Christ and father in the gospel.

When Wingate related his experience to the church, if weeping is a childish thing the crowded house all became children; for the most manly philosophy could not suppress tears. And poor Wingate himself [was] under the same tender sensations. "Glory, glory to that God by whose sovereign grace the loftiness of man is brought down to the dust of humility." This conquered sinner was baptized the next day with his wife and a number of others by the same man he once esteemed a hypocrite.

Thomas Casey and wife are among the young converts at Buck Run, both of them young in years. Casey, being raised in obscurity and to hard labour, has but little learning. He was struck with a great sensibility of his lost state and betook himself to prayer for the first time. And what is very uncommon in such cases, he immediately set up prayer in his family. In a short time he obtained deliverance, while at prayer by himself.

Shortly after, he came to the church for admittance to baptism. Having not lost a sense of the divine goodness to him, he could dwell on nothing but his good feelings. He seemed too good a man (in his own esteem) for the church to receive him, though his wife had been received just before. When

---

[61]The obsolete adverb *strait* means *strictly.*

he took leave of the church, he said to the moderator, "Mr. Boulware, I do know that I love the Lord Jesus Christ."

But the rejection of the church put him almost beside himself. He eat[62] or slept but little for several days, though it was in the midst of harvest. One week after, he came forward and gave the church full satisfaction. He could now talk of the guilt of his sin and [of] his just condemnation under the law. Himself and wife with nine more went into the water next day.

About four months after this, a respectable lady the name of Baid came forward to tell her experience. When asked how she first became concerned about her soul, her reply was, "When Mr. Casey first told his experience to the church." Her reflection was, "This man is going to Heaven. What is to [207,2d]become of me? Lord, have mercy on me." Her relation was so interesting [that] she was received by the church with great joy.

Others being expected, she was rather advised to wait a while for company, to which she assented. But when monthly day came, though there had been a considerable fall of snow and the air very bleak, she desired to be baptized that afternoon. We traveled near four miles to suitable water, and she alone baptized. After which, the same dark evening with her husband [she] went three or four miles to a night meeting. At which place her much-affected husband desired the prayers of the church that mercy might be extended to him. "O Saviour, save his soul."

Buck Run now [1827] has three preachers. [One of them is] Theodoric Boulware, now among the most useful preachers of my acquaintance. But with all his usefulness, he yet knows how to snuff candles and trim the lamps of all kinds of virgins. But one thing makes us mourn: He has sold his place and will probably move away.[63] They have old Uncle Jack, of whom I have said something before, and the poor, old, worne-out [sic] writer hereof.

By estimation, the state of Buck Run Church is as follows. They were constituted with 21 members about nine years ago—8 male members and 13 females, all white people. From the beginning of the church to this time, 50 free, male members have had a place there. Eleven has been dismissed by letter and 7 have died, leaving 32 white, male members in the church, 14 of whom were baptized in our late revival. From the beginning, there have been 57 white females—12 have been dismissed by letter, 1 dead, now 44.

---

[62]Here *eat* is the archaic, dialectal past tense of the transitive verb *eat*.
[63]Theodoric Boulware migrated to Calloway County, Missouri, in October 1827. Spencer, *Kentucky Baptists*, 1:66.

All the blacks that have been in the church male and female [total] 49—1 dismissed, 6 excluded, 42 remaining. It seems about one third of the church are people of colour.

I think no legal complaint has ever been brought into the church against a white person from the beginning. The exclusions have been of the poor blacks.

The number baptized within about eight months has been about 40.

The whole number is at present about 120. This is just the number of the first church at Jerusalem before the Day of Pentecost.[64]

Buck Run Church has never had a particular pastor. All her preachers are on an equality and are servants of the [208,2d]church without superiority in any. Boulware and myself, by turns, have served the church as moderators. A few meetings back the church added two more to act in turn. The brethren appointed Isaac Wilson and Isaac Wingate. Neither of them are preachers. Each man has a tour to serve once in four months.

In the church of Christ there are no masters and servants, no kings and subjects. They all have a King and Master, but He is in Heaven. As in Heaven there is no distinction between one saint and another, for neither there nor here has Christ any distinct relations. All are children, all are heirs and joint heirs with Christ.[65] What a blessed republic is the church of Christ, either militant or triumphant. "Thanks to Almighty God that I have such a home[66] as Buck Run." Reader, will you say "Amen"?

In the late, though partial, revival at Buck Run there is one thing particularly pleasing. Before the revival, perhaps half the members did not pray to God in their families. The revival seemed to begin in prayer. And now there are three prayer meetings in the week kept up in the bounds of the church. On the north side of the meetinghouse a mile or two, several brethren lately baptized concluded to meet every Tuesday night with some of their older brethren for the purpose of conversation, praise, and prayer. On the south side, a number of young and older brethren followed the example of the north side and meet every Saturday night. The church agreed to keep up a prayer meeting every Sunday evening—in long days, before night; in short days, by candlelight.

---

[64]Acts 1:15.

[65]Romans 8:17.

[66]The noun *home* is here an Americanism meaning "the church to which one belongs."

Moreover, the church agreed [that] at those Sunday-evening meetings if any desired to tell their experiences there should be an opening for that purpose. Many happy, Sunday-evening meetings we have had while members were telling the good things the Lord had done for their souls. But [a] few of the brethren are backward to do their part in those prayer meetings. I wish the sisters would be more ready to pray with us also. As I have said, by covering their head they may make free. Paul's not suffering a woman to speak in a church[67] by no means contradicts this idea.

It is very common for these social, prayer meetings to grow lax and dwindle off, against which the greatest care should be taken. The smallest [209,2d]rupture between brethren is a sad drawback on prayer. A little wrath in this case is ruinous. Therefore said Paul, "Pray everywhere, lifting up holy hands without wrath" (1 Tim[othy] 2[d] c[hapter] 8[th] v[erse]). Peter also advises husbands and wives to "dwell together in great harmony that their prayers be not hindered" (1 Pet[er] 3[d] c[hapter] 7[th] v[erse]). The Saviour directs [us] to [have] a forgiving heart when we pray.

In all our commerce and contacts with men, care should be taken that no disputes arise, and thereby our prayers be hindered. By bickering of this kind I have known prayer meetings broken up. "May the Lord preserve our Buck Run brethren that none of those disasters break up their prayer meetings." Communion with God [and] audience in the court above—what can be greater this side of Heaven?

The great likeness in the death of two females, very lately, leads me to take some notice of them. The first was Fanny Neale, the wife of Presley Neale. The other was Theodosia Taylor,[68] the wife of Benjamin Taylor, my oldest son. Between those ladies there was about ten years' difference in age. Both of them [were] of delicate constitution, and both of them died with the consumption. They lived very near neighbors, and each of them [was] delivered of a female child near the same time, after which neither of them recovered. And [both] departed this life after an illness of about seven or eight months.

Mrs. Neale, who was the oldest, died about twenty-four hours before Mrs. Taylor. I had an intimate acquaintance with Mrs. Neale from childhood. She became alarmed of her lost state when a young girl but did not openly profess

---

[67]1 Corinthians 14:34.

[68]Theodosia Payne (1793–1826) became Mrs. Benjamin Taylor about 1815. She was a daughter of Henry Payne (1753–1828) and Anne Lane (1753–1821), who married in 1775. Dorothy Thompson, "Ancestors and Descendants," 32, 33.

the Lord's name till she was the mother of many children. Being very feeble when she related her hope in Christ, I doubted whether it would be proper to baptize her as it was bitter cold weather and the water about a half mile from the house. But by warmth of zeal she preferred taking water at once, after which she immediately recovered better health than for several years before.

With her husband she had been a member at Buck Run about nine years before her death. Her deportment was sedate and grave. [She had] a pleasant voice to sing, and to praise the Lord was her [210,2d] great delight.

She [Mrs. Neale] was often much afflicted with sickness. And when the First-born of Death made his last appearance (though [she had] long [been] bowed down with disease), her resignation to the Lord was uncommon, saying, "I have no trust but the Lord Jesus." She was much more subject to weep than laugh. But she is gone where all tears are wiped from her eyes.[69] Perhaps I never saw any man as much afflicted at the loss of a companion, as [was] her disconsolate husband, Presley Neale.[70] But let him remember [that] he ought not to sorrow as those who have no hope,[71] [and that] his loss is her eternal gain.

I need say nothing more of Mrs. Taylor, as her affectionate husband after her death published what follows, himself being a membe[r] of Buck Run Church:

"Departed this life on the 29th of November [1826], Mrs. Theodosia Taylor, wife of Mr. Benjamin Taylor, of Woodford County, in the 34th year of her age after an illness of ten months.

"She has filled the high relations of dutiful daughter, loving sister, affectionate wife, tender and provident mother, and ardent social friend. She has left a bereaved husband, five children, an aged father, brothers, sisters, relations, and friends to bewail her loss, but whose loss is her gain. She has left a world of affliction and sorrow, has left others to mourn her departure, and has gone to enjoy happiness evermore with her heavenly Father and Saviour.

"To the lovers of religion a short recital of some of the exercises of her mind cannot be uninteresting. Though she had for years been seriously impressed with thoughts relative to her future state and [to] the worth of her

[69]Revelation 7:17.
[70]Presley Neale remarried the following year in Franklin County. His bride was Nancy Calvert Grugin, the widow of Paul Grugin. Darnell, *Forks of Elkhorn Church*, 98, 216.
[71]1 Thessalonians 4:13.

soul, [and] though she had read the Scriptures much, [she] was fond of hearing preaching and of the society of the pious.

"In the habit of prayer, and apparently convinced of the necessity of regenerating grace and a better righteousness than her own to fit her for heavenly bliss, she could not feel a satisfactory assurance of her interest in the great plan of salvation through the righteousness and atoning death of the Redeemer until about nine months before her decease. Since that time reliance on that safe and glorious plan has been her stay and hope. Though wracked with lingering disease, many and rapturous were the transports of her hope of an interest in this sure foundation.

"Twenty-four [211,2d]hours before her death, after appearing to have been engaged two days and a night in almost unremitting, mental prayer, with great earnestness (in a tone that seemed to say she held converse with her God) she exclaimed, 'Thy kingdom come, thy will be done.'[72] Consoling herself with the expression and feeling that 'Jesus can make a dying bed feel soft as downy pillows,' and with extended arms as if almost in reach of her Saviour, [she] often invited the Lord Jesus to come quickly, accompanied with prayer for sufficient strength in passing through the valley of the shadow of death.[73]

"After which, she impressively requested her husband to bring up her children in the 'nurture and admonition of the Lord.'[74] And addressing herself to those that were old enough to weigh her words, [she] exhorted them to 'remember their Creator in the days of their youth.'[75] She retained her right mind as long as she could speak, which was until a few minutes before she expired. Her almost latest words were employed in invocations to her Jesus, with Whom she doubtless reigns.

"The duty of surviving friends is to submit. Though to them [her death is] a heavy dispensation, they should feel that it is of the Lord, Who giveth and Who taketh away."[76]

[303,2d]Two [other] members of Buck Run Church (to our great grief) has lately [1827] been called home by death.

The first is Sister [Catherine] Graves, the wife of Brother John Graves. An amiable woman, [she was] the picture of consummate health and the mother of ten children and not far exceeding thirty years of age. The oldest

---

[72]Matthew 6:10.
[73]Psalm 23:4.
[74]Ephesians 6:4.
[75]Ecclesiastes 12:1.
[76]Job 1:21.

of her last three [children was] not exceeding three years. As [with] many others of Eve's daughters, for her [Eve's] first sin she died in childbed.

She had professed religion, perhaps fifteen years. Her steady, lively devotion in religion much drew the attention of others and particularly in her last illness, [when she was] exhorting those around her to seek the Lord. The morning before her departure she had so bright a manifestation of God's love to her soul [that] she desired to take leave of all weeping friends around her and be with Christ forever.

Perhaps no husband ever sustained a greater loss than in the present case. But with a broken heart [he] resigned her to God without a murmur, considering his loss her eternal gain.

By hasty notice, perhaps a hundred people were gathered at her interment. I do not recollect ever witnessing such a general burst of weeping on the like occasion. Two appropriate discourses were delivered to the people, the last of which was by Br[other] T[heodoric] Boulware, which was interesting indeed. [It came] from these words: "Wherefore comfort one another with these words" (1 Thes[salonians] 4[th] c[hapter] 18[th] v[erse]).

The other death among us was our beloved, young brother Joseph Wilson, son of our well-known brother Isaac Wilson. This choice young man was some of the proceeds of our happy revival at Buck Run last year [1826]. His native modesty and grave deportment with his inoffensive manners in all circles recommended him to all mankind who came into his company.

I am at a loss to describe his worth. If there was any extreme in his composition, [304,2d]it lay in diffidence. There was evidently gift in him. In relating his experience in the church his expressions were short and very pertinent, as also in his prayers to God in public meetings. He seemed to be apprised of his need of all he asked for, and [to think] that many words were needless before an all-knowing God and that repetitions in prayer were superfluous. But above all, his charming voice to sing gave the sweetest sensations in devotion to the Lord. His loud, melodious voice distinguished [itself] from all others who sang with him. And though his modesty mostly led him to take some back seat, he articulated so plainly [when singing] that you understood all the words, by which your mind was edified and every tender feelings of the heart brought into action. But his silence in the grave is no more to be interrupted till the elements melt with fervent heat,[77] and he with all the saints be caught up to meet the Lord in the air.[78]

---

[77]2 Peter 3:10.
[78]1 Thessalonians 4:17.

In his stature he was tall and spare, with a delicate appearance. His countenance [was] solemn and grave, and [it] bore an expression of kindness and good will to men.

He died about ten months after he was baptized, aged about twenty-three years. His complaint was a severe fever of four weeks, in which he suffered much. But his confidence in his Saviour gave pleasure to all his friends.

Stephen French,[79] about such another young man, died about the same time and perhaps [of] the same kind of fever, under which he sunk in about nine days. Mr. French was a son of the well-known James French,[80] of Montgomery County.[81] And though the young man did not profess religion, there is room to think he was a warm friend of that good cause.

If I had any favorite young men in the world, they were Joseph Wilson and Stephen French. And one consolation I have at this time of life is that I shall soon see them again, when we shall all know even as we are known here[82] and ever be with the Lord.[83]

[304,2d]The subscription price of this book is 87½ cents; to non-subscribers, $1.00. The publishers have made considerable additions to the book to what they first intended which has enhanced the cost to them; and consequently they cannot afford it to non-subscribers for less that $1.00.

---

[79]Stephen French was a brother of William French, a son-in-law of the author. Dorothy Thompson, "Ancestors and Descendants," 37.

[80]James French II (1765–1835) migrated from Virginia to Kentucky, where he married Keziah Calloway at Boonesborough in 1783. Ibid.

[81]Montgomery County was erected under a Kentucky law passed in 1796.

[82]1 Corinthians 13:12.

[83]1 Thessalonians 4:17.

# Appendix
## Religious Rhetoric of the Frontier

The two editions of *A History of Ten Baptist Churches* by John Taylor richly illustrate the idiomatic way in which frontiersmen pieced together the words of their language in expressing religious ideas and actions. The tables that follow consist of Taylor's wording that I have laid down in the form of infinitives and have arranged systematically around concepts, organizations, and practices common to his world of religion. Each table of infinitives is given a title, and in turn each group of titles is set down under one or the other of five broad categories. Each infinitive follows an emdash and precedes a reference to one of the two editions of *Ten Churches*. These references are of two sorts: first, a cardinal number standing alone refers to a page of the first edition; second, the use of both a cardinal number and the ordinal number *2d* indicates the second edition as the source.

## A. Salvation and Sinners

### Awakening

—to be struck with a great consciousness of one's guilt (46)
—to become alarmed of one's lost state (110)
—to become alarmed of one's awful danger by sin (170)
—to seek the way to Heaven (37)
—to enquire the way to Zion (179)
—to seek the salvation of one's soul (161, 2d)

### The Travail and Terror of Conviction

—to be under distress of soul (169)
—to be under a sense of the guilt of one's sin (169)
—to be under a great weight of guilt (105)
—to labour under one's long agony of guilt (28)
—to labour a considerable time under a consciousness of one's helpless condition (101)
—to drive one into the extremes of despair for a long time (107)

—to be long under great anguish of soul about one's lost and
   helpless state (171)
—to be almost beside one's self with soul distress (73)
—to go beside one's self (37)
—to be driven to one's wits' end (291)
—to acknowledge the justice of one's doom (292)
—to mourn inwardly over one's hardness of heart (57)
—to feel the wormwood and gall in one's soul (103)

## Conversion

—to believe and trust in the Saviour (103)
—to agonize in birth till Christ be formed within a sinner (102)
—to be born again (57)
—to be born of God (297)
—to have one's standing fixed on the Rock of Ages (108)
—to find the Lord (173)
—to be sent speedy relief (103)
—to obtain the blessing of the Lord (73)
—to receive a very clear deliverance (168)
—to obtain conversion while on one's knees (30)

## Assurance

—to have hope of conversion (278, 2d)
—to have a hope in the Lord (203, 2d)
—to be confident in one's best evidences of eternal life (72)
—to feel a satisfactory assurance of one's interest in the great
   plan of salvation (210, 2d)
—to live in the comfortable hope of eternal life (109)

## The Relation of One's Spiritual Experience

—to relate one's experience to the church (72)
—to profess one's first awakening (163)
—to declare one's faith in Christ (159)
—to profess religion (203, 2d)
—to profess the Lord's name openly (209, 2d)
—to relate to the church one's hope in Christ (164)
—to tell the good things the Lord has done for one's soul (208, 2d)
—to give the church full satisfaction (206, 2d)

## B. New Converts and the Congregation

### Application for Membership

—to be received for baptism (155)
—to be received into the church (152)
—to be under the care of the church (99)

### Receiving Baptism

—to be baptized after obtaining hope in the Lord (47)
—to take water at once (209, 2d)
—to follow the Lord in baptism (102)
—to be led by a proper administrator into water of a proper depth (159)
—to follow the Lord in a watery grave (18)
—to be baptized and join the church (99)

### Taking the Lord's Supper

—to receive the Lord's Supper (140)
—to receive the ministration from [a deacon's] hands (122)
—to commune with one's dying Lord (187)
—to commune at the Lord's table (184)

## C. Ministerial Duties

### Carrying out Missionary Activities

—to have uncommon anguish of heart for the salvation of one's
    neighbors (65)
—to leave appointments [for preaching] (93)
—to preach the gospel far and wide (192, 2d)
—to have a great range (47)
—to take the fire and spread it abroad (113)
—to receive a missionary spirit in its warmest glow (98)

### Examination of Candidates for Membership

—to open a door for the reception of members (141)
—to open the door to hear experiences (167)

—to invite candidates to come forward (99)
—to invite one to come in and tell his experience (296)
—to examine a candidate for baptism (296)
—to admit one to baptism (177)
—to reach out the hand of fellowship to a convert (107)

## Administration of Baptism

—to go to the water (155)
—to attend at the water (164)
—to go into the water to baptize (300)
—to put one in the water (37)
—to pronounce the ceremony (69)
—to dip (17)
—to immerse the whole body under water (139)
—to lean one back and figurate a burial (159)
—to reduce the doctrine of baptism to practice before one's eyes (159)
—to lay on hands at baptism (6)
—to give the hand of fellowship (164)

## Conducting Meetings for Worship

—to keep up the worship of God in decency (137)
—to open meeting (20)
—to devote one's mind to the Saviour's cause (163, 2d)

## Moderating Business Sessions

—to read the business of the day (130-131)
—to give one's light on a subject (141)
—to take the voice of the church (141)
—to lay over an item till next meeting (131)

## Conducting Funerals

—to be requested by the family to address the people (167, 2d)
—to name a text of Scripture (167, 2d)
—to give some ideas that are precious to myself (167, 2d)

## Relationship between Pastor and People

—to take the pastoral care of a church (116)
—to take the watchcare of a church (48)
—to have the pastoral care (128)
—to have the care of several churches (36)
—to administer among the congregation (181, 2d)
—to fulfill the law of Christ (137)
—to fulfill the duty of brethren (137)
—to lay our shoulders to the yoke at once (62)
—to work as a servant of the church on full equality with
    one's sinner brethren (164, 2d)
—to trim hypocrites (145)
—to trim the lamps of all kinds of virgins (207, 2d)
—to yield up one's charge (61)

# D. Ecclesial Functions

## Constituting a Congregation

—to make out at least a semblance of a church (26)
—to begin society (6)
—to go into a new church establishment (133)
—to set up a congregation (134)
—to go into a constitution (135)
—to give themselves in a church compact to one another (137)
—to covenant with and agree to (137)
—to pronounce a church constituted (140)

## Identifying Those Called to Preach

—to begin to speak (20)
—to come forward into the vineyard of the Lord (74)
—to call one forward to preach (298)

## Ordination of a Minister

—to call one to ordination (124, 2d)
—to ask solemn questions of the candidate for ordination (192, 2d)

—to commit the sacred trust to one (119, 2d)
—to give the right hand of fellowship (27)

## Installation of a Pastor

—to put one in the pastoral office in the church (193, 2d)
—to install one into the pastoral care of a church (53)
—to charge one as pastor of the church (192, 2d)
—to give one the right hand of fellowship (53)

## Conducting Business Sessions

—to behave one's self in the house of God (114)
—to bring a query into the church (131)
—to bring forward a matter of complaint (141)
—to give one's voice in the church on an affair (120)
—to pay one's quota of money (119)
—to get the carriage out of the mud (114)

## Administering Discipline

—to treat a complaint in Gospel order (141)
—to watch over one another in brotherly tenderness (137)
—to expel a deacon from office (122)
—to reinstate a deacon in office (75)
—to suspend one from church privilege (194, 2d)
—to restore a member to privilege in the church (194, 2d)
—to give a gentle admonition (130)

## Reception, Dismissal, and Explusion of Members

—to open the door to hear experiences (167)
—to sit to hear experiences (152)
—to open the door to receive members (58)
—to join by letter (202, 2d)
—to come forward to join the church (164)
—to obtain a letter of dismission (132)
—to be turned out of the church (57)
—to expel by a unanimity of voices (76)

## E. Elements of Worship

### Preaching

—to stand up to preach (187)
—to go to the table (20)
—to go forward to preach (119, 2d)
—to go forward in worship (141, 2d)
—to open meeting (20)
—to make a stand (37)
—to open one's mouth (135)
—to speak (20)
—to speak in public (126)
—to take a text (59)
—to communicate (298)
—to speak peace in one's soul (102)
—to speak by example as well as by precept (74)
—to take the tract entertainingly (60)
—to preach with great effect among the people (152)
—to leave off when one is done (187, 2d)

### Prayer

—to go to prayer (12)
—to perform prayer (152)
—to put up a prayer to God (289)
—to kneel down and pray to God (104)
—to go by one's self (104)
—to go into the woods (115)
—to go to prayer in the family (12)
—to pray the Lord to pardon (126)
—to feel a heart to pray for another (92)
—to be afraid to attempt prayer (103)
—to betake one's self to prayer for the first time (206, 2d)

### Singing

—to join in the heavenly melody 164)
—to ring out God's praises with heavenly melody (85)
—to sing the closing hymn with sonorous melody (187)
—to make the lonesome forest ring with the praises of God (25)

## Weeping

—to begin to trickle (100)
—to vent the tender emotions of one's heart (99)
—to give fresh tide to the feelings of sympathy among the people (164)
—to break forth in plaintive sorrow (101)
—to break out into a flood of tears (13)

## Handshaking

—to give one's hand (161)
—to reach out hands to each other (92)
—to reach out the hand of Christian fellowship (28)
—to reach out the hand of love (188, 2d)
—to meet each other with the right hand of fellowship (54)

## Exhortation

—to warn people to flee from the wrath to come (93)
—to give feeling invitations to broken-hearted creatures (25)
—to invite poor sinners to come to Christ (145)
—to invite everyone to come to the supper (188, 2d)

# Bibliography

## A. John Taylor's Works

### Books

*History of Clear Creek Church; and Campbellism Exposed.* Frankfort KY, 1830.
*A History of Ten Baptist Churches of Which the Author Has Been Alternately a Member, in Which Will Be Seen Something of a Journal of the Author's Life for More Than Fifty Years; Also a Comment on Some Parts of Scripture in Which the Author Takes the Liberty to Differ from Other Expositors.* Frankfort KY, 1823. 2d ed.; Bloomfield KY, 1827.
*Thoughts on Missions.* [Frankfort KY] 1820.
*Thoughts on Missions; [and] Biographies of Baptist Preachers.* [Frankfort KY] 1820.

### Other Writings

"Creeds." *Baptist Chronicle and Literary Register* 2 (Aug 1831): 118.
"The Good Man's Rest." *Baptist Chronicle and Literary Register* 2 (June 1831): 81-83.
"The Gospel Supper." *A History of Ten Baptist Churches.* 2d ed., 233-48.
"Intelligence from Kentucky." *The Reformer* 2 (1 Sept 1821): 193-99.
Letter to A[lexander] Campbell. *Baptist Chronicle and Literary Register* 1 (Nov 1830): 164-66.
Letter to [Uriel B. Chambers]. *Baptist Chronicle and Literary Register* 1 (June 1830): 92-93.
"Paul's First Work." *A History of Ten Baptist Churches.* 2d ed., 225-33.
"The Rev. John Taylor's [Religious] Experience." *The Kentucky Missionary and Theological Magazine* 1 (1 May 1812): 33-36.
"Try the Spirits." *Baptist Chronicle and Literary Register* 1 (July 1830): 100-102.

# B. Government Archives

## Virginia Counties

Fauquier County. County Court. Will Books 1 and 2. Office of the County Clerk, Warrenton VA.

Fayette County. Tax Lists, 1787. Microfilm. Kentucky Historical Society, Frankfort KY.

Frederick County. County Court. Deed Book 11. Typescript. Office of the County Clerk, Winchester VA.

_____. Militia. Court Martial Records, 1755–1761. Photostat. Virginia State Library and Archives, Richmond VA.

Northumberland County. County Court. Record Books, 1743–1749 and 1747–1749. Record Books 11 and 12. Office of the County Clerk, Heathsville VA.

Shenandoah County. County Court. Deed Book O. Office of the County Clerk, Woodstock VA.

## Kentucky Counties

Boone County. Circuit Court. Order Book A. Kentucky State Archives, Frankfort KY.

_____. County Court. Deed Books A, B, C-2, D, E, and F. Office of the County Clerk, Burlington KY.

_____. County Court. Marriage Book A. Office of the County Clerk, Burlington KY.

_____. County Court. Order Book A. Office of the County Clerk, Burlington KY.

_____. Quarter Sessions Court. Deed Book A. Office of the County Clerk, Burlington KY.

_____. Quarter Sessions Court. Minute Book. Kentucky State Archives, Frankfort KY.

_____. Tax Lists, 1799 and 1801. Microfilm. Kentucky Historical Society, Frankfort KY.

Campbell County. County Court. Deed Book A. Office of the County Clerk, Alexandria KY.

_____. County Court. Order Book A. Photocopy. Office of the County Clerk, Alexandria KY.

_____. Tax Lists, 1798. Microfilm. Kentucky Historical Society, Frankfort KY.

Fayette County. Circuit Court. Deed Book B. Office of the County Clerk, Lexington KY.

_____. County Court. Burnt Records Book 5. Office of the County Clerk, Lexington KY.

Franklin County. County Court. Deed Books E-2, G-2, I, L, M, N, O, P, and Q. Office of the County Clerk, Frankfort KY.

_____. County Court. Inventory and Sales Book A. Office of the County Clerk, Frankfort KY.

_____. County Court. Order Book K. Office of the County Clerk, Frankfort KY.

_____. County Court. Will Book 2. Office of the County Clerk, Frankfort KY.

_____. Tax Lists, 1816–1835. Microfilm. Kentucky Historical Society, Frankfort KY.

Gallatin County. Circuit Court. Order Books, 1807–1814 and 1810–1814. Kentucky State Archives, Frankfort KY.

_____. Circuit Court. Record of Proceedings, 1802–1810. Kentucky State Archives, Frankfort KY.

_____. County Clerk. Deed Books A-l, B, C, D, E, F, G, H, and J. Office of the County Clerk, Warsaw KY.

_____. Tax Lists, 1803, 1811, 1812, and 1816. Microfilm. Kentucky Historical Society, Frankfort KY.

Woodford County. County Court. Deed Books A, B, C-l, C-2, E, H, M, Q, and R. Office of the County Clerk, Versailles KY.

_____. Tax Lists, 1792 and 1794. Microfilm. Kentucky Historical Society, Frankfort KY.

## Indiana County

Jefferson County. County Court. Corrected Deed Books A, B, C, and D. Original Deed Books E and G. Microfilm. Indiana State Archives, Indianapolis IN.

## Colony and State of Virginia

Brookes-Smith, Joan E., comp. *Master Index: Virginia Surveys and Grants, 1774–1791.* Frankfort KY, 1976.

*Heads of Families at the First Census of the United States Taken in the Year 1790: Records of the State Enumerations, 1782–1785: Virginia.* Washington, D. C., 1908. Reprint ed.; Baltimore MD, 1952.

Hening, William Waller, ed. *The Statutes at Large; Being a Collection of All the Laws of Virginia, from the First Session of the Legislature, in the Year 1619.* 13 vols. Richmond, 1809–1823. Reprint ed.; Charlottesville VA, 1969.

Land Commission. "Certificate Book of the Virginia Land Commission, 1779–1780." *Register of the Kentucky Historical Society* 21 (Sept 1923): [3]-321.

Land Office. Grant Book 15. Office of the Secretary of State, Frankfort KY.

Northern Neck Proprietary. Land Grant Books F, O, and R. Virginia State Library and Archives, Richmond VA.

Robertson, James Rood, ed. *Petitions of the Early Inhabitants of Kentucky to the General Assembly of Virginia, 1769 to 1792.* Louisville KY, 1914.

## State of Kentucky

Court of Appeals. Deed Books H, L, Q, R, and W. Office of the Secretary of State, Frankfort KY.

General Assembly. *Acts*, 1815, 1822, and 1825.

Jillson, Willard Rouse. *The Kentucky Land Grants: A Systematic Index to All of the Land Grants Recorded in the State Land Office at Frankfort KY, 1782–1924.* Louisville KY, 1925.

_____. *Old Kentucky Entries and Deeds: A Complete Index to All of the Earliest Land Entries, Military Warrants, Deeds, and Wills of the Commonwealth of Kentucky.* Louisville KY, 1926.

Office of the Governor. Executive Journals, 1812–1816 and 1816–1820. Kentucky State Archives, Frankfort KY.

## United States of America

Bureau of Land Management, Alexandria VA, Records of Jeffersonville (IN) Land Office. Card File of Final Certificates. Nos. 41, 45, 62, 151, 244-45, 249, and 368.

_____. Records of Jeffersonville (IN) Land Office. Register of Certificates. 3259 and 3263.

Bureau of the Census. Census of 1810, Gallatin County KY, Record Group 29. National Archives, Washington, D.C.

Jeffersonville (IN) Land Office. Accompt of Public Lands Applied for by Individuals, 1808–1811. Sheets 2, 3, 31, and 43. Indiana State Archives, Indianapolis IN.

_____. Applications to Enter Land, 1810–1815. Indiana State Archives, Indianapolis IN.

_____. Register of Certificates, 1808–1816: Public Lands. 2-7, 10-15, 30-31, 36-39, and 52-53. Indiana State Archives, Indianapolis IN.

_____. Register of Receipts Granted to Individuals, 1808–1813. Indiana State Archives, Indianapolis IN.

Pension Office. *Kentucky Pension Roll of 1835.* Washington D.C., 1835. Reprint ed.; Baltimore MD, 1959.

## C. Private Manuscripts

Buck Run Temperance Society, Forks of Elkhorn KY. Minute Book. Kentucky Historical Society, Frankfort KY.

Dozier, Richard. "Historical Notes Concerning the Planting of Baptist Principles in the Northern Neck of Virginia: Text Book from 1711: Sermons Preached from the Within Texts and Heard by Me, Richard Dozier, Son of Thomas, [of] Westmoreland County, Virginia." John S. Moore, ed. *Virginia Baptist Register* 28 (1989): 1387–1442.

Draper Manuscripts, llCC225, llCC228-36, llCC241-45, 12CC147-51, 16CC54-55, and 26CC42. Draper Collection. Wisconsin Historical Society, Madison WI.

Robert Carter III Papers. Daybook 13. Duke University Library, Durham NC.

_____. Daybook, 1789–1790. Library of Congress, Washington, D.C.

_____. Sight Draft, Issued to John Taylor, 22 April 1784. Virginia Baptist Historical Society, Richmond VA.

Thompson, Dorothy Brown. " 'James M. Bradford, Secretary': Pages from an Old Franklin County Minute-Book." *Register of the Kentucky Historical Society* 48 (Oct 1950): 291-314.

## D. Baptist Records and Histories

### Church Minute Books

Bullittsburg Church, Burlington KY. Minute Books A and B. Office of the Church Historian.

Corn Creek Church, Milton KY. Minute Book B. The Southern Baptist Theological Seminary, Louisville KY.

Red River Church, Adams TN. Minute Book, 1791–1826. Microfilm. Southern Baptist Historical Society, Nashville TN.

### Congregational Histories

Bradley, J. N., and Ellis M. Ham. *History of the Great Crossing Baptist Church*. Georgetown KY, 1945.

Campbell, William Bruce, Sr. *Bullittsburg's Ministry of Faith: 175 Years*. N.p., 1969.

Darnell, Ermina Jett. *Forks of Elkhorn Church*. Louisville KY, 1946. Reprint ed.; Baltimore, 1980.

Hofmeister, Kenton C. *A History of Buck Run Baptist Church.* Forks of Elkhorn KY, 1965.

Kirtley, J. S. "History of Clear Creek Church." Elkhorn Association, *Minutes,* 1887.

Kirtley, J[ames] A. *History of Bullittsburg Church with Biographies of Elders Absalom Graves, Chichester Matthews, James Dicken, and Robert Kirtley.* Covington KY, 1872.

Mattingly, Phyllis Sharp. *A Brief History of the South Elkhorn Baptist Church, 1783–1983, Lexington, Kentucky.* Lexington KY, 1983.

Oliver, John P., Jr. "The Baptist Meetinghouse in Front Royal, Virginia, 1830–1868." *Virginia Baptist Register* 13 (1974): 607-19.

_____ . *The Treasure—The Earthen Vessels: A History of First Baptist Church, Front Royal, Virgina, 1839–1989.* [Front Royal VA], 1990.

Ranck, George Washington. *"The Travelling Church": An Account of the Baptist Exodus from Virginia to Kentucky in 1781 under the Leadership of Rev. Lewis Craig and Capt. William Ellis.* Louisville KY, 1891.

Trimble, Dennis E. *Clear Creek Baptist Church: A Church History, 1785–1985.* [Versailles KY], 1985.

## Associational Minutes

Elkhorn Association. *Minutes,* 1820, 1830, and 1831.

_____ . "Minutes, . . . 1785–1805." William Warren Sweet, *Religion on the American Frontier.* 1:417-509.

Franklin Association. *Minutes,* Special Session, July 1830; September 1830; and 1831.

Salem Association. "Minutes, . . . 1802." William Warren Sweet, *Religion on the American Frontier.* 1:617-25.

South Kentucky Association. Minute Book A. Microfilm. The Southern Baptist Theological Seminary, Louisville KY.

_____ . "Transcript of the Minutes of the South Kentucky Association of Baptists from 1787 to 1803, and the Minutes of the North District Association of Baptists from 1803 to 1823, to Which Has Been Added an Index." George F. Doyle, transcriber. Typescript. Margaret I. King Library, University of Kentucky, Lexington KY.

## Associational Histories

Birdwhistell, Ira [V]. *The Baptists of the Bluegrass: A History of Elkhorn Baptist Association, 1785–1985.* [Lexington KY, 1985.]

_____. *Gathered at the River: A Narrative History of Long Run Baptist Association.* Louisville KY, 1978.

Fristoe, William. *A Concise History of the Ketocton Baptist Association.* Staunton VA, 1808. Fletcher ed.; Stephens City VA, 1978.

Gardner, Robert G. "The Ketocton and Philadelphia Associations in the Eighteenth Century." *Virginia Baptist Register* 27 (1988): 1365-82, and 29 (1990): 1482-1500.

Williams, U. V., and F. W. Eberhart. *History of Franklin Baptist Association from 1815 to 1912.* N. p., [1912.]

## Minutes of Societies and Conventions

Baptist Board of Foreign Missions for the United States. "Statement of Monies Received." *Second Annual Report.* Philadelphia PA, 1815.

Baptist Mission Society of Kentucky. *Proceedings of the Board of Managers, 1817–1818.* Georgetown KY, 1818.

General Association of Baptists in Kentucky. *Minutes, 1837.* Louisville KY, 1837.

Kentucky Baptist Convention. *Minutes of the Second Annual Meeting, 1834–1835.* Shelbyville KY, 1835.

_____. *Annual,* 1982, 1985, 1988, and 1989.

## Denominational Statistics

Allen, I. M. *The Triennial Baptist Register: No. 2, 1836.* Philadelphia PA, 1836.

_____. *The United States Baptist Annual Register for 1832.* Philadelphia PA, 1833.

Asplund, John. *The Annual Register of the Baptist Denomination in North America to the First of November 1790.* Richmond VA, 1792. Reprint ed.; Goodlettsville TN, 1979.

_____. *The Universal Register of the Baptist Denomination in North America for the Years 1790, 1791, 1792, 1793, and Part of 1794.* Boston MA, 1794. Reprint ed.; New York NY, 1980.

Edwards, Morgan. *Materials towards a History of the Baptists.* Eve B. Weeks and Mary B. Warren, eds. 2 vols. Danielsville GA, 1984.

_____. "Morgan Edwards' 1772 Virginia Notebook." John S. Moore, ed. *Virginia Baptist Register* 18 (1979): 845-71.

Gardner, Robert G. *Baptists of Early America: A Statistical History, 1639–1790.* Atlanta GA, 1983.

Sweet, William Warren. *Religion on the American Frontier.* 4 vols. Vol. I: *The Baptists, 1783–1830: A Collection of Source Material.* Chicago, 1931. Reprint ed.; New York NY, 1964.

## Denominational Histories

Benedict, David. *A General History of the Baptist Denomination in America and Other Parts of the World.* 2 vols. Boston, 1813. Reprint ed.; Gallatin TN, 1985.

Birdwhistell, Ira V. *Kentucky Baptists, 150 Years on Mission Together: A History of the Roots, Formation, and Development of the Kentucky Baptist Convention.* Middletown KY, 1987.

Cawthorn, C. P., and Norman L. Warnell. *Pioneer Baptist Church Records of South-Central Kentucky and the Upper Cumberland of Tennessee, 1799–1899.* [Brownsville KY,] 1985.

Christian, John T. *A History of the Baptists Together with Some Account of Their Principles and Practices.* Nashville TN, 1922.

Crismon, Leo Taylor, ed. *Baptists in Kentucky, 1776–1976: A Bicentennial Volume.* Middletown KY, 1975.

Ford, Samuel Howard. "History of the Kentucky Baptists." *Christian Repository* 5 (1856).

Lumpkin, William L. *Baptist Foundations in the South: Tracing through the Separates the Influence of the Great Awakening, 1754–1787.* Nashville TN, 1961.

Masters, Frank Mariro. *A History of Baptists in Kentucky.* Louisville KY, 1953.

Newman, Albert Henry. *A History of the Baptist Churches in the United States.* Philadelphia, 1894. Rev. ed.; Philadelphia PA, 1898.

Ryland, Garnett. *The Baptists of Virginia, 1699–1926.* Richmond VA, 1955.

Semple, Robert Baylor. *A History of the Rise and Progress of the Baptists in Virginia.* Rev. ed. Richmond VA, 1894. Reprint ed.; Cottonport LA, 1972.

Spencer, John Henderson. *A History of Kentucky Baptists from 1769 to 1885: Including More Than 800 Biographical Sketches.* 2 vols. Cincinnati OH, 1885.

Tarrant, Carter. *History of the Baptised Ministers and Churches in Kentucky, etc., Friends to Humanity.* Frankfort KY, 1808.

Torbet, Robert G. *A History of the Baptists.* Philadelphia PA, 1950.

## E. Journals

Benedict, David. Journal. Franklin Trask Library, Andover Newton Theological School, Newton MA.

Fithian, Philip Vickers. *Journal and Letters of Philip Vickers Fithian, 1773–1774: A Plantation Tutor of the Old Dominion.* Hunter Dickinson Farish, ed. New ed. Williamsburg VA, 1957.

Fristoe, Daniel. Journal. Morgan Edwards, *Materials towards a History of the Baptists.* 2 vols. Danielsville GA, 1984. 2:38-39.

Rice, Luther. *Dispensations of Providence: The Journal and Selected Letters of Luther Rice with an Introduction and Appendices.* William H. Brackney, ed. Rochester NY, 1984.

## F. Narratives and Reminiscences

Benedict, David. *Fifty Years among the Baptists.* New York NY, 1860. Reprint ed.; Little Rock AR, 1977.

Craig, Joseph. *A Sketch of a Journal of the Rev. Joseph Craig in Which Is Contained His Experience, A Sketch of His Gospel Labors, Travels, Persecutions, Sufferings, Spiritual Conflicts. . . .* Lexington KY, 1813.

Creath, Jacob, Jr. *Memoir of Jacob Creath, Jr.* P. Donan, ed. Cincinnati, 1872.

Hickman, William. *A Short Account of My Life and Travels: For More Than Fifty Years a Professed Servant of Jesus Christ.* N. p., 1828.

Ireland, James. *The Life of the Rev. James Ireland, Who Was for Many Years Pastor of the Baptist Church at Buck Marsh, Waterlick, and Happy Creek, in Frederick and Shenandoah Counties, Virginia.* Winchester VA, 1819. Johnson ed.; West Liberty KY, 1981.

Leland, John. *The Writings of the Late Elder John Leland.* L. F. Greene, ed. New York NY, 1845. Reprint ed.; Gallatin TN, 1986.

Richardson, Robert. *Memoirs of Alexander Campbell, Embracing a View of the Origin, Progress, and Principles of the Religious Reformation Which He Advocated.* 2 vols. Philadelphia, 1868–1870. Rev. ed.; Cincinnati OH, 1897.

Thompson, Wilson. *The Autobiography of Elder Wilson Thompson, Embracing a Sketch of His Life, Travels, and Ministerial Labors in Which Is Included a Concise History of the Old Order of Regular Baptist Churches.* Cincinnati OH, 1873.

Vaughan, Thomas M. *Memoirs of Rev. Wm. Vaughan, D. D.* Louisville KY, 1878.

Young, Chester Raymond, ed. *Westward into Kentucky: The Narrative of Daniel Trabue.* Lexington KY, 1981.

## G. Biographies

*The Biographical Encyclopaedia of Kentucky of the Dead and Living Men of the Nineteenth Century*. Cincinnati OH, 1878.

Crank, Carlysle C. "Life of John Taylor, a Frontiersman, Missionary, Baptist Minister, and Historian." M.A. Thesis. University of Richmond, Richmond VA, 1956.

F[ord], S[amuel] H[oward]. "Pioneer Preachers: John Taylor." *Christian Repository* 8 (June 1859): 400-410.

_____. "William Hickman, Senior." *Christian Repository* 6 (Oct 1857): 600-612.

Freeman, Douglas Southall. *George Washington: A Biography*. 5 vols. New York NY, 1948–1952.

James, Powhatan W. *George W. Truett: A Biography*. Rev. ed.; New York NY, 1945.

Koontz, Louis Knott. *Robert Dinwiddie: His Career in American Colonial Government and Westward Expansion*. Glendale CA, 1941.

Peck, John Mason. "Rev. Jeremiah Vardeman." *Christian Repository* 6 (Jan 1857): 14-24, 104-109.

"A Short Account of the Life and Death of the Late Rev. Absalom Graves." *Hymns, Psalms, and Spiritual Songs*. Absalom Graves, ed. Frankfort KY, 1825.

Simpson, William S., Jr. *Virginia Baptist Ministers, 1760–1790: A Biographical Survey*. Vol. I. Richmond VA, 1990.

"Sketches of Baptists in Missouri." *Christian Repository* 6 (July 1857): 417.

Sprague, William B., ed. *Annals of the American Pulpit*. 9 vols. Vol. VI: *Baptist*. New York NY, 1858–1869. Reprint ed.; New York NY, 1969.

Taylor, James Barnett. *Lives of Virginia Baptist Ministers*. Richmond, [VA], 1837. 2d ed.; Richmond [VA], 1838.

Thompson, Dorothy Brown. "John Taylor as a Biographer of Pioneer Baptist Preachers." *Filson Club History Quarterly* 37 (July, Oct 1963): 258-80, 331-58.

Thompson, Lewis N. *Lewis Craig, the Pioneer Baptist Preacher: His Life, Labors, and Character*. Louisville KY, 1910.

Welch, James Ely. "Early Preachers of Kentucky." *Christian Repository* 5 (May 1856): 289-94.

Williams, John Augustus. *Life of Elder John Smith with Some Account of the Rise and Progress of the Current Reformation*. Cincinnati OH, 1870.

Williamson, Hugh P. "A Chaplain [Carter Tarrant] in the War of 1812." *Daughters of the American Revolution Magazine* 91 (Sept 1957): 1038-40, 1114.

## H. Genealogies

Anderson, Mrs. L. C. "The Taylor Family of Northumberland and Lancaster Counties, Virginia." *Virginia Magazine of History and Biography* 35 (April, July 1927): 211-18, 309-12; 36 (Oct 1928): 388-89; 47 (Jan 1939): 81-84.

Clay, Mary Rogers. "The Genealogy of the Clays." *The Clay Family*. Louisville KY, 1899.

Hiden, [Martha W]. "The Bradford Family of Fauquier County, Virginia." *Tyler's Quarterly Historical and Genealogical Magazine* 27 (Oct 1945): 114-39.

_____. "John Marr of Stafford Co[unty]." *Tyler's Quarterly Historical and Genealogical Magazine* 26 (April 1945): 286-95.

Kemper, Charles E. "The Taylor Family of Fauquier County, V[irgini]a." *William and Mary Quarterly* 6 (Oct 1926): 331-33.

Paxton, M. W. *The Marshall Family: Or, a Genealogical Chart of the Descendants of John Marshall and Elizabeth Markham, His Wife; Sketches of Individuals and Notices of Families Connected with Them.* Cincinnati OH, 1885.

Power, John Carroll, and S. A. Power. *History of the Early Settlers [of] Sangamon County IL: Centennial Record.* Chicago, 1881. Reprint ed.; Springfield IL, 1970.

Thompson, Dorothy Brown. "Additional Notes on the John Taylor Family." *Register of the Kentucky Historical Society* 53 (Oct 1955): 348-54.

_____. "Ancestors and Descendants of the Rev. John Taylor (1752–1835)." *Register of the Kentucky Historical Society* 47 (Jan 1949): 21, 22-51.

Yates, Julie Trabue, and Charles C. Trabue IV. *The Trabue Family in America, 1700-983.* Baltimore MD, 1983.

## I. General Newspapers

*The Commonwealth.* Frankfort KY 1833, 1835.

*Frankfort Argus.* Frankfort KY 1835.

*Lexington Observer and Kentucky Reporter.* Lexington KY, 1833, 1835, 1845.

## J. Religious Newspapers and Periodicals

*Advocate and Messenger.* Front Royal VA 1990.

*The Baptist Banner and Western Pioneer.* Shelbyville KY, 1842, 1847.

*Baptist Chronicle and Literary Register.* Georgetown KY, 1830–1832.

*The Baptist Monitor and Political Compiler.* Bloomfield KY, 1823–1824.

*The Budget.* Lexington KY 1830.
*Christian Examiner.* Lexington KY, 1830.
*Christian Repository.* Louisville KY, 1856.
*The Gospel Herald.* Frankfort KY, 1813.
*The Kentucky Missionary and Theological Magazine.* Frankfort KY, 1812.
*The Reformer.* Philadelphia PA, 1821.


## K. Articles in Religious Newspapers

Leland, John. Letter to John Taylor. Cheshire MA, 10 Dec 1830. *Baptist Chronicle and Literary Register* 2 (Jan 1831): 3-5.
_____. Letter to Uriel B. Chambers. Cheshire MA, 25 June 1830. *Baptist Chronicle and Literary Register* 1 (Aug 1830): 113-15.
Norwood, Joseph G., and Jacob Creath, Jr. "Elder Taylor's Apostacy." *Christian Examiner* 1 (June 1830): 188-89.
_____. Letter to [Jeremiah] Vardeman. *Christian Examiner* 1 (May 1830): 169-71.
_____. "On the Remission of Sins in Baptism." *Christian Examiner* 1 (June 1830): 174-75.
Warder, Walter. Letter to Edmund Waller. Mays Lick KY, 5 March 1836. *Christian Repository* 5 (March 1856): 177-78.


## L. Articles in Periodicals

Gardner, Robert G. "Virginia Baptists and Slavery, 1759–1790." *Virginia Baptist Register* 24 (1985): 1212-20, and 25 (1986): 1225-39.
[Hackley, Woodford B.]. "Baptist Dress in Olden Days." *Virginia Baptist Register* 9 (1970): 425-29.
Holtzclaw, B. C. "The Nine Christian Rites in the Early Baptist Churches of Virginia." *Virginia Baptist Register* 6 (1967): 243-60.
Keyser, C. Dirck. "The Virginia Separate Baptists and Arminianism, 1760–1787." *Virginia Baptist Register* 23 (1984): 1110-38.
Leavy, William. "Memoir of Lexington and Its Vicinity: With Some Notice of Many Prominent Citizens and Its Institutions of Education and Religion." *Register of the Kentucky Historical Society* 40 (1942): 107-31, 253-67, 353-75; 41 (1943): 44-62, 107-37, 250-60, 310-46; and 42 (1944): 26-43.
Lumpkin, William L. " 'Col. Robert Carter, a Baptist.' " *Virginia Baptist Register* 8 (1969): 339-55.

____. "Early Virginia Baptist Church Covenants." *Virginia Baptist Register* 16 (1977): 772-88.

Moore, John S. "Virginia's Three Baptist Apostles." *Virginia Baptist Register* 11 (1972): 498-502.

Morton, Jennie C. "Chronicles of the Old Neighborhood." *Register of the Kentucky Historical Society* 6 (Sept 1908): 57-80.

Polk, Harold G. "John Taylor Gravesite." *Kentucky Baptist Heritage* 12 (July 1985): 14.

Smith, Larry Douglas. "How Old Is the South Elkhorn Baptist Church?" *Kentucky Baptist Heritage* 16 (Nov 1989): 26-30.

____. "John Taylor and Missions: A New Interpretation." *Quarterly Review: A Survey of Southern Baptist Progress* 42 (April–June 1982): 54-61.

____. "The Mission Work of the Elkhorn Association, 1788–1815." *Kentucky Baptist Heritage* 12 (July 1985): 2-5.

____. "The Rise of the Missionary Spirit among Kentucky Baptists." *Quarterly Review: A Survey of Southern Baptist Progress* 40 (April–June 1980): 74-79.

Tarrants, Charles. "Carter Tarrant (1765–1816), Baptist and Emancipationist." *Register of the Kentucky Historical Society* 88 (Spring 1990): 121-47.

Tarver, Jerry L. "Exhortation among Early Virginia Baptists." *Virginia Baptist Register* 5 (1966): 228-36.

Thompson, Dorothy Brown. "John Taylor and the Day of Controversy." *Register of the Kentucky Baptist Society* 53 (July 1955): 197-233.

____. "John Taylor of the Ten Churches." *Register of the Kentucky Historical Society* 46 (July 1948): 541-72.

## M. Entries in Dictionaries and Encyclopedias

B[laikie], W[illiam] G[arden]. "Fuller, Andrew (1754–1815)." *Dictionary of National Biography.* 7:749-50.

Cathcart, William. "Taylor, Rev. John." *The Baptist Encyclopaedia.* Philadelphia, 1881, 1136.

C[ourtney], William P[rideaux]. "Ryland, John (1753–1825)." *Dictionary of National Biography.* 17:544-45.

Crismon, Leo Taylor. "Taylor, John." *Encyclopedia of Southern Baptists.* 4 vols. Nashville TN, 1958–1982. 2:1347-48.

G[ordon], A[lexander]. "Hall, Robert, [Jr.] (1764–1831)." *Dictionary of National Biography* 8:969-71.

H[amilton], T[homas]. "Gill, John (1697–1771)." *Dictionary of National Biography.* 7:1234.

S[weet], W[illiam] W[arren]. "Taylor, John (1752–April 12, 1835)." *Dictionary of American Biography*. 18:330-31.

Welch, James E[ly]. "John Taylor, 1772–1833 [*sic*]." *Annals of the American Pulpit*. William B. Sprague, ed. 9 vols. New York NY, 1860. Reprint ed.; New York NY, 1969. 6:152-59.

W[estby]-G[ibson], J[ohn]. "Booth, Abraham (1734–1806)." *Dictionary of National Biography*. 2:835-36.

## N. Special Studies

Bailey, Kenneth P. *The Ohio Company of Virginia and the Westward Movement, 1748–1792: A Chapter in the History of the Colonial Frontier*. Glendale CA, 1939.

Berkhof, L. *Systematic Theology*. 3rd ed. Grand Rapids MI, 1946.

Billington, Ray Allen. *Westward Expansion: A History of the American Frontier*. 4th ed. New York NY, 1974.

Bishop, Robert H. *An Outline of the History of the Church in the State of Kentucky*. . . . [Lexington KY], 1824.

Bissell, Richard Pike. *The Monongahela*. Rivers of America ser. New York NY, 1952.

Boles, John B. *The Great Revival, 1787–1805: The Origins of the Southern Evangelical Mind*. Lexington KY, 1972.

Carroll, Benajah Harvey, Jr. *The Genesis of American Anti-Missionism*. Louisville KY, 1902.

Clark, Thomas D. *Frontier America: The Story of the Westward Movement*. New York NY, 1959.

————. *Kentucky: Land of Contrast*. Regions of America ser. New York NY, 1968.

Cowing, Cedric B. *The Great Awakening and the American Revolution: Colonial Thought in the Eighteenth Century*. History of American Thought and Culture ser. Chicago IL, 1971.

Davis, Julia. *The Shenandoah*. Rivers of America ser. New York NY, 1945.

Dohme, Alvin R. L. *Shenandoah: The Valley Story*. Washington, D.C., 1972.

Evans, Herndon J. *The Newspaper Press in Kentucky*. Lexington KY, 1976.

Fortune, Alonzo Willard. *The Disciples in Kentucky*. Saint Louis MO, 1932.

————. *Origin and Development of the Disciples*. N. p., 1944.

Garrison, Winfred Ernest, and Alfred Thomas DeGroot. *The Disciples of Christ: A History*. Saint Louis, 1948. Rev. ed.; Saint Louis MO, 1958.

Gewehr, Wesley M. *The Great Awakening in Virginia, 1740–1790*. Durham NC, 1930. Reprint ed.: Gloucester MA, 1965.

Goen, C. C. *Revivalism and Separatism in New England, 1740–1800: Strict Congregationalists and Separate Baptists in the Great Awakening.* New Haven CT, 1962. Reprint ed.; Hamden CT, 1969.

Isaac, Rhys. *The Transformation of Virginia, 1740–1790.* Chapel Hill NC, 1982.

James, William. *The Varieties of Religious Experience: A Study in Human Nature.* New York NY, 1902. Modern Library ed.; New York NY, n. d.

Johnson, L. F. *The History of Franklin County, Ky.* Frankfort KY, 1912.

Kercheval, Samuel. *A History of the Valley of Virginia.* 4th ed. Strasburg VA, 1925.

Kramer, Carl E. *Capital on the Kentucky: A Two-Hundred-Year History of Frankfort and Franklin County.* Frankfort KY, 1986.

Leland, John. *The Virginia Chronicle, with Judicious and Critical Remarks under Twenty-four Heads.* Fredericksburg [VA]: 1790.

Little, Lewis Peyton. *Imprisoned Preachers and Religious Liberty in Virginia.* Lynchburg VA, 1938.

Mullins, Edgar Young. *The Christian Religion in Its Doctrinal Expression.* Nashville TN, 1917.

Olmstead, Clifton E. *History of Religion in the United States.* Englewood Cliffs NJ, 1960.

Railey, William Edward. *History of Woodford County.* Frankfort KY, 1938. Reprint ed.; Versailles KY, 1968.

Rice, Otis K. *The Allegheny Frontier: West Virginia Beginnings, 1730–1830.* Lexington KY, 1970.

Schermerhorn, John Freeman, and Samuel John Mills. *A Correct View of That Part of the United States Which Lies West of the Allegany [sic] Mountains with Regard to Religion and Morals.* Hartford CT, 1814.

Shonkwiler, William Forrest. "The Land Office Business in Indiana." M. A. Thesis. Indiana University, Bloomington IN, 1950.

Sweet, William Warren. *The Story of Religion in America.* 3d ed. New York NY, 1950.

Thomas, David. *The Virginian Baptist: Or, a View and Defence [sic] of the Christian Religion As It Is Professed by the Baptists of Virginia.* Baltimore MD, 1774.

Tristano, Richard M. *The Origins of the Restoration Movement: An Intellectual History.* Atlanta GA, 1988.

Willis, George L., Sr. *History of Shelby County, Kentucky.* Louisville KY, 1929.

Withers, Alexander Scott. *Chronicles of Border Warfare: Or, A History of the Settlement by the Whites of Northwestern Virginia, and of the Indian Wars and Massacres in That Section of the State.* Clarksburg VA, 1831. Thwaites ed.; Cincinnati OH, 1895. Reprint ed.; Parsons WV, 1961.

Wust, Klaus G. *The Virginia Germans.* Charlottesville VA, 1969.

Baptists on the American Frontier

## O. Reference Works

Billups, Edward W. *The Sweet Songster: A Collection of the Most Popular and Approved Songs, Hymns, and Ballads.* N. p., 1854. Reprint ed.; Wayne WV, n. d.

Boatner, Mark Mayo, III. *Encyclopedia of the American Revolution.* New York NY, 1966.

Bogardus, Carl R. "Gallatin County [KY] Marriages." Manuscript. Kentucky Historical Society, Frankfort KY.

Clift, G. Glenn, comp. *The "Corn Stalk" Militia of Kentucky, 1792–1811.* Frankfort KY, 1957.

_____. *"Second Census" of Kentucky, 1800.* Frankfort KY, 1954.

Cowen, Janet C., ed. *Jefferson [IN] Land Entries, 1808–1818.* Utica KY, 1984.

Darby, William, and Theodore Dwight, Jr. *A New Gazetteer of the United States of America.* 2d ed. New York NY, 1833.

Espenshade, A. Howry. *Pennsylvania Place Names.* State College PA, 1925. Reprint ed.; Baltimore MD, 1970.

Gannett, Henry. *A Gazeteer of Virginia and West Virginia.* Washington, D.C., 1904. Reprint ed.; Baltimore, 1975.

Graves, Absalom, ed. *Hymns, Psalms, and Spiritual Songs.* Frankfort KY, 1825.

Gray, Gertrude E. *Virginia Northern Neck Land Grants.* 2 vols. Bowie MD, 1987–1988.

Green, B. W. *Word-Book of Virginia Folk-Speech.* Richmond VA, 1899.

Hanson, Raus McDill. *Virginia Place Names.* Verona VA, 1969.

Heinemann, Charles Brunk, comp. *"First Census" of Kentucky, 1790.* Baltimore MD, 1956.

Hewson, Gertrude Earl, comp. "Marriages, Bonds, Consents [of] Gallatin County, Kentucky, 1799–1835." *Kentucky Ancestors* 13 (1977–1978): 86-89, 116-19, 183-88, and 14 (1978–1979): 9-14, 83-88, 146-51, 203-208, and 15 (1979–1980): 15-20, 79-86, 143-49.

*Illustrated Historical Atlas of the State of Indiana.* Chicago, 1876. Reprint ed. (titled *Maps of Indiana Counties in 1876*); Indianapolis IN, 1968.

Kenny, Hamill Thomas. *West Virginia Place Names: Their Origin and Meaning, Including the Nomenclature of the Streams and Mountains.* Piedmont WV, 1945.

Knorr, Catherine L. *Marriages of Orange County, Virginia, 1747–1810.* Pine Bluff AR, 1959.

"List of Auditors of the State of Kentucky." *Register of the Kentucky Historical Society* 3 (Jan 1905): 37.

Lumpkin, William L. *Baptist Confessions of Faith.* Philadelphia PA, 1959.

McAdams, Edna Wilson, comp. *Kentucky Pioneer and Court Records*. Lexington KY, 1929.

McMurtrie, Douglas C., and Albert H. Allen. *Check List of Kentucky Imprints, 1787–1810*. Vol. 5 of *American Imprints Inventory*. Louisville KY, 1938. Reprint ed.; New York NY, 1964.

Miller, Thomas Condit, and Hu Maxwell. *West Virginia and Its People*. 3 vols. New York NY, 1913.

*New Descriptive Atlas of West Virginia*. Clarksburg WV, 1933.

Rone, Wendell Holmes, Sr., comp. *Chronological Charts of the Baptist Associations of Kentucky since 1785*. [Louisville KY], 1967.

Scott, W. W. "A List of Marriages Recorded in the Back Part of Deed Book No. 17, Orange County, [Virginia]." *Virginia Magazine of History and Biography* 26 (April 1918): 190-200.

Society of Colonial Wars in the Commonwealth of Kentucky. *Year Book, 1917*. [Louisville KY, 1917.]

"Treasurers of the State of Kentucky." *Register of the Kentucky Historical Society* 1 (May 1903): 46.

*Webster's New International Dictionary of the English Language*. 2d ed., unabridged. Springfield MA, 1961.

*Webster's New World Dictionary of the American Language*. 2d college ed. Englewood Cliffs NJ, 1970.

*West Virginia Gazetteer of Physical and Cultural Place Names*. Morgantown WV, 1986.

Wharton, Mary E., and Roger W. Barbour. *Trees and Shrubs of Kentucky*. Lexington KY, 1973.

## P. General Works

Collins, Lewis. *History of Kentucky*. Maysville KY, 1847. Rev. ed. of 2 vols.; Covington KY, 1874. Reprint ed. of 2 vols.; Berea KY, 1976.

Morton, Richard L. *Colonial Virginia*. 2 vols. Chapel Hill NC, 1960.

Smith, Z. F. *The History of Kentucky*. Louisville KY, 1892.

Van Hook, Joseph O. *The Kentucky Story*. Chattanooga TN, 1959.

Walker, Williston, *et al. A History of the Christian Church*. 4th ed. New York NY, 1985.

*Former meeting house of Big Spring Baptist Church, the only such building housing one of the churches to which Taylor belonged. The photograph above was taken by J. Winston Coleman, Jr. (from the photographic archives of Transylvania University, Lexington, Kentucky); the picture below, taken by Charlotte May Young, illustrates the current condition of the building, following a fire of recent date.*

*Title page to Taylor's* Thoughts on Missions *(1820).*

HISTORY

OF

CLEAR CREEK CHURCH;

AND

CAMPBELLISM EXPOSED.

BY JOHN TAYLOR.

FRANKFORT:
PRINTED BY A. G. HODGES, COMMENTATOR OFFICE.
1830

*Title page to Taylor's*
History of Clear Creek Church; and Campbellism Exposed *(1830).*

A HISTORY

OF

TEN BAPTIST CHURCHES,

OF WHICH THE AUTHOR HAS BEEN ALTERNATELY
A MEMBER:

IN WHICH WILL BE SEEN SOMETHING OF

A JOURNAL

OF THE AUTHOR'S LIFE, FOR MORE THAN
FIFTY YEARS.

ALSO,

A COMMENT ON SOME PARTS OF SCRIPTURE:

IN WHICH

THE AUTHOR TAKES THE LIBERTY TO DIFFER FROM
OTHER EXPOSITORS.

BY JOHN TAYLOR.

FRANKFORT, (KY.)

PRINTED BY J. H. HOLEMAN.

1823.

*Title page to the first edition of* A History of Ten Baptist Churches *(1823).*

# A HISTORY

### OF TEN

# BAPTIST CHURCHES,

OF WHICH THE AUTHOR HAS BEEN ALTERNATELY A MEM-
BER: IN WHICH WILL BE SEEN SOMETHING OF

# A JOURNAL

## OF THE AUTHOR'S LIFE FOR MORE THAN FIFTY YEARS.

### ALSO

## *A COMMENT ON SOME PARTS OF*

# SCRIPTURE,

IN WHICH THE AUTHOR TAKES THE LIBERTY TO DIFFER
FROM OTHER EXPOSITORS.

## BY JOHN TAYLOR.

### SECOND EDITION.

### BLOOMFIELD, NELSON COUNTY, KY.

PRINTED BY WILL. H. HOLMES.

## 1827.

*Title page to the second edition of* A History of Ten Baptist Churches *(1827).*

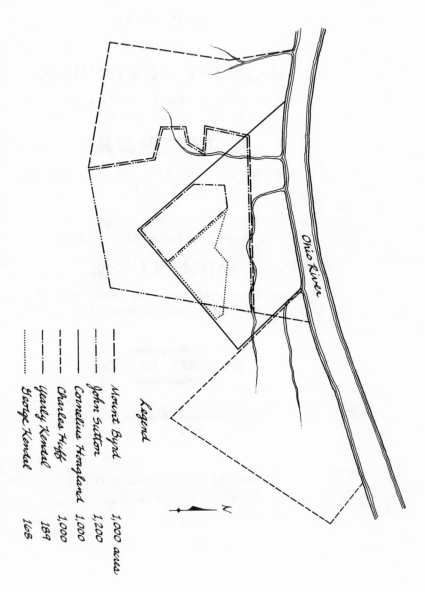

Surveyor's plat of overlapping land claims involved in a lawsuit settled in 1807. Drawn by David Kent Humphreys from a photocopy of a court document (Gallatin Circuit Court Order Book 1, 139, Kentucky State Archives).

Ohio River

N

Legend

| | | |
|---|---|---|
| ——— | Mount Byrd | 1,000 acres |
| — — | John Sutton | 1,200 |
| —·—·— | Cornelius Hoagland | 1,000 |
| – – – | Charles Huff | 1,000 |
| —··—··— | Yearly Kendal | 189 |
| ········ | George Kendal | 168 |

*The house that Taylor built on Mount Byrd, near Milton, Kentucky, in 1803–1804. Drawn by David Kent Humphreys from a photograph by Gregory Scot Rose.*

The house that Taylor built near Forks of Elkhorn, Kentucky, for his youngest daughter, Sally, upon her marriage to Joseph Smith, in 1822. Under later ownership this house was called "Llangollen." Drawn by David Kent Humphreys from a photograph in The Register of the Kentucky Historical Society (July 1948): 540.

# Index

# About the Editor

Chester Raymond Young, Sr., was born at Garlin, in Adair County, Kentucky, in 1920. He received the A.B. degree from Berea College in 1943 and earned graduate degrees from the Southern Baptist Theological Seminary (M.Div., 1949; Th.M., 1959), the University of Hawaii (M.A., 1964), and Vanderbilt University (Ph.D., 1969). During 1949–1964 he and his wife served with the Southern Baptist Foreign Mission Board in the Hawaiian Islands. He was editor of *The Hawaiian Baptist*, 1949–1952; president of the Hawaii Baptist Convention, 1952–1954; and pastor of the Kalihi Baptist Church, 1950–1964.

From 1967 until his retirement in 1985 he taught American history at Cumberland College, Williamsburg, Kentucky.

His first book, *Westward into Kentucky: The Narrative of Daniel Trabue*, which was published in 1981 by the University Press of Kentucky, won a Certificate of Commendation from the American Asssociation for State and Local History. Young's other publications include *"To Win the Prize": The Story of the First Baptist Church at Williamsburg, Kentucky, 1883–1983* (Williamsburg: Centennial Committee, First Baptist Church, Williamsburg, Kentucky, 1983) and numerous journal and dictionary articles.

Professor and Mrs. Young are the parents of three children.

# About this Edition

The annotated third edition is a consolidation of Taylor's two editions that includes only the biographical and historical materials of the previous editions pertaining to Taylor or to the churches to which he belonged. Accordingly, thirteen sermonic and theological pieces and a sketch on Isaac Hodgen have been eliminated. The essay titled "The Author's Conversion and Call to the Ministry," a sketch on Lewis Craig, the "Appendix to the History of Clear Creek Church," and obituaries of Catherine Graves and Joseph Wilson all have been interwoven with the text of Taylor's *Ten Churches*.

The pagination from the first edition constitutes the framework for the contents of this edition. References to the second edition are made here only when its materials are absent from the first edition or appear different in it.

Many of Taylor's lengthy paragraphs have been divided into shorter ones, and many long sentences have been broken up into briefer ones. To some sentences have been added words [enclosed in brackets] that complete the evident meaning or render the reading smoother. Modern capitalization of words and punctuation of sentences have been uniformly used. The spelling of proper nouns has been made to agree with the orthography found in recent atlases or in denominational histories.

An extensive system of annotation has been devised in order to make Taylor's work more understandable and useful.

*Baptists on the American Frontier: A History of Ten Baptist Churches of Which the Author Has Been Alternately a Member by John Taylor.*

---

Mercer University Press, Macon, Georgia 31210-3960. ISBN 0-86554-479-4.
Catalog and warehouse pick number MUP/H373.
Interior and exterior text and design, composition, and layout by Scott Nash.
Illustration from a photograph by J. Winston Coleman, Jr.
Camera-ready pages composed on a Gateway 2000, via WordPerfect 5.1 for DOS and WPWIN 5.1/5.2, and printed on a Hewlett Packard Laser Jet 4.
Text font: TimesNewRoman PS 11/12. Display font: GillSans 14.
Printed and bound in the U.S.A. by
Printed via offset lithography on 50# Natural Smooth. Smyth sewn and cased into Roxite B grade cloth over standard boards, foil stamped, dust jacket printed 2 PMS colors and polyester film lamination, and headbands and matching endleaves.

---